QUALITY CONTROL IN THE FOOD INDUSTRY

Volume 3

FOOD SCIENCE AND TECHNOLOGY

A Series of Monographs

QUALITY CONTROL IN THE FOOD INDUSTRY

Edited by

S. M. HERSCHDOERFER

Formerly of T. Wall & Sons (Ice Cream) Ltd., London, England

VOLUME 3

1972

ACADEMIC PRESS London and New York

ACADEMIC PRESS INC. (LONDON) LTD.
24/28 Oval Road,
London NW1

United States Edition published by
ACADEMIC PRESS INC.
111 Fifth Avenue
New York, New York 10003

Library of Congress Catalog Card Number: 67-19849
ISBN: 12-342903-X

PRINTED IN GREAT BRITAIN AT
THE ABERDEEN UNIVERSITY PRESS

Contributors to Volume 3

H. J. BUNKER, *17 Radnor Road, Twickenham, Middlesex, England* (p. 81)

D. DICKINSON, *Institute for Industrial Research and Standards, Ballymun Road, Dublin 9, Ireland* (p. 1)

E. FELICIOTTI, *Thomas J. Lipton Inc., Englewood Cliffs, New Jersey* (p. 297)

P. LINDLEY, *The Nestlé Company Ltd., St. George's House, Croydon, Surrey, CR9 1NR, England* (p. 259)

J. LLOYD HENDERSON, *117 Oak Shadow Drive, Santa Rosa, California 95405, U.S.A.* (p. 327)

D. MCDONALD, *Schweppes Ltd., Grosvenor Road, St. Albans, Herts, England* (p. 151)

E. G. MULLER, *Tate and Lyle Refineries Ltd., London, England* (p. 229)

W. PRICE-DAVIES, *Schweppes Ltd., Grosvenor Road, St. Albans, Herts, England* (p. 151)

D. A. SHAPTON, *H. J. Heinz Co. Ltd., Hayes Park, Hayes, Middlesex, England* (p. 35)

H. A. SLIGHT, *British Food Manufacturing Industries Research Association, Leatherhead, Surrey, England* (p. 417)

C. L. SMITH, *Continental Can Company Inc., Technical Center 1350 West 76th Street, Chicago, Illinois 60620, U.S.A.* (p. 373)

M. G. TARVER, *Continental Can Company Inc., Technical Center 1200 West 76th Street, Chicago, Illinois 60620, U.S.A.* (p. 373)

G. WELLNER, *International Flavors and Fragrances Inc., Rio de Janeiro, Brazil* (p. 191)

Preface

The food industry covers such an enormous field that obviously no single person would be competent from personal experience to discuss all its quality control procedures. It was therefore deemed preferable to divide the subject into a number of separate chapters and to invite acknowledged experts in those different fields to deal with their quality control aspects. The authors were asked to consider quality control not in the narrow meaning of the term often used and which more suitably should be called "quality audit", a kind of post mortem on the quality of the finished product usually by means of a bacteriological and chemical examination. The authors were invited to look upon quality control as the sum of all those controllable factors that ultimately influence positively or negatively the quality of the finished products, e.g. selection of raw materials, processing methods, packaging, methods of storage and distribution, etc.

In adopting this approach, it was realized that the individual contributions would differ considerably from each other, not only in reflecting the personalities of the authors but also because of the different character and stage of development of the various industries. Some rely greatly on laboratory methods for quality control at all stages of manufacture; one such industry is that dealing with oils and fats. Other industries, e.g. the fishing industry, use laboratory techniques to a very limited extent.

The work has been divided into three volumes, the first being devoted to general aspects of quality control affecting practically all branches of the food industry. It was assumed that most readers would be interested in all the subjects discussed in Volume 1, but might wish to refer in the subsequent volumes only to sections dealing with some specific industries. The contributions were therefore conceived more as a number of separate essays than as consecutive chapters in a text book. While considerable effort was made to reduce overlapping and repetition to a minimum, they could not altogether be avoided.

In spite of the considerable size of this work, it was impossible to deal with any subject exhaustively; however, numerous references to the relevant literature will enable the reader to pursue any enquiries further than could be dealt with within the limited scope of this book. Not included in the book were quality control methods applied to food additives such as organic or inorganic acids, bases and salts, colouring materials, preservatives, antioxidants, etc. The quality control of such additives lies mainly outside the province of the food manufacturer, and the field involved is so wide that its inclusion might have required a further volume.

To the authors of the individual contributions I am indebted for their willing co-operation and for their ready acceptance of the unavoidable delays between submission of manuscripts and publication from which some of them suffered. I am most grateful to these contributors for updating their early submissions. These regrettable delays were especially long in the production of this final volume, but made it possible to include the Chapter on Automatic Control which, I trust, will provide valuable information to the reader, and which forms a useful conclusion to the work.

I gratefully acknowledge the editorial help given to me by some colleagues and my thanks are also due to the staff of Academic Press for their help and advice.

It is hoped that these volumes will be of interest not only to the food scientist and technologist concerned with quality control but also generally to the management in the food industry which is constantly called upon to make decisions vitally affecting the quality of their products. To students in universities or at technical colleges they might serve as a useful introduction to this interesting field of the food industry.

January, 1972   S. M. HERSCHDOERFER

12 Parkgate Gardens
London SW14 8BQ

Contents

Quality Control of Fruits and Vegetables and their Products

D. DICKINSON (with V. D. ARTHEY and D. E. C. CREAN)

Canned and Bottled Food Products (Soups, Mayonnaise, Sauces and Vinegar)

D. A. SHAPTON

Alcoholic Bevereges and Vinegars

H. J. Bunker

Soft Drinks

W. Price-Davies and D. McDonald

Flavouring Materials and Their Quality Control

GEORGES WELLNER

The Sugar Industry

E. G. MULLER

Chocolate and Sugar Confectionery, Jams and Jellies

P. LINDLEY

Quality Control of Prepared Food Mixes

E. FELICIOTTI

Frozen Desserts

J. LLOYD HENDERSON

Quality Assurance of Incoming Packaging Materials for the Food Industry

MAE-GOODWIN TARVER and C. L. SMITH

Automatic Control

H. A. SLIGHT

Contents of Volumes 1 and 2

Quality Control of Fruits and Vegetables and their Products

D. DICKINSON

Institute for Industrial Research and Standards, Dublin, Ireland

with the assistance of V. D. ARTHEY, Ph.D. and D. E. C. CREAN, B.A.

Fruit and Vegetable Canning and Quick Freezing Research Association

1. INTRODUCTION

The desirable characteristics of a fruit or vegetable are dictated largely by the market for which it is intended and the use to which it is to be put. Traditionally, the fresh market is the one to which the grower turns and in order to secure an immediate and ready sale for his produce he tends to give priority to size and "eye appeal". Only rarely do the same properties commend themselves to the food manufacturer seeking raw material for industrial transformation or preservation. It was at one time supposed that fruits and vegetables unsuitable for direct retail markets on account of unattractive size or shape, or perhaps blemishes, would provide raw material for food manufacture, but this is not generally true. Quite apart from the important chemical differences that occur between varieties and materials at different stages of maturity, which are dealt with at length in the following pages, it has been found that a good quality manufactured article cannot be made from poor quality raw material. With increased rate of production, uniformity of size, shape, and composition have become important, and specifications for raw materials for canning and freezing, for example, are now more exacting than specifications for sale on the fresh market.

In many instances selection of vegetables is made at the seed stage and quality control starts at this point, to follow through all the stages of growing and harvesting, transformation and packaging up to the finished article. It would not be possible within the space of a single chapter to cover comprehensively the whole of fruit and vegetable breeding, selection, culture, and transformation. The present account aims at stating principles, illustrated by examples in more detail.

2. CHEMICAL ASPECTS OF THE QUALITY OF FRUITS AND VEGETABLES

It is only of recent years that any detailed exploration of connections between chemical composition and quality has been possible. Previously, chemical analysis was too coarse a procedure involving drastic breakdown of the materials and so-called "proximate" analysis of the resultant solution. The information obtainable by this technique was of severely limited value, although in some few instances it was possible to devise analytical criteria of quality. One of the best examples of this is the Maturity Ratio applied to fruit juices. This ratio is given by

$$\frac{\text{Total solids, g/100 ml}}{\text{Acidity (as citric), g/100 ml}}$$

During the ripening of fruit this ratio changes rapidly, and it has been found that optimum values occur. In the case of orange juice such values have occasionally been written into standards for the product, e.g. California and Israel specify a value of 8; South Africa requires minimum values of 5 for seedling oranges, 5·5 for Valencia oranges and 6 for Navel oranges. Certain U.S. grade specifications for canned fruit juices also include values for acidity and sometimes also for sugar or solids contents, while Dryden and Hills[1] have described the importance of sugar and acid contents in apples.

A similar type of criterion applies to the selection of peas for canning or freezing on the basis of their content of "alcohol insoluble solids" which is that percentage of the fresh weight insoluble in 80% ethyl alcohol after boiling for 30 min. Selection is done in practice instrumentally by means of the tenderometer or some similar device, but it is the chemical composition that determines texture, among other attributes of quality, and the instrument provides a conveniently rapid measure of this composition.

In the case of vegetables the criterion of suitable "ripeness" has been most fully worked out for seeds such as the pea, the broad bean, and sweet corn. Generally these seeds are botanically immature (except in the case of the reconstituted dried or "processed" pea) and suitable criteria must be found to select a point at which texture and flavour are optimum for consumer preference. Soluble carbohydrates are synthesized and reach a maximum at 25/30 days after flowering. Thereafter they decrease and are utilized to form starch, the production of which begins 20 days after flowering.[2] There is a concomitant toughening of the texture. Several excellent reviews on determination

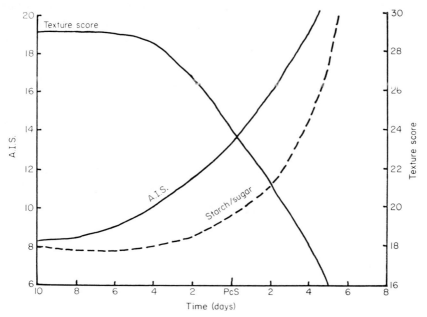

FIG. 1. Changes in Alcohol Insoluble Solids (A.I.S.) content and texture scores.

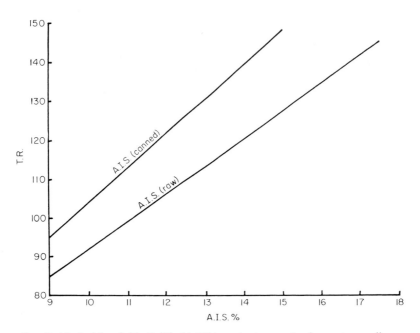

FIG. 2. Alcohol Insoluble Solids (A.I.S.) content *versus* tenderometer readings.

of optimum harvest time have been written notably by Lynch *et al.*,[3] Mackower,[4] and Anthistle.[5]

Neither chemical nor physical measurements actually determine texture; all have to refer to a subjective organoleptic evaluation by a trained tasting panel for its absolute assessment. This is the case in all evaluations of quality. Correlations of chemical and instrumental measurements with tasting panel evaluations are well established. Experiments on peas that have been in progress at Campden Research Station for some years are summarized in Figs 1 and 2 (p. 3). The practical canning stage is a state of maturity judged by

FIG. 3. The Maturometer; a multipoint instrument which measures the texture of peas.

a tasting panel on the basis of texture of skin and flesh, the marks allotted being 24 out of a possible 30. This occurs at an Alcohol Insoluble Solids content of 13·4% and a tenderometer reading of 120. For quick frozen peas which do not have to undergo a long and energetic heat treatment the correct stage for harvesting is at a tenderometer reading of 100. This occurs some three days earlier than the practical canning stage.

For harvest predictions one can take daily small samples and determine their texture by the tenderometer or other allied instrument Figs 3–5. This gives

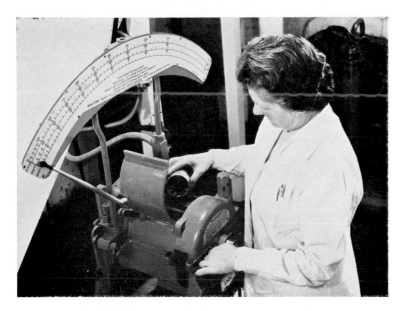

FIG. 4. Measuring the texture of peas with the Tenderometer.

FIG. 5. The Texturemeter: an instrument for measuring the texture of fresh or canned vegetables.

good short term prediction. The actual harvesting dates will depend on the seasonal weather conditions, but a reasonably even flow of peas to the processor can be achieved by arranging the planting dates of individual varieties according to the known number of accumulated heat units (A.H.Us) required to bring them to the correct maturity for canning or freezing. It is first assumed that peas do not grow at temperatures below 40°F and that thereafter growth takes place at a rate proportional to the temperature. The simplest method of assessment is to take a mean of the maximum and minimum daily temperatures, subtract 40°F from this and so obtain the *heat units* for that day. Accumulated heat units have been worked out for many varieties from the time of sowing and give an estimate of the time required for the crop to reach maturity.

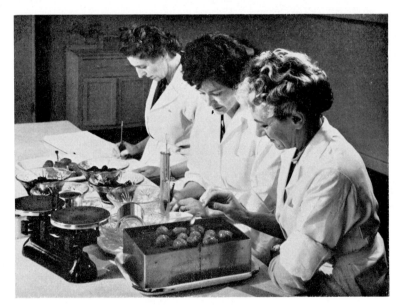

FIG. 6. Assessing the quality of canned fruit at the Fruit and Vegetable Research Association, Campden.

With the development of more refined analytical techniques more knowledge of the *actual* as distinct from the *proximate* composition of the raw materials of food manufacture is now available, and it is increasing rapidly. Among the first of the modern investigations designed to correlate the chemical composition—properly so-called—of fruit with the behaviour and eventual quality of a manufactured article is that begun at Campden Research Station about 10 years ago into the composition of the Victoria plum.[6] The primary object of this work was to discover the cause of acceleration of the corrosion of the tinplate container which has caused serious difficulties in the canning industry from time to time. The first step was to determine the nature of the major compounds actually present in the ripe fruit and these were found to be malic, phosphoric and quinic acids; fructose, glucose, sucrose, and sorbitol; pectins; chlorophyll degradation products; and an anthocyanin—chrysanthemin—which appeared to be the only natural colouring matter present. Having determined the main constituents, it was then possible to attempt to correlate their concentrations in different batches of fruit with the storage life of the canned fruit. It was found that the chrysanthemin concentration and the malic acid content both correlated to a highly significant degree with the storage life, indicating that the more red the fruit and the more acid it contained, the better would the canned fruit keep. These findings involved two other attributes of quality—colour and flavour—and further work was carried out on the development of the fruit on the trees in order to discover if any optimum stage of ripeness could be defined (see Fig. 6).

Rees[7] reported that the composition of the plum does not change very much until the onset of ripening, which is accompanied by an easily visible change from green to yellow; shortly after this stage the plum begins to store sucrose whereas green fruits contain only glucose, fructose, and sorbitol. The plums also begin to increase in size and to soften. By the time the red colour appears the plums have reached their maximum size, the sucrose content has risen to 2·5% by weight, and the acidity has fallen to about 1·5%. Taking account of the total sugars, a red Victoria plum contains from 8 to 10% altogether, which gives a sugar/acid ratio of between 6 and 7. Selection of the fruit for quality, judging ripeness from colour alone, will therefore give fruit containing a useful amount of natural colouring matter (from the point of view of suppression of corrosion) having optimum size and flavour. Underripe plums contain more acid, but if picked and canned at this stage they are of unsatisfactory colour because of the chlorophyll they still contain and which turns brown on heating; they are less than full size, and they contain less sucrose than is desirable. If left to become over-ripe, the plums darken in colour throughout, they lose weight, and although the sucrose content continues to increase, the acidity decreases; and they are, of course, too soft in texture. It is of interest to note that the total pectin content of Victoria plums changes little after the onset of ripening and so is unlikely to be directly connected with the texture of the fruit.

Apparently, since high malic acid content corresponded in the tests with good keeping quality in the canned fruit, there might be some justification, other things being equal, for selecting under-ripe fruit for canning. However, it is now known that all other things are not equal and that the most important factor connected with corrosion is contained in the stone of the fruit and not in the flesh. This is amygdalin, a β-glycoside of mandelonitrile, which is decomposed by enzymic action if the heat process is not sufficient to inactivate the enzyme concerned.[8] Unfortunately, the enzyme system sometimes exhibits a remarkable degree of heat resistance and it is not known at present whether this is due to plums from some sources containing abnormally large quantities of amygdalin, or enzyme, or both, or whether there is some other difference affecting the heat resistance of the system. Further information on this enzyme system has been published by Haisman and Knight.[9]

The chemical composition of rhubarb has been investigated extensively with a view to compiling a list of desirable and undesirable chemical components from the point of view of the canner and consumer. It also provided an opportunity to discover in what way varieties can differ chemically from one another and, perhaps eventually to evolve some chemical "finger-printing" system for varieties which would avoid the recurrent annoyance of rediscovering a variety masquerading under some other name. Contrary to popular belief, oxalic acid is not a major acidic constituent of the common edible rhubarb. As in most other fruits, malic acid is the most important acid. The varieties do not, in fact, differ very greatly in their acid components. All those examined were found to contain precisely the same acids although the proportions varied.[10] Even if, as was at first suspected, oxalic acid had proved to be a major component of some varieties, it now seems that it would not have been possible to breed new varieties free from oxalic acid. Investigations of the acid components of spinach have revealed a very similar acid pattern.[11]

A most important fact that has been revealed by these studies is that the acids found in canned rhubarb are not all derived from the raw material. There is definite evidence that simple organic acids are formed during processing from sugars under the influence—in some way not yet understood—of the natural acids. This may provide the explanation for the observation that accelerated corrosion sometimes follows over-processing. It may also be the reason why the pH values of many canned products, more particularly vegetables, are significantly lower than those of the raw material.[12]

Although the acid components of rhubarb varieties are constant in composition, the phenolic constituents vary considerably. This is obvious from a cursory examination of a collection of varieties, which differ in colour from beetroot red to pale green. The examination of the test varieties for natural pigments and their chemical precursors is not yet advanced to the same extent as the analysis for acids. It is more complex and the number of possible components is greater. Varieties that require no artificial colouring matter when canned, pale green varieties that do not darken on processing, and pale varieties which provide no brown background colour to an artificial colouring matter can, however, be selected.

The inspiration of these researches may fairly be attributed to Dr. E. C. Bate-Smith and the Low Temperature Research Station at Cambridge. His work has been on a much larger scale, covering the whole field of flowering plants, and not concerned at all with the effects of chemical composition on quality. Indeed, he has been mainly concerned with the non-edible parts of plants and with comparison of the chemical constituents of botanically related species.[27,28] It seems at least likely that botanical classification will eventually depend as much on chemical analysis as it has hitherto on physiology.

Returning to quality control one of the earliest successes was the application of a simple chemical test to broad bean seeds to determine their suitability for canning.[13] This test is now widely used, not only in the industry, but by horticulturalists too, and involves simply the detection of the class of plant phenolic substances that discolours severely during processing. Subsequent research on the chemical changes taking place in broad beans during ripening revealed that similar phenolic substances are probably related in this vegetable to the texture. Beans low in extractable phenolics—such as Triple White—are generally more tender than those with a high phenolic content; but the toughening of the green varieties is not simply explained as a transformation of leuco-anthocyanins ("anthocyanogens") to insoluble cell-wall constituents, as it appears that starch and other alcohol-insoluble materials are also involved. This work also established incidentally that texture-measuring instruments may be used to test the maturity of broad beans in the same way as peas.[14] The same test for anthocyanogens has also been advocated for the selection of pears for canning.[15]

Colour is the attribute of quality with the most obvious direct chemical connection. Natural colouring matters which occur most widespread in fruits and vegetables are, however, comparatively few in number. Nevertheless, they behave somewhat differently, especially on processing, presumably because of other chemical substances with which they are associated. Broadly speaking, the same type of compound is found in all red fruits, but its effect on the appearance of the processed fruit is very different in the blackberry and in the Victoria plum. It is not simply a difference in quantity since the addition of extra natural colouring matter is not generally beneficial. Most strawberries and some raspberries, for example, if canned in a syrup coloured with chrysanthemin do not absorb the colouring matter appreciably and remain as pale brown berries floating in a red liquid giving an effect which is far from attractive. There is some mechanism involved which may be compared with mordant dyeing, which fixes a proportion of the natural colouring matters in some fruits and intensifies their colour.

The texture of vegetable tissue is the result of a complicated mixture of chemical and physical effects. The turgidity of raw fruit is due in no small measure to the gases held within the tissues. Cooking causes the expulsion of these gases, among other changes, and there is a consequent softening of the whole structure. The remaining cooked tissue may still be soft or tough according to its composition. Certain varieties of rhubarb are inedible because they lay down woody tissue in their fibres, and other similar instances of lignification could be cited. Bate-Smith has concluded that eight

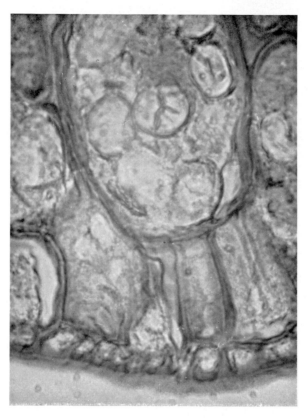

Fig. 7.

phenolic substances are commonly associated with the character of "woodiness" in plants. In vegetables such as asparagus and string beans the fibrousness of the product is the dominating factor in texture. Instruments such as the fibrometer[16] and fibro-pressure tester[17] have been developed to measure this. In the fibrometer an asparagus stalk is put under a standard wire and a standard load applied. Any stalk not cut through in 5 sec is regarded as tough, the recommended limit for tough stalks being not more than 10%. Fibrousness is associated in asparagus with age and with the distance from the tip.

It is apparent that those vegetables and fruits with a tendency towards lignification or woodiness do not usually have a high starch content, and vice versa. The texture of vegetable tissues with a high starch content is very

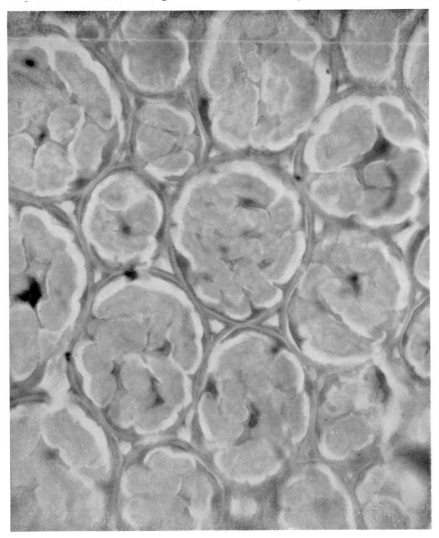

FIG. 8.

greatly modified by cooking, and such materials are not normally eaten in their raw state. The heating of starch grains in water causes them to swell, and in swelling they exert a considerable pressure. As the starch grains are contained within cells, their swelling causes deformation of the cell shape, with a tendency towards the spherical so that the medium that holds the cells together becomes subject to severe strain. This is illustrated by Figs 7 and 8. The cell walls themselves may break under the strain. The adhesion and texture of the cooked vegetable is therefore the resultant of the swelling pressure of the cell contents, the restraining force of the cell walls, and the adhesion of the cell walls to one another. It is widely accepted that the strength of the cell walls is markedly affected by calcium, and to a lesser extent by magnesium, and it is a matter of common knowledge that both these ions affect the texture of cooked peas and potatoes. It is less widely accepted that they also affect the adhesion of the cells, but it is very possible that they do.

The texture of the cotyledons of dried peas has been the subject of study in this connection because of the practical difficulties that follow on variable or unpredictable texture in the canned product.[18] The skins of dried peas are naturally tough and if they are cooked in hard water, they become even more tough, but the softening of the cotyledons exhibits a greater variability. A constituent of peas that is bound up with the chemistry of texture is phytin—inositol hexametaphosphate—which is normally present as a soluble salt of potassium and magnesium. During cooking, a very insoluble calcium–magnesium salt is formed and it was at one time thought that this change could account for observed differences in texture. However, it is now known that even when there is an excess of calcium ions present, as when peas are cooked in hard water, only a proportion of these ions combine with phytic acid. The calcium ions in the pea are distributed between various active constituents, of which phytic acid is only one. Proteins and cell-wall constituents are also involved in the observed effect of calcium on texture. The presence of phytate in peas is important as it ameliorates the effects of soaking, blanching and cooking in hard water, but it cannot be assumed that peas with a high phytate-phosphorus content will necessarily be of good cooking quality.[19]

A. Effects of Processing

In the natural state, fruits and vegetables consist of an agglomeration of biochemical systems and their products. They also carry on their surfaces large numbers of adventitious micro-organisms such as yeasts, moulds and bacteria. The object of any process is to stabilize the product in such a condition that, when eventually prepared for the table, it will approximate as nearly as possible to the same dish prepared from fresh material. This may be done by the application of heat which inactivates the enzymes and micro-organisms which could give rise to undesirable changes on storage, or cold which reduces the rate of metabolic changes to a point where they become insignificant, or a combination of both.

The blanching process has been recognized from the time of Appert as enhancing the quality of canned vegetables and comprises a short treatment in steam or boiling water. Its functions are to remove dissolved and free intercellular gases from the tissues, thereby giving higher vacua in the can, and to shrink the tissue to facilitate handling and filling. In some instances undesirable flavouring materials are removed. It is also important in that it halts surface enzyme reactions. For frozen foods and the pre-treatment of materials for dehydration, much the same considerations apply, only here the inactivation of enzyme systems is of prime importance. It has been shown conclusively that if unblanched peas are stored at 0°F off-flavours develop within two to four weeks of storage and that considerable loss of colour takes place.

Against this desirable retention of quality must be set other factors. In a water blanch especially, there is a considerable loss of soluble nutrients such as sugars, amino-acids and vitamins. These losses are reduced by steam blanching and work in progress on electronic blanching may serve to reduce them still further.

TABLE 1. Loss of sugars and nitrogen in peas as % of total[20]

Treatment	Loss of sugars (%)	Loss of nitrogen (%)
3 min water 212°F	22·6	22.1
6 min water 212°F	34·6	31·5
3 min steam 212°F	17·5	12·2

Soluble minerals tend to be lost to the blanching medium (peas lost 39% of K_2O and 20% of P_2O_5 in 3 min at 212°F), but calcium may be gained to an extent depending on the hardness of the water. These losses are minimized in practice by using the same water over again; the water in a continuous blancher, through which a constant stream of vegetable material passes, is renewed only at infrequent intervals.

Loss of colour is insignificant in the blanching process and an inadequate blanch can lead to chlorophyll degeneration during frozen storage. Texture is inevitably softened and some changes in flavour occur as a result of the partial cooking that takes place.

Heat treatment of fruits generally takes place after filling into cans and during the process known as exhausting. It serves to remove gases from within and between the fruit tissues. The technique of pre-vacuumizing syruping followed by steam flow closure is tending to remove this step with its concomitant cooking.

The thermal processes applied in cooking serve to stabilize the product by killing micro-organisms and inactivating enzyme systems. Canned and bottled fruits and vegetables may be divided into 4 groups depending on pH.

1. Low-acid group (pH 5·3 and above). Most vegetables.
2. Medium-low acid group (pH 5·3–4·5), e.g. carrots.
3. Medium-acid group (pH 4·5–3·7). Tomatoes, pears, cherries, pineapples, peaches.
4. High-acid group (pH 3·7 and below). Apples, plums, berries, etc.

These pH values have an effect on the microflora present in the container and also on their resistance to heat. In the last two groups heating at 212°F for a relatively short time is sufficient to sterilize the product, but in the low-acid and medium low-acid groups the products must be heated at higher temperatures for times designed to minimize the chances of botulism in the can—i.e. to make the chance of survival of a spore of *Clostridium botulinum* as small as practicable. The temperature coefficient or z value (as it is known in thermobacteriology) which is the number of degrees Fahrenheit increase or decrease which will increase or decrease the death rate of bacterial spores by a factor of 10, is in this case 18. Hence a process at 258°F will have ten times the killing power of one at 240°F. Process evaluation is complex as due consideration has to be given to the time necessary for conduction of heat into the centre of the pack. Temperature coefficients for other bacterial spores vary from $z = 15$ to $z = 22$.

The cooking process has, however, a much higher temperature coefficient and, at higher temperatures, a process which gives the same equivalent sterilizing power tends to cook the food less than would be the case at a lower temperature. This may be readily understood from the following table which compares the times at different temperatures to give equivalent sterilization and equivalent cooking as measured by texture:

Peas in A2 cans

Temp. (°F)	240	250	260
Equivalent sterilization times (mins)	30	14½	9½
Equivalent processing times (mins)	30	19	13

Modern techniques using hydrostatic cookers, hot air cookers, and flame cookers favour processing at high temperatures for short times. Agitation of the can contents by spinning reduces also the time required for heat penetration. The latter development is important for soft fruits such as strawberries where processing times at 212°F are much reduced with a corresponding improvement in texture. As regards processing at higher temperatures this can lead to an improvement in products which in the past have tended to be overcooked in the interests of hygiene. In fact shorter equivalent processing times tend to reduce loss of colour, loss of vitamins, and softening of texture.

These advantages could be offset by failure to inactive enzymes. Enzymes vary greatly in their heat resistance. Thus catalase has a temperature coefficient (z value) of less than 10°F while peroxidase has been reported to have temperature coefficients of between 46 and 86, the most reliable value probably being 49·8. A high temperature short time process (HTST) may render a product commercially sterile, but enzymes could still remain active and give rise to off-flavours in the pack during storage.

β-Glucosidase in plum kernels is another enzyme system of high heat resistance which, though not producing off-flavours, leads to accelerated corrosion in the can.

It has further been shown that enzymes, notably peroxidase, can be regenerated and there seems little reason why other enzymes may not exhibit the same property. In the frozen vegetable industry blanching for too short a time in boiling water could lead to enzyme regeneration on storage. The period of regeneration is short and seems to fall off after a time, but the activity during this time may be all that is needed to impair the quality.

B. Some Examples of the Definition of Desirable Characters According to Purpose

Because of the changing habits of the population and the mechanization of farms and growers' holdings, the characteristics of varieties required today are not the same as those that were needed in the last decade. Plant breeders are no longer crossing the best strains of commercial types of fruits and vegetables in the hope that a new and better variety will emerge. The special characters demanded by the machines which harvest and handle the raw materials and the processors who can and quick freeze fruit and vegetables, are being purposely introduced to inbred lines of parent plants so that the new variety is not the result of much guesswork but a planned, if long awaited, certainty. The desirable characters of the most widely appreciated fruits and vegetables do not go unrecognized in plant breeding circles and research workers all over the world are seeking to improve our existing varieties to meet the changing demands of the housewife who, because of education and advertisement, is becoming more critical and selective in her choice of products.

The characters of any one variety which make it superior to another are many and differ widely from fruit to fruit and vegetable to vegetable. In general the producer requires a variety which does not present many growing difficulties, is easy to handle when harvesting and above all yields well, giving him a good return for his financial outlay. The processor is also interested in these broad characteristics especially if he relies on contracts for his supply of raw material. More important to him, however, is the quality of his final processed product and this will depend on the chemical composition, colour, flavour, texture, size, and shape of the raw material.

It is not possible to give a general yet satisfactory account of the desirable characteristics of fruit and vegetables for their various purposes. Those examples given in the following paragraphs have been chosen as illustrations of the characters—physical, chemical, or horticultural—which are important in crops of temperate climates according to the market for which they are intended. Similar considerations may be expected to affect the quality of almost any fruit or vegetable.

C. Fruits

1. Apples

The production of apples falls into two distinct groups—that for the dessert trade and that for the culinary market.

For dessert purposes an apple variety must have an attractive appearance to appeal to the consumer who will only buy brightly coloured fruits for eating in the raw state. Conversely, culinary varieties must be predominantly green skinned and often they are offered to the public undermature. Apples are subject to a number of pests and diseases which, if allowed to attack the fruits, will cause blemishes which may render the crop virtually unsaleable. For this reason many protective sprays are applied while the crop is growing.

Probably the finest flavoured dessert apple which is grown to perfection in Great Britain is Cox's Orange Pippin. This variety is sold by name, it does not colour brightly, but ripens to a mellow golden and red in November and December. Worcester Permain colours brightly and is one of the first dessert fruits to reach the fresh market. Laxton's Superb and Ellison's Orange are also grown as dessert varieties.

The selection of seedlings may be based successfully on sugar/acid ratio.

Culinary varieties are used for both the fresh market and for processing. It is important that apples for processing should be of a size and shape suitable for mechanical peeling and preparation, and have a firm flesh which does not discolour during the heating process. Two varieties which are used widely for processing are Newton Wonder and Bramley Seedling.

2. Blackberries and Loganberries

Both these cane fruits are used for jam, canning, freezing and jelly manufacture.

The hedge blackberry which grows wild throughout Europe is a composite species consisting of many sub-species. It is considered to have a better flavour than most cultivated species, but the seeds are rather woody. In cultivated varieties the seeds are not so noticeable, especially if the fruit is harvested when fully ripe.

It is possible that loganberries may increase in popularity now that new heavier yielding strains are available. This fruit is not grown as much for the fresh market as it is for the processing trade where it gives a very good product.

3. Cherries

The majority of the cherries grown in northern climates are intended for the fresh market and require a skilled team to pick and grade them satisfactorily. They should be treated carefully as when ripe they are a juicy fruit the quality of which can easily be affected by bad handling.

Cherries for processing are mainly of the white fleshed varieties, of which Napoleon Biggareau and Kentish Biggareau are the best. These are coloured red and used for cocktail and glace cherries as well as for dessert purposes. A cherry with an acid flavour is the Morello, which as a culinary variety gives a very attractive canned product.

Black cherries may also be canned, but tend to turn a bluish colour when heated. They make a high-quality preserve when packed in glass containers

Mechanical handling of cherries—stalk removal and pitting—is now universal and the fruit must be harvested with this factor in mind. The selection of varieties must also take into consideration the possible damage to texture resulting from these mechanical processes and from grading machines.

4. Gooseberries

The production of gooseberries might well be divided into two broad groups depending on the purpose for which they are grown: the dessert trade, and culinary and processing trade.

For the dessert trade the red berried varieties are normally grown. These are picked when almost ripe to reach the consumer at the proper stage of maturity. Mention should be made of the specialized production of the green berried variety Leveller. In some districts the berries of this variety are grown to an extremely large size before marketing as dessert fruit. Other green berried varieties are often allowed to ripen for the dessert market.

Varieties for canning differ widely from those used for the dessert trade. No variety which will ripen to a red colour is used as these discolour badly when canned, either as a result of the brown coloration caused by the presence of anthocyanogens or through the formation of blue complexes between tin and anthocyanins. A satisfactory canning variety should have a full sharp flavour, a pale green colour, and the veins on the berry surface should not be prominent. All fruits damaged by insects giving rise to corky areas should be excluded. Unlike fruit for the dessert trade gooseberries for canning should be picked when fully grown, but not ripe. Mechanical handling involves winnowing to remove trash, size grading, and washing, and the berries must be sufficiently firm to withstand these processes without damage. During the

3

snibbing process which removes the "tops and tails" the skins are bruised and the syrup in which the fruit is canned is thus enabled to penetrate the fruit. Without this step, the fruit would shrivel badly when immersed in syrup as a result of osmotic effects.

In common with many other products the berries for canning should be even in size. Fruits less than 10/16 inch (16 mm) in diameter are considered to be too small for canning. Other varieties which are commonly used for canning include Keepsake and Whitesmith.

5. Pears

As with apples, pears are grown for dessert and culinary purposes. They are always harvested in an immature condition and allowed to ripen off the tree.

When they are canned the varieties Williams'. Bon Chretien (Bartlett) and Conference give good results although a disadvantage of the latter is its long thin shape and high pH value. Packham's Triumph is also used for canning but has less flavour than the Williams'. Pears that are prone to discolour when heated may be detected by applying a chemical test for anthocyanogens (see p. 9).

6. Plums and Damsons

Varieties of plums for canning can be divided into three groups (a), Yellow, (b) Red and (c) Purple types. Of the Yellow plums, the Pershore or Yellow Egg is probably most widely used. It should be canned when the colour is just turning from green to yellow.

For both colour and flavour, the Victoria is outstanding amongst the red plums. Unfortunately it suffers from a defect which presents a real problem to the canning of plums, that of stone gum. Fruits affected by this disorder present a most unsightly appearance after the fruit has been processed because a small spot of gum present in the fruit prior to canning swells and causes the processed fruit to break exposing a mass of pink jelly. No satisfactory solution has yet been found to remedy this disorder, the incidence of which in any year correlates with the rainfall during the period when the fruits are developing on the tree.

The greengage and the Cambridge Gage give good results when canned. Regularity of size and freedom from skin blemishes are important for good quality packs.

Whereas plums for canning must be of a good medium size, the damson is a smaller fruit and fruits suitable for canning are consequently much smaller. One variety of damson that is superior to all the rest for processing is the Shropshire Prune: it has a very good flavour and a typical shape which is pointed at one end. Damsons for canning should be deep purple all over with no brown or green areas as these will lead to discoloured patches when heat-processed.

7. Raspberries

The raspberry is an important soft fruit which is grown most widely in Scotland in the counties of Perth and Angus although large acreages are also grown in the southern half of England. Its quality—colour and flavour—is favoured by growth in high latitudes.

For canning the fruits should have a deep crimson colour and a full rich flavour. The size should be even and not less than half an inch (13 mm) diameter and the texture firm enough to prevent the fruit from pulping during the sterilizing process. Lloyd George and Norfolk Giant are two varieties which have been considered as fairly suitable for canning for many years, but neither are grown on a wide scale now. The fruits of Norfolk Giant are rather small and the yield is poor; Lloyd George is susceptible to virus diseases and many stocks are now infected. Probably the most widely used variety of raspberry for canning today is Malling Jewel which has most of the qualities required of a good processing raspberry. Other varieties such as Malling Promise and Malling Exploit have not given good results in canning tests. The former tends to give a product with a brownish hue and in the latter a large hole after the plug has been removed causes the fruit to collapse during heating in the can.

For quick freezing the same qualities are required as for canning and the same varieties have given good results.

The variety Malling Jewel is not so suitable for jam making as it is for canning and quick freezing. This is because of its tendency to give "blind" seeds—the effect of this is to render the seeds almost invisible in the jam product, an effect which is undesirable as the purchaser expects raspberry jam to have clean bright seeds clearly visible and the product not to appear cloudy as is the case with "blindness". The cause of this phenomenon is not known. Lloyd George and Norfolk Giant are also used in jam making.

Research workers both at the Scottish Horticultural Research Institute and at East Malling Research Station are seeking to breed varieties superior to those already in commercial use. The new varieties will have improved flavour and size of fruit and be resistant to the virus vector and other diseases.

8. Rhubarb

The fleshy petioles of this plant are canned in syrup and for this reason the product is considered to be a fruit despite the fact that it is, botanically speaking, a vegetable.

On the fresh market, rhubarb may be either "forced" or natural, the former being presented as a very early spring crop. Forced rhubarb is grown in specially heated sheds from which all light is excluded. The "crowns" are packed tightly in beds and harvesting (pulling) should commence 4–5 weeks after the beginning of forcing. The exclusion of all light, except during harvesting, means that no green colouring matter develops in the stalks. The crop should not be spindly and the desirable colour is a good red on a pale background.

Natural rhubarb grown in the field should be capable of producing heavy crops and the stalks should have an attractive colour. Unfortunately these two characteristics are not found in the same variety at the present time; green stalked varieties crop well, and good, red stalked varieties are often very low yielding.

Canned rhubarb in syrup is one of the most widely packed fruits in Great Britain probably because it is easy to produce and because of the availability of the raw material at a time when no other fruit is in season. The sticks of varieties for canning should be not greater than one and half inches across and should be free from tough fibres. Usually the younger sticks are taken in preference to the older sticks which tend to become coarse as the season progresses. Varieties which are suitable for canning are Prince Albert, Merton Foremost, Victoria, and Timperley Early which produce crops in early spring and can be processed before the true fruits such as gooseberries and strawberries become available.

9. Strawberries

Strawberries must be one of the most popular fruits of temperate zones, not only as a canned and quick frozen product but also as a fresh fruit.

There are many considerations to be taken into account when selecting strawberry varieties for commercial production. Performance both in the field and on processing are equally important. Strawberry plants must be certified virtually free from virus and be resistant to red core disease. For the fresh market the fruit should be fully ripe when it is sold with not more than one third of the surface uncoloured. It should always be picked with the calyx attached and packed in a firm dry condition. Strawberries are packed in different grades according to size.

For processing, the fruit should be a bright even red colour with a good flavour. Uniform shape is required for an even pack and any blemished fruits should be excluded. The core of the berry may present problems as, when the calyx is removed, the core may either leave the fruit with the calyx or remain in the berry. If the core remains in the berry then it should not be tough. If the core is removed, the hole which remains should not be large or the berry may collapse or alternatively an air pocket may be trapped which will interfere with sterilization during heat processing.

New varieties have originated from Cambridge, Invergowrie, Bayfordbury and more recently from Europe and Japan. A popular variety today for the fresh market and the processing trade is Cambridge Favourite. This is a round berried variety with a pale colour (which takes artificial colour well) and a moderate flavour. It crops more heavily than most other varieties in many parts of the U.K. It yields good sized fruits over the whole of its season and husks easily, the plug remaining in the berry. Another Cambridge variety grown fairly widely is Cambridge Vigour which is often used for quick freezing.

The new varieties from Scotland are Talisman and Redgauntlet which were released to replace Auchincruive Climax but neither was up to the standard of this variety which, as is now well known, failed eventually through some genetical weakness. Several red varieties of German origin, e.g. Senga Sengana are being developed for use in the preserving and canning industries.

D. Vegetables

1. Brassica Crops

This large and important group of vegetables includes cabbages, savoys, broccoli, cauliflower, Brussels sprouts and calabrese.

a. Cabbage and Savoy

The cabbage can be produced all the year round in a temperate climate and is rarely expensive to buy on the fresh market.

Winter cabbage and savoys provide green vegetables during the winter months. Spring greens and spring cabbage become available early in the year and these are followed by summer and late autumn cabbages.

There is little demand for canned cabbage although the small firm heads may be canned. Red cabbage is used for pickling. Sauerkraut, which is finely shredded cabbage allowed to ferment and then canned, is popular on the continent and in America.

b. Cauliflower and Broccoli

There is very little difference between a true cauliflower and a broccoli. Broccoli are rather more hardy and the centre leaves curl over the curd to protect it, whereas in a cauliflower the leaves spread causing the curd to be exposed whilst it matures.

Cauliflowers may be produced all the year round although they are in short supply during March and April. They are a popular vegetable on the fresh market. Cauliflowers are sometimes canned but difficulty is experienced in retaining the whiteness of the curd. They are also frozen as whole heads for the catering trade.

Calabrese is a type of broccoli which has increased in popularity in recent years. The small green heads are cut in July, August and September and are quick frozen, when they make a very useful vegetable pack. Desirable heads are about four inches long and have a thick succulent stem. Side shoots do not develop to the required extent.

c. The Brussels Sprout

This is a very popular vegetable in Great Britain from late August through the winter months. Solid sprouts of a size one and quarter to one and a half inches in diameter are required for the fresh market.

This vegetable has received some attention with regard to mechanical harvesting and prototype machines have been built which will do this task satisfactorily. This is especially important for the processing trade as increasing quantities of Brussels sprouts are quick frozen each year. For freezing, sprouts of a deep green colour and with a diameter of three-quarters to one and an eighth inch are required.

2. Carrots

This important vegetable is grown wherever the soil is suitable. Carrots may be grown under glass for the very early fresh market. Carrots grown for these early markets are bunched and the foliage is left on the root. The maincrop carrots are sown in the spring to be harvested during the autumn and winter, the tops being removed before they are sent to market. Large acreages are grown for the canning industry and these too are harvested during the autumn and winter months.

A good carrot should have a clear bright red colour and a tender crisp texture. The core of the root should not be tough and woody and, especially for canning, should possess a good colour similar to that of the flesh.

Varieties suitable for growing for the early market both under frames and in the open are Amsterdam Forcing and Ideal.

The maincrop carrots have been divided into five groups according to their root shape and size by the National Institute of Agricultural Botany (Cambridge)—viz. Nantes, Berlikum, Chantenay, Long Chantenay, and Autumn King.

In the canning industry carrots may be canned whole, diced, or sliced. Whole carrots should have a shoulder diameter of between half and one and a quarter inches and this can be achieved by controlling the plant population by seed rate. For whole carrots the type Red-cored Chantenay is used almost exclusively. For slicing, a carrot with a maximum diameter of two and half inches is used. For slicing and dicing the types Red-cored Chantenay and Autumn King are used; they are allowed to grow to a good size by using a low seed rate per acre.

Carrots of excellent quality are grown on peat soils such as occur in Ireland.

3. Green Beans

There are three main types of green beans grown for processing and market—(1) French beans, (2) Runner beans, and (3) Boad beans.

For processing the French bean is important especially for freezing.

Varieties suitable for freezing and canning are Processor, Tenderlong, and Harvester. The climbing French bean Blue Lake is also used for processing. A bean which is grown exclusively for canning is Keeney's Stringless Green Refugee, which is a pale green variety with purple flecks.

Much work has been done to evolve a method of measuring the maturity of the French bean. So far no entirely satisfactory method is available and beans are harvested when they are considered to be ready. Machines are available which harvest the entire crop at one picking. For mechanical harvesting, varieties are required which hold their beans upright, have straight pods, and which mature together.

Runner beans produced for the fresh market may be grown as pinched beans or by permitting the plants to grow up canes, poles or wire. Pinched beans, where the leading shoots are pinched back regularly, usually mature earlier than poled beans, but are prone to infection by moulds and, as they often lie on the ground, are liable to be soiled. Later in the season, poled beans provide a better quality crop.

Normally scarlet-flowered beans are grown and suitable varieties are Kelvedon Wonder (early), Prizewinner (mid season), Streamline and Princess. For canning the white-flowered variety, Czar, is normally used. This variety gives a good quality product with a satisfactory colour, suitable for artificial colouring.

Unlike the French and runner beans, the seeds of the broad bean only are consumed, the pod being discarded. The broad bean is a hardy annual and is grown for both the fresh market and for processing. For canning only white-flowered varieties are suitable. Varieties which contain anthocyanogens (leucoanthocyanin) have coloured flowers and produce seeds which after processing become brown, and give the brine a muddy appearance. This phenomenon is due to the effect of the heat process on the anthocyanogen content. There are only a few varieties which do not contain these substances. By far the most widely grown variety for canning is Triple White (Threefold White), a variety which is also becoming popular on the fresh market. Other white-flowered varieties are Minerva, Staygreen, and Lux, although Lux is unsatisfactory because of its low yields.

For quick freezing the white-seeded variety Longpod Aquadulce is often used.

4. Peas

The production of peas can be divided into three main parts according to their intended use: (1) Fresh market, (2) Harvesting dry, and (3) Processing (mainly canning, freezing and dehydration).

Peas for the fresh market are picked in an immature condition but when the pods are fully developed. The pickers discard the overmature and undermature pods and pack the remainder into nets which hold 20 lb of peas.

Peas are sown to mature at certain times during the season; thus they are known as first early, second early, maincrop, and late. The most popular British varieties in each of these groups are Kelvedon Wonder, Meteor, and Clipper (first early), Little Marvel, Kelvedon Triumph (second early), Onward, The Lincoln (maincrop) and Kelvedon Wonder (late).

Peas for harvesting dry may be used for retailing as packets of dried peas, or for canning as processed peas. In the latter uniformity of texture is extremely important and most U.K. canners now import dried peas, chiefly from America, because they possess a more even texture than those grown and harvested dry in Europe. The variety normally imported from America is Alaska.

In Britain and N. Europe the varieties Servo, Rondo and Unica (of the Dutch Blue type) are grown for the dried pea market. The Dutch Blues are round, fairly small peas. If a large pea is required Marrowfats, which are wrinkle-seeded, are grown. Varieties are Harrison's Glory and Big Ben.

For direct canning and quick freezing the wrinkled-seeded type of pea is used almost exclusively in Great Britain in preference to the smooth-seeded type, because it is sweeter in flavour. On the contrary, most European countries prefer the smaller round-seeded varieties.

The pea processing industries are very highly organized and varieties are chosen which will mature consecutively throughout the season so that there is no wastage of labour, or equipment which is idle, whilst waiting for the next crop of peas.

In order to produce a pack of top quality the pea crop must be harvested at the correct stage of maturity. In Europe and the U.S.A. the instrument used to measure the maturity of a crop of peas is the tenderometer. This indicates the maturity of a sample of peas by measuring the force required to press it through a standard grid. Peas for quick freezing should give a tenderometer reading of 95–105 and for canning the reading should be 115–120. A similar instrument that has found favour in W. Europe is the Dutch hardness-meter.[21]

Varieties for quick freezing are always dark in colour. Dark Skin Perfection is widely grown, but gives rather large peas and produces a leafy haulm. There is a trend for freezers to select small-seeded types such as Olympic. Other varieties are Kelvedon Wonder, Perfected Freezer, and Lincoln.

For canning, pale-seeded varieties have been widely used in the past, and that which is considered to be the best for this purpose is Gregory's Surprise, a second early with a thin long haulm. Other varieties used for canning are Kelvedon Wonder, The Lincoln, and Charles I. Of the smooth-seeded type European canners favour Roi des fins verts, Serpette nain cent pour un, and Chemin long. A valuable book on pea varieties is "Les variétés de pois cultivés en France" by R. Fourmont, Paris 1956.[29]

During recent years the method of growing pea crops for processing has been gradually changing. With the introduction of efficient weedkillers it has been possible to grow peas at the optimum plant population, considered to be four to seven inches. Mobile viners or strategically placed viner stations separate the peas from the rest of the plant. However, rapid deterioration of quality follows after vining due to enzymic action and the peas must be washed and cooled immediately after vining if serious loss of quality is to be avoided.

5. Potatoes

The potato has become one of the staple foods of temperate climates, and is available in some form during every month of the year. In Britain the first new potatoes to appear on the market are imported from North Africa, the Canary Islands and Spain, and later the Island of Jersey exports new potatoes to the mainland. The first early potatoes grown in Great Britain come from favoured places in Cornwall and Pembrokeshire. Early, second early, and maincrop potatoes then follow from many parts of the country, much of the maincrop being clamped to provide a supply through the autumn, winter, and into early spring.

Potatoes are grown from "seed" which are tubers grown in selected areas, such as Scotland and Northern Ireland, especially for propagation. Seed produced in open districts of good altitude has been shown to give better results than seed grown elsewhere. In addition strict inspections are made of all potatoes being grown for seed to ensure that a minimum of virus infection is present.

Potatoes are not only grown for the fresh market but increasingly for processing in many forms. They may be canned as new or old potatoes. There is not a great demand for canned old potatoes but there is a greater demand for new potatoes even though it is difficult to retain the delicate flavour of this vegetable.

Potatoes are frozen in the form of chips (fresh and partly fried) and cooked and mashed. Other forms of processed potatoes are crisps and dehydrated slices and powder.

The chemical composition of the potato is of importance in regard to the behaviour of the vegetable on processing. Probably most scientific investigation has been directed towards the control of chemical constitution of potatoes for chip or crisp manufacture, and several guiding principles have evolved. The yield of fried crisps depends on the absorption of fat by the potato slices and this is related to the specific gravity of the tubers in such a way that high yields are obtained from tubers of high specific gravity and vice versa. This relationship, however, is only *generally* true; varietal differences have to be taken into account and seasonal variations in specific gravity are important. A similar generality links specific gravity with the texture of the cooked tubers; low specific gravity (1·05) is associated with "soggy" texture and high specific gravity (1·10) with mealy texture.[30]

When fried in fat, potato slices or chips turn brown to a degree related to their sugar content, and perhaps more particularly to their reducing sugar content. Denny and Thornton[22,23] considered that for the production of a light-coloured product, the reducing sugar content of the potatoes should not exceed 0·5%.

The sugar content of potatoes changes during storage, reducing sugars increasing in stored tubers to an extent inversely proportional to the temperature of storage. The maximum practical storage temperature appears to be 45°F and at this temperature the accumulation of reducing-sugars is minimal. Any higher temperature promotes excessive sprouting. Further information on potato chemistry and quality is contained in a review by Brown[24] and in the proceedings of a Symposium on "Potatoes for the Food Processing Industries" published in "Food Trade Review," August 1966, pp. 38–52, September 1966, pp. 41–49.

6. Red Beetroot

Both round rooted and long rooted varieties of red beet are grown for the fresh market and examples of these are Detroit Red Globe and Cheltenham Green Top respectively. For processing, beetroot may be canned whole or sliced. For the former, small round beets are required and a variety which is very popular is Detroit Red Globe. For slicing a variety which is cylindrical in shape is used, Cylindra. This gives much less wastage when sliced transversely for processing or for pickling.

Accidental crossing of red beet with sugar beet gives rise to unsatisfactory seedlings having a pale colour, sometimes uniformly pale, sometimes with very pale rings. Over-mature beet also tends to be unsatisfactory in colour as well as tending towards fibrous texture.

7. Spinach

Spinach may be broadly divided into two types: summer spinach which is round seeded and winter spinach which is prickly seeded. Either of these may be sown in the opposite season and produce a useful crop.

Spinach may be processed satisfactorily although special attention must be given to the canning process to ensure satisfactory heat penetration. It may be canned as whole leaf or purée or it may be quick frozen. It is important to ensure that spinach for processing first receives a very thorough wash as its form of growth makes it prone to contamination with soil.

3. CANDIED AND GLACE FLOWERS AND FRUITS

Many fruits and flowers are preserved by impregnating with sugar to such an extent as to be "self-preserving", that is to say their solids content is so high that spoilage organisms are unable to grow on them. The quality of the more exotic products, such as crystallized roses and violets, is assured by the demands of the consumer; being essentially luxury articles, they are unlikely to sell at their normally high price unless the customer is satisfied. More prosaic materials like candied peel (which is more correctly termed "syruped drained peel") and glace cherries are found in several qualities.

Such materials are not manufactured from fresh fruits; there is an intermediate brining or pickling process upon which much of the ultimate quality depends. Details of the process have been described elsewhere.[25] It is necessary to ensure not only that the finished article contains a sufficiently high concentration of dissolved solids to preserve it from attack by yeasts and moulds, but also that there shall be a sufficient proportion of invert sugars to prevent crystallization. This proportion may vary with the product but is generally similar to that required to avoid crystallization in jams, about 25–30% of the total sugar content. Adventitious metals affect the colour and the texture of glace fruits. The effect may be adverse, as in the case of dark staining by traces of iron, or overall browning induced by concentrations of copper as low as 5 ppm. This is a serious defect in light-coloured products like lemon and orange peel. The effect of calcium and magnesium on the texture, on the other hand, may be advantageous. While too much calcium will toughen the skins of cherries, for example, to an undesirable extent, the fruits have to withstand quite severe conditions during manufacture and calcium is often added in some form to preserve the shape of the fruit.

4. ROLE OF ADDITIVES IN QUALITY MAINTENANCE

Substances added to fruit and vegetables or to their products may be intended to preserve or to improve quality and they include examples of the whole range of food additives. Technically, straightforward preservatives provide the simplest case, since these are intended to prevent undesirable changes of enzymic or microbial origin. Examples are the prevention of the browning of dried fruits (and incidentally of microbial spoilage) by the addition of small concentrations of sulphur dioxide; the prevention of mould growth on dried or syruped products by means of sorbic acid; and, in a rather different way, the use of sulphur dioxide or benzoic acid as preservatives in fruit drinks and sauces. The extent to which such preservatives are used is dictated largely by legislation, deliberate preservation by chemical means being strictly controlled in most countries. National legislation must be consulted in order to ascertain whether such methods may be used in any particular case. As a general rule chemical preservatives should not be used unless there is no alternative means of avoiding the change in question. This is where a precise knowledge of the mechanisms involved in the change becomes indispensable. Enzymic browning of tissues by the intervention of phenol oxidases, for example, can often be inhibited by a reducing agent, and although sulphur dioxide is effective, ascorbic acid, which suffers from none of the objections which apply to sulphur dioxide, is often equally effective. When such an additive is acting as a reducing agent, the usual laws of chemistry apply and it remains effective only until it has itself been oxidized, after which time a shift in the E_h will occur and the undesired reaction will resume.

Colouring matters are a special case of food additives necessary to preserve an attribute of quality. Colouring matters cannot successfully obscure an undesirable off-colour; brown fruits will still be unattractive after colouring; dark-coloured peas can never be made into fresh-looking bright peas by adding a green colour. The use of colouring matters in fruit and vegetable products is quite legitimate if it enhances the appearance of the product and makes it more acceptable to the consumer. In some instances it is very necessary to add colour. Dried peas, for example, if canned without artificial colouring matter have a grey unattractive colour with no appeal to the appetite of any but the ravenous. Slightly coloured green, they are the most popular canned vegetable in the U.K. and contribute materially to the nutrition of the British nation. The alleged toxicity of certain colouring matters is not under consideration in this context; the approval or disapproval of food additives is in other hands. For the manufacturer of food products the principle should be to use artificial colouring matters to enhance the quality of his products and not to attempt to mask any defect, and to use the minimum concentration consistent with this objective.

Flavouring materials, natural or artificial, are used to a lesser extent in fruit and vegetables than are colouring matters. Often their use is dictated by tradition, e.g. mint in canned peas; vegetable extracts in petits pois à l'étuvé. Provided that they meet a demand and improve the product, there is no reason why they should not be used, provided national legislation permits the practice. The principle should be the same as governs the use of colouring matters: added flavours should enhance the quality of a pack in comparison with that of a good quality packed without added flavour. They should not be used to mask an undesirable flavour which is due to poor quality raw material, and indeed it is rarely possible to do this successfully. They can, however, make good a natural deficiency under certain circumstances.

Flavour is one of the properties of food about which very little is known. It is due always to a balance of constituents and the effect of an additive can rarely be forecast. As an example may be quoted the effect of adding a small concentration of saccharin to a mixture of natural lemon juice and sugar. The result is not merely an intensification of sweetness, but an enrichment of the flavour as a whole. Similarly the addition of ascorbic acid to a fruit juice or product frequently restores what may only be called a freshness to the flavour. This is probably the result of the reducing action of the ascorbic acid reversing some of the oxidative changes that have taken place during the conversion of the material from fresh fruit to product.

Calcium salts are used quite extensively to prevent undesirable breakdown of fruits and vegetables during processing. Since calcium is a natural constituent of all foods and is essential to proper nutrition, no serious objection to the use of its salts for this purpose has ever been made. It is most commonly employed as the chloride, but may affect the flavour in this form as calcium chloride is somewhat bitter. Calcium lactate is claimed to be free from this objection. Apples for canning or drying, canned tomatoes and potatoes, among other materials, are commonly "firmed" by the addition of calcium in a suitable form. The addition may be effected by a pre-process soak or dip, hot or cold, or it may be made directly to the liquid in which the material is packed.

5. CONTROL OF QUALITY BY REGULATION

The control of food quality by legislation is both general and specific. In British law, the two general sections of the Food and Drugs Act, 1955 state respectively:

"(1) No person shall add any substance to food, use any substance as an ingredient in the preparation of food, abstract any constituent from any food, or subject food to any other process or treatment, so as (in any such case) to render the food injurious to health, with intent that the food shall be sold for human consumption in that state.

(2) No person shall sell "to the prejudice of the purchaser any food . . . which is not of the nature, or not of the substance, or not of the quality, of the food . . . demanded by the purchaser . . .".

In France the first section of the Law of the 1st August 1905, is of clearly similar intent:

"Quiconque aura trompé ou tenté de tromper le contractant: Soit sur la nature, les qualités substantielles, la composition et la teneur en principes utiles de toutes merchandises; Soit sur leur espèce ou leur origine . . .sera puni de . . .".

Very similar general legislation is no doubt to be found in most countries. This protects the purchaser or consumer against deliberate fraud or accidental misrepresentation, according to the interpretation of the law as practised in the country concerned. It also provides protection against developments in processes or changes in raw materials or packaging practice that might be to the detriment of the consumer and which could not be foreseen at the time the legislation was enacted. For example canned dried peas must not be represented to the purchaser as being canned fresh peas; nor must any other variety of plum be described as Victoria plums; decaffeinated coffee must not be passed as whole ground coffee; no manufactured food may contain any foreign body that would render it *injurious to health* (according to the current interpretation of the phrase) or that would render it of a quality inferior to that expected by the purchaser. Complaints of insect or mould fragments in fruit or vegetable products may be held to contravene either or both of these provisions of the general law. The maintenance of a level of quality is thus assured.

It is, however, necessary to introduce specific regulations in order to improve the quality of food or to assist in the interpretation of the general law, and this is done in different ways in different countries. There may be specific regulations having the force of law to govern the composition and finer quality of certain foods. In many countries, for example, size is used as the prime criterion of quality for fresh peas and regulations have appeared laying down precisely the sizes of canned or frozen peas to which the various popular descriptions may be applied. In Germany, such regulations have evolved from trade standards and are now statutory. They have the character of legal definitions.

Much use is also made of trade standards or "codes of practice" that serve the same purpose, but are not in themselves part of the statute law. The use that is made of such standards of quality depends on the judiciary system of the country, but the object is always the same, to prevent unfair competition by setting a minimum standard of quality to be met by any products sold under a common description. The density of syrup used in the canning of fruit is a factor that is suitable for control in this way. Because of the interchange of water and soluble substances between the fruit and the syrup—initially a simple sugar solution—in which it is canned, the final density of the syrup is very different from the original density. During processing and storage sugar diffuses into the fruit while water, soluble acids, and natural soluble sugars diffuse out of the fruit into the liquid. The attainment of equilibrium takes about 15–30 days, depending on storage conditions. The final density could be calculated with reasonable accuracy if the total weights of soluble solids natural to the fruit, of added sugar, and of water were known, but the natural variation in water content of raw fruit is such that nothing better than a rough estimate is normally possible. In the case of fruit packed in 40° Brix syrup, the soluble solids concentration in the fruit is approximately one quarter or less of that in the syrup used. If, therefore, one can contains 10 g more fruit than its neighbour and consequently 10 g less syrup, the difference in soluble solids content between the two cans is 3 g *from this cause alone.* The difference in water content, also 3 g, aggravates the situation and in cans containing a total weight of fruit and syrup of 300 g, such a variation in filled weight would cause a difference of about 2° Brix in the final density. Variations in the filled weight of fruit depend on the size of the individual units and are greater with large whole fruit than with small fruits or slices, segments, etc. There are also unavoidable variations in the volume of syrup filled into the cans due to air trapped within or between fruit pieces, mechanical difficulties in maintaining a precise filling level, spillage on conveyors and closing machines, and syrup temperature. Add to these the natural variation in fruit composition—which depends on maturity, variety, climate, and even growing area—and it becomes obvious why the precise control of final syrup density in canned fruit is virtually impossible.

Conversely, the estimation of original syrup density from final density is bedevilled by the same variables. The strict legal control of syrup density is, therefore, not practical and control is better left to a less rigid system.

In canned fruit and vegetables the definition of quality is inevitably bound up with considerations of quantity since the product is a mixture of fruit or vegetable with syrup or brine. The vexed question of the proportion of solid to liquid therefore has to be considered and as explained above in connection with canned fruit, this changes during processing and storage. Canned vegetables also change for similar reasons, but not always in the same direction. Starchy vegetables absorb water from the brine during processing and the final weight of "solid" is then greater than the original raw weight. The weight of the solid content of a can is determined by separation from the liquid portion on a sieve and is known as the *drained weight.* Its precise determination is difficult since temperature, the size of the sieve, and time of draining all affect the weight of the drained material. Standardized conditions are therefore necessary in order to obtain comparable results. The drained weight of canned fruit is affected by all the variables that affect equilibrium syrup density, with the addition of the serious effects of processing and transport. Canned vegetables are affected to a lesser extent. The whole subject was considered very fully by Adam[26] who produced the following table summarizing the results of British practice (Table 2). This illustrates very vividly the spread of drained weights obtained in practice even when all factors were controlled to the highest practicable degree.

The conclusion to be drawn from these data is that the control of canned fruit quality by drained weight and syrup density can only be relied upon to show up gross discrepancies and that to be reliable, control over the ingredients filled into the cans must be exercised at the factory. This system has been

D. DICKINSON

TABLE 2. Drained weight of fruit and vegetables in A2 cans

Fruit or veg.	Weight (oz)			Percentage of cans below the weights shown (oz)										
	Prescribed minimum	Average filled	Average drained	6	7	8	9	10	11	12	13	14	15	16
BB	11·5	12·3	9·6	—	—	—	—	—	—	—	—	—	—	—
BC	11.5	12.1	10·3	—	—	—	—	—	—	—	—	—	—	—
C	12·0	12·6	11·2	0	0	0	2	8	37	82	98	100	100	100
D	12·0	13·0	11·4	0	0	0	0	5	31	78	97	100	100	100
G	11·5	12·1	11·4	0	0	0	0	6	28	81	98	100	100	100
L	11·5	12·2	9·1	—	—	—	—	—	—	—	—	—	—	—
P.G	12·0	12·8	10·7	0	0	2	8	27	57	91	100	100	100	100
P.R	12·0	12.9	10·7	0	0	0	4	23	63	91	99	100	100	100
P.V	12·0	12·9	11·6	0	0	0	1	7	25	67	92	99	100	100
R	11·5	12·1	9·7	—	—	—	—	—	—	—	—	—	—	—
RH	11·0	11·8	11·8	0	0	0	2	17	57	89	99	100	100	100
S	11·5	12·2	7·9	0	12	56	91	99	100	100	100	100	100	100
BN.S	10·5	11·1	11·5	—	—	—	—	—	—	—	—	—	—	—
BT.W	12·5	—	13·5	—	—	—	—	—	—	—	—	—	—	—
BT.S	12·5	13·4	13·7	0	0	0	0	0	0	3	23	72	91	100
CT.W	12·5	13·1	13·2	0	0	0	0	0	0	2	36	88	99	100
CT.S	12·5	13·3	13·4	0	0	0	0	0	2	8	48	85	95	100
CT.D	12·5	13·0	13·2	0	0	0	0	0	0	4	33	88	99	100
CL.H	12·5	13·5	12·8	—	—	—	—	—	—	—	—	—	—	—
MC	12·5	13·4	14·1	0	0	0	0	0	0	1	10	45	77	93
P.F	12·5	12·9	13·4	0	0	0	0	0	0	2	30	84	97	100
P.P	9·5	9·8	13·2	0	0	0	0	0	0	10	46	80	94	99
TM	11·0	—	9·7	—	—	—	—	—	—	—	—	—	—	—

Blackberries	BB	Beans, stringless or runner	BN.S
Blackcurrants	BC	Beetroot, whole	BT.W
Cherries	C	Beetroot, sliced	BT.S
Damsons	D	Carrots, whole	CT.W
Gooseberries	G	Carrots, sliced	CT.S
Loganberries	L	Carrots, diced	CT.D
Plums, golden	P.G	Celery, hearts	CL.H
Plums, red or purple	P.R	Macedoine	MC
Plums, Victoria	P.V	Peas, fresh	P.F
Raspberries	R	Peas, processed	P.P
Rhubarb	RH	Potatoes	PT
Strawberries	S	Tomatoes, in brine	TM

adopted by several countries, including the U.K. The information obtainable from the examination of canned vegetables for drained weight is more definite, but again the control of filled weight is preferable.

Optional quality grades for fruit and vegetable products, distinguished by a special mark or label are another useful form of quality improvement. The U.S.D.A. grades for canned products fall into this category. Detailed specifications are published for each grade and products declared to be of a particular grade must conform to the appropriate specification. This type of quality control would appear to be most suitable for international use since no legislation is involved. Products claimed to conform to any published specification and invoiced accordingly could be rejected by the buyer if they were found to be of inferior quality. The specification for tomato puree or paste published by the Comité International de la Conserve is believed to have been used in this way.

Acknowledgement

The authors are indebted to the Director of the Fruit and Vegetable Canning and Quick Freezing Research Association for permission to use the various figures illustrating this chapter.

REFERENCES

1. Dryden, E. C. and Hills, C. H. (1957). *Fd Technol. ii*, 589.
2. McKee, H. S., Robertson, R. N. and Lee, J. B. (1955). *Aust. J. biol. Sci.* **8**, 137.
3. Lynch, L. J., Mitchell, R. S. and Casimir, D. J. (1959). "Advances in Food Research", Vol. 9, pp. 111 (Academic Press, London).
4. Mackower, R. U. (1950). *Fd Technol.* **4**, 403.
5. Anthistle, J. M. (1961). (1961). The composition of peas in relation to texture. *Sci. Bull. No. 4, Fruit & Veg. Canning and Q.F.R.A.*, Campden.
6. Dickinson, D. and Gawler, J. H. (1956). *J. Sci. Fd Agric.* **7**, 699.
7. Rees, D. I. (1958). *J. Sci. Fd Agric.* **9**, 404.
8. Dickinson, D. (1957). *J. Sci. Fd Agric.* **8**, 721.
9. Haisman, D. R. and Knight, D. J. (1967). *J. Fd Technol.* **2**, 241–248.
10. Blundstone, H. A. W. and Dickinson, D. (1964). *J. Sci. Fd Agric.* **15**, 94.
11. Decleire, M. (1961). Le surissement de certaines conserves d'epinards. Rapp. No. 279, Inst. Nat. pour l'amelioration de conserves de legumes, Wesembeek-Ophem, Belgium.
12. Crean, D. E. C. (1966). *J. Fd Technol.* **1**, 55–61.
13. Dickinson, D., Knight, M. and Rees, D. I. (1957). *Chem. and Ind.* 1503.
14. Anthistle, J. M., Ashdown, D. R. and Dickinson, D. (1959). *J. Sci. Fd Agric.* **10**, 412.
15. Luk, B. S., Leonard, S. J. and Patel, D. S. (1960). *Fd Technol.* **14**, 53.
16. Wilder, H. K. (1948). *Nat. Canners Assoc. Res. Lab. Rept.* No. 12313–C.
17. Kramer, A., Haut, I. C., Scott, L. E. and Ide, L. E. (1949). *Proc. Am. Soc. hort. Sci.* **53**, 411.
18. Dickinson, D. (1958). *Chemy. Ind.* no. 486.
19. Crean, D. E. C. and Haisman, D. R. (1963). *J. Sci. Fd Agric.* **11**, 824.
20. Horner, G. (1936). *Rept. Fruit Veg. Preserv. Res. Stn.*, 1936–7, 37.
21. Doesburg, J. J. (1960). *Die indust. Obst. und Gemisseverwert.* **45**, (3), 51–54.
22. Denny, F. E. and Thornton, N. C. (1940). *Contr. Boyce Thomson Inst. Pl. Res.* **11**, 291.
23. Denny, F. E. and Thornton, N. C. (1941). *Contr. Boyce Thomson Inst.* **12**, 217.
24. Brown, H. D. (1960). "Advances in Food Research". Vol. 10. (Academic Press, New York).

25. Dickinson, D. (1955). *Fd Mf.* **30**, 444.
26. Adam, W. B. (1954). Inst. Wts. and Meas. Admin. (U.K.) Monthly Rev. May 1954, Supplement.
27. Bate-Smith, E. C. (1956). *Scient. Proc. R. Dubl. Soc.* **27**, 165.
28. Bate-Smith, E. C. (1962). *J. Linn. Soc. (Bot.)* **58**, 95.
29. Fourmont, R. (1956). Les variétés de pois cultivés en France. Institut National de la Recherche Agronomique, Paris.
30. Heinze, P. H., Kirkpatrick, M. E. and Dochterman, E. F. (1955). Cooking quality and compositional factors of potatoes of different varieties from several different locations. *U.S. Dept. Agr. Tech. Bull.* No. 1106.

Canned and Bottled Food Products
(Soups, Mayonnaise, Sauces and Vinegar)

D. A. SHAPTON

H. J. Heinz Co. Ltd., Hayes, Middlesex, England

1. INTRODUCTION

The aim of this chapter is to present a picture of the way in which basic principles of Quality Control are applied to the relevant packs. The views and methods given are the responsibility of the author as an individual and not necessarily those of H. J. Heinz Company Ltd.

The purpose of the Quality Control operation is to ensure the production of a pack within defined and accepted tolerances at the lowest cost. To fulfil this, the precise objective must be understood, control methods must be available and workers and work organized into a system which is able to achieve reliably the aims set for it. It must be stressed that quality control involves the total manufacturing operation and it is therefore essential to involve and get the co-operation of purchasing, ingredient storage and production planning departments as well as what is normally thought of as the "Manufacturing department".

Taking this broad view of the purpose of Quality Control, it becomes worthwhile to consult literature on Quality Control not directly concerned with food manufacture and to seek to apply such information to one's own circumstances. Reviews such as those of Caplen[1] and Gedye[2] may be found useful as well as the classic text by Juran *et al.*[3] The relationship of the worker to Quality Control is discussed by Stok[4] in a stimulating and original text which emphasizes an aspect which is sometimes overlooked, namely the importance of people in the Quality Control operation. Of direct application to the Quality Control of foods is the chapter on the Organization of Quality Control in Volume I of this book by J. Hawthorn, the text by Kramer and Twigg[5] and the review by Brokaw and Kramer.[6]

At this point it is convenient to refer to three texts which although peripheral to the content of the chapter may be of use to the student. The first is a useful definition of terms by Bender,[7] the second is a discussion of food quality[8] and the third is useful material on food technology by Potter.[9]

It is obvious that Quality Control of the ingredient materials is of considerable importance and it is proposed to deal with this topic before studying individual packs.

2. QUALITY CONTROL OF INGREDIENTS

A. Specification of ingredient materials

1. Principles upon which specifications are based

It is a common practice in many companies to have a specification for each ingredient material. The term "specification" in this context means a technical document used as the basis for a commercial transaction.

Every specification will contain one or more standards. These may be chemical, e.g. the % of butter fat in cream; physical, e.g. the minimum size of potatoes; bacteriological, e.g. the maximum thermophilic spore count of a flour; or organoleptic, e.g. the absence of bitterness in carrots. The standards which a manufacturer will wish to use will depend on the product in which the material is to be used and on the manufacturing processes through which the material will pass. There is therefore no set of standards for each material which has universal application. The practice of writing an existing standard into a specification without giving serious thought as to its appropriateness is to be deplored. The use of unnecessarily strict or lax standards is a clear indication of a lack of thought in the drafting of the specification. As the standards embodied in the specification depend partly on the manufacturing process, when processes change the specification should be examined to see whether revision is required.

The standards which are written into the specification should be realistic, and if met, should make the material acceptable. The practice of stating one standard but of accepting something worse is fundamentally unsound and will result in bringing the specification into disrepute.

It is essential, in order to be fair to the supplier, to describe test techniques in full or to give full literature references. Whenever possible official methods should be used. It is especially important that microbiological techniques should be described carefully since small differences in technique can give widely differing results. It is important that where tolerances are appropriate they should be set down in a clear, explicit manner.

2. Preparation of specifications

The preparation of a good specification is no easy matter. This is especially true when one is dealing with an unfamiliar material. It is often only after some experience in handling a material that one is made aware of precisely what needs to be specified. At an early stage therefore it may be prudent to issue a provisional specification which is described and known as such.

Although the format of a specification will vary according to the practice of the individual company, the contents may be considered under the following headings:

Identity. This is normally a precise definition of the ingredient material. Where variations in origin or composition are intended this should be explicitly stated. In passing, it may be noted here that microscopic tests are often useful to determine quickly the identity of a material.

Purity and Composition. The requirements in this section may be given under the following headings:

Chemical: this gives assay requirements, e.g. % moisture, fat, protein etc. There may also be reference to antioxidants, additives, permitted colouring matter, etc.

Physical: this states requirements for properties such as size, colour, weight, viscosity etc.

Microbiological: this refers to numbers and kinds of organisms of Public Health significance, those used as an index of the sanitary conditions of the material and those of significance in the manufacturing processes.

Filth tests: these tests are a measure of the sanitary condition of the material and include counts of specks, mould fragments, aphids, insect fragments, rot fragments, etc.

Unless legal requirements are given in a separate section, it is appropriate to draw attention here to local statutory requirements.

Packaging. This section states the net weight and form of container required for the delivery of the ingredient, whether bulk handled or individually packaged. In choosing the optimum package there are two considerations to be borne in mind besides that of the cost of the container; firstly that of the quality of the finished product, e.g. fabric sacks are undesirable where fibres may pass through the processes and contaminate the finished product; secondly that of convenience of handling the material in the factory. Having the material in the right form can not only ease the operator's work, it can also mean a saving in costs.

Transport. This section states how the material is to be transported and whether for instance, insulated or refrigerated containers are required. In some cases it may be desirable to specify any substances which *must not* be transported in the same vehicle.

Storage. This section is often for internal use but it may be issued when materials are kept in store outside the factory premises. It states the conditions of storage. These include for example temperature limits for cold stores, the length of time the material may be held in stock, and the frequency and type of checks to be made to ensure that the material remains in good condition. Where fumigation or spraying is required, it is necessary to specify the materials to be used and the method of application. In some cases it may also be desirable to specify the constructional materials of the warehouse and the way in which the ingredient material is to be stowed. It may be noted here that the storage of large quantities of seasonally produced materials through the year until the next season's crop is available requires considerable care and attention, if losses and deterioration of the material are to be kept to a minimum.

Uses. This section is for internal purposes. It is a useful practice when an ingredient material is graded, to include in the specification the usage for each grade. This then provides a central reference for this information and helps to prevent the use of an incorrect grade of material.

3. Changes of Specification

Apart from permanent changes in specifications, changes may have to be made temporarily when an emergency occurs. For example, size gradings may have to be altered or alternative varieties used during a poor vegetable season. Under such circumstances the changes should be notified to the suppliers at once. It is not sufficient merely to suspend existing specifications as this can quickly lead to the discrediting of the specification system.

4. Grading of Materials for Specific Purposes

It may be a matter of Company Policy that grading of an ingredient is not permissible, i.e. only one grade of the material is specified, but where grading as a policy is accepted it may be undertaken for a number of reasons. It may be undertaken to select batches of an ingredient material for a specific purpose without paying the supplier a premium. As an illustration of this, where the thermophilic spore count test is made as a matter of routine, it may well be not only possible but comparatively easy to isolate batches which have a very low thermophilic spore count. These may then be used, for example, in a tropical export pack where the thermophilic spoilage rate must be kept low. This type of grading is often regarded as a normal quality control function.

In those instances where a batch of ingredient material does not meet the specification and no alternative supply is available it is necessary either to cancel the intended production which may or may not result in financial loss, or to grade it for disposal in one of the following ways:

To be used as a standard ingredient in selected products only.

To be used in selected products which will themselves be graded for restricted use.

To be used after modification of the recipe in some or all of the products.

To be used in selected products with increased sterilization.

To be used after suitable treatment has been given to overcome the defect. This might include such treatment as pre-sterilization of the ingredient where excessive numbers of bacterial spores were present or special sorting to remove, for example, stones.

When grading is practised it is absolutely essential to ensure that those responsible for storing and handling the material treat each grade as a separate ingredient material. Unless this is done there is a serious risk of the wrong grade being used in the final product, and this could result in consumer dissatisfaction.

B. Sampling Inspection Schemes

1. Aims of the Schemes

Although it is not always practised, the issuing of any specification standards should always be accompanied by a statement of the relevant sampling inspection scheme. This is because the numerical standards laid down can only be properly appreciated when the sampling system to be used is known.

A Sampling Inspection Scheme details the number of samples to be collected from each delivery and gives the rules by which deliveries will be accepted or rejected. Their aim is to prevent ingredient materials which do not meet specifications from being accepted and therefore used in the finished product. Hill[10] discussed two ways in which the design of Sampling Inspection Schemes can be approached. He defined these as the "curative" and "incentive" standpoints respectively.

The "curative" view is that by sampling and testing materials it is hoped to detect deliveries which are outside the specified limits and by their rejection prevent their use.

The "incentive" view is that only the supplier can change the quality of his material and that since he is in business for profit, he will only take action when there is an economic incentive to do so. On this view, the primary purpose of sampling and testing is to prevent the supplier offering material of inadequate quality. This approach is realistic and providing there is close contact between technical staff of the supplier and the food manufacturer it should be effective.

2. Description of a Scheme

In formulating a Sampling Inspection Scheme each case should be dealt with on its merits. It is essential to get the best statistical advice available and for the technologist to work closely with the statistician. Often the greatest difficulty is not mathematical but to achieve mutual understanding of the situation under discussion.

Quite commonly one meets schemes where the number of samples taken is fixed at a constant ratio to the consignment size (e.g. % of containers that are to be sampled). This is probably because such schemes can be stated simply and also because of the popular fallacy that the degree of protection afforded remains constant when the ratio of sample size to lot size is constant. Actually it is the absolute number of samples taken rather than the relative size of the sample which determines the degree of protection afforded by an acceptance sampling scheme. The real reason for an increase in the number of samples taken as the consignment size increases is that the economic risk is greater, since more money is involved with large consignments than with small ones. One is therefore justified in doing more work, i.e. spending more money, when testing the larger consignment.

It should be noted that bulk delivery of ingredients e.g. by tanker, may pose problems both in the technique of sampling and the design of a sampling inspection scheme. The scheme outlined below would be appropriate for a material delivered in a number of containers, e.g. $\frac{1}{2}$ or 1 cwt sacks.

As an example of an incentive sampling scheme the following is a short account of one by W. R. Hindes (1960, unpublished) used with a thermophilic spore count test. The scheme covers consignments of up to 300 containers. The specification is that the total aerobic thermophilic spore count shall not exceed 150 per 10 g. Since 2 g of material per sample is tested, the "specification limit" is 30 per 2 g. The "control limit" corresponds with a level which will include 95% of all consignments and is commonly 20 or 25 per 2 g.

For each supplier of each material a separate control chart similar to that shown in Table 1 is compiled and used to record results of the test.

TABLE 1. Ingredient material control chart

Material——————— Supplier——————————— Sheet No.———

Sample Number	1								
Consignment Size	100×56 lb								
Date of Sample	1.10.71								

Total thermophilic spore count per 2 g										
	Over 90									
	76–90									
	61–75									
	46–60									
	31–45									
	26–30									
	21–25									
	16–20	X								
	11–15									
	6–10	X								
	0–5	X X X								

Record count by placing "X" in appropriate box, unless it is over 90, when actual figure should be inserted.

Notes: Specification limit at 30 and control limit at 20 have been marked.

The first column has been completed as an example.

The table can, of course, be extended to cover any other relevant test.

At any one time a supplier is on the "REDUCED", "NORMAL" or "TIGHTENED" level of sampling; the supplier with a good record is subjected to reduced inspection, whilst consignments offered by suppliers with a bad record are subjected to intensified inspection. This increases the chance of detecting consignments containing large numbers of defective containers. The control charts also allow warning to be given when supplies of a material begin to deteriorate before they become rejectable. At this stage the supplier can be informed and it is hoped that he will, in his own interest, take steps to improve the position.

The scheme for "REDUCED" level is shown in Table 2 and for "NORMAL" level in Table 3. At the "TIGHTENED" level, ten samples are taken from each consignment, five are tested and the other five held in reserve. The scheme followed is that for the "NORMAL" level in Table 3, but if a re-check is required (see the right hand column) the further five samples are already to hand. Also, when consignments are accepted (see first and second left hand columns) sampling continues at the "TIGHTENED" level.

TABLE 2. Sampling scheme for reduced level with up to 300 containers in consignment

Take 5 samples from every fifth consignment (or once per month whichever is the more frequent)

When average count is below control limit and no individual count exceeds specification limit, ACCEPT consignment. Continue sampling at REDUCED level.	When average count exceeds control limit but is below specification limit, or when 1 individual count exceeds specification limit, collect and test further 5 samples and re-test original 5 samples.	When average count exceeds specification limit, or 2 or more individual counts exceed specification limit, re-check samples.
	If average count below specification limit, and not more than 1 individual count exceeds specification level, ACCEPT consignment, sample future consignments at NORMAL level.	If average count exceeds specification limit or 2 or more individual counts exceed specification limit, REJECT consignment. Sample future consignments at TIGHTENED level.	If original results confirmed, REJECT consignment. Sample future consignments at TIGHTENED level.

When a material from a given supplier is on the "TIGHTENED" level it should be transferred to the "NORMAL" level after six consecutive consignments have the average count lower than the control limit and no individual count above the specification limit. In the same way, a material from a given supplier may be transferred from "NORMAL" to "REDUCED" level after six consecutive similarly low count consignments have been received.

3. Linking of the Scheme with Stock Levels

One further use may be made of the control charts on a practical rather than strict statistical basis. By inspection, a "safe" line may be drawn such that if all counts are below it, the chances of the next delivery being rejected are small. When deliveries are within the "safe" area of the chart, the stock levels should be kept to the minimum practicable. On the other hand, when a material from a given supplier is on the "TIGHTENED" level, the chances of rejection are much greater and stock levels should be kept up to a level where

TABLE 3. Sampling scheme for normal level with up to 300 containers in consignment.

Take 5 samples from all consignments

When average count is below control limit and no individual count exceeds specification. limit, ACCEPT. Continue sampling at NORMAL level.	When average count exceeds control limit but is below specification limit, or when 1 individual count exceeds specification limit, collect and test further 5 samples and re-test original 5 samples.	When average count exceeds specification limit, or 2 or more individual counts exceed specification limit—RECHECK.
	If average count is below specification limit and not more than 1 individual count exceeds specification limit, ACCEPT. Sample future consignments at NORMAL level.	If average count exceeds specification limit, or 2 or more individual counts exceed specification limit, REJECT. Sample future consignments at TIGHTENED level.	If original results are confined, REJECT. Sample future consignments at TIGHTENED level.

the rejection of one or even two deliveries in succession does not cause serious difficulties. In this way the scheme, used with discretion, can help in keeping to a minimum the investment of capital in ingredient material stocks.

3. SOUPS

A. List of typical ingredient materials indicating principal tests applied

1. Introduction

The number and type of ingredient materials with which any one packer is concerned, will of course depend on the range of products he makes. For reasons of space only a limited number of materials can be discussed, but these have been selected to illustrate the ways in which quality control can be applied. It must be re-emphasized that each manufacturer must decide for himself which tests are required and the specific standards which he will apply.

Almost all countries have legislation covering some ingredient materials and finished packs. Because the position is constantly changing, it is not proposed to give specific figures as this might prove misleading. The section on food legislation by Mrs C. S. Burke, in Food Directory, 1971[11] is a most useful guide, as is the guidebook to U.S. Legislation by Gunderson *et al.*[12] Current Food Additives Legislation by the United Nations F.A.O. (ten issues per year, obtainable H.M.S.O.) gives changes in legislation, but to use this one needs additionally the text of legislation. It should also be noted that legislation may not reflect current trade practice or trends. When exporting, this kind of information is of importance and it is prudent to seek expert local advice.

When considering food additives as ingredients, it may be noted that there is a useful text edited by Furia[13] which gives information on properties and uses of a wide range of food additives and that the Food Chemicals Codex[14] has data on standards of identity and purity of a large number of food chemicals.

Since the aim of inspection at this stage is to check the deliveries of material against a specification before the material is used, time is often limited. When controlling quality, the only valuable information is that which enables useful action to be taken. It is better therefore to carry out simple, quick tests on many samples than to carry out complex tests on only a few samples. As the amount of money available for inspection is always finite, careful thought should be given to ensure that tests performed give the best value for the money spent. The methods chosen for control purposes are therefore not necessarily those used in the investigation of specific problems.

At this point it is convenient to give general reference to sources of methods.

For chemical methods, the Official Methods of Analysis of the A.O.A.C.[15] is a book to which frequent reference is likely to be made. Amendments to the text are made in the Journal of the A.O.A.C. This volume gives methods for the determination of extraneous material, more frequently termed "filth tests" for a wide range of materials. The text by Kurtz and Harris[16] on microanalytical entomology forms a useful complement to the A.O.A.C. but is more suitable for the specialist. Other recognized methods may be found in: the Society of Analytical Chemistry's Official Methods[17] and its supplement[18]; Standard Methods of the Oil and Fats section of the I.U.P.A.C.[19]; Analytical Methods for the Soup Industry[20] which deals mainly with the Continental style of soups and broths; the N.C.A. Laboratory Manual[21]; and in two very valuable texts for the bench, The Chemical Analysis of Foods by Pearson[22] and Laboratory Handbook of Methods of Food Analysis by Lees.[23] Some references for microbiological methods are: Canned Foods—An Introduction to their Microbiology (Baumgartner) by Hersom and Hulland,[24] the A.P.H.A. recommended methods,[25] Bacteria in Relation to the Milk Supply by Chalmers[26] which has information on some basic methods, the paper by Mossel[27] on Microbiological Quality Control in the food industry which gives useful techniques and references, another paper by Mossel[28] on the assessment of the hygienic condition of food factories and their products, and a recent discussion by de Figueiredo[29] on the usefulness and limitations of microbial indices for quality assurance. Texts dealing with technique are those of Harigan and McCance,[30] Collins,[31] Baker[32] and Meynell and Meynell.[33] Although not dealing specifically with food microbiology, the Society for Applied Bacteriology's Technical Series is of real value to the bench worker. Nos. 1[34] and 2[35] deal with identification methods, 3[36] and 5[37] deal with isolation methods and No. 4[38] deals with automation and mechanization. When identification of an organism is necessary, reference should be made to Skerman[39] although Bergey[40] remains the classic in this field. For a detailed and extensive work on microbiological methods, reference should be made to Norris and Ribbons.[41]

Tests for pesticide residues and for vitamin content which are only carried out occasionally on batches of soup ingredients are not further discussed here. Bulk sorting tests, to which reference will later be made, consist of taking samples of approximately 10–112 lb weight according to the type of material, and very carefully sorting for defects and contamination. Tests of this sort can also be used to grade individual deliveries for further sorting before use.

General references for equipment are Joslyn and Heid[42] and Jacobs.[43]

The way in which results are recorded is important. The value of control charts compared with the traditional ledger sheet is that the charts assist the comprehension of results and enable trends to be discerned more readily. From a practical point of view trends are of the utmost importance and if they can be seen quickly this enables prompt corrective action to be taken. For a brief account of the selection of raw materials and control of the processing operations, reference may be made to Rose's papers.[44, 45]

2. Fresh and Frozen Vegetables

In soups, vegetables are used for their organoleptic properties. It is important to remember that the interest of the canner is in the quality of the finished pack. The canner is therefore concerned with the colour, texture and flavour of the vegetables after the comparatively severe heat treatment given during sterilization. For this reason, the varieties and grades which are best for canning are not necessarily those which are best for the retail trade. Invariably therefore, acceptable varieties are set out in the specifications.

Pamphlets on individual fruits and vegetables can be found in H.M.S.O. Sectional List No. 1 and in the Ministry of Agriculture, Fisheries and Food Bulletin No. 78.[46] It may be noted that Standards of Quality for British canned fruit and vegetables are set out in an F.V.P.R.A. publication[47] which may be of value if the use of canned vegetables is considered.

For economy in use, the canner wants vegetables which can be conveniently handled by the equipment that he has and which require the minimum of sorting, trimming and inspection.

The choice between fresh, dried and frozen vegetables is made on grounds of the requirements of the finished pack, the initial cost, availability during the year and ease of handling. Frozen vegetables are, of course, very convenient to handle. In general, however, fresh vegetables are chosen and this means that vegetable-using soups are seasonally produced varieties.

There is a common concern in vegetable specifications for those factors which affect general appearance—colour, flavour and texture together with a concern to limit extraneous materials.

The following notes are on individual vegetables and are intended to illustrate the sort of considerations which enter into the making of a specification.

Asparagus

This is used principally for asparagus soup. The stem is often pulped and used to give flavour and body to the soup, whilst the tips are used as a garnish. The ideal is to have fresh, even, medium sized, unblemished full-flavoured spears. Because of its high price it should be carefully cut, packaged and transported to ensure that it arrives at the factory clean and fresh. The acceptable proportion of thin stalks in a delivery is usually specified because thin tips do not make such an attractive garnish as thicker ones. It is also usual to specify the acceptable percentage of damaged or diseased stalks. This is because such stalks will have to be sorted and trimmed and wastage loss is properly regarded as part of the cost of the ingredient.

Green Beans

These are used mainly as a garnish in soups such as "mixed vegetable" and also for flavour. It is therefore important that they should be of a uniform fresh green colour, free from discoloration or blemishes which mar the appearance of garnish, crisp without stringiness and not having any bitterness or off flavour when cooked. It is usual to specify the acceptable percentage of damaged beans and extraneous material such as leaves, flowers or dirt. Insects are most undesirable as they may be difficult to remove, and should not be present.

However, dried green beans are generally used in soups because they are available all the year round and there may well be an overall cost advantage over the fresh beans. Apart from determining the percentage of blemished pieces and the level of extraneous matter, the usual tests are for colour and size of pieces after rehydrating in boiling water for 10 min also a determination of moisture, sulphur dioxide, lead and arsenic on the original material is made, methods given by Pearson[22] may be used.

Carrots

These are used both as a garnish and also for their flavour. Quite large percentages can be used in some soups and they are therefore to be regarded as a major ingredient. As they will probably be used diced or sliced, a deep even colour throughout the carrots is desirable and varieties such as Red Cored Chanteney may be specified. They should have a sweet clean flavour, free from any bitterness. Larger carrots are preferred as trimming losses are lower and dicing is more satisfactory than with smaller ones. Specifications usually cover the size gradings and the acceptable percentages of undersized carrots, cull material such as carrot tops, and damaged or diseased carrots. The presence of woodiness, insect and wireworm infestation are highly undesirable as they result in increased sorting costs and wastage.

Celery

This is used not only in celery soups, but also in others as a garnish and also for its flavour. Although some celery may be pulped, some will be cut into short pieces to provide attractive garnish. For this, long well-bleached stems are the most suitable. Long White Celery is regarded as a good variety. For ease of handling, celery should have a good heart formation and be free from damage, and have the roots and leaves removed. It is usual to specify the acceptable proportion of good hearts and damage.

Onions

These are widely used for their flavour, not only in onion soups, and both English and Spanish types are used. They are normally chopped before use, so that large sizes are preferred, as these have lower peeling and trimming costs. Since the canner may wish to store the onions for some time, they should be mature, dry, sound, and without roots or sprouting. It is usual practice to inspect for signs of rot as its presence can affect storage. Specifications usually cover the acceptable percentages of small, mis-shapen and damaged onions.

Peas

These are used not only in pea soup but in a number of others as garnish; size is therefore of great importance for the appearance of the finished pack, although a deep even colour is of advantage. In order to keep the fresh flavour, peas should be handled quickly. The specification will normally state the degree of maturity required and give acceptable percentages of peas which are yellowed, mechanically damaged, or insect damaged, and of extraneous material.

Potatoes

These are normally added as a garnish and to give body to the soup and are of firm white-fleshed varieties. As they are normally diced, well-shaped, large, shallow-eyed potatoes free from internal disease are preferred as these show the smallest trimming and sorting losses. The specification normally gives acceptable percentages of potatoes which are small, damaged (including frost damage) or mis-shapen, and extraneous material (including soil).

Turnips

These may be used both as a garnish and for their flavour, and variety is less important than size. When they are large they tend to be woody, so that there is both a maximum and minimum desirable size. They are liable to both worm and slug attack and deliveries should be checked for these, as well as for frost damage and internal rot. All of these can cause serious difficulties and losses to the canner. Specifications usually give the acceptable percentages of damaged, wrongly sized turnips and extraneous material.

3. Frozen Meat

For soup making, frozen meat is usually used unless fresh meat can be obtained more cheaply. Normally the meat is inspected as carcase meat and it is not usual to carry out chemical tests.

Useful general references are Martin,[48] Hill and Dodsworth,[49] and Thornton.[50]

When meat has been inspected by the Health Authorities it is not usual to carry out bacteriological tests. Should it be desired to test for the presence of *Salmonella* spp, a number of methods are available. Because numbers of these organisms are low, it is usual to use an enrichment medium before streaking on to selective media. The addition of meat to a medium affects its composition and to some extent its performance. The method of choice may therefore vary but sound basic methods are given by Georgala and Boothroyd.[51]

Many countries have regulations governing the slaughter of animals and the transportation of meat, and attention should be drawn to these in the specification.

One of the difficulties in inspecting frozen meat is that it must be completely thawed before inspection can be effective. This is most important when checking for bone fragments and small objects.

Packaging of meat is usually in a transparent polythene bag in a fibre carton. Should a piece of the polythene tear and become stuck on to the meat block, it can be very difficult to detect, and may find its way into the finished soup. It is possible that coloured polythene would be more easily detected.

The following notes on individual meats are intended to give an indication of the considerations involved when making a specification.

Bacon

This is used mainly for its flavour and as a carrier for smoke flavouring. It should be free from the following defects: bristles, diseased portions, bone and bone fragments, sweating, smoke chamber residues, freezer burn, slime, bacteria or mould growth, insect or rodent contamination, putrefaction or incipient putrefaction, or other deleterious extraneous material such as wood, string, fibre, metal etc.

Beef

This is one of the most usual ingredients in a wide range of soups. It is normally frozen, though chilled meat may occasionally be used. The ratio of fat to lean meat is important, low fat contents being preferred since the valuable protein is in the lean meat and excessive fat is objectionable in many soups. Boneless meat is normally preferred for ease of factory operation, but it *must* be free from bone. Bone splinters in particular present a difficult problem since they can be difficult to detect and remove. It should be free from the following defects: offal, skin, hair, bone splinters, bruised areas, pieces of extraneous fat, loose tendons and sinews, excessive blood, freezer burn, slime, bacterial or mould growth, insect or rodent contamination, putrefaction or incipient putrefaction, discoloration and oiliness or other deterioration, and extraneous materials such as wood, fibre, string, metal, etc.

Kidneys and Liver

These are usually used in some meat soups. They are normally frozen. Beef kidneys and ox or sheep's livers are commonly used. They should be sound, disease-free, not bitter in taste, free from off odours and flavours and from the defects listed under *Beef*.

Mutton

This is used mainly in Scotch Broth. It is normally frozen and may be supplied boneless. The meat should be of good appearance and texture, and free from excess fat. It should be free from the defects listed under *Beef*.

4

Oxtails

These are used mainly in Oxtail Soup. They are normally frozen. They should be free from excessive fat, and from the defects listed under *Beef*.

4. Canned Tomato Puree

A Tomato Puree or paste is normally produced in "single", "double" or "triple" concentration. A "double" concentrate of 28–30% total solids packed in "5 kilo" cans is frequently used for manufacturing purposes. A brief description of production and canning of tomato puree was given in Food Trade Review.[52] More detailed accounts are given by Dickinson and Goose[53] and Goose and Binsted.[54] There is also an extensive review of the literature covering harvesting and utilization of tomatoes, including a section on the factors affecting the quality of Tomato Ketchup, by Ranganna *et al.*[55] Although official laboratories will carry out an examination for metallic contamination by copper, lead, arsenic or tin, for quality control purposes, other tests given below should be carried out on each batch or lot in a consignment. Useful general references are N.C.A. Laboratory Manual[21] and Dickinson and Goose.[53]

Total Solids. The percentage solids clearly influences the purchase price of the puree and is also the basis for computing the amount of puree used per batch of manufactured product. The vacuum oven method given by A.O.A.C.[15] is normally used as the standard or reference method, but the refractometer method is much quicker and accurate enough for control purposes. This is described by Goose and Binsted.[54]

Salt. The importance of salt in the recipe is obvious as its contribution to the total solids figure. The percentage of added salt, if any, should be known to the manufacturer before delivery. For methods of checking this figure, see Pearson[22] and Goose and Binsted.[54] Note that there is a method for estimating salt and acidity on a single weighed sample.

Acidity. The acidity clearly affects the flavour and may affect the amount of lethal heat given to a product. This is normally checked by titration against N/10 sodium hydroxide using phenolphthalein as an indicator and expressing the results as % citric acid. When the puree is to be used in a product where acidity is important in the preservation process, then the pH should be checked also. For methods, see salt references.

Sugar. Invert sugar forms about half the total solids. Dickinson and Goose[53] give a rapid method of estimation.

Black Specks. Large numbers indicate poor sieving of the raw pulp or "burning on" at some stage of the manufacturing process. Dickinson and Goose[53] give a method of examination.

Rate of Spread Test. A good puree, especially if intended for use in ketchup or sauces, should show little separation or "bleeding" on standing. Dickinson and Goose[53] give a description of a rate of spread test.

Colour. This is of considerable importance in a puree to be used in tomato soup or ketchup. Colour may be judged by eye and matched against a standard. It should be noted that women may be better at this than men. Other methods are available. Dickinson and Goose[53] describe the Lovibond Tintometer method; the N.C.A. manual[21] refers to the Munsell method, which MacKinney and Chichester[56] give in more detail. Other references which may be of interest are texts by MacKinney and Little[57] and Burnham et al.,[58] a discussion of basic principles of colour measurement as a quality control tool by Sutton et al.,[59] a description of an objective colour measurement of tomato puree by Younken,[60] and a rapid objective method described by Kramer et al.[61] Although the measurement of colour and the use of colour standards has many difficulties, in general the simplest, quickest method of sufficient reproducibility and accuracy for the purpose in hand is the one to be preferred.

Consistency and viscosity. This is of importance in Ketchup and sauces where a thick product is desired. The whole question of consistency and viscosity is a difficult one. The laboratory handbook of Van Wazen et al.[62] contains a valuable review of basic theory and commercially available equipment. The following references which may be useful are, Dinsdale and Moore[63] who deal with basic principles of viscosity and its measurement; Scott-Blair[64] who edited a standard work on "Foodstuffs—Their Plasticity Fluidity and Consistency" and contributed a chapter to Advances in Food Research.[65] For a terse description of viscosity and consistency measuring instruments, see "Process Instruments and Controls Handbook", Ed. Considine.[66] The use of the Bostwick Consistometer is referred to by Goose and Binsted,[54] however, and the remarks on the choice of the method for colour measurement apply here also.

Flavour. This is of obvious importance and is best judged against an approved standard. Ideally the puree should have a "clean" definite flavour of ripe tomatoes which will give the best flavour in the manufactured product. The most important defect is a caramelized flavour which may be caused either by overheating during the manufacturing process, or more frequently, by insufficiently rapid cooling of the cans after they have been filled with the hot puree. This is more likely to occur when cans are left to cool in the open air than when they are cooled in chlorinated water.

Filth Tests. The most commonly used filth test is the Howard Mould count. In countries where legal standards have been set, the object is to suppress the use of mouldy tomatoes in making the puree. The standard method is set out in A.O.A.C.[15] The Howard Mould count is discussed by Morgan,[67] Field[68] and Dakin[69] and in the Proceedings of the London Conference on Tomato Puree.[52] It should be noted that the technique of this test requires considerable experience before proficiency is attained.

Other filth tests which may be applied are the Rot Fragment Count and the Insect Fragment Count, for which see A.O.A.C.[15]

Microbiological Tests. In most cases, microbiological tests are not carried out as a routine. Occasional checks may be made for thermophilic spore-forming anerobes,[70] and possibly for *Bacillus thermoacidurans* (*coagulans*). It is also useful to check for leaker spoilage organisms and to examine the can seams especially where severe panelling of the can has occurred.

A number of countries have some legal requirements for puree. In general, these govern Howard Mould counts, % tomato solids, the addition of salt, the use of colour and preservatives. Binsted and Devey[71] give an account of the C.I.P.C. standard for tomato puree. Dickinson and Goose[53] give a rating system which is intended to be a practical guide for uses of puree. It is simple, and is valuable for routine purposes.

5. Canned Vegetables

These are generally used as substitutes for fresh vegetables, either to extend the production time of a seasonal pack or for convenience at not too high a cost. Among vegetables which may be used in this way are carrots, sweet corn, celery and peas. The first heat sterilization process will tend to soften the vegetables and allowance should be made for the effect of the second heat treatment. For further information on texture, reference may be made to the paper by Kramer[72] on vegetable products and to the text by Matz[73] which covers a wider field. Apart from examination for colour, texture and flavour, it is usual to check net weight, drained weights and the salt content of the liquor. The salt content is checked because the liquor contains a useful amount of flavour, and it is therefore used as stock for the soup; the amount of added salt in the recipe may need adjustment.

6. Pulses

These may be used either as a garnish or as a main ingredient in the soup. Should they have to be stored for more than a short time they are usually fumigated.

The percentage of water is determined on a comminuted sample either by the vacuum oven method or in a hot air oven.

The thermophilic spore count test may be carried out on water in which a sample of pulse has been thoroughly shaken. This test can give surprisingly high counts especially with lentils.

Beans. These may be of many kinds, e.g. butter beans, large Dutch brown beans, white haricot beans, etc. For an attractive garnish the range of size of the beans is important. This may be assessed either by the % weight retained by each of a series of sieves or by an average count of the number of beans in a convenient weight, e.g. 100 g. The extent of freedom from defects such as discoloration, split skins and insect attack, which mar the appearance of the beans in the finished pack, is best determined by bulk sorting of samples.

Peas. The tests carried out are similar to those for beans, additionally the % water uptake on reconstitution should be measured so that recipe changes can be made. Also the peas should be soaked, cooked and tasted to ensure suitability for the product.

Lentils. Extraneous matter e.g. stones and discoloured material can cause difficulties. The bulk sorting test is a most useful one to apply in order to determine the proportion of extraneous material.

7. Flours and Starches

The flours and starches commonly used include cornflour, farina (potato starch), rolled oats and oatflour, riceflour, wheatflour and various modified starches. It should be noted that there are very considerable differences in the behaviour of different grades of any *one* natural flour. They are all employed to give thickness and body to the soup. Ideally, a starch would form a thin solution which would allow a fast rate of heat penetration during the sterilization process. After this it would thicken and remain unchanged. In practice most starches do not do this and they behave in a complex manner which may partly explain the "broken" heating curve frequently found in heat penetration tests with soups.

Most countries have legal requirements for wheat flour which clearly reflect concern primarily with its use in bread making. The use of bleaching agents and improvers is widely controlled. Some countries, including the United Kingdom and Denmark, require additives to flour such as calcium carbonate. The % of water, ash and protein is also specified in a number of countries.

Rice flour is controlled in a few countries. The main concern seems to be prevention of adulteration, as the addition of foreign material is normally forbidden and the % of ash is specified.

Cornflour is also controlled in some countries. Again the main concern seems to be the prevention of adulteration. The identity of the material (maize starch) is usually specified and there may be limits on the % of moisture and ash. In the U.K. the maximum amount of sulphur dioxide is limited.

A standard text is that of Kent-Jones and Amos,[74] and Pearson[22] has a useful chapter on cereals and starch products. Kerr[75] has a useful chapter on the evaluation of modified starches and gives descriptions of a number of different types of equipment.

Microscopic examination, especially using polarized light, is a useful, quick test for flours and starches and for a wide range of other materials. A great deal has been written on this topic, but Winton and Winton[76] is a classic work. This is unfortunately not readily available. There is a useful text by Wallis[77] which covers a wide field. The text on Pharmacognosy by Hebert and Ellery[78] may also be of value, and mention should be made of a series of 15 papers on food microscopy by Essex and Shelton in *Food*.[79] An older text but one which is still valuable is that of Leach and Winton.[80]

For routine quality control, a microscopic examination provides a quick check of the identity of the material. Moisture measurements may be made to check that the material is in a normal condition. For speed, a moisture meter may be preferred to the air-drying or vacuum oven. These tests together with an occasional filth test are normally considered sufficient.

With rolled oats and oat flour which contain a comparatively large amount of fat and if there is any doubt about the inactivation of lipase, a useful test for rancidity is to extract the fat by the Soxhlet method and then to carry out a Free Fatty Acid estimation on the extracted fat. The two standard methods are given by Pearson.[22]

Modified starches have a very large amylopectin content and a useful quick test for identity is to mix a 0·2% starch suspension with a little N/10 iodine and either judge the colour in a test-tube or count the % of blue starch grains microscopically and compare with a standard sample.

Bacteriological requirements for flours to be used in soups were reviewed in a short article by the science editor of *Milling*.[81] One of the most important practical difficulties is that starches can on occasion have a very high thermophilic spore count. This may be assessed using 10 ml of a 20% suspension, either by the method given in the N.C.A. manual[21] or by that of Shapton and Hindes.[82]

8. *Whole Rice and Pasta Products*

These are used as a garnish in soups. The rice used for soups is of the long grain (Patna) type and is not the same as that used for puddings. The usual checks are for moisture, colour, brokenness of grain, gross defects, extraneous material and the level of stone contamination.

Legislation to control pasta exists in a number of countries. Commonly the moisture content and the amount of egg present in an egg-containing pasta are specified and in some countries the content of ash and salt is also controlled. Regulations also exist governing the addition of colouring matter and preservatives.

The usual tests are for moisture by air or vacuum oven methods, a sorting check for gross defects, and after cooking an organoleptic appraisal.

Bacteriologically, these materials do not usually give trouble. A thermophilic spore count may be made either on the comminuted product or on a quarter strength Ringer's solution in which the product has been thoroughly shaken. The occurrence of a high viable mould count in pasta products is often accompanied by a tendency of the pasta to split or break up on cooking. For this reason a viable mould count is sometimes made even though such mould would be killed very early in the heat sterilization process.

9. Fats and Oils

The most usual fats used in soup are butter and hydrogenated oils. Liquid vegetable oils may also be used. The choice of material may be made as a result of Company Policy, especially where the use of butter is concerned, or by the most economical combination which will give the desired flavour.

Many countries have legislation on butter which reflects concern for the retail distribution of an important article of diet. There is alo a considerable volume of legislation on colouring matter and anti-oxidants for both fats and oils.

The tests considered appropriate will vary with the type of material and the reliability of the supply. It is always desirable to examine the appearance, flavour and odour of the materials.

Chemical methods are described by Pearson[22] and in Richmond's Dairy Chemistry.[83] The fat content is usually determined by the Gerber method, adjusting the weight of material in the cream tube. If unusual values are obtained the results are normally checked by longer but more accurate methods.

The iodine value of the fat is a measure of the degree of its unsaturation and is characteristic for the particular type of material. It is some check on identity and as a general rule the higher the iodine value the greater the liability to go rancid by oxidation. As rancidity is important, the peroxide value and free fatty acid figure are normally obtained. Should the material be stored for any length of time, and in general it is sound practice to use fats and oils as quickly as possible, samples can be taken regularly and the risk of spoilage assessed.

Other tests for rancidity such as the Kreis test may also be carried out if required.

It may be desirable to check from time to time the number of lipotylic organisms present. Nile Blue Sulphate agar or Tributyrin agar is often used for detection of these organisms. It is convenient to add the oil or fat called for in the formula as an inoculum into the medium and then pour the mixture into the Petri dishes.

10. Milk and Cream

Both of these are used extensively in the preparation of soups. Many countries have legislation on these commodities mainly designed to govern the retail trade.

There is a very extensive literature on the testing of milk and cream and details of control methods may be found in Richmond's Dairy Chemistry,[83] Davis, [84, 85] also Pearson,[22] and Chalmers.[26] In addition to other tests it may be advisable to check the thermophilic spore count from time to time. For fresh milk, which is normally pasteurized, it is desirable to know whether the milk is in good condition and whether it is likely to keep for the expected time. It is usually sufficient to check very well mixed samples from the tanker or churn for temperature, acidity (calculated as % lactic acid), 10 min Resazurin readings, and occasionally for fat content. Where supplies are variable it may be necessary to carry out further checks, e.g. to determine the solids not fat and depression of freezing point if adulteration with water is suspected.

With fresh cream, often received as double cream (48% minimum fat content) it must be remembered that it is an expensive material and by its nature perishable. The following tests are usually sufficient if the cream has a good history: temperature, acidity (calculated as % lactic acid), fat by the Gerber method, and Methylene blue reduction time. This may be done according to the method recommended by the working party of the Public Health Laboratory Service,[86] or by mixing 1 ml of double strength Methylene blue with 10 ml of cream and then incubating at 37°C.

Milk powders, both skim and full cream, may be used in soups. As the spray process gives a rather more soluble powder than roller dried material, it is usually preferred.

The main interest in the powder is in whether it will reconstitute to give a good product and whether it can be expected to keep in store for the expected time. The chemical tests usually carried out on material with a good history are moisture by air or vacuum oven method, acidity (calculated as % lactic acid), fat by the Gerber method, and protein by Kjeldahl. The thermophilic spore count should be carried out as some powders may have high counts.

11. Herbs and Spices

Much of the canner's individuality of flavour in his products depends on the balance of herbs and spices. The exact composition of the flavouring materials is, therefore, a closely kept trade secret. An interesting paper in Food Engineering[87] gives a brief description of commonly used spices and typical instances of their use in the U.S.A.

In general, herbs and spices may be used either in the form of the crude materials, or as a spice extract usually suspended on a salt or dextrose base, or in the form of the extracted essential oils or oleoresins.

Synthetic flavourings may be used by some canners often in packs other than soups, but in general it is no easy matter to match the natural product or its extract.

A number of countries have legislation governing the identity of spices, together with the amounts of active constituents, ash, fibre, starch, and sand. It should be noted that the fumigation of spices with ethylene or propylene oxides results in the formation of persistent toxic chlorohydrin residues by the reaction of the fumigant with chlorides present in the spice. For a discussion of this reaction reference may be made to the paper by Wesley et al.[88]

For practical purposes the most important thing is to have a good collection of standard material so that comparisons may be made with the material which is being offered.

Microscopy is used extensively as a means of checking the identity of herbs and spices and the microscopy references given under flours and starches also apply here. A useful book to have in the laboratory is that of Parry.[89]

After checking microscopically, it is usual to compare the flavour with that of the standard. In order to to this it is necessary to dilute the material with an appropriate diluent such as water, a starch gel, or milk. When an alcohol, usually ethyl or possibly isopropyl alcohol, is used as a diluent the mixture is normally further diluted with water before tasting. Alternatively a little of the extract may be taken up on a thin strip of filter paper before being tasted.

Filth tests are important especially with those crude herbs and spices which by their origin and method of handling are susceptible to infestation. The standard methods given in A.O.A.C.[15] may be used.

In order to detect the presence of mites, it may be helpful to sieve the material over a fine screen (18 B.S.) and to examine the material which has passed through.

When further analysis is deemed necessary, the methods given by Pearson[22] may be used.

Bacteriologically, the thermophilic spore count is the most important routine test. This is because some materials, especially the crude herbs and spices, have been found to be very highly contaminated. It must be remembered that some materials contain bacteriostatic substances and it is prudent to carry out the spore count at a series of dilutions. In some cases counts only begin to be appreciable in the one thousandth to one millionth dilutions.

12. Extracts

Vegetable, meat and yeast extracts are used in soups primarily for their flavour. Generally, lighter-coloured extracts are preferred. The usual tests are for colour, flavour, moisture, salt, ash and total nitrogen. With meat extract, it is usual to determine the total creatine and creatinine content. The methods given by Pearson[22] may be used. Since meat and yeast extracts can on occasion have a high thermophilic spore count of very heat-resistant spores it is advisable to test for these using the method of Shapton and Hindes.[82]

Although monosodium glutamate (M.S.G.) is not an "extract" it may be considered here since it is often used as a flavour enhancer. It is a dry, free-running white crystaline powder which when fine will pass a B.S. No. 20 sieve and should dissolve in water to form a colourless solution. Its chemical purity should not be less than 99% calculated as the monohydrate. The assay method given in Food Chemicals Codex[14] may be used.

B. Storage of Ingredient Materials

As a general rule the packer does not wish to store ingredient materials for longer than is necessary, for storage contributes to the overhead costs of the operation. Efficient warehouse operation is therefore essential. Although the use of pallets reduces the amount of material that can be kept on a given floor space it is widely used because it reduces handling costs. For information on general management of stores, reference may be made to the texts of Morrison,[90] or Briggs.[91]

Although very elementary, the principle of using stocks in rotation should be strictly observed. Where goods are received or stored on pallets it is sound practice to mark each pallet load with an identification mark and the date of delivery. If the loads are moved around for any reason this will make stock control easier. There should also be some system of marking the loads to show when laboratory and other examination is completed and the material is ready for use. If grading is practised it is essential that each pallet is clearly marked with the appropriate grade. From the quality control standpoint, efficiency in the warehouse is important, as are the physical conditions in the store area. It is important that buildings are properly designed, kept in good order and that a proper system of pest control is practised. What is required is informed common sense; quality control consists in enforcing this. Information on the quality control aspects of warehousing does not seem to be very well documented, but reference may be made to Parker and Litchfield[92] and to "Sanitation for the food preserving industries".[93] When material is held in cold or cool store similar basic considerations apply. Because refrigerated space is costly, the store must be fully utilized and this often results in more handling than in ordinary storage; also, partly-loaded pallets are more likely to be stowed mixed in a pile. The Ashrae Guide and Data Book[94] has a valuable section on refrigerated warehouse practice to which reference should be made.

C. Can Inspection before Filling

The so-called open topped or sanitary can is normally used to pack soup. As there are many different combinations of tin thickness and lacquer coatings for the can body and end, it is important to choose the combination which gives a satisfactory shelf life at the lowest cost. Most canners buy the cans they fill and do not make them. In such cases it is usual to receive the cans either in wire cages or in cartons stacked on pallets. Since the cans may be expected to be of satisfactory dimensions, examination of the delivery is made for visible defects. These may be classed as major or minor. Major defects are those such as loose solder splashes, heavy solder splashes, badly damaged flanges, faulty plate or rust. Minor defects include slightly damaged cans or scratched lacquer. No definitive list of these defects can be given since the requirements and standards of packers vary. It should however be pointed out that the defects being sought are those which may cause complaints about the pack, e.g. loose solder in the can, and those which may affect the subsequent seaming or performance of the can.

Because of the method of manufacture of cans the entire delivery is likely either to be satisfactory or to have a high proportion of defective containers. It is advisable to inspect a larger number of cans, e.g. 300 taken systematically from the delivery. It is useful to record the results of the inspection on control charts as this simplifies appreciation of the findings. The precise system used depends upon the individual canner's requirements and upon the nature of the supply. As a general rule higher rates of inspection are necessary with poorer supplies. In a sample of 300 cans one would normally expect to find few (less than 6), if any, major faults. As a precaution, it is a good plan to check the dimensions of a few cans, say six per delivery.

The Metal Box Company's Technical Communication No. 15[95] sets out recent ideas on seam composition, and stresses amongst other things the concept of "compactness" of a seam. This term includes the % overlap, seam tightness, and the correct depth of countersink relative to the length of the seam. It also discusses the negative torroid end. This publication is in general use as a source of information amongst U.K. packers.

D. Quality Control of Soup During Manufacture

The aim of quality control is to ensure a product of uniform quality, but there will be variation about the mean of any given aspect of quality such as in colour, flavour, consistency. One of the biggest sources of variation is in the manufacturing process itself, especially where a batch process is operated. In order to reduce this variation it is essential that it is made clear within the factory whose is the responsibility and authority for the maintenance and control of quality. Basically there are two principal systems of organizing responsibility, although the details will vary greatly. The first is to make the factory departmental supervision responsible for output and to have a quality control inspectorate always present to ensure that the quality is satisfactory. The second is to make factory departmental supervision responsible for both quantity and quality of output and to regard the quality control department as a service department which carries out tests and advises the course of action to be taken.

References to the organization of quality control which may be cited are Hawthorn (this Series, Vol. I), Kramer and Twigg[5] and Joslyn and Heid.[42] The basic policy decisions and the practical details are, however, ones for the individual company and the important thing is that they should be effective in practice and not merely look well on paper. Irrespective of the domestic organization it is clear that the men and women on the line who actually manufacture the soup are important. In practice, it is also clear that the training and discipline which they have are a most important part of quality control. It should also be borne in mind that if mistakes are made on the line, although tests may reveal the source of the error, it is frequently too late to take any corrective action. Much of the effective control therefore is in the hands of the line supervision unless a quality control inspector is always present.

One of the most practical ways of controlling quality in a batch process is to taste the product at various stages of manufacture. The taste will not of course be the same as the finished soup, but it should be consistent for any given variety. The basis for comparison is a mental standard and the validity of the judgement is therefore very dependent on the experience of the taster. Nonetheless this kind of testing can be very worthwhile. If a line were continuous this kind of test could clearly not be done and it would be necessary to design the equipment with the necessary automatic controls.

It is common practice in a soup factory to hold frequent tastings of the finished product. Normally the samples are arranged in the form of a triangular test (i.e. out of three samples two are the same, tasters are asked which is the odd one; there can be one or two standards and the corresponding number of test samples), or a range of test samples is set out with a standard. In practice a most important factor is the impartiality and experience of the tasters who should be selected for their ability to discriminate relevant flavours and much of the value of these tests is lost if the tasters are in any way biased or under pressure. As a product fresh from sterilizing often has a different flavour from the one that it will have after a few days storage, the problem of providing a standard is not so simple as it might seem at first sight.

The problem of providing a standard is easier if a line is always making the same product over a period of several weeks or months. In this case the first batch of the week may be made the control batch. On the first day this is used as the standard, a later batch which is comparable will serve as the next day's standard and so on. The tasters in any case will soon have a mental standard which can be surprisingly reliable. Where runs are shorter the importance of the control batch is greater and mental standards become less reliable.

Any laboratory tests carried out during manufacture must be capable of being done quickly. There is time, for instance, to check the refractive index or the salt or acid content. Micoscopic examination and checks on emulsion are also possible but the scope of the tests is limited if quality control rather than quality audit is the aim.

As another illustration of quality control during manufacture, where complex mixtures of spices have to be made, rather than rely on any testing it may be better to have a second person check the weighings and give his signature that the mixture has been properly made.

E. Control of the Filling Operation

Most countries have legislation governing declaration of net weight of a can and this is clearly of great importance to the canner. As Barnard[96] points out, it makes a great deal of difference whether each package must be at or above a stated weight or whether the average may be used. The relation of filling weight to label weight is not determined just by the appearance of the can when opened by the consumer. Consideration must also be given to the chemical reactions of the head-space gas with the interior of the can and/or the pack. When packs are to be sterilized in an agitating or rotating retort, it is essential to fill to a minimum headspace if the correct sterilization is to be achieved, since the amount of agitation in the pack depends on the movement and extent of the headspace bubble. The packer will wish to have as accurate a control of filling weight as practicable. This is because poor weight control costs money. Overfilling means giving the customer extra food which he or she is not conscious of receiving, whilst underfilling may result in legal action and adverse publicity. In this connection it is as well to remember that increasing line speeds makes control of filling weights of increasing financial consequence. It is often instructive to compare filling machine performances because even with the same make of equipment the pattern of filling weights can vary. Ideally, of course, each can would receive exactly the same weight of product, but in practice there is a variation about the mean. Kramer and Twiggs[5] discuss the setting up of control limits on fillers and give a worked example. C. B. Way[97] also refers to this topic and cites a number of useful references. The use of control charts is a valuable method of displaying results and helps those responsible for adjustment of the filler to keep it properly adjusted.

Apart from control of filling weight the filling temperature should be controlled. This is particularly important in the case of thick soups, especially with the larger can sizes which typically have a "Conduction heating" heat penetration curve. This is because the higher the initial temperature the more quickly it will reach temperatures of useful lethal values. Also high initial temperatures may reduce the risk of the product scorching on the inside of the can.

F. Control of the Seaming Operation

Once the seamer has been set up by the fitter it is desirable to make frequent checks throughout the production shift to ensure that a good seam quality is being maintained. The Metal Box T.C. 15 Revised[95] indicates appropriate tests, and if these are recorded on a suitable control chart and positioned prominently and conveniently near the seamer this should help the mechanic to keep good control.

G. Control of Plant Cleaning

1. Introduction

Plant cleaning operations ought always to be regarded as an integral part of production operations, and efficient quality control of cleaning just as important as control of manufacturing.

Because cleaning is not always so regarded it is as well to state the reasons why cleaning is undertaken. Firstly it is carried out for reasons of self-respect and for good employee morale; secondly to maintain the quality of the product in the widest sense; thirdly because bacterial build up in the equipment could cause pre-process spoilage.

It is also advisable to define what is meant by a clean surface of plant. A clean surface is one from which the food material has been removed, from which the detergent and sterilizing agent or sanitizer has been removed, and which has on it a sufficiently low number of organisms not to affect the product during subsequent production. A bacteriologically clean surface is therefore not sterile. The term "sterile" properly means that no living organisms are present.

Information on the establishment and maintenance of a cleaning programme may be found in rather scattered literature. Useful texts are Parker and Litchfield,[92] "Sanitation for the Food Preservation Industries",[93] and McLaughlin's handbook.[98] An article by Jennings[99] may also be of interest. It may be noted that the American term "Sanitation" covers more than plant cleaning. It covers the whole field of hygiene, plant cleaning, pest control, etc.

Chemical sterilization is discussed in a valuable article by Davis[100] and disinfection is the subject of a useful text edited by Benarde.[101]

As control of plant cleaning is an important part of quality control, it is appropriate to outline some of the more important aspects.

2. Establishment of a manual of cleaning methods

The responsibility for each cleaning operation must be clearly laid down. This is even more important when there is a plant cleaning department which does most of the cleaning than when production departments do their own cleaning. In any case, to avoid any possible misunderstanding, and any possible recriminations, it is advisable to have responsibility for each operation written down in a Plant Cleaning Manual.

The manual should also contain specific information on how to clean each piece of equipment. In general the pattern is: a preliminary soak or rinse in warm or cold water according to the product to be removed, followed by the application of detergent. The action of the detergent may be assisted by a hand- or power-operated brush, by an admixture with steam to give a high pressure jet, or by pumping. The Cleaning-in-Place System where pipelines and tanks are cleaned, by a high speed flow of detergent is being used increasingly. A description of the basic principles and application of them to dairy plants are described in "In place cleaning of dairy equipment,"[102] and an article in the International Brewers Journal[103] describes other applications. After the action of detergent a wash or rinse is given to remove detergent and loosened product. At this stage a sterilizing agent may be applied and afterwards the detergent or sterilizing agent must be rinsed away. The plant, after inspection, is then ready for use. It is normal good practice to flush the line with clean potable water immediately before production commences.

Quality control can be very simple but effective. For instance, many cleaners if left to themselves measure detergents in such quantities as "a large handful" or "half a bucket". The provision of proper measures or better still the issuing of correct amounts for a given job can save waste of detergent and also ensure that sufficient is used.

Attention must always be given to likely "trouble spots". This is a sound quality control principle which applies to cleaning. For instance, with cleaning in place methods, the least effective cleaning is on long horizontal lines especially where there is a low "head", i.e. low hydrostatic pressure of detergent. It is necessary to inspect such lines very carefully and it may be necessary to use a mobile pump in the system to get more effective cleaning of this part of the circuit.

It may be noted here that plastic pipework is sometimes used in food plant and if properly used it can be very successful. Plastic pipe lines may however require different treatment from that normally given to stainless steel pipework and it is usual to clean them in place.

In some ways, however, the most effective quality control of cleaning takes place at the design stage and in the siting of equipment. By careful attention to design, by care in the choice of materials and in the installation of equipment, much unnecessary effort and expense on the part of the cleaners can be avoided. Provision of cleaning equipment should always be made before the line is installed. Although this has nothing directly to do with laboratory work, it is nonetheless a major contribution to the quality control of the cleaning operation.

3. Inspection Procedures

The tests are very simple. A strong torch to assist visual inspection is as useful a method of testing as any. Knowing where to look is a much more difficult matter and is one which only comes with experience of a particular plant layout and operation. Cleaning supervision normally inspects work as it is done and in this case the quality control man double checks some items. If the inspection is to determine what the cleaners have done, it should be done immediately the cleaning job has been finished. When it is desired to check the condition of a line before production it is better to leave inspection until the last possible moment. This is because it may happen that alterations are made to a line after it has been cleaned and before beginning production and, although this is unlikely, it is a point to be watched.

4. Laboratory Tests

These fall into two main categories. The first is a check on cleaning. This is normally done by taking a swab or rinse, whichever is appropriate. In

TABLE 4. Numbers of organisms per square foot after cleanup and the corresponding grades

Numbers of organisms per square foot	Grade
0– 5,000	Satisfactory
5,000–25,000	Fairly Satisfactory
Over 25,000	Unsatisfactory

order to avoid the risk of breaking glass test-tubes in the plant, the writer's practice is to use unthreaded aluminium cigar tubes to contain the swabs. It is also useful when swabbing an area to have a swab guide consisting of a 4 in × 1 in hole cut in a piece of thin flexible card about 6 in × $1\frac{1}{2}$ in. This can be sterilized in a hot air oven and it makes it easier to control the area swabbed especially on curved surfaces such as sides of tanks and the inside of pipelines. As a rough guide the standards shown in Table 4 are probably suitable for most soup canneries, although some will think them not sufficiently stringent.

The other main category is that of assessing detergents and sanitizers. In general, once the class or type of a detergent is known, although small scale tests of soil removal may be of some use, conditions are so different in the plant that the only really satisfactory tests is to see what results the plant cleaners obtain under normal working conditions. Care must be taken in the assessment however, since the cleaners' enthusiasm, or lack of it, can profoundly affect the result. Testing of sanitizers is probably also best done in the plant, although Mossel[104] has some interesting proposals for laboratory assessment.

H. Control of Sterilization

1. Factors which must be considered in the Establishment of the Sterilization Process

The first factor that must be clearly understood is that with soups having a pH of 4.5 or above there is a risk of fatal food poisoning by *Clostridium botulinum* unless the soup is properly "sterilized" or "processed". Botulism has characteristic and dramatic symptoms and is often, indeed usually, fatal. The fact that canned soups are universally regarded as safe packs is because canners realize that they have a duty to the public at large and to the industry as a whole to ensure that their sterilization processes are safe with respect to *Clostridium botulinum*.

The second factor is that subject to it being safely processed, the product must be organoleptically satisfactory.

The third factor is that in the establishment of processes one is concerned with spore-forming organisms and that for any given organism in any given substrate at any given temperature the death rate is approximately logarithmic. This means that the more organisms present initially the more chance there is of finding a surviving spore in a can after the process.

To establish a process one therefore needs to know:

(a) The likely number of organisms in the can. This is usually assessed by a spore count on the unprocessed soup.

(b) Thermal Death Time data for the most resistant organism likely to be found in the soup. In practice the "flat sour" 1518 is often used as the test aerobic spore forming organism and P.A. 3679 as the anaerobic test organism. This is because they are both suitably resistant organisms which can be handled relatively easily in the laboratory. It should be noted that the thermal resistance of the organisms varies very considerably from soup to soup and that it is unwise to apply data obtained in one variety to another.

(c) The rate of heat penetration to the slowest heating part of the can. It should be noted that rates of heat penetration vary from soup to soup and that agitation of the can, whether end-over-end or axial, normally increases the rate considerably when compared with that obtained by processing in a stationary retort.

The obtaining and correlation of all this information and the establishment of a process involves much work.

Where one has experience of a particular kind of soup short cuts may be taken after careful thought, and assumptions made. The validity of this depends entirely upon the judgement and experience of the worker. For further reference, Stumbo's text[105] is essential reading for anyone concerned with setting sterilization processes and a useful paper of Charlett[106] contains 114 references. Also of interest is a paper by Richardson[107] which deals with microbial spoilage.

Information, and in some cases process recommendations, may be obtained from Research Associations. Because the soup manufacturer is packing a speciality the answer may not be as quickly available as it would be for some fruit and vegetable packs.

2. Control of the Retort Operation

Heat sterilization of a sealed container is the basis of the canning operation. Sterilization equipment (Retorts) must therefore be properly constructed and operated. N.C.A. recommendations[21] should be closely studied and carefully followed as they are the result of years of successful, widely based experience.

Retorts may either be continuous, in which case good mechanical maintenance is the most effective quality control measure, or of the batch type. Retorts may be vertical or horizontal, the heating medium steam or water, and they may be stationary or agitating. After installation it is wise to check temperature distribution in the retort before it is used, and occasional checks should be made thereafter. "Venting" or "purging" of retorts is of particular importance and it is essential that retort operators know the correct operation and understand its importance.

It is normal practice to have a recorder attached to the retort but as this is usually calibrated to a thermometer, the thermometer itself must be regularly checked. The recorder should not be touched by the retort operator and then it can be used as a check that the correct times and temperatures were given.

The task of ensuring that baskets of sterilized and unsterilized cans are kept separate at all times is one for the factory supervision. The use of tags or tape which change colour on heating has been commended as an aid, and a tally system may also be of value. The knowledge, trustworthiness and reliability of the retort operator however, remain of very great importance.

3. Heat Penetration Tests on Cans

These may be undertaken either in the course of establishing a process or thereafter to ensure that the product is behaving as expected. Changes in recipe or method of manufacture may affect rates of heat penetration.

Thermocouples are normally used for this work with the hot junction placed in the centre of the can, unless experience has shown that another part of the can is slower to heat than the centre.

For general background on thermocouple circuits reference may be made to the paper of Hindes and Croton.[108] Ecklund[109] describes a thermocouple designed for use in canned foods which in our experience works well. Alstrand and Ecklund[110] discuss the mechanics of heat penetration tests and also give their interpretation of these tests. For routine work the method of evaluation of a process given by Patashnik[111] is to be preferred as it is quick and accurate enough for practical purposes. For those wanting further references to process evaluation, the text of Stumbo[105] and the papers by Gillespy[112, 113] and Hicks[114] give a useful lead.

4. Count Reduction Tests

These tests, sometimes referred to as inoculated pack tests, should always be used to confirm that processes are in fact meeting the predictions made on other grounds. The principle is simple, a known number of highly resistant organisms —often "flat sour" 1518 or P.A. 3679, are mixed with a pack and processed. After processing, counts are made either directly on the material or by incubation of a large number of cans. The reduction in count is then estimated and compared with the predictions made.

5. Cooling Water Tests and Cannery Hygiene

It is generally accepted that even very good cans may be subject to micro-leakage during cooling after sterilization and on subsequent handling and that poor cans will leak to a greater extent. For this reason regular checks should be made on the retort cooling water. One would expect that with 0·5–5·0 ppm free available chlorine, providing that the pH of the water is at or slightly above 7·0, the bacteriological quality of the water should be good and that there should be no appreciable corrosion of cans or equipment. With satisfactory chlorination, although spore formers may survive, the total counts on nutrient agar at 30°C may be expected to be less than 50 per ml.

Even though the cans are cooled in good quality water, unless they are dried before they are handled leaker spoilage can occur. Counts on wet runways easily reach the hundreds of thousands or even millions per ml of water. Some causes of leaker spoilage and the uses of a non-destructive large scale incubation test in assessing spoilage rates are discussed by Shapton and Hindes.[115] It is now thought by these authors that 30°C is a better incubation temperature than 37°C.

An invaluable text on Post-Process sanitation in canneries by Thorpe and Everton[116] is based on practical experience over a number of years and should be consulted by anyone dealing with this subject.

6. Incubation Tests of Processed Cans

Apart from the large-scale incubation tests discussed above, it is usual practice in most canneries to take samples from the line for examination. If the expected spoilage rate is as high as 1 in 1,000 a wholly impractical number of cans would have to be examined. If it is accepted that the value of this test is mainly to help good practice on the filling line, then it can be useful. The cans, say 24 per line per shift, should be examined for obvious defects before incubation. As thermophilic spoilage is more likely than mesophilic it is suggested that they are incubated in open mesh crates at 55°C for 14 days, cooled, the vacuums taken, preferably with a B.F.M.I.R.A. (Budenburg) gauge which compensates for headspace variation, and afterwards the pH's measured. As a result of these tests any spoilage should become apparent. Kefford[117] gives information on pH measurement. The principle of this test is that if viable organisms are present they would be expected to produce acid or gas and this is detected by the methods outlined above. When positive results are found it is usual to attempt to isolate and approximately identify the organisms. If the results are plotted on a control chart this is an aid to interpretation, and may give warning of a trend towards higher spoilage rates in time for action to be taken to remedy the trouble.

7. Chemical Tests on the Finished Pack

Whether or not proper quality control has been exercised at an earlier stage these tests are quality audit, not control, and the distinction is important. Occasional checks may be made on total solids, protein, fat, ash, and salt, as well as trace metals. For methods see Pearson.[22] Flavour chemistry on the finished pack is beyond the scope of this chapter but reference may be made to the review by Lea.[118]

I. Control of Labelling and Packaging

The control of packaging material is outside the scope of this chapter. Practical measures which should be taken in the cannery include ensuring that batches of labels match in colour, that labels are "square" on the cans, that excess amounts of paste and glue are not being put on the can, and that case sealing is being done properly.

J. Storage Trials

The object of the quality control described thus far is to ensure, as far as possible, that the product reaches the customer in good condition. It may prove instructive to ship goods out to a distant warehouse and back, and to examine cans and cases for any spoilage or deterioration. Prolonged storage can also be used to test the shelf life of the product and container. Cans may also be sampled from retail stores. The tests that will be carried out at this stage tend with many canners to be investigational in nature rather than quality control measures.

4. MAYONNAISE, TOMATO KETCHUP AND FRUIT SAUCES

A. List of Typical Ingredients Indicating Principal Tests applied to each

1. Vegetable Oils

Apart from the tests discussed in the section on soups, for particular formulations it may be desirable to perform a "cold test". This consists of keeping the oil at a low temperature for a few hours. No sediment or cloudiness should appear. Binsted et al.[119] give the conditions as 0°C for 5½ hr and state that clarity of the oil indicates freedom from stearines and sterols.

2. Eggs

Because dried or frozen eggs are usually cheaper and easier to handle they are normally used rather than fresh eggs. As the egg will impart colour to the finished product it should preferably be a deep, bright yellow.

Chemical tests made on dried egg are usually moisture (vacuum oven), fat (chloroform extract), and alcohol soluble acidity calculated as oleic acid. The Haenni value is also of importance as it relates to the emulsifying power of the egg. The method given by Brooks and Taylor[120] (p. 78) may be used.

On frozen eggs, moisture, fat and free fatty acid content of the fat are usually determined.[22]

Although dried and frozen egg is now pasteurized, since no further heat treatment will be given it may be thought desirable to check for the presence of Salmonella spp. even though the acidity of the product may be high enough to kill Salmonella. Enrichment in Selenite F and streaking on to brilliant green agar is probably sufficient for this purpose. As yeast may cause fermentation in the finished product a yeast count should be made routinely. Acid Malt Peptone (OXOID) is a convenient medium.

3. Vinegar

Often a distilled malt vinegar or spirit vinegar is used for Mayonnaise. It is usual to check total acidity.[22] When malt vinegar is used, as in sauces, the colour and flavour should be checked, and vinegar eels (Anguillula aceti) should be absent.

4. Dried Fruits

These are widely used in sauces. Moisture, filth,[15] and bulk sorting for extraneous material are the usual tests carried out.

5. Fruit Purees

These may be of various kinds, apple puree being one of the most commonly used. Tests for identity, total solids, filth, and preservatives (commonly sulphur dioxide) would be appropriate.

B. Glass Inspection

The objective of glass inspection is to ensure that the bottles received by the packer will be satisfactory both to the customer and when handled on the filling line.

Faults in glass may be classified into "Critical" which are likely to give rise to complaints by the customer, e.g. blisters, bird swings, monkey swings or flanged tops; "Major" which are likely to cause breakage on the line, e.g. cracks, thin or thick spots, or out of shape glass; and "Minor" which are objectionable but not as serious as the above and include black specks, pressure scars, ring joint prominent, etc. Minor faults are probably best removed by inspection on the line before filling.

For a description of glass faults and nomenclature reference may be made to B.S. 1133 Section 18.[121]

In general, as far as "Critical" and "Major" defects are concerned, because of the way in which bottles are produced deliveries are usually either good or have a high proportion of defectives.

The first stage in setting up a sampling system is to define clearly "Critical" and "Major" faults.

The statistics of the sampling scheme which the packer may wish to use can be derived either from Mil. Std. 105A published in the U.S.A.,[122] or from the U.K. Defence Specification DEF 131,[123] and Defence Guide DG 7[124] which is a guide to the use of DEF 131.

As an illustration of a scheme, a packer might define each lorry load as a delivery. A convenient number of bottles to inspect might be 240 per delivery as bottles are normally packed 12 or 24 to a case. Samples would be taken from all parts of the load. With "Critical" defects the acceptance where nil defects were found and the rejection of the delivery if one defect were found, might be deemed a reasonable standard. For "Major" defects one might accept up to five defects and reject the delivery if six or more defects were found.

The details of the sampling scheme used will depend on the needs of the packer, and the kind of the glassware available to him.

In addition, it is advisable to inspect each bottle as it is handled onto the washer and just before filling. The latter is usually done through a large magnifying glass against a green background to improve discrimination of faults. It is usual also to change the inspectors at frequent intervals to avoid fatigue and consequent poor performance. This method is suitable for low line speeds, perhaps up to approximately 100 bottles per minute.

C. Mayonnaise and Salad Dressing

Many countries have legislation governing these products. Several require a declaration of identity and distinguish between Mayonnaise and Salad Dressing. The proportions of oil, egg yolk, acid, and the use of emulsifiers and thickening agents may be controlled. There may also, more rarely, be bacteriological standards, e.g. a maximum count, and absence of *Escherichia coli* or pathogens may be specified. It should be noted that national taste and hence formulation of products vary considerably and here we are concerned mainly with U.K. practice.

There is quite an extensive literature on the subject although it is rather scattered. For example, Bleier[125] gives a brief description of traditional methods. Tritton[126] and Beswick[127] give formulae and an outline of plant operations and packaging; Burrell[128] discusses salad dressing and sauces, and Finberg[129] McCormick[130] and Lipschultz and Holtgrieve[131] give accounts of more modern methods. The series of articles by Devey[132, 133] is also useful and includes a treatment of quality control methods. Flückiger[134] discusses the technology of mayonnaise and similar emulsions in some detail. Smith[135] deals with the factors to be considered when selecting an emulsifier/stabilizer system. The texts of Poultney[136] and Binsted *et al.*[129] give a practical account of mayonnaise and sauce manufacture. Fabian and Wethington[137] give results of bacteriological and chemical analyses of a large number of samples. Harris[138] refers to some lesser-known aspects of emulsion stability. Additionally, Sheets and Lopez[139] present data on total gas, CO_2, O_2 and N_2 in a variety of foods including mayonnaise and salad dressing and Blasco[140] gives a rapid method for determining the content of air in mayonnaise.

During manufacture it is useful to check on salt, acid, viscosity and emulsion as well as for colour, appearance, and flavour. Emulsion size may be checked on a diluted sample by direct microscopic examination.

For examination of the finished product reference may be made to Pearson[22] and Binsted *et al.*[119] In addition, Dickinson and Goose[53] give a method for testing rancidity.

D. Tomato Ketchup

Legislation exists in a number of countries, and in the U.K. for example, the minimum amount of tomato solids is controlled.

There is quite an extensive literature on the subject. Burrell[141] gives recipes for tomato ketchup and discusses the sugar/acid basis of keeping quality and the causes of fermentation. The series of articles by Devey[132, 133] also covers tomato ketchup and includes reference to quality control methods. The texts of Poultney[136] and Binsted et al.[119] give details of the manufacture and control of tomato ketchup.

During manufacture, it is useful to check on salt, acid, viscosity, rate of spread and refractometer solids as well as for colour, appearance and flavour. For examination of the finished pack, reference may be made to Pearson,[22] Binsted et al.,[119] and Dickinson and Goose.[53]

E. Fruit Sauces

From the quality control standpoint these are in many ways similar to tomato ketchup. Legislation often limits the addition of colouring or preservatives and there may, rarely, be a limit on the maximum bacteriological count.

Useful references are Burrell,[141] the series by Devey,[132, 133] and the texts of Poultney,[136] Binsted et al.,[119] and Dickinson and Goose.[53]

During manufacture tests for salt, acid, viscosity, and refractometer solids are useful in addition to colour, appearance and flavour.

For tests on the finished pack, reference may be made to Binsted et al.,[119] and to Dickinson and Goose.[53] It may also be useful to carry out a filth test especially when crude spices and flavourings have been used.

5. Bottling of Vinegar

The bottling of vinegar is essentially a simple process, and the quality control methods are also quite simple.

Most countries have legislation governing the percentage of acetic acid; the origin of the vinegar, e.g. malt or wine, must usually be specified, and if the acetic acid is non-brewed this invariably requires declaration.

The glass should be inspected as indicated in Section 4 B above. Vinegar for bottling is usually tested organoleptically, and for colour. In the case of malt vinegar a comparator with European Brewery Convention Lovibond discs may be used. Examination should also be made for vinegar eels which should be absent. Apart from this, on incoming deliveries the total acidity should be checked.

Before bottling, the vinegars may be blended, filtered, and then either further filtered to remove bacteria or pasteurized. Vinegar can also be pasteurized "in bottle". The time/temperature combinations reportedly in use show considerable variation. For a method of evaluation of pasteurization processes reference may be made to Shapton *et al.*[142] After heat treatment or filtration the bottles are labelled and packed into cases in the usual way.

For examination of the finished pack reference should be made to Pearson.[22]

Acknowledgements

The author wishes to acknowledge the assistance received from his colleagues, especially that of Mr. C. E. C. Hewetson in the Company's Library and Information Service.

REFERENCES

1. Caplen, R. (1969). "A Practical Approach to Quality Control". (Business Books Ltd., London).
2. Gedye, R. (1968). "A Manager's Guide to Quality and Reliability". (John Wiley and Sons, London, New York, Sydney).
3. Juran, J. M., Seder, L. A. and Gryna, F. G., Jr. (1962). "Quality Control Handbook". (McGraw-Hill Book Company Inc., New York, Toronto, London).
4. Stok, Th. L. (1965). "The Worker and Quality Control". (Bureau of Industrial Relations, The University of Michigan, Ann Arbor, Mich.).
5. Kramer, A. and Twigg, B. A. (1970). "Quality Control for The Food Industry". 2 Vols. (The A.V.I. Publishing Company Inc., Westport, Conn.).
6. Brokaw, C. H. and Kramer, A. (1964). *Fd Tech., Champaign*, **18** (9), 73.
7. Bender, A. E. (1968). "Dictionary of Nutrition and Food Technology". (Butterworths, London).
8. Irving, G. W. Jr., and Hoover, S. R., eds. (1965). "Food Quality" (Publication No. 77 of the American Association for the Advancement of Science, Washington, D.C.).
9. Potter, N. N. (1968). "Food Science". (The A.V.I. Publishing Company Inc., Westport, Conn.).
10. Hill, I. D. (1960). "The Economic Incentive Provided by Sampling Inspection". *Appl. Stat.* **IX,** 69.
11. Burke, C. S. (1971). In: "Food Processing and Packaging Directory 1971". (Ed. R. de Giacomi). (I.P.C. Consumer Industries Press Ltd., London).
12. Gunderson, F. L., Gunderson, H. W., and Ferguson, E. R. Jr. (1963). "Food Standards and Definitions In The United States—A Guidebook". (Academic Press Inc., New York and London).
13. Furia, T. E. (Ed.). (1968). "Handbook of Food Additives". (The Cleveland Rubber Co., Cleveland, Ohio).
14. N.A.S.–N.R.C. (1966). "Food Chemicals Codex". Publication 1406 and Supplements. (National Academy of Sciences—National Research Council, Washington, D.C.).
15. A.O.A.C. (1970). "Official Methods of Analysis of The Association of Official Agricultural Chemists". (Published by The Association of Official Agricultural Chemists, Washington, D.C.).

16. Kurtz, O'D. L., and Harris, K. L. (1963). "Microanalytical Entomology for Food Sanitation Control". (A.O.A.C., Washington, D.C.).
17. S.A.C. (1963). "Official, Standardised and Recommended Methods of Analysis". Compiled and edited for The Society for Analytical Chemistry by S. C. Jolly. (Heffer, Cambridge).
18. S.A.C. (1967). "Supplement to Official, Standardised and Recommended Methods of Analysis". Compiled and edited for The Analytical Methods Committee of The Society for Analytical Chemistry by S. C. Jolly. (The Society for Analytical Chemistry, London).
19. I.U.P.A.C. (1966). "Standard Methods of the Oils and Fats Section of The I.U.P.A.C. (Butterworths, London).
20. I.A.B.S.I. (1961). "Analytical Methods for The Soup Industry", (Edited and issued by The Technical Commission of The International Association of the Broth and Soup Industry. Secretariat: Bourse de Commerce, Rue de Viarmes, Paris, 1).
21. N.C.A. (1968). "Laboratory Manual for Food Canners and Processors, Vols. I and II". Compiled by The National Canners Association Research Laboratories. (The A.V.I. Publishing Co., Inc., Westport, Conn.).
22. Pearson, D. (1970). "The Chemical Analysis of Foods". (H. E. Cox). (J. & A. Churchill Ltd., London).
23. Lees, R. (1971). "Laboratory Handbook of Methods of Food Analysis". (Leonard Hill Books, London).
24. Hersom, A. C., and Hulland, E. D. (1969). "Canned Foods—An Introduction to Their Microbiology (Baumgartner)". (J. A. Churchill Ltd., London).
25. A.P.H.A. (1966). "Recommended Methods for the Microbiological Examination of Foods". (Ed. J. M. Sharf). (American Public. Health Association Inc. 1790 Broadway, New York 10019).
26. Chalmers, C. H. (1962). "Bacteria in Relation to the Milk Supply". (Arnold, London).
27. Mossel, D. A. A. (1969). *J. Milk Fd Tech.* **32** (5), 155.
28. Mossel, D. A. A. (1964). *J. Sci. Fd Agric.* **15** (6), 349.
29. de Figueiredo, M. P. (1970). *Fd Tech., Champaign* **24** (2), 157.
30. Harigan, W. F., and McCance, M. E. (1966). "Laboratory Methods in Microbiology". (Academic Press, London and New York).
31. Collins, C. H. (1967). "Microbiological Methods". (Butterworths, London).
32. Baker, F. J. (1967). "Handbook of Bacteriological Technique". (Butterworths, London).
33. Meynell, C. G., and Meynell, E. (1970). "Theory and Practice in Experimental Bacteriology". (University Press, Cambridge).
34. Society for Applied Bacteriology, Technical Series No. 1 (1966). "Identification Methods for Microbiologists, Part A". (Eds. B. M. Gibbs and F. A. Skinner). (Academic Press, London and New York).
35. Society for Applied Bacteriology, Technical Series No. 2 (1968). "Identification Methods for Microbiologists, Part B" (Eds. B. M. Gibbs and D. A. Shapton). (Academic Press, London and New York).
36. Society for Applied Bacteriology, Technical Series No. 3 (1969). "Isolation Methods for Microbiologists" (Eds. D. A. Shapton and G. W. Gould). (Academic Press, London and New York).
37. Society for Applied Bacteriology, Technical Series No. 5 (1971). "Isolation of Anaerobes" (Eds. D. A. Shapton and R. G. Board). (Academic Press, London and New York).

38. Society for Applied Bacteriology, Technical Series No. 4 (1970). "Automation, Mechanisation and Data Handling in Microbiology" (Eds. A. Baillie and R. J. Gilbert). (Academic Press, London and New York).
39. Skerman, V. B. D. (1967). "A Guide to the Identification of the Genera of Bacteria". (The Williams and Wilkins Co., Baltimore, Md.).
40. "Bergey's Manual of Determinative Bacteriology" (1957). (Eds. R. S. Breed, E. C. D. Murray and N. R. Smith). (Baillière, Tindall and Cox, London).
41. Norris, J. R. and Ribbons, D. W. (1969–1972). "Methods in Microbiology"— 8 vols. [Publication is continuing—5 volumes published to date 1971.] (Academic Press, London and New York).
42. Joslyn, M. A. and Heid, J. L. (Eds.). (1963). "Food Processing Operations, Vol. I" (A.V.I. Publishing Co. Inc., Westport, Conn.).
43. Jacobs, M. B., Ed. (1951). "The Chemistry and Technology of Food and Food Products" (3 vols). 'Interscience Publishers, New York—out of print).
44. Rose, H. (1963). Canned Soups, Pt. I—Selection of Ingredient Materials. *Fd Trade Rev.* **33** (4), 39.
45. Rose, H. (1963). Canned Soups, Pt II—Control of the Processing Operations. *Fd Trade Rev.* **33** (5), 36.
46. Ministry of Agriculture, Fisheries and Food. (1958). Bulletin No. 78. "Books on Agriculture and Horticulture". (H.M.S.O. London).
47. The Fruit and Vegetable Preservation Research Association. (1965) (with appendix, 1967—currently under review). "Standards of Quality for British Canned Fruit and Vegetables—Draft of Revised Memorandum Q.C. 6". (The Fruit and Vegetable Preservation Research Association, Chipping Camden, Gloucestershire).
48. Martin, C. R. A. (1969). "Practical Food Inspection, Vols I and II". (H. K. Lewis, London).
49. Hill, H. and Dodsworth, E. (1967). "Food Inspection Notes". (H. K. Lewis, London).
50. Thornton, H. (1968). "Textbook of Meat Inspection". (Baillière, Tindall and Cox, London).
51. Georgala, D. L. and Boothroyd, M. (1969). *In* "Isolation Methods for Microbiologists", (Eds. D. A. Shapton and G. W. Gould). (Academic Press, London and New York.)
52. Proceedings of the London Conference on Tomato Puree (1963). Published in: *Fd Trade Rev.* **xxxiii** (6), 48.
53. Dickinson, D. and Goose, P. G. (1955). "Laboratory Inspection of Canned and Bottled Goods". (Blackie and Son, London and Glasgow).
54. Goose, P. G. and Binsted, R. (1964). "Tomato Paste (Puree, Juice and Powder)". (Food Trade Press Ltd., London).
55. Ranganna, S., Srinath, M. K., and Bhatnagar, H. C. (1964). *Indian Food Packer* **18** (1), 43.
56. MacKinney, G., and Chichester, C. O. (1954). In: *Advances in Food Research* **v**, 301.
57. MacKinney, G., and Little, A. C. (1962). "Color of Foods". (A.V.I. Publishing Co. Inc., Westport, Conn.).
58. Burnham, R. W., Hanes, R. M. and Bartleson, G. J. (1963). "Color. A Guide to Basic Facts and Concepts". (John Wiley and Sons Inc., New York, London and Sydney).
59. Sutton, C. C., Ambler, R. C., and Arkin, D. (1952). *Fd Tech., Champaign* **6**, 190.

60. Younken, S. G. (1950). *Fd. Tech., Champaign* **4**, 350.
61. Kramer, A., Guyer, R. B. and Smith, H. R. (1948). *Proc. Amer. Soc. Hort. Sci.* **51**, 381.
62. Van Wazen, J. R., Lyons, J. W., Kim, K. Y., and Colwell, R. E. (1963). "Viscosity and Flow Measurement". (Interscience Publishers, New York and London).
63. Dinsdale, A., and Moore, F. (1962). "Viscosity and Its Measurement". (Chapman and Hall, London; and Reinhold Publishing Corp., New York).
64. Scott-Blair, G. W. (1953), ed. "Foodstuffs—Their Plasticity, Fluidity and Consistency". (North-Holland Publishing Co., Amsterdam).
65. Scott-Blair, G. W. (1958). In: *Advances in Food Research*, Vol. 8. 1. (Academic Press, New York and London).
66. Considine, D. M. (Ed.) (1957). "Process Instruments and Controls Handbook". See especially section 7: 73–110 by J. L. Hull and A. L. Landesman and section 7: 150–160 by L. E. Cuckler. (McGraw-Hill, New York).
67. Morgan, H. (1963). *Fd Trade Rev.* **xxxiii** (2), 50.
68. Field, H. N. (1963). *Fd Trade Rev.* **xxxiii** (3), 33.
69. Dakin, J. C. (1964). *Fd Trade Rev.* **xxxiv** (6), 41.
70. Gillespy, T. G., and Kenny, G. (1957). "Technical Memorandum No. 18". (Fruit and Vegetable Preservation Research Association, Chipping Campden, Gloucestershire).
71. Binsted, R. and Devey, J. D. (1960). "Soup Manufacture". (Food Trade Press, London).
72. Kramer, A. (1964). *Fd Tech., Champaign* **18** (3), 46.
73. Matz, S. A. (1962). "Food Texture". (The A.V.I. Publishing Co. Inc., Westport, Conn.).
74. Kent-Jones, D. W., and Amos, A. J. (1967). "Modern Cereal Chemistry". (Food Trade Press Ltd., London).
75. Kerr, R. W. (1950). "Chemistry and Industry of Starches". (Academic Press, New York and London).
76. Winton, A. L., and Winton, K. B. (1932). "Structure and Composition of Foods", vols I–IV. (John Wiley and Sons, New York; and Chapman and Hall, London).
77. Wallis, T. E. (1965). "Analytical Microscopy". (J. A. Churchill, London).
78. Hebert, B. E. and Ellery, K. W. (1948). "Textbook of Practical Pharmacognosy" (Baillière, Tindall, and Cox, London).
79. Essex, C. D., and Shelton, J. H. (1956, 1957). A series on food microscopy published monthly in *Food* from January 1956 to March 1957.
80. Leach, A. E. (1920). "Food Inspection and Analysis" (revised by A. L. Winton). (John Wiley and Sons, New York; Chapman and Hall, London).
81. Anon. (1959). *Milling* **133**, 542.
82. Shapton, D. A. and Hindes, W. R. (1963). *Chemy Ind.* **34**, 230.
83. Davis, J. G., and Macdonald, F. J. (1953). "Richmond's Dairy Chemistry". (F. J. Griffin, London).
84. Davis, J. G. (1955). "A Dictionary of Dairying". (Grampian, London).
85. Davis, J. G. (1965). "A Dictionary of Dairying, Supplement". (Grampian, London).
86. Report. (1958). Report of a working party of the P.H.L.S. on "Bacteriological Examination and Grading of Fresh Cream". *Mon: Bulln. of Min. of Health* **17**, 77.
87. Anon. (1970). *Fd Engng* **42** (5), 84.

88. Wesley, F., Rourke, B., and Darbishire, O. (1965). *Fd Res.* **30** (6), 1037.
89. Parry, J. W. (1969). "Spices—Vols. I and II". (Food Trade Press, London; Chemical Publishing Co. Inc., New York).
90. Morrison, A. (1967). "Storage and control of Stock for Industry and Public Undertakings". (Pitman and Sons Ltd., London).
91. Briggs, A. J. (1960). "Warehouse Operations, Planning and Management". (John Wiley and Sons, New York and London).
92. Parker, M. E., and Litchfield, J. H. (1962). "Food Plant Sanitation". (Reinhold Publishing Corp., New York; Chapman and Hall Ltd., London).
93. Association of Food Industry Sanitarians, Inc. in co-operation with The National Canners Association (1952). "Sanitation for the Food Preservation Industries". (McGraw-Hill, New York).
94. A.S.H.R.A.E. (1968). "Guide and Data Book—Applications". (American Society of Heating, Refrigerating and Air-Conditioning Engineers, Inc. 345 East 47th St. New York 10017).
95. The Metal Box Co. Ltd. (1965). "Technical Communication No. 15" and "Amendment to T.C. 15". (The Metal Box Co. Ltd., Research Department, London). Note: A new manual which will supersede T.C. 15 is in preparation.
96. Barnard, G. A. (1963). *Jl. R. Statist. Soc.* **126** (2), series A.
97. Way, C. B. (1961). *Ind. Qual. Control* **17** (11), 30.
98. McLaughlin, T. (1969). "The Cleaning, Hygiene and Maintenance Handbook". (Business Books Ltd., London).
99. Jennings, W. G. (1963). *Fd Tech., Champaign* **17** (7), 53.
100. Davis, J. G. (1968). In: "Progress in Industrial Microbiology, Vol 8". (J. and A. Churchill Ltd., London).
101. Benarde, M. A. (1970). "Disinfection". (Marcel Dekker Inc., New York).
102. Davis, J. G. (1959), Ed. "In-Place Cleaning of Dairy Equipment". (Society of Dairy Technology, London).
103. Anon. (1969). *International Brewers Journal* **105** (1251), 59.
104. Mossel, D. A. (1963). *Lab. Pract.* **12** (10), 898.
105. Stumbo, C. R. (1965). "Thermobacteriology in Food Processing". (Academic Press, Inc., New York and London).
106. Charlett, S. M. (1955). *Fd Mf.* **30**, 299.
107. Richardson, K. C. (1969). *Fd Preserv. Q.* **29** (3), 52.
108. Hindes, W. R., and Croton, L. M. (1956). *J. Inst. Sci. Technol* **2** (3), 1.
109. Echlund, O. F. (1949). *Fd Tech., Champaign* **3**, 231.
110. Alstrand, D. V. and Ecklund, O. F. (1952). *Fd Tech. Champaign* **6**(5), 185.
111. Patashnik, M. (1953). *Fd Tech., Champaign* **7**, 1.
112. Gillespy, T. G. (1951). *J. Sci. Fd Agric.* **2**, 107.
113. Gillespy, T. G. (1953). *J. Sci. Fd Agric.* **4**, 553.
114. Hicks, E. W. (1952). *Fd Tech., Champaign* **6**, 175.
115. Shapton, D. A. and Hindes, W. R. (1965). "Proceeding of the 1st International Congress of Food Science and Technology, 1962" (Ed. J. M. Leitch), Vol 4, 205. (Gordon and Breach Science Publishers, London).
116. Thorpe, R. H. and Everton, J. R. (1968). "Post-Process Sanitation in Canneries". Technical Manual No. 1. (The Fruit and Vegetable Preservation Research Association, Chipping Campden, Gloucestershire).
117. Kefford, J. F. (1957). *Fd Preserv Q.* **17**, 30.
118. Lea, C. H. (1963). *Chemy Ind.* **34**, 1408.
119. Binsted, R., Devey, J. D., and Dakin, J. C. (1962). "Pickle and Sauce Making". (Food Trade Press, London).

120. Brooks, J. and Taylor, D. J. (1955). "Eggs and Egg Products—D.S.I.R. Food Investigation Special Report No. 60". (H.M.S.O., London).
121. B.S.I. (1955). "B.S. 1133 Section 18 Glass Containers". (British Standards Institution, London).
122. U.S. Dept. of Defense (1963). "Military Standard (for) Sampling Procedures and Tables for Sampling by Attributes. MIL-STD 105D". (U.S. Government Printing Office, Washington, D.C.).
123. U.K. Ministry of Defence (1964). "Defence Specification (for) Sampling Procedures and Tables for Sampling by Attributes. DEF–131–A". (H.M.S.O., London).
124. U.K. Ministry of Defence, n.d. supercedes DG7. "A Guide to the Use of Defence Specification DEF–131–A. Defence Guides DG–7–A". (H.M.S.O., London).
125. Bleier, G. (1946). *Fd Trade Rev.* **16** (11), 7.
126. Tritton, S. M. (1948). *Fd Mf.* **23** (118).
127. Beswick, D. R. (1969). *Fd Techn. N.Z.* **4** (10), 332.
128. Burrell, J. R. (1948). *Fd Mf.* **23** 270, 309.
129. Finberg, A. J. (1955). *Fd Engng* **27,** 83.
130. McCormick, R. D. (1964). *Canner/Pckr* **133** (3), 33.
131. Lipscultz, M. and Holtgrieve, R. E. (1968). *Fd Engng* **40** (11), 86.
132. Devey, J. D. (1958). *Fd Trade Rev.* **28** (11) 5, (12), 7.
133. Devey, J. D. (1959). *Fd Trade Rev.* **29** (1) 4, (2) 16, (3) 8, (4) 16.
134. Flückiger, W. (1966). *Fette Seifen AnstrMittel* **48** (2), 139.
135. Smith, V. T. (1969). *Fd Prod. Dev.* **3** (4), 69.
136. Poultney, S. V. (1949). "Vinegar Products". (Chapman and Hall, London).
137. Fabian, F. W., and Wethington, M. C. (1950). *Fd Res.* **15,** 138.
138. Harris, B. R. (1960). In: "Advances in Chemistry Series No. 25" 64. (American Chemical Society, Chicago, Ill.).
139. Sheets, E. H. and Lopez, A. (1962). *Fd Tech., Champaign* **16** (10), 143.
140. Blasco, H. D. (1963). *Rev. Argent, Grasas y Aceites* **5,** 84 (cited in *J. Sci. Fd Agric.,* 1965, **16,** (1), Abstr. p. 47).
141. Burrell, J. R. (1947). *Fd Mf.* **22,** 167.
142. Shapton, D. A., Lovelock, D. W. and Laurita-Longo, R. (1971). *J. appl. Bact.* **34,** 491.

Additional References

The following abstracting journals may be useful sources for readers wishing additional information to that used in the manuscript.

Abstracts of Current Literature. Published by the Fruit and Vegetable Preservation Research Association, Chipping Campden, Gloucestershire.
Analytical Abstracts. Published monthly by The Society for Analytical Chemistry.
B.F.M.I.R.A. Abstracts. Published monthly by The British Food Manufacturers Research Association, Leatherhead, Surrey.
Biological Abstracts. Published semi-monthly by Biosciences Information Service of Biological Abstracts, 2100 Arch Street, Philadelphia, Pennsylvania 19103, United States of America.
British Technology Index. Published monthly by the Library Association. This is a straightforward index of articles from about 400 journals.
Chemical Abstracts. Published monthly by the American Chemical Society.

Dairy Science Abstracts. Published monthly by the Commonwealth Agricultural Bureau and compiled by the Commonwealth Bureau of Dairy Science and Technology.

Food Science and Technology Abstracts. Published monthly by the International Food Information Service, Shinfield, Reading, Berks.

Journal of the Science of Food and Agriculture. Published monthly by the Society of Chemical Industry. It is bound with the Journal but has a separate annual subject and author index.

Metal Box Company, Research Department, Survey of Literature. Published monthly until December 1968.

Packaging Abstracts. Compiled and published monthly by Pira. (The Research Association for the Paper and Board Printing and Packaging Industries) Randalls Road, Leatherhead, Surrey.

Although not an abstract list, current developments in food additive legislation and toxicology are reviewed in the British Industrial Biological Research Association's Information Bulletin which is published monthly by B.I.B.R.A.

For information on the chemical composition of foods, including ingredient materials, reference may be made to McCance, R. A., and Widdowson, E. M. (1960). "Chemical Composition of Foods, M.R.C. Special Reports Series No. 297." (H.M.S.O., London).

Alcoholic Beverages and Vinegars

H. J. BUNKER

Twickenham, Middlesex, England

1. GENERAL CONSIDERATIONS

It might well be argued that the term "quality control" is a misnomer. In the best sense of the term, which implies the maintenance of a standard of good quality, such a thing as quality control certainly exists, but in many products there may be several standards of quality though all perhaps acceptable. In many cases what is called quality control is really consistency control. The maintenance of *consistency* in a product, particularly if it be a food or beverage, is important to the manufacturer in a highly competitive world, and nowhere is this more fully appreciated than in the alcoholic beverage industry. For example, in Great Britain, where there are millions whose favourite is beer, the drinker is normally a very discriminating consumer and his reaction to any beer different from (not necessarily "better" or

5

"worse" than) his usual brand, is immediate. As then consistency, as well as quality, control dominates successful production, it is possible to consider what steps are necessary to achieve adequate control in the fermentation industries. Undoubtedly many of the factors involved are those operating in other food and drink industries and the principles underlying them are widely applicable. If everything we eat and drink consisted purely of chemical compounds such as sodium chloride and distilled water, quality control would resolve itself into a few simple and straightforward analyses. As however our requirements are more complicated, many techniques are involved and consist of a wide variety of operations ranging from numerous analytical procedures which can be operated in the laboratory to trial by the senses: these latter are the final arbiters which continue to be irreplaceable by scientific measurement: the bases of quality control then are both analysis and sensory perception, the senses involved in beverages being sight, taste and smell. (It could be contended that in special instances a fourth sense—sound could be involved: the pop of the champagne cork enhances the consumer's appreciation of this particular beverage, and may assist in activating salivation.)

Beer affords an interesting example of how a factor in "quality" may alter. Today beer drinkers insist on absolute brilliance in their beer, but it was not always so. In bygone days beer was drunk out of pewter or other opaque vessels and the consumer relied on his palate and his nose in judging the quality of the beverage. Nowadays it would be difficult to convince a consumer that because a beer is not brilliant it is not necessarily "off"; it would be fruitless to explain that the haze or cloudiness may well be just precipitated protein and yeast cells which will give him increased nutritional benefit including additional vitamin B1!

In considering quality control of fermented beverages it will be appreciated that, as with other food and drink products, the raw materials employed are all variable and this variability has to be compensated for if consistency is to be achieved.

2. BEER

A. The Brewing Process

The three principal ingredients of beer are malt, hops and water, with yeast as an all-important operating agent. Very briefly, barley is converted into malt which is ground up with water to form a mash. The enzymes in the malt convert the starch into the fermentable sugar maltose. This is the wort, which is then boiled in a copper or kettle with the addition of hops. After straining and cooling, the hopped wort runs into a fermenting vessel into which yeast is added. In the course of a few days conversion of the sugar in the wort to alcohol has taken place and the resulting beer is run off to tanks from which in due course it is "racked" into cask or filled into bottles. Such are the basic principles of beer production with, in practice, many variations in detail.

Malt is made from barley in several ways and not only will these different procedures influence the eventual beer, but the varieties of barleys from which the malts are made will also have important effects. Control operates, then, not only on the original materials but also on the manner of their processing as well as on the finished material.

It is not within the scope of this chapter to describe the details of the malting and brewing process: for these the reader is referred to such textbooks as De Clerck.[1] Furthermore no attempt has been made to list every published paper on quality control in beer or other alcoholic beverages: a selection has been made. Too often a writer, in reviewing a subject feels he must impress by giving a lengthy list of references, thus making the task of his reader more difficult instead of simplifying it.

B. Analytical Methods

Great progress has been made in the past decade in the standardization of analytical methods in the brewing industry and this has resulted in greater uniformity of control over the materials of brewing and their processing. This is due to the activities of such bodies as the European Brewery Convention, the American Society of Brewing Chemists and the Institute of Brewing. These organizations now maintain close liaison and employ, where suitable, many similar techniques. The work of the Analysis Committee of the E.B.C. to which all the major beer-producing countries in Europe adhere, finds fulfilment in "Analytica"[2] the second edition of which appeared in 1963. It is tri-lingual and contains the agreed methods of analysis for barley, malt, adjuncts, hops and beers. In North America the A.S.B.C.[3] have their appropriate committees to recommend standards of analysis and control, and in Great Britain the Institute of Brewing issue Recommended Methods of Analysis.[4] More recently (1967) the Institute revised Recommended Methods[5] to which the reader is referred for exact details of procedure in sampling of raw materials, analyses of barley, pale malts, coloured malts and unmalted grain. In so far as British brewing is concerned, reference to these recommendations is essential.

C. The Raw Materials

1. Barley

Various qualities are looked for in a good malting barley. Appearance and size of the corn and its nitrogen content are less important criteria than

Since this chapter was written a number of papers from the Analysis Committee of the Institute of Brewing on "Recommended Methods of Analysis" have appeared in the Institute's Journal (1971, 77, 181–226). These are available as a collected set.

hitherto, but such factors as ripeness, dormancy, water sensitivity, extract and loss during malting are of real consequence.

The first stage of analysis is careful sampling from bulk and full details are given in "Analytica" and reference [5]. The quantity of mixed samples required for each full analysis is about 500 g. The sample should not be opened at the laboratory until it has reached room temperature, otherwise moisture might be absorbed from the air. The principal data required are (a) moisture, (b) nitrogen, (c) thousand corn weight, (d) germination, (e) percentage of foreign matter and half-corns, and (f) prediction of extract. The methods employed to determine these factors are given in "Analytica" and reference 5, while in A.S.B.C. "Methods of Analysis", prediction of extract is not given but there is a method for "Potential Amylase Activity when Malted". As regards germination, however, it is necessary to distinguish between germinative *energy* and germinative *capacity*. Germinative energy is expressed as "the percentage of grains which can be expected to germinate fully if the sample is malted normally at the time of the test". Moist filter paper or sand is used as a bed and incubation for 72 h (and sometimes for 120 h) at 18–21°C is employed. With poor samples results are apt to be rather varied. Germinative capacity is a measurement of the percentage of living grains in a given sample. The common techniques for this are steeping in hydrogen peroxide for three days or, more rapidly but less reliably with damaged grain, staining with a tetrazolium salt. The prediction of the extract of the malt which should be obtained is calculated using a formula of this nature:

$E\% = A - 4\cdot7\ N + 0\cdot10$ where $E\% =$ Extract percentage on dry malt by the E.B.C. method.

$A =$ Constant for particular variety

$N =$ Nitrogen percentage on dry barley

$G =$ Thousand corn weight in grams of dry barley (see reference 5).

(If nitrogen is calculated as protein, $0\cdot75\ P$ should be substituted for $4\cdot7\ N$, because by convention Protein is taken to be $N \times 6\cdot25$). This is the formula given in "Analytica", which also lists the appropriate constant, A, for the best known European varieties. The figure varies between 84·0 and 86·8, but for most six-row barleys it is 80·0.

For British malts the prediction of extract equation[5] is $E = A - 11\cdot0\ N + 0\cdot22\ G$, and in this case $E =$ Extract in brewer's pounds per quarter of 336 lb on dry basis. N and G have the same meanings but the varietal A, is quite different from the constant in the E.B.C. equation. It normally falls within the range 109·5–113, the latter figure being used for Proctor barley. (For details of constants see references 6 and 7.)

Apart from the analytical data other indications of a good malting barley sample are the uniformity of appearance of the whole corns and also of the transverse or longitudinal sections made with the appropriate cutter. If the cut surfaces are "steely" or vitreous, instead of mealy, or if there are many darkened corns, the barley is not good for malting.

Briefly the malting process consists of steeping the barley corns in water, allowing them to sprout and then kilning. Originally the sprouting stages took place on floors, in "pieces" a few inches deep, and much malt is still prepared in this way, but drums and Saladin "boxes" are replacing floor malting. Furthermore there have been recent developments in three directions; the use of re-steeping techniques, the employment of gibberellic acid, and the development of continuous malting. These newer procedures can affect quality, and considerable economic claims are made for them. With gibberellic acid, whether applied in the steep or later, the claim is for increased extract and the saving of much time "on the floor". Jones and Pierce[8] reported that hopped worts made from gibberellic acid malts showed in most cases increased concentrations of amino acids. These were completely taken up during fermentation so that the final beers had identical analyses with the control beers. An exception is proline, where the figures were much lower than for the control malts without gibberellic acid. The proline content of a malt can indicate the time a malt has been on the floor, provided a depressant such as potassium bromate has not been used. The effect of the use of a high level of potassium bromate together with 1 ppm of gibberellic acid on the production of amino acids during malting varies with the amino acid, the proline content being reduced to one-tenth of that in a normal gibberellic acid malt. Proline is not assimilable by brewer's yeasts and it will therefore still be present in the final beer, and so could affect the stability of the product. Ault[9] did in fact find that beers brewed from malt treated with gibberellic acid were more prone to biological instability than control beers. For a mass of analytical data on the development of the various amino acids during malting and mashing the reader is referred to Jones and Pierce's paper. Püspok and Szilvanyi[10] have published a method for detection of gibberellic acid in malt. After a series of extractions with organic solvents, the substance can be measured spectrophotometrically or by paper chromatography.

The criteria for judging malt are based on analysis, appearance, flavour and texture. Agreed methods are now generally employed. Apart from such items as moisture content, evenness of appearance of the whole corns and of cut cross sections, and thousand corn weight determination of which is described, as for barley, in "Analytica",[2] the efficiency of analysis depends on agreed uniformity of grinding procedure.

A description of the official E.B.C. malt mill has been published[11] together with comparison of results obtained with "classical" mills. Information on the A.S.B.C. mill is given in the Proceedings (e.g. references 12 and 13) and a comparison of the E.B.C. and A.S.B.C. mills is also given.[14] The Analysis

Committee of the Institute of Brewing is working on the comparison of the Seck type mill used in Britain with the E.B.C. mill.[5]

Determination of extract must conform to the exact specifications as given in the method of analysis in use, since it is all important.[5]

In the E.B.C. and A.S.B.C. methods the other factors are nitrogen content, total soluble nitrogen, saccharification rate, character of the mash made from the malt, its speed of filtration, specific gravity, clarity, odour and so forth of the resulting wort. In the E.B.C. method, from the figures obtained for total nitrogen and soluble nitrogen the latter can be expressed as a percentage of the former: this is known as the Kolbach Index. A point to be mentioned regarding nitrogen analyses of malts is that large differences in assimilable nitrogen may be found although the total soluble nitrogen figures may have been similar.

In both the A.S.B.C. Methods of Analysis[3] and the Institute of Brewing Recommended Methods of Analysis[4, 5] there is given a method of determining diastatic activity from the production of reducing sugars from a standard buffered starch solution. The two methods differ in mode of extraction of the malt and the mode of reducing sugar determination. The Institute of Brewing Methods require the determination of "Cold Water Extract".[5]

Hartong's method of measuring degree of modification[1] is very satisfactory but involves mashes at four different temperatures, which is time-consuming.

Attention must be drawn to a report of the E.B.C. Analysis Committee on a revised system for the evaluation of malt modification from the E.B.C. fine-coarse extract difference.[15]

For colour measurement a Tintometer is used which matches the E.B.C. range of standard coloured glasses against the colour of the wort (or beer) in a glass cell. The colour units are based on the Lovibond scale and it must be noted that the values obtained are about twice those used by the A.S.B.C. in their system, because E.B.C. reports colour in 25 mm cell, whereas A.S.B.C. reports in half inch cell, using Lovibond Series 52 glasses. "Analytica",[2] the A.S.B.C. Methods of Analysis, the Institute of Brewing Recommended Methods of Analysis[4, 16] and De Clerck's "Text Book of Brewing" all set out accepted methods for determining colours of caramel malts and roasted malts. These manuals should also be consulted for details of the other official methods for the various items enumerated above. A paper by Walker[17] deals with the development of the British system of malt analysis in relation to Continental and North American systems.

Sometimes acrospire length is required. The acrospire is the structure in the embryo which will eventually emerge as the growing tip of the plant. In malting, however, the germination is arrested while the acrospire is still under the surface of the corn, between the testa and the glume. The method of measurement of the acrospire is given in "Analytica"[2] and consists of a chemical treatment to render the husk translucent so that the acrospire is still visible and its length can be measured.

That malt quality affects fermentation efficiency[18] and beer quality can hardly be doubted: its effect on beer flavour, however, is debated by some. However, the work of Siefker and Pollock[19] and that of Damm and Kringstad[20] indicates that the carbonyl compounds of both barley and malt affect this quality. It is analogous to the undoubted effect on flavour of such substances in food and beverage products.

2. Adjuncts

It is customary in most beer brewing, except where legislation forbids, to use a percentage of unmalted cereals: this may be in the form of barley, rice, maize, wheat and occasionally other carbohydrates. The object is to secure more extract economically, so that this is the factor to be determined in the analysis of adjuncts. Interest in the use of wheat flour has been noticeable in recent years in Britain and it has been claimed that a replacement of up to 25% of the malt by wheat flour gives a satisfactory beer, even improved in some qualities[21] as, for example, in foam character. "Analytica"[2] and the A.S.B.C. have published the latest standardization of methods of analytical methods and both are given in "Analytica": one is based on De Clerck's method[1] and the other on the A.S.B.C. Methods of Analysis.[3] Methods are also given in the Institute of Brewing Recommended Methods.[4] As some cereal adjuncts may have an undesirable amount of fatty substances, the same two sources give methods of estimation. The nitrogen content may also be of importance.

Sugars and syrups of various kinds are used in brewing, the sugars being usually invert sugar, sucrose and glucose. The methods of analysis are those commonly employed and are set out in De Clerck's textbook[1] and in the A.S.B.C. Methods of Analysis. "Analytica" does not set out specific procedures for sugars. Lactose is sometimes added to dark beers to give what is known as "milk stout" but this description is now illegal in Britain. Lactose is not, of course, fermented by brewing yeasts.

The principal amendments in the latest (1967) Recommended Methods of Analysis of the Institute of Brewing[5] are: revised method for estimation of 1000 corn weight, equation of extract prediction (with varietal constants), limits imposed on copper sulphate test for moisture, the preferred method for nitrogen content involving distillation into boric acid and subsequent titration, and the use of Merck's soluble starch for diastatic power determination.

It is further recommended that results should conform to the following scheme:

Moisture as percentage to first decimal place.

Extract of all malts and adjuncts as brewer's lb per standard quarter of 336 lb to the first decimal place.

Colour of all malts in E.B.C. units on the 10% wort in a 25 mm cell to two significant figures.

Diastatic power as degrees Lintner to the nearest whole number.

Cold water extract percent to first decimal place.

Nitrogen as N% on the dry malt, to second decimal place. Total and permanently soluble nitrogen as N% on dry malt to second decimal place. The percentage of the total nitrogen of the malt rendered soluble is the "Soluble Nitrogen Ratio" and is given to nearest whole number.

The percentage of the total nitrogen of the malt rendered permanently soluble is known as "Index of Modification" (more correctly "Index of Nitrogenous Modification").

3. Hops

The principal addition of hops occurs during the boiling of the wort which has come from the mash tun, where amylolytic enzymes have reduced the starchy carbohydrates in the malt and adjuncts, to fermentable sugar. In the copper boil great attention is paid to adequate agitation and aeration of the wort. A good "break" is necessary and consists in the throwing down of large amounts of unwanted protein matter. The hops, a proportion of which may be added at the later stages of the boil, assist in the process besides giving the wort that bitterness which is an essential factor.

The quality of the hops plays a very important part in beer production, not so much because of their preservative value, but because of their contribution to the palate and "nose" of the final beer. The degree and nature of the bitterness of a beer is an overriding factor. The chemistry of hops has become complicated: until two decades ago, the subject more or less started and ended with the conception that the hop resins were divisible into "soft" or α- and β-resins, soluble in light petroleum spirit, and "hard" or γ-resins insoluble in that solvent. While the terms humulone and lupulone were used to apply to the α- and β-resins, it was not realized that both terms really embraced groups of compounds associated with, or derived from these two soft resins. Similarly commercial valuation of hops was based not only on their appearance and "nose" (aroma) on rubbing, but also on their "preservative value" (P.V.) which might variously be expressed as 10 alpha, $10(\alpha + \frac{\beta}{3})$, $(\alpha + \frac{\beta}{9})$, etc. The preservative or bactericidal properties of the hop resins are only active towards certain bacteria, the Gram-positive types. A method of assay depending upon the activity of lactobacilli has largely fallen into abeyance: not only was replication of results between different laboratories difficult, but it has been found that sometimes the test organisms acquire a tolerance towards the hop-resins. In another method, a chemical gravimetric one, the hop resins are extracted by ether in a Soxhlet apparatus. After removal of the ether the residual resinous material is dissolved in pure methanol. The humulone (α-fraction) is then precipitated as the lead salt by the addition of lead acetate, and the total soft resin (humulone and lupulone) is determined by extraction from part of the methanol solution by light petroleum spirit. The difference between the total figure and that for the α-fraction gives the β-fraction. There are variations of the method and descriptions are given in the official books already referred to, also in Lloyd Hind's textbook[22] and more recently in De Clerck's textbook.[1] More modern means of estimation of the α-acids in hops are now available, the three recognized methods being conductometric, spectrophotometric and polarimetric. Details of these are set out in "Analytica", as is also the preliminary operation of determination of moisture content. For a reference method either the use of a vacuum-desiccator (four weeks to final weighing) or a distillation entrainment method is recommended in "Analytica" but for routine work oven drying methods are usual. "Analytica" gives the sources of further information on the above techniques, e.g. Gough[23] on the polarimetric method, Goedkoop and Hartong[24] on the conductometric method, and Alderton et al.,[25] Klopper[26] and Gridgeman[27] on the spectrophotometric method. The above-mentioned sub-committee has made a thorough examination of the methods and found that the chief source of error in all of them has been in the extraction of the sample, and suggestions have been made for reducing the variability. It is agreed that polarimetry should be the reference method, being the only one specific for α-acids; however, for routine control purposes the conductometric method is recommended as being more convenient.

The α-acid content of hops is important on account of its relation to the "brewing value" of the hops and the brewing value is expressed in terms of the bitterness of the beer, which will be discussed later. The α-acid content of a hop is a good guide to its brewing value only in the case of fresh material, when determinations by the three methods mentioned above give similar results. With stored hops the results by the different methods tend to diverge. The brewing value does not, in fact, decrease as much as the analytical figures would indicate. The conductometric method seems to come closest, particularly if chloroform is used as the extractant. The bitterness of beer brewed from old hops is not accountable only to the α-acids: as the hop resins age they give rise to oxidized products more soluble in water and acid solvents. Thus Birtwistle et al.[28] state: "If an iso-octane extract of beer brewed from old hops is washed with acidified methanol, more hop substances are lost from the extract than if similar treatment is given to an extract of beer made from fresh hops. Methods for the estimation of bitterness which did not employ an acid washing stage gave results which agreed with taste evaluation, suggesting that compounds extracted into the acidified methanol are responsible for some of the bitterness of beer brewed from aged hops, although in the absence of precise knowledge of the nature and chemistry of the bitter substances in beer, this is admittedly unproven. Clearly there will be little improvement in control over bitter flavour by adjustment of the hop rate until a chemical means is found of assessing the bitterness of beer which matches the findings of taste panels." The measurement of bitterness is discussed later (pp. 113–115).

4. Water

The composition of the water, referred to in British brewing as "liquor", used in brewing is very important, so much so that the character of many beers is largely due to the type of water used in their brewing. Thus, the well water at Burton-on-Trent is relatively high in gypsum, or in Ca and SO_4 ions, and is considered typical of water for pale ale brewing. Such water requires no treatment beyond a boil and is good also for strong and mild ales. At Pilsen, where the beer brewed is a pale lager, a very soft water with low salt concentration is used and is considered particularly suitable where a delicate hop flavour is involved. At Munich and Dublin, which have water of similar composition there is fairly low content of mineral salts, low chlorides and sulphates and the Ca and Mg ions balance the CO_3 ions. These waters are excellent for the dark lager and stout for which these cities are famous. As Lloyd Hind[22] points out, to brew pale ales with such waters it would be necessary to remove the carbonates and replace by gypsum.

The brewer does not carry out a water analysis every time he brews so that in that sense he does not have a quality control on his brewing liquor: on the other hand, it is recognized that in most cases the mineral content of the water is fairly constant. The brewer does, however, match it to the type of beer he is going to brew. The influence of composition of brewing liquor from mash tun onwards is very marked, but for fuller information on this topic the reader is referred to the standard textbooks.[1, 22] There are, however, certain essential features: thus the liquor supply should be tasteless, odourless and colourless, free from iron and manganese and any suspended matter. It should obviously be free of contamination by micro-organisms. A regular though infrequent examination to test these points is usual.

5. Yeast

(a) *Identification.* The yeasts used in brewing are various strains of *Saccharomyces cerevisiae* and *S. carlsbergensis.* Broadly speaking, in "top" fermentation, as practised in Britain, *S. cerevisiae* strains are used, whilst in "bottom" or lager beer fermentation strains of *S. carlsbergensis* are employed. In recent years however, the systems and strains used have been changing so that clear distinctions have become somewhat diffuse.

The taxonomy or principles of classification of yeasts can be difficult, and except for the broader grouping of types is best left to the specialist. The standard work is the study by Lodder and Kreger-van Rij[29] and a new edition, resulting from collaboration of a number of specialists is in preparation. Meanwhile, for yeasts described in the literature between 1952 and 1958 reference can be made to the Italian monograph by Verona and Monte-martini.[30] Simplified schemes of identification of yeast cultures have been published by Beech et al.[31] For the differentiation of species of the genus Saccharomyces Brady[32] has compared their utilization of amino compounds. Fowell's method[33] of distinguishing the commoner wild yeasts found in the brewery and the yeast factory, is based on colony differences on lysine agar medium. Also of value in identification is the examination of giant colonies on wort gelatin (Richards[34]). The finer differentiation of strains of brewing yeasts is by actual behaviour in fermentation, e.g. head formation, degree and speed of attenuation and separation.

(b) *Pitching Yeast.* In the brewing process the yeast is introduced (or pitched) as a slurry while the cooled hopped wort is run into the fermenting vessel.

A brewer will select—or inherit—the strain of yeast suitable for his particular beer and having done so, he must ensure its consistency, not only its behaviour during fermentation, as regards attenuation and rate of flocculation, for example, but also so that it does not change its character or become infected and hence give a beer differing from his standard. The infection may be due to other strains of *Saccharomyces cerevisiae*, or to so-called "wild" yeasts or to bacteria.

While most lager beer fermentations are conducted with yeast derived from pure cultures, this is not yet the case with much top fermentation beer brewed in this country. As a consequence much attention has to be paid to the condition of the pitching yeast. According to the care taken over plant cleaning and yeast storage, a brewery may carry on with the same yeast for a shorter or longer time; some small breweries need to change perhaps monthly and others may continue for years without change: this latter state of affairs does not necessarily imply that a pure strain is being used: sometimes a mixture of strains is present which seems to maintain a reasonable balance of the different strains which is more or less constant at particular stages of successive fermentations.

The brewing scientist is apt to tire of hearing that a particular pitching yeast has "tired". The older generation brewer was inclined to retain perhaps a too anthropomorphic conception of the yeast cell.

Green and Sullivan[35] have described a technique whereby very small numbers of particular types in a mixed pitching yeast may be quantitatively determined and deviations in the relative proportions of the various types during fermentation demonstrated. The method rests upon plating on various agar media deficient in different growth factors. It is claimed that the method is sensitive enough to detect one yeast cell of one type among hundreds of thousands of cells of another type.

Quality control of yeast, then, does not necessarily imply pure yeast cultivation from a single cell, although this practice, widespread elsewhere, is probably growing in Britain. In some cases cultures of two different yeasts may be deliberately mixed. For example, one strain may be a quick-starting fermenter but a poor attenuator, whilst a second strain may be a slow starter but a good attenuator. (Attenuation is the reduction in specific gravity during fermentation, as the conversion of sugar to alcohol proceeds.) The first strain may be a flocculent type, coming out of suspension and ceasing to operate before completion of fermentation. The second type of yeast, giving good attenuation, may be of the non-flocculating or "powdery" type. For fuller discussion on the subject of yeast flocculation, the reader is referred to various brewing textbooks and particularly to Jensen.[36] The subject is one of some complexity because although numerous theories are in vogue, none appears to be applicable in every case.

Another point about maintenance of particular strains within a brewery is that apart from fermentation efficiency yeast type can have an important effect on the flavour of the finished beer, according to the complexity of the mixture of fusel oil, i.e. higher alcohols and esters.

Several techniques are available for achieving control of yeast quality, which includes viability and freedom from infection. While microscopic examination may, according to the degree of infection (and the experience of the microscopist) reveal the presence of bacteria in a yeast sample, it may not always be adequate to prove absence of infection by wild yeasts, unless the latter, by their difference in size and shape happen to be sufficiently numerous for their presence to be obvious. Microscopically, brewer's yeast in good condition should show cells circular to slightly oval, with a diameter between 5–10 μ. Transparent vacuoles should be evident, with the nucleus visible. The cell walls should be fairly thin and the presence of buds will indicate an active condition. Starved cells may take on an elongated form which could lead to some confusion with wild yeasts.

The Yeast Group of the European Brewery Convention have reported[37] on their combined examination of several methods of estimation of the viability of yeast samples.

A staining technique rests on the fact that healthy cells are less permeable to dyes than are weak or dead cells. Various microscopical stains were employed, and methylene blue was found to be the most useful for reproductibility, although Rhodamine B was also good. With old yeast cultures, however, results were "misleadingly high".

Given a suitable incubation time, a slide culture technique was found to be more applicable for a wider range of viabilities. The basis of the method is the placing of drops of a melted agar medium to which the yeast cells have been added, on to a Thoma haemocytometer slide, and covering with a cover slip. Culturing at 18°C for 16 h was usually adequate.

A third technique in which the number of yeast cells streaked on to a plate was found to give such large variations between different laboratories, and to give such exceptionally low counts, that the Group decided not to continue tests on this method. The procedure is to make a weak saline suspension of the yeast and by haemocytometer or turbidimeter estimate the total number of cells per given volume. By serial dilution a suitable quantity of the suspension, containing a known number of cells (between 50 and 500) is streaked on to the surface of plates of malt extract medium, and the number of colonies subsequently developing is counted and this number as a percentage of the cells streaked on to the plate, gives the viability.

There are now various techniques available for testing purity of a yeast culture. An infection by wild yeasts might well pass undetected microscopically and even "plating" on hopped or unhopped wort agar or malt extract agar may not be effective, since an infecting wild yeast may not give distinctive colonies or may be swamped numerically by the colonies of the primary yeast. Similarly, in the case of bacterial infection, plating on ordinary nutrient agar may be ineffective. The two commonly employed microbiological methods of detecting infection of pitching yeast involve the use of a lysine medium for wild yeasts and an actidione medium for bacteria.

The lysine medium for detection of wild yeasts was initiated by Walters and Thistleton[38] who showed that the normal yeasts *Saccharomyces cerevisiae* and *S. carlsbergensis* differ from some 180 other yeasts examined by them in that these two species are unable to utilize lysine in their metabolism. By employing a medium with this particular amino acid as sole source of nitrogen, therefore, they were able to obtain growth, in liquid medium, where yeasts other than the above two species, were present. Later, by adding agar to the medium Morris and Eddy[39] enhanced its use for the detection and isolation of wild yeasts in pitching yeasts. The medium contains some two dozen ingredients, including the members of the vitamin B complex. The solid medium procedure is to wash and centrifuge a sample of the yeast thrice: it will be appreciated that this is desirable to remove any extraneous nitrogenous nutrient which might otherwise invalidate the test. 0·2 ml of a suspension of the washed yeast containing approximately 10^7 yeast cells/ml on a plate of the lysine medium. The plate is incubated in the ordinary way at 25°C. A point of importance is the concentration of yeast cells in the inoculum because if the numbers are low, say between 100 and 1000, growth of ordinary yeast cells, albeit restricted, does occur. When the cell population exceeds 10 000, the colony count is entirely that of the wild yeasts.

An elegant serological technique for the detection of wild yeast contaminants has been applied to the examination of pitching yeast.[40, 41, 42] The basis of the method is to render fluorescent the cells of the contaminant wild *Saccharomyces* species. A serum of suitable specificity is obtained by cross-absorption with a brewing yeast, and by combining two sera, *Saccharomycetes* contaminants are detected. Other methods for doing this are not easy or as rapid. The only drawback is that a supply of rabbit antiserum is necessary and this would probably have to be obtained outside the brewery.

For the detection of bacterial infections of pitching yeast an actidione medium is commercially available. As actidione is an antibiotic for almost all yeasts but not for bacteria, its incorporation in a nutrient medium with the addition of agar[43] should reveal any contaminating bacteria. Adjustment of the pH of the medium to approximately 6·5 by addition of weak Na_2CO_3 solution is recommended, followed by incubation at 25°–30°C for several days.

With the development of continuous brewing, the use of pure yeast cultures is bound to be of significance. Infection in continuous operations can obviously have serious consequences resulting in the cessation of operations. In continuous brewing the effect of an infection will depend largely on the comparative rates of reproduction of the culture yeast and the infection. It might be contended that the high concentration of culture yeast which is tending to be used in continuous brewing should help towards the suppression of any extraneous infecting organisms. It would not be safe to assume that this always operates: a slight change in environmental conditions (pH, elimination of a nutrient, temperature, etc.) can favour one organism against another.

Contaminated pitching yeast, whether the infection be bacterial or by wild yeasts, may not only lead to unsatisfactory fermentations but can also affect the stability, flavour and appearance of the beer. Worst of all, perhaps, is the fact that infected pitching yeast is a menace in that it is the commonest source of infection of the whole brewery, and that however much attention is paid to brewery hygiene, it may become a losing battle so long as the pitching yeast is infected.

Purification of infected pitching yeast may be effected or attempted by several methods, some of which are at least as old-established as the Pasteur era. They are based largely on dropping the pH to a figure inimical to the infection, but less harmful to the yeast. Culturing the yeast in beer wort to which 0·1% tartaric acid has been added, and repeating the operation a second time, is such a method.[22] The normal pH of beer wort (at any rate top fermentation brewing) is about 5·2, but higher with bottom fermentation worts, and this operation brings the figure down to about 3·9. The treatment is alleged to be effective against the common *Flavobacterium proteus* and *Lactobacillus pastorianus*, but it seems to reduce rather than eliminate the rod infection. Another recommendation is the use of 0·1% phosphoric acid, particularly if the infection consists of lactic acid bacteria: it is claimed that several hours of such treatment is effective without damaging the yeast. Alternatively pitching the yeast into an acid wort (pH 4·5) is claimed to be equally satisfactory.

Various antibiotics such as tyrothricin[44] have been employed, but as they are usually specific for particular bacteria, or even strains, their use is not yet general.

It is not surprising that the methods of pitching ycast purification based on lowering the pH values are not particularly effective against wild yeasts, although this has been claimed for the tartaric acid treatment.

A recently advocated method of disinfection (from bacteria) is by the use of acidified ammonium persulphate.[45] This compound, at 0·75% and pH 2·8 is said to be effective: lactobacilli are resistant to the 0·75% ammonium persulphate adjusted to pH 2·8, the acetic bacteria are resistant to acid unless the pH is brought down at least to 2·4, while "flavobacteria" are sensitive to both treatments, but most rapidly killed by the acidified ammonium persulphate. A treatment time of about 16 h is recommended, although anywhere between 12 and 24 h is said to be safe. A later publication[46] gives a faster treatment: so long as a treatment time of 2 h±20 min is not exceeded, the pH can be dropped to 2·2 without seriously impairing yeast viability. Gram positive lactobacilli appear to be the most resistant forms. Washing with 0·1% H_3PO_4 may eliminate lactic types.

Where laboratory and pilot plant facilities are available this writer prefers to start afresh from a laboratory culture of the brewery yeast or yeasts. Once a pure culture has been worked up to production scale it should be possible with modern plant to retain the yeast in good condition for prolonged periods. The detection of wild yeast contaminants when present in very low concentration compared with the brewer's yeast can be difficult yet important, not only in pitching yeast but also in the finished beer. Thus, when the beer is fined the cells of the culture yeast may be removed but small numbers of wild yeasts may be left behind in suspension in the cask: in this case they can subsequently develop and cause a haze in the beer. A proportion of one single wild yeast cell to 16 million brewer's yeast cells can eventually produce a "commercially significant" haze.[47] One method of detection depends on different thermal death points of the yeasts[48] and a laboratory technique for overcoming the difficulty in so far as pitching yeast is concerned, has been described.[47]

The storage of pitching yeast, pending subsequent re-use, calls for care when the possible effects of autolysis and contamination are borne in mind. Sometimes the pitching yeast is stored "wet", i.e. as a cream, and sometimes pressed. Washing briefly and not repeatedly should be safe if a temperature as near as possible to 0°C for the washing water can be used. Where storage for more than a day or so, say up to a week, is unavoidable, maintenance under very cold water is advisable. Storage in the cold under 2% solution of potassium dihydrogen phosphate has been found satisfactory.[49] For longer periods storage in 10% sucrose has been advocated: certainly this writer has maintained laboratory cultures for periods of years in this way. An alternative, where storage for a period up to four weeks is necessary, is to let the yeast slowly ferment a medium to low gravity wort at a low temperature almost down to 0°C. In culture collections it is nowadays customary to keep the cultures in the freeze-dried state.

(c) *Attenuative power*. This is expressed as the percentage drop of a yeast in specific gravity of the wort during fermentation. The *real* attenuation is the figure obtained by removing the alcohol by distillation and then making the liquid up to its original weight. *Apparent* attenuation is a simpler figure: it is just the above-stated percentage of the O.G. (original gravity) which has been lost during fermentation but measured without removal of the alcohol. It will be a higher figure than that for the real attenuation. Limiting attenuation is determined in the brewery laboratory and represents attenuation achieved under the best conditions. It is usually expressed in the above term as "apparent limiting attenuation", not the "true". The procedure is to inoculate 0·5 g of *fresh* pressed yeast into 200 ml of hopped wort in a conical flask which is then incubated at 25°C with shaking, for three days.

(d) *Chemical analysis*. The actual chemical analysis of yeast is not likely to be of particular interest to the brewer, except when he wishes to dispose of his surplus to makers of yeast extract or compounders of animal feeding stuffs. In such cases the data usually required are moisture content, nitrogen (for protein) ash, vitamins (of the B Group) and some metals, particularly copper, lead and possibly arsenic. Yeasts tend to adsorb these metals readily. Methods for determination of these items are fully set out in textbooks such as that of De Clerck.[1]

D. Process and Plant Control

1. General Considerations

However good the quality of raw materials used in a food or beverage manufacturing process may be, much expense and effort will be wasted if the processing is not of a high hygienic standard. Quality control of processing starts at the reception of raw materials into the factory or brewery and is succeeded by further control, certainly with beer, after it has left the brewery and up to the moment of consumption. This is obvious so far as draught beer is concerned, where handling, storage and dispensing need continued attention, but even bottled and canned beers require consideration, particularly in relation to shelf life and temperature, since although biological stability may have been ensured by pasteurization or other treatment, there is still the possibility of non-biological instability, such as haze development. Strictly speaking, quality control should include such items as the paper and printing of labels, the bottles (as regards colour, dimensions, diameter of locking ring, capacity, both total and at a set filling height, and so forth).[50] Similarly with crown cork closures, the metal and the inserts all call for examination from time to time, and efficiency of closure may be tested by placing in a water bath at 150°F for 20 min and watching for bubbles.

2. Sources of Infection

Discovering the source of microbiological trouble when it arises in the brewery is not always easy, for there are many possibilities and some may be non-recurrent. The infection may be in the materials, the plant, or it may be extraneous. It has already been stated that the worst agent for the spread of microbial trouble on the grand scale can be the pitching yeast itself. It is not unusual to blame airborne infection and this is to some extent understandable: in common with other food and drink factories it is frequently found that trouble develops in spells of hot weather, particularly in regions with conditions of high relative humidity prevailing. Such conditions might well reduce the rate of desiccation and therefore of killing of airborne organisms.

However, most brewing microbiologists are inclined to attach less importance to the incidence of infection by airborne organisms than they formerly did, for various reasons which need not be set out at great length here. Exposure of plates of agar at different places in the brewery will certainly reveal the presence of mould fungi, yeasts and bacteria, but not of such an alarming nature as might be suspected. Moulds are of minor importance in brewing, in so far as beer spoilage is concerned: some of the yeasts, which usually include a relatively high proportion of red forms, (*Rhodotorulae*) are largely harmless types—for less than a dozen of the hundreds of known "wild" yeasts really cause serious trouble: and of bacteria, few species are dangerous from the brewer's point of view; they are almost restricted to certain *Acetobacter* (and *Acetomonas*) species, some *Lactobacilli*, a few micrococci and *Zymomonas anaerobia*. The common airborne aerobic spore-formers, so common in soil and dust, such as *Bacillus cereus*, are not of serious consequence because they are not in a favourable environment at the pH of beer. Bacteria pathogenic to man likewise find beer an uncongenial medium.[51]

While, then, it may be contended that airborne infection has been over-blamed in the past, it would be dangerous to ignore this source of trouble completely. It is only intended here to claim that to attribute any outbreak of trouble to airborne micro-organisms without further attempts at tracking down alternative sources would be irresponsible. A possible source of infection which is sometimes overlooked but which should be borne in mind, particularly where wild yeasts are concerned, and which is akin to aerial infection, is the clothing of operatives, the "turn-ups" of trousers, and even the hair on their heads. Swabs of such possible foci of infection have shown this to be a possibility.

When the boiled wort leaves the copper it is sterile, but infection may recur at any stage thereafter: in the hop-back or hop-strainer, wort cooler, fermenting vessels and storage tanks. Between each of these pieces of plant there will be mains, sometimes of great length, and there will be cocks, valves, sampling taps, sight-glasses and so on—all very easy points for the lodgement of infecting organisms. Conditions may still exist in some breweries where considerable stretches of mains cannot be disconnected into short lengths for cleaning. The passing of ball-brushes through such mains is the only means of cleaning and any assurance of bacteriological cleanliness is difficult. The use of the enclosed heat-exchanger for wort cooling must have done much to reduce the incidence of infection of the wort on its way to the fermenting vessel, particularly when proper attention is paid to the sterility of the air used to aerate the wort at this stage.

From the fermenting vessel stage onwards the fermenting wort and beer are liable to infection from various sources: the matter of aerial contamination has already been considered, but a more formidable source of trouble is the vessel itself. Thorough cleaning is obviously essential, but this is not always perfect: apart from human frailty in the operation, the nature of the vessel surface is important. Bare wood is virtually impossible to sterilize completely and some metallic or treated surfaces are apt to develop pits and scratches. After a time fermenting vessels develop on their inner surface a layer of "beer stone" which consists largely of calcium oxalate, formed during fermentation: some brewers may leave this undisturbed on the grounds that the rougher surface improves fermentation rate. The "pros" and "cons" of various types of surface and their influence on fermentation cannot be discussed here but in general brewers prefer the removal of beer stone in that it may, by its structure, harbour infection. The writer is aware of at least one instance where a bacterial infection was introduced with the paste being used to cleanse the vessel! Another possible source of infection can arise in faulty fermentations which "stick". A sticking or sluggish fermentation is one in which the attenuation fails to go down to its customary level and the fermentation is re-activated by adding powdered material of some sort: this may be malt or baking flour; kieselguhr pumice or bentonite; calcium phosphate or one of the "yeast foods" which are on the market. These materials may well carry infecting micro-organisms so they should be sterilized before use.

After fermentation the beer goes to storage tanks whence it may be "racked" into casks or kegs (draught beer) or it may go to the bottling store. On either journey—and subsequently—it will suffer opportunities for infection or re-infection. With draught beer trouble may come from mains, sometimes lengthy, racking backs (tanks), the racking machine itself, with its several delivery nozzles and the casks or kegs into which the beer is drawn are frequently a source of infection. With the decreasing use of wood and its replacement by metal, cleaning of the casks and kegs has become easier. The difficulty of sterilizing wooden casks or other wooden vessels can be demonstrated by washing and steaming a cask and, when the temperature has fallen, rinsing with sterile quarter strength Ringer solution.* This rinse, on plating out may show no bacterial or yeast colonies and yet if the cask be now closed with a sterile bung and left for a day or two and then re-opened and rinsed again with sterile Ringer solution, when plated will usually show numerous colonies.

Infection can be introduced into a brewery through the return of casks in bad condition or containing stale beer from public houses, etc. The writer has seen "rope" brought into a brewery in this manner, and the man in charge of the "returns cellar" should be on his guard against such an occur-rence. Rope is a bacterial contamination of beer producing a viscous mucila-ginous condition: the infection can readily spread throughout the brewery with disastrous results.

The possibility of wooden bungs being a source of infection has been sug-gested but the writer knows of no proven instance. What can happen, how-ever, is an influence on beer flavour by the variety of wood used. While public house cellar management is outside the scope of this section, it may nevertheless be mentioned that when a cask of beer is set up in the cellar and broached, insertion of a dirty tap can easily result in beer spoilage. The increasing use of metal containers will eliminate much of the public house cellar work and hence reduce infection troubles in that quarter.

For sweeter beers, "primings" of sugar are employed and these can be a source of infection as they constitute such a favourable medium for micro-organisms: when this happens a gummy ropy condition of the beer can result. However, nowadays, the reputable suppliers of sugars and syrups are alive to these possibilities and trouble from this source, should it arise, may originate in the "sweet" or primings room in the brewery.

Finings are added to beer, as also to wines, etc., to clarify them and in beer the commonest agent is isinglass, the product of the swim bladder of fish

---

* Ringer Solution is a solution of mineral salts adjusted to a strength such that it is isotonic with the contents of the yeast or microbial cells.

such as the sturgeon. While sometimes the raw material is infested with insects, the actual preparation of the finings solution is such as to eliminate them as sources of infection. Other types of finings are also employed. The generally accepted theory of their action is a physical one, the charge on the yeast cells and protein particles in suspension in the beer being neutralized by the opposite charge on the finings colloidal matter. This may not, however, be the whole story.

With some draught beers there is the practice of "dry hopping" which consists of adding hops, at a rate of a few ounces per barrel, to the finished beer in cask, the object being to give added aroma and preservative value. To what extent the practice achieves much is possibly open to doubt. Recent indications are that from the point of view of introducing infection with the dry hops, the risk is negligible.

Turning to the processing of beers for bottling: these may be retained until required in tanks for periods varying from hours to weeks. The ordinary light and mild ales may spend little time in tank before fining and filtration. Various types of filter are employed, and the "furnish" of the filter medium may be cellulose pulp, diatomaceous earth or mixtures thereof, and incorporating varying proportions of asbestos. The object of filtration is twofold: to remove all visible suspended matter so that the beer is brilliant, and to remove micro-organisms which, while they may not be numerous enough to be visible at the time of filtration in the form of a haze, may subsequently develop to cause this defect. Filtration is usually in two stages, "roughing" and "polishing", and carbonation of the beer is usually carried out at the same time.

From the filters the beer passes through mains to the bright beer tanks, where it is held until required in the bottling hall. Obviously from the hygienic point of view, the distances between filters and bright beer tanks and between the latter and the bottling units should be as short as possible, to reduce the chance of pick-up of organisms in the beer mains: in some breweries these distances are far too long. Attention is being paid nowadays not only to removing by filtration all suspended matter including micro-organisms but also to potential haze forming substances, largely anthocyanogens, from the beer.

The vast bulk of bottled light and mild beers are pasteurized nowadays: where however, pasteurization is not practised, a final filter actually at the filling unit can be successfully employed. Where in-bottle pasteurization is done the tendency may inevitably be to take less trouble in post-filtration stages on the grounds that if the beer gets re-infected after leaving the filter, pasteurization will deal with any surviving micro-organisms. Besides this attitude being an admission of inefficiency, it can lead to all round slackness in attention to quality control, and is therefore as bad as, for example, having the ceiling of a bottling hall supporting a luxurious growth of black and green moulds, even if they may not often cause much beer spoilage.

The question to pasteurize or not to pasteurize must surely be linked with the shelf-life which is desired for a particular beer. If it is for the local home market with a quick turnover in that particular beer, then a period of two or three weeks' shelf life may be considered adequate, provided the retailer is conscientious in rotating his stock. Where beer is intended to have a long and even indeterminate shelf life, then probably pasteurization is a reasonable policy.

Alternative methods of maintaining biological stability are always being considered: in Britain SO_2 is, at the time of writing, the only permitted preservative for beer. Elsewhere, in U.S.A. for example, diethyl-pyrocarbonate is allowed. Further reference to this material is made in the Wines Section of this chapter. Hot bottling in which the possibility of bacterial infection is greatly reduced is being practised in Germany but does not seem to have developed really extensively elsewhere yet.

A bottle-filling unit is a complicated piece of plant from the microbiologist's point of view and its bacteriological cleanliness is vital: it can be appreciated that if only one of its numerous filling-heads is not sterile, the percentage of bottles which will become infected is such that a very large number of failures can result, because units capable of filling hundreds of bottles a minute are now available. The filler is served by a bottle-washing unit and here again strict biological control is necessary; in fact, it may be contended that among the items of brewing and bottling plant, the filler and the bottler are some of those upon which the most constant biological control is desirable. Bottling stores may nowadays be called upon to handle millions of bottles a week, so it can be contended that it would be quite impracticable for the laboratory to take from the bottle-washing and bottle-filling lines a statistically significant sized sample of the weekly output and retain the bottles for the requisite time to ascertain the efficiency of the units. For the washed bottles several days might be necessary and for the filled beer bottles several weeks retention could be required.

Bottle closures and the machines which deliver them must be watched. In the writer's experience it is the biological condition of the "crowner" which needs attention rather than the crowns themselves, which generally seem to be bacteriologically satisfactory. Nevertheless, very occasionally bacterial trouble has been traced to the cork disc in the crown. As the cork particles are held together by an adhesive which may be bacterially nutritious, e.g. casein, the possibility of microbial multiplication cannot be entirely ignored. Nowadays, however, the foil or plasticized "spot" prevents direct contact of cork and beer. More troublesome from this point of view are the screw stoppers and few brewers will regret their disappearance. It is very difficult to sterilize the stopper and the rubber ring, particularly if they are not separated.

Much could be said about floors as a source of, and particularly spread of, infection. It is a constant problem in all food and beverage factories. Apart from spread by the boots of personnel, the constant traffic of trolleys, etc., not only carries any infection but also gradually causes and subsequently emphasizes uneven floor surfaces, leading eventually to grooves and puddles. In a brewery, where heavy items such as casks have constantly to be moved the problem is probably as difficult as anywhere. Apart from loading and unloading bays, sites where humidities can be high, in cellars, particularly round racking machines, filter rooms, bottling halls and so on, can be a constant source of trouble.

3. System of Brewery Control

In the author's experience there has been a marked improvement in conditions in breweries, etc., in recent years, although control on a systematic basis is still lacking, chiefly in smaller organizations where ignorance rather than indifference prevails. In the absence of a properly devised system of process control there is apt to be a spasmodic and even panic-stricken approach when trouble occurs through, say, an outbreak of wild yeast or bacterial infection. In an organized system all plant and equipment coming into contact with the ingredients of the products during manufacture are periodically examined for bacteriological condition. This does not mean that every day every vessel, every liquor, wort and beer main, every cock, valve and sight glass, every filter, every bottle washing machine and filling unit must be submitted to test. A survey based on initial tests everywhere should reveal in most cases those stages in production or those items of plant which are danger spots from the point of view of spoilage. Such a survey should enable the laboratory to indicate which materials and plant, as well as floors, walls and roofs, need attention daily, weekly, monthly, or even less frequently. This constitutes proper microbiological control* and if such a scheme is not operated either the running of the brewery is, on the one hand, living on the edge of a volcano, or on the other is accumulating a lot of useless information at considerable expense. It is difficult to go far beyond these generalizations into detailed recommendations since each establishment is different. One can only enumerate therefore, general principles. A considerable literature exists on biological control.[52, 53, 54]

* A purist has complained that literally "microbiological control" means control of the study or science of microbes, which is not at all the meaning intended: the purist would presumably prefer "microbial control" but this might convey the idea of control by microbes. The term microbiological control derived from the term biological control which has long been used to indicate control of an animal or vegetable pest by another animal or vegetable. In this sense the meaning is certainly control by an organism, so the purist wins again in his objection to the term. However, this somewhat arid exposition may be left here, since it is most probable that the reader of these chapters knows what is meant by microbiological control in this context.

While different establishments may call for variations in the details of control, these should conform to a schedule which experience in a particular brewery shows, in a relatively short time, to be both efficient and practical. The brewing room, at any rate in a sizeable brewery, has to depend on its laboratory reports for information on the hygienic condition of the plant, equipment and materials and information must be both up-to-date and accurate. It is not of much use to the brewer to know four days after the event, that a piece of plant, say a bottle-washing unit, was working inefficiently on account of the temperature of the liquor being too low, or the concentration of detergent being faulty. Similarly, it is essential that all laboratory results are fully recorded so that in the event of trouble, reference back is facilitated.

As regards plant cleaning, the brewer must appreciate the difference between detergent and germicide. The former may be good for cleaning in the physical sense but may be useless in destroying micro-organisms; the converse applies. A preparation which combines both detergency and germicidal properties is naturally desired in many cases, but indescriminate mixing of the two types of compound must be avoided. For example, mixing of an efficient anionic detergent with an equally efficient cationic germicide will result in a solution which is not efficient in either respect. Another consideration applying particularly to beer is the degree of surface activity of the compound employed: should it be strongly surfactant it may well be suspect in the brewery because unless all traces of the substance are removed after its use on plant, a disastrous influence on the "head" or foaming properties of the beer may result, apart from other undesirable effects.

It is impossible within the compass of this chapter to discuss the relative merits of the various types of compounds available for detergency and sterilization, but lists are compiled for brewers in some countries and for general information the reader is referred to such books as that by Sykes.[55] It is probably safe to say that at the present time the most popular germicides in breweries are the quaternary ammonium compounds and chlorine compounds, but there are various provisos on their use. Many of the relevant considerations were dealt with from both the academic and practical angles in a monograph published in 1964.[56] Other factors affecting efficiency of hygienic treatment are pH, presence of organic matter, period of contact with, and nature of plant, as well as types of micro-organisms involved: some disinfectants are useful against bacteria but useless against yeast and fungi, and vice versa. Apart from the selection of the most suitable sterilizer detergent the manner of its application needs care, both to ensure its effectual use and also its subsequent complete removal. An actual example of ineffectuality may be cited: in a series of fermenting vessels sprays were fixed to the door or placed on the floor of the vessel but failed to achieve sterility because the treatment did not reach the uppermost parts of attemperating coils. Success was achieved when a spray operating as a fixture in the centre of the top of the dome of each vessel was installed, each spray being connected by stainless steel line to the detergent and a portable pump, or to mains liquor if desired. One advantage of a set-up of this nature is in reducing the number of times personnel have to enter the vessel.[57]

Beerstone has been mentioned above and various methods of removal are advocated; most brewers would nowadays favour removal. Sometimes 2·5% solution of metasilicate[58] is favoured and so also is gluconic acid. Another reported formulation is a mixture of 90–92% sodium hydroxide, with 4% sodium gluconate, 0·75% tetraphosphates and a small quantity of wetting agent. Application is for 30 min with 1·5 lb of this mixture diluted with 75 gallons of water.[59] In selecting suitable cleansing and sterilizing agents careful consideration must be given to the materials of the vessel, or their linings, to ensure that no damage is done to them.

As a basic principle of plant hygiene, the fewer valves, taps, sampling cocks, sight glasses and so forth in vessels, the better the chances of achieving sterility, since it is at these places that cleaning is most difficult and where new plant is being installed this point should be borne in mind. Where one entrance or exit from a vessel can be made to serve two purposes, the danger of microbial infection is at least reduced.

Mains, nowadays more usual in detachable sections to facilitate cleaning, need sterilizing at regular intervals, the exact programme being determined by bacteriological swabbing tests, to show whether daily or weekly or monthly attention is required for each line. It could hardly be the same interval for every main. In those mains which are dismantled into lengths which can be immersed, say overnight, in bactericidal-detergent solution, it is most important that total immersion is achieved and that there are no air locks within the sections. This needs attention even more so in the case of flexible hoses used for inter-tank transfers and the male and female elements of the connections need especial care. The writer has found this to be a particularly important point, and even where sterilization has been carried out, the handling of the connections by personnel can often nullify the careful preparation of the parts.

The question is often posed regarding the efficiency of steaming as a means of sterilization of plant and mains. The brief answer is that steam is a good killing agent, but three points need consideration. First, steam should obviously not be used where it can damage any parts of the plant or tackle. Second, it must be employed long enough to heat up the surface which is to be sterilized to a temperature at which organisms could not survive. Third, steam may be a killing agent but not necessarily a cleaning agent. For example, if a beer main has a branch or joint in which yeast and other matter has accumulated, the application of steam will kill the organisms. But it may not *remove* the dead matter and as a consequence when next beer or other liquid which carries any yeast or bacteria flows through the pipe, they will thrive on the excellent food material which the dead matter will provide. Just as in the case of draught beer, particular attention to racking machines and casks is necessary, similarly with bottled beers, the filters, filling units and bottle-washing machines need close observation. Most bottled beers are filtered and on the whole need to have a longer shelf-life than draught beers. Periodic examination of filter efficiency is necessary and for this purpose a membrane filter in the laboratory is desirable because a large quantity, say half or one litre of beer can be passed through and the total count obtained, whereas by ordinary plating technique only one or 2 ml can normally be taken.

While good microbiological control should render pasteurization of bottled beers unnecessary most of them are submitted to this operation. In this case control of the time/temperature relationship is important to ensure that treatment which, while adequate to kill any organisms in the beer, will not be too drastic or prolonged, otherwise the beer will acquire a "cooked" flavour. The "20 min up, 20 min hold (at 140°F) and 20 min down" procedure for half-pint glass bottles is satisfactory, but is unnecessarily long for the small beer can because of the better thermal conductivity of metal: it is inadequate for larger bottles. That part of the cooling period between 140°F and about 90°F should be kept as brief as possible because this it the phase in which "cooking" occurs. A half-pint bottle of beer may, at ambient room temperature of about 20–22°C, take as long as 2 h to drop through this range if not cooled artificially by water immersion or spraying.

The microbiological conditions of washed bottles, particularly when pasteurization is not being employed on the bottled product is very important because a residue of quite a small number of yeasts or bacteria may well in the course of a few days result in a cloudy beer. For the bacteriological examination of washed bottles the method explained by the writer elsewhere[52] is recommended. In effect, the operation corresponds to a roll-tube method. Instead of plating out a rinse of the bottle in Petri dishes the bottle itself is coated internally with melted agar and the bottle rolled backwards and forwards on its side until the agar has solidified. The counts of developing colonies will normally be considerably higher than the counts on a Petri dish inoculated from a Ringer solution rinse. When using the rolling bottle method it is necessary to increase the amount of agar in the medium otherwise it will not set evenly on the bottle surface but will collapse. Figure 1 illustrates the appearance of a badly contaminated bottle subjected to this method of testing.

The value of this technique lies not only in its giving a truer result of the condition of the bottle, but it is more satisfactory for demonstration to bottling personnel than a table of figures conveying little or nothing to the uninitiated.

Occasionally at certain seasons an insect, for example a *Drosophila* fly or related species, may enter a dirty beer bottle and pupate on the inner surface. Normally the detergent will deal with this situation, but sometimes the adhesive material binding the pupae to the bottle wall needs a slightly higher temperature and a slightly stronger solution of the detergent for its removal. In any case the pupa will have been killed by the normal cleaning but its presence could lead to prosecution under food laws.

Fig 1. Imperfectly washed beer bottle, coated internally with agar and incubated for 48 h.

The bacteriological condition of beer cans is usually highly satisfactory and as canned beer is invariably pasteurized there is little likelihood of biological instability arising. Sullivan[60] has set out in great detail the full data of quality control in beer canning.

4. Control of Products

(a) *Biological Stability*. To test the bacteriological condition of a beer ordinary plating techniques can be employed, but membrane filtration is being used increasingly because, as stated above, much larger volumes can be examined, and without resort to centrifugation. The best media to employ for plating depend on circumstances and the beers. Some brewers maintain perhaps that as they are only interested in organisms which may grow in beer, they only want to know what types develop on, say, beer agar or hopped wort agar. This can be misleading. As regards plant, the use of ordinary nutrient agar and wort, or malt extract, agar are desired because all micro-organisms ("total counts") are sought, to see if plant is clean. But with beer itself, the situation is different: nevertheless results based purely on beer agar and wort agar may lead to false conclusions: thus, *Zymonomonas anaerobia* (alias *Saccharomonas anaerobia*, alias *Achromobacter anaerobium*) is not found in bitter beer but is a very serious infection in mild ale where free sugar is present, causing the production of hydrogen sulphide and organic sulphur compounds. Similarly ordinary hopped wort agar plates might fail to reveal the presence of some of the beer-spoilage *Lactobacilli* which are anaerobes. For such organisms as *Pediococci* probably the best medium would be an unhopped wort agar incubated under anaerobic conditions at about 25°C for 7–10 days, since some of these types are slow growing.

An extensive literature on the bacteriology of beer has developed in recent years, and the reader is advised to consult the technical literature from Lloyd Hind[22] onwards. The outstanding types of bacteria are the *Aceto-bacters* (including *Acetomonas* species) the *Lactobacilli* and the *Pediococci*. It is probable that it was species of the last-named genus which were respons-ible in the past for references to "beer sarcinae". No species of true *Sarcina* ever grew in beer although various species have been isolated from a wide variety of hosts.[61] The American Society of Brewing Chemists (A.S.B.C.) has a sub-committee dealing with microbiological controls in the brewery and the reader is referred to their report in the annual Proceedings of A.S.B.C.

(b) *Non-biological Stability.* Apart from instability of a biological nature arising from the presence of micro-organisms there is a number of other causes of deterioration of beer quality: they may manifest themselves by the occurrence of haze, loss of head retention and poor palate.

Non-biological haze can originate from a variety of causes: the commonest almost natural hazes arise from chilling and oxidation. When beer, partic-ularly top fermentation beer, is chilled, it becomes hazy, but on warming this haze disappears and is therefore referred to as reversible. Eventually, how-ever, this haze will become permanent. There are other permanent hazes which are independent of temperature for their appearance. While these may be called "oxidation haze" it is an inaccurate term. The development of per-manent haze is normally hastened by increase of temperature and on this fact are based accelerated tests such as are referred to below, to determine storage life. The tannins or polyphenolic compounds in beer are largely responsible for haze on account of their combining with nitrogenous sub-stances also invariably present. Oxidation accelerates such haze formation as also does the presence of various metals. As little as 0·1 ppm of tin, for example, can produce a haze and about 1 ppm of iron or copper acts similarly though perhaps not quite so rapidly. The effect of copper might be unexpected since copper vessels have in the past been in common use in brewing, but it must be remembered that yeast readily takes out of solution many metals and also other substances including copper. While some hazes may arise from the formation of metallo-tannin-protein complex, in other cases the metal appears to activate the oxygen present and to initiate or accelerate haze in this way. Other metals, besides tin, iron and copper can also cause hazes if present in concentrations in excess of those likely to be found in beer.

A special form of haze not infrequently encountered is due to oxalate: this is readily identified microscopically by the characteristic appearance of calcium oxalate crystals in the deposit.

It is customary to measure haze and haze potential against a "standard haze" and amongst the various systems are two "official" methods, recommended by E.B.C. and A.S.B.C. The E.B.C. method is set out in "Analytica"[2] where exact details are given not only for the sampling and testing but also for the method of making up the standards, known as the Formazin Haze Standards. The A.S.B.C. (1964) have issued addenda to their Methods of Analysis dealing with haze measurement.[3] Procedures for (A) Visual Method and (B) Nephelometric Method are set out in exact detail. In both methods results are expressed in formazin turbidity units. Earlier methods of haze measurements which have met with a considerable measure of success employed suspensions of barium sulphate[67, 1] and of kieselguhr.[63] Various forms of apparatus are available and some of these can be used on bottled beers where shelf life has to be measured and where removal of the beer from the bottle is not desired. In some instruments the measurement of the light scattered at 45° to the incident beam is measured and in others the scattering at 90°, so allowance must be made for this in comparative determinations. An important point is that if a bottle has a seam this must not be in the pathway of the beam of light.

The classic method of following oxidation in a beer is that of Grey and Stone,[64] based on the method of Hartong originally devised for worts, which estimates the reducing power of beer by following the rate at which an indicator, 2: 6-dichlorophenol indophenol is decolorized. The method is known as the Indicator Time Test and the results are expressed as I.T.T. units. A value of less than 200 sec has been suggested as a standard. Details of the method are given in De Clerck.[1] Willox[50] advocates a direct method of determining rH using indigo carmine as indicator. A rapid and, if desired, continuous method based on the use of a Clark electrode is described by Van Gheluwe et al.[65]

So important is the oxygen content of bottled and canned beers as regards stability and avoidance of haze, that great care is taken to ensure that the minimum of air is present. A figure of 1·0–1·5 ml of dissolved air per 12 oz bottle is a good target.[50]

For the details of methods of determining air in the headspace of bottled beer the reader is referred to De Clerck[1] both for his own and that of Mendlik. There are other variants. For further discussion on the various methods of determination of oxygen in bottled beers see Willox.[50]

A rapid gas chromatographic method of estimating the oxygen, nitrogen and hydrogen in the headspace of bottled or canned beers has been described by Brenner *et al.*[66] Interest in hydrogen arises from a use of aluminium for cans and the possible connection between this gas, and nitrogen, in "gushing" beer, the term applied when excessive foaming occurs in opening the bottle.

In view of the importance of shelf life of bottled beer, there is considerable interest in prediction of the life based on accelerated tests in which development of haze is encouraged in various ways, to establish comparative lengths of life. Since hazes have different origins, methods of assessment differ. Hartong showed a relationship between chill haze and the turbidity resulting from saturating to 30% with ammonium sulphate, but De Clerck, as a result of examining 30 different types of beer, found that the best prediction of shelf-life was obtained by storing bottles at 60°C and immersing them daily in melting ice for 3 h. The number of days before haze appears after chilling is noted. By this test, haze develops some eight to ten times more quickly than it would if the same beer were stored at 25°C. Again, it has been shown that if bottled beer be stored at 30°C it is estimated that its life, as indicated by haze development, will be half what it would be at 20°C and may be only a quarter if the storage be at 37°C. These are approximate figures, since there will be variations between different beers. Various shaking devices are also used to accelerate haze. The E.B.C. recommended accelerated test is based on taking about six bottles randomly and storing them upright at 60°C ±1° for seven days if they are stabilized beers, or at 40°C ±1° for normal beers. For draught beers, when putting into bottles for tests, the exclusion of air is extremely important.

(c) *Chemical Analyses.* Many factors are concerned in beer quality apart from susceptibility to biological and non-biological haze formation and some of these are susceptible to chemical analysis.

i. Metals

The effect of certain metals in minute quantities has been referred to and this may manifest itself not only in the production of hazes, but also in "gushing" or "fobbing", and in the production of off-flavours. Various methods of analysis are recommended of which the following are the more important.

ALUMINIUM. The possibility of the increased use of this metal in beer cans as well as in larger containers may make its estimation necessary. Reference to its possible involvement in hydrogen production has been referred to. A method sensitive to 0·01 ppm of Tullo et al.[67] depends on development of a greenish-yellow fluorescence under U.V. light, due to aluminium 8-hydroxy-quinolate. A more recent method is that of Stone et al.[68] in which pyro-catechol sulphonephthalein, which gives a blue colour with aluminium at pH 7. The method is simple and although iron can interfere, a correction factor can be applied for excess of this. Biske and Feaster's[69] simplified and quick spectrometric method, used for tin (see below) is equally applicable to aluminium. A simple direct colorimetric method based on aluminium (the ammonium salt of aurintricarboxylic acid) has been published.[70]

ARSENIC. The usual method of determination is Case's modification[71] of the standard Gutzeit method. The estimation of arsenic in coal which may be used in malt kilns has led to a modification of Case's modified Gutzeit method which is set out in a revised British Standard's Institution Standard no. 1016. The extensive collaborative work involved has been described by Ault.[72]

COBALT. The presence of this metal in beer has been held responsible, like many other factors for "gushing" beer[73] whilst some authorities take the opposite view, that it reduces the trouble.[74] It has been suggested that the conflict in evidence is due to temperature differences. Segel and Lautenback[75] give two methods for detection of added cobalt in beer to improve foam but to eliminate gushing. Such treatment would be illegal in many countries. There has recently been criticism of the practice from the health angle. One of their methods employs the preliminary removal of other cations by ion-exchange and then a colorimetric determination with potassium thiocyanate. Their other method dispenses with the ion-exchange step and uses 1,2,3-cyclohexanetrione trioxime (CHTT) as an indicator, giving a stable yellow complex, with cobalt. A method of Harold and Szobolotzsky[76] said to be adapted from one by Torii[77] is based on a coloured complex of cobalt with 3-methoxy-2-nitrosophenol. Copper and iron do not interfere when present in comparable concentrations with that of the cobalt, but nickel may.

COPPER. Of the several methods of estimation employed, that of Hoste et al. adapted by De Clerck[1] depends on the production of a violet colour with diquinolyl in isoamyl alcohol. Two methods use sodium diethyldithio-carbamate in carbon tetrachloride[78] and zinc dibenzyldithiocarbamate in carbon tetrachloride,[79, 80] the production of a yellow or brown coloration being the indication. Brenner et al.[81] compared four methods and found that one based on the use of oxalyldihydrazide was comparatively easy and time-saving, but that the simplest and fastest method for routine analyses for quantities down to 0·1 ppm was that using Cuprethol, 2-hydroxyethyl dithiocarbamate. This reagent is officially recognized for copper determinations in water and sewage in America. De Clerck[1] gives a method, particularly for use in hop analysis, based on the green colour produced by copper with pyridine and potassium thiocyanate in chloroform solution.

IRON. This is revealed by the interaction with potassium thiocyanate to give a red coloration. Ferrous iron must be oxidized to ferric to show the reaction. A quantitative method by Andrews and Stringer[82] uses thioglycollic acid. A direct method, applicable to pale beers is by use of dipyridyl[83, 84] or *o*-phenanthroline.[84, 85] Full details are given by De Clerck.[1]

LEAD. This is very rarely found in beer nowadays. Sometimes in the past there was a pick-up from leaden pipes in public houses where beer had lain in the pipes overnight: nowadays other metals or materials are used. The metal is estimated by the dithizone method.[1]

NICKEL. With the use in the brewery of alloys containing this metal, its estimation is sometimes important, particularly as it is viewed by some[86] as one of the causes of "gushing" or "wildness" (i.e. excessive foaming) in bottled beers. A colorimetric method of estimation is based on the use of dimethylglyoxime,[86, 87] and a more recent method[88] employs α-furildioxime also for a colorimetric determination. A third method[89] uses dithizone in carbon tetrachloride.[1]

TIN. This is the worst metallic contaminant in beer so far as haze formation is concerned. A method based on the red colour produced with dithiol is a good test for quite low concentrations of the metal.[90] For more exact quantitative estimation spectrography is recommended[1] and a very quick method using this technique has been described.[68] The tin in beer can be precipitated almost quantitatively with tannin and then estimated polarographically or otherwise to a value less than 0·1 ppm.[91] Rooney[92] describes a polarographic procedure revealing as little as 0·007 $\mu g/ml$ of tin.

ZINC. This is seldom met with in beer except in rare cases where beer (or wine) has for some reason been kept temporarily in a galvanized iron vessel. One worker finds that addition of 0·5 ppm of zinc to wort enhances fermentation rate and yeast multiplication.[93] The occurrence of zinc and other metals in wines is referred to in Section IV of this chapter.

Traces of other metals may be readily determined spectrochemically.[94] Trace metals in beer can be chelated wih EDTA (ethylene diamine tetra-acetic acid) to improve stability and reduce wildness.[95] The use of this agent is not permitted in Britain.

Further references to the determination of metals are given in the section of this chapter on Wines.

ii. Non-metals

FUSEL OIL. The fusel oil content of fermented beverages, and not least of beer is of immense importance from several points of view, particularly those of flavour and physiological effect. In the last decade a wide interest has developed in the determination of the higher alcohols and esters by various techniques and a very extensive literature is available. In wines, the methods have largely been improved by such workers as Genevois and his collaborators in France and by Guymon and others in U.S. In beers, and indeed other products of fermentation, there has also been an impressive volume of material emanating from Suomalainen and his colleagues in Finland. Analysis of fusel oil does not form part of the normal procedure of beer analysis, but those interested should consult papers by the above-mentioned authors (e.g. references 96–104).

DIACETYL. Increasing attention is being paid to this substance because of its influence on beer flavour: in general it appears to be produced more abundantly in lager or bottom yeast fermentation. Several methods of estimation have been put forward (e.g. reference 105) and a sub-committee of the A.S.B.C. considered these and reported.[106, 107] Their recommendations are now embodied in the Methods of Analysis (Beer-25).[3] Subsequent contributions and refinements have appeared as well as a method of determination of diacetyl in beer headspace and a method for enzymatic removal of diacetyl from beer.[108–113]

CARBON DIOXIDE. While there may be no "official" EBC method laid down in Analytica for the determination of CO_2 in beer, the A.S.B.C. "Methods of Analysis" describes fully a pressure and a chemical method, as well as a pressure method for beer in tanks together with a chart giving the pressure-temperature relationships for solubility of CO_2 in beer (and a conversion scale for volumes to percentage by weight). Full details of the gravimetric, volumetric, titrimetric and manometric methods of CO_2 determination are given in De Clerck's textbook.[1]

SULPHUR DIOXIDE. This is the most important preservative in beer and, indeed, is the only permitted one in Britain. Methods for estimation of SO_2 are well known to food chemists so they need not be enlarged upon here. Stone and Laschiver[114] have described a direct colorimetric method for beers depending on the red colour formed when acid-decolorized p-rosaniline and formaldehyde are treated with traces of sulphites. The method distinguishes between free SO_2 and the SO_2 complexed (as most of it is) with various beer constituents, e.g. carbonyl compounds. Further reference to SO_2 determinations is made later in this chapter (e.g. Section III, Cider).

CARBONYL COMPOUNDS. The identification of these compounds forms the subject of a paper by Ronkainen et al.[115]

ENZYMES. Proteolytic enzymes are widely used to stabilize beers by removal of breakdown of protein material which may otherwise cause haze development, particularly that which appears when beer is chilled. It is sometimes desired to determine whether any enzyme still remains in the finished beer after treatment. While a quick qualitative method is available by testing for milk clotting, a more accurate quantitative method is described by Salitan *et al.*[116] and further methods of detection and assaying of enzymes in beer have been published.[117, 118, 119]

(d) *Physical Characters.* Apart from constituents of beer susceptible to chemical analysis there are features of immense importance which are of a more physical nature. Colour, head retention or foam stability are such factors, culminating in the really essential features of taste, including bitterness, and aroma.

i. Colour

The necessity for standardization of this feature is obvious. The methods of measurement have been described earlier in dealing with wort. It only needs to be emphasized that trace of haze should be removed before measurement: this can be achieved by mixing the beer with 0·1% kieselguhr and filtering through filter paper, or if a fine haze is still present, through a membrane filter. Alternatively the beer can, after a preliminary filtration, be centrifuged at not less than 5000 rpm.

ii. Foam and head retention

Attention to foaming and ability to retain a "head" is an essential feature of quality control of beer: furthermore, it is not solely a matter of producing a lot of bubbles: the texture, adhesion and life of the head are most important. It is not surprising therefore that a number of methods of measuring foam and head retention are available, and brewers have their own modifications of the various published techniques.[120–131] In Europe, although E.B.C. has not published an "officially" recommended technique, it has more or less adopted Blom's method.[121] The writer has found Helm's Carlsberg method[120] useful because of its simplicity. Blom's method is more elaborate but also more accurate. Some of these methods are described in De Clerck[1] who also gives the modification by himself and De Dijcker[218] of Hartong's[124] method. The latest "official" American method dated 1964, to be found in the A.S.B.C. "Methods of Analysis"[3] under Beer-22 as "Foam Collapse Rate". This gives two methods; one is called a Sigma Value (Modified Carlsberg) method and the other a Foam Flashing method.

(e) Bitterness, Taste and Aroma

Undoubtedly one of the major factors in the quality control of beers is the standardization of measurement of bitterness. While "bitterness" may be due to several factors, it is the character and degree of bitterness due to hops that is important, and here a distinction has to be drawn between good "clean" hop bitterness and "harshness" and "rankness"; much bitterness will

7

depend on the type and age of the hop. The measurement of bitterness is thus of great importance and the brewer will want to know that he is getting good value in terms of bitterness, when he buys his hops; although his brewing methods may also affect the bitter flavour of the finished beer.

Since hop bitterness of beer is due primarily to substances derived from the resin acids of the hops, and chiefly the α-acids, measurement of these acids has long constituted a means of assessing the value of hops. As it is now realized that in the copper boil of the wort, when the hops are added, there is a conversion of the α-acids into isohumulones, the measurement of the latter is of prime importance. The determination of bitterness of a beer has rested chiefly on two principal methods of analysis, that of Rigby and Methune (second method)[132] and the quicker method of Moltke and Meilgaard.[133] These methods determine the isohumulones present but give different results. However, the coordination of results obtained by the Analysis Committee of E.B.C. and by the Isohumulone Sub-committee of A.S.B.C. has shown a relationship between the two methods enabling them to be stated on a uniform scale. As a result the Rigby and Methune calculation has been adopted by both bodies and results are expressed in I.B.U.'s, meaning "Isohumulone Bitterness Units" in America and "International Bitterness Units" in Europe. There are agreed tables for conversion of Moltke and Meilgaard results (or conversion of the U.V. measurements direct) into I.B.U.s.[2, 3, 134] Now (1968) a change to "E.B.C. Bitterness Units" is recommended[135] so that a slight revision of the units of calculation is necessary, but the change is small.*

There are other sources of bitterness in the beer besides the isohumulones as is shown by the fact that old hops, in which the source of isohumulones has virtually disappeared, still give bitterness. In the beers made from old hops, the Moltke and Meilgaard estimation of bitterness is more accurate than the Rigby and Bethune method.

In both these the extraction is with iso-octane: Goedkoop et al.[136] have shown that if extraction is done with chloroform, substances other than iso-humulones are obtained and these may derive from various sources, including malt. Verzele,[137] Verzele and Khokher,[138] and De Mets and Verzele[139] have worked on hop aroma substances and have isolated some twenty-five volatile substances contributing to aroma.

As it is reported that in some countries sorbic acid is being used as a preservative in beer, a point that could be of importance is that, according to Rintala and Arkina[140] the presence of sorbic acid invalidates estimation of

* Recently (1969) the Nomenclature Sub-Committee of the (European) Hops Liaison Committee have published recommendations, agreed and recommended by the main hops Liaison Committee, The European Brewery Convention and the American Society of Brewing Chemists, Normally, except in reference to specific compounds the term "iso-humulone" is to be peplaced by "Beer Bitter Substances" or "Bitterness Units (B.U.)" (*J. Inst. Brew.* 1969, **75**, no. 3, 236).

bitterness depending on extraction of the bitter principles with iso-octane, because of interference with the extinction values in spectrometric determinations.

i. Taste and aroma

The ultimate test of quality and consistency of a beer is by taste and smell. These senses, so interrelated that we may regard them conjointly, may not tell us everything about the wholesomeness of the product, but they will tell whether we have achieved the object we want. The literature on beer tasting is very extensive but it should be sufficient to mention two of the more recent papers.[141, 142]

Tasting panels are used for "preference tasting" and for "difference tasting": broadly, the former may be associated with the projected introduction of a new product and can be done by anyone, whereas the latter, used to ensure consistency or effect of alteration of raw materials or mode of manufacture, is usually performed by experts. It is sometimes difficult to secure the services of a good technical tasting panel since it means dragging reluctant people away from their normal duties. This means that large panels of experts are difficult to employ and this could affect the value of analysis of results. Other difficulties arise from the nature of the beer: the degree of bitterness restricts the number of samples which can be dealt with at one session, since it seems more difficult to clear the palate from hop bitterness than it is from other flavours and aromas: the palate soon tires. Direct difference of single samples, the triangular (one differing from two others) and the pentagonal (two similar and three similar) tests are all employed. It is not necessary to elaborate here on the many factors concerning tasting tests common to other foods and beverages, such as time of day, environment (e.g. noise, onlookers, etc.) lighting, colour, clarity, type of drinking utensil and secrecy: then there are the more subjective influences such as degree of hunger and thirst, age, sex, state of health, emotional condition (including prejudices—likes and dislikes), memory, smoking habits, familiarity with the products (experts on a bitter beer may be poor judges of a lightly hopped lager) and even the possession of dentures and the day of the week!). The writer has time and again noticed a tendency, sometimes subconscious maybe, to cheat. A taster may not like to be "odd man out" as it may be taken as a reflection on ability; similarly a taster may fear giving a verdict which turns out to be the opposite of that of his immediate superiors!

The data provided by the tests have not only to be analysed statistically, but each character upon which opinion has been asked has often to be given a weighting according to its importance *vis-à-vis* the other characters. Then it must be decided whether the final rating is to be by addition or multiplication of the marks for the separate characters: in some instances multiplication may be essential. Thus, a beer may be given 10/10 for each of the characters, colour, "hoppiness", cleanness or "palate-fulness"; but if the beer is very cloudy or "ropey" and is rated 0/10, on such features, they are so important that the sample is entirely rejected because by multiplication of the marks the product is 0. Recent analyses show the complex nature of minor constituents of beer. In the fusel oil part, for example, there are many alcohols, etc., affecting flavour and aroma: here the use of gas chromatography has helped in the identification of many of these compounds. A glance at the gas chromatogram of a typical beer, however, shows the presence of perhaps fifty or more different compounds each of which may be making some contribution to the aroma of the beer. We have learned much about beer with this technique but helpful though it may be, when we realize that the intensity of flavour of each component will differ with different tasters, we can appreciate the complexity of the problem of attempting to devise, by gas chromatography or other techniques, an entirely objective approach to flavour and aroma assessment. We may hazard a guess that it will be a long time before we can eliminate the tasting panel, so sensitive are the human sensory organs.

3. CIDER

A. Introduction

Virtually all commercial ciders are blended and therefore achieve uniformity of the required standards, so that organoleptic tests predominate in quality control of the product. Since the principles of taste testing are similar to those of other beverages and foods, they need not be reiterated here. Nevertheless, certain laboratory analyses are required both on the apple juice and on the fermented product.

B. The Raw Materials

The cider makers are actively engaged in propagating the varieties of apples they require, and these varieties may be classified into four categories according to the relative proportion of acid, tannin and sugar. When the fruit arrives at the factory each load is accepted or rejected both on its being of the required variety and on its condition. This is the first stage of quality control.[143] The percentage of unsound fruit must be less than 10% otherwise trouble will be experienced later in the process when sulphur dioxide is added; this is due to the fact that some of the metabolic end products of acetic acid bacteria will form complexes with sulphur dioxide and result in the removal of SO_2 from the sphere of activity as a preservative. The problem of formation of complexes with SO_2 is by no means confined to cider making.

C. The Process

A detailed description of the cider-making process is not necessary here but during the operations involved various features call for control, since apple juice and cider are readily susceptible to deterioration both chemically, as by oxidation, or microbiologically, as by the action of various bacteria and yeasts. Many wooden vats are still in use and undesirable organisms can lurk in wait to spoil the materials. Other important aspects are the avoidance of access of air and the removal of the cider from the lees at the completion of fermentation. The importance of such measures is enhanced when any lengthy storage is necessary. While the question of maturation does not arise as it does with wines, it is possible to envisage circumstances in which the cider may have to be stored up to two years.

After disintegration of the apples in a high speed mill extraction of the apple juice is still by hydraulic pressure on the pulp which is in cloths, called "hairs", held between a number of slatted wooden boards. The pressed pulp is known as a "cheese" and after pressing contains extremely little apple juice. Since wooden boards are present, this stage of the operation is one at which hygienic control is particularly necessary because, in the author's opinion, any stage or process in food or beverage factories where wood is involved is microbiologically vulnerable and needs constant vigilance and laboratory control.

Whereas in olden times and maybe still in farm house manufacture the apple juice was allowed to ferment "on its own" by chance microflora present on the fruit, nowadays it is customary after the addition of sulphur dioxide to the juice to employ a strongly fermenting SO_2-tolerant yeast. This means a more regular and predictable fermentation as well as more controllable conditions of operation. This procedure is a further factor in facilitating hygienic control.

At the bottling stage careful control is maintained, ensuring not only that the empty bottles are properly washed and sterilized but also that high-temperature-short-time (H.T.S.T.) pasteurized, or sterile-filtered cider goes into the bottles, because cider, like beer, etc. is susceptible to spoilage organisms.[143] Hence as a process control, samples are membrane-filtered as a check on sterility. In good factories a close watch is kept on yeast and bacterial counts of successive samples to detect any trend towards a numerical build-up.

D. Analytical Procedure

1. The Unfermented Juice

The following items receive attention in the laboratory so far as the unfermented juice is concerned:

(a) Original gravity of the fruit juice; (b) Total sugar of the fresh juice; (c) Total acidity; (d) Tannin content; (e) pH (very rarely); (f) Pectin.

Such items as the pectin content of the extracted pomace will only be done when the factory is interested in pectin production. A method recommended involves precipitation by alcohol. 100 ml of cider are evaporated to 10–15 ml and then treated with 60–80 ml 95% alcohol. The precipitate is washed on tared filter paper with 80% alcohol, dried at 20°C, then at 100°C and weighed. The method is crude in that substances other than pectin will be present so a better result is obtained if the material is ashed and the weight of ash deducted.

2. The Fermented Product

Analyses on the fermented cider include:

(a) *Specific gravity*. This is determined by a hydrometer or a weighing bottle, more frequently by the former.

(b) *Alcohol content*. This is determined by distillation. The minimum permitted is 4% actual, by volume.

(c) *Sugar*. This is done by the Lane and Eynon method[144] or a modification.[145]

(d) *Total acidity*. A titrimetric method by Burroughs[146] involves the use of a mixture of the two indicators bromo-phenol blue and phenol red. The natural pigments of the cider do not interfere.

(e) *Volatile acidity*. This is determined by the steam distillation of a de-gassed sample, the distillate being titrated with NaOH.

REAGENTS

1. 0·02N NaOH.
2. Mixed Indicator. Bromothymol blue 0·3 g
   Phenol red   0·9 g
   Cresol red   0·3 g
   Distilled water to 450 ml

METHOD. Pipette 20 ml of the de-gassed cider into the distillation flask; add 15 g of NaCl and 30 ml of distilled water. Generate steam from distilled water and allow the water to boil for several minutes before connecting with the distillation flask. Collect via a water condenser 200 ml of distillate. Titrate rapidly against 0·02 N NaOH, using mixed indicator. The purple colour should remain for 14 sec. Carry out all determinations in duplicate.

RESULTS. Express results as percentage acetic acid. 1 ml of 0·02 N NaoH = 0·0012 g acetic acid. The maximum permitted volatile acidity is 1·4 g/litre expressed as acetic acid.

(f) *Ash*. 50 ml of cider are evaporated in a dish and moderate heating is continued for 30 min until charring is complete, when the material is transferred to a muffle furnace at red heat, followed by cooling in a desiccator and very quick weighing.

(g) *Tannin*

REAGENTS. Folin-Denis Reagents: Heat under reflux for 2 h a mixture of 750 ml of water, 100 g of sodium tungstate, 20 g of phosphomolybdic acid and 50 ml of 85 % phosphoric acid. Cool and make up to 1 litre.

SODIUM CARBONATE: Solution (saturated). For each 100 ml of water add 25 g of anhydrous sodium carbonate. Warm to dissolve and leave to cool overnight. Add to the supersaturated solution a crystal of sodium carbonate. After crystallization decant off the clear liquid.

TANNIC ACID: Dry the solid tannic acid in a desiccator. Weigh out 0·25 g of this, dissolve in water to make up to 500 ml in a volumetric flask. Keep this stock solution in a refrigerator. For the estimation dilute this solution 50 times to give 0·01 g/litre tannic acid.

ESTIMATION

(1) Dilute the cider or apple juice until it contains approximately 0·01 g/litre of tannin.

(2) Pipette 5 ml of diluted cider into a 50 ml graduated flask and add 35 ml distilled water. At the same time pipette 5 ml of the diluted tannic acid solution into a similar flask.

(3) To each flask add 1 ml of Folin-Denis solution, 2·5 ml sodium carbonate solution, make up to the mark with distilled water and shake well.

(4) Place flasks in an incubator at 20–30°C for one and a half hours and then measure the optical density on the Spekker using No. 8 filters and a 2 cm cell. Carry out a blank determination with all reagents except the tannic acid.

$$\frac{\text{Sample reading-blank}}{\text{Standard reading-blank}} = \text{mg/100 ml in cell.}$$

(h) *Sulphur Dioxide*. The determination of SO_2 in cider is of some importance as with other foods and beverages, because SO_2 is apt to lose its efficacy as a sterilant on account of its tendency to form complexes both with substances naturally present in the fruit and with other compounds which may be the end products of the action of acetic bacteria. The statutory maximum for SO_2 is not more than 200 ppm or 200 mg per litre "when delivered for consumption".

Three principal methods are employed for estimation of SO_2 in cider: there is the commonly used Monier-Williams technique, or that of Ripper[147] and more specifically for this commodity, the method of Burroughs and Sparks.[148] These last-named workers studied the rate of removal of SO_2 from aqueous solutions by gas stream to establish the conditions necessary for determining the free SO_2 in cider. The cider is acidified and the free SO_2 removed at room temperature in an air stream under reduced pressure, after which it is absorbed in neutralized hydrogen peroxide and titrated with standard alkali.

(*i*) *Sugar-free extract*. The minimum according to the standard set by the National Association of Cider Makers of Great Britain is 13 g/litre. A total extract is determined from the specific gravity of the alcohol-freed cider as described in A.O.A.C. 9th Edition, 1960. (Method 11.015 (a) page 141 and Table 43.003 for Wines.)

(j) *Metals*. The methods for estimation of metals are the usual ones. The permitted maximum for *iron* is 10 mg/litre; and for *copper* 7 mg/litre. Analyses for *lead* and *arsenic* may be required from time to time to ensure that the product conforms to statutory requirement.

The occurrence of acetaldehyde has been mentioned and the maximum for this is 150 mg/litre.

Finally, for nitrogen estimations the ordinary Kjeldahl method is commonly employed, and occasionally the van Slyke technique.

The publications of A.O.A.C. (U.S.A.) give analytical methods of which some are applicable to cider.

E. Biological and Non-Biological Stability

As with other beverages, cider may suffer from hazes or "cloudiness" and these may be biological or, more rarely, non-biological in origin. Bacterial growth which may take the form of acetification, or less commonly, ropiness or sickness[143, 149, 150] is best checked by hygienic control in the factory particularly by the employment of anaerobic conditions together with the use of SO_2. Chemical or non-biological troubles may be more difficult to eliminate and may take the form of discoloration or turbidity due to the action between aldehydes and tannin. Apart from a change of appearance, undesirable flavours may also result but they are quite rare. For the measurement of hazes various methods such as those described in the beer section of this chapter are available.

As in other fermentation industries, changes are taking place and newer methods leading to increased efficiency and economy are being investigated in the cider factories. Thus, concentration of juice so that it can be stored and cider production become an all-the-year-round operation instead of a seasonal one; improved pulp pressing methods and continuous fermentation are all developments receiving attention. Should they come to fruition, they may call for changes in quality control techniques but eventually, whatever happens, ultimate control on quality consistency will always be organoleptic tests on the final products.[151]

In France the cider industry appears to be under more official control than in some countries. Two of the text-books on the subject are available in English translation.[152, 153]

F. Perry

The methods of perry manufacture are so similar to those used in cider production that the features of quality control do not require separate enunciation here. On account of differences in the polyphenol fraction of perry juice there is a greater chance of running into non-biological haze problems.

4. WINES

A. General Considerations and Basic Approach to Wine Analysis

In so far as laboratory analyses play a part in the quality control of wines, perhaps the most thorough approach is by means of the ' "Receuil des Méthodes Internationales d'Analyse des Vins", Convention internationale pour l'unification des méthodes d'analyse et d'appréciation des vins" '.[154] The methods of analysis are subject to discussion and revision from time to time, as shown, for example, by the report of the eighth reunion of the sub-commission of analytical methods held in Paris in May 1966.[155]

Part 1 of the 1962 Edition (Partie juridique) sets out the text of the International Convention of 13 October 1954 for the above-mentioned unification of methods of analysis and evaluation, while Part II (Partie technique) has three appendices dealing respectively with (A) International methods of analyses; (B) Specimen official certificates of analysis and evaluation; and (C) Maximum acceptable limits of various substances occurring in wine.

Thus, under (C) figures given are 0·6 mg/litre of lead; 100 mg/litre of sorbitol; 5 mg/litre of fluorine; 80 mg/litre of boron (expressed as boric acid; 1 mg/litre total bromine (this is exceptionally exceeded in certain wines from vineyards on brackish sub-soil); *nil* organic bromine; and for volatile acidity 20 Meq/° of alcohol exceeding 10° for wines with more than 10° of fermentation alcohol (added alcohol excluded). The volatile acidity of certain special old wines (subject to Government control and special legislation) can exceed this limit. Since in table wines the volatile acidity, expressed as acetic acid, is a measure of spoilage, its determination is important.

Appendix B gives specimens of two official certificates of analysis and evaluation. The first, comparatively simple, is usually adequate for assessing the quality of a wine. It includes such items as colour, clarity, deposit, taste, stability (in air and at low temperature), microbiological condition and numerous chemical and physical data, including density, residual density without the alcohol, degrees of alcohol and total dry extract; saccharose and reducing sugars, ash and alkalinity of ash, potassium; total, volatile and fixed acidity, pH, tartaric, lactic and citric acids, sulphates and chlorides, total and free SO_2, biological tests for presence of antiseptics or antibiotics, foreign

7*

colouring matter and malvocide (a glucoside of the anthocyanin malvin or malvidin).

Certificate No. 2, which is described as a "detailed analysis", consists of no less than 87 items, which cannot all be enumerated here. Apart from the determinations mentioned above, some eleven metals are listed besides a fuller list of acids and acidities, esters, sugars, alcohols, antiseptics, and other additives. Such an analysis would be very costly and would presumably only be required in special circumstances.

Appendix A, forming the bulk of the volume gives the details of the international analytical methods running to over 170 pages of techniques and tables. The reader must therefore be referred to the original work. It should be noted that the countries which have ratified the International Convention (up to 31 March 1962) are mostly the European wine-producing countries with one or two later additions. The wine-producing regions of North America are not officially covered by the International Convention referred to above.

Perhaps the most widely used textbook outside the European wine-producing countries is that of Amerine and Cruess.[156] This work deals with a number of features of laboratory tests and analyses which are in many cases associated with quality control.

B. Biological Instability

A chapter in the above textbook is devoted to spoilage of wines by bacteria, and to microscopical examination which will indicate whether spoilage is biological or non-biological in origin. The chief types of micro-organisms likely to be found are lactobacilli, including members of the genus *Leuconostoc*, and *Acetobacter* and *Acetomonas* species. An extensive bibliography of wine bacteria has been developing in recent years (see reference 156, Chapter 16) and mention may be made here of the contribution by the workers at Davis, California; Fornachon and Rankine in Australia; and van Zyl, Du Plessis and colleagues in South Africa, who have been producing a series of microbiological papers. Fornachon and Lloyd[157] reported that in Australian wine, production of diacetyl and acetoin is due to *Leuconostoc mesenteroides* and not to the *Lactobacilli* species responsible for the malo-lactic fermentation. It is considered that if a pH below 3·5 can be maintained, the lactic acid bacteria can be suppressed, particularly in fortified wines.

C. Analyses

1. Metals

Coming to chemical analyses, Amerine and Cruess (*loc. cit.*) refer to the need for international agreement on the permissible limit for *lead* (see above).

For *iron*, the orthophenanthroline method appears to be best (Genevois and Larrouquiere),[158] in preference to the thiocyanate method. The French

"Receuil" recommends analysis of the ash when highly coloured red wines are concerned.

Copper estimation by the diethyl dithio-carbamate method is "being studied", with the additional feature of complexing the iron with versene-citrate. The tetraphenyl borate method for *potassium* is being examined, according to Amerine, with a view to comparison with the acid tartrate and flame photometer procedures, and the replacement of the perchlorate method. The tetraphenyl borate method is the method of reference given in O.I.V. Recueil.

Zinc may occur in wines either through its presence in fungicidal or insecticidal spray or if galvanized vessels have been used either for wine or for fortifying spirit. Otherwise the amount present is unlikely to exceed 1 ppm. If this is exceeded, apart from flavour being affected, haze trouble will arise if any protein material is present, due to the formation of a metallo-protein complex, as arises in other beverages and with other metals. An excess of zinc can also arise if the objectionable practice is employed of using zinc sulphate to prevent over "blue fining", where this practice is permitted, but even then its use is illegal.

Tin. While probably non-toxic in small quantities tin is, like copper, zinc and iron, to be avoided in wine because it can, even in minute amounts, cause a haze due to a metallo-protein complex. Nowadays, if examination for the less important metals is required, flame photometry is the most suitable technique. However, from time to time other methods are described in the literature; for example, for such comparatively rarely-occurring metals as nickel (Eschnauer[159]) and antimony (Eschnauer[160]). Karvánek and Silkanova[161] have determined quantitatively various trace metals in red wines.

2. Organic Compounds

Volatile acidity has been referred to elsewhere in this chapter, but a paper by Spanish workers[162] gives a rapid method for the determination of true volatile acidity of a wine containing CO_2, SO_2 and the preservative sorbic acid.

The determination of *tartaric acid* in wines is important and several methods are available, for example, those of Schneyder and Pluhar, Rebelein, Pato, Kling-Reynaud and Kling-Jaulmes *et al.*, but a reference method is not yet official. These methods are at present referred to[155] as "F.V." This symbol, stands for Feuillet Vert (Green Leaflet). Each leaflet describes a method suggested by one of the members of the Commission on Wine Analysis: it may be a member's own method or one which he reproduces from another author, but which in either case he recommends to the Commission. Such a method has to be approved by at least two members of the Commission, and by Professor Jaulmes, for adoption and inclusion in the collection of Methods of Analysis. The green leaflets thus represent methods to be studied and are never recommended by the Commission until a new ruling is given.*

Of the above methods the technique of Kling-Jaulmes *et al.*, appears to be that most favoured. For a quick method, that of Schneyder and Pluhar is accepted, but the commonest procedure is still that of Revelein. The Commission[155] considered all three methods acceptable. A rapid method for the determination of *lactic acid* in wines proposed by Kain and Schneyder was considered by this body but did not commend itself for speed. The usual method is that of Revelein, and as a result of tests on this and three other methods, improvements on the Revelein technique are being considered for adoption.

For the acceptable methods of determination of other organic acids, e.g. citric, malic, succinic, ascorbic and boric, the reader must be referred to the two textbooks, American and French, for details, together with later supplements to the "Recueil" (see, for example, reference 155). The proposed permitted upper limit for boric acid given in the O.I.V. Recueil is 80 mg/litre and the American book mentions 60–80 mg/litre.

Determination of ascorbic acid, used in wines as an antioxidant is not very easy and present methods have been criticized, but an improved technique is hoped for in the near future.[155] According to Haushofer and Rethaller[163] only the best wines benefit from addition of ascorbic acid, and not less than 50 mg/litre is required. For indifferent wines, it may be useful in preventing too rapid maturing. Its addition to long-matured wines is not recommended.

The best methods for the determination of glycerol were discussed in 1966[155] and at present the method of Revelein as given by the "Recueil"[154] is retained. Although it gives an inclusive figure for glycerol, mannitol and sorbitol, the proportions of the two latter are said to be so small as to be of little consequence. The method of van Zyl affording a simultaneous determination of all three was expected to be adopted by 1967.

Where estimation of aldehydes is necessary, the Recueil (reference 154, A. 19b.) mentions the principle of the methods used and Amerine and Cruess (*loc. cit.*) give precise details (p. 638, 1960 edition) of modifications of Jaulmes and Espezel's[164] method.

A useful test is that for hydroxymethyl-furfural because this substance is found when certain sugars, such as sucrose, are heated in acid solution: its presence in dessert wines therefore indicates that they have received heat treatment. The method which gives a semi-quantitative result, depends on the use of Fiehe's solution (0·1 g resorcinol in 10 ml concentrated HC1) which develops a pink to red coloration.

The determination of tannin content is sometimes required as it makes an

* The author is indebted to Professor L. Genevois of the University of Bordeaux for this information.

important contribution to flavour, colour and stability. Amerine and Cruess[156] describe the Neubauer-Loewenthal method, which includes colouring matter, consisting of titrating the de-alcoholized wine before and after decolorizing with carbon. The same authors give a rapid method for tannin estimation based on the Folin-Denis reagent, described in the cider section of this chapter. More recently two methods have been described by Ribéreau-Gayon and Stonestreet.[165]

In wines, as in other fermented beverages such as beers the presence of anthocyanins can affect stability, but their estimation in the laboratory would not be common practice. However, where such determinations are required, references may be made to the work of Ribéreau-Gayon and Stonestreet.[166] Incidentally, they found that in the red wines they studied, the anthocyanin dropped from 385 mg/litre to a half of that figure in the following year and fell progressively at the same rate each year to a constant 20–30 mg/litre.

Other substances, the estimation of which is called for are methanol and hydrogen sulphide. For the latter, which occurs frequently during many yeast fermentations, a method is described by Eschnauer and Tölg,[167] but the substance is considered to be absent from the final wine. Methods for determination of methanol have recently been reviewed by Spanish workers[168] with suggestions for modifications, and a similar chromatropic acid routine method is put forward by Revelein.[169]

(a) *Fusel Oils.* The literature on the occurrence and determination of fusel oils in fermented beverages has during the last two decades become so vast that a really comprehensive survey is impossible within the confines of one section of a chapter. However, the finer determinations of fusel oil constituents do not normally fall within the activities of the practical operations of a commercial laboratory concerned with quality control. The advancement of highly successful techniques during the last ten years or so is responsible for the deluge of information in this field. As an example, in the sphere of wine technology may be quoted a thesis of Boidron,[170] in his investigations he found no less than 240 different peaks in gas chromatograms. To mention but a few of the other contributors to knowledge on the fusel oils there are Suomalainen and his colleagues in Finland; Guymon, Ingraham and colleagues in America; Genevois, Baraud and colleagues in France, and Stevens and colleagues in Britain. Reference has already been made in the Beer Section of this chapter and some references given.[96–104] The profound effect of the fusel oil constituents on the flavour of fermented beverages and on their physiological effects are the principal reasons for interest in these compounds.

(b) *Carbon dioxide.* Methods of determination of this gas in fermented beverages are well known and available in the literature, some being official. See for example, Amerine and Cruess (pp. 643–647, 1960 edition). Recueil d'O.I.V. does not lay down a method. Morrison[171] proposes modifications in the A.O.A.C. manometric method where lightly carbonated wines are concerned.

(c) *Sulphur Dioxide.* The widespread use of this, the most generally employed and legally accepted preservative in the food and beverage industries, makes its determination important, particularly as the substance exists in food and drinks partly "free" and partly combined. The two principal accepted methods of estimation are by distillation or by the classic Ripper method. Both are adequately described in the literature, in particular in the "Receuil"[154] and in Amerine and Cruess.[156]* The Recueil recognizes the Ripper method for speed both for free and total SO_2. The reference method for total SO_2 is recognized as exact but lengthy: the topic was discussed in the Bulletin de l'O.I.V.[155] from which it appears that a decision on a method for free and total SO_2 in red and white wines was deferred. Information on the use of SO_2 in wines as well as methods of estimation are given in the recent textbook by Schroeter.[172] Other contributions to the topic in relation to wine come from Jones,[173] Pataky,[174] and Deibner and Heredia.[175]

(d) *Ageing and Stability.* An essential aspect of quality control in wines is that of stability with avoidance of haze or turbidity, apart from any trouble of this nature due to microbial growth. Characterization of turbidities is dealt with in the usual textbooks and in papers such as that by Beneš.[176] Tests on stability consist of ascertaining the behaviour, for example, of the wine towards heat and cold: heat will bring down protein and chilling will precipitate both the tartar and also protein and colloidal matter. A paper by Berg and Akiyoshi[177] gives a useful comparison between "heat-cold" test and a chemical test involving trichloroacetic acid, indicating that the two methods correlate well. In the "heat-cold" test the wine is stored in 3 oz bottles at 120°F (49°C) for 4 days, then at room temperature for one day, then 23°F (−5°C) for 2 days and a further final one day at room temperature. The wine would only be considered protein stable if no haze or deposit appears at each stage. In the other test, 10 ml of the wine are pipetted into a 19 × 150 mm test tube, 1 ml of 55% trichloroacetic acid added and the tube held in boiling water for 2 min, followed by 15 min at room temperature. This quick method seems to be entirely reliable for protein stability.

Two papers on the stabilization of wines by addition of metatartaric acid may be mentioned as a procedure to prevent the deposition of "wine stone" without impairing the flavour of the wine in any way.[178, 179] The use of ascorbic acid as a stabilizer has already been mentioned. Normal ageing is often accelerated by racking at intervals; this has the effect of aerating and ridding the wine of sediment. Refrigeration and pasteurization are also

* The corrected equation in line 22 is:
$$24{\cdot}1 \times 32 \times 0{\cdot}0196 \times 20 = 302 \text{ ppm approx.}$$

resorted to, but not for good wines, where ageing must be a slow process. Refrigeration also assists in getting rid of the cream of tartar (potassium acid tartrate) of which there is a larger amount in the weaker wines than in the stronger. Cation exchange resins can also be used in this connection (Berg and Keefer,[180, 181]

(e) *Fining*. In regions such as Bordeaux, wine is fined with gelatine during the first year to clarify and remove tannins, protein, etc. In California and Australia, for example, fining after the first racking is with bentonite, but the type of bentonite employed is important. The Wyoming material is considered the best, but Rankine and Emerson[182] have shown that flocculation may be poor, for example, when the wine has been passed through a sodium cation-exchange resin to prevent deposition of potassium bitartrate. From a practical point of view the work of Rankine and his collaborators deserves study. In this field of wine clarification these workers found that dispersion was associated with a high Na and low Ca and Mg proportion, in conjunction with the presence of a dispersing compound, which was shown to be a high molecular weight negatively charged carbohydrate, as revealed by electrophoresis. From this it follows that flocculation in wines treated by a cation-exchange resin will depend on the relative amounts of this carbohydrate dispersing bentonite on the one hand and of protein which flocculates it on the other. Some bentonites flocculate much more readily in low concentrations of divalent cation than do natural sodium bentonites, but were found to remove protein much less effectively. Rankine and Emerson recommend that bentonite fining should be done either before cation-exchange treatment, or a protein such as gelatine can be added to the treated wine to ensure flocculation. The use of Moslinger's "blue fining" (potassium ferrocyanide) is strictly-speaking illegal in some countries but its use under strict analytical control is permitted in others and it is employed to remove very effectively excesses of various metals—copper, zinc, and, in particular, iron from the wine, as well as protein; so it assists generally in fining operations. It is essential, of course, that the use of this reagent does not lead to the residual presence of cyanide in the wine, and to ensure absence thereof the Huback test is employed. A modified form of this test is described by Amerine and Cruess.[156]

(f) *Additives and Preservatives*. In the total absence of SO_2, other preservatives, some permitted in some regions and others not, may be looked for. Where no growth occurs in spite of the apparent absence of known preservatives, the procedure may be adopted of deliberately adding organisms, e.g. yeasts, to the wine in the presence of sugar: the absence of development will indicate the presence of some additive arresting development of microorganisms. Antibiotics would appear at first sight to be an attractive form of preservative, but such substances do not find favour for official permission for several reasons. The most obvious antibiotic to put in wine is actidione, which suppresses yeast growth and has been found to be effective at 0·1–1·0 μg/ml.[183] Several other workers have also reported on the efficaciousness of the substance and of other antibiotics (Ribéreau-Gayon et al., and Kielhofer in reference 156). A drawback to the use of some of these materials is the minute quantities involved, rendering detection and estimation difficult or even impossible.

Benzoic acid, widely used for soft drinks, is not very popular as a wine preservative for several reasons, but a paper by Maurel and Touyé[184] describes how the acid and its derivatives can be detected and determined in wines.

Considerable attention has been directed in recent years to the use of sorbic acid as a wine preservative. It is certainly an effective fungicide and is also useful against yeasts, but apparently at different concentrations for different strains: its efficacy against bacteria does not necessarily follow. The substance is permitted for use for some foods and beverages in some countries, provided the concentration is restricted (e.g. in U.S.A. not more than 0·1%). There is an extensive literature on the detection and estimation of sorbic acid in wines; among the contributions are those of Schmidt[185] based on colorimetry, with suggested modifications by Jaulmes, Mestres and Mandrou,[186] by Prillinger[187] and by Maurel and Touyé.[188] Chromotographic methods have been described by Biol and Foulonneau,[189] Guimberteau,[190] Würdig[191] and by others. Ough,[192] as a result of sensory tests finds the threshold concentration for detection of sorbic acid in wines to be 170± 53·5 mg/litre. Terceli and Adamic[193] find its use unsuitable because at least 300 mg/litre is necessary and this imparts an off-flavour. Yet Haushofer and Rethallen[194] state that 80 mg/litre of sorbic acid is adequate to suppress growth. These apparent discrepancies may well be due to difference in the wines used. The last-named authors report a "geranium-like" flavour following the use of sorbic acid but this was in a wine had been treated with hydrogen peroxide.

Much attention is being given to the use of di-ethyl pyrocarbonate as a bactericide, particularly in wines and beers. The substance breaks down to alcohol and carbon dioxide within a few hours of addition to the beverage, but in the meantime has effected sterilization: it obviously does not prevent subsequent re-infection. The literature on the topic has been voluminous and controversial on certain grounds, as is shown by a discussion reported in connection with its application to wines.[155] To be effective against some yeasts and bacteria it has, it is claimed, to be used as a concentration which makes it detectable to the palate. A further objection is that it does not break down completely to alcohol and CO_2, small quantities of other compounds which may be deleterious to health being reported, although this may not be a serious hazard in its application to wines and beers as opposed to milk, for example. Furthermore the substance has to be handled with great care and its fumes may be dangerous. Some workers (e.g. references 194, 195) support its use together with SO_2, it then being possible to reduce the quantities of the latter. Gas chromatography reveals, by showing the presence of diethyl carbonate, whether the pyrocarbonate has been added to the wine,[196, 197] The legal position at this time is confused. The use of the substance is permitted in the United States, but not yet in Great Britain, although experimentation in beverage laboratories has been widespread here.

The ultimate test of quality of wines being based on flavour, the assessment of this factor far outweighs other considerations as regards contents of the wines measurable by the techniques enumerated on the various analytical tests already discussed. But from the scientific point of view, it is still the most difficult to assess in numerical terms, so many interacting factors being involved. For example, apart from such contributory measurable items as pH, CO_2 content, ethyl alcohol, sugar and so forth, there are the "intangibles", although the nature of many of them, in so far as they are chemical entities measurable individually by modern techniques, are being elucidated. It must further be remembered that minute quantities of chemical substances, whether existing separately or in ultimate combination with others (as may happen in ageing) can contribute not only to the subtle flavour components which constitute "bouquet", but also to undesirable off-flavours which can ruin quality. Since the introduction of such techniques as gas chromatography there have been numerous contributions to the literature on this topic. Carbonyl compounds are of importance in this context as being substances responsible for flavour and taste in foods and beverages. Ronkainen et al.[198] in particular have shown that changes in the carbonyl compounds in wine distillates occur during storage.

(g) *Tasting*. The evaluation of wines by taste, indisputably the overriding criterion of quality, is in general similar to that employed for other beverages and foods; and modern methods, particularly in marking and interpretation of results, have become more accurate. Amerine and Ough[199] have brought out the principal features in a paper on sensory evaluation. A useful point is put thus: "The main problem in the evaluation of the 'expert' tasters is how to determine if they are really 'experts'." This, of course, does not apply where only preference tasting is concerned. The experts deal with such points as difference tasting and ranking, and it is stated by these very experienced workers, so far as Californian wines are concerned, that tasters will deal with 5–25 samples at one session, depending on preference of the taster, type of wine (the number of samples must be less where sweeter types are involved) and how complex is the series. In Professor Amerine's laboratories about one dozen wines is a normal presentation (between 10.0 a.m. and noon) in the form of 4–6 pairs or 3–4 "triangle" sets: this is for difference tests. Other particulars of tasting techniques and scoring are in general similar for evaluation of other commodities. A point requiring comment is that when colour or clarity are not to be assessed, the samples are presented to the taster in glasses painted black (on the outside surface and pre-heated to remove odour). In the experience of some, this procedure seems to have an upsetting effect on the taster, but this is a psychological reaction: it may be compared perhaps to attempting to assess the merit of a cigarette smoked in the dark with neither the glowing tip nor the smoke visible. In both instances the results of such (literally) "blind" tasting should be more accurate but it might be contended that it is not normal drinking or smoking procedure. The reader who is embarking on the setting up of a tasting panel is recommended to consult the contributions to the subject by Amerine and his colleagues. The numerous factors touched upon by Amerine and Ough will not be further enumerated here since they are to be found in other sections of this treatise on quality control.

V. POTABLE SPIRITS

A. General Considerations

It may appear that chemical analyses, and other laboratory methods of assessment play a smaller part in the quality control of potable spirits than in that of beers. In the section of this chapter devoted to beer it was obvious that many methods of analysis and control have become standardized through the efforts of the various committees of the European Brewery Convention and the American Society of Brewing Chemists. Such organization is not so obvious in the spirit industries. Nevertheless, such bodies as the Council of Europe have done much work to achieve agreement on technical specifications for the types of spirits which are marketed in Europe. There is a Consultant Expert of the Council (see below) operating from Berne who has collected a great deal of information and drawn up a scheme for the classification of spirits.

It might be contended that quality and consistency are still more an art than a science and as blending plays a larger part in the spirits industry than it does in brewing, there is something to be said for this view. Nevertheless the ultimate criteria of quality in the brewing industry, just as much as in the potable spirits industry, are taste and smell. It may be that in brewing the achievement of consistency is assisted more than in the spirit industry by laboratory analyses and tests, but the ultimate judgment is by the human sensory organs and not by scientific apparatus. However, since the production of whisky, rum, gin and such spirits depends not only on the raw materials but also on distillation methods, the relative contributions in the two industries made by the scientist may be subjects for debate rather than for dogmatic assertion. As Brandt[200] has pointed out, most industries are aided in control by physical and chemical analyses, but this is not so easy with distilled spirits. While such tests for solids, fusel oil, acids, pH and colour may be regular practice, they do not lead to definite answers for taste and odour uniformity: hence the enhanced importance in the potable spirit industry of physiological and psychological testing procedures coupled with statistical analysis.

As the raw materials for potable spirits vary not only as between different spirits but also within the make-up of the grist for a single spirit, such as whisky, it is not possible here to enumerate analytical procedures. Scotch whisky, for example, may be made from a range of materials from 100% pure barley malt to a mixture of about 16% barley malt and 84% adjuncts of forms of starch.

B. Methods of Analysis

Some of the methods of analysis described or referred to in the Beer Section of this chapter may be applicable to spiritous beverages in general. While practices vary in different distilleries, control starts with usual tests on raw materials, and in particular estimation of diastatic power and extract of the malt. Far less importance attaches to the nitrogen content, both quantitatively and qualitatively, of the barley and the malt than in beer brewing. After mashing, the resulting wort will be examined at pitching for original gravity and perhaps pH. Samples may be taken during fermentation and afterwards for gravity and so forth and the distillate will probably be examined for alcoholic strength, fixed and volatile acidity, total solids and ash. Other analyses on final saleable product may include tests for metals, sugars and colouring matters. Other constituents which may be looked for in certain circumstances would be esters, furfural, aldehydes and higher alcohols. The procedures for such tests are laid down, for example, in the United States.[201] These various tests are in addition or, in most cases, subsidiary to tasting tests, even at this stage.

Brandt (loc. cit.) states that in America before the spirits are put into cask for maturation, the casks themselves are tested for uniformity of charring of the inner surface because the degree or depth of charring affects the ageing characteristics of the spirit. This charring of the white oak barrels to assist in the ageing of the whisky (whiskey in U.S.A. and in Ireland, but whisky in Scotland and in Canada) is an American practice said to date (Marrison,[202]) from a time when old molasses barrels were used. For good Scotch whisky it is believed that maturation is still achieved in old sherry casks, but its colour derives from added caramel.

On the biological side of control, it is usual, though not universal, for the yeast strain in use to be checked regularly for infection: small scale laboratory fermentations may be carried out to note the fermentability of the wort and the condition of the yeast before "pitching", i.e. putting the yeast into the fermenting vessel. It will not be disputed that, with reasonable microbiological control throughout the process, the problems arising in potable spirit production are considerably less than those with which the beer brewer has to contend.

C. Non-biological Instability

Three papers by Warwicker[203–205] dealing with "instability" in potable spirits should be consulted for fuller details and references.

1. Whisky

In Warwicker's first paper he deals with Scotch whisky in its final blended form and indicates that instability is partly inherent, partly due to contamination during maturation and partly to poor filtration techniques. A greying of the spirits appearing at low temperatures but disappearing on raising of the temperature, corresponds to the reversible "chill haze" occurring in beers, but is not necessarily due to the same causes. If, however, the spirit has formed a deposit, a subsequent reversal is not likely to occur and the spirit is designated "thick". Extraction of magnesium salts from filter-pads and filter-aids is a contributory cause of haze and deposit, as also is the presence of zinc and aluminium. The latter and copper are perhaps the most troublesome in the formation of metallic haze. The pH of the blended spirit is a critical factor. Something, believed to be a type of tannin, is extracted from wood during maturation and is deposited if certain metals are present in sufficient concentration and the pH is above the critical value. Reference to the original paper is advised since full particulars are given of methods of analysis and estimation, not only of metals, but also of other constituents, together with the effect of various cations and anions on deposit formation.

2. Rum and Brandy

Warwicker's second paper[204] deals similarly with rum and brandy and again gives details of analyses and effects of metals, wood extracts and added cations. The conclusions reached follow generally those reached in the earlier studies on Scotch whisky.

3. Gin and Vodka

The third paper by this worker[205] deals, on the same lines as for other spirits with gin and vodka, which are not generally matured before use. Fundamentally, in the manufacture of gin, as opposed to brandy and whisky, a "neutral" spirit, that is, a tasteless product is required, with which flavouring substances are subsequently incorporated. It is not required to discuss here the methods of distillation of spirits beyond stating that the "pot-still" is that used for the best brandy and some whisky, but that the Coffee or "patent" still is commoner, particularly for gin. Descriptions of these stills are given in the more specialized books on alcohol (e.g. references 206, 207) and in a more popular form by Marrison.[202]

For gin manufacture, an "essence" of highly rectified spirit is prepared and in it are steeped the various "botanicals" such as juniper berries, orange peel, angelica root, cardamom and coriander seeds and so forth, or oils and essences made therefrom. The steep so obtained is distilled and blended with more spirit and broken down with distilled water to the required degrees of proof spirit. Formulations vary, so there is no standard of analysis, except for the content of spirit. Taste is the essential and ultimate criterion. Nowadays in some distilleries rapid methods have been developed for estimating the essential oils, etc.

Whereas gin has the addition of "botanicals", vodka generally has no additions, although in some countries this is not so. Warwicker found that the deposit which forms in vodka is calcium carbonate, but magnesium carbonate and calcium and magnesium sulphates can also occur. Whereas in the other spirits mentioned above, pH is critical for the formation of deposits, this is not so in vodka but the final concentration of ions *is* critical. The standard of the water used is said to be the most important factor in avoiding a deposit. As with the other potable spirits, contact with zinc, iron and aluminium is to be avoided. Again reference to the original paper is recommended both for information on techniques and on work by other authors.

D. Rum Manufacture

Quality control in rum manufacture does not differ greatly from that in operation for other potable spirits, the organoleptic tests on the product being the principal feature. It is to be noted however, that the use of pure culture yeasts has become general, with a beneficial effect on consistency of flavour. The raw material is almost entirely cane sugar molasses, although methods of fermentation and distillation may vary considerably in different places. Caramel is used, of course, and in some areas (e.g. Jamaica) this must be made only from burnt sugar. As a generalization, Jamaica rum is prepared by a relatively slow fermentation for ten days or so of a high gravity "wash" of s.g. of 1·080 or more, whereas Demerara rum results from a more rapid fermentation, say 36–48 h of a "wash" at a lower s.g., about 1·060.

What may be called a "stretched" rum is made by diluting or "cutting" rectified grain spirit with distilled water to the same strength as a rum of strong flavour and aroma and mixing the two in various proportions. The mixture is then aged in casks at 75°F (24°C). A rum described as "imitation" is prepared in a similar manner, but before ageing it is further diluted with distilled water and redistilled. It is then treated with "rum essence" and aged in casks. This essence consists of a mixture of esters, alcohol and so forth.[206] It is stated, however, that an experienced taster would easily detect the difference from "genuine" rum.

For further information on rum manufacture and the standards for various types, the reader is referred to such text books as Herstein and Gregory[206] and Simmonds.[207]

E. Minor Constituents of Potable Spirits

1. Fusel Oil

Reference has already been made to the presence of these materials in beers and wines and to the extensive literature on the subject. Similar remarks both as to the substances and their importance apply to potable spirits. In particular reference should be made to the contributions to the literature by H. Suomalainen and his colleagues of the State Alcohol Monopoly Laboratories at Helsinki; to those of L. Rosenthaler and colleagues at the Laboratory of the Confederation Alcohol Administration* at Berne, and to such papers as those of Bober and Haddaway,[208, 209] and Maurel-Lafarge,[210] the latter dealing specifically with rum.

2. Dicarbonyl Compounds

A useful paper on the isolation and determination of the compounds comes from Ronkainen and Suomalainen.[211]

3. Other Substances

A simple paper by De Becze[212] enumerates the foreign objects which may be seen in potable spirits or the raw materials from which they are derived: calcium oxalate is said to be the commonest crystalline substance occurring in whiskies and brandies.

4. Taste and Aroma

It is not surprising that there is, with many of the potable spirits, such a considerable degree of blending that particular attention is paid to the organoleptic aspect of control. The procedure laid down in papers such as that by Liebmann and Panettiere[213] are common to many food and beverage products, but, as these authors point out not only are there no real units of measurement in organoleptic determinations, but also in the case of alcoholic beverages there is the additional complication of the influence of the alcohol on the taster, according to its concentration. Hence, it is claimed, especial care is required in the selection of the test panels and consideration has to be

* Laboratorium der Eidgenössischen Alcoholverwaltung.

given to variability in performance on account of the influence of "psycho-physical" forces. Such factors, it may be claimed, can be important in all tasting tests, but it may well be they acquire greater emphasis in the testing of spirituous liquors. Furthermore, it is argued that the effects of the alcohol are more marked in spirits than in wines and beers where the alcohol is normally weaker. Two different methods are employed in difference testing: one is the ordinary triangular test, with two identical and one different sample, the object being to spot the latter. The other procedure is the duo-trio test, in which the taster is first given a "warm-up" sample, followed by one called the standard or control. He then receives two further samples, one identical with the control. It is stated that, using spirits (in this case whiskies) of 86° proof, the triangular test is the more sensitive and easier of the two for testers who have no previous experience of either method. Other points covered in the above-cited paper are similar to those found in general tasting tests, and the actual mechanics of the tests and the structure of questionnaires are also given. In the paper by Brandt[200] details of the duo-trio technique are set out and are given here because it is stated that although it is more difficult to master in the first instance than is the ordinary test, eventually greater con-sistency is achieved. When the taster receives his "warm-up" sample, he wets his tongue thoroughly and then spits out the spirit. After 20 sec he is given 4 ml of the reference standard to identify or register the taste in his mind and then spits out again. After 10 sec he is given sample No. 1, which he tastes and spits out, and after a further 10 sec he repeats the operation with sample No. 2. He then records which, number 1 or 2, he considers to be the same as the reference standard. Now follows a mouth rinse with water and a rest of 20 sec is taken before the tests are repeated. The operations are carried out in cubicles in the usual manner.

The importance which is attached to these tasting tests as the ultimate in quality and consistency control, at any rate in Brandt's Organisation, is indicated by the rigorous "training" given to those picked for testing teams. First there is a four week qualification test, followed by twenty judgments spread over three days, during which pairs of samples of known difference are offered. Then there follows a further four week period of training, terminating in another qualification test. The candidates' daily scores are tabulated and if 75% correct marking in this test is achieved, as well as 58% correctness in the preceding four weeks regular tests and the candidate has participated in 80% of the tests put to him, then he becomes a member or observer of a "control panel". Later tests are made to see whether the observer subse-quently falls below requirements: if he does he returns to a training panel.

It will be noted that this tasting test technique ensures uniformity and is not meant to characterize it. Also it is not to be confused with "consumer preference tasting". This aspect has been discussed above in the section on beer.

Brandt (*loc. cit.*) concludes by drawing attention to the extent to which sensitivity on the part of the taster can be retained: when precautions such as limiting the volume and concentration of the material are taken, at least six consecutive tests are found to be possible. Experienced observers may be expected to respond correctly to at least 58% on samples designed to be the same and some individuals will maintain correct responses of over 70%.

6. VINEGAR

Contributed by Dr John White

A. General Considerations

1. Vinegar and "Non-brewed Condiment"

In England the famous legal case of Kat *v.* Diment [214] conclusively confirmed the definition of vinegar as a product of double fermentation, alcoholic and acetous; it also confirmed that the term "non-brewed vinegar" applied to an imitation product which was a coloured, dilute solution of acetic acid, was a false trade description within the prohibitions of the Merchandise Marks Act 1887, and unlawful.

In vinegar, the fermented liquor may be obtained from malt, wine, cider or spirits. In each case, the first fermentation consists in changing the sugar content of the liquid into alcohol. A second fermentation is then induced in which an organism of the *Acetobacter* group oxidizes the alcohol into acetic acid and also produces a number of secondary changes. The secondary products due to these changes confer on the vinegar a smoothness, bouquet and aroma superior to that of the non-brewed liquor. Esters, higher alcohols and mineral salts (especially phosphates) are characteristic of vinegar but not of the imitation product. Manufacturers of the imitation product, after the decision in Kat *v.* Diment, renamed their product "non-brewed condiment" and as such it is now sold. Both vinegar and non-brewed condiment should contain at least 4% of acetic acid (w/v).

Prior to this somewhat salutary legal case it was possible to market a so-called "Non-Brewed Vinegar" which was normally a dilute (about 5% w/v) solution of "chemically produced" acetic acid suitably coloured with caramel. This cheap imitation has since been re-named "Non-Brewed Condiment" and to a large degree is now known by the food distributive trade (and to a greater or less degree by the public) for what it truly is.

Every young beginner in the Vinegar Industry (indeed in the Food Industry generally) should carry out the very simple test of exhaustively examining the flavour characteristics of a 5% acid content "Non-Brewed Condiment" as distinct from a truly "brewed" vinegar of the same strength.

Flavour and smell of the samples alone will convince him of the astonishing difference in the two products. No words can truly replace the findings of this simple test and it is not the purpose of this short contribution to attempt such a task. Sufficient to say that the 5% acetic acid has its own peculiar sharp clean flavour and smell; the equal amount of acetic acid in the vinegar has its flavour and odour greatly modified by the multitude of other substances present. Some of them are discussed below; when these are carefully examined it will be agreed that it is small wonder that there can be no comparison between acetic acid solutions and truly "brewed" vinegars of equal acid strengths. Such then is the simplest set of two tests for vinegar quality— taste and smell. These are still the best simple preliminary tests to apply. This does not prevent a large quantity of diluted acetic acid from being sold as "Non-brewed Condiment" to Britain's Fish and Chip Trade—the lower end of which still wallows in the stuff!

From the smell and flavour and the analytical data assembled below there is no doubting the differentiation between brewed vinegar and non-brewed condiment (and strong presumptive evidence can be built up to show presence of downwards of half the acetic acid present in a "vinegar" being sophisticated from "chemical" acetic acid).

B. Types of Vinegar

It must be remembered, however, that whilst the predominantly consumed type of vinegar in England is malt vinegar that there are many other types of vinegar made and consumed in other parts of the world. The chief types of vinegar are:

Malt Vinegar. Made from malt "beer" which is prepared from malted barley with or without added cereal adjuncts and brewing sugars.

Cider Vinegar. Prepared from apple cider.

Wine Vinegar. Prepared from wine—red, white or rosé.

Spirit Vinegar. Prepared from a diluted solution of ethyl alcohol which has been prepared by a fermentation process from sugary materials, normally from cereals or molasses.

Blended Vinegar. Made from a mixed substrate, e.g. blended wine vinegar made from a substrate containing diluted fermentation alcohol, with a proportion of wine. *Note:* some blended vinegars are made from fermented molasses mashes containing added fermentation alcohol.

Distilled Malt Vinegar. This vinegar is made by distillation of malt vinegar and is a water-white liquid containing virtually no solid matter but being flavoured with the volatile distillate from the malt vinegar.

Other vinegars. Vinegars can be made from any sugary mash from a variety of fruits and may be prepared, for example, from pineapples, dates, figs, etc.

C. Treatment

It is obvious that the final characteristics of a vinegar must reflect the properties of the substrate from which the vinegar was made. For example, a malt vinegar is made from malted barley (with or without the addition of starchy adjuncts and brewing sugars). The malt beer initially prepared is then acetified (alcohol oxidized to acetic acid) and the subsequent crude vinegar may or may not be stored for "maturing" purposes for many months prior to clarification, filtration and (possibly) pasteurization before bottling or filling into casks or into the various types of plastic containers now being used to get the vinegar to the consuming public.

There is no universally accepted method of carrying out the final stages of presentation of the vinegar to the public. To enable the product to reach the public in good order without growth of infecting micro-organisms, the vinegar must be pasteurized and filled into sterile containers. Alternatively it is legal in Great Britain to resort to two methods of chemical prevention of infection.

(1) To add sodium chloride; addition of about 1.0% w/v of sodium chloride usually prevents growth of *Acetobacter* and other infecting micro-organisms. It does not however, entirely prevent the development of the vinegar eel, *Anguillula aceti*. There is also a tendency for salt additions to "salt out" a protein/iron/(or copper)/phosphate/melanoidin haze which destroys the normally accepted crystal clarity of modern day vinegars.

(2) To add sulphur dioxide; the use of up to 70 ppm is now accepted by law. There is a tendency for this preservative to disappear (probably as a complex with traces of aldehydes, etc., present in the vinegar). Addition of this preservative also has the tendency to produce a "reduction" haze which is a complex protein/copper/phosphate/melanoidin compound and objectionable in that it destroys vinegar brightness.

D. Solid Matter in Vinegars

The solids of the original alcoholic liquor (malt "beer", wine, cider, etc.), are observed as the solid content of the final vinegar with modifications due to the use of the original liquor as substrate for growth of the oxidizing bacteria. Storage of the final vinegar over a period of time also produces slight modifications in solids content.[215]

Prior to the use of the modern deep culture oxidation methods now used in the acetification stages, conversion efficiencies of the alcohol to acetic acid were of the order of 70%; they may now be of the order of 90% or even higher (the British Continuous Culture Method (British Patents No. 878,949 and 963,481) has an efficiency as high as 98%). Consequently solids content of vinegars has been proportionately reduced. For example, a malt vinegar having a solid matter content of 1·8% at conversion efficiency of 70% would contain only 1·29% of solids at the conversion efficiency of 98% (at a standard acidity of 5·0% in the final vinegar).

E. Analytical Characteristics of Malt Vinegar

The pioneer work of Edwards and Nanji[216, 217] and of Whitmarsh[218] in investigating such analytical values as the oxidation, iodine and ester values of various types of vinegars is as valuable today as at the date of publication. Normal analytical values as produced by Edwards and Nanji are shown in Table 1 (calculated at 4% standard acidity):

TABLE 1

	Malt vinegar	Spirit vinegar	Artificial vinegar	Wood vinegar	Distilled malt vinegar
Oxidation value	550–1320	80–224	1·0–6·4	0·8–6·4	840–990
Iodine value	680–1976	8–27	2·4–9·6	26–252	800–1040
Ester value	29–57	6–14	0·4–2·0	0·6–1·2	30–35
% Acetic acid	4·3–5·1	4·3	4·2–5·9	4·5–5·8	5·0

The low values given by acetic acid solutions are as could be expected; the values given by spirit vinegar (a product of bacterial oxidation of a "fermentation" alcohol solution to which salts and traces of organic substances are added as bacterial nutrients) are noteworthy.

The values which would be obtained for adulterating genuine malt vinegars with acetic acid or spirit vinegars can be calculated and these are values which a Public Analyst might reasonably expect to use in such cases of suspected sophistication!

Morgan and Voelcker[208] have examined such analytical values in the light of modern high-yield technological methods and their figures have shown the following range of values for malt vinegars:

Oxidation value	505–1,770
Iodine value	180–1,600
Ester value	72–152
Total solids %w/v	0·8 –2·0
Ash %w/v	0·12 –0·37
Phosphate %w/v	0·041–0·086
Nitrogen ppm	434–791
Albuminoid nitrogen ppm	252–470

A typical analysis of *spirit vinegar* would show the following:

Total acidity %w/v	10·0
Volatile acidity (acetic acid) %w/v	9·98
Non-volatile acidity %w/v	0·02
Total solids %w/v	0·28
Phosphates (P_2O_5) %w/v	0·01
Nitrogen (N) %w/v	0·006

1. pH Values

The pH value of a precisely 5% (total acidity) vinegar is of interest in assessing its "genuine" nature. Typical values are as shown in Table 2.

TABLE 2

Substance	pH of solution of 5% w/v total acidity
Acetic acid (5%)	2·46
"Spirit" vinegar (5%)	2·52
*Blended vinegar (5%)	2·60
"Wine" vinegar (5%)	2·82
"Cider" vinegar (5%)	2·88
Malt vinegar (5%) Sample A	2·82
Malt vinegar (5%) Sample B	3·18

* Blended mixture of spirit vinegar and wine vinegar (South African).

2. Total Acidity

This is a total value of true volatile acidity (largely acetic acid) together with "non-volatile" acidity (a mixture of *inorganic* acidity from acid phosphates and other acid salts together with often significant amounts of lactic acid and traces of, for example, gluconic and other organic salts.

A genuine malt vinegar of total acidity of 5·0% may contain from 0·1 to 0·35% of non-volatile acidity. Of this, up to 0·1% can be due to the *inorganic* acidity due to acid inorganic salts, the balance is of non-volatile organic acidity.

Much work remains to be done in investigating the composition of the volatile matter in genuine vinegars. A study by Suomalainen and Kangasperko[220] has demonstrated the presence in wine vinegars of a number of volatile substances including iso-amyl acetate, iso-amyl alcohol, acetoin, iso-butyl alcohol, sec-butyl alcohol, diacetyl, and ethyl acetate.

In addition to the acetic acid and volatile flavour- and odour-producing substances such as the above, the flavour and properties of vinegars are influenced by the non-volatile substances left in the vinegars from the original alcoholic substrates, e.g. carbohydrate residues, amino acids, proteins, gums, mineral salts, colouring substances (anthocyanins, tannins, flavones, etc.), vitamins, glycerol, lactic acid, etc. The action of the buffering substances on the nature of the vinegar has already been referred to above when the pH of a 5·0% acid product was examined.

3. Analysis of Vinegar for Special Groups and Constituents

A quite voluminous literature now exists for estimation of specific constituents in vinegars of all types.

4. Amino Acids

Bergner[221] and Bergner and Petri[222] have discussed the amino acids of brandy and spirit vinegars. Bourgeois[223] has described chemical and microbiological methods for amino acid determination in various kinds of vinegar. Similar work has been done by Schander.[224]

5. Acetylmethyl carbinol, Diacetyl and 2–3 butylene glycol

The presence of acetylmethyl carbinol, diacetyl and 2–3 butylene glycol in vinegars has been the subject of much investigation and among others should be mentioned the methods of Doro and Sadini,[225] Kniphorst and Kruisbeer,[226] Happold and Spencer,[227] Serini,[228] Curzel,[229] Barnicoat[230] and Whitmarsh.[218]

6. Free Mineral Acids

Mention must be made of work by Jenkin,[231] Leibov,[232] Oliviera and Castiel,[233] O'Neill and Henry,[234] Pratolongo,[235] Rokita and Henry,[236] and Scurti.[237]

7. Caramel

Among the most important work in estimation and properties of caramel in vinegar should be mentioned that of Gulick[238] and Mallory.[239]

White and Munns[240] have described how the colouring matters of caramels behave as amphoteric electrolytes and have shown how various types of caramel may be selected for commercial use.

8. Glycerol

Glycerol estimations in vinegars of various types have been made by Englis and Wollerman[241] Hromatka,[242] Hromatka and Steiner,[243] Jackson and Rammamurti[244] and Marconi.[245]

9. Inorganic Ions

Mecca[246] has discussed the estimation of various ions in vinegar; an older paper of Shuman[247] for estimation of ash content should also be mentioned.

F. Microbiological Stability of Vinegars

A stated volume of the sample should be incubated at 30°C in a sterile bottle closed by means of a loosely-fitted sterile cotton wool plug. Growth of the characteristic film or haze of *Acetobacter* organisms clearly demonstrates presence of infection. Commercially the presence of only one single infecting cell of *Acetobacter* may be detected in this manner (in 1 litre, 1 gallon or whatever volume of liquor is taken for this purpose). Nowadays, well bottled vinegars will show no growth of infection in bottles of consumer sizes.

Presence of the vinegar eel, *Anguillula aceti*, is also detected most easily by the above methods.

Very few other organisms than the above can grow in vinegar of commercial strengths although strains of *Candida* and *Oidium* which have adapted themselves to the stringent conditions have very occasionally been detected in commercial vinegar samples.

G. Non-biological Stability of Vinegars

Several types of non-biological hazes are encountered in vinegars and these are usually caused by the presence of small quantities of metallic contamination; in most cases, such contamination is unpreventable due to presence of small concentrations of metallic ions in raw materials. Such hazes in malt vinegars are similar in constitution to the non-biological hazes of beers.

1. Reduction Hazes

These are normally complexes of protein fragments with anthocyanins or tannins and phosphates, complexed with traces of copper (as little as 0·5 ppm of copper is sufficient to precipitate such a haze). The haze is detected by incubating a *full* bottle of vinegar at 30°C, reduction hazes often forming in a few weeks.

2. Oxidation hazes

These are formed by the complexing of traces of ferric iron with the protein-phosphate-anthocyanin (tannin) type complex and are demonstrated by incubating vinegar in a bottle fitted with a cotton wool plug (to allow admission of oxygen). Such a haze will often form inside a few weeks.

Tin will produce an immediate oily haze quite impossible to precipitate or filter out, if as little as 0·1 ppm of tin gains entrance to the vinegar.

Caramels either protect the product from haze formation or bring about a rapid precipitation of haze depending upon the iso-electric point of the colouring matters of the caramel (White and Munns,[240]).

Acknowledgement

The author wishes to express his thanks to the following who gave advice and assistance during the preparation of the sections. Mr. J. F. Walker, Section II; Mr. G. B. Nelson of Messrs. H. P. Bulmer and Company Limited of Hereford, Section III and Dr. P. F. Fraser, Section IV.

REFERENCES

1. De Clerck, J. (1957, 1958). "A Textbook of Brewing." 2 Vols. (Trans. by K. Barton-Wright). (Chapman & Hall, London).
2. De Clerck, J. (1963). "Analytica—E.B.C." 2nd Edn. (Elsevier, Amsterdam).
3. De Clerck, J. (1944 *et seq*). Methods of Analysis of *Am. Soc. Brew. Chem.* Pub. by A.S.B.C. Inc.
4. De Clerck, J. (1961). *J. Inst. Brew.* **67**, 351.
5. De Clerck, J. (1967). *J. Inst. Brew.* **73**, 233.
6. De Clerck, J. (1958). *J. Inst. Brew.* **64**, 469.
7. De Clerck, J. (1965). *J. Inst. Brew.* **71**, 470.
8. Jones, M. and Pierce, J. S. (1963). *Proc. Eur. Brew. Conv.*, p. 101. (Elsevier, Amsterdam).
9. Ault, R. G. (1965). *J. Inst. Brew.* **71**, 376.
10. Puspok, J. and Szilvanyi, A. (1962). *Mitt. Vers. Sta. Gärungsgw.* **16**, 139. Through *J. Sci. Fd Agric. Absts.* 1963, ii, 199.
11. Bishop, L. R. (1963). *J. Inst. Brew.* **69**, 228.
12. Bishop, L. R. (1964). *Proc. Am. Soc. Brew. Chem.* 275.
13. Bishop, L. R. (1965). *Proc. Am. Soc. Brew. Chem.* 274.
14. Meredith, W. O. S. and Bettner, R. E. (1964). *Proc. Am. Soc. Brew. Chem.* 119.
15. Kolbach, P. and Zastrow, K. (1966). *J. Inst. Brew.* **72**, 257.
16. Analysis Committee. Inst. Brew. (1965). *J. Inst. Brew.* **71**, 471.
17. Walker, J. F. (1959). *Proc. Am. Soc. Brew. Chem.* 133.
18. Scriban, R. and Biserte, G. (1963). *Proc. Eur. Brew. Conv.*, p. 151. (Elsevier, Amsterdam).
19. Siefker, J. A. and Pollock, G. E. (1956). *Proc. Am. Soc. Brew. Chem.* 5.
20. Damm, E. and Kringstad, H. (1964). *J. Inst. Brew.* **70**, 38.
21. Hudson, J. R. (1963). *Proc. Eur. Brew. Conv.*, p. 422. (Elsevier, Amsterdam).
22. Lloyd Hind, H. (1943). "Brewing Science and Practice." 2 Vols. (Chapman and Hall, London).
23. Gough, W. H. (1956). *J. Inst. Brew.* **62**, 9.
24. Goedkoop, W. and Hartong, B. D. (1957). *J. Inst. Brew.* **63**, 386.
25. Alderton, G., Bailey, G. F., Lewis, J. C. and Stitt, F. (1954). *Analyt. Chem.* **26** (6), 983.
26. Klopper, W. J. (1955). *Brauwissenschaft* **8** (5), 101.
27. Gridgeman, N. T. (1951). *Bull. photoelect. Spectrom. Grp.* No. **4**, 67. Through "Analytica" (see reference 2).
28. Birtwistle, S. E., Hudson, J. R. and Whitear, A. L. (1963). *J. Inst. Brew.* **69**, 239.

29. Lodder, J. and Kreger-van Rij, N. J. W. (1952). "The Yeasts: a Taxonomic Study". (North-Holland Pub. Co., Amsterdam).
30. Verona, O. and Montemartini, A. (1959). *Atti Ist. bot. Univ. Lab. crittogam. Pavia* Serie V–17.
31. Beech, F. W., Davenport, R. R., Goswell, R. W. and Burnett, J. K. (1968). In: "Identification Methods for Microbiologists", Part B. (Ed. B. M. Gibbs and F. A. Skinner). (Academic Press, London).
32. Brady, B. L. (1965). *Ant. van Leeuwen.* **31,** 95.
33. Fowell, R. R. (1965). *J. appl. Bact.* **28,** 373.
34. Richards, M. (1967). *J. Inst. Brew.* **73,** 162.
35. Green, S. R. and Sullivan, P. J. (1959). *Proc. Am. Soc. Brew. Chem.* 154.
36. Jensen, H. E. (1958). In: "The Chemistry and Biology of Yeasts." (Ed. A. H. Cook), p. 635. (Academic Books, Ltd., London).
37. E.B.C. Yeast Group. (1962). *J. Inst. Brew.* **68,** 14.
38. Walters, L. S. and Thistleton, M. R. (1953). *J. Inst. Brew.* **59,** 401.
39. Morris, E. O. and Eddy, A. A. (1957). *J. Inst. Brew.* **63,** 34.
40. Campbell, I. and Allan, A. M. (1964). *J. Inst. Brew.* **70,** 316.
41. Campbell, I. and Brudzynski, A. (1966). *J. Inst. Brew.* **72,** 556.
42. Richards, M. and Cowland, T. W. (1967). *J. Inst. Brew.* **73,** 552.
43. Green, S. R. and Gray, P. P. (1950). *Wallerstein Labs Commun.* **13,** 357.
44. Gray, P. P. and Kazin, A. D. (1946). *Wallerstein Labs Commun.* **9,** 115.
45. Bruch, C. W., Hoffman, A., Gosine, R. M. and Brenner, M. W. (1964). *J. Inst. Brew.* **70,** 242.
46. Brenner, M. W. (1965). *J. Inst. Brew.* **71,** 290.
47. Ellison, J. and Doran, A. H. (1961). *Proc. Eur. Brew. Conv.*, p. 224. (Elsevier, Amsterdam).
48. Ault, R. G. (1954). *Brewers' Guild J.* **40,** 391.
49. Bishop, L. R. (1955). *J. Inst. Brew.* **61,** 150.
50. Willox, I. C. (1964). *Brewers' Guard.* **93,** No. 3, 49.
51. Bunker, H. J. (1955). *Proc. Eur. Brew. Conv.*, p. 330. (Elsevier, Amsterdam).
52. Bunker, H. J. (1952). *Lab. Pract.* **1,** 354.
53. Bunker, H. J. (1953). VI Internat. Microbiol. Congr. Absts. 7, Session 19, p. 26.
54. Bunker, H. J. (1956). *Wallerstein Labs Commun.* **19,** 143.
55. Sykes, G. (1958). "Disinfection and Sterilization". (E. & F. N. Spon, London).
56. Sykes, G. (1964). Monograph No. 19. Surface Activity and the Microbial Cell, Soc. Chem. Ind., London.
57. Osborne, P. W. (1962). *Proc. 7th Convention, Austral. Sect., Inst. Brew.*, p. 246. (Adelaide, S. Australia).
58. Turnbull, D. T. (1962). *Proc. 7th Convention, Austral. Sect., Inst. Brew.*, p. 251. (Adelaide, S. Australia).
59. Neilan, G. (1962). *Proc. 7th Convention, Austral. Sect., Inst. Brew.*, p. 253. (Adelaide, S. Australia).
60. Sullivan, B. J. (1962). *Proc. 7th Convention, Austral. Sect., Inst. Brew.*, p. 119. (Adelaide, S. Australia).
61. Buchanan, R. E., Holt, J. G. and Lessel, E. F. Jr. (1966). "Index Bergeyiana". (Williams & Wilkins, Baltimore).
62. Helm, E. J. (1938). *Woch. für Brauerei* **51,** 105 and in J. de Clerck (see reference 1), **2,** 379.
63. Gray, P. P. and Stone, I. M. (1939). *J. Inst. Brew.* **45,** 443.
64. Gray, P. P. and Stone, I. M. (1939). *J. Inst. Brew.* **45,** 253.

65. Van Gheluwe, J. E. A., Buday, A. and Stock, A. L. (1963). *Proc. Am. Soc. Brew. Chem.* 58.
66. Brenner, M. W., Vigilante, C. and Arthurs, M. J. (1963). *Proc. Am. Soc. Brew. Chem.* 158.
67. Tullo, J. W., Stringer, W. J. and Harrison, G. A. F. (1949). *Analyst*, **74**, 296.
68. Stone, I. M., Gantz, C. S. and Salitan, L. T. (1963). *Proc. Am. Soc. Brew. Chem.* 149.
69. Biske, V. B. and Feaster, J. F. (1964). *Proc. Am. Soc. Brew. Chem.* 189.
70. Etian, H. O. and Rovella, M. A. (1966). *Proc. Am. Soc. Brew. Chem.* 177.
71. Case, A. E. (1938). *J. Inst. Brew.* **44**, 362.
72. Ault, R. G. (1961). *J. Inst. Brew.* **67**, 14.
73. Gray, P. P. and Stone, I. M. (1957). *Wallerstein Labs Commun.* **20**, 355 and *J. Inst. Brew.* **63**, 512.
74. Thorne, R. S. W. and Helm, E. J. (1957). *Wallerstein Labs Commun.* **20**, 307.
75. Segel, E. and Lautenback, A. F. (1964). *Proc. Am. Soc. Brew. Chem.* 49.
76. Harold, F. V. and Szobolotzsky, E. (1963). *J. Inst. Brew.* **69**, 253.
77. Torii, T. (1955). *J. Chem. Soc. Japan*, Pure Chem. Sect. **76**, 328, through *Chem. Absts.* (1956), **50**, 4717b.
78. Andrews, J. S. and Stringer, W. J. (1953). *J. Inst. Brew.* **59**, 52.
79. Marthens, R. I. and Githens, R. E. (1952). *Analyt. Chem.* **24**, 991.
80. Stone, I. M., Ettinger, R. and Ganz, C. (1953). *Analyt. Chem.* **25**, 893 and *Wallerstein Labs Commun.* 1955, **18**, 27.
81. Brenner, M. W., Mayer, M. J. and Blick, S. R. (1962). *Proc. 7th Convention, Austral. Sect., Inst. Brew.*, p. 80 (Adelaide, S. Australia); and 1963, *Proc. Am. Soc. Brew. Chem.* 165.
82. Andrews, J. S. and Stringer, W. J. (1953). *J. Inst. Brew.* **59**, 211.
83. Gray, P. P. and Stone, I. M. (1938). *Ind. Engng. Chem., analyt. Edn.* **10**, 415; and 1948, *Wallerstein Labs Commun.* 10 years Res. record, p. 37.
84. Stone, I. A., Alexander, O., Bockelmann, J. Henry, R. E., Rolner, R. and Sigal, A. (1950). *Proc. Am. Soc. Brew. Chem.* 169.
85. Stone, I. A. "Official Methods of Assoc. Offic. Agric. Chem." (8th Edition, p. 157. (Washington, 1955).
86. Stone, I. M. and Gray, P. P. (1955). *Proc. Am. Soc. Brew. Chem.* 145 and *Wallerstein Labs Commun.* **18**, 291.
87. Hagues, G. (1931). *J. Inst. Brew.* **37**, 366.
88. Andrews, J. S. and Harrison, G. A. F. (1954). *J. Inst. Brew.* **60**, 133.
89. Kenigberg, M. and Stone, I. M. (1955). *Wallerstein Labs Commun.* **18**, 285.
90. Stone, I. M. (1941). *Ind. Engng Chem. analyt. Edn.* **13**, 791 and 1948, 10 years Res. record, p. 115.
91. Franken-Luykx, J. M. M. (1963). *Proc. Eur. Brew. Conv.* p. 516. (Elsevier, Amsterdam).
92. Rooney, R. C. (1963). *Analyst* **88**, 959.
93. Densky, H., Gray, P. P. and Buday, A. (1966). *Proc. Am. Soc. Brew. Chem.* 93.
94. Steiner, R. L. and Oliver, R. T. (1963). *Proc. Am. Soc. Brew. Chem.* 111.
95. Gray, P. P. and Stone, I. M. (1960). *Proc. Am. Soc. Brew. Chem.* 166.
96. Genevois, L. and Baraud, J. (1956). *Inds. aliment. agric.* **76**, 837.
97. Stevens, R. (1960). *J. Inst. Brew.* **66**, 453.
98. Hudson, J. R. and Stevens, R. (1960). *J. Inst. Brew.* **66**, 471.
99. Ingraham, J. L. and Guymon, J. F. (1960). *Archs Biochem. Biophys.* **88**, 157.
100. Boruff, C. S. (1961). *J. Ass. off. agric. Chem.* Washington, **44**, 383, through *J. Sci. Fd Agric. Absts.* (1962), **i**, 143.

101. Webb, A. D. and Ingraham, J. L. (1963). In: "Advances in Applied Microbiolology". (Ed. W. W. Umbreit), **5**, 317. (Academic Press).
102. Suomalainen, H. and Kahanpaa (1963). *J. Inst. Brew.* **69**, 473.
103. Sihto, E. and Arkima, V. (1963). *J. Inst. Brew.* **69**, 20.
104. Nykänen, L. (1963). *Teknill. Kem. Aikak.* **20**, 129.
105. Owades, J. L. and Jakovac, J. A. (1963). *Proc. Am. Soc. Brew. Chem.* 22.
106. Owades, J. L. and Jakovac, J. A. (1963). *Proc. Am. Soc. Brew. Chem.* 205.
107. Owades, J. L. and Jakovac, J. A. (1964). *Proc. Am. Soc. Brew. Chem.* 269.
108. Brenner, M. W., Blick, S. R., Frenkel, G. and Siebenberg, J. (1963). *Proc. Eur. Brew. Conv.*, p. 233. (Elsevier, Amsterdam).
109. Gjertsen, P., Undstrup, S. and Trolle, B. (1965). *Brygmesteren.* **22**, 21, through *J. Sci. Fd Agric. Absts* (1965), **ii**, 88.
110. Portno, A. D. (1965). *J. Inst. Brew.* **71**, 9.
111. Harrison, G. A. F., Byrne, W. J. and Collins, E. (1965). *J. Inst. Brew.* **71**, 336.
112. Canales, A. M., Paniagua, L. and Gallindo, F. (1965). *Proc. Am. Soc. Brew. Chem.* 214.
113. Bavisotto, V. S., Shovers, J., Sandine, W. E. and Elliker, P. R. (1964). *Proc. Am. Soc. Brew. Chem.* 211.
114. Stone, I. M. and Laschiver, C. (1957). *Proc. Am. Soc. Brew. Chem.* 46.
115. Ronkainen, P., Arkima, V. and Suomalainen, H. (1967) *J. Inst. Brew.* **73**, 567.
116. Salitan, L. T., Gantz, C. S. and Gray, P. P. (1963). *Proc. Am. Soc. Brew. Chem.* 74.
117. Brenner, M. W., Messing, R., Streifer, S. and Golyzniak, R. (1966). *Proc. Am. Soc. Brew. Chem.* 236.
118. Weissler, H. E., Eigel, J. A. and Garza, A. C. (1966). *Proc. Am. Soc. Brew. Chem.* 215.
119. Weissler, H. E. and Eigel, J. A. (1966). *Proc. Am. Soc. Brew. Chem.* 221.
120. Helm, E. (1933). *Wochschr. für Brauerei*, **50**, 241.
121. Blom, J. (1937). *J. Inst. Brew.* **43**, 251.
122. Ross, S. and Clark, R. (1939). *Wallerstein Labs. Commun.* **2**, 46.
123. Gray, P. P. and Stone, I. M. (1940). *Wallerstein Labs. Commun.* **3**, 159.
124. Hartong, B. D. (1941). *Wschr. Brau.* **58**, 183.
125. Brenner, M. W. (1952). *Proc. Am. Soc. Brew. Chem.* 113.
126. Klopper, W. J. (1954). *J. Inst. Brew.* **60**, 217.
127. Ziliotto, H. L., Bockelmann, J. B. and Tirado, W. (1962). *Proc. Am. Soc. Brew. Chem.* 77.
128. De Clerck, J. and De Dijcker, G. (1957). *Proc. Eur. Brew. Conv.*, p. 43. (Elsevier, Amsterdam).
129. Rudin, A. D. (1957). *J. Inst. Brew.* **63**, 506.
130. Harvey, J. V. and Pope, N. H. (1962). *Proc. 7th Convention, Austral. Sect. Inst. Brew.*, p. 246 (Adelaide, S. Australia).
131. Glenister, P. R. and Segel, E. (1964). *Proc. Am. Soc. Brew. Chem.* 55.
132. Rigby, F. L. and Bethune, J. L. (1955). *J. Inst. Brew.* **61**, 325.
133. Moltke, A. B. and Meilgaard, M. (1955). *Brygmesteren* **12**, 23.
134. Bishop, L. R. (1964). *J. Inst. Brew.* **70**, 489.
135. Bishop, L. R. (1967). The E.B.C. Scale of Bitterness. *J. Inst. Brew.* **73**, 525.
136. Goedkoop, W., Hartong, B. D. and Klopper, W. J. (1963). *Proc. Eur. Brew. Conv.*, p. 343. (Elsevier, Amsterdam).
137. Verzele, M. (1968). *Proc. Eur. Brew. Conv.*, p. 77. (Elsevier, Amsterdam).
138. Verzele, M. and Khokher, A. (1967). *J. Inst. Brew.* **73**, 255.
139. De Mets. M, and Verzele, M. (1968). *J. Inst. Brew.* **74**, 74.

140. Rintala, P. and Arkima, V. (1961). *Brauwissenschaft*, **14**, 397, through *J. Inst. Brew.* 1962, **68**, 83.
141. Trolle, B. (1964). *Lab. Prac.* **13**, 720.
142. Klcdal, S. (1965). *Proc. Eur. Brew. Conv.*, p. 439. (Elsevier, Amsterdam).
143. Carr, J. G. (1964). *Brewers J.* **100**, 244, 324, and 390.
144. Lane, J. H. and Eynon, L. (1923). *J. Soc. Chem. Ind.* **33** T, 42.
145. Lane, J. H. and Eynon, L. (1963). *Rep. agric. hort. Res. Stn Univ. Bristol* 150.
146. Burroughs, L. F. (1946). *Rep. agric. hort. Res. Stn Univ. Bristol* **122.**
147. Ripper, M. (1892). *J. prakt. Chem.* **46**, 428.
148. Burroughs, L. F. and Sparks, A. H. (1964). *Analyst* **89**, 55.
149. Burroughs, L. F. and Sparks, A. H. (1963). *Int. Bottler Pckr.* **37**, 85.
150. Tavernier, J. (1960). *Revue Ferment. Ind. aliment* **15**, 103.
151. Tavernier, J. (1964). *Brewer's J.* **100**, 682.
152. Warcollier, G. (1928). La Cidrerie, 3rd edn. Trans. by V. L. S. Charley as "Principles and Practice of Cider-making". (Leonard Hill, London, 1949).
153. Warcollier, G. (1953). "The Cider Factory: Plant and Layout". Trans. by V. L. S. Charley *et al.* from Tech. Pub. no. 2 of Royal Engng Service of French Min. of Agric.
154. Warcollier, G. (1962). Recueil des Methodes internationales d'analyse des vins. Convention internationale pour l'unification des methodes d'analyse et d'appreciation des vins. Limited edition pub. by Office internationale de la Vigne et du Vin. 11 rue Roquepine, Paris 8ᵉ.
155. Warcollier, G. (1966). *Bull. off. int. Vin.* **39** (427), 1035.
156. Amerine, M. A. and Cruess, W. V. (1960). "Technology of Wine Making". (Avi, Westport, Conn.).
157. Fornachon, J. C. M. and Lloyd, B. (1965). *J. Sci. Fd Agric.* **16**, 710.
158. Genevois, L. and Larrouquiere, J. (1961). *Bull. Soc. chim. Fr.* **1905.**
159. Eschnauer, H. (1965). *Z. Lebensmittel unters. u. -Forsch.* **127**, 268: through *J. Sci. Fd Agric. Absts.* (1966), **i**, 193.
160. Eschnauer, H. (1966). *Z. Lebensmittelunters. u. -Forsch.* **128**, 337: through *J. Sci. Fd Agric. Absts.* (1966) **ii**, 137.
161. Karvánek, M. and Silkanova, J. I. (1966). *Sb. Praz. vys. Šk. chem.-technol. potravin. Technol.* no. E.9, 65, through *J. Sci. Fd Agric. Absts.* (1967) **i**, 141.
162. Sandoval Puerta, J. A. and Hidalgo Zabollos, T. (1965). *Boln Inst. nac. Invest. agron. Madr.* **25**, 417: through *J. Sci. Fd Agric. Absts.* (1966). **ii**, 293.
163. Hauschofer, H. and Rethallen, A. (1965). *Mitt. höh Bundeslehr-u. Versanst. Wein- Obst- u. Gartenb. Series A. Rebe u. Wein*, through *J. Sci. Fd Agric. Absts.* (1966), **i**, 193.
164. Jaulmes, P. and Espezel, P. (1935). *Ann. Falsif.*, *Paris* **28**, 325.
165. Ribéreau-Gayon, P. and Stonestreet, E. (1966). *Chim. analyt.* **48**, 188: through *J. Sci. Fd Agric. Absts.* (1966) **ii**, 293.
166. Ribéreau-Gayon, P. and Stonestreet, E. (1965). *Bull. Soc. chim. Fr.* **2649.**
167. Eschnauer, H. and Tölg, G. (1966). *Z. Lebensmittelunters. u. -Forsch.* **129**, 273: through *J. Sci. Fd Agric. Absts.* (1966). **ii**, 182.
168. Feduchy Marino, E., Sandoval Puerta, J. A. Hidalgo Zaballos, T., Rodriquez Matia, E. and Horsche Diez, T. (1964). *Boln. Inst. nac. Invest. agron., Madr.* **24**, 453: through *J. Sc. Fd Agric. Absts.* (1966) **i**, 193.
169. Rebelein, H. (1965). *Dt. LebensmittRdsch.* **61**, 211: through *J. Sci. Fd Agric. Absts.* (1966). **i**, 193.
170. Boidron, J. (1966). Thesis "Identification des Constituents de l'Arome des Vins de Vitis vinifera". Univ. de Bordeaux.

171. Morrison, R. L. (1965). *J. Ass. off. agric. Chem.* **48**, 471, through *J. Sci. Fd Agric. Absts.* (1966). **i**, 32.
172. Schroeter, L. C. (1966). "Sulphur Dioxide (Applications in Food, Beverages and Pharmaceuticals)". (Pergamon Press, Oxford).
173. Jones, G. T. (1964). *Analyst* **89**, 678.
174. Pataky, B. (1963). *Mitt. Wein u. Obstbau, Wien,* **13A**, 232.
175. Deibner, L. and Heredia, N. (1966). *Chim. analyt.* **38**, 66 and 143.
176. Beneš, V. (1963). *Kvasný Prům,* **9**, 86, through *J. Sci. Fd Agric. Absts.* (1963), **ii**, 145.
177. Berg, H. W. and Akiyoshi, M. (1961). *Am. J. Enol. Vitic.* **12**, 107.
178. Beneš, V. and Krumphanzl, V. (1964). *Kvasný Prům.* **10**, 258, through *J. Sci. Fd Agric. Absts.* (1965), **i**. 261.
179. Manchev, K. (1961). *Sborn Praž. Vys. Škol. chem. Technol., Potravin Technol,* through *J. Sci. Fd Agric. Absts.* (1964), **i**. 151.
180. Berg, H. W. and Keefer, R. M. (1958). *Am. J. Enol. Vitic.* **9**, 180.
181. Berg, H. W. and Keefer, R. M. (1959). *Am. J. Enol. Vitic.* **10**, 105.
182. Rankine, B. C. and Emerson, W. W. (1963). *J. Sci. Fd Agric.* **14**, 685.
183. Ford, J. H. and Klomparens, N. W. (1960). *Antibiotics Chemother.* **10**, 682, through *J. Sci. Fd Agric. Absts.* (1961). **i**, 142.
184. Maurel, A.-J. and Touyé, S. (1963). *C. r. Acad. Agric. Fr.* **49**, 150, through *J. Sci. Fd Agric. Absts.* (1963). **ii**, 198.
185. Schmidt, H. (1962). *Dt. Lebensmittel Rundsch.* **58**, 1 and *Anal. Absts.* **9**, 4486, through *J. Sci. Fd Agric. Absts.* (1962). **ii**, 1962.
186. Jaulmes, P. Mestres, R. and Mandrou, B. (1964). *Ann. Falsif., Paris* **57**, 119.
187. Prillinger, F. (1964). *Mitt. Wein u. Obstbau, Wien,* **14A**, 193, through *J. Sci. Fd Agric. Absts.* (1965). **i**, 152.
188. Maurel, A.-J. and Touyé, S. (1962). *Ann. Falsif., Paris* **55**, 297, through *J. Sci. Fd Agric. Absts.* (1963). **i**, 32.
189. Biol, H. and Foulonneau, C. (1961). *C.r. hebd. séanc. Acad. Agric. Fr.* **47**, 957, through *J. Sci. Fd Agric. Absts.* (1962). **ii**, 104.
190. Guimberteau, G. (1962). *Industr. aliment. agric.* **79**, 99.
191. Würdig, G. (1966). *Dt. LebensmittRdsch.* **62**, 147, through *J. Sci. Fd Agric. Absts.* (1966). **ii**, 240.
192. Ough, C. S. (1964). *Mitt. Wein u. Obstbau, Wien,* **14A**, 260, through *J. Sci. Fd Agric. Absts.* (1965). **i**, 152.
193. Tercelj, D. and Adamic, J. (1965). *Mitt. höh. Bundeslehr. u. VersAnst. Wein-Obst- u. Gartenbau Ser. A. Rebe u. Wein,* **15A**, 279, through *J. Sci. Fd Agric. Absts.* (1966). **ii**, 38.
194. Van Zyl, J. A. (1962). *S. Afr. J. agric. Sci.* **5**, 293.
195. Minarik, E. and Laho, L. (1962). *Kvasný Prům.,* **8**, 86, through *J. Sci. Fd Agric. Absts.* (1963). **i**, 258.
196. Kielhöfer, E. and Würdig, G. (1963). *Dt. LebensmittRundsch.* **59**, 224, through *J. Sci. Fd Agric. Absts.* (1963). **ii**, 93.
197. Prillinger, E. (1964). *Mitt. Wein u. Obstbau, Wien* **14A**, 29, through *J. Sci. Fd Agric. Absts.* (1964). **ii**, 40.
198. Ronkainen, P., Salo, T. and Soumalainen, H. (1962). *Lebensm. u.-Forsch.* **217**, 19.
199. Amerine, M. A. and Ough, C. S. (1964). *Lab. Pract.* **13**, 712.
200. Brandt, D. A. (1964). *Lab. Pract.* **13**, 717.
201. Brandt, D. A. (1960). *Official Methods of Analysis of A.O.A.C.*
202. Marrison, L. W. (1957). "Wines and Spirits", Pelican Books, A383. (Penguin Books, Ltd., Harmondsworth).

203. Warwicker, L. A. (1960). *J. Sci. Fd Agric.* **11**, 709.
204. Warwicker, L. A. (1963). *J. Sci. Fd Agric.* **14**, 365.
205. Warwicker, L. A. (1963). *J. Sci. Fd Agric.* **14**, 371.
206. Herstein, K. M. and Gregory, T. C. (1935). "Chemistry and Technology of Wines and Liquors". (Chapman & Hall, London).
207. Simmonds, C. (1919). "Alcohol: its production, properties, chemistry and industrial applications". (Macmillan, London).
208. Bober, A. and Haddaway, L. W. (1963). *J. Gas. Chromato.* **1**, 8.
209. Bober, A. and Haddaway, L. W. (1964). *J. Gas Chromato.* **2**, 76.
210. Maurel, A-J and Lafarge, J-P. (1963). *C.r. hebd. Séanc. Acad. Agric. Fr.* **49**, 332.
211. A. Ronkainen, P. and Soumalainen, H. (1966). *Acta chem. Journ.* B **39**, 280.
212. De Becze, G. I. (1962). *J. Ass. off. agric. chem.* **45**, 645.
213. Liebmann, A. J. and Panettiere, B. R. (1957). *Wallerstein Labs Commun.* **20**, 27.
214. Liebmann, A. J. and Panettiere, B. R. (1956). "Bell's Sale of Food & Drugs", 13th edn., 887. Ed. J. A. O'Keefe. (Butterworth, London).
215. White, J. (1958). *Fd Mf.* **33** (March), 95.
216. Edwards, F. W. and Nanji, H. R. (1938). *Analyst* **63**, 410.
217. Edwards, F. W. and Nanji, H. R. (1938). *J. Inst. Brew,* **44**, 392.
218. Whitmarsh, J. M. (1942). *Analyst* **67**, 188.
219. Morgan, R. II. and Voelcker, E. (1963). *Fd Process Packag.* p. 207.
220. Suomalainen, H. and Kangasperko, J. (1963). *Z. Lebensmittunters. u. -Forsch,* **120**, 353.
221. Bergner, K. G. (1960). *Z. Lebensmittunters. u. -Forsch.* **112**, 319.
222. Bergner, K. G. and Petri, H. (1960). *Z. Lebensmittunters. u.-Forsch.* **112**, 494.
223. Bourgeois, J. (1957). In Proc. 1st. Internat. Vinegar Cong., the Hague, publ. by CONAF (Combinatie van Nederlandse Azijnfabrikanten) 's-Gravenhage.
224. Schander, H. (1956). *Z. Lebensmittunters. u. -Forsch.* **100**, 26.
225. Doro, B. and Sadini, V. (1953). *Boll. Laboratori. chim. prov. (Bologna),* **4**, 85.
226. Kniphorst, L. C. E. and Kruisbeer, C. J. (1938). *Dt. Essigind.* **42**, 133.
227. Happold, F. and Spencer, C. (1952). *Chem. Zentr.* **123**, 7036.
228. Serini, G. (1958). *Chimica* **34**, 245.
229. Curzel, V. (1955). *Rev. Viticultura e Enologia* **8**, 93.
230. Barnicoat, M. (1942). *Deutsch. Essigindustrie* **46**, 94.
231. Jenkin, D. C. (1941). *Analyst.* **60**, 328.
232. Leibov, Z. M. (1938). *Chem. Zentr.* **109**, 94.
233. Oliviera, J. and Castiel, V. (1961). *Revta Quími. ind., Rio de J.* **30**, 19.
234. O'Neill, R. E. and Henry, A. M. (1944). *J. Ass. off. agric. chem.* **27**, 263.
235. Pratolongo, U. (1949). *Annali. Sper. agr.* **3**, 607.
236. Rokita, P. and Henry, A. M. (1946). *J. Ass. off. agric. chem.* **29**, 304.
237. Scurti, F. (1951). *Ann. Ist. sper. chim. agr.* **17**, 35.
238. Gulick, M. (1941). *J. Ass. off. agric. chem.* **24**, 691.
239. Mallory, G. R. (1945). *Ind. Engng Chem.* **17**, 631.
240. White, J. and Munns, D. J. (1947). *J. Inst. Brew.* **53**, 305.
241. Englis, D. and Wollerman, L. (1952). *Dt. Anal. Chem.* **24**, 1983.
242. Hromatka, O. (1962). *Branntweinwirtschaft* **102**, 608 and 703.
243. Hromatka, O. and Stainer, J. (1962). *Branntweinwirtschaft* **102**, 507.
244. Jackson, G. P. and Rammamurti, K. (1958). *J. Sci. Fd Agric.* **9**, 787.
245. Marconi, M. (1952). *Chimica* **7**, 336.
246. Mecca, F. and Calabrese, F. (1958). *Chimica Ind. Milano* **40**, 537.
247. Shuman, H. (1938). *J. Ass. off. agric. chem.* **21**, 430.

Soft Drinks

W. PRICE-DAVIES and D. McDONALD

Schweppes Ltd., St. Albans, Herts., England

1. INTRODUCTION

Soft drinks are refreshing non-alcoholic beverages. In Europe there is considerable activity to establish standards for soft drinks and the Council of European Communities in 1970[1] issued a draft directive concerning soft drinks. The directive excludes products derived exclusively from water, saccharides or fruit juice, and specifies three categories:

Fruit Juice Drinks
Natural Extract Drinks
Flavoured Drinks

A. Definition of Soft Drinks

In the United Kingdom the Soft Drink Regulations 1964[2] define a "soft drink" as any liquid intended for sale as drink for human consumption either without or after dilution, and they include:

(i) Any fruit drink and any fruit juice squash, crush or cordial.

(ii) Soda water, Indian or Quinine tonic water and any sweetened artificially carbonated water whether flavoured or unflavoured.

(iii) Ginger beer and any herbal or botanical beverage.

This definition excludes natural spring waters, fruit juices, intoxicating liquor as defined in the Licensing Act 1953(a).

Prior to the implementation of these Regulations, soft drinks consisted of a range of loosely defined products covering such long established names as:

Ginger Beer

Sparkling Orange

Lemonade

Lime Juice Cordial

to name but a few. From a compositional and labelling point of view, the Soft Drinks Regulations for the first time sub-divided the principal soft drinks into specifically defined groups and laid down the minimum compositional requirements for each group. In addition obligatory descriptive names were defined for certain types of product.

For example, citrus-type products are grouped under five named headings:

Category	Obligatory name	Definition
Ready to drink	CRUSH	A soft drink containing fruit juice.
Ready to drink or to be diluted	DRINK (This description is confusing as it also covers a concentrated product requiring dilution)	A soft drink produced by a process involving comminution of the entire fruit.
Ready to drink or to be diluted	CORDIAL (Another misleading description as this name covers both ready to drink and concentrated products	An alternative name to crush for clear citrus crushes but is also alternative name for clear citrus squashes.
To be diluted	SQUASH	A soft drink containing fruit juice for consumption after dilution.
Ready to drink or to be diluted	FLAVOUR or "ade"	An artificially flavoured soft drink which does not meet the minimum compositional requirements of fruit juice or fruit content.

The anomalies in defining the "drink" and "cordial" categories created considerable initial confusion to the trade and it can be questioned whether the general public, even now, is fully conversant with these various product categories. In many cases, the brand name is used by the public when defining their requirements, rather than the actual legal name.

Soft drinks can be broadly grouped into three main categories:

Carbonated drinks	Ready to drink
Squashes	To be diluted
Bottled fruit juices	Ready to drink. Although not soft drinks by legal definition, this group is normally included in soft drinks manufacturing and marketing categories.

In the U.S.A. carbonated beverages have been designated as "Soda Water". Soda Water may contain optional ingredients in such proportions as are reasonably required to accomplish their intended effects and include:

1. Nutritive sweeteners consisting of the dry or liquid form of sugar, invert sugar, dextrose, corn syrup, glucose syrup, sorbitol, or any combination of two or more of these.

2. One or more of the following flavouring ingredients may be added, in a carrier consisting of ethyl alcohol, glycerin, or propylene glycol:

   (i) Fruit juices (including concentrated fruit juices), natural flavouring derived from fruits, vegetables, bark, buds, roots, leaves, and similar plant materials.

   (ii) Artificial flavouring.

3. Natural and artificial colour additives.

4. One or more of the acidifying agents acetic acid, adipic acid, citric acid, fumaric acid, lactic acid, malic acid, phosphoric acid or tartaric acid.

5. One or more of the buffering agents, consisting of the acetate, bicarbonate, carbonate, chloride, citrate, lactate, orthophosphate, or sulphate salts of calcium, magnesium, potassium or sodium.

6. (i) One or more of the emulsifying, stabilizing or viscosity-producing agents, carob bean gum (locust bean gum), glycerol ester of wood rosin, guar gum, gum acacia, gum tragacanth, hydroxylated lecithin, lecithin, methylcellulose, mono and diglycerides of fat-forming fatty acids, pectin, polyglycerol esters of fatty acids, propylene glycol alginate, sodium alginate, sodium carboxymethylcellulose, sodium metaphosphate (sodium hexametaphosphate).

(ii) When one or more of the optional ingredients in subdivision (i) of this subparagraph are used, diocyl sodium sulphosuccinate may be used in a quantity not in excess of 0·5% by weight of such ingredients.

7. One or more of the following foaming agents: ammoniated glycyrrhizin, gum ghatti, liquorice or glycyrrhiza, yucca (Joshua tree), yucca (Mohave).

8. Caffeine, in an amount not to exceed 0.02% by weight of the finished beverage.

9. Quinine in an amount not to exceed 83 ppm by weight of the finished beverage.

10. One or more of the chemical preservatives, ascorbic acid, benzoic acid, BHA, BHT, calcium disodium EDTA, erythorbic acid, glucose-oxidase-catalase enzyme, methylparaben or propylparaben, nordihydroguaiaretic acid, propyl gallate, potassium or sodium benzoate, potassium or sodium bisulphite, potassium or sodium metabisulphite, potassium or sodium sorbate, sorbic acid, sulphur dioxide, or tocopherols; and in the case of canned soda water, stannous chloride in a quantity not to exceed 11 ppm calculated as tin (Sn), with or without one or more of the other chemical preservatives listed in this subparagraph.

11. The defoaming agent dimethylpolysiloxane in an amount not to exceed 10 ppm.

B. Identity

1. The name of the beverage for which a definition and standard of identity is established which is neither flavoured nor sweetened, is soda water, club soda or plain soda.

2. The name of each beverage containing flavouring and sweetening ingredients as provided for above is ". . . soda" or ". . . soda water" or ". . . carbonated beverage", the blank being filled in with the word or words that designate the characterizing flavour of the soda water; for example, "grape soda".

3. If the soda water is one generally designated by a particular common name; for example, ginger ale, root beer, or sparkling water, that name may be used in lieu of the name prescribed in 1 or 2. A proprietary name that is commonly used by the public as the designation of a particular kind of soda water may likewise be used in lieu of the name prescribed in 1 and 2.

2. MATERIALS USED IN THE MANUFACTURE OF SOFT DRINKS

A. Water

As carbonated beverages may contain up to 90% water, the treatment and quality control of water supplies for soft drink plants is of prime importance in the production of high quality beverages, to a consistent standard. The natural variations in water supply—both in the U.K. and abroad pose many difficult problems for both local authorities and industrialists, as indicated by the tables opposite which illustrate the high purity requirements for potable water.

In the U.K., soft drink manufacturers usually obtain their supplies of water from mains supply (normally of good potable quality in the U.K.) but occasionally from private wells, which lessens the degree of treatment required to remove interfering substances which may affect product quality. As even mains supplies may have a high natural colour (such as soft peaty

TABLE 1

Chemical quality	Maximum allowable
Substances affecting potability:	
Total dissolved solids	1500 mg/litre
Iron	50 mg/litre
Manganese (assuming that the ammonia content is less than 0·5 mg/litre)	5 mg/litre
Copper	1·5 mg/litre
Zinc	1·5 mg/litre
Magnesium plus sodium sulphate	1000 mg/litre
Alkyl benzyl sulphonates (ABS: surfactants)	0·5 mg/litre
Substances affecting health:	
Nitrate as NO_3	45 mg/litre
Fluoride	1·5 mg/litre
Toxic substances:	
Phenolic substances	0·002 mg/litre
Arsenic	0·05 mg/litre
Cadmium	0·01 mg/litre
Chromium	0·05 mg/litre
Cyanide	0·2 mg/litre
Lead	0·05 mg/litre
Selenium	0·01 mg/litre
Radionuclides (gross beta activity)	1000 $\mu\mu$c/litre

	Minimum indicative of pollution
Chemical indicators of pollution:	
Chemical oxygen demand (COD)	10 mg/litre
Biochemical oxygen demand (BOD)	6 mg/litre
Total nitrogen exclusive of NO_3	1 mg/litre
NH_3	0·5 mg/litre
Carbon chloroform extract (CCE; organic pollutants)	0·5 mg/litre
Grease	1 mg/litre

BACTERIOLOGICAL QUALITY STANDARDS

Classification	MPN/100 ml Coliform bacteria*
I. Bacterial quality applicable to disinfection treatment only	0–50
II. Bacterial quality requiring conventional methods of treatment (coagulation, filtration, disinfection)	50–5000
III. Heavy pollution requiring extensive types of treatment	5000–50 000
IV. Very heavy pollution, unacceptable unless special treatments designed for such water are used; source to be used only when unavoidable	> 50 000

* When more than 40% of the number of coliform bacteria represented by the MPN index are found to be of the faecal coliform group, the water source should be considered to fall into the next higher category with respect to the treatment required.

waters in Scotland and northern England) or alternatively a residual hardness (e.g. southern England) the treatment of water in U.K. soft drinks plants consists, essentially, of:

(a) Removal of colour and suspended matter.
(b) Reduction of hardness (if present).
(c) Elimination of undesirable bacteria.

Where water of high purity is already available, such as mineral springs, "polishing" by filtration may be the only treatment necessary. Highly coloured or hard waters require a full chemical treatment and general practice is to employ coagulation systems, where the impurities in the water are removed by treatment with either ferrous sulphate or alum and lime (particularly if softening is required). Sodium hypochlorite or gaseous chlorine is included in the treatment to assist the chemical coagulation conditions and to provide an excess of chlorine sufficient to sterilize the water. The chlorine is then removed by carbon filtration (which also removes any undesirable off-taste) and this is normally preceded by sand filtration to ensure no contamination or blockage of the carbon by fine sludge particles of ferric or aluminium hydroxide. These plants are reliable and provide a first class water provided their operation is supervised by regular laboratory checks at intervals during production. These checks include pH, free chlorine, alkalinity and sludge content.

To achieve a final "polish" to the water, ultra-filtration is carried out using either resin-impregnated paper candles or discs, or porous porcelain candles. These filters remove any trace of suspended matter from the carbon filter.

It is also current practice in a number of companies to utilize monochromatic ultra-violet radiation to sterilize process water—either with or without complementary chemical treatment. The UV light is most effective at a wavelength of 265 nm.

In the coagulation process, the bicarbonate alkalinity is converted to the insoluble calcium carbonate, which is precipitated with the sludge.

$$Ca(HCO_3)_2 + Ca(OH)_2 = 2\ CaCO_3 + 2H_2O$$

A treated water from a coagulation plant operating on a reliable mains water supply should meet the following basic standards:

Taste and odour	Nil
Suspended matter	Less than 2 ppm
Colour	Max. 10 Hazen units
Alkalinity	Max. 100 ppm as calcium carbonate (50 ppm for Cola drinks)
Free Chlorine	Less than 0·05 ppm
Iron or Aluminium in solution	Less than 0·3 ppm
Nitrate	Max. 5 ppm
Bacteriological quality	Free from coliform bacteria

Alternative methods of treatment are available, including reduction of alkalinity by hydrogen ion exchange, sterilization and colour removal by ozone treatment; and more recently, the development of membrane filtration, and the reverse osmosis process for demineralization, offer a wide range of complementary treatments to the soft drinks bottlers. The final selection of the optimum treatment required will essentially relate to (a) the quality of the water supply to be treated and (b) the economics of the alternative systems available.

In addition to process or "in-bottle" water, the quality of the water used in certain other factory operations requires to be of a suitable quality. For example:

Operation	Standard required	Treatment employed (if required)
1. Warm/cold water rinsing jets in bottle washing equipment	Low total hardness	Base exchange softening
2. Boiler water	Low hardness chloride and total dissolved solids content	Ranges from complete de-mineralization by ion exchange, to chemical in-boiler conditioning
3. Factory/domestic hot water systems	Low hardness	Base exchange softening
4. Plant sterilization	Low hardness and good bacteriological quality	Base exchange softening or full coagulation treatment, if necessary

The laboratory control of these types of treatment is much simpler; in general, control of hardness, i.e. efficiency of softeners, is the principal requirement. In-line monitoring devices, both chemical and electronic, are now available for continuous checking of hardness by chemical indicators or conductivity measurement.

It is appreciated that the main text of this section relates more directly to U.K. operations where, in general, good mains water quality provides an excellent "platform" on which to build water treatment requirements. Overseas conditions inevitably are significantly more difficult, particularly in hot climates where water is scarce. Major problems in controlling water quality arise in these areas—principally where the presence of high dissolved solids (particularly chloride) makes treatment more difficult and expensive. The application of reverse osmosis membrane filtration could be an important development overseas.

It is quite clear that close control of water for a wide range of operations is essential in soft drinks plant and the chemist therefore has a vital part to play in this work.

B. Carbon Dioxide

Carbon dioxide can be delivered to the bottler in solid form as cardice, or under pressure in cylinders at atmospheric temperatures or in refrigerated tankers as a liquid. The latter method is that most commonly used by larger manufacturers. After discharging into the customer's storage system, the liquid CO_2 is converted into the gas via a heater. It is essential that a sample of gas is smelled and some carbonated water prepared for tasting each delivery by experienced tasters to confirm that the gas is not tainted in any way, before being accepted for use.

CO_2 in the U.K. is now produced to a very high quality but overseas supplies may vary considerably, depending on the method of producing the gas and the degree of control applied to impurities. No gas other than CO_2 is used in soft drinks manufacture.

C. Sugar

Sugar is delivered in granulated form or in solution as "liquid" sugar. Granulated sugar is packed in sacks, paper bags or received in bulk and should be dry, free from foreign matter, and in solution neutral to litmus, clear and colourless. It can be conveniently prepared (by dissolving in water, boiling and cooling) as a concentrated syrup of 66–67° Brix (between 8 and 9 lb/gal). Alternatively, liquid sugar can be purchased—ready to use—usually at a strength of about 9 lb/gal, i.e. 67° Brix. The highest grade is required for clear, colourless, ready to drink products such as certain carbonated soft drinks. A typical specification for this product is % invert sugar 0·0015, % ash 0·017, pH 7·0, colour water white. A slightly lower grade is normally suitable for use in squashes and cordials, and a typical specification for this quality might be % invert sugar 0·15, % ash 0·10, pH 7·5 and colour pale straw. For both qualities of sugar, freedom from preservative should be specified together with maximum limits for heavy metals. Microbiological standards may vary with the type of product being prepared from the sugar and according to the local conditions for high quality soft drinks. A supplier should be able to meet the following levels, using the media specified:

(i) *Nutrient Agar*—less than 400 colonies per 10 ml of sugar after 3 days at 37°C.

(ii) *Wort Broth*—less than 20 colonies per 10 ml after 2 days at 33°C.

(iii) *Osmophilic medium*—less than 1 colony per ml after 2 days at 33°C.

Liquid sugars will not support the growth of many micro-organisms at the solids concentration at which they are normally delivered. Some condensation, however, is liable to occur inside storage tanks, and this can dilute the surface layer of the syrup, resulting in a reduced concentration, at which many organisms will grow. To prevent this, a germicidal ultraviolet lamp should be installed in the top of the tank to irradiate the surface. Alternatively, the tanks may be ventilated with sterile air from special filters. Subject to the storage facilities available, lengthy storage of liquid sugars is undesirable and they should normally be processed within a few days of receipt from the supplier. It is also imperative for liquid sugar to be delivered to the soft drink manufacturer at an acceptably cool temperature (e.g. 85°F max), otherwise subsequent finished product filling problems may arise because of high flavoured syrup temperatures, making full CO_2 gas saturation difficult.

D. Artificial Sweeteners

(a) Saccharin is the only permitted artificial sweetener allowed in soft drinks in the United Kingdom, United States of America, and in the majority of countries in the world, and in many cases it is only permitted for use in drinks prepared for diabetics. It has been in use for decades, during which it has been subjected to many biological tests. It is obtained either as the sodium derivative of saccharin (which is readily soluble in water) and is about 450–500 times sweeter than an equivalent weight of sugar, or as saccharin which can be dissolved in dilute ammonia or, with the evolution of carbon dioxide, in solutions of alkali bicarbonates. Its presence in a beverage can be quickly determined qualitatively by mixing a portion of the beverage with ethyl ether to extract the saccharin, evaporating the ether, and tasting the resulting residue. If saccharin is present in the original beverage, it can be tested in the residue.

(b) Cyclamates. Until 1970 this type of sweetener was permitted in soft drinks in the United Kingdom, United States of America, and in many other countries. It was added as the acid or as the sodium or calcium salt, but very few countries now permit the use of this material.

(c) Although a few other artificial sweeteners are available, very few countries now allow any artificial sweetener other than saccharin. It is therefore essential to consult the respective food laws before any artificial sweeteners are considered for use in soft drink formulations for or in overseas countries.

E. Preservatives

Benzoic acid and sulphur dioxide are the only preservatives permitted in soft drinks in the United Kingdom. In some other countries additional preservatives include sorbic acid and diethylpyrocarbonate (Baycovin). Before considering a preservative for use in a soft drink, the relevant regulations should be consulted to find out if the particular preservative can be used and to determine the maximum concentrations allowed.

(a) *Benzoic acid* is used as the soluble sodium salt in soft drinks processing. It is essential to add this ingredient, where possible, to the batch prior to any additions of acidic materials, to avoid the less soluble benzoic acid coming out of solution. Though tasteless in the beverage, benzoic acid is less effective than sulphur dioxide.

(b) *Sulphur dioxide* can be added as the sodium or potassium metabisulphite or, where it is undesirable to increase the sodium or potassium content of the beverage, a solution of sulphurous acid can be used. All these materials are unstable and should, therefore, be stored in airtight containers. Because of this, it is necessary to know the SO_2 strength in the supply being used.

F. Colours

Food colours must comply to the British Standards Institute specifications in the U.K. and to the Food & Drug Administration specifications in the U.S.A.

The colouring materials used in soft drinks manufacture can be prepared from the basic colours permitted in the country in which the beverage is sold. The colours may be of natural origin such as caramel, or synthetic, e.g. "coal tar" colours. Each batch of colour from a supplier should be simply checked against the previous batch delivered by dissolving both samples in distilled water in the proportion in which they are used in the finished beverage. Some colours are unstable in the presence of sulphur dioxide or when exposed to light, and these factors must be taken into account when deciding on the colour to use in soft drink formulations. Solutions of colours should not be kept as they are particularly susceptible to microbiological spoilage. In general a high consistent quality is obtained from United Kingdom manufacturers and errors of significant colour variations are unlikely from reputable manufacturers.

G. Acids

In the United Kingdom ascorbic, citric (normally the monohydrate), lactic, malic and tartaric acids can be used in soft drinks. In addition, acetic and phosphoric acids may be used if fruit or juice is *not* present. In general, citric acid is nearly always used, with the exception of Cola drinks, where phosphoric acid is used. Where additions of Vitamin C are required in fruit juices and squashes, ascorbic acid is added.

H. Fruit Juices

Citrus juices are obtained from many parts of the world and may be delivered at various concentrations and pulp contents, preserved or unpreserved, and packed in many different types of container. These juices are normally pasteurized. To achieve a uniform finished product, it is necessary to blend the juices received from the differing processing areas in order to eliminate normal seasonal and source variations.

Orange, lemon and grapefruit juices for soft drinks production should conform to the following specifications and be subjected to the following tests:

The juice should contain no additions of sugar, colouring matter, flavour and unspecified preservative, and must possess a uniformly bright natural colour, free from any traces of browning. The juice must be sterile and give a negative result when checked for yeasts by mixing one part of juice with nine parts of sterile 10% w/v sucrose solution and placing the mixture in an incubator for 14 days at 26·5°C. The absence of gas bubbles and a white deposit of yeast cells indicates a yeast-free juice. The juice must also contain no core, skin, grubs, or foreign matter. Fruit cells must be of the required size and concentration. The degree of concentration of concentrated juices can be determined by measuring the refractive index and comparing the results with the published tables. By incubating samples of juice in plugged test tubes in

TABLE 2. Range of Acidity in Citrus Fruits

	Minimum %	Maximum %	Average %
Grapefruit			
Florida	0·70	2·43	1·42
California	0·85	2·64	1·77
Arizona	1·24	1·92	1·61
Palestine	1·82	2·44	2·13
Oranges			
U.S. (all varieties)	0·39	1·00	0·68
California	—	—	1·23
Florida	—	—	1·11
Palestine	0·70	1·5	1·2
Lemons			
California	4·20	8·33	5·96
Palestine	5·56	7·25	6·40
Limes	6·10	8·32	7·20

From Braverman, J. B. S. (1949). "Citrus Products." Interscience.

an incubator at 26·5°C and noting the physical condition of the samples, at daily intervals, for fourteen days, juices with a permanent cloud will maintain their homogeneous condition throughout the incubation period, while unpasteurized juices and juices which have not been correctly processed become clear. To determine accurately the SO_2 content of a citrus juice use the Monier Williams method. Ascorbic acid is determined by titration with 2·6 dichlorophenol-indophenol. Other characteristic features which can be determined by the published methods are specific gravity, acidity, recoverable oil, ash, alkalinity of ash and P_2O_5.[3]

Lime juice, unlike other citrus juice, requires specialized processing before it can be used in a soft drink and is usually received as a settled or filtered juice from Ghana, Dominica and Mexico. The fruit used in its preparation should be clean, sound, fresh limes and should be prepared by passing the whole fruit through suitable pressing equipment so adjusted that excessive pressure on the fruit does not result in juice of inferior flavour as might happen if the pips were crushed. Immediately after expression the juice must be freed from pips, peel and excessive pulp by passing through a suitable sieve.

If the juice is a settled juice it should be allowed to stand for at least 14 days in a suitable container to allow the juice to clear. After standing the lower layer of clear settled juice is drawn off. Preservative must be added to the cleared juice to a level of at least 400 ppm. w/v sulphur dioxide if the juice is to be stored and transported. The acidity of the juice should be specified and it should have the following characteristics: After polishing filtration should give a sparkling clear product, possess a bright natural greenish yellow colour, a good distinct characteristic lime flavour free from bitterness, metallic taste or any off flavour and be free from contamination by heavy metals.

If the juice is a filtered rather than settled juice the sieved juice must be passed to rotary filtration equipment for pulp removal, followed by addition of sodium metabisulphite to preserve the juice. Both types of lime juice must be guaranteed to contain no addition of acid, sugar, colouring or flavourings other than the specified preservative; must not be subjected to any heat treatment during or after processing and the juice must be sterile. Settled or filtered lime juice can be obtained in concentrated form. The temperature of the juice must not exceed 48°C, during the concentration process, to avoid inactivation of the pectic enzymes.

Pineapple Juice is usually obtained in cans without the addition of chemical preservatives but pasteurized to ensure that it will keep until it is required for bottling. Routine quality control includes regular sampling from incoming shipments, the samples being checked as follows:

Volume in can, taste and appearance, freedom from foreign matter, acidity, pulp content, sugar content, Vitamin C, esters (which are the main flavouring compounds), refractive index and specific gravity.

Tomato Juice. When received in cans it is free of chemical preservatives and pasteurized. The juice must be unadulterated and extracted from firm unbroken and properly mature fruit of red varieties of tomato and must comply with the relevant food and health regulations, including content of trace metals. The juice must be free from seeds, stalks, pips, skin, or any foreign matter, and must be a uniformly bright red clean colour, free from traces of browning. Tomato juice must possess a characteristic natural flavour and aroma free from bitterness, traces of scorching, any metallic taste and any off flavour or unripe taste.

It must not contain additions of colour or any other substance unless these are specified. The pulp content, limit of acidity, refractive index, and minimum ascorbic acid content should be specified.

As tomato juice is highly susceptible to mould contamination, close control of this feature is essential before accepting juice for processing. The "Howard Mould Count" on any sample should not exceed 15% positive fields.

I. Comminuted Fruit Bases

The rapid popularity of "whole orange" drinks since 1953 (when early processing methods utilizing the whole fruit were introduced) has seen the progressive development of comminuted base production at source, i.e. in Israel, South Africa, and the Mediterranean countries. These bases have proved more economical and more consistent in quality when used in the preparation of comminuted carbonated drinks and squash concentrates, than the fresh fruit previously used. The fresh fruit was susceptible to wide variations in quality and price due to seasonal fluctuations and periods of shortage.

The bases are normally hot filled into cans or pasteurized, cold filled and preserved (with benzoic acid) into wax lined casks, and essentially consist of a homogeneous mixture of fruit tissue and juice—the latter including the emulsified fruit peel fraction.[4] The bases are produced at source by a range of processing methods to a number of specifications and fruit concentrations, as required by the purchasing companies. Cool transportation and storage of comminuted citrus bases is desirable (but not essential) for the maximum retention of flavour and character.

As with citrus juices, close technical control of comminuted bases is necessary by soft drink manufacturers in view of the major importance of these materials as a basic raw material. Regular sampling of deliveries followed by analyses of Brix, acidity, pulp and oil content, flavour, colour and cloud, as well as bacteriological quality.

The introduction of the Soft Drinks Regulations 1964, which, for the first time, included legal standards for whole fruit content of soft drinks, has posed new analytical problems for industrial laboratories and public analysts alike in determining the fruit content of comminuted bases and whole fruit soft drinks.

To summarize this important section—it is obvious that citrus juice technology is a science in its own right and the systematic sampling and detailed analytical control of citrus juice deliveries is essential in the production of consistent citrus beverages of high quality. Allied to this is the considerable skill required in "blending out" the wide natural variations in these bases and juices. The role of the chemist in the quality operation of this sector of soft drinks processing is obviously a vital one.

J. Flavours

Soluble citrus and lemonade flavours are prepared from either essential oil extracts from citrus fruits or synthetically. Great care is needed in selecting the oils and flavours to be used to achieve the best results and a standard repeatable flavour. The solvents used must be permitted by the country's food regulations. Ginger Ale essences can be prepared from Gingerine, obtained from Jamaican ginger root. Ginger Beer essences can be prepared from special processing of the ginger root.

Emulsions are prepared from essential oils which are intimately mixed into an emulsion with water and an emulsifier, which may be a gum or other permitted material. This emulsion when added to the beverage will form a cloud flavoured product. The U.K. and U.S.A. Governments ban in 1970 on the inclusion of brominated vegetable oil (B.V.O.) in soft drinks has posed major problems for manufacturers producing cloudy "flavoured" soft drinks (which exclude fruit juice or fruit base from their formulation). No alternative material to B.V.O. has been as yet approved by the U.K., U.S.A. or Canadian Governments. B.V.O. acts as a weighting oil or stabilizer in emulsion preparations.

The manufacture and technical control of essences and emulsions is a very skilled operation—a combination of both science and art—and high quality flavours form an integral part of first class soft drinks. Quality control includes physical, chemical, organoleptic and olfactory testing of both raw materials and final flavour and close comparison with a "standard" sample. Flavours should be stored under cool, dark, conditions, and should keep for over one year before any deterioration. Emulsions are less stable—two to four months can be maximum "life".

3. MANUFACTURING PROCESSES

A. Carbonated Soft Drinks

1. Preparation of Bottling Syrups

The bottling syrup contains all the ingredients of the finished product except the carbon dioxide and most of the treated water. The ingredients may include sugar, fruit juices or comminuted fruit base, essences, citric or other permitted acid, artificial sweeteners, preservatives, colours and emulsions for cloudy products. Clear drinks prepared from partially soluble essences are filtered before use and many methods of filtration can be employed, such as sheet filtration with or without additional filter aids and other pressure filters using septa of metal or porcelain etc., in conjunction with diatomaceous earth filter aids.

The ingredients must be added carefully, taking into account their behaviour in the presence of the other ingredients already added to the batch; e.g. sodium benzoate is added before the acid materials and to as great a volume of liquid as possible to prevent the less soluble benzoic acid from separating out of solution. To confirm that the flavoured syrup contains all the specified ingredients in the correct quantities, chemical, physical and organoleptic tests should be carried out. These will include the percentage of soluble solids by refractometer or hydrometer, acidity by titration or pH determination, sulphur dioxide by direct titration or distillation methods, sodium benzoate by flame photometry or direct quantitative methods (the latter methods are only used for final confirmation of presence of preservative). The taste and appearance test should be carried out on each batch in comparison with a standard product sample to confirm the absence of "off" flavours and foreign matter, and the correct amounts of artificial sweeteners, flavours and colours etc.

2. Bottle Washing

One trip bottles do not normally require full comprehensive detergent washing as they are usually received in a clean and almost sterile condition from the glass works. Warm detergent rinsing in the following typical sequence is fully adequate to meet most conditions:

A pre-rinse—water at about 85°F.
A detergent rinse—$\frac{1}{2}$% Caustic detergent at about 120°F.
Softened water rinse at about 85°F.
Softened water rinse at mains temperature.

This treatment ensures elimination of carton or storage dust and loose foreign matter, and by eliminating any residual greasiness in the bottle interior, ensures smooth even filling with minimum "fob" at high speeds. Some manufacturers rely on internal air blowing, or brief water rinsing to prepare the bottle for filling.

Returnable bottles from the trade require more rigorous treatment to remove product residues, old labels and foreign matter, and the following sequence is typical:

Water pre-rinse.
2–4 stage detergent soaking sections—up to $2\frac{1}{2}$% caustic detergent in each section at temperatures rising to 160°F.
Internal brushing (optional) plus jetted softened water section.
Low strength detergent jetting.
Softened warm water rinsing by jetting.
Softened water rinsing by jetting at mains temperature.

In both washing treatments, care is taken to adjust detergent and water temperatures to enable the bottles to pass through the washer without being subjected to excessive thermal shock. The necessary high standard of bottle cleanliness is maintained by closely controlling temperatures and detergent strengths in conjunction with frequent microbiological tests on the bottles emerging from the washer.

3. Syrup Dosing and Filling

Two-stage systems. By this method, the washed sterilized bottle receives an exact dose of flavoured syrup from a rotating syruper followed by filling to a predetermined height in the bottle, with chilled carbonated water, under pressure on a filling machine. To confirm that the bottled soft drink meets specification, four parameters are controlled. These are:

Syrup dosing.
Carbon dioxide gas content or "carbonation".
Volume of product in each bottle.
Flavour and appearance.

The syrup content (and therefore flavour) of the finished product may be influenced by variation in machine speeds, syruper settings, incorrect fill, and in the case of highly pulpy drinks, blockage of syruper or filler tubes. A Brix check on the mixed finished product in conjunction with the volume of product in the bottle confirms whether the bottle received the correct syrup dose. Carbonation is the volume of carbon dioxide gas contained in the bottle relative to the volume of the contents at normal temperature and pressure, e.g. "$3\frac{1}{2}$ volumes of CO_2". Carbonation is determined by measuring the temperature and pressure of gas in the bottle and consulting tables to convert these to volumes of CO_2 gas. The volume of product, or capacity, is measured either by weight or by measuring the volume of the liquid. The organoleptic assessment is made by comparing with known standard samples, and includes "nose", flavour and appearance.

Premix systems. This system is preferred for higher speed bottling plants (above 200 bottles per min) and consists of proportioning into a CO_2-pressurized mixing chamber the exact ratio of flavoured syrup and water required then cooling and carbonating this mixture, and filling it in a single operation into the bottle. This system enables the bottler to employ more in-line automated quality control than is possible with the two stage system, as the beverage at finished product strength is piped under pressure to the filler and thence into the bottle. The first quality control parameter of the two stage system, the flavoured syrup content, is now independent of the filling levels and capacity of the contents, and the syrup strength in the finished product can be measured by in-line refractometers prior to the product being fed to the filler. The in-line refractometer activates warning systems if the syrup concentration of the finished product deviates from the standards laid down, and, therefore, the proportioners can be adjusted immediately, thus enabling tight product standards to be met consistently. The other parameters (carbonation and capacity) are identical to the two-stage systems, and require control in the same way.

Statistical control both two-stage and premix systems. Three of the four parameters mentioned (Brix, carbonation and volume of contents or capacity) can be recorded in graphical form[5] to enable simpler interpretation of results for both quality control and production staff who will be taking action on the results achieved. A typical system could be introduced as follows: estimate the desirable frequency of testing finished products from the production line and at these times, check three bottles and average the results obtained (Fig. 1). Plot these mean results on a simple graph as shown, and continuous

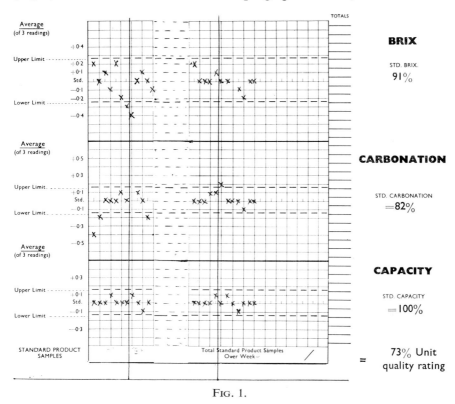

FIG. 1.

simple interpretation of product quality can be quickly achieved. An overall statistical quality control index can be calculated and which can be expressed as the number of bottles tested which fall completely within the specification for all the three parameters being considered.

4. Sealing

The type of closure used will determine the method of sealing. The seal may have to retain product liquid and gas for long storage periods under considerable pressure at ambient temperatures. The specifications for the areas of contact between the bottle finish and the closure are of prime importance in producing an effective seal.

a. Crowning. Crowning, although the simplest of soft drinks manufacturing operations, still requires close maintenance and quality control supervision for optimum performance. Regular maintenance and replacement of crowner throats, accurate setting of crowner height, and simple gauging of crimp diameter of crowned bottles should ensure reliable sealing without excessively tight (or over-crimped) crowns. The recent general replacement of cork liner by a plastic insert has also improved crown performance. Excessive lacquer loss during crowning should be avoided because of rapid corrosion in storage of exposed tinplate surfaces.

b. Seals. A more recent innovation is the threaded aluminium seal for carbonated beverages. In this sealing operation, the thread is applied to the seal whilst it is on the bottle and if the tensions are set correctly, the seal can be removed easily by the consumer and yet be sufficiently tight to retain product liquid and gas under the storage temperatures and pressures experienced. Closer quality control of the capping operation is needed with this type of seal than with crowning, to ensure that this is achieved. Frequent torque tests are made throughout production both at the time of sealing as well as after a period of time, to ensure that specification torque results are achieved which are consistent with good sealing performance and consumer convenience.

This seal has been developed both in the United States and in the United Kingdom, largely on lightweight one-trip bottles, and is the first major competitor in the beverage industry to the reliable crown closure which has been used for many years. It would appear that there is now considerable room for closure development and modification in the soft drinks industry in parallel with glass finish design improvements.

5. Labelling

Good labelling enhances the appearance of the product, particularly on supermarket shelves. To achieve a high standard under modern high speed labelling conditions, labellers must be maintained in a clean and sound condition. The choice of adhesive will be influenced by the quality of the paper being used, its removability when used on returnable bottles, the condition of the bottle being labelled—whether it is wet or dry, hot or cold—and by the type of packing used to convey the bottle to its destination. For soft drinks, the adhesive needs to be quick drying, ice proof (for refrigerator storage), not subject to mould growth, easily handled and virtually colourless. Dextrin based (jelly gum) adhesives can give good labelling performance using a very thin film of adhesive, whereas the "wetter" starch-based adhesives tend to require a greater quantity, which can give rise to unsightly excess gum smearing. Labels should be date coded to enable the bottler to achieve better stock rotation and follow up consumer complaints more effectively. On high speed labelling units particularly, labelling checks should be included in the overall product/container routine quality control programme.

6. Inspection Systems

The in-line system adopted will depend to a great extent on the speed of the filling line and the type of container and products being filled. High speed lines filling returnable bottles cannot economically (or practically) utilize full manual sighting of bottle and contents. Therefore, electronic inspection devices have been developed as an essential alternative. Devices are available which sight electronically the complete bottle interior or the area of the bottle base only, for foreign matter, and will automatically reject contaminated bottles before they reach the filling machine. This may be supplemented by a sighting operator inspecting for specific reject features such as chipped necks or foreign bottles. Although these electronic sighters are consistently more effective than human inspectors when inspecting a wide range of fault features at high speeds, they still require regular efficiency checks by passing standard defect bottles through the system. If these are not rejected, or the electronic sighter rejects satisfactory bottles, the sensitivity of the sighter requires adjustment to the correct level. Electronic filling height inspectors have been developed which will accurately monitor for under-filled bottles (and if necessary over-filled ones). This relieves the packer to concentrate on inspection of the product, for labelling faults and general appearance.

On slower speed units where electronic sighting methods are not economically justified, visual inspection of each bottle by operatives, before and after filling, is normally employed. The effectiveness of sighting systems may be monitored by drawing at regular intervals a case of finished products from the end of the production line and checking carefully the general quality of the product, e.g. freedom from foreign matter, short-filled or leaking bottles, labelling standards and other visible faults. If faults are found, the stock concerned can be isolated for re-inspection and the sighting operation corrected. When bottle breakage occurs during the filling operation, it is essential that any residual glass fragments are completely removed from the filling heads, using high pressure water hoses, to prevent glass entering subsequent bottles filled on the same head. For obvious reasons, freedom from glass fragments is essential in soft drinks bottling practice and forms an important part of any inspection system.

7. Packing

Packing of soft drinks into the final trade case or carton can be carried out automatically or by hand, depending on the nature of the pack and the speed of operation. Quality control of this final stage of the process should ensure that no damage to the label occurs during packing, and that the final pack reaches the ultimate consumer in a clean and attractive condition.

In the case of cartoned goods, a simple code can be used on the sides of the cartons in order that warehousemen and shopkeepers can check when stock was produced and rotate their stocks correctly, thus ensuring that the drinks reach the consumer in the freshest condition possible.

The shelf life of carbonated products varies, but under normal storage conditions, there is little evidence of deterioration within six to twelve months after bottling. However, most soft drinks, and especially those containing quinine, deteriorate considerably if exposed to excessive sunlight, strong artificial light or heat. Although canned products have a similar shelf life, Cola type drinks with a low pH can develop "off" flavours if kept for more than six months.

B. Concentrated Soft Drinks

1. Processing

The method of preparation will depend on the type of beverage manufactured—squash, comminuted drink, or cordial. The blending of the ingredients is carried out normally on a batch basis in a similar manner to that used for bottling syrups in carbonated drink manufacture. The product is also tested in the same way as carbonated bottling syrups (i.e. Brix, acidity, flavour and appearance). In most cases, additional processing is necessary to complete the process prior to bottling, e.g.—

a. Pasteurization. Flash pasteurization of fruit squashes and comminuted drinks is necessary to ensure a stable fruit cloud and product. To achieve this, the temperature of the product is quickly raised to 200–202°F and held for thirty seconds, then cooled to ambient temperatures, using a heat exchanger and holding section.

b. Homogenization stabilization. The appearance of squash or comminuted drinks may be improved by passing the fruit juice or base through a homogenizer and/or the addition of a chemical stabilizer, as this assists in the retention of the fruit particles in suspension, improving its shelf appeal.

c. Filtration. Filtration through a powdered diatomaceous earth of paper–cellulose medium is necessary to prepare a sparkling clear cordial. The grade of filter aid required will be determined by the nature and particle size of the material to be removed from the product and the clarity of filtrate required. The degree of clarity achieved can be seen by eye but electronic instruments are available which will determine the clarity in standard EBC units. Where the unwanted material is the insoluble fraction of an essence or essential oil, an absorbent filter medium is used.

2. Filling

The processed product is filled into the container (normally detergent-sterilized glass bottles) by a vacuum one-stage filling machine, the containers being filled to a standard filling height to achieve the quantity required. Tests on the filled product will include: refractometric solids, acidity, determination of the preservative content, clarity or cloud stability and micro-biological tests (including shelf life tests) and in addition, the volume of the contents is measured. The acceptable appearance of the product and container and the effectiveness of the seal must be confirmed. A taste comparison with a known standard is also made.

3. Sealing

The product may be sealed with aluminium seals, plastic caps, or corks, and even though the bottle does not have to retain a pressure, a good seal is essential to retain the gaseous SO_2 preservative (if used) and to prevent ingress of air and spoilage.

4. Labelling

The containers are labelled, coded and packed (normally into cartons) in a similar manner to carbonated soft drinks.

In general, squash filling speeds are substantially lower than carbonated drinks units and the key to consistent high quality squash manufacture is reliable processing and hygiene. Very high standards of hygiene are quite essential otherwise trade spoilage of benzoate preserved squashes can occur, particularly during the higher summer ambient temperatures.

C. Fruit Juices

Bottled pure fruit juices are prepared in the U.K. from unpreserved blended juices in cans and may contain additional sugar, vitamins and flavourings where these are necessary. Although cans of pineapple and tomato juices can be stored at room temperatures, cans of orange and grapefruit juice should preferably be stored at 38–40°F until required for use because of colour deterioration. Any juice from rusting or leaking cans is rejected and the juice from sound cans smelled prior to its addition to the juice batch. Juice having a sour, metallic or otherwise abnormal smell is not used. The blended juice is then tested to see if it is satisfactory before processing further. Before use, all plant used in processing fruit juices must be perfectly clean and sterile. First rate plant hygiene is essential if spoilage of the finished product is to be avoided.

Once the juice has been emptied from the cans, it should be bottled within 4 h, to ensure that there is no bacteriological pick-up. Two methods of pasteurization are in use and determine the bottling process used. In one process (in-bottle pasteurization) the juice is filled into cold, washed and sterilized bottles which are crowned and the whole finished product raised to the pasteurization temperature of the particular juice concerned, usually in the range 160–200°F for up to 20 min, cooled and then labelled and packed.

In the other (more favoured) process, the juice is flash pasteurized for half a minute at 200–202°F and filled into hot, washed sterile bottles, which are crowned and the bottle immediately inverted to bring the hot juice into direct contact with the crown to sterilize it. Providing the temperature of the juice does not drop below 180°F before the bottle is crowned and inverted, and the temperature of the juice in the inverted bottles is maintained above 175°F for at least $2\frac{1}{2}$ min, the product will remain sterile until opened by the consumer. After this high temperature treatment, the bottle is cooled to room temperature as quickly as possible, but without inducing thermal shock in the glass. The product is then labelled and packed for despatch. Good temperature control is necessary throughout either method to prevent incomplete pasteurization and bottle breakage. The juice can also be de-aerated before pasteurization to reduce flavour oxidation risks.

Quality control includes frequent inspection of process temperature, testing the juice in the blending vats for correct flavour and level of added ingredients, and ensuring that the correct time intervals between each stage are being observed. In order to confirm a satisfactory product shelf life, frequent control samples are removed from the production line and stored for:

two weeks at incubation temperatures (55°C for tomato, 27°C for other flavours),
two weeks at room temperature,
the shelf life of the product (6 months plus),

and then tested and smelled to confirm that the finished product is free from fermentation, mould growths and off flavours. In addition, routine batch quality control tests for refractive index (or Brix), acidity, flavour and appearance, and special tests for any added ingredients ensure that the finished product is being processed correctly to consistently high chemical, organoleptic and bacteriological standards.

4. EFFLUENT

A. Treatment of Effluent

As with many other major users of water in the food processing industry, soft drink manufacturers have had to re-examine carefully water usage in their factories because of rising costs of intake water and of effluent disposal to the local sewerage system. The implementation of the Rivers (Prevention of Pollution) Act 1961 and the Public Health Act 1961 meant that industry had to comply with volume and compositional limitations for their effluents discharged to the local sewers and was now charged for this service. If discharging to a river or stream, the limitations were particularly stringent and in many cases required, for the first time, treatment of effluent at the factory to ensure these standards could be set. Generally, for food processors the treatment required included settling, simple filtration, cooling, pH adjustment and in more polluted effluent, B.O.D. reduction.[6] The latter requirement meant provision of suitable equipment for biological oxidation of the effluent by either activated sludge treatment, or more recently, the use of biological filters constructed from corrugated PVC sheets, such as I.C.I.'s Flocor material.[7] For B.O.D. loadings of the order of 1000–2000 ppm in the combined factory effluent, a B.O.D. and suspended solids reduction down to Royal Commission standards could quite readily be obtained.

The biological filtration system using corrugated P.V.C. sheets is simple to maintain and operate and only requires adjustment of pH and the provision of nutrients in suitable form to supply the nitrogen and phosphorus for optimum operation. The disposal of the separated sludge presents certain problems in the biological oxidation systems, but a range of alternative types of processing equipment is now available for this purpose, including concentration by filter pressing and vacuum filtration, chemical conditioning, and final disposal to farm land or by incineration.

The present system of using potable water once only, then discharging it as effluent, could appear to be now a matter of growing concern in the United Kingdom with the rapid rise in water consumption for industrial purposes. The comprehensive treatment of effluent to such a standard that re-use in factory processing is feasible, is under study in a number of industries, including the Soft Drinks Industry with its particularly high water consumption (although a large percentage of this is used in the actual product). There are, however, a considerable number of additional technical problems if a high quality "second grade" water is required for re-use in food or drinks processing. (This would not be used in the product.) High bacteriological purity is essential for this type of processing water and even after attaining very low suspended solids and B.O.D. figures by suitable biological filtration, chlorination above "break-point", following by sand and then carbon filtration is necessary. The use of final polishing ultra-filtration or heat treatment systems may also be required because of the problems of maintaining carbon filters in a consistently high degree of sterility.

Finally, in typical Soft Drink Plant effluents, the problem of de-salination may arise because of possible corrosion effects on the process plant from the treated effluent, or perhaps second grade water may contribute an undesirable flavour to the product or intermediate raw material, under certain processing conditions. De-salination can be an expensive problem requiring provision of either demineralization, electrodialysis or reverso-osmosis equipment and although the latter two systems are only capable of handling essentially low saline effluents, they would normally be adequate for typical Soft Drinks Plant effluent saline levels, e.g. under 4000 mg/litre. These methods hold out considerable promise in the long term, as an alternative solution to the water shortage or cost problem, by being capable of providing re-usable water from effluent, for specific processing purposes.

The provision of potable water from sewage for human consumption is a major research project both in the United States of America and South Africa. In the latter country a large scale pilot plant is already in operation[8] and is technically quite feasible although commercial implications are problematic at this stage.

B. Control

This will be applied to the discharger:

(a) By the Local Authority, if discharging to a sewer.

(b) By the appropriate River Board if discharging to a river.

But in each case by

(c) The manufacturer himself by regular sampling and analysis as well as recording and control of volume discharged.

Depending upon the size and complexity of the effluent treatment plant, chemical, biochemical, and, in some cases, bacteriological control is necessary to ensure that appropriate standards are being met. Where simple filtration and pH adjustment only is being carried out, daily checks on suspended solids and pH are sufficient for monitoring purposes. In more complex plants equipped with biological oxidation or filtration systems, daily checks are also required on B.O.D. and nutrient dosage.[9]

Where re-use of effluent in food or drinks processing is contemplated, strict chemical control of both chlorination and de-chlorination efficiency is necessary, as well as bacteriological testing of the final treated effluent. In view of the 3–5 day delay incurred in both bacteriological testing and B.O.D. analysis, this imposes particular problems in ensuring reliability of plant performance to prevent the contamination of process plant, raw materials or finished product, particularly where the latter is not subject to a heat treatment or sterilizing process. Some progress has recently been made in developing monitoring devices for on-line analyses of dissolved oxygen, ammonia, phosphate and pH by electrochemical methods but this equipment is of more direct interest to large scale effluent processors.

As yet, the development of advanced effluent treatment systems and their control is in its comparative infancy in the Soft Drinks Industry, but as mentioned earlier, the rising costs of accepting and discharging water and the seasonal shortages occurring in certain areas are influencing major manufacturers to look again at the commercial implications of effluent treatment and re-use of water.

5. PLANT HYGIENE

A. Introduction

Although bacterial growth in soft drinks is inhibited by low pH, preservative content and carbon dioxide (in the case of carbonated drinks), yeast

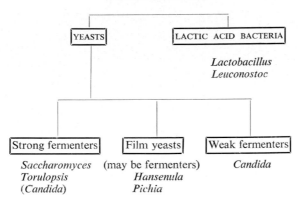

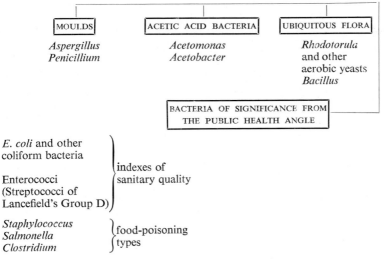

Typical spoilage organisms
(Organisms which cause macroscopically
detectable changes)

YEASTS   LACTIC ACID BACTERIA

Lactobacillus
Leuconostoc

Strong fermenters   Film yeasts   Weak fermenters

Saccharomyces   (may be fermenters)   Candida
Torulopsis   Hansenula
(Candida)   Pichia

Organisms which do not usually
cause macroscopically detectable changes

MOULDS   ACETIC ACID BACTERIA   UBIQUITOUS FLORA

Aspergillus   Acetomonas   Rhodotorula
Penicillium   Acetobacter   and other
                                             aerobic yeasts
                                             Bacillus

BACTERIA OF SIGNIFICANCE FROM
THE PUBLIC HEALTH ANGLE

E. coli and other
coliform bacteria
                    indexes of
Enterococci   sanitary quality
(Streptococci of
Lancefield's Group D)

Staphylococcus
Salmonella   food-poisoning
Clostridium   types

FIG. 2. Microflora of soft drinks.

From Sand, F. E. M. J. (1969). Proc. Soc. Soft Drink Technologists, 16th Annual Meeting, Colorado.

infection from plant or ingredients can lead to progressive fermentation with product off-flavour and generation of CO_2 gas, and therefore, bacteriological control and hygiene standards in soft drinks factories must be to a similarly high level as, for example, the dairy and brewing industries (see Fig. 2, p. 175).

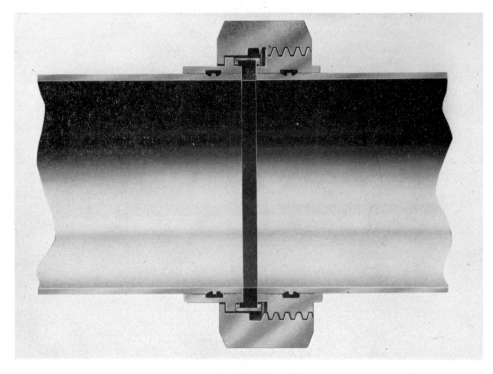

FIG. 3a. I.S.S. pipe union made by the APV Co., showing the T-shaped sealing ring flush with both pipes and the "Lok Ring" inserts connecting the male part and liner to the pipe ends.

Soft drinks do not normally support pathogenic food poisoning organisms, because of their low pH range. In general, provided ingredients are purchased from reputable suppliers and to a high specification, they do not provide a normal source of product spoilage organisms. Ineffective plant cleaning is the most frequent cause of soft drinks spoilage, about 90% being due to yeast contamination. With the increasing range and complexity of both processing and filling plant in the soft drinks industry, the establishment of effective closely supervised hygiene practices has become paramount to ensure satisfactory product shelf life is maintained in the trade. In addition, to be fully effective, these procedures must be monitored throughout production so that appropriate action can be taken to improve a deteriorating situation before an actual spoilage situation develops.[10] At filling speeds approaching 600 bottles/min, the economic importance of avoiding spoilage is quite clear.

Soft drink plant hygiene can be divided into three important areas:

(a) Cleaning of equipment
(b) Sterilizing of equipment
(c) Control systems.

B. Cleaning of Equipment

In parallel with both dairy and brewing industries, *in-place cleaning* of pipework and processing tanks has been adopted by the large soft drinks manufacturers, principally because of its reliability and efficiency rather than for labour saving reasons. The reliability of these systems is dependent on establishing a closed circuit of pipework, valves, and tanks (which are normally manufactured from stainless steel (Figs 3a, 3b, 4).[11]

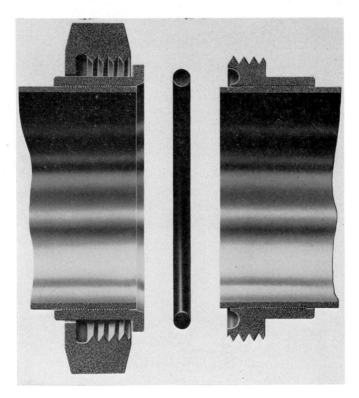

FIG. 3b. Pipe union of the ring-joint type, showing the crevice between the two pipes, that makes the union unsuitable for cleaning in-place.

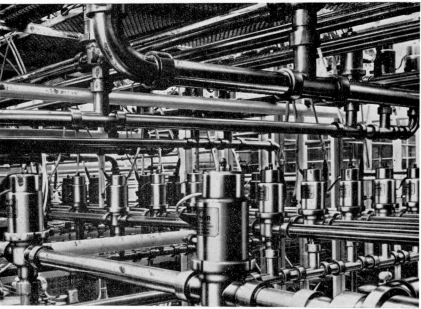

Fig. 4. (Top) APV paravalves installed in the beer mains at Molsons Brewery, Montreal, Canada.

(Bottom) Soft Drinks factory of Schweppes Ltd. at Sidcup uses APV Zephyr valves to control circuit-selection and cleaning in-place.

The general principle is to provide a pumped circulation detergent cleaning cycle (including spray-balls for internal tank cleaning) followed by chemical sterilization, for a sequential hygiene programme as follows:

(a) Cold water pre-rinse to remove product residues such as fruit pulp.

(b) Hot detergent circulation (normally caustic-based).

(c) Cold water rinse to remove detergent.

(d) Sterilant circulation—normally cold halogen-based sterilant used.

(e) Final cold water rinse.

For maximum efficiency, it is essential that the circuit is carefully designed with full consideration of optimum pressures and flow rates required. These systems are understandably expensive but eliminate the possibility of operator error and expensive loss of materials, and in fact, provide an essential solution to the very complex cleaning problems which arose with the development of Benzoate preserved fruit squashes and carbonated drinks in the mid-late fifties.[12]

Unfortunately modern bottling fillers do not lend themselves readily to in-place cleaning methods. As sterilization of equipment can only be undertaken if complete effective physical cleaning has preceded it, this has posed important new hygiene problems in the bottling industry, particularly in contemporary high speed bottling fillers of the "Premix" type, where the finished product is fed to the bottle in a single operation via the filler (Fig. 5). In the older "two-stage" (or Postmix) systems, a concentrated flavoured syrup was dosed into the bottle through a comparatively simple and cleanable device, and the main filler then added carbonated water only, to the syruped bottle. This minimized cleaning problems considerably on the main filling equipment.

Although some progress has been made recently in developing a degree of automatic recirculation in-place cleaning (and sterilization) of certain types of Premix fillers, these methods require much more development work before they can be adopted for even limited use. In the meantime, *manual* stripping and cleaning of fillers and certain process plant (which cannot be cleaned in-place) is essential to remove pulp particles, flavour resin deposits, etc., prior to sterilization procedures.[13] Despite the detailed tedious nature of these manual operations, they perform an essential function in the hygiene programme and if not carried out properly, would soon reflect in product spoilage, owing to accumulated product deposits in valves, pipeline joints and other less accessible places.

The use of specially designed brushes is advisable for these operations to ensure maximum efficiency of soil removal, and in addition, a detailed programme must be established for step-by-step equipment dismantling, cleaning, and re-assembly; the staff engaged in this work should be carefully trained and re-trained at regular intervals to maintain effective operating

standards. After dismantling, each component is brushed with either detergent or cleaning paste, thoroughly rinsed in water, then carefully re-assembled
in correct sequence (the use of explanatory diagrams for detailed components
is particularly helpful in training new staff, or for reference with particularly
complicated pieces of equipment) ready for inclusion in the sterilization
programme.

Fig. 5. 500 bottles/min Ortmann and Herbst Premix type soft drinks filler at the
Schweppes Ltd. factory, Fareham, Hants.

C. Sterilizing of Equipment

Sterilization of plant cannot be fully effective unless preceded by complete
removal of physical debris and soils by thorough cleaning, and in most food
operations, sterilization is the final stage in a sequential hygiene programme.
Sterilization of soft drinks plant can be effected by:

   (i) Application of heat in a suitable form.

       and/or

   (ii) Chemical treatment.

1. Sterilization by heat has, of course, been in use for many years in bottling
operations such as dairies and has the advantage of simplicity, economy, and
reliability. Heat is normally applied as low pressure steam at 5 p.s.i. but for

certain applications, hot water at 180°F or hot detergent at 160–180°F at appropriate strengths may be used. Until the more recent development of the Premix type high speed bottling fillers, cold chemical sterilization of carbonated drink filling plant was effective in maintaining suitable bacteriological standards, as carbonated water only passed through the system of filling valves. The larger, more complex modern fillers have required the development of specialized sterilization procedures to eliminate spoilage organisms, etc. from the working parts in contact with the beverage, and certain bacteriologically sensitive beverages such as shandy and unpreserved fruit juices have only achieved suitable commercial shelf life and bacteriological stability by establishing daily advanced hygiene systems of physical cleaning, chemical sterilization followed by a final "polish" using hot water at not less than 180°F, immediately prior to production.

When benzoic acid (which is odourless and tasteless) gained popularity as a preservative some years ago, its lower efficiency compared with SO_2 meant that a higher bacteriological standard in the bottled product was necessary— particularly in uncarbonated products of the squash type. For many years previously, thorough washout of plant after bottling, followed by cold chemical treatment with sterilants such as sodium hypochlorite was quite sufficient. Improved, more detailed hygiene procedures for squash plant were developed by necessity, covering dismantling of pipework and fillers, thorough physical cleaning followed finally by steam sterilization of components in suitable industrial autoclaves. These procedures proved to be fully effective in maintaining biological stability consistent with good product shelf life. Where low pressure steam is readily available at low cost, the high efficiency of heat as a sterilizing medium gives it considerable preference over cold sterilization methods. The advantages of either system must be carefully assessed when establishing hygiene procedures.

2. Sterilization by Chemicals

A bewildering range of chemical detergents, sterilants, biocides and sanitizers are now available to manufacturers of soft drinks for plant sterilization (see Table 3 and Fig. 6).

In general, processing equipment such as mixing tanks and pipework require cleaning and sterilization by either combined detergent/sterilizer chemicals or separate two-stage treatment by detergent followed by sterilant. Bottling plant, particularly fillers, are generally sterilized by cold halogen-based chemicals such as hypochlorites, iodophors, and brominated compounds, but the effectiveness of these chemicals under the more stringent bacteriological conditions referred to earlier must be examined closely by plant trials. Iodophors (which are acidic detergent/sterilizers) have gained some favour for specific hygiene operations but the majority of these newer

TABLE 3. Sterilizer and Detergent Sterilizer Properties

Type	Chemical and biocidal properties	Typical applications
Iodophors	Always in acidic medium and blended with synthetic detergents. Rapid broad spectrum biocidal activity. Solutions are high and low foaming. Max. operating temperatures about 120°F. Liquid.	Main uses in milk handling plant where acid controls milkstone. Applications in "Acidic" foods, i.e. mineral bottlers and breweries where similarity to soils is an advantage. Functional in manual, soak and low velocity circulation.
Phenolic compounds	Supplied as sterilizers only or blended as detergent sterilants. Excellent residual activity. May have unpleasant odour or are perfumed. Usually high foam. Liquid.	Rarely used in food vessels. Manual procedures in environmental hygiene are most efficient.
Quaternary ammonium compounds	These are sterilizers or detergent sterilizer blends in liquid or granular form. Compounds are generally of neutral pH. Foam produced in solution. May be blended with other sterilants. Biocidal activity good in limited spectrum. Good residual activity.	Very wide use in meat industries and shop hygiene procedures. Some application in production vessels in soak and manual cleaning. Not spray or circulation due to foam. Not normally recommended for brewing use due to effect on beer head.
Ampholytic detergents	Compounds are detergents with bactericidal activity. May be blended with QAC and other detergents to broaden kill spectrum. These are neutral liquids with high foam characteristics. Good residual action.	General use in manual operations and environmental hygiene. Limited use in cleaning and sterilizing production vessels. Not generally suitable for spray or high velocity circulation.
Hypochlorite and hypobromite compounds	Sterilants based on inorganic chlorine release agents with pH adjustment for corrosion control. Organic chlorine release agents also used where balanced with detergent materials. Formulations may be low alkalinity and high foam for hand use or high alkalinity low foam for circulation. Rapid broad spectrum biocidal activity is increased by combination with bromine release materials. Low residual effect. Completely compatible with food matter.	This is the broadest group of sterilizers available. Used in all industries for manual, soak, spray and circulation cleaning. May be applied as combined detergent sterilizers where lighter residues are encountered or follow a detergent clean in terminal sterilization.

From R. Hill (1949). *Food Proc. Ind.* **38** (October 1949).

sterilizing chemicals are more expensive than sodium hypochlorite which has been used for many years for bottling plant sterilization.

In conjunction with the development of these chemicals, more advanced equipment is now available for applying these chemicals by circulation, spraying or "fogging" (i.e. as a fine mist). Considerable interest has been

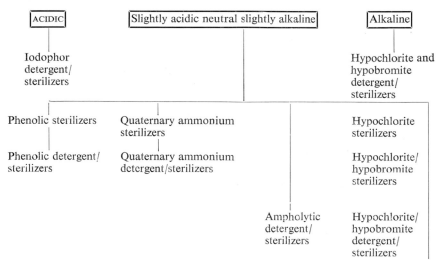

FromR. Hill (1949). *Food Proc. Ind.* **38** (October 1949).

FIG. 6

shown in the recent development of centralized systems for sterilant supply whereby detergent or sterilant is pumped from a central consol to all points required in the factory and can be tapped with minimum effort and maximum flexibility to suitable pressurized spray guns for easy access to all soiled plant.

D. Control Systems

Continuous monitoring of hygiene procedures is quite essential in large soft drinks factories (as in dairies) to ensure that bacteriological infection during processing or bottling does not reach a level which will overcome the product inhibitory conditions of pH and preservative, thereby causing spoilage in the trade and adverse reaction from consumers. Wherever possible, either local or centralized systems of product sampling, bacteriological testing and plant cleanliness evaluation by swabbing, should be established and suitable maximum acceptable bacteriological standards set. A typical systematic scheme is shown below:

Detection of Plant or Ingredient
Infection of Soft Drinks

Bacteriological counts in soft drinks are derived from the following:

A. Postmix System (i.e. Flavoured syrup and carbonated water dosed separately into the bottle)

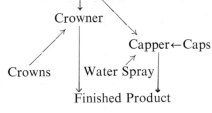

Raw Materials (sugar, water, essence, fruit base, etc.)
↓
Syrup Manufacture
↓
Syruper & Pipework
↓
Carbonated Water→Filler←Washed bottles   Aerial contamination
↓   between bottle washing and
Crowner   capping/crowning areas

Capper←Caps

Crowns   Water Spray

Finished Product

B. Premix system (i.e. flavoured syrup and carbonated water blended, then injected simultaneously via the filler, into the bottle).

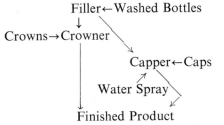

Raw materials (sugar, water, essence, fruit base, etc.)
↓
Syrup manufacture
↓
Carbonated Water   Chilling/Carbonating system and Pipework
Filler←Washed Bottles   Aerial contamination
↓   between bottle washing and
Crowns→Crowner   capping/crowning areas

Capper←Caps

Water Spray

Finished Product

In view of the wide range of variables, the system must be rationalized into specific sections as follows:

    I. Syrup Manufacture
   II. Syruper and Pipework
  III. Carbonating System and Pipework
  IV. Filler
   V. Crowner/capper

I. Syrup Manufacture

Collect a sample of syrup in a sterile container from the top of the batch tank prior to bottling. Plate this sample out, 1 ml of syrup to 15 ml of Potato Dextrose Agar (remember to mix carefully in view of the high viscosity). Incubate for 5 days at 27°C. (Plate counts should be below 10 organisms/ml). If not, check the following:

(1) Liquid Sugar.
(2) Treated water (used both for cleaning as well as for syrup).
(3) Plant Hygiene.
(4) Fruit Juice or Base (if used).

No. (3) would require swab tests of pieces of equipment and the walls and valves of tanks.

II. Syruper and Pipework

Sterilize several bottles of the same size as the production run and pu them through the syruper. Plate out 1 ml of the syrup to 15 ml of Potato Dextrose Agar and incubate for 5 days at 27°C.

At the same time, plate out production samples ex syruper. Difference between these two sets is the washed bottle count. In efficient bottle washing, this count should be virtually zero. If not, investigate bottles *ex* washer.

Should there be a count between Sections I and II and it is *not* caused by bottle washing, this would suggest:

(i) Syruper not cleaned effectively.
(ii) Lines to syruper not being rinsed free of pockets of dilute syrup.
(iii) Inadequate general plant cleaning.

To check which of these factors is the cause, it is necessary to strip plant and linework and swab various pieces of equipment.

III. Carbonating System and Pipework

Sterile sampling may be somewhat difficult from the outlet side of carbonating equipment. Make sure that any sampling cock to be used has been thoroughly cleaned and sterilized so as to eliminate this as a variable:

High counts on outlet side of carbonating system indicate contamination from:

(i) Treated Water.
(ii) Carbonating system and pipework.
(iii) Inadequate general cleaning.

Stripping of plant and lines followed by swabbing of various pieces of equipment should be carried out to check (ii) and (iii). Plate count of treated water may show that the water line has not been sterilized for a long period, or has been inadequately treated.

IV. Filler

Collect bottled samples prior to crowning or capping.

In the case of the *Postmix System* increased counts over the syruper samples would be due to:

(i) Carbonated water.
(ii) Filler.
(iii) Inadequate general cleaning.

In the case of the *Premix System* increased counts over those from the carbonating syruping system would be due to:

(i) Filler.
(ii) Inadequate cleaning.

V. Crowner or Capper

In the case of increased counts in this area, this would be due to:

(i) Crown Seal Dust.
(ii) Crown Seal Throats needing regular stripping, cleaning, sterilization and re-greasing.
(iii) Water spray by Capper contaminated.
(iv) Capper chucks need cleaning.
(v) Inadequate general cleaning.

It is generally considered that infection from crown seals and caps is minimal and can be neglected, particularly with the modern development of plastic crown and cap liners.

Plant hygiene is an important factor in all four sections and, if inadequate, this is likely to show itself as counts in most sections of the operation. In this case, independent investigation of procedures or method of operation of Plant Hygiene is required to determine the major reason for contamination.

Significant deviations from standard require prompt investigation before product spoilage develops or deep-rooted plant infection develops. It is also advantageous in these bacteriological control schemes to select the product found from experience to be the most bacteriologically sensitive, since hygiene procedures maintaining acceptable low yeast counts in this product should prove perfectly adequate for the complete product range bottled. A suitable soft drink for this work should have a pH over 3·5 and be unpreserved.

In addition to checking the initial yeast, mould and bacterial count on the bottled product, these control systems can give an early indication of product shelf life and stability by incubating at 80°F for 1–4 months, depending on product composition and use. This accelerates yeast development to fermentation of the product (where initial infection is high) and the absence of fermentation gives a useful guide as to the product performance in the trade.

6. PACKAGING OF SOFT DRINKS

A. Carbonated Beverages

The traditional container for carbonated beverages is the returnable (multi-trip) glass bottle with a crown cork closure.

In the past decade marketing requirements have demanded greater flexibility in packaging, and carbonated beverages are now sold in returnable bottles, non-returnable bottles sealed with convenience closures, and in cans. The bar and catering trades are also supplied with carbonated beverages in Premix and Postmix systems for dispensing soft drinks.

Moody[14] has presented a comprehensive review of glass packing technology and Price-Davies[15] has reviewed developments in packaging of soft drinks.

In 1970 attempts have been made in the United States to pack carbonated beverages in plastic containers, but owing to cost, such developments are making slow progress.

B. Glass Containers

Although attempts have been made by glass manufacturers, trade engineers, and representatives of the soft drinks industry to standardize bottle shapes, no general agreement has been reached because most users insist on retaining the shape of their own bottles. A British Standards specification is in being for the crown finish,[16] and one has recently been issued for non-returnable soft drink bottles.[17]

Essentially the glass manufacturer and the user must agree on the bottle specification and the user's quality control system involves taking a random selection of bottles from deliveries and subjecting the samples to gauging and physical checks such as weight, capacity and, in particular, glass strength. These characteristics received particular emphasis by the glass manufacturers and users during the development of the one-trip bottles and it is now general practice to supplement the normal design strength characteristics by applying a permanent external coating, such as stannate treatment. In addition certain manufacturers include a further non-permanent coating which is actually removed in the bottle washing process, but which increases the resistance to the glass-to-glass contact. New bottles progressively lose their strength in handling and studies have established that bottles could lose up to a quarter of their initial strength in the handling process from the glass manufacturers, through the bottle filling and packing process, in a high speed bottling line.

C. Closures for Glass

The crown cork has been the standard closure for carbonated drinks for many decades. More recently convenience closures have been introduced. Increased use of convenience closure in the range of such closures has been reviewed by W. C. Williams in a paper to the 17th Annual Meeting of the Society of Soft Drink Technologists in Orlando, Florida, in May 1970.[18] Closures made from a wide range of materials are now being subjected to much more intensive research and general interest by manufacturers and users. The British Standards Institution has also reflected this interest in their activities.

D. Cans

It is essential to conduct evaluation storage tests prior to introducing canned soft drinks to the market, to ensure full compatability between can and product. The test cans are filled with product under evaluation and subjected to up to 6 months storage at ambient temperature and examined frequently during this period for signs of deterioration in either can or product. Checks include metallic pick-up (iron and tin) flavour assessment and detailed physical examination of can interior. SO_2 *must be excluded* from the product formulation. If satisfactory over the 6 months storage period, the cans are normally suitable for commercial use *for the category of product tested.* This is due to the widely differing effect of product on can (or vice versa) according to product formulation, e.g. highly coloured drinks, Colas, clear Lemonade and Soda Water have shown to be particularly corrosive beverages and may require a higher specification tinplate or lacquering system to guarantee shelf life, whereas a number of other coloured, low carbonated fruit drinks have been found to be perfectly satisfactory 2–3 years after filling.

In the factory canning operation the cans may require to be internally rinsed with cold or hot water jetting to remove dust or small pieces of carton material, then the rinsed can is filled normally by the single operation Premix system described earlier. The next stages of the production line are then significantly different from bottling lines. In canning, it is vitally necessary for the headspace air in the filled can to be purged with CO_2 gas *immediately* prior to applying the can lid (or end), otherwise the high air content will accelerate corrosion of can and deterioration in contents during storage. After CO_2 purging and application of the can end on the seamer, the can is heated to ambient in a warm water jetting tunnel, then air dried, to remove adhering moisture which would cause corrosion, is then coded, individually check-weighed, and packed into cartons for sale. Frequent close control of the end seaming operation is essential to ensure no product leakage in the trade and it is advisable that, in addition to seaming control by line maintenance staff, can seam checks be included in the Quality Control Department daily programme.

The beverage can has seen many development changes in the past 10 years, most of which have been motivated by the need to maintain a low priced container for the beverage industry. Changes have included successive light-weighting of the basic tinplate, frequent redesign of the important side-seam area, improved lacquering systems and standardization of the plastic compound systems used on the can ends to achieve a pressure seal after application to the can body. It was also found necessary to replace the lead solder used on the side seam by pure tin solder, because of lead pick-up on certain varieties over lengthy storage periods.

The latest can development is a particularly significant one—adoption of the easy-open end, in parallel with similar convenience developments in the bottling industry. The can easy-open end exists in a number of alternative designs but in the United Kingdom is principally an all-aluminium end with a scored opening section attached to an aluminium ring, which is pulled by the consumer, to open the can. This avoids the irritating need for an opening device, as on the old design. This can required detailed evaluation by beverage canners, covering storage tests and high speed handling trials, before being adopted.

Further important specification changes are envisaged, including the cemented side seam (which eliminates the present wide side seam and provides virtually all-round decoration facility), the all-aluminium can and the interesting use of various combinations of tinplate, aluminium plastic or paper laminates, to achieve radically new composite beverage containers.

As can be seen, beverage can technology and quality control has become a highly developed specialized aspect of soft drinks quality control.

E. Packaging of Squash

The traditional container is glass with a resealable closure but in recent years there has been increasing use of P.V.C. bottles for these products.

ACKNOWLEDGEMENTS

The authors wish to express their thanks to G. A. Rogers for his assistance in preparing original drafts, to the APV Co., Crawley, Sussex and the Permutit Co., London for permission to reprint illustrations of their equipment.

REFERENCES

1. E.E.C. (1970). Draft Council Directive on Non-Alcoholic Refreshing Beverages. COM(70) final, Brussels, 10th April 1970.
2. Soft Drinks Regulations (1964). S.I. 1964: No. 760. (H.M.S.O. London).

3. Dupaigne, P. (1961). *In*: "Fruit & Vegetable Juice Processing Technology" (Eds. Tressler, D. K. & Joslyn, M. A.), p. 538.

4. Charley, V. L. S. (1963). *Food Technol.* **17,** 987.

5. Steiner, E. H. (1967). In: "Quality Control in the Food Industry". Vol. 1 (Ed. Herschdoerfer, S. M.), p. 121. Academic Press, London and New York.

6. Dahlstrom, D. A. and Dlouhy, P. E. (1969). Waste Treatment and Water Circuit Control to Maximize Profitability. Effluent & Water Treatment Convention, London, 1965.

7. Askew, M. W. (1968). Plastics in Water Treatment. Effluent & Water Treatment Convention, London, 1968.

8. Stander, G. J. and Funk, J. W. (1967). *Chem. Eng. Progr. Symp. Series* 63 (78), 1.

9. Min. of Technology (1969). Notes on Water Pollution, No. 44.

10. McDonald, D. (1969). Quality Control of Soft Drinks. Royal Society of Health (Leeds Branch), 1969.

11. Blois Johnson, W. J. (1965). *Soft Drinks Trade J.*, Sept. 1965, 734.

12. Price-Davies, W. and Chandler, B. M. (1960). *Ann. Inst. Pasteur Lille*, **11**, 59 (3me Symp. Int. de Microbiologie Alimentaire, Evian-les-Bains, Sept. 1960).

13. Rice, F. G. R. (1967). *J. Appl. Bact.* **30** (1), 101.

14. Moody, B. E. (1963). "Packaging in Glass". (Hutchinson.)

15. Price-Davies, W. (1962). Recent Advances in the Packaging of Soft Drinks. Inst. Packaging Conference Guide, 108.

16. British Standards Institution (1970). Glass Container Finishes, B.S. 1918: Part 2: 1970. Crown Finish.

17. British Standards Institution (1970). Specification for $\frac{1}{3}$ litre (12 fl. oz.) non-returnable soft drink glass bottles. Part I—bottles with crown finish, B.S. 4590.

18. Williams, W. C. (1970). Proc. Soc. Soft Drink Technologists, 17th Ann. Meeting, Florida, May 1970.

Flavouring Materials and Their Quality Control

GEORGES WELLNER

International Flavors and Fragrances Inc., Rio de Janeiro, Brazil

1. INTRODUCTION

Flavouring is an important quality of products intended for consumption by humans and animals. It is a valuable aid in making them enjoyable, in exciting the appetite, and to a certain degree, in stimulating the activity of the digestive tract.

The flavour of a food is the result of a combination of many sensations and of their effects upon the human senses of taste, smell, feel and sight. There are four basic tastes which, individually or in combination with each other, are detected by the taste buds located on the tongue. They are sweetness, saltiness, sourness and bitterness. The sense of smell detects the aroma of the volatile constituents of food products when they are smelled or swallowed. The sense of feel detects sensations of texture, cold and warmth. The sense of sight distinguishes colours and appearance. It is by the judicious combination of the effects upon the senses that the food producer can increase the palatability of his product. He formulates the composition of his merchandise by expertly balancing nutritive ingredients with the above mentioned factors.

This chapter will describe the most important categories of flavouring materials and consider problems of their quality control, which vary from type to type. Flavouring materials may be processed or unprocessed natural products, blends of synthetic materials, or combinations of natural and synthetic products. They can be used to transfer to a food the flavour of the natural products from which they derive or to simulate an aroma which cannot otherwise be imparted. Owing to short supply seasonal availability, or inefficient results obtained from some natural flavouring products, manufactured flavours have a very important place in consumer goods. These manufactured materials may be natural or synthetic.

Flavouring materials are supplied to the food industry in many forms. They may be liquids, in alcohol, oil or aqueous solutions; emulsions; solids in powder or in pieces; or resins. They may be soluble or insoluble in water or in other solvents.

Many of the flavour values are difficult, if not impossible, to measure by any but the subjective human instrument. However, the discussion and description of taste testing, panelling, and other such approaches to the evaluation of flavours is not the concern of this chapter. The taste value is only one among the various sets of physical and chemical criteria which should be tested in flavour quality control laboratories. Many of these tests are described below.

In the United States, the Food and Drug Administration is the agency enforcing the Federal Food, Drug and Cosmetic Act. Flavouring materials are covered by this legislation when used in interstate commerce, and many states possess legislation covering the use of flavours in intrastate commerce.

The Association of Official Analytical Chemists, known as the AOAC, is the professional organization of state and federal scientists devoted to developing, testing and approving methods for the analysis of foods, feeds, fertilizers, pesticides, drugs, cosmetics, etc. The AOAC has accepted the responsibility for providing the regulatory agencies' scientists with the accurate and reproducible methods of analysis that are required for the enforcement of laws and regulations. The U.S. federal definitions and standards of identity for many foods incorporate AOAC methods into their requirements. These analytical methods are published in the Official Methods of Analysis of the AOAC.[1]

Many of the products used as flavouring materials have been described in the U.S. service and regulatory announcements, the U.S. Pharmacopoeia and the National Formulary as well as in the British Pharmacopoeia and the British Pharmaceutical Codex. Many of the criteria and methods cited below have the above mentioned publications as their sources.

2. SPICES AND HERBS

A. Whole and Ground

These consist of many parts of various plants—leaves, roots, barks, flowers, fruits or buds. They are often incorporated in foods, in rather small amounts, after being ground or pulverized. The contribution they make to the taste of food is due to a large extent to the presence of volatile oils. Spices and herbs are generally collected at that period of maturity when their development has reached its fullest. The collected plant portions are dried, ground, and the largest impurities, such as stems, are removed.

According to the U.S. federal specifications, spices are made from the true aromatic vegetable substances from which no portion of any volatile or other flavouring principle has been removed and are free from artificial colouring matter, adulterants and impurities. The aroma must be true to the name. There are few British standards for herbs and spices. (Only mustard[2] and curry powder[3] have been the subject of Food Standards Orders.) The standards for spices used for pharmaceutical purposes which are prescribed in the British Pharmacopoeia and the British Pharmaceutical Codex and the numerous U.S. standards are most useful as a guide to quality.

1. Routine Methods of Analysis

(*a*) Moisture should be determined by distillation from an inert solvent such as toluene (AOAC 28.002).

(*b*) Total ash should be determined by conventional methods (B.P. 1968, p. 1276) or (AOAC 28.003).

(*c*) Soluble and insoluble ash (AOAC 28.004).

(*d*) Acid insoluble ash (AOAC 28.005).

(*e*) Volatile and non-volatile ether extract (AOAC 28.009).

(*f*) Volatile oil (AOAC 28.017-18-22 and 23).

2. Specific Methods of Analysis

A number of specific tests should be performed in addition to the above:

(*a*) For black and white pepper—nitrogen in non-volatile ether extract to determine the amount of piperine (AOAC 28.008).

(*b*) For cloves and allspice—tannin determination (AOAC 28.015).

Adulterants of vegetable origins are best detected by microscopic examination.[4, 5] A number of specific tests help to detect specific adulterations, such as the presence of turmeric in mustard,[6] of starch in mustard,[7] of rice and other adulterants in pepper[8] and many others.

The results of the various tests should conform to the standards or average figures given in Table 1. A number of adulterant analyses are also listed.

B. Soluble Spice and Herb Extracts

Soluble spice and herb extracts are the flavouring constituents of the natural spices and herbs incorporated either in a solvent such as alcohol, or on a soluble dry edible carrier. These extracts are intended for use as alternatives for natural whole or ground spices and herbs in many foods. The odour

TABLE 1. Spice and herbs

Name	Moisture %	Total ash %	Acid insol. Ash %	Vol. oil %	Crude fibre %	For. org. matter %	Stalks %	Remarks
Allspice	8	5 U.S. max.	0·3 U.S. max.	3.5	25 U.S. max			
Aniseed		9 U.S. max.	1·5 U.S. max. 1·5 B.P. max.	1·5-4 2 B.P. min.		1 B.P. max		Fixed oil 8-20%
Basil		11-5	0·3	1·8				
Bay leaves	7	4·5 U.S. max.	0·5 U.S. max.	1·0 U.S.		3 U.S. max.		
Capsicum	5-8	8 B.P. max.	1-3		14-23	1 B.P. max.		Non volatile ether extract 12% B.P. min.
Caraway seeds	9	4·8-7·5 8 U.S.	1·5 B.P. max. 1·0 U.S.	2·5-7 3·5 B.P. min. (2·5 powder)	17-22	2 B.P. max. 3 U.S. max.		Water insol. ash. 2-2·3% Cold water extract 20-25%
Cardamom seeds	9	6 B.P. max. 5 U.S.	3·5 B.P. max. 3 U.S.	4 B.P. min. 3 U.S.				
Celery seeds	10	12 U.S. max.	2 B.P. max. 1·5 U.S.	1·5-3 1·5 B.P. min. 2·0 U.S.	1 B.P. max.			Fixed oil 15-30%
Cinnamon	7·5-10 10	7 B.P. max. 5 U.S. max.	2 B.P. max. 2 U.S. max.	1 B.P. min. (0·7 for ground)	30-35	2 B.P. max.		Alcohol extract 8·5-13·5% Fixed oil 1·3-1·7
Clove	5-11 8	7 B.P. max. 6 U.S. max.	1 B.P. max. 0·5 U.S. max.	15-20 14 B.P. min. 15 U.S. min.	10 U.S. max.		U.S. 5max.	Not less than 12% Quer-citannic acid U.S. standard

Spice								Remarks
Coriander	9	7 U.S. max.	1·5 B.P. max. 1·5 U.S. max.	0·3 B.P. min. (0·2 powder)		2 B.P. max.		Fixed oil 12–20%
Cumin	9	6–10 9·5 U.S. max.	1·0 U.S.	2–4 1·0		2 B.P. max. 5 U.S. max.		Fixed oil 10–14%
Dill		10 U.S. max.	3 U.S. max. 8 B.P. max.	2·5 B.P. min. (2 ground)		2 B.P. max.		Fixed oil 15–18%
Fennel	8	9 U.S. max.	1 U.S. max. 1·5 B.P. max.	1·4 B.P. min. (1 ground)		2 B.P. max.		Cold water extract 22–27% Fixed oil 12–20%
Ginger	8–14	6 B.P. max.	1·5 B.P. max.	1–3	8 U.S. max.			Not less than 42% starch (U.S.)
	12	7 U.S. max.	2 U.S. max.		2·5			Not more than 1% lime U.S. Not less than 12% cold water extract
Mace	3·5–7	3 U.S. max.	0·5 U.S. max.	4–15 8 U.S. max.	5–8 12 U.S. max.			
Marjoram	10	16 U.S. max.	4·0 U.S. max.	0·7–2·5			2–12 10 U.S. max.	
Mixed mustards	4–7	6 U.S. ground 5 U.S. max.	1·5 U.S. max.	0·5–1	5 U.S. max.			Flour 1·5% Starch (U.S. max.)
Nutmeg	4–8	3 B.P. max. 5 U.S. max.	0·5 U.S. max.	4 B.P. min. 6 U.S. min.	10 U.S. max.			Non volatile ether extract 25% U.S. min.
Parsley	12–18	1–6		4–7			2–3	

TABLE 1. Spice and herbs—contd.

Name	Moisture %	Total Ash %	Acid insol. Ash %	Vol. oil %	Crude fiber %	For org. matter %	Stalks %	Remarks
Pepper Black	8-12 12	6 B.P. max. 7 U.S. max.	1 B.P. max. 1·5 U.S. max.	0·5-1·8 2·0	10-15 15 B.P.C. max.	2 B.P.C. max.		Non-volatile ether extract 6·75% U.S. min. starch 30% U.S. min.
Pepper cayenne	10	8 U.S. max.	1·0 U.S. max.		28 U.S. max.			Non-volatile ether extract 15% min. starch 1·5% U.S. max. Scoville pungency 35 000-55 000
Pepper red		8 U.S. max.	1 U.S. max.					Scoville pungency 15 000-35 000
Pepper white	8-15 13	5 B.P.C. max. 2 U.S. 3·5 U.S. max.	0·5 B.P.C. max. 0·3 U.S. 0·3 U.S. max.	0·5-1·8 1·5 U.S.	6 B.P.C. max. 5 U.S. 5 U.S. max.	2 B.P.C. max.		Non-volatile ether extract 7% min. U.S.-starch 52% min. U.S.
Paprika		8·5 U.S. max.	1 U.S. max.					Iodine number of extracted oil 125 U.S. min. 136 U.S. max.
Pimento	11	8·5 U.S. max.	1 U.S. max.	1·5 U.S.		21 U.S. max.		Non-volatile ether extract 18% max.
Sage	10	10 U.S. max.	1 U.S. max.	1·5 U.S.	25 U.S. max.	4-14 12 U.S. max.		
Thyme	9	7-19 8 U.S. max.	4 B.P.C. max. 2 U.S. max.	0·4-2·5 1·5 U.S.	4-6	2-8		
Turmeric	8-10 9	6-9 7 U.S.	0·5 U.S.	2-5 4	6			Color power 5·0 expressed as % curcumin.

Table 1.—Adulterants

Almond shells ground		2·5–3	0·1–0·2	45–50	
Cocoa shell ground		8–9	1–1·5	14–15	
Walnut shell ground		1·2–1·5	0·1–0·2	55–60	
Olive stone ground		0·5–1	0·5–0·75	50–60	
Corn flour	13–14	1·4–1·6			Carbohydrates 60–70%
Wheat flour	13–14	0·6–0·8			Carbohydrates 70–75%
Rice flour	10–12	0·5–0·6			Carbohydrates 83–87%

TABLE 2. Specifications for soluble spice and herb flavourings

Name	Total extractives on carrier or in solution %	Nonvolatile ether extractives % of total extractives	Essential oil % vol./wt.	Odour	Taste	Remarks
Allspice (Pimento berry)	4·5	40 max.	60 min	Reminiscent of mixture of cloves, nutmeg and cinnamon	Clovelike, pungent, astringent, slightly bitter	
Basil	2	60 max.	40 min	Sweetish, fragrant and strongly suggestive of anise	Warm and somewhat pungent	
Caraway	5	40 max.	60 min	Agreeable, spicy	Warm, pleasant, slightly sharp with sweet fruity undertone	
Cardamom	4	50 max.	50 min	Pleasant, aromatic, cineole-like	Camphorous, followed by a cineole-like taste	
Celery	3	90 max.	10 min	Characteristic celery odour	Characteristic celery taste, warm and slightly bitter	
Cinnamon	6	50 max.	50 min	Agreeable, aromatic	Sweet, pungent	
Clove	6	30 max.	70 min	Strong, aromatic.	Strong, biting, burning, pungent	
Coriander	3	67 max.	33 min	Pleasant, fragrant, aromatic	Pleasant	

Cumin	3	40 max.	60 min	Strong, aromatic	Warm	
Dillseed	5	40 max.	60 min	Aromatic, faintly resembling caraway but flatter and less agreeable	Warm, slightly sharp, akin to caraway	
Fennel	5	50 max.	50 min.	Aromatic and sweet	Sweet and resembling anise	
Ginger	4	75 max.	25 min	Agreeable, aromatic and slightly pungent, biting	Spicy, sweet, pungent and biting	
Mace	7·5	50 max.	50 min	Fragrant, nutmeg-like	Slight warm, nutmeg-like	
Marjoram	3	60 max.	40 min	Pleasant, aromatic	Warm, slightly sharp, bitterish with a camphorlike taste	
Nutmeg	6	20 max.	80 min	Fragrant, strongly aromatic	Sweet warm and slightly bitter	
Pepper black	4·5	55% piperine min.	15% min	Characteristic, penetrating	Hot, biting, pungent	
Pepper red	5			Sharp and pungent	Hot, sharp, pungent	Pungency rating of 15 000 to 35 000 Scoville units
Sage	5·5	35 max.	65 min	Fragrant, aromatic	Somewhat bitter with a slight camphorous undertone	Addition of propylene glycol is permissible in processing provided it does not exceed 2% of soluble sage flavouring
Thyme	4	50 max.	50 min	Aromatic, fragrant	Warm, slightly pungent	

and taste of the soluble extracts should conform to the odour and taste of the original plant material.

The soluble dry edible carrier can be salt, sucrose, dextrose, or any combination thereof. The extractives from the plant material are the sum of the non-volatile ether extract and volatile oil content.

1. Routine Method of Analysis

The quality control tests described in the Methods of Analysis of the AOAC are:

(a) Alcohol determination (19.095).

(b) The detection of iso-propyl alcohol as solvent (19.097).

(c) Determination of amount of oil (19.098).

(d) Volatile and non-volatile ether extracts (28.099).

2. Specific Methods of Analysis

(a) The detection of the presence of capsicum in ginger extracts (19.102).

(b) Nitrogen in non-volatile ether extracts (for black and white peppers) (28.008) to determine the amount of piperine present.

(c) The U.S. federal specifications on soluble spice flavourings describe the Scoville method for pungency determination used in quality control of red pepper extract.

Scoville method. 1·0 g of the flavouring is weighed accurately and mixed with 50 ml of ethyl alcohol. This mixture is allowed to stand 24 h with occasional shaking. Serial dilutions are prepared of the clear supernatant liquid with a 5% solution of sugar in distilled water. 5 ml of the diluted solution are swallowed, and the presence or absence of a distinct sensation of pungency in the throat or mouth is noted. The value in terms of the greatest dilution at which such a sensation is detected is noted. Thus, if 1 ml of the clear supernatant extract is diluted to 140 ml with 5% sugar solution and this was the dilution which produced a barely perceptible sensation of pungency, this would have a Scoville value of $50 \times 140 = 1\,000$. It is desirable to approach unknown samples from the dilute side.

The specifications in Table 2 for soluble spice flavourings have been published by the agencies of the U.S. federal government and should serve as criteria for quality control on this type material.

3. ESSENTIAL OILS

A. Unprocessed

Essential oils are volatile oils derived from plants and usually have the odour and flavour of the plant. They are obtained by various processes such as distillation, steam distillation, extraction, expression, adsorption, enfleurage and similar means. These oils are rarely produced by the user of flavouring materials. Many of the essential oils originate in parts of the world remote from the centres of their use.

Essential oils consist, generally speaking, of: (a) Compounds of the general formula $(C_5H_8)n$ where n can be 2 or 3. When n = 2, the various compounds are called terpenes, and when n = 3, they are known as sesquiterpenes. These compounds possess the characteristics of relative insolubility in dilute alcohol and are of little flavour value. They are, on the other hand, excellent solvents for

(a) oxygenated compounds carrying the odour and taste of the oil. Many classes of chemicals are represented, the most important ones being

Alcohols: such as menthol found in peppermint oil, linalool in bergamot oil, geraniol in rose oil.

Phenols: such as eugenol found in clove oil and thymol in thyme oil.

Aldehydes: such as citral found in lemon oil, and benzaldehyde in bitter almond oil.

Esters: such as linalyl acetate in lavender and bergamot oil and menthyl acetate in peppermint oil.

Ketones: such as carvone in caraway oil.

Ethers: such as anethole in anise oil and safrole in sassafras oil.

(b) Waxes and resinous materials of low solubility and low flavour value.

The quantities of the compounds present in essential oils determine, to a great extent, the value and quality of the oil. The most important among the essential oils, as far as the flavour industry is concerned, are the citrus oils, with lemon and orange oils at the head of the list, also anise and cinnamon oils, peppermint and spearmint oils, and to a lesser degree, nutmeg, clove and bitter almond oils.

The best of the citrus oils, with the exception of lime oil, are obtained by expression of the peels. The raw oil obtained is then freed from pectinous matter and water by, for instance, filtration or centrifugation. Since expression releases only part of the oil from the peels, they are then subjected to thorough distillation which yields second quality oils. These are cheaper than the expressed oils and are therefore sometimes used by unscrupulous producers to adulterate good quality oils. Terpenes obtained as by-products of the concentration of essential oils are also used as adulterants.

Organoleptic qualities of essential oils should always be the paramount preoccupation of the flavour control laboratory. Odour of the oil and its taste in diluted sugar syrup should be evaluated as a standard procedure. A new, fresh sample should always be compared to a vault sample, regularly replaced from acceptable batches, usually kept under refrigeration, and normal variances found in nature should be taken into consideration.

10*

TABLE 3. Typical physical standards of some essential oils

Name	Specific gravity 25/25	Ref. index n_D^{20}	Rotation degrees	Solubility in alcohol	Remarks
Allspice (Pimento)	1·018–1·048	1·5270–1·5400	0– –4	2 vol. 70%	As much as 80% eugenol
Angelica root	0·850–0·930	1·4735–1·4870	0– +46	1 vol. 90%	
Angelica seed	0·853–0·876	1·4800–1·4880	+4– +16	4 vol. 90%	
Anise Star U.S.P.	0·978–0·988	1·553–1·560	1– –2	3–5 vol. 90%	Solidifying point 15–18°C
Aniseed	0·975–0·990	1·555–1·559	0– –2		Solidifying point 16–19°C
Bergamot	0·875–0·880	1·4650–1·4675	+8– +24	1 vol. 95%	Esters as linalyl acetate 34–42%
Bitter almond FFPA	1·040–1·050	1·5410–1·5442	0– +0·25″	2 vol. 70%	Detection of halogens shows addition of benzalde-hyde
Caraway	0·900–0·910	1·4840–1·4880	+70– +80	8 vol. 80%	Carvone 50–60%
Cardamom	0·917–0·947	1·4630–1·4660	+22– +44	5 vol. 70%	
Cassia	1·055–1·072	1·600–1·607	–1– +7	2 vol. 80%	As much as 85% cinnamaldehyde
Cinnamon bark (Ceylon)	1·010–1·030	1·5730–1·5910	0– –2	3 vol. 70%	55–78% cinnamaldehyde
Cinnamon leaf (Ceylon)	1·030–1·050	1·5290–1·5370	+1– –2	1·5 vol. 70%	80–88% eugenol
Cinnamon leaf (Seychelles)	1·040–1·060	1·5330–1·5400	0– –2	1 vol. 70%	87–96% eugenol

Oil	Specific gravity	Refractive index	Optical rotation	Solubility	Requirements
Clove U.S.P.	1·038–1·060	1·527–1·535	0– –1·30"	2 vol. 70%	75–95% eugenol
Coriander U.S.P.	0·863–0·875	1·462–1·472	+8– +15	3 vol. 70%	45–65% coriandrol
Dill seed	0·890–0·915	1·483–1·490	+70– +82	2 vol. 80%	42–60% carvone
Fennel U.S.P.	0·953–0·973	1·528–1·538	+12– +24	1 vol. 90%	Congealing point +3–+10°C. 50–60% anethole
Ginger	0·871–0·882	1·488–1·494	–28– –45		
Grapefruit exp. Fla.	0·848–0·856	1·475–1·478	+91– +96		Evaporation residue 5–10% CD value not less than 0·58 at 319 μ (50 mg/100 ml alcohol)
Juniper berry	0·854–0·879	1·474–1·484	0– –15	4 vol. 95%	
Lavender French	0·875–0·888	1·459–1·470	–3– –10	4 vol. 70%	25–45% esters as linalyl acetate
Lavender English	0·875–0·902	1·462–1·471	–4– –10	4 vol. 70%	6–15% esters as linalyl acetate
Lemon oil Cal. U.S.P. expressed	0·849–0·855	1·4738–1·4755	+57– +65·6	3 vol. 95%	Aldehyde as citral 2·2–3·8%. CD value not less than 0·20 (315 μ±2) 250 mg/100 ml alcohol. Rotation of 1st 5 ml distilled (see foreign oils test) not more than 6° less than original oil. Ref. index of this not less than 0·0010 and not more than 0·0027 lower than that of original oil
Lemon oil Italian	0·854–0·862	1·474–1·476	+54– +66	3 vol. 95%	Aldehyde as citral 3–5·5% CD value not less than 0·49 (315 μ±2) 250 mg/100 ml alcohol
Lime expressed	0·872–0·881	1·482–1·486	+35– +41	0·5 vol. 95%	Aldehyde 4·5–8·5% as citral CD value not less than 0·45 (315 μ±2) 20 mg/100 ml alcohol evaporation residue 10–14·5%

TABLE 3. Typical physical standards of some essential oils—contd.

Name	Specific gravity 25/25	Ref. index n_D^{20}	Rotation degrees	Solubility in alcohol	Remarks
Lime distilled	0·855–0·863	1·4745–1·4770	+34– +47	5 vol. 90%	5–2·5 aldehyde as citral
Neroli	0·870–0·885	1·468–1·477	0– +55	3 vol. 80%	Esters as linalyl acetate 7–20%
Orange, bitter	0·845–0·851	1·4725–1·4755	+88– +98	4 vol. 95%	Evaporation residue 2–5% Aldehyde content 0·5–1% as decylaldehyde CD value not less than 0·63 (320 μ±2) 100 mg/ 100 ml alcohol
Orange, sweet U.S.P. expressed	0·842–0·846	1·4723–1·4737	+94– +95	1·5 vol. 95%	Aldehyde as decylaldehyde 1·2–2·5% CD value not less than 0·13 for California oil and not less than 0·24 for Florida oil (325–330 μ) 250 mg/ 100 ml 3 ml evaporated leave at least 43 mg residue Rotation of first 5 ml distilled (see foreign oils test) does not vary more than 2° from original oil. Re-fractive index of this not less than 0·0008 and not more than 0·0015 lower than that of original oil
Orange mandarin expressed	0·854–0·860	1·474–1·478	+67– +75	1·5 vol. 95%	CD value not less than 0·83 (323–343 μ) 250 mg/100 ml alcohol
Origanum Spanish	0·935–0·960	1·502–1·508	−2– +3	2 vol. 70%	60–75% phenols.
Peppermint English	0·900–0·912	1·460–1·466	−23– −33	4 vol. 70%	55–70% menthol 3–15% esters as menthyl acetate

Peppermint U.S.A.	0·900–0·920	1·459–1·465	−18– −35	4 vol. 70%	50–62% menthol 6–10% esters as menthyl acetate
Peppermint U.S.A. Rect. U.S.P.	0·896–0·908	1·459–1·465	−18– −32	3 vol. 70%	More than 5% esters as menthyl acetate. More than 50% menthol free and as esters
Spearmint	0·917–0·934	1·4840–1·4910	−48– −59	1 vol. 80%	At least 50% carvone
Tangerine expressed	0·844–0·854	1·4731–1·4752	−88– +96		CD value not less than 0·46 (325 μ—2) 250 mg/100 ml alcohol aldehyde 0·8 to 1·9 as decylaldehyde Evaporation residue 2·3–5·8%
Thyme	0·910–0·935	1·4950–1·5050	0– −3	2 vol. 80%	20–40% phenols as thymol

Essential oils are usually costly substances and, therefore, subject to adulteration. The simplest tests for quality control are those based on the properties of the standard, genuine oils and should serve as guides for the acceptance or rejection of these flavouring materials.

1. Routine Methods of Analysis

(a) Specific gravity is determined with a pycnometer. The specific gravity may vary but slightly from standards. Its measure is of great value because the terpenes sometimes used to adulterate essential oils have a lower specific gravity than the oil. A low reading should arouse suspicion.

(b) Refractive index is obtained with any standard instrument. The readings are usually made at 20°C. Here again, a low reading may point to a high terpene content.

(c) Optical rotation is determined on any standard instrument, using a 50 mm tube and sodium light. The results are given in angular degrees on 100 mm basis. A high positive rotation generally denotes a high terpene content.

(d) Solubility in alcohol of various concentrations.

2. Specific Methods of Analysis for Citrus Oils

(a) Spectrophotometric absorbance characteristics. The addition of distilled oil, terpenes, or so-called washed oils to cold pressed oils can be detected by spectrophotometry in the ultraviolet range.[9]

Method

Place a known amount of oil, accurately weighed, in a 100 ml volumetric flask; add alcohol to volume, and mix. Determine absorbance of this solution in the UV region from 260 to 400 nm with a suitable recording or manual spectrophotometer, against alcohol in matched silica cells of 1.00 cm or known thickness. If a manual instrument is used, read absorbances at 5 nm intervals from 260 to 315 nm, at 3 nm intervals from 315 to 336 nm and at 10 nm intervals from 340 to 400 nm. At points of maximum or minimum absorbance, read absorbances at 1 nm intervals. From these data, plot the absorbances as ordinates against wave length and draw a smooth curve.

Draw a straight (base) line (AB), tangent to the curve, either plotted or recorded, at the point of minimum absorbance and at the inflection point where the curve levels off. Drop a vertical line (CD) from the absorption peak to the base line. Subtract the absorbance at intersection of line CD with line AB from the peak absorbance to obtain the CD value. Correct this value to exact amounts oil/100 ml solution and to 1·00 cm thickness.

The CD value varies according to oils, but is specific for each of them. (See Table 3).

(b) Residue after steam distillation (AOAC 19.074).

(c) Total aldehydes (AOAC 19.076, 78, 80, 82).

(d) Esters determination (AOAC 19.084).

(e) Pinene detection (AOAC 19.087).

(f) Foreign oils. Place 50 ml of orange or lemon oil C.P. in a 4 bulb Ladenburg flask (lower bulb 6 cm in diameter, smaller ones 3·5 and 2·5 cm respectively in diameter; distance from the bottom of the flask to side arm 0·20 cm). Distil the oil at a rate of one drop per second until distillate measures 5 ml. Measure optical rotation and refractive index of distillate. (See Table 4.)

(g) Detection of washed citrus oil in orange oil CP. Evaporate 3 ml orange oil in a tared 40 × 80 mm glass dish on steam bath for 5 h. Continue heating for 2 hr. Cool in desiccator and weigh. Not less than 45 mg of residue should remain after evaporation. (USP XVI).

(h) Determination of peroxides in citrus oils. A variation of Nozaki's[10] method for the determination of organic peroxides has been described by Flores and Morse.[11] A mixture 1:1 by volume of acetic anydride and chloroform and sodium iodide are added to orange oil; water and an emulsifying agent are added, and the liberated iodine is titrated with sodium thiosulfate using starch as an indicator. From this work, it is felt that the critical peroxide values are about 20 millimoles per kg of oil. It also proves that a low peroxide value in a citrus oil is an added asset to its quality.

3. Specific Methods of Analysis for Anise, Fennel and Rose Oils

(a) The congealing point is determined by immersing a tube containing a sample of the oil in a cooling bath at 10°C. When the oil begins to solidify, the tube is removed and placed in a bath at 14°C. The temperature of the oil rises and then falls. The maximum point reached is the congealing point. (For fennel oil, the temperature has to be lowered to 0°C by a mixture of salt and ice.)

(b) The melting point is determined by placing the congealed oil contained in a tube in a water bath at a temperature approaching that at which the oil should melt and increasing the temperature slowly. The temperature is read off when the oil just melts.

4. Specific Method of Analysis for Peppermint Oil

(a) Identification. Mix 3 drops peppermint oil with 5 ml HNO_3 in glacial acetic acid (1 in 300) and place container in boiling water. Within 5 min, the mixture develops a blue colour which deepens on continued heating and shows copper coloured fluorescence, then fades leaving a golden yellow solution. This reaction is characteristic of peppermint oils.

TABLE 4. Physical constants of most common deterpenated oils

Name	Approx. conc.	Specific gravity 25/25	Rotation degrees	Solubility in alcohol	Remarks
Angelica	20	0·950	−30	1·4 vol. 80%	
Aniseed	1·5–2	0·970–0·980		10 vol. 80%	
Bergamot	2·5–3	0·883–0·890	−7– −10	2 vol. 70%	Esters as linalyl acetate 50%–60%
Caraway	2	0·960–0·965	+50– +60	1·5 vol. 70%	
Cassia	1·5–2	1·05–1·06		2 vol. 70%	
Cinnamon	1·5–2			1·5 vol. 70%	
Clove	1·5			1·5 vol. 70%	
Grapefruit		1·03–1·04	−2– +1		Aldyhydes as nonylaldehyde about 17%
Lemon	20	0·895–0·899	−5– −9	1·5 vol. 80%	Aldehydes as citral—35–45% ref. index 1·477–1·484
Lime distilled	10–15	0·920–0·930	−2– +1	35 vol. 70%	
Mandarin	55–65	0·92–0·96	+10– +22	1·5 vol. 80%	
Orange	30–45	0·882–0·897	0– +30	1·5 vol. 80%	Aldehydes as decyl aldehyde about 20–25%

5. Gas Liquid Chromatography

The supplementation by gas liquid chromatography (GLC) of traditional methods for quality control of essential oils has greatly increased the scope and capabilities of the flavour control laboratory.

Most of the common and many exotic essential oils have been examined by GLC. Published data include both "finger-print" charts and qualitative and quantitative information on the constituents of the oils. The biannual reviews in "Analytical Chemistry" by Guenther et al.[12] provide a convenient source of collected short abstracts of articles on GLC analysis of essential oils. When read from the first part published in 1949 to the most recent issue these reviews show the dramatic increase in the use of GLC for all phases of essential oil work. The Gas Chromatography Abstracts edited by Knapman[13] cover all phases of gas chromatography including analytical control and specific applications to essential oils and related products. Teisseire[14] gives an account of the application of GLC techniques to the examination of essential oils and other materials of interest to the perfumer and flavourer. He includes an extensive bibliography.

Smith and Levi[15] used GLC effectively to examine a large number of samples of Mentha piperita and Mentha arvensis oils. The qualitative and quantitative data obtained, when ingeniously grouped into a series of component ratios, allowed the authors to classify the oils systematically as to type and geographical origin. They also were able to evaluate processes for oil production, to recognize the biochemical relationships governing the formation of essential oils in the plant and to detect even subtle adulterations.

Theile et al.[16] pinpointed fortification and adulteration of bergamot oil through the use of GLC in conjunction with other physical and chemical methods. Montes[17] used GLC to determine the presence of 1% or more added lemongrass citral in lemon oil. Ikeda et al.[18] conclusively demonstrated the formation of p-cymene from γ-terpinene during the deterioration of lemon oil by the use of GLC.

So far, GLC techniques have not been found to be the full equal of the nose in sensitivity to many specific materials or in discriminating between mixtures varying only slightly in trace components. However, as methods and equipment are improved the ability to correlate GLC data directly with organoleptic findings should increase. For instance, the development of the electron capture detector with its specific sensitivity to conjugated carbonyls, nitro compounds, halogenated compounds and some sulphur compounds, opens a new order of magnitude in the GLC sensitivity range.

The use of GLC in the examination of essential oils will assist the control chemist to:

1. Establish the identity and/or origin of the oil.
2. Detect adulteration.

3. Detect composition changes due to environmental effects.
4. Maintain uniformity of raw materials and finished products.
5. Critically examine other methods of analysis.
6. Investigate causes of odour and/or flavour differences and changes in raw material or product.

It is through the intelligent interpretation of the results obtained by the various methods of analyses the comparison against known standards, the relationships between the various results, and the all-important taste and odour evaluations that one can decide whether a suspect sample is adulterated, fraudulent, or of poor quality.

B. Concentrated Essential Oils

Among the hundreds of essential oils used in the flavouring industry, only a small number are used as such, or in simple mixtures, without prior processing, to flavour the many foods sold to the consumer. The processing might consist of concentrating, extracting, solubilizing, or other processes which alter drastically the appearance and characteristics of the oil.

Terpenes present in oils expressed from peels are far less soluble in dilute alcohol than the oxygenated compounds. They also have a tendency to oxidize readily in contact with air, being unsaturated hydrocarbons. This oxidation results in the development of unpleasant odours and tastes. The terpenes usually have only a slight aromatic, but not specific odour, and therefore their total presence contributes very little to the flavour of an oil. Their partial or total removal is indicated when the oils are to be used in consumer goods apt to be stored for a long time. An added advantage is the smaller space needed to keep large stocks. The concentrated oils should also be used when high solubility in dilute alcohol is required.

The manufacture of concentrated and terpeneless oils is a matter of considerable difficulty. When heat is carelessly applied to a delicate oil, the fine aroma may be spoiled. It is generally recognized that it is inadvisable to carry a concentration too far, the oxygenated constituents being particularly susceptible to high temperature and to the general conditions involved in the concentration process. The concentration or fold of an essential oil is calculated from the actual yield of the concentrated oil obtained from a known weight of whole oil. The choice of concentration of the oil and the need for the removal of resins and waxes depends on the ultimate use intended. The method used to concentrate the oil would, by the same token, be chosen according to the quality of oil required. Various methods are commonly used to effect partial or total removal of terpenes, sesquiterpenes, waxes and other nonvolatile residues. The principal methods are distillation in vacuum, with or without subsequent steam distillation, alcoholic distillation, solvent extraction, polysolvent extractions, chromatographic separation and combinations of the above processes.

Quality control of the concentrated essential oils is based upon their physical and chemical examination and, of course, organoleptic evaluation. The physical constants should be measured before chemical analysis if desired.

1. Routine Methods of Analysis

(a) Specific gravity gives valuable clues to the amount of terpenes left in the concentrate. The terpenes have generally a specific gravity of 0·84 to 0·86, and the specific gravity of a concentrated oil will vary according to the amount of terpenes remaining. Most terpeneless oils have specific gravities of 0·88 to 0·96.

(b) The determination of the optical rotation also provides excellent information about the extent of the removal of the terpenes. Most very highly concentrated terpeneless oils possess rotations under +5°. Nearly all terpenes have a high positive rotation.

(c) Since the refractive index of terpenes is fairly low, this figure will also help in evaluating the concentration of the oil.

(d) Solubility in dilute alcohol is a very important criterion. The higher the concentration of an oil, the better is its solubility. One has to keep in mind that a concentrated oil will have physical and chemical constants which may vary considerably, depending on the process used and also on the constants of the original oil. A wax- and resin-free essential oil is more soluble than oil containing wax and resin, although both oils may be of the same concentration.

(e) The chemical examination of concentrated oils is an added tool. By careful interpretation of analytical results and combining that information with the physical constants, it is possible to detect adulteration, poor concentration and mislabelling. A very good indication of the genuine nature of a terpeneless lemon oil, for example, is the ratio existing between esters and aldehydes. Jensen[19] has shown that the value of the citral/linalyl acetate ratio is 2·5. If this value is higher, the oil should be suspected of having been adulterated.

The set of tests recommended for quality control of essential oils should also be used on the concentrated oils, but it should be noted that a method which is used for determining small amounts of a constituent in a whole oil may not be suitable for the determination of a large amount of this substance; chemicals which do not interfere when present in small amounts may have an inhibiting action on analytical processes when present in appreciable amounts.

The determination of peroxides by the method described previously is of great value, as is any other method to determine the oxidation potential of oils. To measure the oxidation potential, a known amount of concentrated oil is placed in a clean glass container which is connected to an inverted "U" shaped tube immersed either in water or in a hydroquinone solution. The oil is heated to approximately 60°C for 5–10 h, and the rise of liquid in the inverted "U" tube is measured. The values and permissible maximum rise have to be determined experimentally for each oil and every specific concentration.

Table 4 give constants for highly concentrated oils only as an indication of their order of magnitude. The degree of removal of the terpenes, or the concentration of the essential oils, can be calculated from the relationship between specific gravities and optical rotations of the straight oils and their concentrates.

2. Antioxidants

A word should be added here about the use of antioxidants. The U.S. Food and Drug Administration has permitted the use of a number of antioxidants in essential oils, but has specified the limits at which these antioxidants may be present in finished foods. The manufacturer of concentrated oils has to keep in mind that through his process he runs the risk of concentrating proportionally the amount of antioxidant which was originally present in his oil. It is therefore advisable to process only oils which contain no synthetic or natural antioxidants or, at the most, the amount which when concentrated will not exceed allowed proportions.

C. Essential oil extracts and emulsions

Essential oil extracts and emulsions are generally obtained by dissolving the oil in alcohol or oil, or suspending it in water. These extracts are used by the food manufacturer in preference to the undiluted essential oils or their concentrates because of the ease of handling. The essential oils are generally extremely potent and therefore should be diluted to a practical flavour strength, and this may present difficulties for the flavour user. These extracts may be prepared by dissolving the requisite quantities of oil in strong alcohol or by extracting or shaking the oil out with more dilute alcohol. By the use of this last process, two layers are formed, the top one being the less soluble terpenes, the bottom one containing most of the flavourful components of the oil in alcohol and water. Some extracts are also made by dissolving essential oils in vegetable oil, such as cottonseed or corn oil. Emulsions are generally used because they are less expensive than the alcoholic extract, their principal component being water, and they are ideally suited for use in the beverage industry. An emulsifying agent has to be used in addition to water. Gum arabic or acacia, gum tragacanth, algin and alginates and synthetic cellulose derivatives are most commonly used for this purpose.

The method used to prepare emulsions yielding clear beverages when diluted with acidified sugar syrup and still or carbonated water is as follows. Highly soluble oils, such as concentrated or terpeneless dewaxed oils usually solubilized by the addition of solubilizing agents, are mixed with the emulsifying agent, sometimes sugar syrup, glycerine, or propylene glycol, mixed thoroughly with water and the blend is passed through a homogenizer. The addition of colour is optional. When non-concentrated dewaxed oils are used, the low solubility of the terpenes and the larger amount to be used causes clouding in the finished drink. It is evident that clear beverages can also be obtained using the more expensive terpeneless extracts obtained by shaking out essential oils with dilute alcohol and subsequently separating the terpenes forming the upper layer.

The cloud-yielding flavours are emulsions containing the weaker and less soluble oils. The specific gravity of these oils, being lower than the specific gravity of the finished product, has to be adjusted. Otherwise, they would separate rapidly, and either drop to the bottom of the container if heavier than the liquid in which they are suspended, or form rings at the top of it if lighter. The adjustment consists in equalizing the specific gravities of the oil and water phases. In the United States, this is often done by the use of brominated vegetable oils, which have such high specific gravities that the amounts needed are small. They are almost tasteless and odourless and relatively inexpensive. Their specific gravities generally vary from 1·23 to 1·34 at 25°C for the more common brands on the market.

The required amount of brominated oil to be used is calculated from the specific gravity of the essential oil or mixture of essential oils, the specific gravity of the finished beverage, and the specific gravity of the grade of brominated oil used. It is then added to the oil phase. Glycerine, propylene glycol, fruit juices, if necessary, and then water are added. The mix is thoroughly emulsified, care being taken not to ruin the quality of the oil phase by overheating during the process. However, the use of brominated vegetable oil is prohibited in a number of countries. The manufacturer then has to rely on fruit cellulosic material or natural waxes to obtain a cloud in combination with oils and juices. These emulsions or suspensions are usually less stable.

1. Routine Methods of Analysis

(a) Specific gravity, which is measured by usual methods.

(b) The determination of proportion of volatile oil present is obviously of primary importance. The procedure is different for clear extracts and for emulsions.

(1) *Clear alcoholic extracts.* An official AOAC (19.056) method prescribes the reading in degrees sugar of a polarized sample and dividing the result by 3·2 for lemon extract and 5·2 for orange extract. In the absence of other optically active substances, the result of the division gives the percentage by volume of the oil present. If cane sugar is present, its percentage is determined independently, and the result is corrected accordingly. A simpler method has been proposed. It consists in pipetting 10 ml or 5 ml of sample of the extract into a Babcock milk test bottle; adding 0·5 ml of a mixture of equal parts of U.S.P. mineral oil and water-free kerosene with 1 ml of HCl (1 + 1), and then filling to the shoulder with a saturated salt solution; shaking the bottle, and bringing the column of oil within the graduated area in the neck of the bottle by the addition of more salt solution. The bottle is then centrifuged at high speed, and the volume of oil separated is read. The reading is from the extreme bottom of the lower meniscus to the extreme top of the upper meniscus except for allspice, peppermint and pimento when it is from the bottom of the lower meniscus to the bottom of the upper meniscus. The percentage of oil is obtained after subtracting 2·5 divisions and multiplying the remainder by 2, where a 10 ml sample is used, and by 4, if 5 ml are used.

(2) *Clear oil base extracts.* Lemon, orange and lime oils are removed from an oil base extract by steam distillation. After completion, the volume of recovered oil is read, and the percentage by volume is calculated by dividing the reading by 0·9 for lemon oil in cottonseed or corn oil, by 0·95 for orange oil, and by 0·78 for distilled and expressed lime oils in these oils. Where the menstruum is mineral oil, 0·3 ml is substracted from the reading before the calculation.

(3) *Emulsions.* The recovery of essential oils from emulsions is also accomplished by steam distillation, using an oil separator trap, connected to a round bottom flask and equipped with a tight-fitting finger condenser having a projection at the bottom to facilitate the return of oil to the trap. The sample of emulsion is mixed with about 200 ml water (sample size to contain about 2 ml of oil) and carefully boiled for at least 1 h. The separated oil is allowed to cool in the trap. The volume is read from the bottom of the lower meniscus to the highest point of the upper meniscus.

(c) Variations of the above listed methods for specific application to almond, cassia, cinnamon, clove, ginger, peppermint, spearmint and wintergreen oil extracts, as well as specific tests, such as detection of benzaldehyde, benzoic acid, hydrocyanic acid and nitrobenzine in almond extract, and capsicum in ginger extract, are thoroughly described in AOAC (19.088 to 19.108).

(d) The percentage of alcohol in extracts consisting of oil, alcohol and water is calculated from the oil content and the specific gravity. (AOAC 19.046).

(e) Tests for detection of methanol and isopropyl alcohol are also recommended. (AOAC 19.047–19.048).

(f) The size of the oil droplets suspended in an emulsion is an important feature contributing to its stability. A very finely and regularly divided oil phase is much to be preferred, and a microscopic examination of an emulsion is therefore quite valuable.

D. Entrapped Essential Oils

The last fifteen years have witnessed the development of a large number of entrapped, encapsulated, or sealed flavours. This was triggered by the tremendous increase in the number of powdered, dehydrated, prepared and prepackaged foods. These products are purchased by consumers who add only liquid ingredients at the time of use. The liquid may be water, as in the case of drink powders, water puddings, gelatin dessert powders, drugs and over-the-counter pharmaceuticals and powdered soups, or milk for baked goods, instant puddings, etc. The number of applications for powdered, entrapped flavours is increasing at a fast rate. Before the wide use of these flavouring materials, the food industry was limited to the use of flavours of low volatility. Essential oils were mixed as such or in concentrated form directly with the powder or carrier, with particularly poor results. They lost their light, volatile esters and aldehydes, and the citrus oils oxidized and developed obnoxious terpenes. These drawbacks are partially overcome by sealing these oils in natural or synthetic water-soluble colloidal materials.

The process of entrapping, with all its variations, is well known by now. A colloidal suspension of gum, starch, dextrin, gelatin or synthetic colloid, mixtures of sugars, or combinations of any of these, is prepared; a known amount of oil or mixture of oils is added; the suspension is emulsified and dried by one of the conventional methods. The shelf life of the entrapped oils is a function of the quality of the oil entrapped and also of the protection afforded by the coating material to the penetration of oxygen or reaction with components of the mix. Since the coating is water-soluble, it is of the greatest importance that the moisture content of the flavouring material be kept at a practical minimum.

The organoleptic qualities of the entrapped flavours have to be tested on their suspension in water. The only odour noticeable in the powder is due to a small amount of surface oil and is not indicative of the quality of the entrapped oil.

1. Routine Methods of Analysis

(a) Particle size examination. The size of the particles should be compatible with the packaged end product. The danger of stratification during storage should be kept at a minimum.

(b) Moisture content is determined by submitting a known quantity of the flavouring material to a toluene or toluene/benzene distillation and measuring the amount of water recovered.

(c) Determination of amount of oil entrapped by recovery of the internal phase by steam distillation should be performed using the method described for recovery of oil from emulsions. Some of the essential oils cannot be recovered by this method and should then be extracted by an organic solvent. The non-volatile inner phase is separated from the sealing material in water suspension and its amount weighed after evaporation of the solvent. This method will not, of course, yield a truly representative sample of the entrapped oil. It will, however, give a good indication of the proportion of inner phase to colloid, especially if performed routinely on batches of identical material. Any oil recovered by distillation, extraction or separation methods will not be identical with the oil originally entrapped, owing to temperature of treatment, partial solubility in water phase, etc. Therefore, the final and most important quality tests are the organoleptic tests performed in comparison with an accepted vault sample. This should be done either in water, sugar or, possibly, in the end product.

4. Vanilla and its Extracts

Among all the natural products used by the food industry to impart flavour, vanilla is undoubtedly among the most important. In some countries, such as Germany and France, vanilla beans are frequently used by the manufacturers of finished goods, whereas in the United States extracts are preferred.

Vanilla beans are cultivated in Mexico, Java, Malagasy, Guadaloupe, the Comores and Reunion, the Seychelles, Mauritius, Tahiti and a few other minor locations.

The beans are cured after picking, and this process develops the flavour through enzymatic action. The curing processes vary from one geographical location to another, and this, in addition to variations in weather conditions and soils, accounts for the quality differences. However, the Tahitian bean is completely different, being another variety of vanilla called *Vanilla tahitensis Moore,* whereas the beans grown in the other areas are *Vanilla planifolia Andrews.* Only the cured Tahiti bean contains heliotropine in detectable amounts.

After curing, the beans are graded according to their appearance, moisture content, length and thickness, and the appellations given to each classification vary with the country of origin.

A. Classification

1. Mexican Beans

Prime, good to prime, good, fair and ordinary whole beans and cut beans. The prime (superior) are the choicest beans, without blemishes. They are dark in colour and measure not less than 15 cm and not more than 25 cm. The good (buena) are slightly lighter in colour, tougher and harsher, and also usually lower in moisture content.

2. Bourbon Beans (Indian Ocean Production)

Extra, first, seconds, third, fourths and bulk (en vrac). The extra are usually excellent mature beans, having an oily appearance and a dark colour, rather high in moisture. Firsts do not have the nice appearance of the extras, and seconds are harder and drier. Thirds are even drier, with deformities, and are lighter in colour. Fourths are much smaller, still lighter, and rather low in vanillin content. The beans in bulk are very dry and woody, with cut or broken ends.

3. Tahiti Beans

Tahiti beans are labelled as pink, white, yellow or green.

Mexican and Bourbon beans make the best extracts; the Java beans have a somewhat harsher flavour, and the Tahiti beans usually produce a cloudy, resinous extract low in vanillin. Prices vary greatly among the various grades, the differences being greater than the flavouring values would warrant.

The purchaser of vanilla beans should inspect them for mould or the presence of foreign matter, and if he considers purchasing the chopped beans, he should make sure not to buy partially extracted beans. A very low moisture content may be an indication that the merchandise had been stored for a long period of time and/or under unfavourable conditions. This condition may be indicative of a low vanillin content owing to the tendency of this product to sublime. Since vanillin is without doubt the most important, although certainly not the only contributor to the flavour and aroma of extracts, it is important that it be present in amounts characteristic of the beans.

B. Standards of Identity

The Food and Drug Administration in the United States has issued definitions and standards of identity for vanilla extracts and related products such as vanilla sugars and powders. (F. R. Doc. 62–8816.) The term "vanilla bean" is reserved for the properly cured and dried fruit pods of *Vanilla planifolia Andrews* and of *Vanilla tahitensis Moore*. The term "unit weight of vanilla beans" is defined as 13·35 oz or 378·6 g of beans containing not more than 25% moisture. If their moisture content is higher than 25%, the weight has to be adjusted proportionally.

A "vanilla extract" is the solution in aqueous ethyl alcohol of the sapid and odorous principles extracted from vanilla beans. The alcohol content must not be less than 35% by volume and the content of vanilla constituents not less than the total sapid and odorous principles extractable from one unit weight of vanilla beans per U.S. gallon (3785·3 ml) of extract. Concentrated vanilla extracts are solutions in aqueous ethyl alcohol of the total sapid and odorous principles extractable from two or more units by weight of vanilla beans.

Vanilla powders and vanilla sugars are mixtures of ground vanilla beans or vanilla bean extracts containing in each 8 lb (3628·5 g) not less than one unit of vanilla constituents. Vanilla flavouring conforms to all the above definitions with the exception that the ethyl alcohol content is less than 35% by volume.

It is therefore clear that, under these standards and definitions, the addition of vegetable extractives other than those of vanilla and/or chemicals obtained synthetically or extracted from natural products is adulteration under the meaning of the law in the United States. It is said that the adulteration and misbranding of vanilla extracts has reached great proportions owing to the high price of vanilla beans, the low cost of synthetics and other vegetable materials, and the fact that the world supply of beans cannot normally fill the demand. The primary concern for the control chemist, besides the flavour value of vanilla products, should be their authenticity.

The adulteration of vanilla extracts may consist in the partial or total substitution of some other natural extract having a flavour resembling or compatible with that of vanilla, or in the use of entirely factitious mixtures which resemble in appearance, taste and odour the genuine extract. These mixtures include dilute alcoholic solutions of vanillin, coumarin or other synthetic chemicals—sometimes with the addition of a fruit juice, such as prune, to give some body to the mixture and caramel for colour. Weak tinctures, obtained by re-extraction of spent beans, are many times the basis for adulterated extracts. These are usually enhanced by St. John's bread (locust bean) extract, liquorice, cascara or many other natural products and chemical additives.

Methods for the detection of adulteration have been developed in the United States and in Europe. These methods, which include detection of foreign botanicals and of flavour additives, make the detection of any type of misbranding or adulteration possible when their results are interpreted judiciously and used in conjunction with the classical methods of analysis.

1. Foreign Plant Material

The detection of foreign plant material is based on paper chromatographic methods which consist in separating various constituents of vanilla beans by the action of specific solvents and then observing the resulting chromatograms under UV light. If the fluorescent patterns vary from characteristic patterns obtained from known, genuine extracts, the authenticity of the extract should be questioned because other plant materials also form their characteristic patterns and do not in any way resemble those obtained from genuine vanilla extract. Thus, the observation of complicated chromatograms permits identification of materials of botanical origin. In addition, the intensity of the fluorescence is proportional to the concentration so that the relative amounts of vegetable additives can be evaluated. The relative intensities of the vanillin spot and other spots in the fluorescent patterns might indicate, to an experienced operator, whether the amount of vanillin is exceptionally high, and if so this would shed doubt on the authenticity of the extract. Since different systems of solvents produce different fluorescence patterns, a number of solvent systems have been recommended. Stahl[20] has shown that the use of two-dimensional paper chromatography with various solvent systems permits better definition of the fluorescent patterns and the detection of foreign botanicals in a concentration as low as 10% of the amount of vanilla extractives present.

It is noteworthy that authentic vanilla extracts prepared either from Mexican or Bourbon cured beans give chromatographic patterns, whether one-dimensional or two-dimensional, which vary only in minor details, no matter which system of solvent is used. The pattern obtained using Tahiti bean extracts is different from the others when developed by isobutanol-acetic acid solvent[21] and can thus be distinguished.

If an extract is chromatographed in two- or three-solvent systems, by one- and two-dimensional methods, and conforms to the patterns of authentic extracts, it is fair to draw the conclusion that no vegetable extractives other than those of vanilla are present. Propylene glycol, sugar and glycerine, whose use is permitted, may interfere in the development of the patterns, and it is best to extract the flavour with chloroform or a chloroform-amine mixture and to spot this rather than the original liquid.

2. Chemical Additives

Many synthetics are used to intensify the flavour of weak extracts. Vanillin is, of course, the most common, being present naturally in the extracts, but others, such as coumarin (banned in the U.S. and in many other countries), heliotropine, and ethyl vanillin have been used.

The identification of these chemical additives in extracts has been the subject of thorough research. Stoll and Bouteville[22] have shown that para-hydroxybenzaldehyde is always present in natural vanilla extracts and that the relation between the amount of vanillin and that of para-oxybenzaldehyde is rather constant. It is therefore clear that a method permitting excellent separation and identification would be a great asset in determining whether synthetic vanillin has been added to an extract.

Such a method was published by Horst and McGlumphy in 1962.[23] It describes in detail a chromatographic procedure for the separation and identification of para-oxybenzaldehyde, vanitrope, coumarin, ethyl vanillin, anisaldehyde, vanitrope, coumarin, ethyl vanillin, anisaldehyde, maltol, heliotropine, vanillin and methyl vanillin.

C. Methods of Control Analysis

1. Specific gravity at 20/20 with pycnometer. (AOAC 19.001.)

2. Alcohol content by distillation, the sample being measured at $15.56°C$ in a pycnometer calibrated at that temperature. (AOAC 19.002.)

3. Percentage of glycerine (AOAC 19.003).

4. Percentage of propylene glycol (AOAC 19.004).

5. Percentage of vanillin is determined either by a gravimetric method[24] or by the official photometric method. (AOAC 19.008.)

6. Lead number (Wichmann) is determined by the official method (AOAC 19.021).

7. Total solids (AOAC 19.023).

8. Ash (AOAC 19.024).

9. Vanilla resins (AOAC 19.026). An additional qualitative semi-official test was published in the Journal of the AOAC in 1960 by Fitelson.[25]

10. Colour solubility in amyl alcohol (AOAC 19.030) is a valuable indicator. The natural colouring matter of vanilla beans is rather soluble in acid amyl alcohol, whereas caramel colour is almost completely insoluble. In genuine extracts, the proportion of insoluble colour rarely exceeds 35% and is generally below 25%.

11. Besides total solids and total ash, the water-soluble and water-insoluble ash should be determined (AOAC 29.015) in a thorough control.

12. Acidity of extract is determined by diluting 10 ml of the extract to 200 ml and titrating with 0.1 N of alkali using phenolphthalein as indicator.

13. Foreign plant material by:
one-and two-dimensional paper chromatographic method described in detail in the AOAC (19.031 and following).

14. Chemical additives are detected by the chromatographic method.[23]

15. The addition of acidic material to vanilla extract in order to increase the lead number can be detected by a paper chromatographic method used to separate organic acids in the extracts.[26, 27, 28]

The choice of the number of tests to be performed should be left with the analyst. The information obtained should be sufficient to make a judgment concerning the quality of the extract analyzed.

The following limiting values have been suggested for genuine vanilla extract:

Vanillin: 0.10–0·35 gm in 100 ml (0·19 average)

Neutral lead number: 0·40–0·80 (0·55 average)

Acidity: not less than 28 ml 0·1 N alkali per 100 ml

Total ash: 0·20–0·43 gm in 100 ml

Water soluble ash: 0·17–0·35 gm in 100 ml

Water insoluble ash: 0·03–0·08 gm in 100 ml

Alkalinity of water soluble ash: 21–40 ml 0·1 N acid per 100 ml

Alkalinity of water insoluble ash: 7–18 ml 0·1 N acid per 100 ml

Colour insoluble in amyl alcohol: less than 35%, usually below 25%

Resins: 0·09 to 0·12 gm per 100 ml

5. FRUITS AND THEIR EXTRACTS

The food manufacturer who utilizes fruits for their flavouring properties and not to merchandise fruit products such as jams, jellies or preserves, prefers using extracts or concentrated juices rather than the fruits themselves, be they whole, comminuted, crushed or pureed. The insoluble fibrous, cellulosic materials present in fruits, their low flavouring power, and the problems encountered in keeping and storing fresh or frozen foods are all reasons for the preference for extracts which are quite convenient to use. These extracts may be concentrated juices, distillates, powdered juices, etc.

The aromatic fractions of fruits are complex mixtures of organic volatile materials such as alcohols, esters, ketones, aldehydes, acids, which are present in very small proportions but, nevertheless, give each fruit its characteristic aroma. This flavour is formed only when the fruit reaches its maturity through complex mechanisms still generally unknown to chemists. Enzymatic action on non-volatile constituents seems to be a factor in the development of aromas, specific for each species and quality of fruit.

The flavour manufacturer should therefore extract and concentrate fruits at the time when they have reached full ripeness. Fruits are purchased at the time of the harvest, and processing is scheduled according to the facilities and equipment available. If the amount of fruit is greater than the quantities that can be processed, the excess has to be stored, deep frozen, until processing time.

Fruits are usually first crushed and pressed. The juice is clarified either by filtration or centrifugation and then concentrated. The most important volatile aromatic constituents should be recovered from the juice and returned to the concentrated extract. Many methods are used to perform this concentration, including distillation, vacuum distillation and lyophilization. The removal of water can also be total, and solid, usually powdered, products are obtained. Strashun and Talburt[29] dehydrated juices in a puffed form and then added back volatile flavourings. Sinnamon et al.[30] describe a method whereby apple juice concentrate was prepared by drying in a vacuum tray dryer. Many other methods are utilized, such as continuous foam-mat drying, spray drying, etc. The quality of the concentrate is a function of the quality of the raw material, the care taken during processing, and the method used. Damage to the fine flavour occurs if the amount of heat applied is high, and this is usually evidenced by colour and flavour changes in the juices stripped of their essence as well as in their concentrates. The point where such changes are obvious is defined by both time and temperature. High temperature and very short time of exposure may be less critical than a lower temperature exposure for a long time. If high temperature contact is lengthy, both the stripped juice and the essence might have a cooked, scorched taste. It is therefore important to use extremely rapid flash evaporation for the stripping and low temperatures, preferably under vacuum, for the concentration of the stripped juice.

After the concentration process, the juice is depectinized. Pectins are those bodies in fruit juices which go into colloidal suspension in water and are derived from pectose through hydrolysis. They gell under certain conditions, denature on ageing and precipitate after standing in liquid products and in the presence of alcohol and certain metallic salts. The use of non-depectinized concentrates is therefore contraindicated in liqueurs, cordials and non-alcoholic beverages. This depectinization may be performed by removing the alcohol or salt-precipitated pectins by filtration or centrifugation or by hydrolyzing the pectins through the action of enzymes.

The concentrates should be kept frozen unless their soluble solids content is sufficiently high (65–68° Brix) to prevent fermentation or other degradation, or are preserved by the addition of at least 12% alcohol or 25% propylene glycol.

A fruit extract, theoretically, if processed under ideal conditions, would possess a flavour equal in strength and quality to that of the original fruit. This is not the case in reality. Fruit flavours are elusive and delicate, and 25 to 50 lb of fruit are usually needed to produce one U.S. gallon of flavouring. Many fruits, and consequently their extracts, are in short supply and therefore too high in price for use in low cost foods. Also, their quality, taste, solid content, sweetness and flavour vary more widely than in most other categories of natural products. Enhancers are added to overcome all the above listed short-comings, and this is performed through the addition of cheaper and more powerful vegetable extractives, essential oils, manufactured, synthetic flavours, or combinations of these.

Quality control should determine whether fruit products are genuinely or deceptively identified. The U.S. Food and Drug Administration has stated that a flavour may be labelled with the "name of a fruit with other natural flavours" provided that at least half the flavour strength is derived from extractive materials whose name appear in the title and not more than half from other natural flavours. If any synthetic or artificial additives are used, the extract becomes an imitation product.

The detection of fortifiers and adulterants to fruit extracts can be helped by judicious use of paper and gas-liquid partition chromatographic methods. Each fruit extract contains combinations of various constituents which can be separated by action of specific mixtures of solvents, and the resulting chromatograms viewed under UV light have characteristic patterns. They are greatly deformed by the addition of extraneous materials.

Another method yielding good results consists in submitting a concentrate to careful steam distillation, followed by extraction of the distillate with a solvent system (ether-isopentane for example) and examination of this extract by gas chromatography. Fractions may be trapped for identification by spectrophotometric methods. A control, genuine extract of identical concentration is analyzed by the same procedure, and the results are compared.

Jorysch[31] has applied the gradient elution technique to investigating organic acids in juices. He has shown that the acid profiles are rather characteristic for each fruit and that the profiles of blends containing 70% black raspberry juice and 30% grape or apple juice were distinctly different from that of either the black raspberry alone or the other two.

Bayer et al.,[32] described a general method for the analysis of natural and synthetic flavours applicable to fruit extracts. A large number of papers concerning gas chromatography of fruit flavours has been listed by Mehlitz and Gierschner.[33]

If great differences in profiles or in the patterns of the chromatograms appear or if chemicals are shown to be present in amounts greater than could logically be contributed by the amount of fruit used in making the concentrate, the authenticity of the extract is at least questionable.

Concentrations are roughly determined by the amount of solids in extracts compared to the solids normally present in juice before concentration. The amounts vary greatly from year to year and also according to locations and

varieties. A few ranges characteristic for one year are given here in percent
solids in single-fold juice:

Apple	11–16%
Blackberry	9·5–12·5%
Grape (Concord)	17–20%
Raspberry (red)	9–11%
Raspberry (black)	9–12%
Strawberry	6–8%

A. Routine Methods of Control Analysis

1. Alcohol content is determined (AOAC 11.004).
2. Total solids (AOAC 29.009).
3. Soluble solids.
4. Ash (AOAC 20.017).
5. Fruit and sugar content (AOAC 20.007).
6. Sucrose and commercial glucose (AOAC 20.068 and 20.071).
7. Pectins. Alcohol-precipitable pectins are tested by adding approximately
90–95 volumes of 40% volume ethyl alcohol to 5–10 volumes of extract and
holding at 40°C for at least 4 h.

B. Specific Methods of Analysis

1. Detection of β-ionone in Fruit Extracts

While the presence of β-ionone has been shown in a number of natural
products, the amounts present in the most commonly used fruits and fruit
extracts are extremely small.

β-ionone is one of the most popular chemicals for the reinforcing or adulteration of various raspberry extracts, and when used in combination with
other chemicals, it can be utilized to reinforce strawberry, currant and other
berry extractives. The presence of relatively large amounts of β-ionone in a
fruit extractive should be considered at least suspicious.

A qualitative and quantitative method based upon a reaction between the
β-ionone and m-nitrobenzhydrazide, the formation of crystals, their identification by a microscopic method, and the process used to identify β-ionone
in a food product is described in AOAC 10th ed., 19.115–118.

2. Detection of ethyl methyl phenyl glycidate (strawberry aldehyde)

This product, used commonly in the adulteration of strawberry extracts,
has never been identified in pure natural products. Its detection in a strawberry extract is possible through saponification to the acid, which is then
distilled to obtain the corresponding hydrotropic aldehyde. This is then
combined with m-nitrobenzhydrazide. This method is applicable only in the
presence of relatively large proportions of the glycidate.

6. SYNTHETIC FLAVOURS

The use of synthetic aromatic chemicals in the manufacture of flavouring materials has greatly increased since the development of new, efficient analytical chemical methods. These new methods helped to identify a large number of chemicals present in natural products. The organic synthesis laboratories of the large flavour manufacturers synthesized and put these at the disposal of the flavour creators.

The flavour creators then mix and blend these raw materials with the aim of reproducing the flavours of naturally-occurring products or creating new combinations which would appeal to the taste of the consumers.

The larger producers of flavours keep a big research staff on their payrolls. The members of this staff, flavour creators, analytical chemists, organic synthesis chemists, etc., join forces to create and manufacture flavours tailor-made for the specific purposes of the food manufacturers.

The products used by the flavour chemists belong to many categories of organic chemicals, such as alcohols, acids, amino-acids, esters, ketones, aldehydes, ethers and hydrocarbons. The composition of a flavour will be dictated to a large extent by the intended end use. The flavour might be a liquid or a solid, entrapped or not. The flavourist must gear its composition to the end requirements. A bakery product, for example, would profit from a low proportion of highly volatile materials, although at the same time, it would be advantageous to create a pleasant kitchen odour at the time of baking.

The flavour creator must also consider the interactions which will occur when all the various chemicals are put in the presence of each other, when they will be heated together and when they are eaten.

Ageing before testing is an important step in the organoleptic evaluation of a flavour. The number of possible combinations is, of course, tremendously high when even as few as ten reactive chemicals are used, and this is greatly increased when, in addition to relatively pure chemicals, essential oils are used. They are themselves, obviously, combinations of a large number of components which individually contribute to the final complex result.

The use of synthetic raw materials in flavours is regulated by law in the various countries. These laws vary in severity and principles from country to country and will not be detailed here.

The quality control of synthetic flavours is handled differently from that of the natural flavours. Whereas the quality control of the latter is, in the main, the responsibility of the user, who must watch for mislabelling, adulteration, or inferior quality merchandise; the synthetic flavours should be thoroughly evaluated by the manufacturer before delivery. A vanilla extract can, after all, be manufactured by any supplier having vanilla beans, alcohol, water and the necessary equipment at his disposal. The created flavours are often the result of many months and sometimes years of effort, experimentation, testing, evaluation by the combined talents of a flavour house and finally testing and evaluation by the purchaser who cannot go on the open market and shop around for such a product. It might take years for a competitor to submit a counter-sample or an acceptable duplication. This quality control of synthetic flavours is performed on the raw materials utilized as well as on the blend.

A. Routine Methods of Analysis on Raw Materials

The flavour creator is more interested in the flavour values of an item than in its purity, its specific gravity and other statistics. This does not mean that quality control should discard all physical and chemical testing and limit itself to the all important organoleptic evaluations. On the contrary, the classic tests described previously should be carefully and routinely applied according to the class in which the chemical belongs.

Aldehydes should be tested for proportion of non-aldehydic compounds present, esters for the amount of acid unreacted, etc. Such tests should be performed to detect gross deficiencies in the purity of raw materials which might be indicative of differences in flavour. Even though purity is not synonymous with flavour value, standards should be maintained within narrow bounds.

1. Chemical tests determining purity (for aldehydes, ketones, acids, esters, alcohols, etc.)

2. Physical tests determining specific gravities, melting points, refractive indexes, etc.

B. Routine Methods of Analysis on Finished Compounded Synthetic Flavours

1. Specific gravity, on liquids.
2. Particle size, on powdered products.
3. Moisture content, on solids.
4. Alcohol or other solvent.
5. Extraneous materials and clarity.
6. Colour intensity and shade when flavour is intended to supply it to end product, etc.
7. Organoleptic—in comparison with standard samples kept in a vault and replaced from time to time by fresh, accepted lots.

C. Specific Methods of Analysis

The quality control laboratory will devise its own set of tests for specific flavours. Where aldehydes form the bulk of the flavour-giving materials, for example, a determination of total aldehyde value might be useful.

It is the responsibility of the flavour control chemists to determine which tests best apply to a specific combination of raw materials. He realizes that, in all probability, a flavour has been tailor-made for a customer, for use in a specified product, and it is expected that he releases only the production batches which impart uniform flavour intensity and quality. This chemist should therefore, be fully aware of manufacturing processing involved, as well as of the condition under which the consumer utilizes the food flavoured with the product under scrutiny.

In addition to these tests, gas chromatography has become a most useful tool in the control of synthetic flavours. It is used to prove that successive lots of certain flavours show substantially similar chromatograms. Only gross differences in the general pattern of the peaks might indicate errors in the composition of the lots.

A reliable flavour supplier normally submits to a customer a set of standards, chemical and physical, applicable to each specific synthetic flavour. These should be determined by the flavour control laboratory after measurements on a number of acceptable batches and thus allow the purchaser of the finished flavour to double check the material at the time of reception of the goods.

REFERENCES

1. Official Methods of Analysis of the Association of Official Agricultural Chemists. 10th Ed. 1965.
2. Food Standards (Mustard) (No. 2) Order 1944. S.R.O. 1944–275. Amended by S.R.O.'s 1946–157 and 1947–650 and S.I. 1948–1073.
3. Food Standards (Curry Powder) Order 1949. S.I. 1949–1816. Amended by S.I. 1956–1166.
4. Winton, A. L. (1916). "Microscopy of Vegetable Foods". (John Wiley, New York.)
5. Winton, A. L. & Winton, K. B. (1932–1939.) "The Structure and Composition of Foods", Vols. I–IV. (John Wiley, New York.)
6. Bohisch, P. (1904). *Analyst, Lond.* **29**, 372.
7. Kreis, H. (1910). *Chemikerzeitung* **34**, 1021–1023.
8. Stoddart, F. W. (1889). *Analyst, Lond.* **14**, 37.
9. Sale, J. W. (1953). *J. Ass offic. Anal. Chem.* **36**, 112–119.
10. Nosaki, K. (1946). *Ind. Engng Chem. analyt. Edn.* **18**, 583.
11. Flores, H. and Morse, R. S. (1952). *Fd Technol.* **6**, 6–8.
12. Guenther, E. *et al.* (1949).– *Analyt. Chem.* (Essential Oils and Related Products).
13. Knapman, C. E. H. (1958). *Gas Chromat. Abstr.* pp. 59–62. Butterworths, London.
14. Teisseire, P. (1962). *Recherches* **12**, 54–73.
15. Smith, D. M. and Levi, L. (1961). *J. agric. Fd Chem.* **9**, 230–244.
16. Theile, F. C. *et al.* (1960). *Perfum. essent. Oil Rec.* **51**, 535–40.
17. Montes, A. L. (1962). *An. Asoc. quím. argent.* **50**, 111–119.

18. Ikeda, R. M. *et al.* (1961). *Fd Technol.* **15,** 379–380.
19. Jensen, H. R. (1927). *Perfum. essent. Oil Rec.* **18,** 510.
20. Stahl, W. H. *et al.* (1960). *J. Ass. Offic. Anal. Chem.* **43,** 606–610.
21. Burchfield, H. P. *et al.* (1958). *Amer. Perfumer Arom.* **71**(4) 49.
22. Stoll, S. and Bouteville, Y. (1954). *Annls Falsif. Fraudes* **47,** 183–6.
23. Horst, P. and McGlumphy, J. H. (1962). *Annls Falsif. Expert. chim.* **55,** 264.
24. *U.S. Dept. Agr. Bur. Chem. Bull.* No. 312 (1910).
25. Fitelson, J. (1960). *J. Ass. Offic. Anal. Chem.* **43,** 600–601.
26. Prill, E. A. *et al.* (1960). *J. Ass. Offic. Anal. Chem.* **43,** 96–107.
27. Sullivan, J. H. *et al.* (1960). *J. Ass. Offic. Anal. Chem.* **43,** 601–605.
28. Way, R. (1961). *Proc. Flav. Ext. Manuf. Assn* p. 52.
29. Strashun, S. I. and Talburt, W. F. (1953) *Fd Engng.* **25** (3) 59–60.
30. Sinnamon, H. I. *et al.* (1954). *Fd Engng* **26**(7) 78–79.
31. Jorysch, D. (1963). *J. Ass. Offic. Anal. Chem.* **46,** 365–371.
32. Bayer, E. *et al.* (1958). *Analyt. Chem.* **164,** 1–10.
33. Mehlitz, A. and Gierschner, K. (1962). Rep. Scient. Tech. Comm. Intern Fed. Fruit Juice Prod.

The Sugar Industry

E. G. MULLER

Tate and Lyle Refineries Ltd., London, England

1. INTRODUCTION

In 1970 the world output of the sugar industry amounted to over 73 million metric tons. The reason for this vast output becomes clear when one considers the following facts. Sugar is just about the cheapest form of food available, in terms of calories obtained per unit cost. Refined sugar is manufactured to a purity of over 99·9 %. High food value and high purity are sufficient to make sugar a desirable food. Add to this the very pleasant, sweet taste and the combination becomes irresistible.

It is, therefore, not surprising that the consumption of sugar per head in various countries is closely related to the standard of living and that it is one of the first products which a developing country wishes to make on gaining independence.

There are quite a number of plants which contain sucrose, amongst them the maple tree, certain palm trees and sweet sorghum but they are comparatively unimportant commercially. The two plants that synthesize and store sucrose in abundant quantity are the sugar cane and the sugar beet and these have become the major sources of sugar.

2. SUGAR MANUFACTURE

A. Cane Sugar Manufacture

Cane accounts for nearly 60% of the total production of sugar. The sugar cane (*Saccharum officinarum*) is a giant grass which grows to a height of 12–15 ft and resembles bamboo. It thrives under conditions of high temperature and plentiful rainfall (65 in./year). It is grown commercially in most tropical countries, the principal suppliers being Cuba, Brazil and India.

The manufacture of refined sugar from cane is done in two stages:

1. the extraction of sugar from the cane and its conversion into raw sugar
2. the purification of raw sugar, resulting in refined sugar.

Although mechanical harvesting is technically feasible, much of the cane is still cut by hand. After cutting, the top leaves are removed and the bundles of stalks are transported to the factory situated near the plantations.

In order to extract the juice, which contains up to 16% sugar, the cane is passed through shredders or crushing rollers, followed by squeezing rollers under high pressure and a spray of water. The juice is clarified by the addition of milk of lime and heating which coagulates some of the impurities, entraps suspended solids and allows sedimentation of the mud.

The clarified juice is concentrated in multiple effect evaporators to a solids content of about 65% and is then boiled in steam heated vacuum pans. The removal of water by evaporation results in the crystallization of sucrose, producing "massecuite", a dense mass of sugar crystal and mother syrup. The raw sugar crystals are separated from the syrup in centrifugal machines. These are, essentially, cylindrical drums with perforated sides, lined with fine wire mesh. When rotated at high speed the syrup is thrown off and removed while the raw sugar crystals are retained by the wire mesh. The mother syrup is returned to the vacuum pans to extract further crops of crystals which are combined with the main crop.

Eventually two products result:

1. cane molasses or "blackstrap", a heavy, viscous, dark liquid containing water and some sucrose together with other sugars, decomposition products, gums, waxes, colouring matter, etc., in fact all the accumulated impurities and
2. raw sugar which is an aggregate of sticky brown crystals, containing about 96–99% sucrose. It consists of comparatively pure crystals of sucrose surrounded by a residual film of molasses.

Some raw sugar is consumed locally but the majority of it is transported in bulk carriers to highly developed countries for refining. There are many reasons for carrying out this operation near the centres of consumption rather than in the producing countries. The refining processes require large amounts of high grade fuel and pure water. They involve more complex operations, requiring skilled supervision and maintenance. All these commodities are more readily available near large centres of population. Moreover, while the transport of raw sugar in bulk is comparatively cheap, the handling, distribution and marketing of packed refined sugar is more economically and conveniently managed in highly developed countries.

B. Beet Sugar Manufacture

The other main source of sugar is the sugar beet (*Beta vulgaris*). It grows in temperate climates, including the United States and Canada, most European countries and the U.S.S.R.

The sugar beet stores sucrose in its large root. It is harvested mechanically in the autumn. The green tops are cut off on the farm and the roots are transported to the factory, where they are washed to remove adhering soil and are then cut into thin V-shaped slices called "cossettes". These are passed to continuous diffusers, large slowly rotating drums in which the sugar is extracted by diffusion into water. The resultant raw juice is carbonatated, i.e. it is treated with milk of lime and carbon dioxide bubbled through it in order to coagulate and precipitate some impurities which are filtered off.

After further treatment with sulphur dioxide the thin juice is treated in a manner similar to cane sugar, i.e. it is evaporated and boiled under vacuum and the massecuite of crystals and syrup is centrifuged. The sugar in the centrifugal machines is washed with a spray of hot water. The resultant white sugar is dried and can be used directly for consumption. The lower crops boiled from the mother syrups resemble raw cane sugar and can be recycled, or else sent to a refinery as raw sugar.

3. SUGAR REFINING

Refineries are normally situated at deep water ports so that the raw sugar can be unloaded directly into the store. Most refineries operate on cane raw sugar as their main raw material but they may use beet raw sugar as well. Whatever the origin of the sugar, it will be in the form of sticky brown crystals consisting of comparatively pure sucrose crystals surrounded by a thin film of impure syrup.

A. Raw Sugar Quality

The quality of the raw sugar is very variable. Owing to differences of soil, climate, technological development, etc., the amount and nature of the impurities of sugars produced in various countries shows marked differences. The sucrose content of Australian raws, for example, often exceeds 98·7% while West Indian sugars sometimes contain less than 96·2% sucrose. Since the job of a sugar refinery is to produce virtually pure sucrose, all the impurities have to be removed. The throughput of a refinery is limited by its capacity to eliminate impurities. The difference between 98·7% and 96·2% sucrose represents an almost threefold increase in the impurity load. Quite apart from the amount, the nature of the impurities differs between various types of raw sugar. Raw beet sugar, for example, contains much less reducing sugar than cane raws but has a larger ash content. Even for a single country of origin the sugar produced at many small factories may differ widely.

Differences of sugar content are taken into account when a parcel of raw sugar is finally paid for. The price per ton is adjusted if the sugar content differs from that laid down in the standard contract. Moreover, in some countries, notably the United States, the contract may provide for penalties and premiums for various aspects of quality such as filterability, grain size, colour, ash, moisture and the presence of osmophilic yeasts. The price paid for the raw sugar takes account of the yield of refined sugar that can be obtained from it and of the difficulty of refining but these adjustments, made eventually in the company's accounts, do not reduce the difficulties which the technical manager of the refinery has to overcome from day to day when faced with a variable raw material. Processing conditions have to be adjusted to ensure that the standard quality of the final product is maintained.

There are two ways in which the difficulties arising from fluctuating raw sugar quality can be minimized. One approach is to keep the various types of raw sugar separate and process them sequentially. This means a large disturbance when the sugar is changed. However, by trial and error, the optimum processing conditions can be determined in a few hours and the refinery may then run under stable conditions for several days or even weeks. This approach is more common in the United States, particularly in refineries which get their raw sugar from one country of origin only.

The other alternative is the deliberate mixing of origins to produce, as near as possible, an average raw sugar. Some sugars contain starch and filter badly, others are difficult to decolorize, yet others have a lot of impurity included in the crystal making removal difficult. These difficulties would create bottlenecks in different parts of the process and it is clearly advantageous to avoid the extremes. Such an approach is used in British refineries which take their raw sugar from a very wide range of countries. This policy has some disadvantages. The types and amounts of sugar available for blending at any one time are limited and the mixed input is not completely uniform. It results in less violent but more frequent fluctuations of quality and the problems of process control are made more difficult. The size of plant, however, can be substantially reduced if the unit processes do not have to deal with the extremes of composition. The policy of mixed melts represents savings of capital expenditure for a given throughput.

An accurate analysis of each raw sugar parcel is required for three purposes:
1. to determine the price to be paid for the sugar;
2. to adjust the processing conditions;
3. to compare the input and output of the refinery for the preparation of loss balances.

The most important analysis carried out in a sugar laboratory is the measurement of the polarization of raw sugar. The polarization is closely related to the sucrose content of the sugar and the commercial contract is based on it. In Great Britain alone several million pounds worth of sugar are bought every week, the price paid depending on the polarization.

The methods of raw sugar analysis are described in Section 5.A.

B. Refining Processes

The object of refining is to extract the maximum amount of pure sucrose. The residue from the process, refinery molasses, contains some sugar and all the impurities present in the raw sugar.

Although refinery operations are more sophisticated than those of the raw factories, some of the unit processes are essentially similar. The major refining processes are shown in Table 1.

TABLE 1. Refining Processes

Process	Purpose
Affination	To remove the outer syrup film surrounding the crystals
Melting	To dissolve the affined raw sugar
Defecation	To remove suspended solids and some dissolved impurities
Decolorization	To remove most of the colour
White sugar boiling	To crystallize the sugar and separate it from the mother syrup
Granulating	To produce dry, free-flowing sugar
Recovery	To extract the excess sugar from the syrup produced in affination and eliminate the impurities as refinery molasses

Although all refineries follow this general scheme there are many variations because the processes of defecation and decolorization can be carried out in a number of ways. The milk of lime added in defecation can be neutralized by carbon dioxide (carbonatation), by phosphoric acid (phosphitation) or even by sulphur dioxide (sulphitation). The decolorization can be done using bone charcoal, granular carbon, powdered carbon, ion exchange resins or combinations of more than one adsorbent. Finally, there are many different boiling schemes that can be used in recovery. As a result, the number of possible combinations is endless. The refining scheme described below is a

11*

typical one which is in use in Great Britain and Canada and is increasingly gaining acceptance in the United States.

The degree of purification achieved by refining can be seen from the typical analyses of raw sugar, refined sugar and refinery molasses shown in Table 2.

TABLE 2. Typical Analyses of Sugar Products

	Raw sugar (%)	Refined sugar (%)	Refinery molasses (%)
Sucrose	98·0	99·95	33
Reducing sugars	0·6	0·01	18
Ash	0·4	0·01	11
Water	0·5	0·02	25
Organic non-sugars	0·5	0·01	13

1. Affination

The actual crystals of raw sugar are comparatively pure. Some of the dissolved impurities are contained within the sugar crystals but the bulk of them is present in the syrup surrounding the crystals. Affination is aimed at removing as much as possible of this syrup film. The raw sugar is mingled with a warm, saturated syrup of intermediate purity which softens the syrup film adhering to the crystals. The resultant magma is spun in centrifugal machines and the crystals are washed in the rapidly rotating machine by a spray of hot water. The washed raw sugar goes forward for further processing. Affination is an effective process and most of the impurities are removed. However, the application of wash water dissolves some of the sugar crystals and the excess syrup has to go to the recovery process.

The quality of the washed raw sugar can be improved by increasing the wash in the centrifugal machines. The greater the wash the more sugar is dissolved. This decreases the yield of sugar going forward and, more seriously, it greatly increases the load on the recovery process. Normally, it is the capacity of the recovery process to deal with extra syrup which determines the extent to which washed raw sugar quality can be improved.

The work of the Affination Station is greatly affected by the quality of the raw sugar grain. A uniform grain of adequate size and the absence of crystal conglomerates makes the purging of the syrup much easier.

2. Melting

Washed raw sugar and recovered sugar are dissolved in hot water to give a solution containing about 69% solids, at about 65°C, and after passing through coarse strainers go forward to defecation.

It is very important to maintain the solids content at the required value. Fuel costs are a major refining expense and every gallon of water added to the process has to be evaporated, eventually, at great cost.

3. Carbonatation and Filtration

Milk of lime (about 0·5% CaO, on solids) is added to the solution and carbon dioxide (scrubbed boiler-flue gas) is bubbled through until the pH is 8·4. This results in the coagulation of some organic impurities and the flocculent precipitate of calcium carbonate formed entraps the gums, waxes and some other impurities. Up to one half of the colour is also removed from the solution by adsorption. Moreover, the precipitate of calcium carbonate acts as a filter aid so that the mud can easily be removed in pressure leaf filters.

Successful carbonatation depends on maintaining the final pH at the required value. Although 0·5% CaO is normally sufficient the process can be improved, slightly, by larger doses of lime. The limiting factor is often the amount of carbon dioxide gas available or rather the rate at which it can be pumped to the carbonatation tanks.

The presence of starch in some raw sugars can cause serious difficulties in filtration and it can quickly bring the filter station to a standstill. The only remedy is to reduce the viscosity of the liquor substantially, by decreasing the solids content of the melter liquor. This greatly increases the costs of evaporation.

4. Decolorization

The filtered liquor is sparklingly clear but is still brown in colour. More than nine-tenths of the colour is removed by passing the brown liquor through cylindrical filters filled with granules of bone charcoal. Bone char consists primarily of a porous framework of calcium phosphate (hydroxyapatite). The large internal surface is coated with a very finely divided, active form of carbon. When sugar liquors are passed through it, some of the inorganic impurities and virtually all the colour are adsorbed. After running for three days or so the decolorizing power deteriorates to below 90%. The liquor in the filter is then displaced by water and the bone char washed *in situ* for several hours to remove the adsorbed ash. It is then dried and regenerated in a kiln at a temperature of about 550°C in a controlled amount of air, to destroy the adsorbed organic matter. The bone char is used over and over again. A small amount of dust is formed in each cycle owing to attrition. This is made up by the addition of new char.

In order to reduce the fluctuations of the quality of output liquor and also to keep the size of the filters to reasonable proportions, the stock of bone char is divided amongst a large number of filters. These are run in parallel, with staggered starts. If, for example, there are 20 filters, and it is decided to operate a 100 h total cycle, then every 5 h the oldest filter would be taken out of service and its liquor supply switched to a filter containing freshly regenerated char.

If the quality of the brown liquor deteriorates the remedy is to "shorten the starts". If a new filter is started every 4 h, then the total cycle time becomes 80 h, i.e. each filter is regenerated earlier. This increases the total amount of char that has to be burnt and kiln capacity is usually the limiting factor.

In the long term, good decolorization depends on maintaining the quality of the char stock by:

1. adequate washing of the char before regeneration.
2. careful control of the kilns with respect to temperature and access of air.
3. a sound char replacement policy. As the char gets older, it gradually deteriorates because some ash is irreversibly adsorbed and some of the pores get blocked. The rate of removal of spent char and its replacement by new char should be such that the whole stock is renewed in two years.

5. Boiling and Finishing

The decolorized white liquor is concentrated in multiple effect evaporators and then boiled in steam heated vacuum pans. Owing to the use of high vacuum the boiling point of the solutions is reduced, resulting in less decomposition of sucrose and reduced colour formation. The massecuite is spun in centrifugal machines as described above and washed with a spray of hot water. The refined crystals are dried in hot air, being tumbled in slowly rotating drums (granulators) and are then weighed and packed.

The mother syrups are reboiled for two further crops of crystals and the three crops are mixed together. The yield of crystals from a white sugar pan is over 50%. The removal of over half of the solids in the form of virtually pure sucrose means that the concentration of the impurities in the mother syrup is more than doubled. After three boilings the impurities have multiplied nearly tenfold and the syrup is too impure to be boiled into high quality, refined sugar. The final syrup can be used in a number of ways depending on what specialities are manufactured (table syrups, brown sugars, etc.) or else they go to the recovery process.

6. Recovery

The excess sugar contained in the affination syrup is recovered by a series of boilings similar to those used in raw sugar factories. The quality of the recovered sugar (1st crop) is comparable to that of the washed raw sugar and it is added to the mainstream of sugar going forward. The mother syrups are reboiled to give further crops of sugar. These lower crops of sugar are used as feed to the 1st crop pans, either after being dissolved in water or in the form of crystalline seed. Whatever the scheme employed, the mother syrup from the lowest quality boiling is rejected from the process as refinery molasses.

This is the residue from the whole sugar refining process, containing all the impurities, those originally present in the raw sugar or added during processing and also decomposition products.

The efficient operation of the recovery process is of very great economic importance. In addition to the impurities, molasses also contain substantial amounts of sucrose. This is so because the crystallization of sugar from the recovery syrups becomes more and more difficult as their purity decreases. In fact, molasses is the syrup from which no more sucrose can be economically extracted. The price of molasses is but a small fraction of that obtainable for refined sugar. The refiner will, therefore, strive to minimize both the quantity of molasses formed and the percentage of sucrose contained in it.

With respect to the latter, good exhaustion is achieved by the careful control of the purities of the various boilings and by ensuring that the crystals grown in the pan are of adequate and uniform size, leading to the efficient separation of the mother syrup in the centrifugal machines. Leaks, spillages and washings from all parts of the refinery are collected and sent to the recovery process. The production of this sweet water should be minimized.

The amount of molasses formed depends mainly on the total amount of impurities in the raw sugar. It can increase, however, if chemicals or other non-sugars are added anywhere in the process or if non-sugars are formed by the decomposition of sucrose.

By contract, molasses have to contain over 50% total sugars. The additions of ash or other non-sugars to the process will, in effect, take sucrose with them into the molasses since the limit of 50% total sugars must be maintained.

If the non-sugar has resulted from sucrose decomposition the situation is even worse. Decomposition reduces the total amount of sucrose available and further amounts of this reduced total are then carried into the molasses by the decomposition products.

The progressive removal of two important impurities, ash and colour, by the various refining processes, is shown in Table 3.

TABLE 3. Refining Effect of Various Processes

Process	Product	Ash (% solids)	Colour*
—	Raw sugar	0·4	3000
Affination	Washed raw sugar	0·12	1000
Carbonatation	Brown liquor	0·11	500
Decolorization	White liquor	0·09	50
Crystallization	Refined sugar	0·01	10

* For units see Section 5.B.8.

C. Technical Control

1. Process Control

The need for process adjustments arises because a product of constant composition has to be made from a raw material of variable quality. The problem is intensified when, owing to a variety of reasons, one or other of the individual processes is working below optimum efficiency and produces a substandard intermediate product. This necessitates frequent adjustments to processing conditions to ensure that the successive steps of purification do finish up at the desired level.

Fortunately there is a certain amount of overlap between the processes. Colour, for example, is removed both by carbonatation and by charring and the deficiency of one process can be made up by the other to some extent. Moreover, the quality of the final product can be improved substantially and rapidly in the last purification step, by increasing the wash in the white sugar centrifugal machines. Thus, unlike many other industries, product quality control does not have to be of the acceptance/rejection type but can be used as a positive control of the process. Increasing the white sugar wash is, how ever, a strictly short term remedy. It reduces the yield substantially and the recirculation and reprocessing of the syrup generates colour and may in the long run make the problem worse. The only real solution is to improve the earlier processes so that the steps of purification are adequate.

Some of the other changes that can be made to alter the performance of intermediate processes were described in the previous section but these corrective adjustments always lead to increased costs. Because there is a great deal of recirculation of materials and the process is complicated, it is difficult to calculate precisely what the effect of a process alteration will be on the costs of all the other processes. A number of companies are now trying to develop mathematical models of the sugar refining process which will aim at minimizing the total cost and place the technical management of the process on a more rational basis than is possible now.

Two major items of cost which are influenced by technical control are fuel consumption and sugar loss. The need to avoid unnecessary evaporation by maintaining a high solids content in the syrups has already been mentioned. An additional reason to avoid adding water unnecessarily is that dilute sugar solutions are prone to microbiological attack. The most important problem is to prevent the loss of sugar.

2. Sugar Loss

The major proportion of the value of refined sugar is represented by the cost of raw material. A relatively small loss of sugar can wipe out the rather narrow margins on which the industry operates. The losses of most refineries are within the range of 0·5–3 % of the input. In this context the sucrose present in the molasses is not counted as a loss.

(a) Physical losses. These can be measured fairly accurately and account for about half the total loss. They include overweights, arising from the need to comply with Weights and Measures Regulations, the washings of bone charcoal and filter-press cake which it is not economical to recover, losses to sewer from spillages and other small items.

(b) Chemical losses. Sucrose solutions are readily hydrolyzed to form invert sugar. The rate of inversion is lowest at a pH of about 8. Invert sugar is decomposed under alkaline conditions. Both reactions are greatly accelerated at higher temperatures. To minimize chemical losses, "cool and neutral" are a good general policy. There are many tanks of syrup, all at different temperatures and pH so that an exact calculation of loss is difficult but all the syrups are decomposing to some small extent and it is very important to minimize the liquid stock-in-process.

(c) Microbiological losses. Dilute sugar solutions are liable to attack by a variety of micro-organisms and are easily fermented by airborne osmophilic yeasts. The only remedies are to avoid the creation of light, sweet waters and to insist on scrupulous cleanliness and plant hygiene.

An additional penalty of decomposition is the increased amount of molasses formation.

3. Ash Ratios

Ash analysis is very useful to the technologist because the amount of ash does not alter during processing, so that changes in the quantity of the other ingredients can be related to the constant yardstick of ash.

All the other ingredients are liable to change. The quantity of sucrose, for example, may be decreased by inversion. Large amounts of sucrose are removed from solution by crystallization. Invert sugar may be decomposed under alkaline conditions. Water is evaporated from solutions or may be added from the tap. The amount of ash on the other hand remains constant. To demonstrate the use of ash ratios, let us assume that one has a solution from which virtually pure sucrose is removed by crystallization. By comparing the ash concentration of the mother syrup with that of the feed syrup, the yield of crystals obtained can easily be calculated. The concentration of invert sugar will also have increased in the mother syrup. If, however, the invert sugar has increased more than in proportion, i.e. if the invert/ash ratio of the mother syrup is greater than that of the feed, then this would show that some hydrolysis of sucrose had taken place. The rise in the invert/ash ratio may give an incomplete measure of sucrose hydrolysis because invert sugar may also be decomposed and only the net change will be apparent.

However, decomposition will be revealed by an increase of the organic non-sugars/ash ratio. Thus, three important technical parameters—yield, inversion and decomposition can be obtained from simple ash ratios.

4. REFINED SUGAR QUALITY

Table 2 showed the composition of some typical sugar products. The subdivison into five items (sucrose, reducing sugars, ash, water and organic non-sugars) is the standard form in which sugar analyses are normally set out, both for intermediate factory materials and for final products.

Sucrose has the empirical formula $C_{12}H_{22}O_{11}$. It is a disaccharide formed by the condensation of dextrose (glucose) and laevulose (fructose). Extensive data on the physical and chemical properties of sucrose have been collected by Bates et al.[1] and Hirschmüller.[2]

The outstanding characteristic of refined sugar is its exceptionally high purity. A purity of 99·95% is, perhaps, not remarkable in itself. It is, after all, achieved in fine chemicals manufacture. The remarkable thing is that this degree of purity is achieved on a vast output. A modern sugar refinery is capable of producing over 3000 tons of sugar of this quality, every day.

It may be thought that the impurities remaining are so small in amount as to be negligible. This is not the case. The general remarks about the nature and importance of the impurities will demonstrate why such a very high standard of purity is required for refined sugar.

Apart from the impurities there are other properties which are of importance to the purchaser. The appearance of the sugar is influenced by the colour and the grain size. These attributes also affect the technological properties of the sugar and they are, therefore, of interest to all purchasers be they housewives or manufacturers. The presence of micro-organisms can also present special problems.

The quality requirements discussed below apply primarily to granulated sugar which is the principal product of most refineries. The analytical methods are described in Section 5, which also deals with some of the problems arising in the manufacture of specialities.

A. Impurities

1. Reducing Sugars

Reducing sugars are so called because they are able to reduce polyvalent ions. The most important reducing sugars are dextrose and laevulose. Invert sugar is the equimolecular mixture of dextrose and laevulose formed by the hydrolysis of sucrose. Although "reducing sugars" is strictly speaking more correct, the simpler term "invert sugar" is normally used in the sugar industry.

Dry, crystalline sucrose is a stable substance but in the presence of acid or some enzymes, aqueous solutions of sucrose are easily hydrolyzed. Invert sugar does not crystallize easily and it is rather hygroscopic. If more than traces of invert are present in the final product, the sugar is liable to go sticky. Once this has happened the extra moisture attracted by the invert sugar will dissolve more sucrose in the syrup film surrounding each crystal, thereby facilitating further inversion of sucrose and so on, leading to the deterioration of the product.

Invert sugar is not without value. It is a wholesome food, it is sweeter than sucrose and it contributes to the "total sugars" in molasses. However, it is an undesirable impurity in the refined sugar and one must try to operate the refining process in such a way as to minimize the conversion of sucrose into invert and to eliminate it from the product as far as possible.

2. Ash

Refined sugar contains very small amounts of inorganic salts. These do not represent a disadvantage or hazard to its use as a foodstuff or to its technological properties. In spite of this, the estimation of ash is the analysis most frequently carried out both during processing and on the final refined sugar. The reason for this is that the ash content is the most general indicator of the degree of refining. There are wide variations in the level of the other impurities, dependent on the origin of the raw sugar, but all raw sugars contain significant amounts of ash and the quickest way of judging the general purity of a refined sugar is by the measurement of its ash content. In the European Economic Community, for example, the official grading of white sugars is based on a points system which depends primarily on ash (and colour).

3. Water

The water content of crystalline sugar at equilibrium is closely related to its purity. The syrup layer on the crystals will give up water vapour to its surroundings, depending on its vapour pressure until, eventually, the sugar reaches its equilibrium water content. For a high purity refined sugar this equilibrium water content is very low.

The fact that the sugar will eventually attain its equilibrium does not mean that the water content, as delivered, is unimportant. On the contrary, the changes which would have to take place to attain equilibrium are of great importance to the user. Since the crystals are closely packed, even a small amount of crystallization may lead to bridging between adjacent crystals, causing the sugar to cake in storage.

Another hazard due to the presence of water is that of moisture migration. The vapour pressure of a sugar solution increases with temperature. If there are temperature gradients in a large bulk of sugar, the net effect of the resultant vapour pressure gradients is a transfer of water, via the atmosphere, from the warm sugar to the cold sugar. If the total amount of water in the bulk of sugar is large enough and the temperature gradients persist, the cold sugar may become quite wet. The dangers of subsequent caking and other deterioration are obvious.

All these hazards are reduced if the water content is low, i.e. if the sugar has been refined to a high degree of purity.

4. Organic Non-sugars

This is an omnibus term and it includes the other components present such as sugar decomposition products, organic acids, colouring matter, etc.

There are so many organic compounds present, in such minute amounts, that the individual, quantitative analysis of them is inappropriate.

5. Extraneous Matter

Specifications written by company buyers often contain such statements as "extraneous matter shall be absent". This is pointless since the requirements can never be met. Any manufactured product will contain some atmospheric dust, minute traces of rust or scale, a few fibres deriving from the paper or other packing material, etc. No system of quality control can ensure the complete absence of these traces of insoluble matter. The task of the quality control chemist is twofold. He has to ensure that the total insoluble material does not exceed a realistic, quantitative limit and further he has to exclude completely any contaminant, however little in amount, which could be harmful.

6. Trace Elements

Analyses of trace elements (arsenic, lead, sulphur dioxide) are necessary because of legal limitations. Small amounts of these substances are present in raw sugars. They are nearly all eliminated by the refining process but, since many chemicals are used in the refinery, the possibility of contamination cannot altogether be excluded. The batches of raw sugars and of the chemicals are checked for lead and arsenic on arrival and the regular testing of the refined sugar is a necessary precaution. In fact, high quality refined sugar normally contains less than 0·02 ppm of lead and less than 0·05 ppm of arsenic.

B. Colour

Pure sucrose crystals are colourless and transparent. The juice extracted from the sugar cane and sugar beet, however, contains colour bodies and more colour is formed during processing by the breakdown of sugars (caramelization), by the interaction of reducing sugars with amino compounds (Maillard reaction) and in other ways.

The weight of colouring matter is minute, but if present in more than trace quantities, the high intensity of the coloured compounds imparts a yellowish tinge to the refined sugar crystals.

The retail customer judges the quality of the sugar by the appearance of the crystals themselves. The human eye and brain are surprisingly tolerant. Because the observer expects sugar to be white, he will accept as white, sugars which are quite yellow or grey, when compared side by side with a highly refined sugar. The manufacturer, on the other hand, is more interested in the colour obtained when the sugar is dissolved in water as it is the latter which will influence his product. Although the appearance of the crystals is taken into account, the quality control of colour is primarily based on the measurement of solution colours.

In the past sugar colours were measured in a colorimeter, by visual comparison against standards, either coloured solutions or, more usually, brown coloured glasses. These methods had the virtue of simplicity and the various systems ("Stammer" on the Continent, "Horne" in the United States and "Lovibond" in Great Britain and elsewhere) are still in use. However, the use of visual comparison against arbitrary standards has a number of serious drawbacks:

1. The hue of sugar solutions is variable and if it differs from that of the standard it is difficult to get an accurate match.
2. A personal error may be introduced by the human observer.
3. The colour scales are not always linear and additive.
4. The results of the various systems are not comparable.
5. In the case of highly refined sugar the amount of colouring matter is so small that the cells required are inconveniently long.

Recent work is based on optical measurement and on units which have absolute significance. The reference instrument for such studies is the spectrophotometer. This is an expensive instrument and the use of spectrophotometers is limited to research laboratories. The normal quality control work of sugar laboratories is done by means of photoelectric colorimeters.

C. Grain Size

The grain size has an obvious effect on the appearance of the sugar. It is interesting to note that the preferred size seems to increase as one goes round the world from West to East. The American consumer prefers a sugar smaller than the granulated sugar sold in Great Britain while for export to the Far East special, large grained sugar is required.

Even more important than the average grain size is the distribution of sizes. The visual appearance of a sugar having a large spread of sizes, containing fines and oversize crystals, is very inferior to one where the spread is narrow and the grain even.

Quite apart from the aesthetic appeal, the size distribution, both average size and spread, has an important bearing on the suitability of the sugar in use. Whether one considers the making of icing paste or the sprinkling of caster sugar on fruit or again the large crystals used to decorate biscuits and buns, it is clear that the correct average grain size is a fundamental requirement. The average grain size is most important for certain sections of the baking industry, where in addition to sweetening, the sugar performs a mechnical function and, indeed, in any field where the sugar is used dry or in an incompletely dissolved state.

As to the distribution of sizes, for most technological applications the requirement is for a narrow size range. An excessive amount of fines is undesirable since these may segregate from the rest and the accumulation of dust could cause caking or uneven flow.

Sieving analyses giving the percentages retained on various meshes are difficult to visualize and interpret. The MA/CV notation introduced by Powers[3] is very convenient. It is based on the fact that the weight frequency distribution of a granular sugar plotted against particle size conforms very closely to the Gaussian normal distribution. The MA/CV nomenclature has the advantage that it defines the size distribution in terms of two parameters only which, with a little practice, convey a complete picture of the size distribution.

The mean aperture (MA) describes the general size of the grain. It is the aperture of the sieve which would retain 50% by weight of the sample.

The coefficient of variation (CV) is a measure of the spread of the sizes. It is the standard deviation of the distribution expressed as a percentage of the mean aperture.

The method cannot be applied if the distribution has been drastically altered, for example by screening, milling or by mixing of two batches of sugar of different size.

In connection with size analysis, reference must be made to the importance of sampling. The difficulties of drawing representative samples from a large bulk of granular material are well known. While the necessity of ensuring that the sample is a true one is important for all items of analysis, it is of overriding importance in size analysis. For it is the variations of size, the very property one is trying to measure, which brings about the errors of sampling. Whenever sugar is moving along an inclined plane, segregation may occur. If, for example, sugar is poured from a bag so that it forms a cone, the larger crystals will run down the surface of the cone to the bottom. Thus, if a hopper has been filled up, a sample drawn from the irregular surface of it will bear little relation to the size distribution of the bulk of the sugar. The only satisfactory way of obtaining a representative sample is by drawing rapid cross-sections from a freely falling curtain of sugar. The end of a conveyor band, where the sugar is falling off, is usually a convenient point to sample the shallow curtain under free fall. It is important that the complete width of the curtain is traversed and that a sufficient number of samples is taken to represent the whole consignment. Having produced the sample it must be reduced in size to that used in the analysis. This can be done properly only by means of a riffle or rotary divider and the whole sample must be used. Much work can be saved and argument between manufacturer and consumer avoided by adhering to these principles.

5. METHODS OF ANALYSIS

Before dealing with the actual methods a few words are necessary about I.C.U.M.S.A. (International Commission for Uniform Methods of Sugar Analysis). The sugar industry is fortunate in having established a body to which all the major producing countries except the U.S.S.R. and China belong. Adherence to I.C.U.M.S.A. and acceptance of its methods is voluntary and because of this a method is adopted only when approval is unanimous. This is, indeed, a source of its strength but the process of obtaining universal acceptance for a method is slow. Usually, a method is at first adopted tentatively and at the next session, four years later, it may be adopted officially.

The methods adopted, either tentatively or officially, up to the 13th Session (1962) have been summarized in "I.C.U.M.S.A. Methods of Sugar Analysis".[4] Frequent reference will be made to this book and shown thus: (I.C.U.M.S.A. 1964; page number). Some of these methods have been modified at the 14th Session (1966) and 15th Session (1970).

A. Raw Sugar

1. Polarization

Solutions of sucrose, like those of other optically active substances, have the power of rotating the plane of polarized light. The degree of rotation depends on the concentration of optically active substance in the solution, the length of the light path through the solution, the wavelength of the light and the temperature. If the conditions are standardized the rotation is proportional to the sucrose concentration, provided that no other optically active materials are present. A saccharimeter fitted with the International Sugar Scale is a polariscope such that if the "normal weight" (26·000 g) of pure sucrose is dissolved to 100 ml, in water, and read in a 200 mm tube, at 20°C, a reading of 100°S will be obtained. Thus, if a raw sugar containing, say, 97% sucrose and no other optically active material were polarized under standard conditions, the reading would be 97°S. In practice, various optically active substances such as dextrose, laevulose, etc., are always present and the polarization does not equal the sucrose content. Nevertheless, the polarization has become the commercial criterion by which raw sugar is bought and sold.

Because of the enormous commercial importance of polarization measurements it has been extremely difficult to get international agreement.

The method described in the I.C.U.M.S.A. Method Book (I.C.U.M.S.A. 1964; 67) is a simplified version of what was finally adopted at the 15th Session (1970).[5]

Most of the saccharimeters used are manually adjusted and depend on visual observation. It is probable that they will be replaced by automatic, photoelectric instruments which are being perfected at the present time.

2. Sucrose

The polarization of raw sugars differs from the true sucrose content because of the presence of other optically active compounds. The most important of these is invert sugar which reduces the polarization. If pure invert sugar were the only contaminant it can be shown that $S = P + 0.333\ I$ where S, P and I are sucrose, polarization and invert sugar respectively. In practice, owing to the presence of other optically active compounds such as raffinose and also because dextrose and laevulose may not be present in equal proportions, the polarizing constant $\left(\dfrac{S-P}{I}\right)$ is usually less than 0.333.

The exact estimation of sucrose requires rather elaborate methods involving multiple polarization before and after hydrolysis by various enzymes (I.C.U.M.S.A. 1964; 7).

For routine control purposes an empirical constant is used. Many refineries use the value of 0.22, so that:

$$S = P + 0.22\ I.$$

3. Reducing Sugars

The basic method for the determination of reducing sugars in sugar solutions is the volumetric method of Lane and Eynon[6] which consists in determining the volume of test solution required to reduce a given volume of Fehling's solution from the cupric state to cuprous oxide. The end point is shown by the decolorization of methylene blue which is reduced to its leuco-form in alkaline solution if no cupric salts are present. The reaction is not stoichiometric and, from the volume of sugar solution required, the concentration of invert sugar is found by reference to the appropriate table (I.C.U.M.S.A. 1964; 13).

Since the estimation is one of reducing power one is, strictly speaking, determining not invert sugar but total reducing sugars expressed as invert. Traces of other reducing sugars present are included.

4. Ash

The ash is determined gravimetrically as sulphate (I.C.U.M.S.A. 1964; 36). The salts originally present are converted to sulphate by concentrated sulphuric acid, the organic matter is burnt off and the sample is ignited in a furnace at 800°C, in a platinum dish, to constant weight. Although the weight of sulphated ash is different from that of the salts originally present, this difficulty also applies to direct incineration, owing to the uncontrollable loss of chlorine, sulphur, etc. The sulphated ash method gives more reliable results.

5. Water

The analytical methods for determining the water content of sugars by drying in an atmospheric oven are very unsatisfactory. The amount of water to be driven off is small and there are many sources of error unless the conditions of drying and details of the oven are standardized. Even under standardized conditions, the results may not reflect the true water content because carbohydrates and some of the other organic compounds present are not completely stable at high temperatures. The ratio of sugars to water is over 100:1 and even a small change in the weight of the sugars or other components present will be a serious source of error.

The reference method (I.C.U.M.S.A. 1964; 41) uses a precision vacuum drying oven developed by Gardiner.[7] The design of this oven, manufactured by Griffen and George Ltd., London, eliminates some of the errors due to the unequal temperature distribution and excessive air space inherent in ordinary ovens and, above all, it uses a lower temperature (60°C). The method takes several hours and is not suitable for routine control.

At the 15th Session (1970) a chemical method based on the reaction between water and the Karl Fischer reagent was adopted as a rapid method. The method was originally developed for the analysis of refined sugars and is described more fully under that heading. With minor modifications it can be used for raw sugars.[8]

6. Organic Non-Sugars

The organic non-sugars are calculated by subtracting the sum of the other ingredients (sucrose, reducing sugars, ash and water) from 100%.

7. Colour

The method used is as for refined sugar (Section 5.B.8).

8. Grain Size

Before analysis the sugar has to be made free-flowing. The 15th Session of I.C.U.M.S.A. (1970) tentatively adopted a method based on washing the sugar with a saturated sucrose solution followed by methyl alcohol, isopropyl alcohol and drying under vacuum.[9] The grain size is then determined as for refined sugar (Section 5.B.9).

B. Refined Sugar

1. Sucrose

One of the consequences of the high purity is that the quality of sugar is controlled not by estimating the sucrose content but by analysis of the impurities. The accuracy of a routine determination of polarization is of the order of 0·05%. A much more precise estimate of the sucrose content is obtained by analysis of the impurities and subtracting from 100%. The principle of impurity control is applied not only to the final product but also to the control of the production process.

2. Reducing Sugars

The volumetric method of Lane and Eynon,[6] in general use for raw sugars and syrups, is unsuitable for refined sugars because the invert sugar content is too low. For amounts up to 0·15% the I.C.U.M.S.A. reference method is the colorimetric one of Emmerich[10] using 3:6–dinitrophthalic acid. For highly refined sugars, containing up to 0·02% invert sugar, the method of Knight and Allen[11] was adopted as the routine method in which the invert sugar reacts with an alkaline copper reagent and any unreduced copper is titrated against a standard E.D.T.A. solution (ethylene diamine tetraacetic acid).[12]

3. Ash

The ash content of refined sugar is too low to be measured gravimetrically. It can be determined rapidly and accurately by a conductometric method (I.C.U.M.S.A. 1964; 38) which can also be used for impure materials. The electrical conductivity of an aqueous solution of sucrose is very low compared to that of mineral electrolytes and the conductivity of a sugar solution is due almost entirely to the dissolved ash. The apparatus used consists of a glass cell with two platinum electrodes approximately 1 cm square whose leads are fused into the sides of the cell so that the electrodes are a few millimetres apart. The cell is standardized with 0·01 M KCl at 20°C. The conductance of the sugar solution, measured at 20°C, is multiplied by the cell constant to obtain the specific conductivity.

The concentration of the sugar solution used in the measurement has to be specified. For refined sugars, the 15th Session of I.C.U.M.S.A. (1970) adopted 28 g per 100 g. Having determined the conductivity, a correction has to be made for the conductivity of the distilled water used for the preparation of the solution. One half of the conductivity of the water is subtracted. To calculate the ash content (% solids), the corrected conductivity (μ S cm^{-1}) is multiplied by 6×10^{-4}.

For products other than refined sugar a concentration of 5 g per 100 ml was adopted. The water correction is then nine-tenths and the factor used to convert conductivity to ash content is 18×10^{-4}.

4. Water

The methods used are similar to those mentioned above under raw sugar analysis.

The disadvantages of the conventional oven drying method apply even more in the case of refined sugar. The amount of water to be driven off is much smaller and the ratio of carbohydrates to water is enormous (5000:1). The effect of possible decomposition is much more serious. A special difficulty arises in the case of freshly manufactured sugar. Immediately after manufacture, only a part of the water is in an "available" state. If water is evaporated from a saturated sucrose syrup, the state of saturation is restored, in normal circumstances, by the removal of sucrose from the solution by crystallization. In an oven, however, the initial removal of water is very rapid and the rate of crystallization is insufficient to keep pace with it. As a result, a highly supersaturated, glassy layer of syrup is formed, which is so viscous and has such a low vapour pressure that the removal of further water is inhibited. This difficulty does not arise in the case of conditioned sugar. During the initial handling and storage of the sugar after granulation, the loss of water, by diffusion into the atmosphere at normal temperature, takes place sufficiently slowly for a commensurate amount of crystallization to take place. The formation of the glassy layer is avoided. It is probable that despite its shortcomings non-specialist laboratories will continue to use oven drying because of the simplicity of the apparatus.

For specialist work and as a reference method the vacuum oven method (I.C.U.M.S.A. 1964; 41) is used.[7]

A rapid control method based on the chemical reaction between water and the Karl Fischer reagent was developed by Bennett et al.[13] Methanol is rendered water-free by titrating it with Karl Fischer reagent. A known quantity of sugar, containing not more than 50 mg of water, is added to the methanol and shaken for 25 min. As a result, the water is extracted from the sample by the dry methanol and it is then titrated with more Karl Fischer reagent. The endpoint is detected by an electrometric method which depends on the depolarization of a pair of platinum electrodes as soon as there is an excess of Karl Fischer reagent in the reaction mixture. For details of the apparatus and method, "Analytical Methods used in Sugar Refining" should be consulted.[14]

5. Organic Non-Sugars

In impure sugar products the percentage of organic non-sugars is calculated by estimating the sucrose, invert, ash and water and subtracting the total from 100%. This procedure is not practicable for the routine analysis of refined sugars since the errors of the sucrose estimation are greater than the amount of organic non-sugars.

It has been established that in refined sugars there is a fairly constant relationship between the organic non-sugars and the ash. For routine control purposes it is assumed that the organic non-sugars amount to 1·25 times the ash.

6. Extraneous Matter

Hitherto the estimation of extraneous matter was carried out by filtration through paper and visual comparison against previously prepared, standard filter discs. The standards were prepared by depositing on them weighed quantities of artificial "dirt" such as atmospheric dust, powdered bone charcoal, etc. The method was simple and inaccurate. The 15th Session of I.C.U.M.S.A. (1970) tentatively adopted the gravimetric method of Hibbert and Phillipson[15] based on filtration through membrane filters. A 1000 g sample of sugar is dissolved in distilled water and filtered through a previously weighed membrane (5 μm pore size). After thorough washing the membrane disc is dried and reweighed. Owing to the small weight of the membrane itself, the small amount of insoluble matter can be estimated accurately. The pore size of 5 μm ensures a rapid filtration rate. The insoluble material is retained on the surface so that it can be examined qualitatively under a low powered microscope.

7. Trace Elements

(a) *Lead.* The method (I.C.U.M.S.A. 1964; 46) is based on the colorimetric estimation of the red, chloroform soluble complex formed by lead with Dithizone and is suitable for refined sugars having a maximum lead content of 0·5 ppm.

(b) *Arsenic.* The well known Marsh–Berzelius test is carried out in a conventional Marsh apparatus, with standard interchangeable ground glass joints.

(c) *Sulphur dioxide.* The method (I.C.U.M.S.A. 1964; 52) depends on SO_2 being displaced from an aqueous solution of sugar by phosphoric acid, distilled under vacuum, collected in an alkaline solution as sulphite and finally determined by iodine and thiosulphate.

A more rapid colorimetric method by Carruthers *et al.*,[16] based on the decolorization of rosaniline hydrochloride has been adopted by the 15th Session (1970).

8. Colour

Until recently a number of methods using photoelectric colorimeters were in use. This arose from attempts to separate the effects of colour and turbidity. In dark solutions the presence of a small amount of turbidity is unimportant but in a refined sugar, containing very little colour, it may amount to 20% of the total absorption. Attempts to use the differences between the spectral absorption curves of colouring matter and turbidity, by measurement at two different wavelengths, have not been entirely successful. At the 15th Session of I.C.U.M.S.A. (1970) the two-wavelengths methods were abandoned and Method 4 (I.C.U.M.S.A. 1964; 57), slightly modified, was adopted. It is based on the measurement of the attenuancy of a filtered solution, at 420 nm, against distilled water as the standard. For refined sugars the concentration used is 50% solids, the solution is filtered through a membrane filter (pore size 0·45 μm) and the cell length is 10 cm. Different combinations of concentration and cell length are used for syrups and dark products.

$$\text{COLOUR} = 1000\frac{A}{bc} = 1000\frac{-\log T}{bc}$$

where A = Attenuancy

T = Transmittancy

b = cell length in cm

c = concentration of solids in g/ml

9. Grain Size

A weighed sample (50 g) is placed on top of a graded nest of sieves (8 in. diameter) and shaken mechanically for 15 min. The fractions remaining on each sieve are weighed and expressed as a percentage of the total weight (I.C.U.M.S.A. 1964; 94). If the cumulative percentages are plotted against particle size on arithmetic probability paper a straight line is obtained. From it the MA and CV are easily determined.[17]

C. Specialities

Specialities range in purity from pure sucrose to dark treacle. All these products present special problems depending on their purity and on their intended use.

1. Canners Sugar, Bottlers Sugar

These are high quality granulated sugars. Because of their use in the canning of fruits and vegetables and for the manufacture of soft drinks they are made to conform to special microbiological standards and are discussed in Section 5.E.

2. Cubes

Cube sugar is a very pure, refined sugar and its chemical analysis is as for high quality granulated sugar. Additional tests are required to measure the mechanical properties of the cubes.[18] The abrasion resistance is important in order to minimize damage during transport. It is measured by placing a known quantity of cubes in a rotating drum and weighing the dust formed under standardized conditions. The strength of the cubes is also measured by applying an increasing, static load on individual cubes until they are crushed. Cubes should disintegrate quickly in water and this can be checked by placing a number of them on a coarse mesh, immersing the assembly in water and measuring the time required for the bulk of the sugar to disappear from the mesh. The mesh used is a coarse one so that it will pass small aggregates of crystals. This is desirable because the object of the test is to measure the disintegration time of the cubes rather than the time required for complete dissolution.

3. Powdered Sugars

These are produced from granulated sugar, by milling. Milled products do not conform to the normal particle size distribution. Hill and Muller[19] have shown that the distribution is log-normal. Straight lines are obtained if the cumulative percentages are plotted against particle size on logarithmic probability paper. The dry sieving of finely powdered sugars presents difficulties and the routine method of control is based on the measurement of the specific surface area (cm^2/g). The specific surface is inversely proportional to the average particle size and it can be estimated by a measurement of the air permeability. If a known amount of powdered sugar is compressed into a pad of fixed size, then the time required for a quantity of air, under slight pressure, to pass through the pad, is related to the specific surface. The suitability of powdered sugar depends not only on having a small average size (large specific surface) but also on the absence of large particles which could spoil the smooth surface of the prepared icing. Since the normal dry sieving methods are not applicable, an additional test is used, based on wet sieving with water-free acetone on a 150 mesh sieve. The apparatus used for the determination of the specific surface and the wet sieving method are both described in a paper by Hill and Muller.[20]

Powdered sugars are prone to caking and in order to improve the keeping quality, small amounts of anti-caking agents are usually added. Those in most common use are starch and tricalcium phosphate. The proportions added have to be declared on the packet, and frequent sampling is necessary to ensure that the amount of additive is within the declared limits. The starch is estimated by a polarimetric method, based on the difference between the polarization and the total solids.[21] Tricalcium phosphate is determined by the addition of hydrochloric acid and titration with sodium carbonate solution using screened methylorange as an indicator.[22]

4. Soft Brown Sugars

The analysis of soft brown sugars follows, broadly speaking that of raw sugar. Some refiners prefer to estimate the sucrose content by the chemical method, as described for molasses. The main difficulty in the quality control of refined brown sugars is to maintain a constant product colour despite the large variations of colour in the raw sugar input.

5. Liquid Sugar

Liquid sugars are, in effect, refined sugar dissolved in water in the form of almost saturated solutions. They are analyzed accordingly. The solids content is determined refractometrically (I.C.U.M.S.A. 1964; 44), no correction being necessary for the small amounts of impurities (Section 5.D.3). The main problems are microbiological ones and they are discussed more fully in Section 5.E.

6. Table Syrups

High quality table syrups are specially refined, partially inverted sugar solutions which have been evaporated to over 83% solids. In addition to the sugars present they also contain about 3% of non-sugars, deriving from the raw sugar, which gives them their characteristic colour and flavour. In order to achieve the desirable high viscosity the syrups must have a high solids content, much higher than could remain in solution if sucrose were the only sugar present. By the controlled, partial inversion of sucrose it is possible to make a syrup which can be evaporated to contain over 80% sugars and which, though supersaturated, will not crystallize easily. An important feature of the best quality syrups is the very low colour/non-sugar ratio. Very careful control of the refining process is necessary to achieve the high non-sugar content which gives the product its flavour and yet retain the characteristic golden colour of the syrup. The methods of analysis used for molasses are inherently more accurate than those which have to be employed to estimate the minute amounts of impurities in refined sugars. The high non-sucrose content of table syrups makes it possible to use the molasses type analyses, Section 5.D.

D. Molasses

After several crops of sugar crystals have been extracted the purity of the resultant syrup is so low that the extraction of further quantities of sugar becomes very slow and difficult. The precise point where it ceases to be economic to extract more sugar depends on the composition of the impurities but, as a very rough guide, molasses are reached when the non-sugars (ash and organic) have increased to one third of the total solids in the syrup. The water content of molasses, as delivered, is usually of the order of 25% and an approximate molasses analysis would, therefore, be:

$$\text{sugars (sucrose + invert)} \quad = 50\%$$
$$\text{non sugars (ash + organic)} = 25\%$$
$$\text{water} \quad\quad\quad\quad\quad\quad\quad = 25\%$$

Commercial contracts for molasses usually specify a minimum of 50% total sugars and also a range of water contents since below about 16% the viscosity of molasses is so high that it cannot be pumped easily and above 27% there is the possibility of fermentation.

1. Sugars

The method for the determination of sucrose and invert in molasses is the Tate and Lyle Invertase Method (I.C.U.M.S.A. 1964; 71). It consists of estimating the reducing sugars, by the Lane and Eynon method, both before and after inversion. Having determined the original invert sugar content, another determination is carried out after the sucrose has been hydrolyzed to invert sugar by invertase. The difference between the original and the total invert sugar content is due to the invert sugar formed from the sucrose by hydrolysis. 342 parts by weight of sucrose produce, on inversion, 360 parts of invert sugar. To calculate the original sucrose content, the difference between the original and total invert sugar is multiplied by 342/360 or 0·95.

The reference method to determine sucrose is based on an isotope dilution technique.[23]

2. Non-Sugars

The ash is determined gravimetrically, as described in Section 5.A.4.

The organic non-sugars are calculated by subtracting the sum of the other ingredients (sucrose, invert, ash and water) from 100%.

3. Water

The disadvantages of oven drying methods for the determination of the water content of sugar products have already been noted. Moreover, because of the viscous nature of molasses and the likelihood of skin formation, aluminium powder, sand or some similar extender has to be mixed with the sample so as to present a large surface for evaporation. To facilitate the mixing of the extender with the molasses the latter has to be diluted by the addition of a weighed quantity of water. The reference method (I.C.U.M.S.A. 1964; 42) specifies the use of the precision vacuum oven already described.[7]

Although oven drying methods are often specified for commercial transactions they are clearly unsuitable for process control purposes. The control of the water content of molasses and syrups is based on the measurement of the refractive index (I.C.U.M.S.A. 1964; 44). The refractive index of pure sucrose solutions of various concentrations has been determined with great precision,[24] resulting in the new (1966) International Table of Refractive Indices of Sucrose solutions.[25] The refractive index of the impurities is, of course, quite different from that of sucrose. If the refractive index of an impure sugar solution is looked up in the International Table, the corresponding "refractometer solids", will be in error. For comparatively pure sugar liquors the error is small and the solids content of most process syrups is determined by refractometer. In the case of molasses, however, the true solids content could be 3% less than the refractometer solids. The difference varies widely with the type of raw sugar (cane or beet) and the composition of the impurities. Empirical formulae are used.

Molasses are usually diluted for pumping and delivery. This operation is also controlled refractometrically. Because of the simplicity and precision of the refractive index measurement, the range of permitted water contents has, in some commercial contracts, been specified by a range of refractive index readings.

E. Microbiological Standards

The microbiological control of the refining process is necessary for two reasons. The micro-organisms introduced with the raw sugar and by airborne contamination may cause deterioration and loss of sugar. More importantly, the presence of certain organisms in the refined sugar may damage the food products to which the sugar is added. Owing to the high temperatures encountered in sugar refining the microbial population of refined sugar is small but there are customers to whom micro-organisms are of special interest: canners, bottlers and other users of liquid sugar.

The main classes of micro-organisms which need to be controlled are: thermophilic bacteria, mesophilic bacteria, yeasts and moulds.

In the United States the National Canners Association and the American Bottlers of Carbonated Beverages have imposed restrictive standards on refined sugar products and, with modifications, these have become accepted in other countries.

1. Canners Sugar

The reason for the very high standard imposed is that thermophilic bacteria, because of their spore forming characteristics, may survive the high processing temperatures during canning. The spores of Flat sours (*B. stearothermophilus*) produce acid, the presence of Sulphide producers (*Cl. nigrificans*) may result in the blackening of cans while the Hydrogen swells (*Cl. thermosaccharolyticum*) may cause blown cans.

Control is based on the count of the number of spores remaining after steam treatment to kill off the vegetative forms. After steaming, the sample is cultured on specific agar based media, on plates or in tubes, incubated at 55°C for 3 days and the resultant colonies are counted. The complete standard[26] of the National Canners Association, Washington is rather complicated and statistical difficulties arise because of the small numbers of organisms involved and their unequal distribution. A rather strict interpretation of it by one refiner permits the following counts in 10 g of sugar:

Flat sours and other aerobic spores 50
Sulphide producers 0
Hydrogen swells 5

2. Bottlers Sugar

The most important organisms relating to the manufacture of soft drinks, mineral waters, etc. are mesophilic bacteria, yeasts and moulds. Although they will have been destroyed when the sugar was boiled, they may be reintroduced into the product by atmospheric contamination. Since they can multiply at moderate temperatures, the quality of the beverage could be adversely affected by fermentation and clouding.

For control purposes the sample solutions are mixed with nutrient agar or other appropriate specific culture media, plated, incubated at 30°C for 3 days and counted. The standard prescribed by the American Bottlers of Carbonated Beverages, Washington[26] can be interpreted as permitting the following maximum counts in 10 g sugar:

Mesophilic bacteria 100
Yeasts 10
Moulds 10

3. Liquid Sugar

Because of the high water content of liquid sugar the danger of microbiological action is much greater than it is for solid sugars. Airborne yeasts and moulds present the most serious problem. In liquid sugar the sucrose concentration is too high for the organisms to develop but they can survive in it. Dilution of the sugar solution, either by localized condensation or during further processing, can produce conditions in which the organisms could multiply. Great care is required, therefore, at all stages of manufacture, storage and transport.

The standards, self imposed by the refiner or agreed with the customer, are more strict than those relating to solid sugars. Mesophilic bacteria should not exceed 100 per 10 g of sample. Yeasts and moulds should be absent.

4. Membrane Filtration

Because the counts are meaningful only in relation to the method used and the intended use of the sugar in a particular product, the details of procedure are often specially agreed between the refiner and the user. This is often based on a new technique which depends on the use of micropore membrane filters capable of retaining micro-organisms. A sample of sugar is dissolved and filtered aseptically through the membrane which is subsequently supported on or immersed in the appropriate culture medium prior to incubation and counting. This method is simpler and it makes possible the use of much larger samples, making the results more reliable statistically. The membrane method is more expensive but its real advantages are so great that it is replacing the conventional method in the sugar industry.[27,28] The membrane filtration method has been adopted by I.C.U.M.S.A.[29]

F. Process Control

The type of analysis used for control purposes on intermediate products depends on the level of the impurities.

1. Sucrose

In high quality syrup sucrose is not determined at all and control is exercised by measurement of the impurities. For lower syrups the molasses type analysis is used. Some refiners use polarization measurements for all syrups but this is rather inaccurate for low quality materials.

2. Ash

For high purity solutions conductometry is the only practicable method. Low purity syrup ashes are determined gravimetrically for experimental and statistical purposes while conductometry is used for routine control.

3. Solids Content

Plant operators rely on density measurements. Most of the syrups are hot and special metal hydrometer spindles are used which have been calibrated at high temperatures and read directly in per cent solids. The laboratory method for the routine determination of solids is refractometry (Section 5.D.3.).

4. Books

There are a number of excellent reference books on sugar technology and analysis. A selection of them follows:
Technology: Honig,[30] Lyle,[31] Meade.[21]
Analysis: Browne and Zerban,[32] Meade,[21] Plews,[8] de Whalley.[4]
Reference Tables: Bates et al.,[1] Norrish.[25]

REFERENCES

1. Bates, F. J. and Associates (1942). "Polarimetry, Saccharimetry and the Sugars". (National Bureau of Standards, Washington).
2. Hirschmüller, H. (1953). In: "Principles of Sugar Technology" (P. Honig, ed.), Vol. I, pp. 1–74. (Elsevier, London).

3. Powers, H. E. C. (1948). *Int. Sug. J.* **50**, 149–150.
4. de Whalley, H. C. S. (ed.) (1964). "I.C.U.M.S.A. Methods of Sugar Analysis". (Elsevier, London).
5. Wilson, R. A. M. (1970). *Int. Commn. unif. Meth. Sug. Analysis*, **15**, 91–105.
6. Lane, J. H. and Eynon, L. (1923). *J. Soc. Chem. Ind.* **42**, 32–37T.
7. Gardiner, S. D. (1953). *Analyst*, **78**, 709–711.
8. Plews, R. W. (ed.) (1970). "Analytical Methods used in Sugar Refining", p. 57. (Elsevier, London).
9. Payne, J. H. (ed.) (1968). "Sugar Cane Factory Analytical Control", pp. 85–86. (Elsevier, London).
10. Emmerich, A. (1957). *Zucker*, **20**, 603–611.
11. Knight, J. and Allen, C. H. (1960). *Int. Sug. J.* **62**, 344–346.
12. Plews, R. W. (ed.) (1970). "Analytical Methods used in Sugar Refining", pp. 76–79. (Elsevier, London).
13. Bennett, R. G., Runeckles, R. E. and Thompson, H. M. (1964). *Int. Sugar. J.* **66**, 109–113.
14. Plews, R. W. (ed.) (1970). "Analytical Methods used in Sugar Refining", pp. 47–57. (Elsevier, London).
15. Hibbert, D. and Phillipson, R. T. (1966). *Int. Sug. J.* **68**, 39–44.
16. Carruthers, A., Heaney, R. K. and Oldfield, J. F. T. (1965). *Int. Sug. J.* **67**, 364–368.
17. Plews, R. W. (ed.) (1970). "Analytical Methods used in Sugar Refining", pp. 80–84. (Elsevier, London).
18. Plews, R. W. (ed.) (1970). "Analytical Methods used in Sugar Refining", pp. 87–88. (Elsevier, London).
19. Hill, S. and Muller, E. G. (1958). *Int. Sug. J.* **60**, 128–132.
20. Hill, S. and Muller, E. G. (1958). *Int. Sug. J.* **60**, 194–197.
21. Meade, G. P. (1963). "Spencer–Meade Cane Sugar Handbook", 9th ed., pp. 581–582 (Wiley, New York).
22. Plews, R. W. (ed.) (1970). "Analytical Methods used in Sugar Refining", pp. 88–90. (Elsevier, London).
23. Sibley, M. J., Eis, F. G. and McGinnis, R. A. (1956). *Anal. Chem.* **37**, 1701–1703.
24. Rosenhauer, K. (1966). *Int. Commn. unif. Meth. Sug. Analysis* **14**, 65–73.
25. Norrish, R. S. (1967). "Selected Tables of Physical Properties of Sugar Solutions", Scientific and Technical Surveys No. 51, pp. 57–59. (B.F.M.I.R.A., Leatherhead).
26. Meade, G. P. (1963). "Spencer–Meade Cane Sugar Handbook", 9th ed., p. 315. (Wiley, New York).
27. Coleman, M. C. and Bender, C. R. (1957). *Food Technology*, **11**, 398–403.
28. Attenborough, S. J. and Scarr, M. P. (1957). *J. appl. Bact.* **20**, 460–466.
29. Weidenhagen, R. (1966). *Int. Commn. unif. Meth. Sug. Analysis*, **14**, 120–124.
30. Honig, P. (ed.) (1953). "Principles of Sugar Technology". Vols I–III. (Elsevier, London).
31. Lyle, O. (1957). "Technology for Sugar Refinery Workers", 3rd ed. (Chapman Hall, London).
32. Browne, C. A. and Zerban, F. W. (1941). "Physical and Chemical Methods of Sugar Analysis", 3rd ed. (Wiley, New York).

Chocolate and Sugar Confectionery, Jams and Jellies

P. LINDLEY

The Nestlé Company Ltd., Croydon, Surrey. England

1. INTRODUCTION

Manufactured products containing a large proportion of sugar cover a vast field. In this chapter it is proposed to deal with the following main types of product:

> Chocolate Confectionery
> Sugar Confectionery and
> Jams, Jellies and Marmalades

In considering the quality control of these products it is convenient to divide it into (A) Raw materials control (B) Control over the manufacturing process (C) Finished product examination, and (D) Defects occurring in the stored products. The production and sale of goods of satisfactory quality is always the objective and results from the co-ordinated efforts of all sections of a manufacturing company. Thus the Quality Control Department must maintain very close liaison with Research and Development, Purchasing, Production, Marketing and Distribution departments. In many instances it will adopt a co-ordinating and advisory role although some functions such as laboratory testing and the inspection of raw materials, sources of supply and incoming goods may be a direct responsibility.

2. CHOCOLATE CONFECTIONERY

Convenient Definitions for chocolate products are proposed by the Food Standards Committee (Report on Food Labelling September 1965).

These are as follows:

CHOCOLATE means any product made by grinding roasted cocoa beans, whether or not cocoa butter had been added or partially removed and with or without the addition of carbohydrate sweetening matter or dairy products, but does not include cocoa powder.

CHOCOLATE CONFECTIONERY means any solid or semi-solid product complete in itself and suitable for consumption without further preparation or processing, of which the characteristic ingredient is chocolate or cocoa, with or without the addition of nuts and fruit and includes products made by enrobing sugar confectionery and other ingredients in chocolate but does not include chocolate, chocolate coated filled or flavoured biscuits, flour confectionery, any type of ice cream or pharmaceutical products.

A. Raw Material Control

The three essential raw materials required for the manufacture of chocolate products are cocoa beans, cocoa butter and sugar, to which may be added milk, since milk chocolate represents a large proportion of chocolate manufacture, particularly in the U.K.

In addition there are a number of secondary materials such as dried fruit and nuts and technological aids such as lecithin. Many different flavourings are used in the chocolate itself and in centres.

Probably the most important single factor in maintaining product quality is the quality of raw materials supplies. Goods that arrive for processing at the food factory should be of consistent quality, properly packaged and free from foreign materials. One of the biggest practical headaches in the food factory is to prevent the entry of unwanted foreign materials in the finished product, consequently the less that comes in with the raw materials the easier is the problem. To ensure satisfactory raw material supplies, clear, precise and practicable specifications should be used and these should be understood and accepted by suppliers.

It is pointless to produce detailed technical specifications which are quite impossible to meet, although they can be just as unsatisfactory if they are written too loosely. The point of a specification is to lay down clearly the quality attributes which are really important as far as the user is concerned. Particular care is required when considering bacteriological standards and their application as regards the rejection of consignments.

Close technical liaison with suppliers of both natural and manufactured raw materials is by far the best way to deal with the quality control of raw materials. In this way the problems of vendor and purchaser are fully understood. This is not always possible and purchase may at times be based upon the approval of a sample which should be be retained as a standard for comparison with the bulk supply.

When bulk consignments arrive at the factory or store they should be examined and sampled. Signs of infestation should be especially looked for and any damage to packages noted—it is sensible to put aside any damaged packages for special examination and possible rapid use or disposal. In the case of infested goods care must be taken to prevent any cross infestation of other stored materials and arrangements should be made for fumigation. A careful check must be made on stock control and proper rotation maintained according to age.

1. Cocoa Beans

Cocoa beans are the basis of all chocolate products. These beans, each about $\frac{3}{4}$ in. long, grow in pods on the tree genus *Theobroma*, *T. cacao* being the commercially important species.

There are two main types of bean used in chocolate manufacture: "bulk" beans which grow largely in West Africa and Brazil and make up a substantial part of the world harvest, and "fine" beans which are grown in Ecuador, Venezuela, Central America, the West Indies, Ceylon and Samoa. These latter types are prized for their flavour, and in some cases, special colour characteristics. "Fine" cocoas should always be selected after making small sample lots of chocolate and carrying out tasting tests. The usual procedure adopted for the evaluation of "bulk" beans is that of cutting the beans and noting the internal appearance.

During the process of fermentation, which is carried out to facilitate the removal of the pulp surrounding the beans and which plays a vital part in flavour development, the colour of the interior of beans changes from a slate grey, through a deep purple and finally becomes a reddish brown colour. Consequently colour may be taken as an indication of the degree of fermentation. Of equal importance is the texture of the cut surface; poorly fermented beans have a waxy cut surface, whilst the cut surfaces of well fermented beans exhibit a broken appearance. This is the basis of the "cut-test". Full details are given in a very useful booklet issued by the Cocoa, Chocolate and Confectionery Alliance.[1]

Beans may conveniently be sampled using the square root number, i.e. samples being taken from that number of sacks equal to the square root of the total number of sacks in the consignment.

The sample of beans to be examined is thoroughly mixed and then "quartered" to leave a heap of about 200 beans. The first 200 beans, irrespective of size, shape and condition, should then be counted off, leaving the dross behind. The weight is recorded and the beans are cut longitudinally. The halves are then examined and put into the following eight categories:

(a) Fully fermented—rich brown colour.
(b) Partly brown and partly purple.

(c) Fully purple—a stage in the fermentation when the violet pigments spread throughout the bean.
(d) Slaty—the colour of the unfermented bean.
(e) Mouldy.
(f) Infested.
(g) Germinated.
(h) Shrivelled.

Thus the sample is being examined to indicate the general degree of fermentation which has taken place and to assess the defects present.

Also important is the size of the bean because of the corresponding influence on shell content which is economically important. In addition the size range of a batch of beans is important. Beans of varying sizes will cause problems in roasting. If the roaster is set to give a correct roast for the largest beans, the smallest will be grossly over-roasted and vice versa. Size may be assessed adequately by a count of a given weight of beans.

The fat content of the beans should be determined by solvent extractions after digestion with hydrochloric acid.[2] This, however, has the disadvantage of being a rather long procedure and a more rapid refractometric method has been proposed.[3] A factor of economic importance is the amount of shell present. This may be determined by shelling the beans and weighing the fractions. Such an examination can also help reveal the characteristics of the bean, such as a tendency of the shell to adhere to the nib (cotyledon).

Moisture is important in relation to mould growth in the stored beans. Eight per cent is a reasonable maximum working figure, unless immediate use is envisaged. Moisture is determined on a mixture of the ground beans with sand by oven drying for 4 h at 100–102°C.

Interesting information on cocoa bean quality is given by Kleinert[4] and in the book, "Cocoa Bean Test", 1961–62.[5]

2. Cocoa Butter

Cocoa butter is removed from cocoa beans by pressing or by solvent extraction. Pressed butter is generally extracted from nib only, while extracted butter is often obtained from residues or from whole substandard beans. For this reason pressed butter is generally regarded as the higher quality article. At a temperature of 20°C it is a pale yellow, hard, brittle substance with an oily surface, and the break is clean with a waxy surface. When heated to about 35°C it melts to a golden yellow oil. It has the characteristic chocolate aroma and faint chocolate flavour which is difficult to remove. Under satisfactory conditions of storage it has excellent keeping properties. Prolonged exposure to light, however, causes the development of a rancid taste and smell and bleaching of the colour.

Chemically cocoa butter is a mixture of glycerides of fatty acids (largely oleic, palmitic and stearic). It is this range of compounds which gives cocoa butter its special melting characteristics so important to the eating quality of chocolate.

The tests carried out on cocoa butter are flavour, colour measurement, melting point and tests for the presence of adulterant fats such as hardened palm kernel oil, or hardened coconut oil. These would include refractive index, iodine value, saponification value, Reichert–Meissl value, Polenske value and acidity. The detection of low levels of adulteration of admixture with so called cocoa butter alternatives such as Illipe butter (Borneo Tallow) and other "tailor made" alternatives now on the market requires the use of chromatographic techniques. Sometimes a cocoa butter reputedly pressed, is mixed with butter extracted from cocoa waste such as shell. An extracted butter differs mainly in the increased content of unsaponifiable matter and in a decreased extinction value of a 1 % solution. However, when the extracted butter is admixed with a pressed one, detection is difficult—particularly in small quantities.

The flavour and cleanliness of the product are important and after approval of a sample, checks should be made to ensure a satisfactory general standard in the whole consignment.

The production of an international standard for cocoa butter is one of the tasks being undertaken by the Codex Alimentarius Commission.

3. Chocolate Crumb

Chocolate crumb is made by drying a mixture of sweetened condensed milk and cocoa mass (ground nib) under vacuum. The moisture content is reduced to a low level of about 1–2%. The evaluation of a sample of crumb would include taste testing, analysis for fat and sugars (sucrose and lactose) to indicate composition and the determination of moisture. The product should be well packaged in multiwall bags, preferably polythene lined, and stored under clean dry conditions free from infestation.

The cocoa mass present has an antioxidant effect and this enables the manufacturer to store milk in this form for subsequent use in chocolate some months later.

4. Commercial Lecithin

Commercial lecithin, a phosphatide complex, is added to chocolate to lower the viscosity. It does so by reducing the surface tension between the solid and fat. It is used for economic reasons as it enables the quantity of cocoa butter to be reduced with financial advantage. The addition of lecithin is also said to increase the resistance of the resulting chocolate to fat "bloom" formation.

When sampling lecithin it is important to warm it to 40°C for some hours, then thoroughly mix the sample. Examination would comprise a test of acetone insoluble materials,[6] benzene insoluble matter[6] and moisture by toluene distillation.

To estimate the practical value of lecithin, small batches of chocolate must be made and examined. Some samples of lecithin contribute most unpleasant flavours and it is obviously essential that such lecithins are not used in any form in chocolate production.

5. Nuts

Nuts must be carefully selected and sorted before use. Sub-standard nuts are particularly objectionable when eaten, and consequently great care must be taken to exclude them from the finished pack.

Small nuts are often required for chocolate products and these are liable to be hard. Quality examination of nuts includes cutting them to look for infestation or discoloration, a roasting test to assess the final roasted nut flavour, a test for rancidity and a size count.

Nuts are susceptible to the development of rancidity and should preferably be kept in chill storage before use. In recent years considerable attention has been focused upon the problem of aflatoxin. Although the chief source of this toxic material, produced by a strain of the fungus *Aspergillus*, is to be found in groundnuts, any mouldy nuts must be suspected. Tests are outlined by Coomes and Sanders,[7] Coomes, Crowther, Francis and Shone[8] and Coomes, Crowther, Francis, and Stevens[9].

As a practical point care must also be taken to eliminate all pieces of shell from nuts. These are very unpleasant and are very likely to lead to consumer complaints.

6. Packaging Materials

In the manufacture of modern packaging materials volatile products are used which are liable to taint chocolate products very seriously.

In view of this, very careful selection and testing of all packaging materials is essential. For this reason the Robinson test has been devised and details are given in the O.I.C.C. handbook.[2]

B. Process Control

Quality control in the factory is based upon clearly specifying all procedures which are likely to affect the quality of the product and carrying out any tests necessary to give a running record of performance. In this way important quality attributes can be kept within defined limits and remedial action taken where necessary. The most vital factor in process control is speed: speed in carrying out tests, speed in reporting results and speed in taking remedial action when this is indicated. The graphical recording of results and the use of statistical control charts are most important in following trends and in ensuring that time is not lost in making unnecessary adjustments to machinery.

1. Bean Cleaning

Beans are cleaned to eliminate various extraneous matter such as sticks, string and nails and to remove dust and loose shells. This is accomplished by the use of screens, magnets and air streams incorporated in a cleaning machine. A visual check should be maintained on the efficiency of this machinery.

2. Roasting

The cocoa beans are roasted to develop the full chocolate flavour. This also facilitates the removal of the shell and renders the nib suitable for grinding. Careful control over this process is required in order to ensure that under-roasting (with insufficient flavour development and difficulty of shell removal) or over-roasting (with destruction of flavour and undue loss of weight) do not occur.

The roasting temperature is normally 100–130°C and the time and temperature set according to the equipment in use and the properties of the beans being roasted. After roasting the beans are cooled rapidly to about 50–60°C to prevent further uncontrolled roasting and the migration of cocoa butter into the shell which will become waste.

Interesting information on cocoa bean roasting is given by Kleinert.[10]

3. Winnowing

The roasted beans are cracked and broken between adjustable toothed rollers so as to loosen the shell from the nibs. Separation of the shell and nib is by an air flotation process, where a controlled air current separates the heavy/small surface area nibs from the light/large surface area shell, the separate particles falling on to conveyers on opposite sides of the machine. This is a most important stage and careful control must be maintained. The retention of too much shell with the nib is undesirable (in some countries there is a legal limit) and the inclusion of nib with the shell waste incurs a financial loss.

One method of checking is to hand pick samples to separate the larger pieces and use liquid flotation to separate smaller ones.[11] The separated portions are then weighed.

The determination of fat content on the two portions should also be carried out. It is then possible to calculate the percentage of nib in the shell waste, and the percentage of shell in the nib on the basis of an average fat content of 55% in the nib and about 5% in the shell. In the factory it is possible to

12*

determine by analysis the fat content of the pure nib and shell in a particular batch, so making this method quite accurate.

4. Milling

The cocoa nib is ground between rollers or pin mills, to produce a smooth "liquor". The breakage of the tissues releases the contained fat which melts because of the frictional heat produced and the mass flows from the grinder at a temperature of 60–80°C. The temperature of the mass must not be allowed to rise too high because of the danger of loss of aromatic flavour, consequently the grinding machines are usually water cooled. The mass produced solidifies at a temperature of approximately 35°C.

A constant check must be maintained on the particle size. (This may be determined by microscope or by sedimentation.) The final particle size will depend upon individual requirements.

The cocoa liquor produced by milling the nibs may be used for making chocolate, chocolate crumb or for pressing to remove cocoa butter leaving cocoa cake. Consideration is given here only to the manufacture of chocolate which may be sold in bar form or used as a couverture for some kind of fancy filling.

5. Mixing Operation

According to the individual formulation the cocoa liquor is mixed with sugar and perhaps chocolate crumb and a proportion of the cocoa butter in order to form a stiff paste suitable for refining.

Dark chocolate is manufactured from cocoa mass, sugar and cocoa butter and milk chocolate from either full cream milk powder, cocoa butter, cocoa mass and sugar, or chocolate crumb and cocoa butter.

Mixing is usually carried out in large vessels with stone rollers called melangeurs. These and other equipment are described by L. Russel Cook.[12]

In order for a manufacturer to produce a standard item, close control of the mixing operation must be maintained. If liquids are pumped and metered volumetrically, temperature must be reasonably constant. All scales used must be frequently checked and weighings carefully made, especially of small quantities, e.g. flavouring.

6. The Refining Operation

The purpose of refining is to reduce the particle size of the mix, particularly the sugar, to the required size according to individual specification. This is usually between 25 and 30 μm for the largest particles. If finer than this the texture in the mouth tends to be "slimy", and if above it becomes "gritty". Refining to a very small particle size is also to be avoided for economic reasons, e.g. increased wear on rollers, increased power consumption and increased cocoa butter usage. The operation of a chocolate refiner is carried out by a skilled operator and frequent laboratory testing for particle size is carried out to ensure that accurate setting is maintained across the width of the rollers. This is usually done by examining a suspension in oil, of refined chocolate, on a microscope fitted with a size graticule. The use of a polarizer is recommended as this shows up the sugar particles and makes them easier to measure.

During refining, the chocolate, which is in a finely divided state, is exposed to the atmosphere and in this state is particularly susceptible to the pick-up of unwanted moisture. The relative humidity of the refining room can, with advantage, be controlled to below 65%.

7. *Conching*

Conching is a final mixing process which has great influence on the flavour and aroma of the chocolate. In the conventional equipment the chocolate is placed in a conch pot with a granite bed upon which heavy granite rollers are moved backwards and forwards. The chocolate is thus mixed with a rolling splashing action.

This operation which is used in the manufacture of high class chocolate can take anything from 12 to 72 h. During this time, complex chemical and physical changes take place which affect the flavour and aroma, the process favouring oxidation changes and the removal of some undesirable volatile products. The conditions for conching will be determined during the product development stage. Friction during conching produces heat and checks on the temperature cycle are made throughout. The working range is likely to be within 70–90°C for dark chocolate and 50–70°C for milk chocolate.

Conching is a costly and time-consuming process and obviously a continuous search is being made to understand further the changes taking place in order to produce a more efficient and economic process of chocolate manufacture. This has led to the development of newer types of conches and to the search for entirely new processes.

If volatile flavourings are used in the formulation and manufacture of chocolate, a suitable time to add them to the mix is towards the end of the conching cycle together with the balance of the cocoa butter. Laboratory checking of the conched mix includes the determination of viscosity and fat content. Reference will be made later to analytical methods.

8. *Tempering*

Tempering is a process of controlled cooling of the chocolate to ensure crystallization of the stable crystal forms in the fat component giving an end product with the required appearance and texture. Liquid chocolate is usually stored at between 40 and 50°C and in the case of dark chocolate is cooled or tempered to between 29 and 31°C and in the case of milk chocolate to 28–30°C. The lower temperature range for milk chocolate is due to the lower solidification point of the milk fat present. Without correct tempering it is impossible to demould the subsequently chilled chocolate blocks, owing to limited contraction. Unsatisfactory tempering will lead to poor texture and a dull finish and can lead to the subsequent formation of an unsightly fat bloom on the surface of the chocolate.

Once the best tempering conditions for a particular chocolate product have been determined, they must be carefully controlled. The continuous checking and maintenance of recording and controlling equipment is important. Temper can be checked with special meters with a thermistor head giving a complete recording of the cooling curve. Bracco *et al.* give interesting information on all aspects of tempering.[13]

9. Bar Moulding

The chocolate may be required for moulding into bars or for enrobing on to fancy centres. In the production of bars the tempered chocolate is deposited into pre-heated metal (or plastic) moulds of the required shape and at the correct temperature. The moulds then pass through a cooling chamber gradually reaching ambient temperature. Careful control of temperature and humidity is required in the packing room where the chocolate will emerge from the cooling chamber. The entry to the tunnel is usually in one room and the exit in another allowing easier control over conditions.

A very important control at this point is that of the weight of the product. This is of great importance from an economic and legal point of view. Statistical methods are used to control the deposition weights and these should be very closely applied.

The finished bars, by means of a moving belt, are usually passed through a cooler before passing through a metal detector. Proper maintenance of this equipment is vital and any excess lubricating oil must be carefully removed if contamination of the finished product is to be avoided. If at any stage in the procedure it is necessary to handle chocolate great care should be taken to prevent finger marking. Clean, light cotton gloves free of loose fibres can be used to advantage.

10. Chocolate Coated Confectionery

In the past assorted chocolates were made by hand dipping the centres in tempered chocolate. Today, the coating is carried out by enrobing machines which pass the centres for chocolate assortments or bar confectionery through a "curtain" of molten chocolate. Controls must cover tempering, viscosity and temperature. A continuous coating is essential—with many centres any break may lead to "weeping", i.e. the formation of syrup on the chocolate due to moisture absorption by the centre. A breakdown of the chocolate covering of the sweet can be caused by development of osmophilic yeasts in the centre unless appropriate control measures are in operation, e.g. ensuring an adequate sugar solids content.

C. Finished Product Examination

The routine examination of chocolate products includes organoleptic assessment, chemical and physical examination. Few bacteriological problems arise with chocolate because of very low moisture content and the presence of inhibiting substances.

1. Organoleptic Assessment

The following attributes should be noted:

(a) *Appearance.* The appearance of the pack as sold—i.e. in box or wrapper —is important and should not be neglected. Appearance of the product is more important with some packs than with others. It is of prime importance with boxes of chocolates when presentation is vital, finger marks or scuffing having a very detrimental effect.

A full assessment of all aspects of presentation would be made according to laid down standards for acceptance.

(b) *Flavour.* For routine daily control in the factory flavour is usually judged by trained tasters using their own memories as a reference. Periodic checks should be made that there is no gradual change in product quality by testing against approved standards.

(c) *Texture.* The chocolate should melt agreeably in the mouth without becoming sticky. There should be no "grittiness" due to high particle size, or "sliminess" due to low particle size.

It is preferable to examine chocolate samples under standardized temperature conditions.

2. Chemical and Physical Examinations

The examinations carried out on the finished product act as a further check on process control efficiency as well as providing some information not obtained during production.

Testing carried out would be as follows:

(a) Moisture content
(b) Fat content
(c) Particle size
(d) Sugar analysis
(e) Cocoa bean shell content
(f) Viscosity
(g) Any tests concerned with special attributes of the particular product (e.g. chocolate containing alcohol derived from the addition of spirits such as rum).

It is assumed here that the only testing carried out will be concerned with the maintenance of the quality of the company's products, that is to meet market demands and legal requirements. Formulation would be known and tests selected accordingly. It may additionally be required that the Quality Control Department examines competitors' products.

(a) *Moisture content* of chocolate is important. In bars it is usually between 0·8 and 1·3% and rarely exceeds 1·5%. High moisture content unfavourably affects texture and flavour (deterioration of cocoa flavour with the danger of development of "off" flavours increased) and makes the product more liable to infestation by insects.

Water is determined by mixing with sand and oven drying[2] or sometimes by the Karl Fischer method. Solvent distillation is little used because of the low amount of water present.

(b) *Fat determination.* The most precise method[2] is unfortunately rather time consuming. This involves treatment with HCl prior to extraction of the fat. The rapid refractometric method, based upon the variation of refractive index of a fat solvent according to the dissolved cocoa butter present, can be used, but is really more applicable to process control when speed is vital. The A.O.A.C.[11] method is basically similar, and may be utilized.

(c) *Particle size.* This has already been mentioned under process control when the miscroscopic method would most likely have been used. For the rather more leisurely analysis of the finished product sieve analysis, sedimentation or cone measurement methods may be used. Kleinert in 1964[14] reviewed these methods.

(d) *Sugar analysis.* Recommended[2] are polarization methods for sucrose, the Luff–Schoorl method for lactose, and the Potterat–Eschmann complexometric method for sucrose and lactose together in the absence of other sugars.

(e) *Viscosity* is basically important during process control but may be conveniently considered here. Factors affecting viscosity are conching, water content, particle size and lecithin content. The complex rheology of chocolate is outside the scope of quality control and only some of the most used methods of viscosity measurement are considered.

For quality control purposes comparative results are often adequate. Much used is the McMichael instrument. This apparatus uses a mechanically driven cylinder rotating in a vessel containing molten chocolate.

Also useful is the Koch viscometer of the falling sphere type. Although perhaps not quite as accurate it is particularly valuable for process control because it may be used by semi-skilled assistants.

(f) *Milk components.* Determination is of butter fat and non-fat milk solids.

The total fat may be extracted by the Roese–Gottlieb method[11] and butter fat estimated by the Reichert–Meissl index.[11] Non-fat milk solids estimation is generally based upon lactose content.

D. Defects Occurring in Stored Chocolate Products

Manufacturers take a great deal of care to ensure that finished goods are kept under closely controlled conditions. Temperature (55–65°F) and relative humidity (55–65%) are carefully controlled and any deterioration invariably occurs after the goods have left the manufacturers' care.

1. Heat Damage

This most commonly observed defect is an unsightly white fat "bloom" on the chocolate surface. It is perfectly harmless but gives rise to a considerable number of consumer complaints. It is usually caused by unsatisfactory handling such as leaving it in a motor car in the hot sun or placing by a warm radiator.

The design of bulk stores requires considerable care. Controlled ventilation is essential. Sometimes the need for refrigeration may be overcome by the judicious opening of doors and windows to permit the entry of cool night air. Chocolate in outer shipping containers is quite well isolated from the environment and this procedure may with care and attention avoid undue spoilage of stored goods. However, most large manufacturers do have properly conditioned stores.

2. Moisture Damage

A high relative humidity may permit the formation of dissolved sugar on the surface which dries out to a bloom showing a crystalline structure. If coated centres are left long enough under conditions of high relative humidity mould growth can occur. However, before this stage, the appearance of the produce would have made it unsaleable.

3. Infestation

The danger of infestation of cocoa products has already been emphasized. Thus stores must be scrupulously clean and no dust allowed to gather or bad stock rotation to conceal old stocks.

3. SUGAR CONFECTIONERY

A variety of products are known under this heading. Some, like fruit drops, are hard and clear, while others, like fudge, are soft and crystalline. Solid ingredients such as fruit and nuts are often added for further variety.

In such forms as fondant creams, caramels and toffees, sugar confectionery is extensively employed as centres for chocolate bars and chocolate assortments. Although differing so widely in eating qualities, sweets are basically sugar mixes and the texture variation is due to varying water content and to varying proportions of liquid and crystalline sugar, a clear hard sweet being a super-cooled liquid like glass, and fondant being well crystallized. Variations are introduced by addition of colloids and by aeration. The texture is thus controlled by initial formulation and by manufacturing procedures. When sugar syrup is concentrated and allowed to cool, crystallization will take place. If other sugars are present this crystallization is slowed down or altogether prevented. This delayed crystallization may be effected by the presence of invert sugars, possibly through addition of acid to the boiling to promote inversion, or more usually by adding confectioners' glucose (hydrolyzed corn starch). The formation of very fine sugar crystals in confectionery is termed "graining".

Examples of sugar confectionery are:

Low Moisture Content

Uncrystallized	Boiled sugars	Mixed sugars with or without other ingredients e.g. butter, boiled and cooled with minimum stirring.
Crystallized		Sugar syrup dried out with continuous friction through rolling in a revolving pan.
Powdered	Tablets	Icing sugar with some additives compacted by pressure.

High Moisture Content

Uncrystallized	Jellies and Gums	Mixed sugars with jellifying agents such as gelatine, pectin, sugar and starch.
	Caramels	Mixed sugars with fat and milk protein.
	Liquorice	Mixed sugars including raw sugar and molasses with flour as gelatinizing agent.
Crystallized	Fondant Cream	Mixed sugars rich in sucrose boiled to give supersaturated syrup cooled with vigorous agitations.
	Fudge	Caramel somewhat supersaturated with sucrose possibly seeded with fondant cream.
	Montelimar Nougat	Mixed sugars including honey boiled and whipped with albumen and seeded with icing sugar.
Powdered	French Pastes and Marzipans etc.	Icing sugar and other ingredients including humectant and fat held together with gelatine gum etc.

A. Raw Material Control

1. Sugars

This is the most important group of raw materials associated with sugar confectionery manufacture. It is largely the proportions of sugars that donate the various degrees of texture to the final product, depending on the formulation or recipe and method of manufacture. Broadly speaking, there are three main types of sugars used and these are now described.

(a) *Sucrose.* This disaccharide sugar is extracted and refined from natural sources. It occurs in different forms, the most important being:

(i) Granulated sugar—pure white sucrose in crystalline form suitable for manufacturing purposes.

(ii) Caster sugar—a smaller crystal size than granulated sugar, mostly used for crystallized work.

(iii) Icing sugar—very finely ground sugar used for tablets, lozenges and pastes, e.g. marzipan.

The quality of the three types mentioned above is by necessity of high standard and is assessed by the crystalline properties and colour of the resulting solution particularly after boiling. The highly refined sucrose is to be a free running, clean, white coloured crystalline substance, readily soluble in water to give a colourless syrup which can be simmered without developing colour. Lower grades of sugar are available commercially and may be used for reasons of flavour, colour, or economy; an example is the use of dark sugar in liquorice confectionery. The less refined sugars are very pale yellow to brown in colour and are "sticky" owing to the presence of uncrystallizable syrup or invert sugar adhering to the crystals. Another important aspect is the presence of dirt or other extraneous matter in the raw material which may ultimately result in its appearance in the final product. To control this problem, a "dirt test" is carried out by passing a known concentration of a sugar solution through a filter pad. The resulting pad is then examined and compared with a standard series of pads. Nowadays sugar is of a high quality, and is rarely suspect, but some analysis of the sugar as received should nevertheless be made.

The methods available include: Sucrose content, Moisture content,[11] Ash (sulphated),[11] Invert sugar,[11,15] Colour of Solution.[11]

Sugar is frequently delivered in bulk and stored in large bins. To be sure of high standards the receiving bins and bulk distribution lines must be regularly cleaned and the bins must be placed in a dry environment. In the case where sugar is delivered in packages, these should preferably be multiwall paper bags. They must be stored in a cool dry place free from infestation. If the relative humidity is high then there is the possibility that the sugar will become damp; if it is palletized and the pallets are stacked high, cementing of the sugar can occur in the lower pallet layers. Sugar stocks should be used as quickly as possible and supplies should be obtained according to demand.

2. Invert Sugar

Invert sugar consists of equal parts of the monosaccharides, laevulose and dextrose, obtained by acid or enzymatic hydrolysis or inversion of the disaccharide sucrose. It also occurs as a result of heat:

$$C_{12}H_{22}O_{11} + H_2O \xrightarrow[\text{Acid}]{\text{Heat}} C_6H_{12}O_6 + C_6H_{12}O_6$$

Sucrose + Water   Dextrose   Laevulose

The main properties of invert sugar are twofold. Firstly, unlike sucrose, invert sugar will not readily crystallize out from solution, and when added to a supersaturated solution of sucrose slows down the rate of crystallization of the sucrose. Secondly it is of a hygroscopic nature and is advantageous in paste work where it prevents the paste from becoming hard. However, excess use will lead to a sticky product. Commercial invert sugar is viscous and slightly yellow in colour and is delivered either by bulk road tanker or in large metal drums. Moisture content should be frequently checked by refractometer.

3. Glucose Syrup

Glucose syrup, often known as confectioners' glucose (or liquid glucose) is produced by acid or enzymatic hydrolysis of edible starch. It is a complex substance consisting of an aqueous solution of variable quantities of dextrins, maltose, dextrose, and different oligosaccharides, (isomaltose, maltotriose, maltotetrose etc.). It is a viscous, colourless or almost colourless, sweet tasting liquid, similar to invert sugar in most of its properties, i.e. hygroscopic in nature and with the power to decrease crystallization rates, but it is much less sweet. It has an additional important property in that it is of a gummy nature being stable during boiling. This substance will therefore promote some chewiness in products such as toffees. Excess will cause toughness and stickiness and as a result its addition must be properly controlled. The degree of degradation of the corn starch is measured by the reducing power of the glucose syrup expressed as dextrose (D.E. = Dextrose equivalent) in the solids. The D.E. Value is the percentage of reducing sugars as dextrose based on the solids content. Liquid glucoses with a range of D.E.s are available commercially.

4. Honey

This naturally occurring substance has found a place in sugar confectionery ever since the industry began. It is a complex substance containing hexoses (laevulose and dextrose) and oligosaccharides, and possesses a very distinctive flavour. It is employed for this flavour, e.g. in nougat and marshmallows, since commercially it is not practicable on cost grounds to use it merely to replace glucose or invert sugar. It has a very high invert sugar content, approximately 75% and as such is hygroscopic and therefore useful as a moisture retainer, although this is, of course, overshadowed by its distinctive flavour property.

It is a variable substance and its flavour will depend on the locality of the hive and the source of nectar. In the quality control of honey, water content is important. It is generally in the range of 15–25% but to ensure good keeping quality and to avoid fermentation, 18–20% is the practical maximum. High water content may indicate adulteration or lack of maturation and to determine this, methods given for the examination of sugars are utilized.

Honey should be free from any extraneous matter such as wax and animal debris, and should be stored in a cool dry place in tightly packed containers, preferably in darkness.

Tests should be made to ascertain to what degree the distinctive flavour will stand heating as honeys vary considerably in this respect.

5. Milk and Milk Products

Milk is a popular ingredient in confectionery as it promotes texture and flavour development, and is an ingredient in caramels, toffees and fudge. The use of fresh milk is not practical, owing to the time needed to boil away the water, and the flavour changes and increased sugar inversion brought about by the long boiling. Other milk products are therefore used: sweetened condensed milk, evaporated milk, and dried milk, each being manufactured from either full cream or skimmed milk. Each of these products adds its own distinctive flavour and texture. The milk most widely used is sweetened condensed milk. There are many problems relating to milk and milk products and these are described in the "Dairy Products" chapter.

6. Fats and Oils

Fats and oils are very important ingredients as they contribute to the required body, smooth soft texture and free eating properties which are so desirable. In some cases where the product is cut after manufacture, the addition of fat gives lubricating properties, and aids cutting. There are two main types used in confectionery, hard or high melting point fats and soft or low melting point fats. Soft fats such as butter fat and coconut oil are used in high boil products such as butterscotch and toffees where the firm consistency is not dependent on the presence of a hard fat. Higher melting point fats such as hydrogenated vegetable and animal fats are used where their firmness will prevent collapse of a product which would be otherwise too soft. Examples are cream pastes and fudge. In all cases where fats are used the melting point of the final mixture in the sweet from all sources should ideally be a few degrees below body temperature so that the product "melts" in the mouth.

The fat therefore must have a suitable melting point and must be properly packed. Rancidity is a major problem which arises mainly in the soft fats. By and large fats with low Reichert and Polenske values are the most reliable in confectionery.

Analyses carried out on the fats and oils include flavour assessment, melting point, colour assessment, refractive index, iodine value, saponification value, Reichert–Meissl value, Polenske value, acidity and peroxide value (the results can then be compared with standard tables or specifications and the quality assessed). The standard methods mentioned above are described in the "Edible fat and oils" chapter where the information concerning fats may be obtained.

7. Acids

Acids are utilized for such purposes as sugar inversion, flavour development or pH adjustment. Standards for food acids are given in the B.P.[16] and the Food Chemicals Codex.[17]

(a) *Citric acid and tartaric acid.* These acids are utilized to enhance flavours, tartaric acid being particularly suitable for sherbet. They may be used for sugar inversion but control has to be very strictly enforced to prevent over-inversion, discoloration, and excess flavour development. For flavour development the acids are added as late as possible in the manufacturing process.

(b) *Lactic acid.* This has been proposed for use in confectionery when the sharp flavour of citric or tartaric acid is undesirable. It can be employed in the production of clear fruit boilings of mild flavour and with gum arabic which remains clear in its presence.

(c) *Cream of tartar.* Available as white powder with a pleasant acidic flavour, and mild in its inversion properties, it can therefore be used with high boiled sugars, e.g. in the preparation of Montelimar nougat.

8. Setting Agents

These materials provide a setting medium, for low boil products, such as gums, jellies, pastilles, marshmallows, pastes and lozenges.

(a) *Gelatine.* This has strong setting powers and when used enables solutions of glucose and sugar to set at a relatively high water content.

These gels can be of varying textures and firmness according to the amount of gelatine used.

Gelatine can be purchased in either powdered or sheet form. In both cases the product must be tightly packed with exclusion of air and moisture, the moisture causing lumpiness in the powder. The pure gelatine can be estimated by determining nitrogen by the Kjeldhal method and the gel strength measured by using the Bloom gelometer or the F.I.R.A. jelly tester. Taste and colour are important items in the specification.

(b) *Agar Agar.* This is a product obtained from seaweed, producing firm jellies without the chewiness and elasticity of gelatine, but it cannot stand heating in the presence of acid. It can be obtained in powdered or strip form and the exclusion of moisture is again important.

(c) *Pectin*. There are several types of pectin, obtained from citrus fruits and apples. By chemical action on the basic pectin, different setting times are produced and the products are graded as such. It is usually obtained in a powdered form, packed in tightly closed containers. It is not used extensively in confectionery because pH and solids requirements are difficult to achieve and control in many confectionery products.

In all three cases mentioned above, the setting or gelling power may be measured by trial batch manufacture. This is sometimes the only satisfactory way of estimating the power of a setting agent.

(d) *Starches*. There are two distinct uses of starch in the confectionery industry. The first is as a moulding medium for which it is specifically prepared and the second use is as an ingredient in the manufacture of confectionery, as in Turkish Delight. For this latter use the starch is pre-treated with acids that will render it almost soluble giving the starch a thin boiling property.

(e) *Albumen*. Albumen is a naturally occurring substance, its main source being the white of eggs, especially hens' eggs. It is purchased in either flake or powder form and before processing is soaked in water. It is important to soak only the required daily amount as albumen will not keep in its liquid state.

9. Emulsifiers and Humectants

These ingredients can give a product an increased quality and shelf life, and are frequently to be found in a recipe. Emulsifiers, such as commercial lecithin and glyceryl monostearate will promote a uniform distribution of fat throughout the product and by doing so improve the texture considerably. An example that may be cited here is the manufacture of toffee and caramel. Glyceryl monostearate besides its emulsifying property is an anti-foaming agent and, it is often claimed, reduces the tendency of the product to stick to metallic surfaces.

Humectants, such as sorbitol, give the product an increased shelf-life by slowing the "drying-up" process which occurs during storage of products such as fudge and pastes.

10. Other Ingredients

Under this heading come ingredients such as fruit, nuts, fillers and cereals. The control of their quality is important, especially the organoleptic qualities. Careful control is required during storage of the materials, particular attention being paid to prevention of infestation which is dealt with in the section on chocolate.

11. Wrapping

Two types of wrapping much utilized in the confectionery industry are waxed paper and moisture-proof synthetic films, used either alone or as laminates with or without foil. These materials are important because of the property of being moisture-proof. The wrappers will prevent moisture gain and will retain moisture in the product. If the wrapper is inadequate, the product, depending on the variety, will lose or gain moisture, leading to unsatisfactory quality in a very short time. As a consequence, checks must be made on the wrappers as soon as they are received from the manufacturers. These checks include:

> Size.
> Strength.
> Thickness.
> Correct type of material.
> Quality of print.
> Permeability to water vapour.
> Absence of smell and taste.

If any of the above are found to be incorrect then it is pointless to use the wrappers, as the product will spoil under storage or give unsatisfactory appearance.

B. Process Control

As already stated there is an almost unlimited variety of sugar confectionery, much of which is now produced by continuous processes employing purpose-built automatic plants. Most aspects of production quality control apply equally to both batch and continuous production; in the interests of conciseness, therefore, most of the following paragraphs deal mainly with batch processing.

1. High Boiled Sweets

These are produced in vast quantities on plants varying in scale from a single pan on a gas fire to continuous lines which take in sugar and glucose at one end and deliver wrapped sweets at the other at the rate of many tons per day.

Whatever the size of the plant it is of great importance that the services required such as gas, steam, water, vacuum and refrigeration are both adequate in quantity and amenable to fine control and that the instrumentation, thermometers, pressure gauges, etc., are of suitable design. It will otherwise be impossible to maintain top quality production.

These sweets have a very low moisture content, probably less than 3.5%. The mixture of sugars used must be accurately controlled and be such that the final product does not contain too much sucrose, which would cause graining. The actual figure will depend upon the nature of the sugars used and the processes through which the boiled mass will have to pass in the course of producing the final sweet. For instance a deposited sweet may be allowed a higher sucrose content than one subjected to much pulling and forming. Probably the sucrose will be in the region of $65\pm5\%$.

In all cases it is imperative that all the sucrose is dissolved and that no crystals are allowed to survive on the sides of the vessels, as this would give rise to "graining" and other troubles.

If inversion during the boiling process is to contribute substantially to the final composition, as for instance by the inclusion of cream of tartar in the recipe, very great care must be taken to ensure that this is accurately dispensed and that the boiling time as well as the final temperature are thoroughly under control.

Colours and flavours must also be accurately measured whether in small batch quantities or by automatic injection into a continuous stream, and the temperature of the batch at the stage at which the addition is made should be standardized. Some are so stable that they can be added before the boiling process but others must be added after the batch has cooled a little and is becoming plastic.

If "buttered" boilings are to be made it is important that the plant includes adequate mixing devices so that the butter is maintained evenly distributed, otherwise some sweets may contain less butter fat than is legally required to justify the appellation "butter".

The boiled mass may be formed into sweets by a number of processes. For instance it may be deposited into moulds or poured on to slabs and then divided by knives set in a frame. It may be cooled and then have various additives, such as citric acid, kneaded into the plastic mass and then be passed in sheets through drop rollers bearing sunken depressions which form the sweets. It may be formed into ropes which can be fed into dies which automatically close together to form the sweet and then open to release it. It may simply be formed into sticks which can be broken into suitable lengths for sale as "rock".

The mass after cooling to a plastic condition may be "pulled" by repeated folding and pulling so as to entrap a lot of air, giving the sweet an opaque appearance and an easily crushed texture. Such a mass may have thin layers of clear unpulled product wrapped around it to give it a "satin" effect. Various centres may be introduced into boiled sweets, some based on fats such as chocolate, some based on boiled syrup such as jams, some consisting of powder such as sherbet. It is essential that the centre material should be so formulated that it will be in equilibrium with the solid casing, especially so far as moisture retention is concerned, otherwise graining and deterioration will rapidly arise from the inside of the sweet. Such sweets may be made by wrapping a sheet of cooled plastic mass round a quantity of the centre material, which must be at a suitable temperature to allow the whole "package" to be pulled out in a conical fashion to form a rope, with a core in the centre, which may be fed into dies for shaping into sweets. This is usually carried out automatically and continuously by pumping the centre through a pipe, which forms the axis around which the plastic mass rotates with a reciprocating motion in a batch roller. For success the mass has to be properly formulated so as to be of the right consistency at the operating temperature and attention must be paid to the height of the boil, quality and proportion of glucose, and amount of invert sugar present at the time of handling. Low D.E. glucose has a toughening effect and invert sugar gives fluidity, so a nice balance must be struck between them.

The formed sweets must be kept separate until they are cooled and solid, and attention must be paid to the humidity of the air used for this purpose as stickiness may ensue if conditions are not right. Drying of the air will almost certainly be called for if production is to be carried out in all atmospheric conditions, the moisture being removed according to well known air-conditioning techniques.

The cooling must be thorough or trouble will ensue when the sweets are packed in airtight containers, through "sweating".

If the sweets are wrapped care must be taken to ensure that the wrapping material is suitable both for the product and for the particular wrapping machine which is to be used. Slipperiness, stiffness, brittleness, tearing strength and resistance to adhesion to the sweet are among the factors involved. A special air-conditioned wrapping material store may be called for, since wrapping machines demand very narrow tolerances in the condition of the materials they handle, and these are very susceptible to temperature and humidity conditions.

2. Nougat

High boiled sugars are also employed in the manufacture of nougat. The mixture often includes honey and cream of tartar. The high boiled sugar is poured slowly into whipped albumen solution or other foaming material. Nuts, dried fruit and fat may be added. The sucrose content in the final product must be controlled to give the desired consistency. If a somewhat grained nougat is required the sucrose must be over 40% and a little icing sugar may be dusted in the last stage of mixing to initiate crystallization in the mass. The nougat may be spread on slabs and cut by rotating knives, the fat content being important to prevent sticking to the knives.

3. Marshmallow

Marshmallows are softer and lighter than nougat, which they resemble in that they too are basically an aerated sugar mix with added setting agents to retain air spaces and donate chewiness. The setting agents can be used individually or in combination with others, i.e. gelatine and albumen.

The process involves boiling sugar and glucose in water to 260°F, adding soaked gelatine and flavour, and then adding this boil to soaked albumen, beating whilst doing so. This is then poured into starch moulds.

It can be seen that both gelatine and albumen are soaked prior to use, and this soaking must be closely controlled, since the water content is critical to both keeping and eating quality.

4. Gums, Pastilles and Jellies

This group of products is of the range soft fluid jellies, through fruit gums to Turkish Delight. By careful choice of setting agents, any texture between the above range of products may be obtained. They are essentially high water content sugar solutions which depend for their set entirely on the action of the setting agents. The sugar and glucose are boiled, the previously soaked setting agent added and the whole mixed. The resulting foam scum is removed, flavour and colour added, and the liquid confectionery run into starch moulds to set. The main control of importance is that of setting agent addition as it is this that determines the final texture and appearance. It is very important that the moulding starch is kept clean and dry. The product may need prolonged storage to give the required texture. The stores must be well designed and controlled to give an even distribution of air movement at the required temperature.

If starch or pectin are the setting agents then these are boiled with the sugar batch. The final moisture content before pouring is critical and some means of controlling it by suitable thermometers or refractometers must be employed. The time taken in boiling must also be under control. In the case of pectin the pH is critical, the exact value depending upon the type of pectin used. It may be around 3·5; lower values tend to give a curdled crumbly consistency, higher values may ultimately prevent setting altogether.

5. Fondant

Fondants are prepared from a solution of sugar, glucose and water, which after processing has a soft, paste-like opaque appearance and smooth texture quite free from grittiness. The success or failure of fondant manufacture is dependent on crystal size, the crystals should be small and of constant size. These minute crystals are suspended in a non-crystallizable syrup and minute air spaces are incorporated into the product during manufacture. In fondant manufacture the sugar is important and should be of the best quality, especially in colour. The mix is boiled to 238°F (for centres) or 246°F (for crystallized) and cooled to 100–115°F as quickly as possible, without agitation, in order to prevent crystallization, further inversion and discoloration. When the sugar mix has reached the required temperature it is creamed. Creaming is a very vigorous process whereby the sugar mass becomes white due to crystallization and entrapped air, the sugar being extremely finely grained. The fondant is poured into stainless steel containers, covered with a damp cloth or wax paper to prevent crust formation and left to mature for 24 h. After this time the fondant mix is remelted with the other ingredients. It is then poured into the starch moulds. The remelting method and temperature are very important. If the temperature is too high or there is a lack of mixing, then coarse crystallization will occur on cooling. The starch moulds consist of depressions in boards of specially prepared cornflour. The starch must be dry, and the moisture content can be easily lowered to 3–4% by drying, about 6% being the working maximum. Above this figure the starch will tend to stick to some products and the detrimental effects can be easily imagined. The starch moulds may be cleaned by sieving, and prepared in drying rooms where the humidity and temperature are strictly controlled, with the object of drying out the moulds at a temperature of 100–120°F in the shortest time. The humidity of the room is important as the rate of drying depends upon it. It is controlled by means of ventilation to give minimum humidity with minimum loss of heat. After the drying of the starch the moisture content is checked and it is only used when the moisture is deemed to be low enough. These processes take place automatically and continuously in modern depositing machines which incorporate a cleaning and drying unit.

6. Toffees and Caramels

The dividing line between these products is one of texture. Caramels are usually soft eating while toffees are hard and chewy, these characteristics being determined by boiling temperatures and ingredients. The boiling temperature differs, from 245°F for a soft caramel to 300°F for a hard toffee. The main ingredients are sugar, glucose, milk and fat, the quality and quantity of the individual ingredients determining the final flavour. The sucrose content of the final caramel must not be too high or graining will ensue. There are many methods for manufacturing toffees and caramels and these can be found in any confectionery textbook. Essentially, the sugar, glucose, fat and condensed milk are boiled together according to the method and temperature specified. The sweetened condensed milk donates a delicate, subtle flavour as well as giving the chew and body required in the sweet. An important requirement is constant stirring during cooking, to avoid burning on the pan and to ensure complete emulsification of the fat.

Caramels may be deposited in starch, cut by knives or fed, when cooked and plastic, into a cut-and-wrap machine.

7. Fudge

Basically the manufacture of fudge consists of the mixing of fondant cream and caramels, with the attainment of a finely grained milky flavour product. Fudge can be manufactured by mixing in fondant cream with cool caramel boil, pouring into a frame and scoring. To produce a fine grain the final mix must be stirred adequately. Coarse grain will result if the hot mix is poured on to a cold surface, or if the fondant cream is added to an insufficiently boiled batch.

8. Liquorice Goods

These are produced in purpose-built plants in which a mixture of raw sugar and molasses can be boiled with a suspension of wheat flour in water, the liquorice being added in the form of broken blocks of liquorice root extract. The equipment is of very robust construction to allow stirring of the heavy mass during the boiling process, which is fairly prolonged. When the cooking is complete, as judged by the character of the stirred mass, it is extruded into the form desired, for instance sheets, rods, tubes, etc. These must be subjected to a very hot stoving to achieve the final chewy consistency. The stoves must be constructed to give even drying with forced ventilation, and the operation must be amenable to control if consistent uniform results are to be obtained.

9. Pastes, Tablets and Lozenges

This class of products is based on icing sugar mixed with varying amounts of other sugars, gelatine, gum and fat to produce pastes, which may be extruded into sheets or granulated for feeding to compressors. The sheets may form part of large sandwiches, e.g. liquorice allsorts, or may be cut into individual pieces for storing as lozenges. Pastes which are required to remain soft will have a considerable addition of humectant such as glucose, and also fat. Pastes for lozenge making will be mostly icing sugar and gum arabic mucilage or gelatine solution. Granules for compressing will require admixture with a lubricant such as powdered stearic acid. The moisture content calls for careful control, and air-conditioning may be required in the compressing room.

10. Panned Goods

These are so-called because they are made in wide-mouthed rotating tilted pans in which the goods can be maintained in continual movement rolling over each other. The pans may be steam jacketed, and have pipes through which a stream of air can be blown over the contents. This air must be controllable in volume and temperature. Any centre which will roll can be fed into these pans for coating with sugar. This is formed by a combination of a dusting of icing (or fine caster) sugar together with the application of sugar syrup. Cocoa powder may also be incorporated into the added coating. In the main the application of hot strong syrup to a hot pan gives a coarse coating, the fine smooth finishing coats requiring weak syrups and low temperatures. Centres may range from caster sugar grains for small items up to whole large nuts or large thick lozenges for giant mint imperials. Best quality sugar is needed for the syrup, and the skilled operator must be provided with adequate means of controlling all the factors involved such as temperature and strength of syrup, volume and temperature of air and temperature and speed of the pan.

11. Sugar Syrup Crystallization

A slightly supersaturated sugar syrup can form a strong, moisture proof shell on a surface which acts as a seed bed for crystallization. This property is made use of for finishing such goods as peppermint creams, and for forming the small globules of syrup which are an attractive feature in some jellies and chocolates. Good quality sugar must be used for making the syrup for the crystallization process. It must be allowed to cool without agitation, and flow very gently over the creams held in suitable baskets. It should not be too cold or the crystallization will be too prolonged. The syrup must be allowed to drain off freely as soon as the crystallization has advanced far enough. This may take a few hours. When the surfaces dry they possess a fine sparkle, and the crystal shell will retain moisture in the creams giving a very long shelf life provided it remains uncracked.

It should be emphasized that sugar confectionery is so varied that it forms a continuous spectrum, of which the items mentioned in these eleven paragraphs will form distinctive guide lines.

C. Finished Product Examination

For various reasons confectionery products are often made in relatively small quantities. Very large batches could lead to problems of darkening or changes in composition during handling; again in some cases the same article is required in several different flavours. Because of the small batches it is difficult to have any extensive analytical control of goods in process; it is usually more satisfactory to have checks on factory procedure such as weighings and temperatures. It is nevertheless desirable to examine analytically samples of each day's production from each line. For high boilings the moisture content is important—methods for testing include adding a solution of the sweet to filter paper for drying in a vacuum and calculating moisture on a solids basis, and the Karl Fischer method. Again, in the case of fondant creams to be enrobed with chocolate, it is essential that the sugar content of the liquid phase be high enough to prevent the development of osmophilic yeasts.

This can be controlled by determining the E.R.H. of the centre. Sucrose content is critical for caramels, fudges and nougat and should be checked.

Besides chemical examinations, physical examinations are carried out. These include flavour, texture, general appearance, quality of the wrappers and net weights. In addition to such tests it is very important that regular inspections are made of the product during storage, as so many factors are involved in ensuring a long shelf life for confectionery products.

D. Defects Occurring in Stored Products

Very important aspects to consider are storage conditions. The ideal temperature for storage is between 55 and 65°F and relative humidity 65% maximum. If either of these conditions is increased above these values then all manner of faults may occur in the products under storage. Fluctuation and extremes of temperature and humidity will also cause faults. Sweating, softening, and graining may be the result of departure from these standard conditions, so it becomes quite apparent that strict control of these factors is necessary.

As a consequence of storage the product may exhibit faults caused by in-correct manufacturing procedures. Common faults include the appearance of graining at a much quicker rate than anticipated, cracking of the product owing to lack of moisture and sticking of the sweet to the wrapper owing to over-inversion, or poor moisture-proof wrapping.

The shelf-life of sugar products is variable and is dependent upon the type of product being stored. In general it is in the range 9–15 months if stored under proper conditions.

During storage by the manufacturer the products are frequently inspected for quality and the possible deterioration of storage conditions. The store is constantly under close scrutiny and there is continuous recording of humidity and temperature values. At certain times of the day, checks are made and if either the humidity or temperature has varied from the norm, remedial action is immediately taken in order to restore the correct conditions.

4. JAMS, JELLIES AND MARMALADES

Although perhaps not strictly correct it is convenient for our purposes to classify these items in two groups:

Jams. Comprising jams, marmalades, jelly jams, and jelly marmalades which are basically sugar–pectin gels, containing either fruit, or fruit juice. Marmalades are essentially jams made from citrus fruits, and jelly jams are those without the insoluble fruit fibres characteristic of normal jams. Jelly marmalades may or may not contain fine cut shreds of peel.

Jellies. These differ from jams in composition and texture. Like jams they have a high sugar content, but the texture characteristic depends upon gelatine or other gelling agent, and not pectin. There is usually no natural fruit content, and the flavour is achieved either by the addition of fruit juice or by the use of a flavouring agent. Colour is normally included in order to achieve a colour characteristic of the fruit flavour chosen.

A. Raw Material Control

1. Fruits

These are purchased for use in the manufacture of jams and marmalades, either fresh, frozen, or as sulphited pulps. Processed fruit pulps are dealt with in a separate section. Notes on storage and handling of some common fresh fruits are given below:

Strawberries. These should be of uniform colour, reasonably firm texture, full flavour, and should become tender without disintegrating on boiling in the jam. Being readily damaged they are best transported in shallow, well ventilated trays holding some 14–21 lb. At the factory the trays of fruit should be kept in a cool place. Considerable juice loss is likely to occur if they are stored for any length of time.

Raspberries. These should be of uniform colour, reasonably firm, and the seeds should not be too large, nor too numerous, and they should not be tough or gritty.

This fruit is particularly susceptible to mould growth, and, if picked in humid conditions, it may exhibit extensive mould within a few hours.

Raspberries are best transported in chips or punnets holding no more than about 4 lb; wood is undesirable due to a foreign matter hazard. For general purposes, however, they may be carried in bulk containers, or in polythene bags within plywood drums. The fruit (up to 100 lb. in each container) may be chilled, or preserved with SO_2 and should preferably be handled promptly on arrival at the factory.

Blackcurrants and Red Currants. A satisfactory method of dealing with these fruits is to pick when just ripe, when they are sufficiently firm to travel well and without undue loss of juice. The currants are normally then frozen in well-ventilated trays holdings about 20–28 lb of fruit. When the fruit is required for use, the stalks are removed from the frozen berries by machine. By this method the loss of fruit and juice is reduced compared with the handling of fresh fruit direct from the farm.

Stone Fruits. The handling of these fruits such as plums, greengages, damsons, and cherries generally follows the same pattern, except that stones have to be removed before use. This is usually done by cooking and then sieving, or by a pitting machine.

The fruit should not be over-ripe if maximum pectin value is to be obtained. Greengages are best delivered slightly under-ripe for a jam of good colour.

Gooseberries. These are usually picked in an under-ripe condition, when pale green and hard, in order to obtain a jam of good colour, flavour, and set. Gooseberries tend to travel rather better than other fruits and are often packed into sacks holding up to about 80 lb.

Citrus Fruits. Citrus fruit is susceptible to mould growth and diphenyl has been added to wrapping papers as a mould inhibitor, and the sodium salt of o-phenylphenol has been used as a dip. In the U.K., amounts of 100 and 70 ppm respectively are permitted by the Preservatives in Food Regulations, 1962, any excess likely to be carried over to the finished product must be avoided.

In order to take full advantage of the pectin in citrus fruits, the cut fruit, peel and hearts, should be processed without delay to avoid degradation of the pectin by pectolytic enzymes. Cut fruit should certainly not be left overnight.

The functions of the Quality Control Department would generally be to supply specifications for the fruit, to ensure compliance with these, to control proper storage in the factory, and to check satisfactory inspection by the factory personnel prior to use.

The specifications should be based on experience, or published information, and include a statement of the varieties required or alternatively the varieties unacceptable. Such specifications would usually result from a close liaison between the production, control and purchasing departments. Some difficulty may be encountered in compiling these specifications owing to the natural and seasonal variations which may occur in the fruit. Under these circumstances the fruit may have to be purchased on the understanding that its quality compares favourably with that of a buying sample.

In order to produce a finished preserve of good colour, flavour, and appearance, a blend of varieties of fruit may be specified.

There is an increasing tendency for manufacturers to obtain their fruits direct from farms, either by ownership, or more commonly by crop contracts. This enables the manufacturer to watch the fruit during growth, and to control the use of fertilizers and insecticides. By choice of the harvesting time, losses due to spoilage may be minimized.

The fruit should be examined on arrival at the factory. Of particular concern must be the degree of ripeness, the presence of spoiled fruit, and of foreign material such as stalks and leaves. There may be considerable variation in the ripeness of fruit on delivery, under-ripe fruit will have a poor colour and flavour, and over-ripe fruit will additionally be difficult to handle. Generally, with the exception of greengages and gooseberries, which should be used when slightly under-ripe, only sound medium-ripe to ripe fruit should be used. The quality control inspector may consider it necessary to advise the use of new consignments out of delivery rotation.

A small boiling pan in the laboratory is most useful in enabling trial boilings to be made, for assessing the quality of fruit and for deciding a recipe for factory use.

The factory procedure for dealing with the fruit would usually be an inspection on a table or conveyor belt, where the de-stalked fruit is examined for foreign matter and this and any blemished, bad or mouldy fruit is removed.

2. Processed Fruit Pulps

While the finest quality jams are made from fresh fruits, the manufacturer has to use preserved fruit or pulp for production out of season. Frozen and canned fruit may be employed, but the most common method is preservation of fruit pulp with sulphur dioxide. These pulps are put down during the fruit season, and stored in metal drums with semi-rigid polyethylene inners, or more recently high density polyethylene drums which are rapidly rendering the old wooden casks obsolete. Some fruits are stored in bulk.

Soft fruit, such as strawberry and raspberry is put down cold. Stone fruit, as well as other hard fruit such as blackcurrant, goes through a cooking process first, as do oranges for marmalade. Blackcurrants should be cooked sufficiently to rupture the skins, otherwise they behave as semi-permeable membranes on jam manufacture, and the water passes from inside the fruit by osmosis leaving tough, shrivelled blackcurrants which collect near the surface of the jam.

The sulphur dioxide may be added either as a gas from cylinders, as a 6% aqueous solution, or as a solution of sodium metabisulphite, or calcium bisulphite.

The strength of the SO_2 solution must be checked before it is added, since it takes some time for equilibrium to be reached after addition to the fruit. The pulp should then be checked for SO_2 content at intervals of a few months and reinforced if necessary.

Fruit is generally rich in pectin which is utilized in the jam manufacture and must, therefore, be cooked sufficiently to eliminate any pectin-destroying enzymes. This is especially so with marmalade oranges. Any residual enzyme left after cooking will hydrolyse the pectin, resulting in the formation of gelatinous masses of calcium pectate. As long as the minimum boiling time required is correctly determined, there is no risk of this. Tests are available for detecting the presence of such natural enzymes. The pulp may also be tested for toxic trace metals (arsenic, copper, and lead), and any other tests which would be difficult to apply to the whole fruit.

Fruit pulps should be prepared to a standard specification to ensure uniform fruit content, but in any case of doubt it may be necessary to perform tests to establish fruit concentration (soluble solids by refractometer, acidity and insoluble solids). At the same time a useful purpose can be served by the occasional determination of the natural trace elements potassium and phosphorus. This does not strictly come under the heading of direct quality control, but the figures obtained are useful for establishing standards for pulps of normal fruit strength.

To these tests must be added a general inspection of the pulp for quality. Important points to look for are consistency, and freedom from foreign matter or blemished fruit. Colour is not such a good guide, owing to the bleaching effect of the sulphur dioxide. An exception to this is orange marmalade pulp, in which a clear orange colour is an excellent guide to quality.

Before use there should be examination of the pulp by factory operatives, and if canned fruit is employed it should be similarly examined. A convenient way of doing this is to pass the fruit over a trough with a Perspex base, illuminated from below and fitted with a magnet. In dealing with sulphited pulps in this way attention has to be given to ventilation.

3. Sugar

This was mentioned in some detail in the previous section on sugar confectionery, and it is not proposed to discuss it further.

4. Setting Agents

Pectin and gelatine have also received a brief mention in the section on confectionery, but, in view of the significant part which they play in the manufacture of jams, jellies, and marmalades, they are considered worthy of further mention.

(a) *Gelatine.* When used in the manufacture of jellies this should possess a high gel strength and good clarity. For use in jellies the Bloom strength should be 250; this may be measured using the Bloom gelometer or the F.I.R.A. Jelly tester.[18] It is important that this value be determined under conditions similar to those likely to be experienced in jelly manufacture. pH is particularly important since the gel strength is pH-dependent, and should always be checked at the pH at which it is to be used.

Before use the gelatine must be soaked in water to swell. Cold water should be employed for soaking since hot water reduces the gel strength, and warm water promotes microbial growth. High quality gelatines require more water since they are more difficult to disperse. Lengthy soaking should be avoided owing to the possibility of microbial growth. The quality of gelatine for food purposes is specified in the U.K. by the Food Standards (Edible Gelatine) Order 1951.

(b) *Pectin.* The common forms of pectin commercially available are citrus and apple pectins in powder form, and apple pectin as a liquid, either preserved with sulphur dioxide, or pasteurized in tins. These varieties are available in a number of different grade strengths, and are modified by controlled de-esterification to give a slow or fast set. The grade strength indicates the

13

amount of sugar required to produce a satisfactory jelly with a given quantity of pectin under chosen conditions. Methods of checking the strength of pectins have been published by the British Food Manufacturing Industries Research Association,[18] modified by Olliver et al.[19] See also "Methods of Analysis adopted by the Technical Committee of the International Association of Confectionery Manufacturers" (1961). As with gelatine, the set is dependent on a number of factors including pH, and the concentration of sugar and other solids, set should therefore be determined under the required conditions by the manufacture of trial batches.

5. Acids and Other Additives

The success of jam and jelly manufacture depends, to a considerable degree, upon obtaining the required pH for a correct set. The pH may be reduced by the addition of small quantities of acid. Citric and tartaric acids are commonly being used for this purpose. Lactic and malic acids may also be used. Similarly the pH may be raised by the addition of alkaline salts such as sodium bicarbonate, sodium citrate, and sodium potassium tartrate. Care should be taken in selecting an acid suitable for use in jellies, since the manufacture of gelatine may involve the use of an alkali, and some of this alkaline residue may be carried over. On the addition of acid, this may result in the formation of a precipitate of an insoluble calcium salt which imparts an undesirable cloudy appearance to the jelly. Other additives which may be used are colour and flavour.

Quality Control should ensure that the additives employed are of the required standard of purity, and that they are on the permitted list of the country concerned. Colours should additionally be examined, to determine whether they will withstand the processing conditions, and, in particular, whether they are stable in the presence of sulphur dioxide.

6. Packaging

There should be agreed specifications with the supplier for the containers and closures. From the economic point of view it is particularly important to check the capacity of the jar as this often governs the fill of preserve.

Jellies are generally wrapped in either waxed paper or in transparent plastic film and often packed in sealed cartons. The wrapping material should be somewhat permeable to water vapour because of the problems of mould growth. If, however, the permeability is too great, there is the possibility that the jelly will dry out with a significant loss in weight.

B. Process Control

1. Jams

Although some preserves are made by vacuum boiling, many are still made by the old open pan method. Prepared fruit, liquid pectin and syrup are delivered by pipeline to the boiling pans to give a mix with a pH of around 3·0. The mix is then boiled to a standard value of total soluble solids by raising the temperature to a pre-determined figure, generally about 221°F (105°C) for open pan, and rather lower, of course, for vacuum boiling. The lower temperatures required for vacuum boiling mean that much of the caramelization which would occur at atmospheric pressure is avoided. The boiling operation should be sufficient to destroy yeasts, moulds, and other spoilage organisms, and should be long enough to ensure penetration of sugar into the fruit and partial inversion of the sucrose. Either batch or continuous processes may be employed, batch sizes being generally between 90 and 150 lb. The boiling may take from 5 to 15 min, after which the product is filled hot.

Quality Control checks during the processing will include:

(a) *Appearance and flavour*. Each batch should be sampled and the appearance and flavour compared with those of samples from an approved batch. These standard samples should have cool and dark storage to minimize colour and flavour changes and should be replaced about every two months.

(b) *Total solids by refractometer*. As the boilings come off, they are checked for total solids on a robust projection-type refractometer located in the manufacturing department or on in-line equipment. The samples taken are cooled before testing, and the figures thus obtained are liable to small errors, owing to temperature and incomplete equilibrium of the preserve. The errors are not likely to be large, and experience will indicate what differences are to be expected between such results and those of tests carried out on the jam after 24 h storage.

On the basis of the first few tests the boiling temperature is adjusted, if necessary, to obtain the required solids content.

(c) *Filling checks*. If filling is by an automatic filling machine, samples should be removed from the line at intervals for net weight checks. The limits should be decided statistically, based on the performance of the filling machine. For recording results it is convenient to use conventional charts showing warning and action lines. Information on filling control is given in the joint Confederation of British Industry and Institute of Weights and Measures Administration document; "Guide to Good Practice in Weights and Measures in the Factory".[20] Other filling controls would include ensuring the correct filling temperature, generally 185°F (85°C) and checking capping and labelling standards.

(d) *Invert sugar*. Action of the fruit acids on sugar results in the formation of invert sugar. A final invert sugar content of some 30–40% gives a stable preserve, depending on the type of jam and its soluble solids content. If the figure falls outside these limits, the product may show crystallization of sugar on standing. Since, however, inversion proceeds even after the preserve is boiled and continues until it has finally cooled down, and even slowly during storage, it is advisable to aim at an invert sugar content of 25–30% for the hot, freshly boiled preserve. In the case of open-pack preserves (i.e. closed with paper or parchment caps after cooling) there must be close adherence to these figures. When hermetically closed packs are used, crystallization is far less likely, and more variation is permissible.

(e) *Set*. Samples of the preserve are placed on cool plates as soon as production is under way. With experience, a finger tip test will tell fairly soon whether the set is satisfactory. Later, cooled filled jars can be turned out and examined. Instruments have been devised for testing the set, but owing to the lack of homogeneity of the preserve, very accurate results cannot be expected. The advantage of an instrumental measurement is that it is objective and reproducible. The F.I.R.A. Jelly Tester[18] (previously known as the "B.A.R. Jelly Tester" used for pectin assay) has been recommended for measuring the strength of fruit jellies. When the preserve contains pieces of fruit the Exchange Ridgelimiter described by Cox and Higby[21] could be considered. Factors involved in testing pectin jellies with this instrument were the subject of a paper by Olliver.[22]

It should be noted that reliance cannot be placed on a test made immediately after manufacture since the strength of set may alter appreciably during the first 24 h.

(f) *Sulphur dioxide*. Determination of sulphur dioxide is another important test to be performed, particularly if the preserves are being manufactured for export markets having a low limit for SO_2 content, or from a pulp containing many seeds or tough skins which tend to hold SO_2 (such as raspberry or blackcurrant). High SO_2 can usually be dealt with by adding more water to the batches, and so increasing the time of boiling.

(g) *Acidity*. The acidity, either as free acid or combined acid, may be determined by titration. It is usual to fix standards for the acidity of each line of preserve manufactured, and these should be adhered to for the sake of uniformity of quality.

(h) *pH*. The pH may be most conveniently determined on a 50% dilution of the preserve with water. Dilution does not greatly affect the pH, but should nevertheless be recorded when reporting the result. It is advisable to check the pH at regular intervals, and to keep a record of the results, since the figures may be of use if trouble occurs. The normal pH range is 3·1–3·2, with extreme values of 3·0–3·4.

(i) *Copper*. If Copper equipment is used, and not, as is now more common, stainless steel, occasional tests must be carried out for copper content. Contamination is only likely to occur in the first round of batches, and then only in the case of strongly acid preserves.

When any of the above tests show abnormal results, they may often be corrected by slight alterations to the basic recipe and process, or by the addition of small portions of acids or buffer salts.

2. Jellies

The manufacturing process used for table jellies is similar to that employed for jams. A mixture of sucrose and glucose syrup is boiled in either a vacuum pan or open pan evaporator until a total solids content of 90% is achieved. The syrup is allowed to cool to around 210°F (98–99°C), and then added to the soaked gelatine, with the acid and buffer providing the required pH. Colour and flavour are also added, and the batch is deposited either in large slabs or in individual moulds constructed from metal or plastic.

The control checks which are suggested for jams may equally well be applied to the manufacture of jellies, i.e. appearance, flavour, total solids by refractometer, filling checks, invert sugar, set, acidity and pH. Sulphur dioxide may also be determined since it is often used as a preservative in glucose syrups and in gelatine.

C. Finished Product Examination

It is likely that in future increased attention may be given to mould and "filth" contamination. Although mainly of concern to firms exporting to the U.S.A., such tests may well be applied in Europe.

Mould counts are usually made by the Howard test described by the A.O.A.C.[23] but the liability of the method to give a wide range of figures for positive fields should be appreciated. The so called "filth" test is also described in the A.O.A.C.[24] and involves separation and a microscopic examination for the presence of material, such as rodent hairs, indicating undesirable contamination of the raw materials.

As previously mentioned, preserves take several hours to reach a condition of equilibrium. A final quality check can therefore, with advantage, be carried out on the day following manufacture. Since uniformity of quality should already have been well assured by the production control tests, one or two samples per day may be all that is required.

For the determination of total solids on a comminuted sample of the finished preserve, the Abbé type of refractometer should be used. The results are more accurate than those obtained with the projection refractometer under process conditions.

Detailed methods for the analytical examination of preserves have been proposed by Chatt,[25] these have particular application in the examination of competitive products.

D. Defects Occurring in Stored Products

Jams, being hermetically sealed products, should be stored under the normal conditions for food storage, i.e. cool, clean and dry. The jars are generally packed in open-topped cartons with dividers, or shrink-wrapped. If shrink-wrapped it is advisable to store them in a dark place to avoid the possibility of colour fading.

During the period of storage, defects may become apparent in the products as a result of incorrect manufacturing procedures. Faults most likely to occur are spoilage and crystallization.

Spoilage may arise from insufficient processing, inadequate sealing, or contamination during cooling. The heat processing should be sufficient to destroy all spoilage organisms, but since the boiling of jams is generally at a temperature of around 220°F and the filling at about 185°F the jam must be cooled before filling. Overcooling must be avoided because of the possibility of infection by spoilage organisms.

Similarly, if the jars are not properly sealed, there is the possibility that spoilage organisms may enter from the atmosphere. The most likely forms of spoilage to be encountered are those arising from yeasts and mould contamination. Low solid content and a large headspace are favourable to mould growth. Jellies are also susceptible to mould growth in the air spaces, and a little acetic acid is sometimes incorporated in an attempt to prevent this.

For long term storage, jams rely on hermetic sealing for their preservative effect, and for shorter periods, when opened, they rely upon the low pH and high solid concentration to prevent spoilage. A suitable means of determining whether spoilage is likely to occur on storage is to incubate samples from a cross-section of each day's production for a period of 7 days at 25°C.

The problem of crystallization on storage may occur as a result of an incorrect ratio of sucrose to invert sugar, either excessive or insufficient boiling or incorrect pH.

During the manufacture of jams and jellies, some of the sucrose employed is inverted by the acids to form reducing sugars, or invert sugar. The finished product should not be supersaturated with respect to either of these sugars as an excess will lead to crystallization. The pH of the preserve is very important in this respect since it controls the rate of inversion. As previously mentioned, the inversion process continues slowly after cooling and during storage, and in time, therefore, after lengthy storage, crystallization of invert sugar is likely to occur.

REFERENCES

1. "Raw Cocoa, Manufacturers Quality Requirements" (1959). The Cocoa, Chocolate and Confectionery Alliance.
2. Methods of Analysis (1962). Office International du Cacao et du Chocolat.
3. Kleinert, J. (1955). *Int. Choc. Rev.* **10** (11), 440.
4. Kleinert, J. (1965). *Int. Choc. Rev.* **20** (7).
5. "Cocoa Bean Test" (1961–62). Gordian Publishing House, Hamburg.
6. Food Chemicals Codex (1966). **1**, 377. National Academy of Sciences, National Research Council, Washington, D.C.

7. Coomes, T. J. and Sanders, J. C. (1963). *Analyst*, **88,** 209.
8. Coomes, T. J., Crowther, P. C., Francis, B. J. and Shone, G. (1964). *Analyst*, **89,** 436.
9. Coomes, T. J., Crowther, P. C., Francis, B. J. and Stevens, L. (1965). *Analyst*, **90,** 492.
10. Kleinert, J. (1966). *Int. Choc. Rev.* **21** (5), 16.
11. A.O.A.C. (1970). Official Methods of Analysis of the Association of Analytical Chemists.
12. Cook, L. R. (1963). "Chocolate Production and Use". Magazines for Industry, New York.
13. Bracco, U., Schubiger, G. F., Egli, R. H. (1965) *Int. Choc. Rev.* **20** (7), 299–305.
14. Kleinert, J. (1964). *Int. Choc. Rev.* **19** (12), 582.
15. Potterat, M. (1955). *Int. Choc. Rev.* **10** (1), 4–14.
16. British Pharmacopoeia (1963). Pharmaceutical Press, London, 183, 434, 811.
17. Food Chemicals Codex (1966). 1st Edition
18. B.F.M.I.R.A. (1951). *Analyst*, **76,** 536.
19. Olliver, M., Wade, P. and Dent, K. P. (1957). *Analyst*, **82,** 127.
20. "Guide to Good Practice in Weights and Measures in the Factory". (1969). Confederation of British Industry.
21. Cox, R. E. and Higby, R. H. (1944). *Food Inds.* **16,** 441.
22. Olliver, M. (1950). *Food Technol.* **4,** 370.
23. A.O.A.C. Official Methods of Analysis (1970). 824.
24. A.O.A.C. Official Methods of Analysis (1970). 822.
25. Chatt, E. M. (1957). B.F.M.I.R.A. Research Report 80.

Quality Control of Prepared Food Mixes

E. FELICIOTTI

Thomas J. Lipton Inc., Englewood Cliffs, New Jersey

1. INTRODUCTION

The end of the Second World War marked the beginning of a new era in food manufacture and marketing. The advent of so-called "convenience foods" to fit the changing needs of the consumer gave rise to a number of new product forms. Among the more prominent entries which have successfully gained a major position in the modern consumer market are the prepared food mixes.

Prior to World War II, mix products had gained only limited acceptance. Substitution products, i.e. those which offer single package convenience in place of ingredient and recipe use, were generally considered to be artificial in character and inferior in quality to that which could be prepared by the housewife. In many cases such criticism was justified since manufacturers lacked an adequate knowledge of the many controls required to maintain high quality standards in such products. The stigma which had developed as a result of lack of awareness of basic quality requirement has been virtually erased, and the credit for this achievement must lie with the many scientists and companies who expended considerable effort to the investigation and solution of complex chemical, physical and microbiological problems. This presentation will attempt to summarize the results of these efforts and relate them to quality control requirements and practices.

Prepared food mixes may be defined as "formulated food products, consisting in part or totally of free-flowing dried ingredients, which, when rehydrated and prepared according to instructions, yield finished products which serve as substitutes for recognized home-prepared foods". The number of products which fit this definition may be conveniently divided according to the following general categories: (1) bakery product mixes (cakes, cookies, coffee cake, pancakes, waffles, corn bread, muffins, biscuits, doughnuts, bread, rolls, etc.); (2) dried soup mixes (consommés, bouillons, etc.); (3) dried sauce mixes (cooked and instant); (4) gelatin dessert mixes; (5) custard and pudding mixes (cooked and instant); (6) beverage mixes (sugared, non-sugared and artificially sweetened); (7) casserole mixes; (8) frosting and topping mixes and (9) salad dressing mixes.

A fundamental knowledge of the principles involved in preservation by dehydration is essential to the discussion of the control requirements for such products. The following is presented as a guide to be used in establishing definitive criteria for specific applications and is not intended to serve as a treatise on the subject.

A review of the underlying scientific principle of food dehydration is beyond the scope of this presentation and the reader is referred to one of many excellent and complete treatises on the subject ([1, 2, 3, 4]).

2. GENERAL INGREDIENT CONTROL

The stability of a prepared food mix is intimately dependent on the establishment of adequate ingredient control to insure that each component meets specific performance requirements. In addition, each ingredient must possess an inherent preservative to assure that it does not, either as a result of inherent instability or through reaction with other ingredients, contribute to any deleterious changes.

The causative agents of food spoilage, micro-organisms, the enzymes elaborated by them or those present in the food *per se,* and the chemical reactions between natural constituents of the food, are unable to carry out their usual activity when the moisture content is reduced to certain prescribed levels. At the same time, reduced moisture content can result in the establishment of an environment where there is increased susceptibility to certain oxidative reactions which can cause rapid product deterioration. Although many of the factors associated with degradation reactions in dehydrated foods have not been elucidated, the control mechanisms have been the subject of considerable study.

A. Enzymatic Control

Possibly the most significant single factor which retarded the growth of the dehydration industry was lack of recognition of the role played by the naturally occurring enzymes in foods. For some time it was assumed that the mere reduction in moisture content was adequate to insure against the deleterious effect of these vital biochemical constituents. Nelson and Schubert[5] and Matheson and Penny[6] pointed out that reduction in moisture content does decrease the activity rate of enzymes, but there is little knowledge as to the level at which such activity ceases, since this value can vary with each enzyme and the physical form of the material where the reaction is occurring. Kuprianoff[7] in discussing bound water in foods pointed out that low moisture content results in a reduction in contact surface of the liquid phase to decrease the amount of reactive surface. The modern theories on the adsorption of vapors on surfaces indicate that they are condensed to liquids, first in the small capillaries and gradually in the larger. In a system containing many capillaries an enzyme could be in contact with water although the material is apparently dry.

Several workers have studied the effect of moisture level on enzyme activity in various dried food materials. Glass et al.[8] stored wheat for 48 weeks at 20°C and found no significant increase in reducing sugar at 14% moisture, but a definite increase was observed when the wheat contained 16% moisture. Kiermeier and Coduro[9] found no amylase activity in a starch/amylase mixture at 14% moisture, but activity was apparent above this level. When the reaction was carried out on impregnated filter paper, amylase was active below 10% moisture and it was concluded that this could be attributed to the structure of the filter paper which allowed free water to persist on capillary surfaces at relatively low relative humidities.

Pre-cooking or blanching improves the shelf-life of dehydrated vegetables, meat and fish. Sharp and Rolfe[10] reported that dehydrated cooked meat containing 12·5% moisture on a non-fat solids basis had a shelf-life of one year at 37°C, whereas comparable dehydrated raw meat of 11·0% moisture was scarcely edible after one month at the same storage temperature. They postulated that the freeze-dried raw meat has a capillary structure and that the moisture is condensed in the capillaries where enzymes are active during storage to produce a supply of sugars which enter the non-enzymatic browning reactions. The inactivation of enzymes, as a result of precooking, prevents this reaction.

In general, standard ingredient moisture levels which have been established for non-heat-treated products have been found to be adequate for preventing enzyme activity. The fact that such materials can undergo enzymatic degradation as a result of increase in moisture content requires the maintenance of careful control of relative humidity during storage. In the case of ingredients subjected to heat for the purpose of inactivation of enzymes prior to dehydration, control storage is equally important because of the potential that enzyme regeneration may occur.

B. Control of Non-Oxidative Deterioration

During prolonged storage at relatively low temperature most dehydrated foods undergo slow deterioration in quality. The tissues may become tough, the ability to take up water during reconstitution is reduced and the flavor becomes "stale". The cause of these changes is not fully understood, but it is generally recognized that several factors can play an important role. Among the more critical are: chemical composition, moisture content and storage temperature.

As the storage temperature increases there is a pronounced reduction in the shelf life of dehydrated foods. This is characterized by the development of brown discoloration which involves a series of complex chemical reactions initiated by the condensation of the initial products of the Maillard or non-enzymatic browning reaction. These are colorless at first, but as the reaction continues the products are brown. There has been a vast amount of literature on the chemistry of the browning reaction.[11, 12, 13, 14] Acceleration of browning with increased temperature is most striking. A dehydrated ingredient which contains the necessary precursors for the browning reaction might keep for 2 years at 15–20°C (60–70°F), but will last only about 6–8 months at 38°C (100°F.) The Q_{10}, or temperature coefficients, for the rate of loss of reducing sugar and the development of brown discoloration in dried meat over the range 15–50°C, are identical and lie between 3·2 and 4·3.[15] Although this general relationship is true, a given dehydrated food may have longer or shorter storage life due to the influence of other factors, the most important of which is moisture content.

The lower the moisture content of a dehydrated product the longer its shelf-life at a given temperature. Reduction in moisture content of certain dried vegetables from say 5 to 3% will double their storage life at 37°C (98·6°F). Further reduction to 1–2% moisture, as can be achieved through use of accelerated freeze drying procedures, results in a three to four-fold increase in high temperature storage life compared to air dried food at 5–6% moisture content. The browning reaction increases with moisture content up to a R.H. of 60%.

C. Control of the Browning Reaction

The most generally applicable method for controlling the browning reaction in dried foods involves dehydration to sufficiently low moisture content, maintaining these low moisture contents during storage, and avoiding
exposure to high storage temperature. Special techniques have been developed for particular cases to retard or prevent the deteriorative browning
reactions.

Dried egg white, which contains 83% protein and 3% glucose, becomes
brown and insoluble on storage and develops a fluorescence. These changes
were traced to the occurrence of the Maillard reaction between the protein
and the glucose. A similar, but somewhat more complex series of reactions
occurs in dried egg yolk.

One successful procedure for delaying the browning reaction in dried egg
involves acidification with hydrochloric acid to pH 5·5 before dehydration
to a low moisture content. Sodium bicarbonate is then added to the powder
to restore the pH, on reconstitution and cooking, to a value of 7·5–7·8.[16]
This procedure reduces the browning reaction rate to one-third or less of that
in untreated egg powder.

A somewhat more successful technique involves fermenting away the
glucose either with yeast[17, 18] or with glucose oxidase and catalase enzymes
in the presence of hydrogen peroxide[19] and dehydrating the powder to a
moisture content below 2·3%. The addition of a high concentration of
sucrose (15%) to the liquid egg before drying improves the aerating power of
the dried egg.[20] This is of considerable importance when spray-dried egg is an
ingredient in prepared cake mixes.

The only chemical inhibitor of browning which is used in dehydrated foods
is sulfur dioxide, in fruits and vegetables. In formulated foods it may be
possible to segregate a reactive component by means of encapsulation, enrobing or fat coating.

D. Control of Oxidative Degradation

Among the several types of oxidative deteriorations which can occur in
dehydrated foods are: (a) fat rancidification; (b) pigment degradation; (c)
vitamin destruction; and (d) development of stale flavor.

The removal of water during dehydration tends to leave a sponge-like
structure which is now richer in all other original components. The increase in
relative proportion of fat makes the material seriously more susceptible to
oxidative rancidity reactions. In contrast to the situation which exists in the
case of other deteriorative reactions in dehydrated foods, the greater the
amount of residual moisture, the more stable the product will be against

oxidation. Although this is often cited as a potential method for the preservation of dehydrated ingredients and mixes, the manufacturer finds it difficult to balance the opposing reaction possibilities and generally must resort to other control techniques.

The only really practical protection against oxidative spoilage is limitation of access of oxygen to the product. This can take the form of inert gas packing, vacuum packing, minimal headspace and encapsulation of the oxidizable material in hardened fat, gelatin or starch. In addition to elimination of available oxygen, which may often present difficulty, several other techniques are available. These include: Low temperature storage; preservation of natural antioxidants during processing; and addition of approved antioxidants.

It is important that quality control procedures be established to ensure that ingredients which are potentially susceptible to oxidative deterioration, are carefully checked on receipt to establish the adequacy of packing. The materials should not be stored for long periods of time since this can have a disastrous effect on the shelf life of the mix. The use of old or partially degraded ingredients deprives the product of its full potential storage capability and can lead to severe consumer dissatisfaction.

The most useful measurement for the study of the rate or extent of deterioration of an ingredient which contains fat is the peroxide value which is the ratio of peroxide to fat. In general, the higher the peroxide value the more oxidized or rancid the fat, but in some cases the test can prove misleading. It is a wise general principle to regard all dehydrated foods as liable to oxidative deterioration and to utilize every means available to protect them accordingly.

E. Microbiological Control

The ability of a micro-organism to grow and multiply in a particular food system usually depends on the activity of the water present. Morris[21] lists six factors which determine the amount of protection afforded by reduced moisture content: (a) the amount of moisture actually available to the organism; (b) the hydroscopic nature of the material; (c) whether the material is open to the atmosphere; (d) the nature of the gaseous atmosphere around and inside the material; (e) whether desiccation is confined to the outer crust; and (f) the time and temperature of storage.

In a given food, the amount of moisture above which spoilage can be expected is known as the "alarm level". This is defined[21] as the total moisture content or the relative humidity expressed as the ratio of the actual water vapor pressure to the saturated water vapor pressure at the same temperature. The "alarm" value varies with different materials and is dependent on the condition of storage. Wheat for example is stored with a moisture content of 14–15%, but mold growth can occur at 13·5% at 65–70% relative humidity at the same temperature.

Molds can grow on food substrates with as little as 12% moisture content whereas bacteria and yeast require higher moisture content, usually over 30%. Mossel and Ingram[22] believe that the measurement of the equilibrium relative humidity (E.R.H.) is a more reliable means of determining the amount of moisture needed to permit the growth of micro-organisms.

They report that the lowest E.R.H. values which will permit growth of the common spoilage micro-organisms are:

Organisms	E.R.H.
Most bacteria	0·91
Most Yeast	0·88
Most Molds	0·80
Halophilic bacteria	0·75
Xerophilic bacteria	0·65
Osmophilic bacteria	0·60

3. EFFECT OF MOISTURE CONTENT ON KEEPING QUALITY

From the foregoing it should be apparent that moisture content is the fundamental factor associated with the keeping quality of dried foods such as the prepared mixes. A knowledge of certain fundamentals is required to understand the influence of moisture on the components of a mix.

A. Equilibrium Relative Humidity

The equilibrium relative humidity (E.R.H.) of a dried ingredient, i.e. the relative humidity at which the substance will neither gain nor lose moisture at constant temperature, is an important factor in determining the storage requirement. Humidity equilibrium tests provide data for which moisture equilibrium curves, or sorption isotherms, may be prepared to show the relationship between storage relative humidity and ultimate moisture content of the product. Applications of the information developed from studies of the relationship between E.R.H. and equilibrium moisture content for ingredients can be used for: (1) determination of optimum dehydration conditions (e.g. temperature and pressure of vacuum areas); (2) establishment of safe moisture limits for storage of ingredients to prevent deteriorative reactions; (3) specification of safe limits for the humidity of the air in processing, mixing and packaging areas; (4) provide a reliable basis for computing moisture transfer among the components in a mixture of dried ingredients; and (5) determination of package structure required to assure product protection during projected shelf-life.

There are several methods available for determining E.R.H. values, and each can give essentially identical results and can be used satisfactorily. A description of each method, as well as an analysis of the advantages and disadvantages of each, follows:

1. Weight Equilibrium Method

The weight equilibrium method as developed by Wink[23, 24] involves placing small samples (1–2 g) of the material in small closed vessels in which the atmospheric relative humidity is controlled by use of saturated salt solutions, the number of test units being determined by the number of points desired on the sorption isotherms. The initial moisture content of the sample is determined by the Karl Fischer method or by vacuum oven drying as outlined

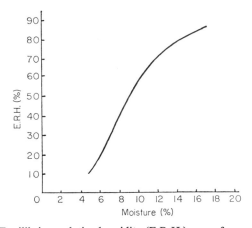

FIG. 1. Equilibrium relative humidity (E.R.H.) curve for egg noodles.

Method: Weight Equilibrium at 75°F.
Initial Moisture: 7·7%
Initial E.R.H.: 32·0%

E.R.H. (%):	10	20	30	40	50	60	70	80	90
Moisture (%):	4·0	6·4	7·4	8·3	9·3	10·4	12·0	14·5	19·5

Notes: Mold growth at 90% and 100% E.R.H.
         Tackiness at 80% E.R.H.

by the Association of Official Agricultural Methods.[25] The samples are weighed periodically until they neither gain nor lose moisture during three successive weighings. Equilibrium moisture content at each relative humidity is calculated from the initial moisture content and the weight changes. The equilibrium percent moisture content is then plotted on the *y*-axis against the percent relative humidity of the control atmosphere on the *x*-axis and the points are connected to yield the humidity moisture equilibrium curve or sorption isotherm for the specific material under test. The initial moisture content, temperature at which tests were conducted, method used to determine moisture content and the critical moisture content (i.e. point at which deterioration in the form of caking, mold growth, browning, etc. is observed), should be included with the curve. Figure 1 shows a representative sorption isotherm for egg noodles. Details regarding the procedure to be used in the weight equilibrium method and others to be described later in the text are presented by Wink,[23, 24] Makower and Dehority,[26] Packaging Institute Food Committee,[27] Landrock and Proctor,[28] Stokes and Robinson[29] and Carr and Harris.[30]

The advantages of the weight equilibrium method are as follows: (1) simple and accurate; suitable for routine use because of minimum attention required; (2) does not require highly skilled technicians; (3) there is ample time for true equilibrium to be reached; (4) simulates practical conditions and gives supplementary information about caking, mold growth, browning, liquefaction, etc., and (5) the rate of adsorption or desorption can be measured.

The disadvantages, though not serious in actual practice are: (1) each determination requires 10–14 days or longer, although, several tests may be conducted simultaneously; (2) true E.R.H. values are often impossible to attain at humidities greater than 80% because of mold growth.

2. Graphical Interpolation Method

The so-called Landrock[28] method involves exposure of small samples to atmospheres of controlled humidity for 1 h. Weight increase is then plotted against relative humidity and a point on the humidity axis is found, by interpolation, where no increase or decrease in weight has taken place; this is the E.R.H. at the initial moisture content of the sample.

Advantage of the graphical interpolation method include: (1) results are available in a few hours for the product at its initial moisture content; and (2) results can be obtained when the E.R.H. is high since there is not sufficient time for spoilage to occur.

The disadvantages of this method are: (1) only one point on the E.R.H. moisture content curve is determined; (2) moisture may not completely permeate some products; and (3) requires more experienced and technically trained operator.

3. Vapor-Pressure Measurements

The sample is allowed to come to equilibrium with the surrounding atmosphere in a closed system and the water vapor pressure is measured by one of several methods. These include: the mercury manometer technique as described by Vincent and Bristol[31]; Dew Point determination by Grover[32]; and electrical methods by Mossel and Van Kuijk.[33] The E.R.H. is determined by dividing the water vapor pressure by the saturation water pressure at the given temperature. Although there are several advantages to the use of this technique, the severe disadvantages of requiring elaborate equipment and technically skilled personnel and the unreliability of results unless test procedures are carefully followed, have limited the application of the procedures as routine methods. Salwin and Slawson[34] reported the results of tests carried out to compare the various methods and concluded that the weight equilibrium method yielded data which were comparable to those obtained by direct manometric measurement or with an electric hydrometer. Their study indicated that equilibration in atmospheres of known relative humidity was the most satisfactory procedure from the point of view of the amount of data per hour of laboratory manipulation.

B. Application of E.R.H. Data to Ingredient Control

The initial E.R.H. of an ingredient is that which corresponds to the initial moisture content and can be read directly from the sorption isotherm. This value is the humidity existing in a well sealed container. As previously outlined the initial E.R.H. should be less than that at which mold can grow, and the relative humidity and temperature of storage as well as package protection should be such that the E.R.H. does not correspond to a moisture content at which other deteriorative changes can occur. For example, if a product is susceptible to the browning reaction the initial moisture content should be less than 5%, the actual value depending on temperature and humidity of storage and anticipated moisture pick-up.

The shape of the E.R.H. curve guides the choice of packaging to be used for storage of ingredients. If the curve is shallow, i.e. large moisture change with small humidity change, the product requires more protection than one which has a steep curve. For example, the chicken noodle soup mix formulation shown in Fig. 2 stored at 50% relative humidity requires more protection than that typified by the instant pudding mix in Fig. 3 stored at the same humidity.

If the initial E.R.H. is higher than the storage humidity, the product will dry out whereas, if the E.R.H. is lower than the external storage humidity the product will absorb moisture. The greater the differential between initial E.R.H. and the humidity of storage the more is the packaging protection required because of greater vapor pressure differential between the inside and outside of the package.

Salwin[35] studied the sorption properties of a number of ingredients to determine: (a) whether or not there was a common moisture behavior pattern; (b) whether a minimum moisture content or vapor pressure, as well as a maximum could be established; and (c) whether an optimum moisture range could be established from the sorption isotherms, thereby eliminating the need for empirical storage studies.

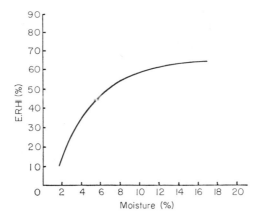

FIG. 2. Equilibrium relative humidity (E.R.H.) curve for chicken noodle soup intermix.

Method: Weight Equilibrium at 75°F.
Initial Moisture: 2·2%
Initial E.R.H.: 19·0%

E.R.H. (%):	10	20	30	40	50	60
Moisture (%):	1·8	2·4	3·5	4·9	6·8	11·0

Notes: Caking at 50% E.R.H.
Liquefaction at 65% E.R.H.

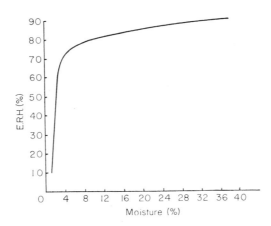

FIG. 3. Equilibrium relative humidity (E.R.H.) curve for instant pudding mix.

Method: Weight Equilibrium at 75°F.
Initial Moisture: 2·0%
Initial E.R.H.: 40%

E.R.H. (%):	10	20	30	40	50	60	70	80	90
Moisture (%):	1·6	1·7	1·8	1·9	2·3	2·5	2·9	8·9	35·6

Notes: Low moisture content below about 70% R.H. Above this humidity there is a large moisture uptake due to high proportion of sugar in mixture.
Mold growth at 90% and 100% E.R.H.

Application of the Brunauer, Emmet, Teller (B.E.T.)[36] absorption theory for gases in multimolecular layers to vapor pressure data indicated that there was good correlation between that amount of moisture which represents a statistical monolayer of adsorbed water and the moisture content generally specified for good stability. Although there were some exceptions, Salwin[35] concluded that the amount of water which represents a monomolecular layer according to the B.E.T. theory may be regarded as a protective film which protects the particles of food from attack by oxygen, Citing a number of fundamental references by Stadtman,[37] Uri,[38] Klotz and Heiney[39] and Shaw,[40] he states that the monomolecular layer may not in fact, represent a continuous film, but rather corresponds to the number of available absorption sites in the various materials which undergo oxidative reactions. The combinations of water with these functional groups results in protection from reaction with oxygen.

4. FORMULATION CONTROL

All of the problems associated with the individual dehydrated ingredients become substantially more critical when they are mixed in the formulation of prepared food mixes. The many deteriorative reactions responsible for browning, lumping, caking, crystallization, microbial growth, enzyme activity, color changes, rancidity, flavor loss, vitamin destruction, etc., become the subject of considerably more concern when the various ingredients are combined to form the complex number of mixes which are required to fit the consumer needs.

A. Moisture Distribution in a Mixture

In a system consisting of a combination of dehydrated ingredients, the difference in moisture vapor pressure (MVP) results in the transfer of water from items of higher MVP to those of lower MVP until a pressure equilibrium is reached. The percentage of water in each ingredient may be different although the E.R.H. values are the same. Once the E.R.H. of the mixture is known from the sorption isotherm of the system, the percentage moisture content of each of the ingredients can be determined from the E.R.H.-moisture content curves for the ingredient. Knowledge of the moisture distribution among the ingredients is more helpful than the moisture content of the mixture. For example, a mixture may have a low moisture content yet individual components of the mixture which are responsible for browning reactions may have high moisture content.

Suppose we wished to find the moisture content of each ingredient when the moisture content of a prepared mix is 6% and the E.R.H. of the mix, as determined from the sorption isotherm at this moisture content, were 50%.

Since all of the ingredients will have an E.R.H. of 50%, the corresponding moisture contents can be found from the E.R.H.-moisture curves for the individual ingredients. The moisture content of the mix at 6% would indicate that it will not be subject to accelerated browning, but specific constituents may be found to hold 10–15% moisture which can prove to be most critical for the reducing sugar-amino acid reaction.

B. Determination of the E.R.H. in a Mixture

The E.R.H. of a mixture of two ingredients in a closed system can be determined by use of the following equation:

$$H = \frac{\dfrac{W_1 h^\circ_1}{K_1} + \dfrac{W_2 h^\circ_2}{K_2}}{\dfrac{W_1}{K_1} \quad \dfrac{W_2}{K_2}}$$

where H is the E.R.H. of the mixture, h° is the initial E.R.H. of the ingredient, K is the slope of the E.R.H.-moisture content curve, and W is the dry weight of the ingredient. K is calculated from two convenient points on the sorption isotherm in the range where it is approximately linear.

Salwin and Slawson[41] studied the relationship between moisture and moisture-vapor pressure for the purpose of predicting the extent of moisture transfer in a system containing several ingredients. Since it is not possible to predict the direction or extent of transfer in a system of as many as 4 or 5 ingredients a series of equations are presented for use in calculating the final E.R.H. and equilibrium moisture content for typical combinations of ingredients. The calculated values were compared with equilibrium moisture content determined experimentally. This was done by placing weighed proportions of the ingredients in a mix in separate stainless steel baskets in a tin can sealed under vacuum. After storage for periods up to 5 months at 40°, 72° and 100°F (4·4°, 22·2° and 37·8°C), the cans were opened and the moisture content of each ingredient was determined. Data are presented which show that there is close agreement between final moisture content as calculated by the formula and the values determined experimentally.

The difficulties associated with the development of stable formulations for prepared mixes have given rise to a number of specialized techniques. In addition to those cited for control of specific degradation reactions under the discussion of ingredient control, the manufacturers of such products have developed a technique whereby one or more of the ingredients act as a moisture "sink". This is accomplished by using materials which can be dried to extremely low moisture content without affecting either their functional or stability characteristics. Starches, flours, salt, sugar, leavening agents, milk powders, egg products, and a number of other ingredients can be dried to relatively low levels and used in adequate proportion to function as formulation stabilizers. In the case of soup mixes, the noodles, rice and freeze dried meats can serve a similar purpose when dried to levels below that which is common for the standard packed product. In several cases the technique of redrying components for this purpose have resulted in the issuance of patents, e.g. Seltzer and Saporito.[42]

The use of low moisture content ingredients in formulations requires the establishment of careful controls to prevent moisture pick-up during storage, mixing and filling. A number of the materials which can be treated in this manner show extremely high hygroscopic tendencies, therefore, purchasing specifications should include adequate packaging requirements and storage control.

5. MANUFACTURING CONTROL

Once all of the required ingredients which are to be used in the manufacture of a prepared food mix have been tested for quality and compliance with specifications, the assembly of the components for the formula is begun. The ultimate objective is that of producing individual packages of product which are consistent with the established product image.

A. Weighing and Mixing

The first operation of weighing or measuring of ingredients may be done by hand or may be completely automated in the larger volume plants. In the former method, the ingredients are generally brought to a weighing station and each component is successfully weighed or metered into the batch. The materials are conveyed to a suitable mixer where they are blended for sufficient time to achieve a homogeneous dispersion of the ingredients. In those cases where the mix is composed entirely of dried powders, each should be as uniform in sieve size as possible to prevent segregation between coarse and fine materials during subsequent transport and filling operations. In those cases where the ingredients vary appreciably in size it is generally preferable to prepare separate mixes and then multiple stage fill into the packages. This procedure may also be applied when relatively small amounts of a costly raw material is incorporated into a formulation. The type of mixers used varies appreciably with the composition of the mix.[43]

In larger scale operations the major ingredients are stored separately in a series of bins which are fitted with various types of discharge mechanisms. The valves or gates are generally actuated automatically to deliver ingredients into a tote bin which travels along under the bin and serves as a weighing mechanism.[44, 45] More highly automated plants utilize an electronic computer system in which each formula is entered on a punch card. The cards are fed into a computer and any given number of batches are automatically scaled off. The tote bin containing the weighed ingredients is conveyed by overhead trolley to the mixer. The blended mix is then dumped into another tote bin and conveyed to a hopper which feeds the filling machines.[46, 47, 48]

One of the most important elements of a good quality control program in a prepared mix manufacturing operation is that of continuous maintenance of the weighing and mixing equipment. A malfunction of a bin mechanism, an error in scale operation, failure to include an ingredient or any of a number of other errors can result in the packaging of a large batch of unacceptable product. The quality control personnel in a well organized prepared mix plant are constantly taking batch samples for chemical, physical, micro-biological, functional and organoleptic evaluation. It is not uncommon to find representatives of the quality control department obtaining early samples to make specialized checks before a batch is moved to the packaging area.

B. Packaging

The complexity of the problems associated with the packing of prepared mixes can vary appreciably with the character of the product. Homogeneous mixes (e.g. bakery products) are generally easier to handle than multiple component products (e.g. soup mixes). The proportioning and filling of components to yield uniform blends presents a number of difficulties. Some packers have found it to be desirable to have several streams feeding the filler head whereas in other cases, each of the components is discharged separately into the package. Free-flowing powdered materials are generally proportioned volumetrically to give more uniformity in weight, while particulate material, especially that which has a bridging tendency often requires special techniques. Manufacturers have generally developed highly specialized procedures for solving individual problems to ensure product uniformity and weight control.

1. Environment of the Packaging Area

The basic requirements for the packaging area where prepared food mixes are packed include: (1) low relative humidity; (2) dust control; and (3) sanitation.

Kupersmit[49] listed the following specifications for an ambient atmosphere in a dehydrated foods packaging room:

Bacteria Count	"O" colonies
Dust Particle Count	38·4
Dust Particle Size	0·3 μm
Temperature	74°F
Relative Humidity	28%
Free of Noxious Gases	

2. Package Protection Requirements

There are several criteria which must be considered in the selection of the package for prepared mixes. Some of the requirements are as follows: (1) all elements of the package should be odorless and not generate odors from heat-sealing or other processing operations; (2) at least one element of the package should be substantially impervious to water vapor, foreign odors, air and micro-organisms; (3) the primary barrier layer in contact with the foodstuff should be resistant to the product and there should be no interaction; (4) the package must be able to withstand processing, warehousing, shipping and retail handling; (5) the packaging material should be maintained as free as possible from contamination by micro-organisms; (6) the package should be a barrier to insect attack; and (7) the package should be adaptable to automatic machine operation.

Once a satisfactory package has been developed for a specific prepared food mix it is essential to maintain a constant check on the integrity of the finished package. In the final analysis, the keepability of a product is entirely dependent on the protective quality of the package. Defects in the material as received, inadequacy of the seal and damage during filling and shipping are the more common causes of failure.

6. SPECIFIC INGREDIENT SPECIFICATIONS AND CONTROLS

The numerous individual ingredients used in the formulation and manufacture of prepared food mixes defy any attempt at discussion of specific quality standards and procedures. The functional requirements for ingredients will vary with the quantity used and the type of product, but there are a number of general characteristics which can be considered for the various categories of material. The following is a basic discussion of the major ingredients and is intended as a basis for development of more specialized techniques.

A. Farinaceous Products

Cereal grains are the basis for a number of ingredients which are used in the formulation of prepared mixes. Among the most common grains which are processed to produce flour, meal, semolina, bran, middlings, grits, shorts, starch, syrups, sugars, etc., are corn, wheat, oats, sorghum, barley, rye, rice, and buckwheat.

1. Flours

Wheat flour is the most commonly used of the cereal flours because of its unique property of forming an elastic sponge which is capable of holding gas and setting to a spongy structure when heated in an oven.[50, 51] The chemical composition, particularly the protein and ash content, of wheat flour is adjusted to satisfy specific requirements of use in prepared baking product mixes. For example, angel food cake mixes are made with a low protein flour, running around 5·0–6·0% whereas a general purpose cake flour may run 7·5–9·0% protein.

The testing of flour can be divided into four categories, as follows: (a) chemical tests; (b) physical tests; (c) organoleptic tests; and (d) performance tests. Many of the tests which are used have been established by the American Association of Cereal Chemists.[52]

Chemical tests include: moisture content; ash content; protein content; crude gluten content; starch content; fat content; reducing sugars content; pH; fat acidity; gas production; particle size and chlorine content.

A number of devices have been developed for the purpose of evaluating flour quality in terms of physical measurements to give an indication of their hydration and mixing characteristics. These include: (1) the Brabender Farinograph which is used to give information on absorption of water, mixing time and mixing tolerance of flour; (2) the Brabender Extensograph which measures the extensibility and resistance to extension of flour dough; (3) the Brabender Amylograph which is used to record viscosity changes on a flow-water suspension being subjected to a uniform increase in temperature; and (4) the Mixograph which yields data relative to dough development, stability, absorption, mixing time, and mixing tolerance.

Standard organoleptic evaluation is made to ensure that the flour is free from foreign or undesirable odors and also for evaluation of flavor of the baked product.

Performance testing has a number of shortcomings, but it is still the best method for overall evaluation of the quality of flour. There are several standard procedures outlined by the American Association of Cereal Chemists.[52]

The stability of a farinaceous material is of principal interest where the storage life of a mix is critical. A number of flours contain enzymes known as lipases, or fat splitters, which catalyze the splitting of fat on storage to yield free fatty acids. This reaction can give rise to "soapy" off-flavors. In a mix not only the natural flour fat, but also the added fat may be affected in this manner. The lipase value of a flour can be determined by incubation of a sample of flour mixed with fat at 80–100°F for a period of time, and then measuring the free fatty acid content by titration with alkali.

2. Starches

Starches are important ingredients in all prepared mixes and are used to improve texture, consistency, shelf-life, etc. There is a great deal of variety in sources, modifications and properties of starches, therefore, processors need to know the product which is best suited for the specific application. Commercial sources include the grains: regular (dent) corn, waxy maize, wheat, sorghum; certain roots and tubers: white potatoes, sweet potatoes, cassava (tapioca-mannioca) and arrowroot; and a trunk, the Sago palm.

Starches from each source differ in several important respects, but they all have one thing in common, the same general chemical composition. All can be broken down into dextrose, a single sugar containing 6 carbon atoms, 12 hydrogen atoms and 6 oxygen atoms. The dextrose units are combined in straight chains (amylose chains) or branched chains (amylopectin chains). Corn starch, the most commonly used starch, is composed of 27% amylase and 73% amylopectin, whereas, tapioca starch has 80% of the branched chain form and only 20% of the straight chain type.

Since starch is often employed as a thickener and stabilizer, the gelling, flow and clarity of its solutions are of prime interest. Each property will depend on how the starch units are held together.

The evaluation of starches for use in prepared food mixes includes: moisture content, thickening power, ash content, sieve analysis, extraneous matter and bacterial examination. The procedures outlined under the section on flours are generally applicable to the testing of starches. The thickening power of starch may be determined by viscometric techniques using the Brookfield or Redwood viscometer under controlled conditions.

3. Alimentary Pastes

Macaroni, spaghetti and noodles are used in soup mixes and casserole mix products. Standard chemical and physical tests include: moisture content, ash, protein, bacteriological examination, salt content, extraneous matter, egg solids content and bulk density,[25, 53] Special tests to evaluate cooking quality include: tenderness of cooked product, volume increase on cooking, water absorption and resistance to disintegration.[54] As indicated in the general discussion on the effect of moisture content on the keeping quality of prepared mixes, moisture determination and control are most important quality considerations in the evaluation of alimentary pastes. The ability to reduce the moisture content below that of standard macaroni and noodle products affords the opportunity to utilize this ingredient as a moisture "sink" for formulation stabilization. Care must be taken to minimize breakage during redrying of such products.

B. Sugars

Sugar, in some form or other, is the most common single ingredient used in prepared food mixes. By common usage as well as definition, sugar means sucrose. The term "sugars" however, refers in the chemical sense to the family of carbohydrates known as saccharides, any member of which may be called "sugar", but not simply "sugar". The most familiar sugars are milk sugar (lactose), corn sugar (dextrose) and malt sugar (maltose).

1. Sucrose

Although sweetness is the quality most commonly associated with sugar, in prepared mixes this is no more important than certain of its chemical and physical characteristics. To name only a few: the ease with which it hydrolyzes to form single sugars, its high degree of solubility in water, its ready crystallization from supersaturated solution, its reaction to heat (caramelization), its ability to disperse protein and its preservative action. The refined granulated sugar of commerce is at least 99·9% sucrose, is highly uniform in quality, contains no waste and has infinite keeping quality under suitable storage conditions.

Standard tests on sugar include: moisture content, sucrose assay, ash content, color, clarity, particle size, microbiological evaluation and extraneous matter.[25]

2. Other Sugars

Other sugars used in prepared mixes include: dextrose (corn sugar); corn syrup solids, lactose, maltose, dextrins, etc. Each differs in carbohydrate composition and as a result possess different chemical and physical properties.

Dextrose is the most commonly used and is available to the prepared mix manufacturer in two forms: hydrous, containing 8·5% water of crystallization; and anhydrous, containing essentially no moisture. This choice affords the opportunity to achieve optimum moisture balance in given formulations, but considerable care must be taken in the storage of the anhydrous form to prevent hydration. The sweetening power of dextrose and other sugars, when compared to sucrose, is primarily dependent not only on the percentages of sweetener solids, but also upon the combination of sweeteners. A two percent solution of dextrose is about two-thirds as sweet as a sucrose solution of equivalent concentration, but as the concentration is increased, the difference in sweetness in less apparent. In fact, at a level of 40% solids, sucrose and dextrose solutions appear to be equally sweet. Standard testing of this class of sweeteners includes: moisture content, dextrose equivalent, pH, ash, trace elements and color.[25]

C. Fats and Oils

Fats when used in prepared food mixes serve a number of functions. Shortenings are essential ingredients of almost all types of bakery product mixes. Hydrogenated vegetable oils and animal fats are used in substantial quantity in dehydrated soup mix, sauce mixes and other products. The materials are processed by a number of methods to change the characteristics of the original fats and they may have emulsifiers, antioxidants and other ingredients added to improve and adopt them for specific purposes.

Fats to be used in prepared mixes should be fresh, pure and free from foreign odors, flavors and any sign of rancidity. The most common tests performed on fats and oils include: free fatty acids, color, iodine value, stability tests (AOM or Schaal test), peroxide value, congealing point, melting point, smoke point and flavor and odor testing.[55, 56] Special tests applied to fats which function as shortenings include: plasticity,[57] cake tests, icing volume, water absorption and creaming volume.[58]

1. Antioxidants

Synthetic antioxidants commonly used to improve the keeping quality of fats and oils include: Nordihydroguaiaretic acid (NDGA), Propyl Gallate, Butylated Hydroxyanisole (BHA), Butylated Hydroxytoluene (BHT), and Tocopherols. While these are all effective, they are not equivalent and it is common practice to utilize a combination of antioxidants and acidic synergists such as citric acid and phosphoric acid. These latter materials function as chelating agents which scavenge metals to minimize their effect in oxidative rancidity reactions.

2. Emulsifiers

Emulsifiers used in prepared mixes are generally monoglycerides and diglycerides of fatty acids and of certain other organic acids. Lecithin and Polyoxythelene sorbitan monostearate are also used either individually or in combination with other emulsifiers.

D. Milk Products

Milk products, particularly non-fat dry milk, dry buttermilk and whey solids, have become widely used ingredients in prepared mixes. Non-fat dry milk content in bakery mixes will typically vary between 5 and 10%, based on the flour weight. When added to such formulations, milk solids perform a number of functions which are extremely beneficial. These include: strengthening agent for flour proteins, increased tolerance to over-mixing, improved flavor and eating quality and moisture retention.

Standard tests on dehydrated milk products include: butterfat content, moisture, titratable acidity, solubility index, scorched particles, bacterial examination, extraneous matter, flavor and odor.[25, 53, 59] One special test which is not a grading requirement, but which is of considerable value in indicating the suitability of spray dried non-fat milk for various uses is the whey protein nitrogen.[59]

E. Egg Products

Dried egg products are used principally in prepared bakery mixes. According to Pyler[60] there are at least six functions performed by eggs in cakes and similar products. These are: (1) binding action; (2) leavening action; (3) emulsifying action; (4) flavor; (5) color; and (6) nutritive value.

1. Egg White Solids

A number of patents have been issued on the use of additives to improve the whipping properties of dried egg white. These include the addition of anionic surface active agents,[61] triethyl citrate, [62] and bile salts.[63] An unintentional additive which has a pronounced effect on the whipping quality of egg white is fat. The fat of egg yolk significantly retards the formation of foams and decreases their stability and although the whipping aids can overcome a portion of the damage caused by fats, their effectiveness is limited. Fats from other sources such as flour can also contribute to the instability of egg white foams.

2. Egg Yolk Solids

The most critical factors associated with dried egg yolk are microbial growth and deterioration resulting from chemical reactions. The development of both spoilage type and health hazard type organisms may occur during the pre-drying handling of the material. Predominant spoilage organisms are of the *Pseudomonas* or similar types which attack the protein material resulting in off-odors and flavors. Primary pathogens are of the Salmonella species although generally found in very low numbers. Pasteurization effectively reduces total microbial populations and is especially effective for the pathogenic types.

The storage life of dried egg yolk is determined primarily by two factors: (1) the reaction between glucose and proteins (the Maillard reaction) which can be retarded effectively as indicated earlier by removal of glucose; and (2) the typical oxidation of fat which is retarded by low temperature storage, inert atmosphere packaging and the original bacterial population.[64]

3. Dried Whole Egg

Processing variables have essentially the same effect on dried whole egg as described for dried yolk. There is somewhat greater resistance to the deterioration of fat since the fat content of whole egg solids is 41% compared with yolk at 57%.

Standard tests applied to all dried egg products include: moisture content, pH, fat content, bacterial examination, extraneous matter and color.[25, 53, 65] A number of special tests are not considered official, but are commonly used by the industry for evaluation. The most important of these are the standard whip test for dried egg white and sensory evaluation techniques.[66]

F. Dehydrated Vegetables

Many types of vegetables are used in dehydrated form in soup mixes and casserole mixes. A low moisture content, preferably of the order of 5% is recommended, although this is subject to variation since each dehydrated material has its own equilibrium moisture characteristic and moisture may be absorbed or given up by the other ingredients in the mix.

Standard tests on dehydrated vegetables include: moisture content, size, extraneous matter, microbiological examination, defects, organoleptic evaluation, and reconstitution ratio. On occasion a number of special tests are performed to determine the presence or absence of enzymes and sulfur dioxide.

G. Dried Meats

The commercialization of the freeze dehydration technique for food products has resulted in the development of a number of dried meat ingredients for use in soup mixes and similar products. Prior to that time the meat content of such products was limited to very minute pieces because of problems associated with rehydration of the resultant dense shrunken structure. Freeze drying which involves removal of water by sublimation from the frozen state, results in a sponge-like porous structure with excellent rehydration properties. As a result of this technique it is possible to utilize larger pieces of meat which exhibit superior color, flavor and texture.

The open structure of freeze dried meat and the exposure of fat which results requires care in storage of this raw material. Freeze dried products are generally stored under inert gas atmospheres to retard deterioration reactions. In general the tests performed on freeze dried products are similar to those applied to fats and dehydrated vegetables.

H. Protein Products

A number of animal and vegetable proteins are hydrolyzed under special techniques and then neutralized to form liquids, paste and powders which yield flavor and flavor-enhancing compounds. These materials include monosodium glutamate, hydrolyzed animal and plant proteins, ribonucleotide derivatives, etc. Additional materials which are used for similar purposes are: beef extract, whale meat extract, and autolyzed yeast extract.

Standard specifications and tests on the materials in this grouping include: moisture content or total solids, total nitrogen and amino nitrogen content, total ash, salt, monosodium glutamate content, ammonium chloride content, microbiological examination, extraneous matter, sieve analysis and organoleptic evaluation.

I. Miscellaneous Ingredients

Among the many other ingredients which are used in prepared food mixes are: salt, flavors, colorings, herbs and spices, leavening agents, gums, acids, alkalis, etc. The majority of these materials are highly specific in character and special tests have been developed to suit individual requirements. The general criteria are applicable in all cases to ensure proper function in formulation. Standards of moisture content, microbiological control, absence of extraneous matter and purity are among the most important for this grouping of ingredients.[25, 52]

7. FINISHED PRODUCT SPECIFICATIONS AND QUALITY CONTROL

A complete and effective quality control program requires the establishment of adequate specifications and testing procedures at all stages of manufacture. Examination of ingredients, evaluation of materials at various stages of preparation and the testing of packaging components culminates in the examination of the finished product. The establishment of comprehensive specifications for the packaged product and the tests performed at this point constitute a major portion of the entire program. The more common physical, chemical, microbiological and organoleptic tests performed on finished prepared food mixes are: (1) moisture determination; (2) equilibrium relative humidity studies; (3) weight checks; (4) color measurement; (5) reconstitution and preparation tests; (6) sieve analysis; (7) extraneous matter determination; (8) ingredient analysis (e.g. salt content); (9) bacteriological examination; (10) packaging seal efficiency; (11) bursting strength of packages; (12) accelerated storage studies; (13) package permeability determination; (14) gas analyses; (15) flavor and odor evaluation.

The specific tests which are applicable to a given prepared mix will vary with the composition and nature of the product. There are a number of standard references available to the manufacturer for use in establishing individual requirements.[25, 64, 67]

A. Performance Evaluation

Performance evaluation is an extremely important part of the quality control program. The use of chemical, physical and microbiological tests alone does not ensure that a product will perform up to expectations when prepared by the consumer. This phase of testing should include evaluation of minor and major deviations from standard preparation instructions to determine the degree of variability which might be encountered. It is not possible to build in a high degree of protection against mishandling and/or deviation from preparation instructions for the many complex formulations which are placed on the market, but the products should allow for minor variations in technique.

1. Bakery Product Mixes

Performance evaluation is very important in the case of this class of products. A slight error in the batch resulting from any of several manufacturing malfunctions can cause failure. The standard scoring procedures for cakes include: specific volume, contour, crust color and character, texture, grain and flavor and aroma. Numerical values are generally assigned to several factors in accordance with relative importance. A sample scale as outlined by the American Association of Cereal Chemists[52] for coffee cake is as follows: softness (0–25 points); color of crust (0–10); grain (0–10); texture (0–20); color of crumb (0–10); and eating quality (0–25). Scoring is often done the day following preparation. Cookie mix and pancake and waffle mix performance testing involves measurement of width and thickness of the cooked product to calculate spread factors. Performance test score for bread, rolls, muffin and biscuit mixes include: general appearance (0–25 points); crust color (0–10); grain (0–20); texture (0–20) and odor and flavor (0–25).

2. Soup Mixes

Performance testing products in this grouping involves reconstitution according to the stated instruction, cooking and evaluation of the appearance, color, aroma and flavor of the prepared product. The material should not stick to the sides or the bottom of the cooking vessels. The noodles, rice, vegetables, meat or other particulate components should be adequately rehydrated and there should be no undissolved lumps of mix. In the case of a cream style soup, there should be no separation on standing after a reasonable period of time and in all cases, the viscosity should not change appreciably with temperature variation following cooking.

3. Sauce Mixes

The prepared product is evaluated for homogeneity, viscosity, absence of undissolved fragments, proper rehydration of particulate matter, absence of surface film formation, general appearance, flavor and aroma. Reconstituted and prepared sauce mixes are generally subjected to flavor and aroma evaluation on products for which they are intended to insure that the proper effect is achieved.

4. Gelatin Dessert Mixes

The standard performance tests include evaluation of solubility of ingredients, setting time, gel strength, texture, flavor, aroma and consistency. The gelled dessert must be firm and tender and not soft, runny, tough or rubbery.

5. Custard and Pudding Mixes

Following preparation in accordance with standard instructions the finished product is scored on the following points: texture, consistency, color, appearance, flavor and resistance to separation or weeping after standing at room temperature. The products should be creamy and smooth, tender in consistency, free of lumps and graininess.

6. Beverage Mixes

Beverage base powders should be free-flowing and readily soluble, or dispersible in cold water. The prepared beverages are evaluated for color, flavor and aroma, and stability after standing. The products should be free of undissolved or foreign material, have characteristic color and flavor typical of the respective fruit juice of the specified type.

7. Casserole Mixes

Prepared casserole or dinner mixes are evaluated for reconstitution efficiency, yield, flavor and aroma and other points in the same manner as indicated for soup mixes.

8. Frosting and Topping Mixes

Performance testing for products in this grouping is principally that associated with overrun evaluation (i.e. quantity of air which can be incorporated into the material), stability of the foams produced, flavor and aroma, appearance, consistency and texture.

B. Storage Studies

All products in the prepared mix category, for reasons previously outlined, are tested for storage stability. The conditions of temperature and humidity for storage studies are extremely variable and depend on a knowledge of the potential environmental conditions in the marketing area. The more common test procedures involve storage at: 100°F/50–100% R.H.; 70°F/50% R.H.; 32°F°/ambient R.H.; −10°F/ambient R.H.; and cycling conditions of two or more of the above. Frequency of testing varies with the character of the product and the storage test conditions. At elevated temperatures samples may be evaluated on a weekly, bi-weekly or monthly basis, whereas at ambient or refrigeration temperatures one to three month intervals are common.

14

Tests on stored samples consist of: (a) moisture determination; (b) rancidity determinations (peroxides and free fatty acids); (c) sensory evaluation of the prepared product; and (d) examination of packages, although other special procedures may be used.[69, 70]

8. SUMMARY

Prepared mixes have become a strong factor in the present day food marketing picture. This success stems from the fact that the products which comprise this segment of the "convenience foods" are of excellent quality and can be used by the consumer to prepare products which are indistinguishable from, and in many cases superior to, those which she is able to prepare in any other way.

The acceptance of prepared food mixes has been achieved as a result of concerted efforts on the part of manufacturers to understand and correct the many deficiencies which are inherent in standard ingredients. The development of tailor-made materials to suit the individual needs of the prepared mix producer has played a major role in overcoming problems.

A step-by-step continuing program of quality control is essential to the maintenance of the recognized high quality of the products in this segment of the industry. Although the progress to date has been considerable, the efforts being made constantly to improve and to broaden the scope of products foretells a bright future for prepared food mixes.

REFERENCES

1. Van Arsdel, W. B. and Copley, M. J. (1963). "Food Dehydration". 2 Vols. (Avi Publishing Co., Westport, Conn.).
2. Charm, S. E. (1963). "Fundamentals of Food Engineering". (Avi Publishing Co., Westport, Conn.).
3. Von Loesecke, H. W. (1955). "Drying and Dehydration of Foods". (Reinhold Publishing Co., New York).
4. Burke, R. F. and Decareau, R. V. (1964). Recent advances in the freeze-drying of food products. In: "Advances in Food Research". Vol. 13. (Academic Press, New York).
5. Nelson, J. M. and Schubert, M. P. (1938). Water concentration and the rate of hydrolysis of sucrose by invertase. *J. Am. chem. Soc.* **50**, 2188–2193.
6. Matheson, N. A. and Penny, I. F. (1961). Storage of dehydrated cod. *Fd Process. Packag.* **30**, 87–91, **98**, 123–127.
7. Kuprianoff, J. (1958). Bound water in foods. "Conference on Fundamental Aspects of the Dehydration of Foodstuffs". Aberdeen (London Society of Chemical Industry).
8. Glass, R. L., Ponte, J. G., Christiansen, C. M. and Geddes, W. F. (1959). The influence of temperature and moisture level on the behaviour of wheat stored in air or nitrogen. *Cereal Chem.* **36**, 341–356.
9. Kiermeier, F. and Coduro, E. (1954). Diastatic hydrolysis of starch in air-dried substances. *Biochem. Z.* **325**, 280–287.

10. Sharp, J. G. and Rolfe, E. J. (1958). Deterioration of dehydrated meat during storage. "Conference on Fundamental Aspects of the Dehydration of Foodstuffs". Aberdeen (London Society of Chemical Industry).
11. Ross, A. F. (1948). Deterioration of processed potatoes. "Advances in Food Research". Vol. 1. (Academic Press, New York).
12. Hodge, J. E. (1953). Dehydrated foods; chemistry of browning reactions in model systems. *J. agric. Fd Chem.* **1**, 928–943.
13. Reynolds, T. M. (1963). Chemistry of nonenzymic browning 1. The reaction between aldases and amines. "Advances in Food Research". Vol. 12. (Academic Press, New York).
14. Jones, N. R. (1959). Browning reactions and the loss of free amino acid and sugar from lyophilized muscle extractives of fresh and chill-stored codling. *Fd Res.* **24**, 704–710.
15. Regier, L. W. and Tappel, A. L. (1956). Freeze-dried meat. IV. Factors affecting the rate of deterioration. *Fd Res.* **21**, 640–649.
16. Military specification. Stabilized dehydrated egg. QMC Mil-e-10006 (Sept. 12, 1959).
17. Kline, L. and Sonoda, T. T. (1951). Role of glucose in the storage deterioration of whole egg powder. I. Removal of glucose from whole egg melange by yeast fermentation before drying. *Fd Technol.* **5**, 90–94.
18. Kline, L., Hanson, H. L., Sonoda, T. T., Gcgg, J. E., Feeney, R. E., and Lineweaver, H. (1951). Role of glucose in storage deterioration of whole egg powder. III. Effect of glucose removal before drying an organoleptic, baking and chemical changes. *Fd Technol.* **5**, 323–331.
19. Military specification. Egg powdered. QMC Mil-r-1075A (May 17, 1950).
20. Brooks, J. and Hawthorne, J. R. (1943). Dried egg. IV. Addition of carbohydrates to egg pulp-method of retarding the effects of storage at high temps. and of improving the aerating power of spray-dried egg. *J. Soc. chem. Ind., Lond.* **62**, 165–167.
21. Morris, E. O. (1962). Effect of environment on microorganisms. Recent Advances in Food Science, Vol. 1. (Butterworth's, London).
22. Mossel, D. A. A. and Ingram, M. (1955). The physiology of the microbial spoilage of foods. *J. appl. Bact.* **18**, 232–268.
23. Wink, W. A. (1964). Determining the moisture equilibrium curve of hydroscopic materials. *Ind. Engng. Chem. analyt. Edn* **18**, 251–252.
24. Wink, W. A. (1947). Moisture equilibrium. *Mod. Packag.* **20**, (6), 135–138.
25. Assn. of Official Agricultural Methods. (1960). "Official Methods of Analysis". 9th Ed., Washington, D.C.
26. Makower B. and Dehority, G. L. (1943). Equilibrium moisture content of dehydrated vegetables. *Ind. Engng. Chem. analyt. Edn* **35**, 193–197.
27. Anon. (1953). Moisture equilibria of food products. *Mod. Packag.* **26** (4), 133–137.
28. Landrock, A. H. and Proctor, B. E. (1951). A new graphical interpolation method for obtaining humidity equilibria data with special reference to its role in food packaging studies. *Fd Technol.* **5**, 332–339.
29. Stokes, R. H. and Robinson, R. A. (1949). Standard solutions for humidity control at 25°C. *Ind. Engng. Chem. analyt. Edn* **41**, 2013.
30. Carr, D. S. and Harris, B. L. (1949). Solutions for maintaining constant relative humidity. *Ind. Engng. Chem. analyt. Edn* **41**, 2014–52015.
31. Vincent, J. F. and Bristol, K. E. (1945). Equilibrium humidity measurement. *Ind. Engng. Chem. analyt. Edn* **17**, 465–466.

32. Grover, D. W. (1947). The keeping properties of confectionery as influenced by its water vapor pressure. *J. Soc. chem. Ind., Lond.* **66**, 201–205.
33. Mossel, D. A. A. and Van Kuijk, H. J. L. (1955). A new and simple technique for the direct determination of the ERH of foods. *Fd Res.* **20**, 415–423.
34. Salwin, H. and Slawson, V. S. (1958). Moisture transfer in combinations of dehydrated foods. *Fd Technol.* **12** (4), abstract.
35. Salwin, H. (1959). Defining minimum moisture content of dehydrated foods. *Fd Technol.* **13**, 594–595.
36. Brunauer, S., Emmett, P. H. and Teller, E. 1938. Absorption of gases in multimolecular layers. *J. Am. chem. Soc.* **60**, 309–319.
37. Stadtman, E. R. (1948). Nonenzymatic browning in fruit products. "Advances in Food Research". Vol. 1. (Academic Press, New York).
38. Uri, N. (1956). Metal ion catalysis and polarity of environment in the aerobic oxidation of unsaturated fatty acids. *Nature, Lond.* **177**, 1177–1178.
39. Klotz, I. M. and Heiney, R. E. (1957). Changes in protein topography upon oxygenation. *Proc. natn. Acad. Sci U.S.A.* **43**, 717–719.
40. Shaw, T. M. (1944). The surface area of crystalline egg albumen. *J. chem. Phys.* **12**, 391–392.
41. Salwin, H. and Slawson, V. S. 1959. Moisture transfer in combinations of dehydrated foods. *Fd Technol.* **13**, 715–718.
42. Seltzer, E. and Saporito, F. (1956). Dryer for granular materials. U.S. Patent 2 740 204.
43. Anon. (1963). Batching and mixing. *Fd Engng* **35** (6), 75–90.
44. Slater, L. E. (1951). Electronic systems turns out food product in quantity and quality. *Fd Engng.* **23** (6), 80–84, 185–187.
45. Anon. (1964). Computer directs ingredient batching. *Fd Engng.* **36** (11), 70.
46. Anon. (1961). Swiss firm's use of punched card technique. *Fd Process. Packag.* **30**, 365–369, 377.
47 Evans, H. S. (1965). How digital blending does better job. *Fd Engng* **37** 2, 105.
48 Finn, R. (1964). Mechanized formula handling. *Fd Process. Packag* **26** (11), 79–81.
49. Kupersmit, J. B. (1961). New concepts in protective packaging. *Mod. Packag. Encycl.* 704–710.
50. Halton, P. and Scott-Blair, G. W. (1937). Study of some physical properties of flavor doughs in relationship to their bread-making qualities. *Cereal Chem.* **14**, 210–219.
51. Swason, C. O. (1938). The colloidal structure of dough as a means of interpreting quality in wheat flour. *Cereal Chem.* **15**, Spec. Supplement.
52. American Association of Cereal Chemists. (1962). "Cereal Laboratory Methods" 7th Ed., St. Paul, Minn.
53. American Public Heath Association. (1960). "Standard Methods for Examination of Dairy Products". 11th Ed., Washington, D.C.
54. Binnington, D. S., Johannson, H. and Geddes, W. F. (1939). Quantitative methods for evaluating the quality of macaroni products. *Cereal Chem.* **15**, 149–167.
55. American Oil Chemists Society. 1958. "Official and Tentative Methods". 2nd Ed., Chicago, Ill.
56. Evans, C. D. (1955). Flavor evaluation of fats and oils. *J. Am. Oil Chem. Soc.* **32** 596–604.
57. Rich, A. D. (1942). Methods employed in expressing the consistency of plasticized shortening. *J. Am. Oil Chem. Soc.* **19** 54–57.

58. Woerfel, J. B. (1960). Shortenings. "Bakery Technology and Engineering". (Avi Publishing Co., Westport, Conn.).
59. Anon. 1963. "Standards for Grades for the Dry Milk Industry". Bulletin 916. American Dry Milk Institute, Inc., Chicago, Ill.
60. Pyler, E. J. (1952). "Baking Science and Technology". (Seibel Publishing Co., Chicago, Ill.).
61. Mink, L. D. (1939). Egg material treatment. U.S. Patent 2 183 516.
62. Kothe, H. J. (1953). Egg white composition. U.S. Patent 2 637 654.
63. Kline, L. and Singleton, A. D. (1959). Egg whites. U.S. Patent 2,881,077.
64. Kline, L., Cegg, J. E. and Sonoda, T. T. (1951). Role of glucose in the storage deterioration of whole egg powder. II. A browning reaction involving glucose and cephalin in dried whole eggs. *Fd Technol.* **5** 181–187.
65. Anon. 1958. "Recommended Methods for the Microbiological Examination of Foods". (American Public Health Association, New York).
66. Forsythe, R. H. (1960). Eggs. "Bakery Technology and Engineering". (Avi Publishing Co., Westpot, Conn.).
67. Kramer, A. and Twigg, B. A. (1962). "Fundamentals of Quality Control for the Food Industry". (Avi Publishing Co., Westport, Conn.).
68. Anon. (1956). "Bread Baking". Department of the Army Technical Manual TM 10–410, Washington, D.C.
69. Dawson, E. H. and Harris, B. L. (1951). "Sensory Method for Measuring Differences in Food Quality". Agr. Inf. Bulletin 34, Washington, D.C.
70. Cecil, S. R. and Woodruff, (1952). "Long-Term Storage of Military Rations". Department of the Army, Washington, D.C.

Frozen Desserts

J. LLOYD HENDERSON

*Dairy Consultant, Formerly Dairy Technologist, University of California, and Quality Control Manager, Foremost Dairies Inc., San Francisco, U.S.A.**

1. INTRODUCTION

Quality control in the frozen dessert field is essential to the conduct of a profitable enterprise. The public purchases frozen desserts largely because they enjoy eating them and are confident that the regulations of the public health authorities and the company specifications control the composition, sanitary quality, and the environment in which they are produced to the point where they can have assurance of the quality and safety of the products. The processor then has a legal obligation to fulfil with respect to composition, bacterial standards and sanitation of the manufacturing plant. Customer satisfaction results in increased sales and thus the potential for greater profits. The pride of employees working in the plant is another reason for maintaining a strict quality control program.

2. COMPANY-WIDE RESPONSIBILITY FOR QUALITY

Quality control in the frozen dessert field, as with all food products, requires teamwork and the cooperation of all segments of the business. The purchasing, production, sales and quality control departments are all involved in an effective program. A really successful program, however, requires a company policy made at a high level that recognizes the importance of quality in the success of the business and which actively supports an effective program.

The procurement, or purchasing, department is involved in the program in connection with the purchase of quality ingredients.

Price should not be the only criterion on which supplies and ingredients are purchased. The purchasing agent should have "guide lines" in terms of

* Present address: 117 Oak Shadow Drive, Santa Rosa, California 95405 U.S.A.

quality requirements for ingredients such as milk solids, sugars, stabilizers, emulsifiers, fruits, nuts, berries, flavorings, containers and equipment. The purchase of dairy ingredients is one of the most important responsibilities in procurement with respect to the quality control of frozen desserts. The quality control manager, or laboratory superintendent, depending upon the type of organization, must be closely associated with this activity. Specifications must be provided for the "guide lines" with respect to alternate sources of fat and milk-solids-not-fat.

The production department is also one of the key units in a program to supply customers with high quality products at all times. In order to function effectively, this department must be provided with adequate equipment in terms of capacity, construction and sanitary features. Pasteurizers, flavor tanks, homogenizers, storage tanks, freezers and packaging equipment must be designed to perform properly and must be maintained in good repair.

The quality control manager or director, working usually with production and sales managers, should be responsible for the preparation and issuing of specifications for basic mixes, and for flavored frozen desserts. This function is especially important for a multi-plant operation since the procurement of ingredients and the uniformity of product cannot be maintained if each plant "goes it alone".

The final link in the chain to quality products from raw material to the finished frozen dessert supplied to the ultimate consumer are the sales and distribution departments. Policies with respect to types and servicing of delivery equipment, inspection of trucks and stores with respect to temperatures and to the rotation of product to prevent over-age merchandise in distribution channels are all important functions in a total quality control program.

3. ORGANIZING FOR QUALITY CONTROL

An organization chart should be prepared showing the lines of authority and responsibility in order to avoid confusion and frustration on the part of department heads. Written specifications, processing procedures, testing schedules and testing methods should be the corner stones in the organization of the program.

The specifications should include the basic mix formulae, the flavored mix formulae, and the sources and all types of ingredients and material used to produce the final product. The sales policy of the company with respect to market requirements will largely influence the decisions as to the gross composition requirements of the specifications. The quality control manager and the production manager should have joint responsibility for the selection of ingredients and supplies. The specifications should be formally issued by the quality control manager and should be supplied to personnel who have need for their use in the performance of their duties. When specifications are changed, each holder of the original specifications should be supplied with the new copy and instructions given to destroy the replaced copy in order to avoid its use in current production.

TABLE 1. Summary of the microbiological control of raw materials in ice cream manufacture[1]

Raw material	Sampling frequency	Resampling frequency	Bacteriological tests	Principal organisms causing faults
Milk	Each tanker	—	Total count Coliforms	Spores Coliforms
Milk powder	Each delivery	3 months	Total count	—
Chocolate	Each delivery	—	Total count Coliforms Yeasts and moulds	—
Vegetable oil	Each delivery	—	Yeasts and moulds Coliforms Lipolytic organisms	—
Sugar	Each delivery	—	Total count Coliforms Yeasts	Osmophilic yeasts
Stabilizers	Each delivery	3 months	Total count Coliforms	—
Fruit: Purees Canned Dried	Each delivery	—	Total count Coliforms Yeats and moulds	Yeasts
Nuts	Each delivery	1 month	Total count Coliforms Yeasts and moulds	Moulds
Confectionery products	Each delivery	1 month	Total count Coliforms Yeasts and moulds Staphylococci	Yeasts and moulds

Processing procedures should also be specific as to the essential procedures to use in pasteurization, homogenization, storage and freezing the mix. Care of equipment, such as the frequency of sharpening freezer blades, purging freezer barrels and the maintenance of all equipment should be provided in written form for the guidance of personnel responsible for the operation of the equipment.

Testing schedules should be established for the guidance of plant personnel responsible for securing and testing the samples. A minimum testing schedule should include the number, source and frequency of sampling to assure essential information on the composition, flavor and bacteriological quality

14*

of the ingredients and the finished frozen desserts. If problems are encountered, the frequency of sampling may be increased until the problem is solved.

The amount of testing of raw material will depend primarily on the effectiveness of the quality control program of the supplier. When the supplier has demonstrated that his products will uniformly meet company standards, the testing program for that supplier's products can usually be reduced. Table 1 shows a suggested program for sampling and testing the microbiological quality of raw ingredients to be used in frozen dessert manufacture.

When the raw materials are under control with respect to bacteriological content and composition standards, the quality of the finished frozen desserts is dependent to a large degree on the effectiveness of the quality control on the production line.

Tests determined on the production line and in the mix making department are usually made in the plant at the point of production by either a plant operator or by a member of the laboratory staff assigned to production line control. The principal tests are: (a) drawing temperature of the frozen dessert, (b) net weight or overrun, (c) record of mix temperatures in storage tanks, (d) heat treatment as shown on the pasteurizer charts, (e) organoleptic tests of all ingredients used in the mix, (f) report on equipment sanitization, (g) fat and total solids tests to confirm standardization.

Tests on the finished product should be performed in the laboratory. Representative random samples should be secured from the production plant by a member of the laboratory staff. The samples may be tested for (a) plate count (Standard Plate Count in the U.S.A.),[2] (b) coliform count—supplemented by *E. coli* confirmation if indicated, (c) Methylene Blue tests (England and Wales),[1,3] (d), fat and total solids determination, (e) grade samples for flavor, texture, color and package, (f) slice samples of strawberry, nut and candy ice cream to determine particle distribution.

The actual laboratory program established by a processor will normally be influenced by legal requirements, the degree of control required to maintain its quality standards, competition, and perhaps cost factors.

A. Testing Methods

Where standard testing methods are available and are recognized in a court of law they should be used. The results of such tests will be comparable to those obtained in other laboratories and if court action occurs they will be recognized as official. In the U.S.A. "Standard Methods for the Examination of Dairy Products",[2] and "Standard Methods of Analysis of the Official Analytical Chemists"[12] are used in most private and commercial laboratories as well as by the regulatory authorities laboratories. The above references present tests for the determination of fat, solids-not-fat, and bacteria.

The most common tests for fat are, the Gerber used in most European countries, the Babcock (various modifications) used in the U.S.A. and Canada, the Mojonnier or extraction method and the new Milko tester.

The bacteriological tests consist of the Total Plate Count (The Standard Plate Count in the U.S.A.), the Direct Microscopic Count (for manufacturing milk supplies), the coliform count and the *E. coli* confirmatory count, Methylene Blue on finished ice cream by regulatory authorities in England and Wales.[1,3]

Miscellaneous other tests run on the raw products or processed mixes are acidity, phosphatase, and sediment. In some jurisdictions dairy ingredients are tested for the presence of certain pesticides and antibiotics. Other control tests that may be run in the laboratory include quality of water, and strength of sterilizing solutions after passing through equipment.

The report forms, their distribution and use after being prepared are very important in the operation of the quality control department. To be effective, the records should be in the hands of personnel who can correct the situation as soon as possible after the tests have been completed. Essential paper work should be employed but not for the sake of accumulating reports but for the purpose of evaluating quality. When a report form has been found to be no longer useful and the information of little value, the form should be discontinued. Testing schedules should be reviewed from time to time to make certain that tests have not been "frozen" into the program and are no longer supplying useful information.

The laboratory staff will vary in number depending upon the size and complexity of the operation. In a small plant the technician may perform all of the bacteriological and chemical tests and also monitor the quality control function in the processing plant. In larger operations the chemical, bacteriological and plant quality control function may be separated and a number of technicians used. In a very large plant the quality control activity may be staffed by 10–15 or more workers. The Standard Methods previously referred to should be available in the laboratory as well as text books on ice cream such as Arbuckle's[4] and Volumes I and II of "Quality Control in the Food Industry."[5,6]

B. Housekeeping and Sanitary Inspection

These inspections are very important functions of the quality control department. It is essential to have a prepared form to facilitate the inspections. The inspection should include all areas of the plant and premises and should serve as a guide to make corrections of errors in the cleanliness and orderliness of each area and also to point out where corrections should be made in the repair and finish of buildings and equipment. Good house-keeping depends upon knowledge of good practices and requires systematic and regular inspection to determine that company policy is being followed in this function.

It is desirable to appoint a "sanitary" committee to evaluate the program. The committee should consist of personnel having responsibility in this area: for example, the committee may include the production manager, the chief engineer, the plant superintendent and the quality control manager. It has been found that when the committee system is used, housekeeping and maintenance of the premises are taken seriously by employees and they co-operate so that a clean, orderly, sanitary and well maintained environment is provided for the manufacture of high quality products.

In addition to an attractive plant and premises, the truck fleet should receive regular inspection with written reports. The inspection of the truck fleet is ordinarily under the control of the sales department. The trucks should be kept in good repair and washed at regular intervals. The public may never see the production plant but the trucks on the street are a constant reminder of the plant and its products. It is essential that a good impression be made—quality is often associated in the mind of the customer with attractive delivery equipment. The drivers should wear clean and attractive uniforms and present a neat and clean personal appearance. It is a good practice to have a full length mirror in the drivers' room in a position where it cannot be avoided. The driver can then get a preview of his appearance as it will be presented to the customer—clean uniform, shoes shined, haircut and fresh shave.

C. Insect and Rodent Control

Insects and rodents cannot be tolerated in a food plant. The quality control department has a responsibility in this area. Two approaches are available—the plant personnel can apply the necessary insecticides, baits or traps or a professional rodent control contractor can be employed to inspect the plant and premises on a regular basis and apply the indicated control measures. The latter is often the best solution since special knowledge of control material is required with respect to effective agents and legal procedures. Only approved insecticides should be applied.

The plant should be built to prevent the entrance of rodents and have all doors, windows and other openings screened or fitted with an air curtain or other device.

4. WORLD FROZEN DESSERT STANDARDS

In a free society, standards are necessary to ensure fair competition between processors and to supply consumers with a product that is safe and healthful. A survey of the frozen dessert standards in 25 countries shows the wide variations that exist.[7] As companies grow in size and expand into world markets the trend for many major food standards has been toward international standards.[5] The proposed Frozen Dessert Standards of the European Economic Community (Common Market) is a step in this direction.[8] The International Dairy Federation and the FAO/WHO Codex Alimentarius programs are other steps toward international standards.

TABLE 2. Statutory requirements for major contents
Minimum content of major ingredients[7]

	Total solids %	Total milk solids %	Fat %	Milk-solids not-fat %	Sugar %
Austria	—	—	10		
Belgium	—	—	8	*11, 10, 9,	—
Denmark	—	—	9	7	—
Eire	—	—	5	9	10
Fiji	—	—	8	—	—
Finland	30	—	12	10	—
France	31	—	7	—	14
Germany (Federal)	—	—	10	—	—
Greece (Code of Practice)	35–36	16–17	3·5–4·5	—	16–18
Holland	—	—	12	—	—
Israel	—	—	3·5	8	13
Italy (Code of Practice)	—	—	9–10	10	15–18
Norway	—	15	12	—	—
Portugal		No figures			
Spain	—	—	8	6	10
Sweden	—	—	12	—	—
Trinidad	36	—	8	—	—
U.K.	—	—	5	7·5	—
U.S.A.	—	20	10	—	—
U.S.S.R.	34	—	10	—	14

* Belgium requires a minimum of: 11% MSNF for fat content between 8% and 10%. 10% MSNF for fat content between 10% and 12%. 9% MSNF for fat content between 12% or more.

The U.S.A. frozen desserts standards are the most detailed standards in this field with respect to ingredients permitted, labeling regulations, minimum composition and other factors. The proposed E.E.C. standards are also very detailed concerning classification, minimum standards of composition, approved ingredients, labeling, processing procedures, health of employees and adequacy of facilities for the production and transportation of frozen desserts.

The wide variations in frozen dessert standards, shown in Tables 2, 3 and 8, emphasize the need for more uniform standards as trade between the Common Market countries and others concerned with import and export markets expand.

TABLE 3. Bacteriological standards for ice cream in countries whence information has been received[7]

Country	Maximum total count	Maximum count *B. coli*
Australia	50 000 per gm	None in 0·1 gm—No pathogenic bacteria
Belgium	100 000 per cc	1 in 0·1 cc
Canada	100 000 per cc	—
Czechoslovakia	100 000 per cc	100 in 1 cc
Denmark	100 000 per cc	150 in 1 cc
Eire	No standards	—
Fiji	50 000 per gm	None in 0·1 cc
Finland	50 000 per gm	5 in 1 gm
France	300 000 per cc	No pathogenic bacteria
Germany (Federal)	No Federal standards—each State has its own standard	
Greece	No standards—but stated "as for pasteurized milk"	
Holland	100 000 per cc	None in 0·1 cc. No pathogenic bacteria
India	No standards given	—
Israel	100 000 per cc	20 in 1 cc
Italy	No standards. Variation between communities	
Japan	50 000 per cc	None in 1 cc
New Zealand	No standards	None in 0·1 cc
Norway	According to Local Authority Regulations	
Portugal	100 000 per cc	10 in 1 cc
Sweden	100 000 per cc	1 in 0·1 gm
Switzerland	25 000 per cc	None in 0·1 cc—No pathogenic bacteria
Spain	100 000 per cc	No faecal, gelatin-liquefying or pathogenic bacteria
South Africa	200 000 per cc	None in 0·1 cc
Trinidad	No standards	—
U.K.	No standards	Control by Methylene Blue Test
U.S.A.	No Federal standards	States have their own standards
U.S.S.R.	No standards reported	—

Some of the provisions in the proposed E.E.C. standards are:

1. Total mesophile count—not to exceed 100 000.
2. Coliform count not to exceed 100.
3. Absence of pathogens and their toxins.
4. Minimum ice cream composition—fat 9 %, m.s.n.f. 7 %, total solids 31 %.
5. Minimum composition for vegetable fat ice cream—5 % fat, total solids 28 %.

It is reasonable to expect the E.E.C. standards to become the standards for all members of the Common Market and that they will doubtless be adopted by other countries that trade extensively with the Common Market members.

The wide variations in minimum content of major ice cream ingredients are shown in Table 2.

The bacterial standards for 27 countries are presented in Table 3. Nine of the standards have total counts of 100 000 as the maximum. The coliform standards range from not more than 1 in 0·1 cc to 150 in 1 cc.

5. CONSIDERATION OF BASIC FORMULAE

The basic formulae used for frozen desserts have an important bearing on the final quality as observed by the customer. Many potential defects are avoided or minimized by the proper selection of the gross composition of the mix and by the selection of the critical ingredients such as milk solids, sweeteners, stabilizers and emulsifiers. The selection of the basic formulae

TABLE 4. Representative frozen dessert formulae (U.S.A.)

Ingredient	Ice cream competitive %	* %	Ice cream good grade %	* %	Ice cream de luxe %	Ice milk %	* %	Ice milk high quality %
Milkfat	10·0	10·0	12·0	12·0	16·0	2·2	2·2	5·0
MSNF	10·2	7·7	11·0	9·0	9·0	12·0	9·5	13·5
Whey (dried)		2·5		2·0			2·5	
Sucrose	15·0	13·0	15·0	13·0	15·5	10·0	10·0	12·0
42 DE, corn syrup solids		4·0		4·0		8·0	8·0	6·0
Stabilizer†	0·3	0·3	0·3	0·3	0·3	0·5	0·5	0·4
Emulsifier†	0·12	0·12	0·12	0·12	0·12	0·2	0·2	0·2
Total solids	35·62	37·62	38·42	40·42	40·92	32·9	32·9	37·1

* Alternative formula.
† Depends upon type and composition.

with respect to fat, total solids percentages, flavor levels and overrun are largely based on such factors as: (a) legal requirements, (b) local practices, (c) market conditions, (d) type of operation, i.e. concentration on high quality or on mass production of highly competitive products. The final decision, however, must take into consideration the manufacture of products that are consistently uniform in quality and highly acceptable in a particular market.

A. Ice Cream

The minimum compositions of frozen desserts in most countries are set by ordinances and regulations. The formulae shown in Table 4 for ice cream and ice milk are similar to those used in many U.S.A. plants. As Table 2 indicates, the wide variations in standards make it impossible to consider formulae from all countries where frozen desserts are manufactured. The compositions shown in Table 4 will be referred to in connection with the selection of ingredients for ice cream mixes. The factors considered would apply to ice creams of all compositions.

B. Ice Milk

Ice milk is a product that has been growing in popularity in recent years in the U.S.A. The product is lower in fat and higher in milk-solids-not-fat than that usually found in ice cream. The product ranges in fat from 2 to 7%. Table 4 shows two different ice milk compositions, one low in fat and solids and another higher in fat. Where vegetable fat ice milk is permitted a considerable proportion of the product is made with vegetable fat.

C. Vegetable Fat Frozen Desserts

During recent years a growing percentage of frozen dessert products are made with vegetable fat. Factors concerned with quality of the fat are discussed in Section 6. When vegetable fat frozen desserts are permitted the fat content is usually lower than in those made with milkfat.

D. Soft-serve Ice Milk

Soft serve products—ice milk and ice cream are important in the frozen dessert industry. In some countries most of the soft serve products are ice milk. A typical soft serve ice milk formula is shown in Table 5.

Partially frozen ice cream or ice milk drawn from the freezers into cones or cups requires special consideration from the standpoint of public health. Operators should be instructed in the proper and sanitary way to handle the mix and to operate and clean and sanitize the freezer.

E. Sherbets

The definition of sherbets differs in various countries and even in parts of the same country. A good typical fruit sherbet contains 1–2% milkfat and 3–4% milk-solids-not-fat. Good quality whey solids may be substituted for all or part of the milk-solids-not-fat in some jurisdictions. A typical sherbet formula is shown in Table 5. The sherbet base is blended with fruit or puree, fruit concentrate or juice to yield the desired flavor. In the U.S.A. the minimum amount of fruit that must be used in the preparation of fruit sherbet is specified. In relation to the weight of the finished dessert, the following fruit must be used: citrus 2%, berries and cherries 6% and other fruits 10%. Water may be added to the concentrated fruits to re-establish the original moisture content.

In most definitions of sherbets, the acidity must be adjusted to at least 0·35% calculated as lactic acid. In practice, a 50% citric acid solution is usually used to adjust the acidity in the flavor tank just before the freezing. Color is added at the flavor tank.

TABLE 5. Representative formulae for soft serve, milk shake base, sherbet base and water ice base

Ingredient	Soft serve %	* %	Milk shake base %	Sherbet base %	Water ice base %
Milkfat	4·0	4·0	4·5	2·0	0
MSNF	11·0	8·5	11·0	4·0†	0
Whey (dried)		2·5			
Sucrose	13·0	11·0	8·0	22·0	23·0
42 DE corn syrup solids		4·0		6·0	7·0
Stabilizer‡	0·4	0·4	0·4	0·5	0·4
Emulsifier‡	0·15	0·15	0·15		
Total solids	28·55	30·55	24·05	34·5	30·4

* Alternative formula.
† May be partially or all dried whey solids.
‡ Amount depends upon type and composition.

F. Ices (Sorbets)

This class of frozen desserts is differentiated from the fruit sherbets in that they do not contain dairy products. A typical ice formula is shown in Table 5. The water ice is blended with fruit, purees or juices to produce the desired flavored ice (sorbet). In the U.S.A. ices must have the minimum fruit content as previously indicated for sherbets.

G. Novelties

Many types of fancy ice cream and novelties are manufactured in frozen dessert plants. The two principal types that are made in volume on a machine production line basis are bars and cups.

1. Bars

Bars are frozen desserts produced on a number of types of equipment. The Gram, the Eskimo–Nelson and the Vita-Line companies are the principal suppliers of equipment. The bars may be made under franchise from a company that supplies the bags, sticks, flavors, molds, advertising promotion and sometimes the freezing equipment. In many countries, U.K. and Germany in particular, the frozen dessert manufacturer purchases the supplies and equipment independently. The bars may be ice cream, ice milk, sherbets, ices (iced lollies) or various combinations of these products. Bars may be enrobed with chocolate or other coating or sold with no coating. Some are provided with center sticks and others are extruded into equipment that conveys them directly to a hardening tunnel (Eskimo–Nelson machine).

Quality control problems in a bar operation vary with the type of freezing equipment. If a brine tank is used the molds must be checked frequently to determine that brine is not leaking into the mold. Steel wool sponges should not be used in cleaning the interior of the molds—nylon pads are preferable. A mold washer and sterilizer is essential when molds are used to form the bars. When chocolate coating is used, care must be taken to maintain the coating at the proper temperature for coating the bars.

2. Cups

Equipment is available for the rapid filling of cups of various sizes—3 oz, 4 oz, etc. Cups are filled with ice cream, ice milk or sherbet alone or in various combinations. Chocolate and other syrups may be variegated into the cup or a sundae topping may be applied.

6. SOURCES OF DAIRY INGREDIENTS

A. Milk fat

Milk fat used in frozen desserts may be selected from a number of products. In any production area the manufacturer should check with the regulatory authorities on the approval of the fat source. The most common sources are: whole fresh milk, fresh cream, frozen cream, plastic frozen cream, sweet (unsalted) butter, anhydrous milkfat, butter oil, sweetened condensed whole milk and powdered whole milk. The choice for quality is roughly in the order listed above provided each product meets the quality standards within its own classification. The decision as to alternatives that may be used is usually made on the basis of a number of criteria, such as (a) quality of finished product required for a particular market, (b) availability of ingredients, (c) processing facilities available and (d) cost.

It is desirable to establish a basic policy for the procurement department to adhere to in securing dairy ingredients for use in frozen desserts. For example the specification of a de luxe catering ice cream (Table 4) may contain provisions that all of the fat be derived from whole milk and sweet cream. The specification for a 12% fat ice cream (Table 4) may be written to permit the utilization of frozen cream, frozen plastic cream or a percentage of sweet butter (unsalted) of a specific grade. A highly competitive "traffic brand" ice cream or one made for a private label account (Table 4) may be written to permit any source of fat that will meet minimum standards accepted by the regulatory authorities and by the customer. It is important with this type of product to make the quality at the level decided upon uniform from day to day; that is, do not use fresh cream one day as the major source of fat and butter oil the next day. A distinct difference should be maintained between ice creams of different compositions and price levels.

The milkfat content and the solids-not-fat content of all sources of milk-fat in the mixes should be determined in order to facilitate mix making and to reduce the amount of mix restandardization.

B. Vegetable Fats

Vegetable fats or oils may be used in many of the countries of the world. It is important that the oils used be of good quality—bland in flavor and low in peroxide and acid numbers. If oils are stored in bulk tanks it is desirable to empty and clean and sanitize them before more product is put into the tank. A small amount of aged and deteriorated oil can trigger the oxidation of a large volume.

C. Milk-Solids-Not-Fat

The quality of the sources of milk-solids-not-fat for use in frozen desserts is equally important as are the sources selected for milkfat. The most commonly used products are: whole milk, fresh skimmed milk, fresh condensed skimmed milk, low or medium heat non-fat dry milk, sweet dry buttermilk, sweetened condensed skimmed milk, specially treated milk solids (Nutrimix) delactosed milk and sodium caseinate.

As previously discussed in connection with the source of milk fat, the list above is roughly in the descending order for contribution to the flavor quality of the finished product, provided the ingredients meet the quality specifications within their own classification. For example; The specification for a de luxe catering ice cream may require that all of the milk-solids-not-fat be derived solely from whole milk, fresh skimmed milk and fresh condensed skimmed milk. A standard grade of 12% fat ice cream may permit a percentage of the solids-not-fat be secured from low or medium heat non-fat dry milk or sweet cream dry buttermilk, or whey. A "traffic" or private label ice cream with 10% fat may be written with a specification that will permit any source of milk-solids-not-fat that will meet regulatory authority requirements, company specifications and customer acceptance. If a product with increased solids-not-fat is desired, one of the specially treated milk solids should be used to delay "sandy" development in storage.

High quality U.S. Extra Grade Dry Whey solids may be used where available in all except the top grades of ice cream and ice milk. Condensed whey is less dependable as a source of solids. The amount of whey used should not exceed 2·5% of the weight of the mix or approximately a 25% replacement of milk-solids-not-fat. This limitation is due primarily to two factors, the high lactose of whey and the possibility of an off flavour or salty flavor if too much whey is used. New whey products are beginning to be available for use in ice cream that make them more acceptable—reduced salt content and reduction in lactose content are some of the developments.

The discussions relative to the quality of the sources of fat and solids-not-fat also apply to ice milk. If it is desired to increase the milk-solids-not-fat in ice milk from 13·5 to 15·0% or more it is necessary to use specially treated milk solids in order to avoid "sandiness" owing to lactose crystallization. Sandiness is further discussed under the section on frozen dessert defects. A product known as Nutrimix may be used to replace 40% of the regular solids-not-fat. Nutrimix is specially treated milk-solids that delays the onset of sandiness. It is prepared by treating milk solids in concentrated form with sodium phosphate and calcium hyroxide under specific conditions. The condensed product is then dried. Another method of maintaining a high protein content in ice milk is to replace some of the milk solids with food grade sodium caseinate. This procedure will also assist in maintaining a good body and texture and will tend to avoid sandiness.

D. Blends of Fat and Milk-Solids-Not-Fat

In addition to the sources of fat and solids-not-fat mentioned earlier, combinations of blends are available in many areas in the U.S.A. The blend of fat and solids-not-fat will vary depending upon the requirements of a particular ice cream plant. If most of the production is a 10 or 12% fat mix the blend may consist of 20% fat and 25% solids-not-fat. The milk is usually standardized and condensed in a country plant and hauled by tanker to a city ice cream plant. The blends are less useful if a great number of mixes of varying composition are processed.

7. SOURCES OF NON-DAIRY INGREDIENTS

While emphasis has been placed upon the importance of dairy ingredients in securing a high quality frozen dessert, the non-dairy ingredients can also have a significant influence on the flavor as well as other characteristics, such as body, texture, appearance and general appeal.

A. Sweeteners

Since frozen desserts are desserts, the degree of sweetness is an important factor in their acceptance by the consumer. In many areas 15% sucrose or equivalent sweetness is considered optimum. There are areas, however, where consumers apparently prefer 16% or more in sweetness. The equivalent of sucrose in the formulae are in terms of the effective and relative sweetness of corn sweeteners as compared to sucrose.

Absolute values of sweetness cannot be established precisely since individuals vary in their taste perceptions. Other factors such as concentration, temperature, presence of non-sugar substances and the combination of two or more sugars also influence the evaluation. Table 6, however, indicates the average values that may be used in estimating the sweetening level in frozen desserts when sucrose and a corn sweetener are used.

TABLE 6. Relative sweetening power of corn sweeteners and lactose as compared with sucrose

Sweetener	Relative sweetness
Sucrose (cane or beet)	100 Standard
High conversion corn syrup (62 DE)	65*
Regular conversion corn syrup (42 DE)	50*
Low conversion corn syrup (36 DE)	45*
Dextrose (91% solids)	80
Lactose	15

* Solids basis.

1. Sucrose

Sucrose (cane or beet) is available in dry (granular) form or as a 66–67% solids liquid sugar or as a blend with dextrose or corn syrup solids. There are few quality problems associated with the use of dry sugar. It must be stored in a dry environment and protected from contamination and dust. The product may be secured in 100 lb bags and in some localities as bulk shipments. If the operation has suffcent volume to utilize bulk shipments of dry sugar it is likely that a liquid product would be more suitable from the standpoint of convenience and cost. Where liquid sugar is not available and the convenience of handling the liquid product is desired, the granulated sugar may be liquefied in special equipment to 67% solids and stored in a sugar tank.

When the frozen dessert volume warrants the use of liquid sugar, that is, when a tank delivery can be used in a few days (or, as is the case with some large installations, in one day), this type of operation is applicable to an automated or semi-automated operation. In order to prevent fermentation it is desirable to test all tanker deliveries for total solids, clean the tank at intervals and use a "sterile" lamp in the headspace.

2. Dextrose

Dextrose, as Table 6 shows, has a sweetening value (at 91 % solids) of 80 as compared to sucrose. Dextrose generally sells for a lower price than does sucrose and is often used in sherbets, ices and occasionally in sucrose blends. Dextrose has a lower molecular weight than that of sucrose and hence has a greater effect in depressing the freezing point of the mix. If too much dextrose is used this can be a factor in the temperature that must be maintained in dealers' cabinets.

3. Corn Syrup Solids

Corn syrup solids that are available in different parts of the world vary in composition. The 42 DE (dextrose equivalent) product with a sweetness (relative to sucrose of 50–60 %) (Table 6) depending upon the composition of the mix and other factors, has an apparent molecular weight of approximately 400 and hence has little effect upon the freezing point of the ice cream or other frozen dessert when it is used to replace a portion of the sucrose which has a molecular weight of 342. The 42 DE corn syrup solids is the one most commonly available and is apparently the best one to use if only one tank is available for liquid sugar. The 36 DE product with an apparent sweetness of approximately 45 as compared with sucrose is available in some localities and has application for use in ice cream or ice milk where the milk-solids-not-fat is reduced and the total solids and sweetness are to be maintained. In some areas the 55–65 DE product is available.

The amount of corn syrup solids or corn sugar (dextrose) that may be used in a mix is dictated by a number of factors:

(a) Body and texture considerations: if 36 or 42 DE corn syrup solids are used in reasonable amounts there is generally an improvement in the body and texture—all other ingredients in the mix remaining constant. The possible effect on flavor is discussed under the section on defects in frozen desserts.

(b) Economy: the second reason for considering corn syrup solids in the mix is the effect on costs. If the milk-solids-not-fat content is reduced from 12 to 10 % and corn syrup solids are used to maintain the solids and sweetness, total cost of the mix can be reduced. The cost of corn syrup solids varies with corn prices, business conditions, and other factors but often there is a differential of two cents per pound on the solids basis as compared with sucrose.

4. Blends of Sucrose and Corn Sweeteners

Blends of liquid sucrose and different corn sweeteners are available in many locations. The increased use of blends has been accelerated by increased labor costs and the trend to the automation of the mix-making operation. With this system only one storage tank is required and one less product must be metered into the mix tank. There are, however, certain disadvantages. The most important one is that it is more difficult to vary the amount of corn sweetener in the various mixes. Dry sugar or dry corn syrup solids must be inventoried if different ratios of corn sweetener are specified for certain frozen desserts.

Blends are available in different compositions and products. A blend of 70% sucrose and 30% 42 DE corn syrup solids is probably the most acceptable product. Some blends may contain 62 DE corn syrup solids and others may contain dextrose or invert sugar. Some blends even contain three liquid sugars. There is probably little advantage in these more complex mixes. The blends should be pasteurized and standardized at the sugar plant to avoid fermentation during storage in the ice cream plant.

B. Stabilizers

Stabilizers are used in frozen desserts to improve the body and texture and to minimize the adverse effects of unfavorable storage temperatures and fluctuating temperatures. The primary function of stabilizers is to bind and hold the water in the mix (water of hydration) in a manner to avoid the formation of large ice crystals. Until recent years gelatin was the principal stabilizer used in ice cream and most frozen desserts. It is still important in some areas but it is being largely replaced by mixtures of gums. In addition to binding water, gelatin establishes a gel structure in the mix. The stabilizer ingredients now most commonly used are: locust bean gum (carob gum), guar gum, sodium alginate, carrageenan (Irish moss extract) and sodium carboxymethyl cellulose (CMC, a synthetic gum).

The selection of the stabilizer to use in a particular ice cream or other frozen dessert is dictated largely by the type of body desired, by the processing facilities available and by the storage conditions likely to be encountered in the channels of trade. The commercial stabilizers are usually made up of a mixture of gums. Since the gums vary in their properties, a stabilizer can be blended to suit mix composition or processing procedures. Locust bean gum, for example, will bind water very tightly even through the freezing and thawing cycles encountered in a storage cabinet. The stabilizer mixture is selected on the basis of the properties of the individual ingredients used.

Guar gum is in many ways similar to locust bean gum but differs in some side chains in the molecular structure, making it soluble in cold mixes, while locust bean gum requires heat for hydration. CMC hydrates rapidly in cold mix and gives good protection against heat shock in storage cabinets and home refrigerators.

A common stabilizer mixture is as follows: locust bean gum, CMC and carrageenan mixed with dextrose as the diluent.

The amount of each ingredient is varied according to the purpose of the stabilizer. It is generally the best policy to purchase the mixed stabilizers from a reliable manufacturer who maintains a quality control department and regularly tests each batch of stabilizer compounded.

A sherbet stabilizer may contain pectin, locust bean gum and dextrose as a diluent. Many frozen dessert manufacturers use locust bean gum as the only stabilizer in ices.

C. Emulsifiers

Emulsifiers play an important role in modern frozen dessert manufacture. Emulsifiers are used to secure a stiff, dry product from the freezer, to improve the body and texture and when judiciously used to improve the resistance to melting down of the frozen product. It has generally been considered that the emulsifiers probably function through their ability to orient themselves at the fat–plasma interface and thereby increase the permanence of the oil-in-water emulsion and the foam produced during whipping. The concentration in the interface reduces the surface tension of the system. Ice creams containing emulsifiers appear to have somewhat smaller air cells and therefore a smoother texture.[4] The stiffer and drier appearance of the ice cream discharging from a continuous freezer is physical evidence of its action.

According to Keeney[9] all emulsifiers used in ice cream as drying agents accelerate the agglomeration of the fat. They do not stabilize the fat. Emulsifiers provide a means of controlling the dryness of ice cream as it leaves the freezer.

The rate and degree of fat agglomeration depends upon the amount and type of emulsifier used and upon the processing conditions. Excessive use of emulsifiers promotes the formation of visible churned fat which is an undesirable defect.[10]

Before modern emulsifiers were available, egg yolk was used for this purpose and it still provides most of the emulsification in French type (egg) ice cream. Modern high speed fillers and the emphasis on high production rates with the attendant higher drawing temperatures from continuous freezers have resulted in the more frequent use of emulsifiers at higher rates.

The most common emulsifiers now in use for ice cream manufacture (U.S.A.) are the monodiglycerides and Tween 65 and Tween 80. These emulsifiers are approved for use in frozen desserts in the United States at the following maximum levels:

1. Mono-diglycerides—0·20% of the weight of the finished product.
2. Tween 65 (polyoxyethylene (20) sorbitan tristearate).
3. Tween 80 (poly sorbate 80).

The Tweens may be used at a level not to exceed 0·1 % of the weight of the finished product when used separately or together.

A series of mono and diglycerides are available with varying amounts of the "mono." The greater the mono content the greater the drying action. Also the type of fatty acid in the mono is important; the greatest drying action is imparted when the mono is derived from unsaturated and medium molecular weight fatty acids. The polyoxyethylenes or "polys" (Tween 65 and Tween 80) are more potent drying agents than are the mono-diglycerides. Blends of mono-diglycerides and polys are available with approximately 20 % derived from the poly. This type of product is used at the rate of 0·12–0·15 %. Tween 80 is very effective and when used alone the usual rate is 0·03–0·04 %.

Extruded products such as sandwiches require additional emulsification and this can be secured by adding additional emulsifier (usually Tween 80) to the mix in the flavor tank.

The excessive use of emulsifiers can cause a number of ice cream defects. If the emulsifier is high in free fatty acid (due to improper refining) shrinkage may be promoted. An excess of emulsification may cause a slow and curdy melt down.

It is often necessary for the frozen dessert manufacturer to experiment with his stabilizer–emulsifier combination to secure the desired results with his particular mix and market. The manufacturer of these items can usually provide technical assistance. Once the desired result is obtained it is recommended that the identification of the ingredients and the amounts of stabilizer and emulsifier be included in the formal product specifications and then changed only for a good reason. It is not advisable from a quality standpoint to be constantly changing the type and amount of stabilizer and emulsifier. These two ingredients constitute a minor part of the mix cost but have important functions in maintaining uniformity and the general quality of the frozen desserts.

Blends of ready-mixed stabilizer–emulsifier combinations are available for processors who prefer to use one rather than two products.

D. Colors

The standards for color in the different countries range from none permitted to no regulation. In the U.S.A. the Food and Drug Administration issues a list of approved colors. In some countries the use of colors is covered by the general food laws. Colors when used should be characteristic of the product being colored—pastel rather than deep shades are usually preferred.

Colors can be a source of bacterial contamination if not properly handled. Prepared liquid colors are available and small operators may find them more convenient than the dry colors. Large operators generally prepare colors from dry approved powders (generally using 4 oz/gal). The dry colors are dissolved in recently boiled water and stored in clean containers. Sodium benzoate may be added at the rate of 0·1 % where permitted by food laws.

Uniformity of color in frozen desserts is important and can be attained only if the amount of color is carefully controlled.

8. SELECTING SOURCES OF FLAVORING INGREDIENTS

The quality of the flavoring ingredients used in ice cream and other frozen desserts is very important from the standpoint of making a product highly acceptable to customers and is an important factor in their continued purchase of your brand rather than that of a competitor. Flavoring ingredients should be selected with care and used at the proper levels.

A. Vanilla

Vanilla is the most popular ice cream and ice milk flavor. Many surveys have shown that in some countries vanilla accounts for over 50% of the flavored ice cream. It has been estimated that when one counts the vanilla used in parfaits, chocolate, eggnog and many other flavors that 70–75% of all ice creams contain some vanilla. The Bourbon beans of Madagascar and the Mexican beans of Mexico are the most important sources of the types of vanilla beans used for flavoring frozen desserts. Tahiti, South America and Java supply the market with smaller amounts of vanilla beans.

Types of Vanilla Flavoring Extracts used for Frozen Desserts

1. Pure Vanilla Bean Extracts

Bourbon beans and Mexican beans or a blend of the two are used most frequently to produce pure vanilla extracts. Tahiti beans are used by some manufacturers at a level of 5–25% of the extract to yield a characteristic flavor.

In the U.S.A. a single fold vanilla contains the extract from 13·35 oz of vanilla beans per gal when the beans have a moisture content of 25%. The standard then means that the extract is derived from 10 oz of bean solids per gal. A twofold pure vanilla extract contains the extract from 26·7 oz of 25% moisture beans per gal or 20 oz of bean solids. A twofold product is about the maximum that can be made by direct extraction. Four-, six- and higher fold extracts are usually made by concentrating the direct extract.

In the U.S.A. a vanilla ice cream flavored with the pure extract may be labeled "Vanilla Ice Cream".

2. Vanilla–Vanillin Extract

In the U.S.A. a vanilla extract made with 1 oz of methyl vanillin and the extract of 13·35 oz of beans per gal may be used to flavor ice cream which must be labeled "Vanilla Flavored Ice Cream". The extract is referred to as a twofold extract onefold is from the beans and onefold is from the added methyl vanillin. Methyl vanillin is the naturally occurring vanillin of vanilla beans where it occurs in amounts ranging from 0·11 to 0·35 g per 100 ml of extract.[11] The vanillin is a product of the curing process.

3. Artificial or Imitation Vanilla Extract

In the U.S.A. a vanilla flavored extract that has more than 1 oz of methyl vanillin to the extract from 13·35 oz of vanilla beans must be labeled "Artificially Flavored or Imitation Flavored Vanilla Ice Cream". When once this amount of vanillin has been exceeded there is no limitation on the amount of methyl vanillin that may be used. Some commercial products contain up to 8 oz of vanillin per gal with little or no vanilla bean extractives. Many products may be added to imitation vanillas such as heliotropine, piperonal, anisyl aldehyde, ethyl vanillin and others.

4. Control of Vanilla Quality

The first step in the selection of a dependable supply of vanilla is to select a reliable supplier. Such a supplier will have contact with the vanilla bean market, he will have laboratory and quality control facilities and programs and will have demonstrated by his years in business that he is conducting a successful enterprise. It is desirable to obtain the supplier's advice on the amount of vanilla extract required for the frozen desserts to be manufactured. Samples of the ice cream should be made with the recommended amounts and if these do not prove suitable the amount should be varied until one is satisfied that the ice cream is flavored to the requirements of the market. The amount to use will vary with the amount of flavor in the extract. the total solids of the mix, the quality of the mix ingredients and the strength of flavor required in a particular market.

In the selection of the vanilla extract to use consideration must be given to the requirements of the market, the labeling laws of the area, availability of the product and finally the cost. A top quality of ice cream or ice milk deserves a good vanilla, either a pure one or one with not more than 1 oz of methyl vanillin to the extract of 13·35 oz of good grade vanilla beans. For highly competitive frozen desserts an imitation product with 5 oz of methyl vanillin per 13·35 oz of beans may be satisfactory. In addition to the three types of vanilla mentioned, powdered, ground and paste products are available.

Before the chromatographic methods of analysis, tests for the detection of adulteration and for evidence of the amount of bean solids present were chemical tests that in most instances could be altered by the addition of foreign substances which could not easily be detected. The vanillin content, the lead number and the resin content could easily be altered to render the analysis valueless.

The analysis of vanilla extracts using one- and two-dimensional fluorescence chromatography, paper chromatography for organic acids, thin-layer chromatography for the detection of added substances such as ethyl vanillin, piperonal and other "sophisticated" additions, and the gradient elution method for the detection of organic acids makes the adulteration of vanilla extracts more difficult. The tests are too time-consuming for routine use but are available in some commercial laboratories and can be used in the selection of a vanilla supply or for spot checking at intervals to make certain that the supplier is maintaining his standards. Most of the tests mentioned are now "official" or "first action" tests of the Association of Official Analytical Chemists.[12]

B. Chocolate

Chocolate ice cream and ice milk are manufactured in a variety of forms: regular chocolate, fudge (syrup), chip (chocolate pieces in vanilla ice cream), rockyroad (added pieces of nuts and marshmallow) and many other variations. This family of chocolate frozen desserts have been found in many surveys in the U.S.A. to be the second most popular flavor after vanilla and to account for about 15% of the total production. The purchase of the proper chocolate products for the particular market requirements is an important procurement and quality control function.

The flavor is due to the chocolate solids contained in the chocolate product. The various sources of chocolate contain different amounts of cocoa fat due to the amounts removed by processing and hence vary in chocolate solids. It is generally considered that at least 2·5% chocolate solids is required to flavor the ice cream mix. This amount will vary with type and quality of the beans, the amount of processing and the amount of flavor desired in the ice cream. The principal sources of chocolate flavor for ice cream are:

1. Chocolate liquor—50–55% cocoa fat.
2. Granules—36–38% cocoa fat.
3. Breakfast-type cocoa—22–26% cocoa fat.
4. Low fat cocoa—12–18% cocoa fat.

In selecting the source of chocolate solids it is necessary to consider the requirements of the market with respect to degree of flavor and color. The price of the product to use is influenced by the market for cocoa fat which varies over a wide range. When cocoa fat is high in price, cocoa is relatively low in price and when cocoa fat is low in price cocoa is high since the chocolate solids must then bear a larger proportion of the entire cost.

Table 7 shows the chocolate solids, the cocoa fat and the pounds of chocolate product required to yield 2·5 lb of chocolate solids or the amount to flavor 100 lb of mix.

TABLE 7. Cocoa fat and chocolate solids content of various chocolate products

Product	% Cocoa fat	% Chocolate solids	lb product to Yield 2·5 lb solids
Cocoa	16	84	2·97
Cocoa	22	78	3·20
Cocoa	26	74	3·38
Granules	38	62	4·03
Liquor	53	47	5·32

Chocolate products may be obtained in either the natural or Dutched form. The Dutched product has been treated with one of the alkalies—sodium, potassium, ammonium or magnesium carbonate or hydroxide, while the natural product is untreated. Authorities are not in complete agreement as to the value of Dutching.[4,11] Some hold that it increases the color, brings out the flavor, makes the product more soluble, and mitigates the bitter taste that is sometimes found in the natural product. Most authorities will agree on two points, i.e. increase in color and increase in solubility. The natural products generally range in pH from 5·7 to 6·3 whereas the Dutched products range from 7·0 to 7·8. The pH and color can be modified by blending the natural and the Dutched product.

Chocolate products are often modified in flavor by the addition of vanillin, cinnamon, anise and other compounds. It is frequently the custom of ice cream manufacturers to add vanilla to chocolate mixes. About half of the amount in vanilla ice cream is added to the flavor tank. If a good mix is used there is some question as to the need for modifiers for chocolate ice cream. If vanilla is used it should be a good product and not a rank imitation which detracts from the chocolate flavor.

After the selection of the desired chocolate source, the major quality control programs are in the processing and in enforcing rules to prevent chocolate ice cream from becoming a dumping ground for re-run or re-worked ice cream or for the salvaging of ice cream returned by dealers who have experienced cabinet failures. Strong flavored ice creams such as maple-nut, walnut, mint and the like should not be added to the chocolate mix. If the amount of approved re-run exceeds 10–15% of the weight of the mix, a restandardization should be made to adjust the amount of chocolate solids and sugar. Re-run ice cream should not be returned directly to the flavor tank since it may contaminate the mix if it is not properly handled; because of the air in the product, it will also interfere with the normal operation of the freezer. All re-run should be added to a fresh chocolate mix and pasteurized.

When the volume of chocolate ice cream is sufficiently large, a separate chocolate mix should be processed rather than a chocolate syrup being added to the white mix.

In the selection of the source of chocolate for frozen desserts, a first approximation in the evaluation can be obtained by preparing a syrup of the chocolate product and sugar, adding it to the unflavoured white mix and freezing it in a small laboratory freezer. This test will indicate the flavor and color the chocolate will impart to the finished ice cream.

Top grades of ice cream are often made with chocolate liquor or granules. Standard grade and private label brands may well be made with low-fat cocoa. The sugar level in chocolate ice cream is especially important and the general practice is to standardize the chocolate mix with about 2% more sugar than that of the vanilla mix.

C. Fruits for Ice Cream

After vanilla and chocolate, strawberry has been found in many surveys to be the third most popular flavor. Fruit ice creams in general are popular with many customers. In selecting the fruit to use, it is important that careful consideration be given to the kind of fruit used, the variety and form (i.e. whether it is frozen, dried, pureed, concentrated or juice). The frozen fruit used in ice cream, whether whole, sliced or pureed, should have 20–25% sugar added at the time of preparation for freezing. The sugar tends to preserve the color and flavor during the thawing period and reduces the "iciness' when fruit pieces are added to the ice cream via the fruit feeder.

1. Strawberry Ice Cream

The quality of strawberry ice cream is greatly influenced by the quality of the fruit and the amount that is used for flavoring the frozen dessert. When available, fresh unfrozen strawberries make a superior ice cream. Since a supply of fresh berries is seldom available, the most popular type of strawberry is the sliced frozen 4+1 or 3+1 pack, that is, with 20 or 25% of sugar. Quality problems with the frozen type of berry consists in the variability in freedom from coliform organisms and in the color and flavor of the fruit. Stabilizers may be added at the fruit freezing plant to compensate for the stabilizer dilution of the mix when the fruit is added.

Strawberries should be used at a level that will adequately flavor the ice cream and give it a character that customers associate with strawberry ice cream. In the U.S.A. if a product is to be labeled "Strawberry Ice Cream" without any qualifications it must have no artificial flavor added and have enough berries to impart the characteristic flavor. It will ordinarily require 15% of sugared berries to give a pleasing characteristic strawberry flavor. Top grades of ice cream are often flavored with 20–25% sugared fruit.

To be labeled "Strawberry Flavored Ice Cream", at least 6% fruit must be added in relation to the weight of the finished product and when once this amount is met, artificial flavor may be added in any quantity. The package requires subsidiary flavor label declaration such as "Strawberry and Artificial Strawberry Flavor" or other wording to indicate that artificial flavor was added.

When less than 6% of fruit is used, added flavor is considered to predominate and the product must be labeled "Artificially Flavored Strawberry" or "Artificial Strawberry".

In order to meet the label requirement for "Strawberry Ice Cream", a combination of fruit sources may be used in order to impart the characterizing flavor. Frozen berries plus a concentrate of berries with true fruit flavor derived from strawberries or in combination with other natural fruit flavors may be used. In the imitation classification there are many sources of flavors to use. It is recommended that for top grades of ice cream the imitations be avoided.

Frozen strawberries should be thawed in a room at 40°F before use. An attempt to thaw berries quickly at a higher temperature results in darkening of color and in a "mushy" texture, and generally results in increases in bacterial counts. When specifications call for not more than 10 coliform organisms/g, the need for hot-pack fruit may be indicated. Most strawberries have a high natural content of 1-ascorbic acid (vitamin C) and do not respond noticeably to further additions of the acid at the time of freezing as do some other fruits such as peach and bananas.

2. Other Fruits for Ice Cream Flavoring

Peach flavored ice cream is becoming one of the most important flavors, especially for a summer special. Peach ice cream by definition in the U.S.A. must have enough fruit to impart the characteristic flavor of the fruit but no minimum is specified for this class or category. Some varieties of peaches, the cling stone type in particular, have very little flavor and 30–35% fruit will not give a good peach flavor. With this type a fortifier is required and if it is not true fruit it cannot be labeled "Peach Ice Cream". With this amount of fruit the fat content of a 10 or 12% fat white mix would have to be increased to meet a minimum standard of 8% fat in the finished ice cream. Many freestone peaches have enough flavor so that 20% fruit with some true fruit flavor will produce a good peach ice cream. In actual practice apricot or nectarine puree is often used for one third of the fruit in peach ice cream. Peach ice cream with a minimum of 10% fruit can have artificial flavor in any amount. This product must be labeled "Peach Flavored Ice Cream" with subsidiary label declaration of the added artificial flavor.

All other fruits except berry and cherry ice cream require a minimum of 10% fruit and are labeled "Flavored" preceded by the name of the fruit, when artificial flavoring is also added. Banana and pineapple are among the most popular flavors in this category and approximately 20% of the fruit is used to avoid the term artificial. Banana ice cream is usually a banana-nut or banana-bisque.

For recipes for many other types of other fruit ice cream see Turnbow et al.[11] and Arbuckle.[4]

D. Nuts

Many kinds of nuts are used for flavoring frozen desserts either alone or in combination with other materials such as fruits, candies and chocolates. Almond, Pecan and Walnut probably account for 75% of the nut ice cream manufactured. Other types of nuts used for flavoring ice cream are: Brazil, Cashew, Filbert (Hazel), Macadamias, Peanut and Pistachio.

In the U.S.A. an ice cream carrying the name of the nut without further qualifications must have sufficient nuts to characterize the flavor. Some nuts require 4–5% to give a good product. A background flavor is often added to the mix.

In order to label an ice cream for example "Almond Flavored" it must contain a minimum of 2% nuts by weight in relation to the weight of the finished ice cream. When this level is met any amount of artificial flavor may be added with the appropriate subsidiary flavor declaration. When less than 2% nuts are added, any amount of artificial flavor can be added and the name of the product, for example would be "Artificially Flavored Almond" or "Artificial Almond".

The manufacture of good quality nut ice cream requires careful attention to the source of supply and to the proper handling of the nuts in the ice cream plant. The most satisfactory supply is one secured from a specialist in this field rather than to try to operate a nut shelling, roasting and cleaning department in the ice cream plant. The nuts as purchased should be thoroughly cleaned and free from shells, stones and other foreign material. They should be handled in a sanitary manner and most kinds should be roasted to sterilize them. The nuts should be packaged in a container that will prevent contamination and moisture pickup during shipment and storage.

When the nuts are received at the frozen dessert plant, the cartons should be spot checked to determine if the nuts meet sanitary and other quality standards. The cartons should be stored in a cold room in sealed containers until used.

E. Candy

Candy for flavoring ice cream is a fairly recent development and is growing in customer acceptance. Until recently suitable candies were not available—they were dense, glossy, hygroscopic, and difficult to eat. Manufacturers who specialize in making candies specifically for ice cream have developed crunches that are "tender", that is, they contain small air pockets and thus have more bulk per pound than do ordinary hard candies. These candies retain their identity in the ice cream for many weeks.

The candies are made in many flavors and in combination with nut meat pieces (pecan, almond, filbert, etc.). They are also available in chocolate flavored crunches. Candies may be used alone in mixes flavored with vanilla, butterscotch or other background flavor or in combination with other pieces such as cherry bits.

Candies, like nuts must be stored in a cold room in sealed containers that will prevent moisture pick up. And as with nuts they should be purchased as required and not inventoried for a long period of time.

9. CONTROL OF PROCESSING FACTORS AFFECTING QUALITY

A. Preparation of the Mix

The first step in the processing of a high quality frozen dessert is the assembly and proper combination of ingredients of known composition and quality. If the ingredients are all liquid—milk, cream, condensed milk, sugars and stabilizers, the mix can be compounded in the makeup tank via a series of pumps and meters. The mix could also be assembled in tanks mounted on scales or load cells. If the calculations have been accurately made and the indicated quantities of the ingredients are blended, the resulting mix should closely meet company standards and the need for restandardization be reduced. A test for fat and total solids on the final mix should be made to confirm the accuracy of the composition.

B. Pasteurization

One of the three following methods are generally used for the heat treatment of the mix: batch or vat method, high temperature short time (HTST), and ultra high temperature (UHT).

The following time–temperatures (in U.S.A.) are considered adequate for the proper heat treatment of frozen dessert mixes:

155°F held for at least 30 min.
160°F held for at least 15 min.
165°F held for at least 10 min.

15

170°F held for at least 5 min.
175°F held for at least 25 sec.
194°F in the vacreator process.
200°F holding at least 3 sec.
210°F or higher with no holding time required.

In HTST pasteurization it is usual to use a temperature of 175°F and to
hold the product 25 sec or longer at this temperature. UHT pasteurization
may be considered to require 210°F or higher with no holding time but with
a heat-up time of 6 sec or longer. Proper heat treatment is essential in the
preparation of an acceptable mix since all pathogens that might be present
must be destroyed, as well as most of the other bacteria.

TABLE 8. Minimum heat treatment standards in different countries[1]

Australia*	155°F (68°C) for 30 min. Others may be approved.
Canada	None. 160°–165°F/71°C for 20–30 min most commonly used.
Czechoslovakia	155°–158°F (68–70°C) for 30 min
Denmark	149°F (65°C) for 30 min or equivalent
Eire	None
England and Wales	(a) 150°F (65·6°C) for 30 min ⎫ All followed by cooling to (b) 160°F (71·1°C) for 10 min ⎪ below 45°F (7·2°C) within (c) 175°F (79·4°C) for 15 sec ⎬ 1½ h of heating† (d) 300°F (149°C) for 2 sec ⎭
Finland	None
France	(a) 176°–185°F (80°–85°C) for 3 min (b) 145°–149°F (60°–65°C) for 30 min (c) Or other authorized method
India‡	None
Italy	None
Japan	68°C for 30 min or equivalent
Netherlands	More specified. Must pass the Storch test
New Zealand	156°F (69°C) for 20 min or 165°F (73·9°C) for 10 min or boiling
Norway	(a) 158°–161·6°F (70°–72°C) for 15 sec (b) 174·2°F (80°C) or above momentarily
South Africa	None
Spain	None
Sweden	176°F (80°C)
Switzerland	None. Usual practice is 167°F (75°C) for 15–40 sec
USA‖	155°F (68·3°C) for 30 min, 175°F (79·4°C) for 25 sec, or some other approved method.

  * Commonwealth Food Specification: each of the six Australian States has its regulations,
but this specification is usually close to the State requirements.
  † If the mix is canned under aseptic conditions—"sterile"—no cooling is required.
  ‡ A comprehensive sanitation code is under preparation which proposes compulsory mix
heat treatment.
  ‖ For a comprehensive survey State-by-State, see *Ice Cream Field* (1958), 72 (6), 70–76,
and (1959), 73 (1), 44.

Table 8 prepared by Lloyd[1] lists the minimum heat treatment for pasteurization of frozen dessert mixes in 19 countries. As the table indicates there is no uniformity in the requirements and the range is from no standards to 300°F for 2 sec.

The control of the pasteurization process has a definite effect on the mix quality. If vat pasteurization is used and the malfunctioning of the jacket permits steam to leak into the jacket, milk solids will "burn on" the inner surface of the jacket and the mix will have an appreciably cooked or scorched flavor. This effect is accentuated if a high percentage of the milk solids are derived from powder, non-fat, buttermilk or whey. Another potential source of flavor defect when using vat pasteurization is an excessive holding period when the surface cooler is of too low capacity. It is desirable to put water into the jacket to reduce the temperature to 150°F if the homogenization and cooling will require excessive time.

The HTST system avoids the above two problems and will usually result in a better flavored mix (using the same ingredients). The HTST system also results in economies such as less floor space required and a better utilization of manpower. The UHT system and the HTST method are adopted to an automated operation.

The pasteurization of the mix if properly done will result in a mix with a low bacterial count. It is important that all equipment in the plant be properly cleaned and sanitized before use. The cleaning-in-place system (CIP) has aided quality and especially in reducing post-pasteurization contamination.

C. Homogenization

The purpose of homogenization is to make a permanent and uniform suspension of the fat by reducing the average size of the fat globules to a very small diameter, preferably not more than 2 μm. When butter, butter oil or vegetable oils are used efficient homogenization is especially important.

The temperature of homogenization influences the efficiency. When the HTST system is used the mix may go to the homogenizer at 175°F or higher. With vat pasteurization the mix may be homogenized at 150°F (reduced from 160 to 170°F if the cooling and homogenization process will require more than 30 min to complete). The higher temperatures result in less fat clumping and in a lower viscosity.

The pressure to use for homogenization depends upon a combination of factors, the principal ones being: type of equipment, temperature of homogenization, viscosity of the mix, and the fat content. When other factors are held constant, the higher the fat content the lower the pressure required. A pressure of 2000–2500 lb with one valve or 2500–3000 lb at the first stage and 500 lb at the second stage will usually give good results for the average mix of 10–12% fat. High fat or chocolate mixes will usually require a reduction in pressure of 500 p.s.i.

Efficiency of homogenization is an important factor in the production of a high quality frozen dessert. The testing schedule should include the requirement that mixes be checked regularly for the efficiency of homogenization and corrective measures taken if defective or improper homogenization is detected. The most convenient test is to examine a sample of the mix with a microscope and determine the average size of the fat globules and the extent of fat clumping. The care and maintenance of the homogenizer is important from the standpoint of the efficiency and uniformity of performance.

D. Cooling and Storage

The mix should be cooled to as low a temperature as practicable following pasteurization. A cooling temperature of 34–35°F is desirable. The mix should be stored in a clean and sanitized storage tank equipped with cooling facilities and with a recording thermometer. The mix should be held at 35–36°F until it is pumped to the flavor tank. Some jurisdictions limit the time that a pasteurized mix can be held in storage before freezing. Only clean and sanitized pumps and lines should be used in transferring the mix from the storage tank to the flavor tank. If a manifold is used for a number of tanks, precautions must be taken to see that contamination is avoided. When the gum type of stabilizers are used it is not ordinarily necessary to age the mix—storage of 2–4 h or until a test for accuracy of the standardization has been made is usually adequate. If a stabilizer is used in a HTST process and if it is not completely hydrated by the time it reaches the storage tank, some additional holding time may result in more complete hydration. Stabilizers, however, are now available that are completely hydrated during HTST pasteurization. If gelatin is used as a stabilizer, an ageing period of at least 24 h is recommended.

Storage tanks should be cleaned and sanitized before a new mix is put into the tank.

E. Flavoring

Flavor tanks with a capacity of 50–500 gal or more are used as surge tanks just before the mix goes to the freezer. Flavors and color are added to the tanks just before freezing of the mix. The flavors added to the flavor tank are primarily the liquid ones such as vanilla, coffee, peppermint and the like and small pieces of fruit, nuts and candies that can pass through the freezer barrel. Larger pieces of these ingredients are introduced into the ice cream via special equipment known as a fruit feeder. Syrups, fudges and parfaits are introduced into the ice cream by means of a pump and a special nozzle.

It is not desirable to add vanilla to the mix before pasteurization for at least two reasons—one, the "top" or more volatile compounds contained in the extract are lost, and secondly, it is not economical to add vanilla to fruit and other flavors that may be made with the mix.

It is essential that flavor tanks be provided with agitators to maintain a uniform composition and to keep particles of fruit and other discrete flavoring material in suspension.

When fruit feeders are used to introduce material such as candy, nuts and fruit pieces into ice cream emerging from the freezer, it is essential that this material be as cold as practicable in order to minimize the effect of adding a warm ingredient to the partially frozen ice cream. It is desirable to have the shortest possible lines connecting the freezer to the fruit feeder and the fruit feeder in turn to the packaging equipment. The friction from the passage of the ice cream through long lines and the increased exposure of the product to the warmer air in the room will have an adverse effect on the texture of the ice cream. Many of the smaller ice crystals will be melted and the resulting water will freeze on the larger ice crystals in the hardening process and thus result in still larger crystals which cause a coarse or icy texture.

F. Coloring

If color is used in the ice cream it should be added in the flavor tank. If the mix is colored in the bulk storage tanks, non-characteristic colors will be produced in some of the flavored ice creams made with the mix. The exception is when all of the mix is used for one flavored ice cream such as vanilla. If the vanilla colored (usually cream color) mix is used for peach ice cream, the resulting color will be on the purplish side when peach color is added to the flavor tank.

G. Freezing

Two types of freezers are available, the batch and the continuous. Most manufacturers with an appreciable volume of frozen desserts use continuous freezers. The freezing process has a definite effect on the quality of the finished product. If the mix is supplied to the freezer at a temperature of 50°F rather than 35°F, the freezer capacity is reduced or the frozen dessert is drawn at a higher temperature than is desirable. This condition will adversely affect the texture and especially will do so in the absence of a hardening tunnel to complete the freezing process rapidly. A drawing temperature of 20–21°F is desirable. Current developments in freezer design will permit even lower temperatures.

Satisfactory freezer operation requires that a regular schedule be followed by the plant engineers in a program of maintenance that will ensure that the dasher blades or mutators, depending upon the type of freezer, receive proper care at regular intervals. All gauges, valves and pumps should be inspected regularly to determine that they are operating correctly. The freezer operators must understand the correct operation of the freezers in order to maintain the desired drawing temperature and to secure the specified overrun (weight per gallon). Whenever possible, long runs rather than short runs should be scheduled. This procedure results in more uniformity of operation and reduces the amount of ice cream that has to be reworked.

H. Maintaining and Control of Overrun

Overrun of ice cream may be defined as the volume secured in excess of the volume of the mix. The increased volume is due to the air incorporated in the freezing process and is referred to as the percent overrun. For example, if the mix weight is 9 lb/gal and the frozen ice cream weight 4·5 lb/gal, the overrun is 100%.

For a profitable operation and for a uniform product with respect to overrun, it is essential that the product specifications state the net weight or overrun per gallon required for all products and all types of containers used, and that effective programs be instituted to see that specifications are being adhered to. Tolerances may be set for variations in overrun from the standards. Bayer,[13] however, believes that tolerances too frequently permit errors, carelessness and poor performance. Experience has shown that a specific standard weight per gallon and an evaluation of performance with respect to attainment of the standard is more likely to result in greater uniformity of weight than if a ± number of ounces per gal is given as a tolerance. The lower weight of the tolerance too frequently becomes the standard weight. Control charts used on the production line may be of assistance.[5]

The operation of the freezer determines the amount of air incorporated in the mix and hence the overrun. A freezer in good mechanical condition and operated properly will produce an ice cream with fairly constant overrun. An operator who constantly adjusts the air and refrigerant pressures will generally secure a product that varies considerably in weight per gallon.

Scales should be provided at all packaging stations, and cartons checked frequently for net weight. It is desirable to provide a form for recording weights at scheduled intervals. The drawing temperature may also be recorded on this form. Equipment is now available that will reject packages that are over or under a set weight standard. In many plants in U.S.A. 75% of the product is in half gallon cartons and this type of operation lends itself to the use of automatic weight monitoring equipment.

I. Packaging the Frozen Dessert

This operation is related to the appearance of the final package and to the uniformity of net weight. Various types of containers are used for packaging frozen desserts. Tinned metal cans of 1 gal and ½ gal capacity are extensively used in the United Kingdom, the continent of Europe and in Australia and New Zealand. In the U.S.A. bulk ice cream was formerly packed in 2 and 3 gal tinned metal cans. Currently bulk ice cream is largely packaged in 3 and 5 gal fiber containers. Single service containers for pints, quarts, half gallons and gallons are available. The single service containers up to the ½ gal size are available in both fiber and plastic. The first type is most commonly used and may be secured in the Philadelphia type or the round carton.

Efficient packaging machines have been developed for filling the Philadelphia linerless carton. Machines of lower capacity are also available for filling the pint, quart and half gallon round carton.

When it is necessary to fill the containers manually from the discharge tube of the freezer, it is difficult to secure uniform weights and a neat carton. Hand-filling also greatly increases the labor cost for filling packages. This is one of the most costly single operations in the production of frozen desserts and machine filling, where the volume warrants, presents the best opportunity to reduce and control production costs.

The quality of the packaging material is definitely related to the quality of the product and to packaging costs. The proper selection of the thickness of the board used for the linerless type carton and the coating used on the board depends somewhat on the method used for hardening the frozen dessert. If cartons are stacked in the hardening room where a hardening tunnel is not available, a thin board used in the manufacture of the carton will permit serious distortion of the shape of the container before the ice cream has hardened sufficiently to give the package sufficient rigidity to prevent this distortion. Where a tunnel is used or where the frozen dessert is not stacked in too high layers before hardening, it is possible to use a much thinner carton which consequently incurs less cost. Inferior packaging material can be one cause for "shrinkage", a defect discussed in the section on defects in frozen desserts. Laminated cartons are available with a thin aluminium foil in the center of the board. It is reported that a better texture can be obtained by reduction of temperature fluctuations in the package when the cartons are stored in dealers' cabinets.

Lack of uniformity in packaging material—variations in board thickness and in dimensions—can cause the loss of many cartons by the malfunctioning of the filler when the cartons jam the machine.

Cups and novelties are filled on special equipment.

J. Coding the Cartons

It is desirable to equip all packaging equipment with coding devices. Many large supermarket customers require that all frozen desserts be dated or coded for a 60-day "pick-up". This may be an actual date or a code devised to indicate the date. In the U.S.A. there is a trend towards "open" or actual dating of all food products.

To be effective the code must be legible—worn dies, lack of ink, or ink that dries too slowly often result in codes that cannot be read and hence are valueless. When tracing complaints the codes on the package are of great value in identifying when the product was made. Proper rotation of frozen desserts in customers' cabinets or on delivery trucks is facilitated when an effective coding program is used.

K. Hardening the Frozen Dessert

The hardening process is one of the most important factors in producing a high quality product with respect to texture. Careful formulation of the mix and its processing can be largely nullified with respect to texture if proper hardening facilities are not available. The ice cream will have the best texture if it is drawn from a continuous freezer at 20–21°F and immediately conveyed to a hardening tunnel where the freezing process is completed within 2–4 h. Such ideal conditions are not available in many frozen dessert plants and precautions must be taken to permit existing conditions and practices to approach the ideal situation as closely as possible. The drawing temperature of 20–21°F can usually be attained—the product should then be conveyed as rapidly as possible to the hardening room and placed in front of fans that blow air at −25 to −35°F. This procedure will result in a shorter hardening time as compared with storage in a room with still air.

Packaged ice cream should not be placed in the hardening room in a solid stack that will limit the circulation of air. An air space should be left between each row of packages. After the ice cream has hardened it may be moved to a −10 to −15°F room. Here the packages should be piled closely together to delay changes in temperature. This policy of close stacking should also apply to transport trucks and inventories held in branch plants. The temperatures in hardening and storage rooms should be monitored and recorded daily. Hardening and storage room temperatures should not be permitted to fluctuate.

Hardening time depends upon many factors such as: size and shape of packages, drawing temperature from the freezer, temperature of the air in the hardening room or tunnel and the velocity of the air. Mix composition and overrun cause slight variations in the hardening time. Arbuckle[4] reports that one degree higher in drawing temperature will cause a 10–15% increase in the hardening time.

When ice cream is drawn from the freezer at approximately 21°F about 55% of the free water has been frozen. After being stored in the cold room about 90% of the available water is in the form of ice crystals at −13°F.

Thus 35% of the water must be frozen in the hardening room or tunnel. The more rapid the hardening process the better the texture.[11]

L. Transportation of Ice Cream and other Frozen Desserts

The methods used in the transportation of frozen desserts in local delivery trucks and in large over-the-road transport trucks are very important from a quality control standpoint. Ice cream may be carefully processed and have its texture ruined if care is not taken in handling the product after it leaves the hardening or storage rooms. Trucks should be properly refrigerated and maintained so that the ice cream will not rise above $-10°F$ during shipment.

Large over-the-road transport trucks that serve large customers or branch plants especially must maintain the ice cream at the proper temperature. The method used for loading and for unloading trucks has an important influence on the texture of the ice cream. Trucks that are loaded with pallets on fork-lift trucks or by the use of carts can be loaded in a few minutes as compared to $1\frac{1}{2}$–2 h when the conveyer system is used. The rapid handling of the product protects the texture.

Dry ice is sometimes used in the shipment of small orders or for specialty items shipped in insulated cartons. Dry ice should not be used to ship ice cream that has not been thoroughly hardened, owing to the possibility of shrinkage as discussed in connection with frozen dessert defects (Section 10).

10. DEFECTS IN FROZEN DESSERTS

Proper formulation of the mix, selection of quality ingredients and proper processing and handling of the products in the manufacturing plant will tend to limit the defects that may be observed in the channels of trade. When all of these factors have been controlled, the responsibility for preventing defects falls largely upon the sales and delivery departments. How they handle the frozen desserts in the channels of trade and how they educate and monitor the operations of the drivers and dealers influences the texture and the appearance of the product as it is offered to the customer. With all of the above factors under control, the customer may still illtreat the product if precautions are not taken in transporting the frozen dessert to the home and in the manner in which it is stored and served in the home. Many supermarkets now provide an insulated bag for ice cream purchases and this has aided texture control. Many texture complaints are due to poor home refrigerators or to heat shock when the package is left in a warm room at the time of serving a portion of the dessert.

Some defects are due to milk products, others to chemical or bacteriological changes or to inferior flavoring ingredients or too little or too much flavoring. In addition to flavor defects, body, texture, melting characteristics

15*

and package defects are important in the total evaluation of the quality of frozen desserts.

In order to put the evaluation of the quality of ice cream on a factual rather than on a conversational basis many score cards have been developed and used in the evaluation of ice cream.[14] Most of the score cards have been developed for student judging and serve a useful purpose in developing score ratings for various defects. Most of the score cards use the following values for perfect scores:

	Points
Flavor	45
Body and texture	30
Melting quality	5
Color and package	5
Bacteria	15
	100

The following chart indicates the score for defects:

Class	Range in score	Specific description
Flavour		
Excellent	45–40	No criticism
Good	39·5–37·5	Slightly cooked, storage, slightly salty, distinctly egg, slightly to distinctly lacking in flavor or freshness.
Fair	37·5–35·5	Slightly old ingredient, oxidized, slightly to distinctly unnatural flavour, distinctly cooked or lacking in flavour or freshness.
Poor	35·5–31·0	Slight to strong neutralizer, rancid or unclean, slightly to distinctly old ingredient, oxidized, high acid or unnatural flavouring.
Body and Texture		
Excellent	30·0–29·5	Firm, smooth, velvety.
Good	29·0–28·0	Slightly coarse, crumbly, soggy or gummy.
Fair	27·5–26·5	Coarse, crumbly, fluffy, weak, soggy or gummy
Poor	26·0–25·0	Icy, Sandy.
Melting Quality		
Excellent	5·0	Smooth, creamy.
Fair	4·5	Slightly curdy, slow melting.
Poor	4·0	Curdy, very slow melting.
Colour and Package		
Excellent	5·0	No criticism.
Fair	4·5–4·0	Slightly unnatural or uneven.
Poor	3·5–3·0	Extremely unnatural or uneven.

A. Flavor Defects Due to Dairy Products

1. Feed Flavor

This defect is not common but it can be a source of complaints, particularly in vanilla ice cream which does not contain strong flavoring ingredients that could mask the feed flavor. When they occur feed flavors are more likely to be onion, bitter or cabbage-like in character.

Feed flavors are not entirely removed by processing. The control is to test organoleptically all dairy ingredients to be used in the mix and to reject those that have objectionable flavors.

2. Rancid Flavors Due to Fat Hydrolysis

When rancid flavor is encountered in frozen desserts its cause can usually be traced to dairy products, particularly to cream or butter that has developed this flavor before the mix has been prepared and processed.[15] The organoleptic test of all fat sources used in the mix will detect the defect if the taster is sensitive to and familiar with the flavor. The acid degree determination will indicate the extent of the hydrolysis.[2]

3. Oxidized Flavor

In the dairy industry, oxidized flavor is distinguished from hydrolytic rancidity in that the former is an oxidation of the unsaturated bonds in the fatty acid constituents in the glyceride molecule, whereas the latter is the hydrolysis and liberation of free fatty acids from the glyceride molecule. The lower (short chain) acids are principally responsible for the rancid flavor defect.

The flavors referred to as metallic, cappy, cardboard, oxidized and tallowy are variations in the degree of oxidation. Contamination of fat-containing dairy ingredients with copper or iron or oxides of these metals are the most common sources of oxidized flavor.[15]

The use of stainless steel surfaces on equipment in contact with dairy products from the farm to the final package is the most effective means of eliminating or minimizing oxidized flavors in frozen desserts. The inherent stability of the fat is also a factor to consider. The susceptibility of the fat to oxidative changes is related to the fatty acid composition of the glycerides, the presence of natural or added antioxidants and to the temperature and time of holding the products.

Frozen cream, frozen plastic cream, sweet butter and butter oil that have not had adequate heat treatment in processing are the most common ingredients of frozen desserts that develop oxidized or tallowy flavors on holding in storage. The processing of these products for storage must have a treatment that will result in the development of sulfhydryl groups from the milk proteins which will function as antioxidants and delay the onset of oxidation, or in other words prolong the induction period or the time before rapid absorption of oxygen takes place. Stored fat-containing products should be re-examined before use in frozen desserts.

4. Old Ingredients

As the name implies, the defect is due to the use of ingredients that are not fresh and which impart this characteristic flavor to the frozen dessert, particularly to vanilla ice cream or ice milk. Plain condensed milk that has developed some acidity or has been contaminated after pasteurization and not held below 40°F is a common cause of this flavor defect. Sweetened condensed skim milk that has been held in storage under unfavorable conditions, that is, at relatively high temperatures or for considerable time may result in this flavor defect. The use of stale milk powder in the mix will also impart this flavor defect to the processed mix.

5. Stale Flavor

Some authorities have considered stale flavor as a prelude to oxidation. Others have felt that milk powder with a high moisture content or sweetened condensed milk that had undergone some darkening of color in storage gave flavors that were more characteristic of this defect. It is important that all processed and stored dairy products be inspected for flavor defects at the time they are received, and that they are stored at proper temperatures and the inventory rotated to make certain that the oldest products are used first. Such products should be re-examined just before use.

6. Cooked or Scorched Flavors

The cause of these flavor defects were discussed in connection with the pasteurization of the mix. The control of these defects at the point of processing is obvious—avoid equipment surfaces and temperatures that result in "burn on" of milk solids or use time and temperatures for pasteurization that will not result in excessively strong cooked flavors, for example avoid 170°F for one hour.

The use of non-fat dry milk made with the high heat process (whey protein nitrogen below 1·5 mg/g) may impart cooked flavors to the mix if the powder is used for a large percentage of the serum solids. The effect of the powder will be further exaggerated if vat pasteurization at too high a temperature or for too long a time is practised.

A slightly cooked flavor is not ordinarily regarded as a serious flavor defect.

7. Neutralizer Flavor

This is not a common flavor defect in modern ice cream manufacture. In the United States it is now illegal to use neutralizers to adjust developed acidity in ingredients used in the manufacture of ice cream. When this flavor defect is observed it is the result of using too much neutralizer or the wrong kind of compounds to neutralize the acidity of milk or cream that has been improperly handled and has developed acidity.

B. Flavor Defects Due to Non-Dairy Ingredients

1. Syrup Flavor

A flavor defect often referred to as "syrup flavor" is observed in ice cream or ice milk in which too large a percentage of the sweetening value is derived from some form of corn syrup solids. This defect is more noticeable in vanilla ice cream than it is in flavored ice cream such as peach or strawberry. The type of corn solids used as well as the percentage will influence the extent of the flavor defect. When 25% of the sweetening value is derived from 42 DE (dextrose equivalent) corn syrup solids, this defect is not usually observed. If the syrup is not heated above 105°F during a reasonable storage period, it will not darken significantly in color and will remain bland. If, however, the syrup is held above 115°F for a period of time, it will become dark amber in color and will impart a molasses-like flavor to the mix even if the amount is limited to 25% of the sweetening value. If as much as 40% of the sweetening value is derived from 42 DE corn syrup solids the criticism of "syrup-flavor" may apply.

If 55–60 DE corn syrup solids is used the flavor defect may be observed at a lower percentage. Corn syrup solids of lower DE values such as 36, 28 or 15 are usually more bland than the higher DE products. The 28 and 15 DE solids are dry products and at this time are not available as syrups. The 42 DE product is available as either a syrup or as a dry product. The dry product is very hygroscopic and care must be taken in handling and storing it in the bags in which it is shipped to avoid tearing of the bags and the exposure of the product to the atmosphere.

2. Lacks Fine Flavor

This is considered a minor flavor defect. The cause may be that it is deficient in vanilla or flavored with an imitation vanilla or one that is high in vanillin. Unnatural fruit or other flavors as well as old dairy products will produce an ice cream that is lacking in fine flavor.

3. Too High in Flavor

If too much or too strong flavoring ingredients are used the product is not pleasing to most customers. Imitation flavors that may have a bitter note are most often the cause of high flavored frozen desserts. Harsh flavor as a rule may be considered to be high in flavor.

4. Unnatural Flavor

Pronounced flavors not associated with the expected flavor are unnatural. Strong imitation vanilla or strong terpene flavor in citrus frozen desserts are unnatural. Rancid nuts and overripe fruit products produce unnatural flavors.

C. Body and Texture Defects

It is usual in the literature to consider body and texture defects under the same heading and there is some justification for this approach since the same factors tend to affect both properties. The body refers to the firmness and resistance when the ice cream is spooned or eaten and the texture is more concerned with smoothness and is related to air cell size, to ice crystal size and to certain constituents of the mix such as lactose which can produce a "sandy" texture.

The mix formulation, composition of the ingredients used, method of processing, freezing and thawing procedures and storage conditions in the plant, in trucks and in sales outlets can all play a role in causing body and texture defects. Perfect body and texture conditions are attained only if all of the above factors are controlled to the optimum degree. This condition seldom obtains and it is rare that any frozen dessert is given a perfect score on the score card for body and texture.

1. Icy or Coarse Texture

This defect is probably objected to by more customers than is any other defect including flavor. A coarse or icy texture is due to large ice crystals, lack of uniformity in size of crystals and too large air cells. The discussion on selection of ingredients and the processing and freezing of the mix has indicated some of the causes of an icy texture; slow freezing in the freezer and in the hardening room, insufficient stabilization and fluctuating temperatures over a long storage period are the factors responsible for much of the coarse textured ice cream. The evaluation of stabilizers by holding the frozen dessert samples in the hardening room is not sufficient evidence to use in establishing the optimum level of a particular stabilizer. Heat shock tests and evaluation of samples secured from channels of trade are essential.

2. Sandy Texture

The sandy texture of ice cream is due to the crystallization of lactose contributed by the milk-solids-not-fat ingredients in the mix. Lactose is less soluble than other sugars that may be in the mix and will crystallize out of solution under certain conditions. The powdery or gritty crystals are highly objectionable to most customers. Sandiness should not be confused with icy texture—the lactose crystals in sandy ice cream do not melt as do the ice crystals and persist after the ice cream is in the mouth.

Theoretically, a milk-solids-not-fat content of 10% should produce sandy ice cream but experience has shown that 12% can usually be safe from this defect.[11] In ice milk with lower total solids, 13–13·5% of milk-solids-not-fat is usually safe.

When sandy ice cream is encountered it is usually due to one or a combination of the following conditions: (a) high milk-solids-not-fat content, (b) normal milk-solids-not-fat product (10–12%) held at fluctuating temperatures for a long period of time, (c) nut ice cream where the nuts have not been oil-roasted or otherwise treated to protect the surface. Any ingredient that can absorb moisture and provide a surface for lactose crystallization is a potential cause for sandy ice cream if it is held for a long period of time under storage conditions that permit wide fluctuations in temperature.

3. Buttery Texture

This defect occurs when small lumps of milk fat can be detected in the mouth. The defect is due to churning of the fat to form butter particles. Poor homogenization of the mix is the most common cause, especially if it is a high fat mix and one that is largely derived from butter or frozen cream. The defect is more common with batch freezers where the defect can occur during the freezing and whipping process. Other contributing factors may be: (a) too low milk solids-not-fat content in the mix, (b) dull freezer blades, (c) high acidity in the mix. This defect is usually an indication of a poor and ineffective quality control program.

4. Fluffy Texture

This defect is characterized by an open texture and large air cells. The principal causes for this defect are: (a) high overrun, (b) an excessive amount of emulsification, (c) low total solids. Proper mix formulation and control of overrun at a reasonable standard will limit the occurrence of this defect.

5. Weak Body

If the ice cream lacks "chewiness" and has rapid melting characteristics, it is said to have a "weak" body. Insufficient stabilization and low total solids are the principal causes for this defect. This may be considered as a defect caused by poor mix formulation.

6. Crumbly Body

This defect is more common in sherbets and ices than it is in ice cream. In this defect the body breaks or tears apart when it is dipped or spooned. Conditions that result in crumbly body usually are one or a combination of two or more of the following factors: (a) excessive overrun, (b) low total solids, (c) inefficient homogenization, (d) insufficient stabilization, (e) excessive emulsification, (f) use of certain vegetable stabilizers such as gum karaya or agar. As with most frozen dessert defects, proper mix formulation and processing will limit its occurrence.

7. Soggy Body

This defect is most likely to occur in ice cream that is low in overrun and high in milk-solids-not-fat. The product is usually dense and "wet" in appearance. Hand packaging after hardening can result in a soggy body due to the reduction in the overrun. Soggy bodied ice cream usually resists melting.

8. Gummy Body

This defect is most often due to high total solids and excessive stabilization.

D. Defects in Melting Characteristics

In some proposed score cards for evaluating the quality of frozen desserts, the melting characteristics are considered as a part of the score on body and texture while in others it is considered as a separate classification. While many of the causes for poor melting characteristics are among the ones listed for body and texture defects, a separate listing is useful in summarizing the causes for the defects.

When ice cream is exposed to room temperature it should melt fairly rapidly and smoothly to resemble the original mix. An ice cream that melts to form a foamy, flaky or curdy liquid is considered by many customers as a serious defect and they may think the product is adulterated. The following are the most common defects in melting characteristics and their probable causes:

1. Does not melt. The major cause is the use of excessive amounts of stabilizer and/or emulsifier. Other contributing causes may be: (a) excessive mix viscosity, (b) homogenizing the mix at excessive pressures or at too low a temperature, (c) high milk fat, (d) low overrun.

2. Flakiness. This defect is characterized by a dull wrinkled film on the surface of the melted ice cream which may be caused by a combination of the following factors: (a) use of an excessive amount of emulsifier, (b) inefficient or incomplete homogenization, (c) freezing to a very stiff consistency,

(d) operation of continuous freezers at reduced capacity, (e) prolonged storage.

3. Curdy melt-down. In this defect finely divided curd particles appear in the melted liquid. The contributing causes may be: (a) use of stabilizers which react with and cause precipitation of milk proteins, (b) homogenization of mix at excessive pressures or at too low a temperature, (c) development of acidity in the mix, (d) excessive calcium salts in relation to citrates and phosphates in the mix, (e) prolonged storage, (f) destabilizing effect of the freezing process on the proteins of the mix.

4. Whey separation. Clear whey or liquid appears during the melting. This is often seen in samples that show slow melt down or curdy melt down but this defect may be caused primarily by (a) high milkfat ice cream homogenized at too high a pressure, (b) type of stabilizer used.

5. Foamy melt-down. This defect results in a distinct foamy appearance. The principal causes are: (a) excessive amount of stabilizer and/or emulsifier, (b) excessive mix viscosity.

E. Miscellaneous Body and Texture Defects

1. Shrinkage

This defect refers to the condition found in ice cream when well filled packages exhibit decreased volume of product. The specific causes of shrinkage are not well documented in spite of much research on the problem. It is very difficult to produce at will ice cream that will shrink in volume. Shrinkage can occur, however, when least expected and in some cases it is difficult to correct. It may occur in only a portion of the frozen packages from the same mix frozen under identical conditions. Arbuckle[4] lists the following conditions as possible causes: (a) neutralization of the mix or some of the ingredients used, (b) containers that are porous to air such as paper not properly coated on the side in contact with the ice cream, (c) abnormally low temperatures either when freezing, drawing from the freezer, hardening in tunnels or hardening by dry ice before storage, (d) conditions favoring bleeding or pancakes, (e) excessive overrun as in fluffy texture where the air content is greater than can be contained at conditions to which the product is to be exposed, (f) excessive smoothness where the texture is too fine grained, probably because of a unique combination of conditions such as too rapid freezing which favours small-sized particles and a combination of emulsifiers which favor small air cells, (g) textures that favor curdy melt-down caused by partial destabilization of milk proteins.

Most frozen dessert plant operators have observed the above factors in relation to shrinkage and have experienced difficulty in correcting the situation which may reach "epidemic" proportions. More research is required on this problem.

Cream with a high fatty acid content and a rancid flavor has been found to favor shrinkage. Any other source of free fatty acids such as poorly refined emulsifiers and chocolate products that have a high acid degree also favor this defect since the fatty acids act as foam breakers.

2. Pancakes

This defect refers to the taffy-like deposit that sometimes occurs at the bottom of a container of bulk ice cream. The defect is associated with ice cream with a high sugar content which has been slowly hardened. The defect is more likely to be found in batch frozen than in continuous frozen ice cream.

F. Color and Package Defects

When a customer selects a package of ice cream from a store cabinet the appearance of the carton has a great influence on his decision. If the package is clean, free from smudges of ice cream on the sides, free from concave or convex surfaces and is attractively printed the appeal will be greater than if one or more of these defects is present.

The principal color defects are uneven or unnatural color. These are regarded on the score card as minor compared to flavor and texture defects.

REFERENCES

1. Lloyd, T. P. (1969). *Dairy Ind.* **34,** 1.
2. American Public Health Association (1967). "Standard Methods for the Examination of Dairy Products". 12th Ed. (A.P.H.A., New York, U.S.A.)
3. Herschdoerfer, S. M. (1970). *J. Soc. Dairy Tech.* **23,** 60.
4. Arbuckle, W. S. (1966). "Ice Cream" (Avi Publishing Co., Westport, Conn., U.S.A.)
5. Herschdoerfer, S. M. (ed.) (1967), "Quality Control in the Food Industry". Vol. I. (Academic Press, London and New York).
6. Herschdoerfer, S. M. (ed.) (1968). "Quality Control in the Food Industry". Vol. II. (Academic Press, London and New York).
7. Bogod, Mark (1968). Mimeographed Manuscript.
8. Proposition de directive du Conseil relative au rapprochement des legislation des Etats membres Concernant les glaces alimataries (1970). Journal official des Communautes européennes, 13/10/70.
9. Keeney, P. G. (1961). *Ice Cream Field*, **78,** 20.
10. Webb, B. H. and Johnson, A. H., "Fundamentals of Dairy Chemistry". (Avi Publishing Co., Westport, Conn., U.S.A.)
11. Turnbow, G. D., Tracy, P. H. and ¡Raffetto, L. A. (1947). "The¦ Ice Cream Industry". (John Wiley & Sons, New York, U.S.A.).

12. A.O.A.C. (1965). "Methods of Analysis of the Assoc. of Offic. Analytical Chemists". (New York, U.S.A.).
13. Bayer, A. H. (1963). "Modern Ice Cream Plant Management". (Ruben Donnelly Corp., Chicago, U.S.A.).
14. Nelson, J. A. and Trout, G. M. (1964. Rev.). "Judging Dairy Products". (Olsen Publishing Co., Milwaukee, U.S.A.).
15. Henderson, J. L. (1971). "The Fluid-milk Industry". (Avi Publ. Co., Westport, Conn., U.S.A.).

Quality Assurance of Incoming Packaging Materials for the Food Industry

MAE-GOODWIN TARVER[a] and C. L. SMITH[b]

Continental Can Company, Inc.

1. INTRODUCTION

During the ten years following the introduction of statistical quality control (*c.* 1942) in the metal-working and precision industries in the U.S.A. there was a very limited use of statistical methods by food processors in process control and in appraising the quality of purchased raw materials. This fact is shown in the results of a survey conducted in the U.S.A. in 1955 by Hoskins to determine the extent to which statistical quality control was used by food processors.[1] An analysis of the returned questionnaires indicated that about 35% of the food processors replying to the survey made some use of statistical quality control methods in plant operations. About 38% of the food processors using statistical quality control employed these methods in varying degrees to evaluate conformance of purchased materials to specifications.

a Continental Can Company, Inc., Technical Center 1200 West 76th Street, Chicago, Illinois 60620.

b Continental Can Company, Inc., Technical Center 1350 West 76th Street, Chicago, Illinois 60620

Four years later, a second survey was published, reporting upon the use of statistical quality control by food processors in the U.S.A.[2] Approximately 70% of the replies indicated that statistical quality control was used in the food processing industry. The survey respondents reported that better vendor relations, reduced raw material losses, and improved raw material delivery times were among the benefits of using statistical quality control.

A survey published by Brokaw and Kramer in 1964 showed that in the U.S.A. approximately 95% of the food processors were using statistical quality control in their operations.[3]

The above information indicates that the use of statistical sampling methods in the food processing industry has been increasing rapidly in recent years. This growth of incoming quality assurance programmes in the food industry in the U.S.A. has been influenced (a) by rising raw material and production costs,[4] (b) by the fact that the individual consumer in many instances has become increasingly quality conscious,[5a] and (c) by the development of new materials with relatively unknown quality characteristics.[6]

In the past few years, rising production costs have encouraged food processors to install high-speed equipment and to automate food processing operations wherever possible, e.g. in filling, check-weighing, and casing operations. Excessive variation in container weight or capacity is critical in high-speed packaging operations because automatic filling equipment must continually be adjusted to compensate for this variation. Since the empty package weight is the tare weight when food products are packaged by weight, consistency of empty package weight is an important factor in fill control.

Consistency of finish and shape of containers is also desirable because a single improperly shaped container or one with poor mobility may cause filling-line difficulties, resulting in costly down-time. It is therefore necessary for food processors to place additional quality requirements upon standard packaging materials and to develop quality assurance systems to determine whether or not incoming packaging materials conform to these requirements.

Packaging materials for food products must meet the following general quality standards:

(1) Reliability of Performance (Quality of Performance). The food container or package must adequately perform its packaging function for a *specified* time under *specified* conditions with a *specified* degree of success.

(2) Compatability of Product and Package (Quality of Performance). The package or container must not impart a foreign flavour or odour to the food product. It must not change the colour, texture or appearance of the food product from the required standard of quality.

(3) Dimensional Characteristics (Quality of Conformance). The dimensional quality characteristics of packaging materials must meet the container

specifications. Deviations from these specifications are often related to on-line problems encountered in packaging processes.

(4) Appearance of Visual Quality Characteristics (Quality of Conformance). These characteristics affect the ultimate consumer's attitude when a specific food product competes with other food products for shelf space at retail centres. The appearance of a food package is often responsible for both initial sales and repeat sales.

(5) Public Health Aspects of Packaging Materials (Quality of Conformance). Some form of Government regulation exists throughout most of the world in regard to the public health requirements of packaging materials. These regulatory requirements protect the ultimate consumer from food contamination by materials associated with known public health hazards.

In some instances, the installation of a quality assurance system by a food processor has resulted in the adoption of a formal incoming sampling programme. In other cases, small sample groups are selected from occasional shipments in order to detect obvious non-conformance to specifications and the functional quality of the shipment is evaluated by observing the performance of the packages in the processing operations. Testing for functional defects is mandatory with many types of packaging materials. However, many kinds of *critical* functional defects such as microscopic flaws in solder bonds, incipient checks in glass finishes, and minute perforations in plastic films cannot be detected until the material (a) has passed through a "pilot" or "preproduction" run or (b) has passed through the food processor's operations.

Consumer attitudes also affect the quality standards of food containers. In the past 15 years the individual consumer has become increasingly quality conscious and is demanding higher quality of food products in safe, convenient, and attractive packaging. This consumer attitude reflects the usefulness of the application of statistical quality control in the food industry. When SQC methods were employed, processors were able to market a higher quality food product and one which was more attractively packaged—without increasing the price. This fact was indicated in the 1959 survey conducted by Stier,[2] since the greatest single benefit of statistical quality control was the improvement of product quality. This improvement appealed to the consumer and his reaction, or "feed-back", resulted in an adaptive quality cycle. Consumers, during this time period, have also become "package" oriented and food processors must now utilize new packaging concepts and new types of packaging materials in order to retain their fair share of the market.

The development of packaging materials such as lightweight tinplate, aluminium plate, plastics suitable for semi-rigid containers, plastic films, thin metal foils and metallic-plastic-paper laminates has required a high degree of quality collaboration between package fabricator and food processor.[6] This extensive cooperation was essential for the following reasons:

(1) Because of time limitations it was not possible, during the pilot production stage, for the manufacturer or fabricator to explore all of the quality characteristics of these newer packaging materials. The appraisal of the degree of importance of these quality characteristics became a joint effort of supplier and food processor as the packaging materials were initially marketed. The packaging industry, at the present time, judiciously combines research and the development activities with industrial operations in order to meet the ever-quickening demand for new packaging materials.

(2) In the U.S.A. and also in many other countries throughout the world, government or ministerial regulations specify that no material injurious to human health shall be in contact with foods designed for human consumption. This requires extreme caution in developing new packaging materials since, in many instances, there is little or no prior public health information on some of the proposed materials. The packaging materials supplier and the food processor collaborate to some extent in this area, although in certain instances the responsibility for public health certification is placed upon the fabricator.

In these introductory pages, we have commented briefly upon the growth of statistical quality control in the U.S.A. food packaging industry. It is obvious that the appraisal of incoming packaging material quality is, and will continue to be, an integral part of quality control in the food industry. Therefore, the following subjects will be discussed in this chapter: (a) the general quality considerations of packaging materials, (b) the major quality characteristics or rigid, semi-rigid and flexible packaging materials, (c) legal restrictions and regulatory requirements for food packaging materials, (d) sampling systems for incoming packaging materials.

2. GENERAL QUALITY CONSIDERATIONS OF PACKAGING MATERIALS

A. The Value of Quality Versus the Cost of Quality

In the U.S.A. in 1962, the value of packaging materials used in the food industry was approximately 6 billion dollars.[7a] This total dollar value was divided in the following manner among the four primary packaging materials classifications:

Rigid Containers: 49% or about 2·9 billion dollars
Semi-rigid Containers: 39% or about 2·4 billion dollars
Flexible Packaging Materials: 8·4% or about 0·5 billion dollars
Closures: 3·6% or about 0·2 billion dollars

The above figures were calculated from the statistics presented in the 1964 edition of the "Modern Packaging Encyclopedia."[7a]

The inference can be made from the above list that the monetary value of the packaging materials also represents their tangible quality value. This statement is correct only if the fabricated packaging materials received by the food processor are completely free of defects, i.e. if no quality loss occurs.

We shall, therefore, define the *quality value* of packaging materials as the proportion of satisfactory packaging units in a shipment multiplied by the monetary value of the shipment. As a corollary, we shall define the *quality loss* of packaging materials as the proportion of defective units in the lot multiplied by the monetary value of the lot plus an additional cost for removing defective units in the lot multiplied by the monetary value of the lot plus an additional cost for removing defective units. If the shipment of packaging materials received by the food processor contains a high proportion of satisfactory units, then the *quality value* of the packaging material is high and the *quality loss* is low. Obviously, as the proportion of defective packages increases, the *quality loss* increases and the *quality value* decreases, but not necessarily at the same rate.

Because the food industry is highly competitive and the margin of profit per unit is low, quality losses owing to defective packaging materials are a major concern to both fabricator and food processor. The reduction of quality losses must be the objective of incoming sampling programmes and this is the key to the successful operation of all acceptance sampling programmes. We shall continually emphasize this fact throughout this chapter: THE VALUE OF INCOMING PACKAGING MATERIAL QUALITY MUST ALWAYS EXCEED THE COST OF A QUALITY ASSURANCE PROGRAMME.

Defective containers, detected by the food processors' incoming inspection system, constitute a quality loss primarily for the fabricator. Defective containers passing undetected through the food processor's incoming inspection system but detected by the packaging process constitute a quality loss for both fabricator and food processor. In order to achieve an economic balance between the value of quality and the cost of quality, it is imperative for the fabricator and the food processor to agree upon the following points: (a) the fabricator must build quality into the packaging material by regulating and controlling his high-speed process within its natural capability, (b) the food processor must accept the fact that the fabricator's process capability is his economic limit of quality and (c) the *cost* of inspection must never exceed the *value* of quality under normal profit-and-loss operations. A cardinal principle of all profitable quality control systems is that, *economically, quality cannot be inspected into the product*—it must be an inherent characteristic of the product.

The out-going defect level of packaging materials from the fabricator's process in the U.S.A. is normally quite low in regard to critical defects. Depending upon the nature of the packaging material, the proportion of critical defects is sometimes as low as 0·002% (1 in 50 000) and frequently a defect level of 0·050% (1 in 2000) is easily maintained under normal operating conditions. Generally, it is not a profitable practice for the food processor to establish costly incoming sampling procedures if the primary purpose is to detect an infrequent shipment containing a higher than normal percentage of defective material. When a supplier's out-going defect level is satisfactorily low, it usually is sufficient to sample occasional shipments for obvious defects, i.e. to "spot-check" shipments, and then to use the packaging operations as a "100% inspection device" to detect small numbers of functional defects present in a normal shipment. This approach is profitable from the food processor's viewpoint if the cost of a formal incoming sampling programme is high in relation to the cost of packaging line down-time. If, however, the cost of packaging line down-time exceeds the cost of the sampling programme or if the presence of defective packages constitutes a production or a consumer hazard, then it is economically sound to establish a formal sampling system for critical defects which are detectable by simple inspection methods.

Many kinds of functional defects are detected only under actual food processing conditions (microscopic flaws in seams, incipient checks in glass finishes, perforations in plastic films, etc.) and cannot be detected by simple non-destructive methods of visual and dimensional inspection. In this particular instance, there are two solutions to the problem. First, a preproduction sample of packages is selected from the shipment, packed, and then examined critically for functional defects. Based upon the evidence obtained from the sample, the lot or shipment is classified as acceptable or rejectable. Secondly, the entire shipment can be packed, and a sample can then be selected for critical examination. The level of functional defects in the packed lot is based upon the results of the sample evaluation.

In either instance, the observed defects must be categorized as (a) those arising from deficiencies in the incoming shipment, thus establishing its quality level or (b) those which bear no relation to the quality of the incoming shipment.

The food processor's economic limit for objectionable quality is the highest level of defects that his process can tolerate when it is operating in a normal manner. The theoretically desirable limit of "0·0%" defective cannot be maintained by the container fabricator in the continuous operation of this high-speed process. Therefore, the food processor must periodically review his quality requirements in order to set realistic quality criteria.

B. Defect Definition and Quality Standards—Joint Effort of Fabricator and User

The nature of the quality relationship between packaging material vendor and food processor is generally informal since few formal vendor certification programmes are in existence in the food industry. Because of the informality of the vendor/vendee quality relationship, it is essential for the fabricator and the food processor to develop mutual agreement upon defect definitions, specifications, and quality standards.

The first step in a quality assurance programme for packaging materials is to define defects and to classify them according to severity or degree of occurrence. It is impractical to develop specifications and quality standards until this step is taken. Defect definition is dependent upon the kind of packaging material (metal or glass containers, folding cartons, plastic pouches, etc.) and it is unrealistic to specify an acceptance sampling system for a defect which has not been clearly defined in the same language and with the same intent by both supplier and food processor.

The primary cause of quality misunderstandings, when they arise, is poorly worded or incorrect defect definitions.

This is particularly important when visual quality characteristics are considered. It is not sufficient merely to state that a scratch upon a printed or lithographed surface is objectionable and must be classed as a major defect. In order to define the defect properly, the severity classification of scratches must be enumerated as well as stating that the scratch is objectionable. For example, "deep, heavy scratches through coated surface to base material and scratches over 2 in long and $\frac{1}{8}$ in wide are classified as major defects". A defect definition of this type specifies the yardstick for visual inspection systems and mitigates the subjective tone of such a system. Unless visual defect definitions are clearly stated in incoming quality appraisal systems it is possible, as Juran points out, for inspectors at the bottom of the industrial organization to make policy decisions on quality which should be made at the top of the organization.[5b]

The chaotic condition described above seldom occurs when quality characteristics of packaging materials are dimensional and are capable of being defined in terms of dimensional specifications, e.g. spot board caliper shall be 0.018 ± 0.002 in. If an individual sample is above or below these limits, it is by definition—*not by opinion*—a defective sample. If go/no go gauging is used to appraise the quality of packaging materials, an inspector's decision is clear-cut and objective because these gauges are based upon dimensional limits and the inspector's decision is not in terms of what constitutes a defect but whether or not the sample meets the gauge limits.

Whenever packaging materials are examined for visual or sensory quality characteristics, primary or secondary standards must be available.[5b] The visual quality standards for degree of denting of metal surface, degree of surface or printing blemish, watermarking, surface scuffing, scratches and other visual defects in packaging materials are usually illustrated by "limit samples" and represent the maximum degree of deviation which is acceptable for the quality classification. These quality standards may be samples of the actual conditions (primary standards) or they may be photographs or drawings (secondary standards) of the defects.

When visual quality standards are set for colour, shape, blemishes, etc., maximum and minimum limit samples must be available. In some instances, the limit samples age or deteriorate and must be replaced with fresh samples from time to time. Limit samples, for this reason, must be carefully handled and stored to preserve their integrity.

In appraising the visual or other sensory quality characteristics of packaging materials there are several conditions beyond the actual quality characteristic which must be considered: (a) established ability of inspection personnel to discriminate between acceptable and unacceptable sensory quality characteristics, (b) standardization of testing conditions, such as lighting for visual characteristics, proper environment for flavour and odour testing and so forth. J. M. Juran in his "Quality Control Handbook" gives an excellent discussion of the factors which must be considered in appraising sensory quality characteristics and the reader is referred to this volume for specific details.[5c]

C. The Specification of Quality for Packaging Materials

1. Quality of Conformance to Specifications

In developing specifications for incoming packaging material, it is important for the supplier and the food processor to co-operate in the development of these specifications.[8] Some of the dimensional characteristics are easily measured.[7b, 9, 10, 11] Incoming sampling procedures can be established for these dimensional characteristics provided that the food processor has ascertained that quality losses can be related to these characteristics and that the cost of incoming inspection is less than these quality losses. The quality loss sustained within the food processing plant and the quality losses owing to the defects found by the ultimate consumer of the food product must be included in this costs analysis. It is possible to establish mutually agreed specifications for the physical dimensions of a container, a carton, or a pouch; for weights of containers; for capacity of containers; for tin coating weights; for thickness of metal plate, of fibre board, or of plastic films; or for finish dimensions of glassware. It is also possible to establish quality specifications for the esthetic or subjective characteristics such as appearance defects, colour, odour, taste, etc. However, it will not be practical for the food processor to establish a formal incoming inspection programme for all of these quality classifications because (a) many of these cause insignificant quality losses, (b) adequate tests for some of these characteristics are time-consuming and costly (often the shipment is used before the results of the quality inspection is known), and (c) examination of the packages for some of these characteristics requires destructive testing procedures.

Frequently, incoming shipments of packaging materials are unloaded directly on to the packing lines. Under these circumstances, when quality tests are time-consuming, a post-mortem examination is conducted in the quality control laboratory after the production run to estimate shipment quality rather than using sample results to classify the shipment as acceptable or as rejectable. When tests are not time-consuming it is possible to sample incoming shipments and to classify them as acceptable or rejectable prior to use.[8, 12, 13a]

In establishing esthetic quality specifications it is highly important to consider the ultimate consumer preferences, and to appraise consumer acceptance of particular esthetic characteristics. These specifications must be based upon market research techniques such as Home Use Tests and Consumer Preference Panels.

2. Quality of Performance within the Food Processor's Plant

Functional quality characteristics of packaging materials which can affect the food processors operations are listed within this category. For example, excess glue on folding cartons may cause cartons to stick together resulting in feeding jams in the filling operation—loose particles such as chips or dust in plastic or fibre containers may interfere with filling operations—out-of-round metal containers which do not roll smoothly may cause jams in gravity-feed runways—and plastic containers with rocker bottoms may tip over, causing runway or feeding line jams. When difficulties similar to these occur, the processing line must be shut down. Line down-time caused by defective packaging materials is a quality loss for the food processor. It is also an obvious fact that the inherent quality characteristics of packaging materials greatly affect in-plant performance, but it is difficult to develop specifications which correlate percentage of defectives and in-plant performance with a high degree of assurance. Other factors such as condition of plant equipment, machine adjustment and operator techniques enter into this relationship and the severity of defects in a particular lot is very difficult to assess under these conditions. Furthermore, the incidence of critical defects in this category is generally low in packaging materials—well under 1%. It is frequently more economical to run the packages through the food processing operation than to sample each shipment extensively and make pre-production runs. If trouble develops in the food processing operation, then the quality of the packaging material can be thoroughly investigated. However, the in-plant performance of a shipment is often sufficient to establish the quality level.

3. Quality of Performance—End Use

Functional quality characteristics of packaging materials are often based upon the results of test packs of food products. These test packs are made both by the fabricator in developing the material or container and by the food processor in approving the package. The resulting end-use specification states the quality performance characteristics which are required for adequate product protection. End-use specifications cover all of the components of the completed package and frequently specify the shelf-life or service-life, or, as it is popularly known, the *reliability* of the packed container for a particular product.

Quality characteristics of packaging materials which are functions of time of contact with food products cannot be appraised on incoming inspection of packaging materials. Service-life defects show up only after the container has been packed and stored for a considerable length of time. For example, thin spots in glass containers for carbonated beverages frequently show up only after the internal pressure rises on storage in an overheated warehouse during the summer months; minute leakage of closures on pressurized products is a function of time—internal corrosion of metal containers by food products is a function of time and temperature of storage—drying-out of plastic films is also a time/temperature function.

Evaluation of quality of end-use performance in the above examples is similar, in some respects, to the reliability concept of electrical components. However, unlike electrical component reliability, it is not generally possible to specify an exponential failure distribution and to use sampling systems for this type of failure.[13b] This situation exists because the probability of failure is usually not constant but depends upon a *wearout* reaction occurring between the food product and the packaging material. It is possible, however, to set a minimum standard of performance for a particular package-product combination and to appraise the quality of performance of the package upon this basis.

D. Quality Rating of Packaging Material Suppliers

Since there are usually comparatively few suppliers of a particular kind of packaging material, the suppliers of these materials are usually rated on their quality performance rather than on a vendor rating system. When food processors have two or more suppliers of the same packaging material, the orders are frequently divided among the suppliers and based upon these quality performance ratings.

Regardless of how he rates a vendor, the food processor must clearly understand his quality requirements from which he prepares his specifications. He must evaluate the relative importance of individual specifications and pass this information along to his supplier. He must also have clear-cut policies for adherence to specifications. In addition, he must have an organization for making independent decisions on quality. It is also helpful for the supplier to prepare Vendors' Manuals. If formal acceptance plans exist, the food processor must be prepared to assume the user's risk connected with such plans.

3. QUALITY CONSIDERATIONS FOR SPECIFIC PACKAGING MATERIALS

A. Rigid Containers

In the *Glossary of Packaging Terms* a rigid container is defined as: (a) "a package or container made of difficulty yielding materials that require tools and power or high temperatures to change their configurations, chiefly metals or ceramics (which includes glass)" and (b) "a package that, after filling and closing, requires a force greater than manual strength to change its shape or configuration, even if the package has been fabricated from materials that, like paperboard, would normally be regarded as somewhat flexible."[14a] In accordance with these definitions, we have chosen to discuss, for illustrative purposes, the significant quality characteristics of metal, glass, composite containers, and fibre drums. They will be listed in the order of their economic significance.

As stated in Section 2, rigid packaging materials in 1962 accounted for 49% (about 2·9 billion dollars) of the total value of packaging materials used for food products in the U.S.A. The 49% is broken down as follows:

$$
\begin{aligned}
&\text{Metal containers} &&= 34\cdot0\% \\
&\text{Glass containers} &&= 12\cdot7\% \\
&\text{Composite containers} &&= 1\cdot4\% \\
&\text{Fibre drums} &&= 0\cdot9\%
\end{aligned}
$$

1. Metal Containers

An incoming quality appraisal of metal containers at a food processor's plant might include all possible dimensional, visual, and performance characteristics of the package. However, as indicated in Section 2, if shipments are examined for all possible characteristics, the cost of quality very soon exceeds the *value* of the incoming packaging material. The quality characteristics of metal containers must, therefore, be carefully examined in regard to economic significance and frequency of occurrence. Acceptance sampling systems must be applied only to those quality characteristics which are economically important or to those materials which show a significant incidence of defectives. In addition, it is practicable to apply incoming sampling procedures for those characteristics relating to quality of conformance that can be measured visually or dimensionally. Functional quality characteristics can be appraised only by (a) packing a pre-production sample or (b) sampling the finished product after the packaging operations.

In the U.S.A. the sales contract for metal containers frequently specifies such plate characteristics as the thickness or basis weight, temper or hardness, chemistry, weight of tin coating, as well as lacquer coating type and double seam compound type. The contract also includes a statement that the containers will be relatively free of obvious fabricating defects (quality of workmanship). The food processor is, therefore, purchasing a product which is legally certified to conform to the specifications stated in the contract and the container fabricator is usually penalized for excessive quality failures of packed containers for which he is responsible.

Generally, when quality failure occurs, a supplier is liable only for the value of his particular product. If metal containers fail when they are packed with food products and if this quality failure is attributed to a fabricating defect, the container producer is responsible not only for the value of the container but also for the value of the contained food product. This liability concept obviously encourages a high degree of excellence in fabricating practices and the use of proper raw materials.

Since the quality standards for finished containers are exceptionally high, it is generally not profitable for food processors to install formal incoming sampling programmes to detect an occasional non-conforming shipment. For example, if the average percent defective in incoming shipments is 0.05%, then 6000 metal containers per shipment must be inspected in order to have 95% assurance of finding *at least* one defective container per shipment. It is, however, advantageous for the food processor to audit the quality of all incoming materials in order to establish an unbiased quality rating for each supplier. In addition, it is highly desirable for the food processor and the container fabricator to make a joint quality investigation when an occasional shipment of metal containers does not perform satisfactorily.

The critical quality characteristics of metal containers are dependent upon the end-use of the containers. This means that a defect can be classified as "minor" for non-food products but when food products are considered, this same defect may be classified as "critical". The following list is a partial summary of the quality characteristics of metal containers considered to be critical for a large proportion of food and beverage products:

(1) End seam, or side seam defects which predispose containers to leakage.

(2) Defective lacquer coatings or incomplete lacquer coverage for specific products which require metal-free container surfaces.

(3) Potential product contamination by the container (solder pellets, grease, oil, and other extraneous substances).

(4) Alien labels in the case of lithographed container.

(5) Dimensional characteristics which adversely affect in-plant performance.

Visual or dimensional defects which occur at the end seam or side seam area indicate a potential non-hermetically sealed container. Metal containers exhibiting these defects are potential performance failures since these defects can result in product leakage or in microbial contamination of the food product. When fabrication defects are suspected at the end seam or side seam area, the metal containers are disassembled at these areas for visual or dimensional inspection. Obviously, this is a destructive test. The sample sizes for such tests must remain as small as possible and still yield adequate quality information. The results from non-destructive tests, such as air pressure or vacuum tests are time-consuming and costly and frequently do not show a high degree of correlation with spoilage or leakage performance results.

Some products, such as beer, carbonated beverages, and some highly-coloured fruits and vegetables must be protected against contact with metal. These products require as complete freedom from internal metal exposure as fabrication and equipment capabilities permit.

In order to avoid contamination of food products, the internal portion of the metal container must be relatively free of loose or easily dislodged solder. In addition, the internal portion of the container must be clean; that is, free from dust, dirt, grease, oil, and other contaminants. These critical defects are easily found by non-destructive visual examination. Explicit defect definitions, however, must be established for these quality characteristics since they are not readily measured. The cost of an acceptance sampling system for these characteristics is dependent primarily upon the cost of sampling. The cost of inspection is of minor importance in this instance since visual inspection is quite rapid.

Quality characteristics of metal containers which often interfere with the food processor's operations are usually classified as major functional defects, e.g. out-of-roundness or lack of mobility of lithographed containers. These functional defects are frequently significant quality factors in high speed food processing operations because a few containers having these undesirable characteristics can cause costly line slow-downs, interruptions, and other operational difficulties. Major functional defects which cannot be detected by simple incoming sampling are detected either (a) by running a pre-production sample or (b) by the food processor's operations.

16

2. Glass Containers

The conformance of glassware to dimensional specifications, e.g. capacity, wall thickness, and so forth, is generally too time-consuming for routine acceptance purposes. Other dimensional characteristics such as the outside diameter of the thread (T dimension) and the inside diameter of the neck (I dimension) can be inspected by go/no go gauging methods.* It is, therefore, practicable to include these and similar quality characteristics of glassware in routine sampling inspection of incoming shipments.

Critical functional characteristics of glassware, such as resistance to thermal shock and resistance to high internal pressures, are certified by the producer as part of his routine quality control procedures.[16a, 16b] In this instance, the food processor has a choice between two approaches to quality assurance: (a) he depends upon the integrity of his supplier for assurance that the shipment is relatively free of critical dimensional and functional defects or (b) he must run pre-production samples before classifying the shipment as acceptable or rejectable. If he accepts the first approach, the food processor should periodically select samples from incoming shipments in order to audit the quality level of these characteristics and to obtain quality performance information for vendor ratings.

In general, the food processor can profitably institute acceptance sampling of incoming ware only for visual or non-destructive dimensional quality characteristics which, in his experience, have had a past history of quality difficulties. The following is a partial list of quality characteristics which may cause trouble in food processing operations and for which it is practicable to install routine acceptance sampling procedures:

VISUAL DEFECTS*

Checks	Stuck Glass
Crizzles	Tears
Blisters and Stones	Unfilled finish
Bird Swings	

DIMENSIONAL DEFECTS BY GO/NO GO GAUGING

Finish Dimensions (T and I)*
Weight of Containers (Direct Reading Scales)

Checks are minute, difficult-to-observe fractures at critical points on the glass container, e.g. on the principal bearing surface, finish or shoulder, and are due to temperature differentials or to mechanical fractures. Checks are important quality characteristics because they reduce the inherent strength of

* This is the standard terminology of the Glass Container Manufacturer's Institute of the U.S.A.[15]

the ware. Checks do not result in breakage until the ware is subjected to stresses and strains generated by heat and by mechanical factors present in the food processing operations. Checks are, therefore, considered to be critical functional defects.

Crizzles occur as a maze of tiny cracks upon the finish of ware. This defect is usually due to temperature differentials or to mechanical stresses. When the finish is subjected to mechanical or thermal strains, breakage can result. Crizzles are, therefore, considered to be critical functional defects.

Blisters and Stones in glassware are the results of improper melting of raw materials in the tank or furnace. These defects also reduce the inherent strength of the ware but are more easily seen than checks. Blisters and stones often result in functional or operational failures. For this reason, they are generally classified as major defects.

Bird Swings describe the presence of glass filaments or needles within the ware and are due to defective forming operations. Since dangerous food contamination will result if this defect passes unnoticed, it is classified as a critical defect constituting a public health hazard.

Stuck Glass describes the presence of glass fragments or needles on the outside of the ware and this defect is also due to faulty forming operations in the fabrication process. This condition also is defined as a critical defect since it constitutes a safety hazard in handling the ware as well as interfering with the smooth performance of the ware in the food processor's operations.

Tears are similar to checks in regard to factors in the glass-making process which cause these defects, but tears are found only in the seam. Since fracture of the glassware or leakage can occur when tears are present, this defect is classified as a critical functional defect.

An *unfilled finish* is a depression in the finish and occurs during the forming operation. This defect results in poor sealing efficiency when the cap or cover is applied to the ware. Any unfilled finish is classified as a critical defect since it can result in leakage or microbial contamination of the food product.

The dimensional characteristics known as T and I dimensions can be appraised by go/no go gauging methods. These are critical dimensions since, if they are out of specification, filling and sealing efficiency of the container is reduced. Defective T and I dimensions are the result of conditions occurring during the forming operations.

Generally food processors select a small number of containers from each incoming shipment of ware and these samples are appraised for weight and capacity. The data resulting from these quality tests are seldom used for acceptance or rejection purposes but are frequently used to adjust automatic weighing and filling equipment and to appraise supplier performance.

3. Composite Containers

For the purposes of this chapter, a composite container is defined as one having a fibre or paperboard body and metallic ends. Composite containers are used in the U.S.A. food industry principally for refrigerated bakery products, for frozen fruit juice concentrates and for low moisture content foods such as grated cheese.

The container for refrigerated bakery products is designed by the fabricator to be opened by bursting at a specified externally applied impact force. The bursting strength of the container is, therefore, classified as a critical functional characteristic. In order to evaluate shipments for this critical defect, the food processor can make small pre-production runs. Since generally this is not practicable, the processor usually selects a small sample of composite containers after packing in order to appraise the fabricator's performance for ease of opening.

In general, formal incoming sampling systems can be used advantageously by the food processor to classify shipments as acceptable or rejectable on the basis of major visual defects such as excessive dust, label registration and label "float" (up-and-down shift of label from container to container).

The composite containers used for frozen fruit juice concentrates are subject to many of the same quality requirements as the all-metal containers employed for these products. Formal incoming sampling systems can be used by the food processor to detect the presence of critical defects such double seaming defects, unsatisfactory glue bonds, and crushed containers. Formal sampling systems can also be used to evaluate critical or major appearance defects such as dust, label registration and label float for frozen citrus juice containers.

In general, critical functional characteristics of composite containers for frozen fruit juices leading to product leakage can be appraised only after the containers are packed. For this purpose, pre-production runs can be made or small sample groups ("spot-checks") can be selected after the packing operations are completed in order to appraise the performance of the fabricator.

4. Fibre Drums

Typical food products packaged in fibre drums are dried milk or eggs, dehydrated vegetables (onions, garlic, and so forth) citric and phosphoric acids, shortenings, meat seasonings, brined meat, and vegetables and fruits in either brine or syrup. The major quality requirements of fibre drums for food products in the U.S.A. are (a) the container must hold the product and protect it from outside contamination. In doing so, it must not adversely affect the inherent properties of the food product, and (b) the drums must comply with current shipping regulations established by the American Association of Railroads[17] and by the National Motor Freight Traffic Association (U.S.A.)[18] in regard to the physical strength of the completed drums.

The first quality requirement is functional in nature and a deviation from this requirement constitutes a critical defect. For obvious reasons, it is generally not practicable to evaluate shipments for functional defects by making pre-production runs of fibre drums. The food processor, therefore, generally relies upon the producer to supply drums which are relatively free of obvious fabricating defects.

The second quality requirement is concerned with quality of conformance to fabricating specifications. Test procedures for drums have been established in the U.S.A. by the American Society for Testing Materials (ASTM), by the Packaging Institute, and by the Technical Association of the Pulp and Paper Industry (TAPPI).[7b] In addition, quality standards for drums have been developed by the U.S. Government (Federal Specification PPP-D-723E, 6/1/61). The fibre drum fabricator has both a legal and a moral obligation to certify to the food-processor that the quality, materials, and workmanship of the drums supplied for a particular food product are acceptable. In order to appraise the long-run quality level of each supplier, food processors often test a few drums from occasional shipments. This procedure is worthwhile only if the monetary value of the quality information obtained is equal to or greater than the cost of sampling and inspecting the drums.

B. Semi-Rigid Containers

In the *Glossary of Packaging Terms* semi-rigid containers are defined as "containers that have the configuration of a rigid container but will yield on application of manual forces and return to their original shape after the force has been removed."[14b] In accordance with this definition, some general and also some unique quality characteristics of corrugated cartons, folding cartons and plastic containers will be discussed.

Semi-rigid packaging materials in 1962 accounted for 39% (about 2·4 billion dollars) of the total value of packaging materials used for food products in the U.S.A. This 39% is apportioned among the three categories of semi-rigid packaging materials as follows:

Corrugated cartons	26%
Folding cartons	11%
Plastic containers	2%

The special quality characteristics of the above generic examples will be discussed in the order of their economic importance in this subsection.

1. Corrugated Cartons

In the U.S.A., there are relatively few food products packaged directly into corrugated cardboard cartons. Corrugated cartons are primary containers for products such as dried prunes, dried apples, and dried apricots for institutional purposes. Corrugated cartons, however, are used in large quantities in the food industry as overpacks or shipping packages for primary containers.

Because corrugated cartons are designed, in general, to act as "sacrificial" packages, their critical quality characteristics are more functional than esthetic in nature. The carton manufacturer, therefore, is responsible for using the proper raw materials and for guaranteeing quality of workmanship in order to supply functionally satisfactory corrugated cartons. Since it is usually not practicable to make pre-production runs to detect functional defects, the food processor usually selects a few sample cartons after packing in order to audit functional quality. The functional characteristics which are important to the great majority of food processors and which are often appraised by audit sampling are as follows:

(1) Compression strength
(2) Bursting strength
(3) Puncture resistance
(4) Impact resistance
(5) Shipping damage resistance

A list of the standard U.S.A. tests for the above functional quality characteristics was published in the 1961 edition of the "Modern Packaging Encyclopedia".[7b]

Bursting strength and puncture resistance of the paperboard are normally part of the carton specifications. The quality of the basic raw materials is certified by the fabricator's stamp which is placed upon each finished carton. This stamp legally certifies that the raw materials from which the carton was fabricated meet minimum quality requirements for bursting strength and puncture tests. Therefore, only "spot-checking" of incoming carton shipments for conformance to specifications of these characteristics is required. However, when cartons show functional failure, a thorough investigation of the failure is advisable in order to determine the principal cause of failure.

When corrugated cartons are used to advertise the food product to the ultimate consumer the significance of visual or esthetic quality characteristics increases In these instances, smeared or illegible printing, off-register printing, and off-colour or odour-emitting inks are considered to be major visual and subjective defects The food processor can establish formal acceptance sampling programmes for visual characteristics when these programmes are expected to result in decreasing quality losses.

Dimensional characteristics of corrugated cartons are critical quality problems particularly when the variation in finished carton dimensions affects the operation of carton set-up or sealing equipment, resulting in excessive machine down-time, or poorly registered flaps lead to out-of-square and otherwise poorly sealed cartons.

2. Folding Cartons

In the U.S.A., frozen foods, bakery products, cereal products, dry cooking mixes and dry or semi-dry miscellaneous food products are commonly packaged directly into folding cartons. The increased consumption of frozen foods and dry cooking mixes has resulted in a marked increase in the use of folding cartons by the food processing industry in the past 15 years.

The following quality problems are associated with folding cartons:
(1) functional quality characteristics, including packaging efficiency;
(2) visual or esthetic quality characteristics.

The current trend in the manufacture of folding cartons in the U.S.A. is for the food processor to specify the desirable functional characteristics of the carton and for the fabricator to specify the weight and grade of board required to make a satisfactory carton to meet these conditions.

If it is desirable, a pre-production run can be made to appraise the functional quality of a shipment of cartons. Frequently, however, critical functional quality is appraised by audit sampling of the packed cartons. The functional characteristics which are important to consider in preproductions runs or in quality audits of packed cartons are:
(1) Moisture vapour resistance of the completed package.[7b]
(2) Compression strength of the package.[7b]
(3) Carton bulge resistance.
(4) Grease resistance of paperboard
(5) Carton sealability.
(6) Sift resistance of cartons.
(7) In-plant running efficiency of cartons.

At the present time, general testing methods for functional defects are developed by joint agreement between carton fabricator and food processor. Standard methods will undoubtedly be developed by the American Society for Testing Materials (ASTM) and by the Technical Association of Pulp and Paper Industries (TAPPI) in the future for testing the functional quality characteristics of folding cartons.

It is practicable at the present time to establish formal sampling inspection systems for folding cartons for the following visual and dimensional characteristics:
(1) Physical appearance of carton.
(2) Quality of printing and lithography.
(3) "Squareness" of carton set-up.

However, a formal incoming inspection system will be profitable for the food processor *only* if packaging material quality losses or operational losses are reduced by a programme of this type.

3. Plastics Containers

At the present time, the use of plastics containers for food products is limited by the physical characteristics of the currently available materials. As plastics materials are developed that are heat-resistant after moulding, as the permeability of plastics materials is reduced and as the flavour characteristics of these materials are improved, the use of plastics containers for food products is expected to expand at a rapid rate. This rapid expansion is illustrated by the following figures: from 1960–62, the monetary value of plastics materials used for packaging food products jumped from approximately 0·01 billion to approximately 0·14 billion dollars, more than a ten-fold increase in the two-year period.

Semi-rigid plastics containers are used principally for: (a) liquid or semi-solid food products such as prepared milk, orange juice, honey, prepared mustard, cottage cheese, and ice cream and (b) dry foods products such as cornstarch, sugar and grated cheese.

In general, the dimensional quality characteristics of plastics containers such as container weight and capacity, neck dimensions or opening diameters, finished container height, and wall thickness are specified by the customer. These critical quality characteristics must be within the fabricator's process capabilities before he can satisfactorily manufacture plastics containers to customer specifications. It is imperative for the customer and the supplier to have the same defect definitions in order to maintain a harmonious quality relationship. In addition, it is highly desirable for both parties to agree upon mutual inspection procedures and testing methods for quality appraisals of plastics containers.

When the food packer is establishing formal incoming sampling systems for plastics containers, he may wish to accept shipments or to classify them as rejectable, based upon critical dimensions appraised by go/no go gauging. Examples of these characteristics are T and I dimensions, H dimension (height of the bottle neck measured from the shoulder), and finished container height.* Frequently, container weight is considered to be a quality attribute since direct reading scales permit rapid evaluation of this dimension on a go/no go basis.

The inspection procedures for the other dimensional characteristics of plastics containers are generally too time-consuming to be used in routine

---

* These terms have been formally adapted by the Society of the Plastics Industries, U.S.A., Plastics Container Division.[19]

incoming sampling. However, small sample groups ("spot-checks") are selected from occasional shipments for appraising the supplier's quality performance in regard to container capacity, wall thickness, axial load ("crush" resistance), stress-cracking, drop-testing, and similar dimensional or performance characteristics.

It is, however, economically practicable to establish incoming inspection procedures for critical visual characteristics, that is, for those characteristics which affect in-plant or end-use performance. A summary of some of these critical visual characteristics is as follows:

(1) Bulged or "rocker" bottoms—causes containers to sway and to fall on conveyor lines, resulting in jammed feeder lines.
(2) Unfilled finish,[19] causes poor sealing efficiency of caps, resulting in secondary spoilage; may prevent filling equipment from shutting off, resulting in product spillage.
(3) Large dents in sidewalls—may cause difficulty with the feeding system, resulting in filling line slow-downs; can also reduce capacity of the container.
(4) Chips or loose particles of foreign materials within container—may interfere with filling operations resulting in costly line down-time; may also result in contamination of food products since the inherent electrostatic properties of the material tends to retain loose particles in spite of incoming cleaning operations.
(5) Visible cracks or perforations in container walls—may result in product leakage and microbial contamination of food product.

Some esthetic quality characteristics are frequently classified as major defects. It is profitable to inspect incoming shipments of plastics containers for esthetic characteristics, provided that the value of the quality information obtained from the sample exceeds the sampling and inspection costs. The following list is a summary of the general esthetic characteristics that are important in regard to plastics containers:

(1) Colour—it is desirable to have as little variation in colour as possible from shipment to shipment; incoming inspection personnel should have available colour limit samples showing the colour tolerance range. This is especially important for containers which must match labels, caps, and so forth.
(2) Labelling of Container—if container is directly printed the printing must be legible, in register, and not smeared; if a label is applied, the label "float" must not be excessive.
(3) External Dirt—the container exterior must be relatively free of dirt or dust particles and grease smears.

16*

C. Flexible Packaging Materials and Containers

A flexible container is defined in the "Glossary of Modern Packaging Terms" as "a package or container made of flexible or easily yielding materials that, when filled and closed, can be readily changed in shape or bent manually, without the aid of tools."[14b, 14c] Flexible packages are at the present time used in the U.S.A. for a variety of frozen, refrigerated, and dry food products and the use of these packages for food products is expected to continue increasing. As indicated in Section 2, in 1962 flexible packaging materials in the U.S.A. accounted for about 8·4% (0·5 billion dollars) of the total monetary value of packaging materials used for food products. As the use of flexible packaging materials is expanded in the food industry and as new materials appear on the market, the incoming quality assurance problems of the food processor are also expected to increase.

When a food product is to be packed in plastics or laminated foil pouches, the food processor usually purchases his packaging materials in the form of rolls or coils. The roll stock is frequently imprinted, decorated, and cut to width, but the actual pouches are formed, filled, and sealed in the food processor's plant. However, when food products are to be packaged in bags fabricated from flexible materials, finished bags are generally shipped by the supplier to the food processor.

Many of the critical quality characteristics of flexible pouches are inherent properties of the material or are in-plant and end-use functional characteristics. Routine inspection and testing of incoming shipments for these critical characteristics is time-consuming and, therefore, may not be profitable for the food processor. However, when it is desirable to classify incoming shipments of pouches as acceptable or rejectable, a representative sample is selected from the shipment and is tested under natural or simulated packaging conditions. Depending upon the results of this preproduction sample, the shipment is accepted or classified as rejectable.

The following is a list of critical functional characteristics which are influenced by the fabricator's process:

(1) Sealability—the heat or adhesive seal must be satisfactory to prevent product leakage and possible contamination of the food product. Cook-in pouch seals must not yield under the internal pressures generated during cooking.

(2) Ease of opening during filling—each unsealed pouch must open easily for filling using either manual or automatic opening devices. Failure to do so results in a slowing-down of the filling operation.

(3) Perforations in the film, imperfect lamination, or delamination of the foil—when present, these defects may result in product contamination and leakage.

(4) Flavour and odour characteristics—the completed pouch must be free from objectionable flavours and odours.

When flexible packaging material is received as roll stock by the food processor, routine acceptance sampling of incoming shipments is profitable for the following critical functional quality characteristics that are influenced by the fabricator's process:

(1) Slip Characteristics of Film—If film does not slide easily enough or if it slides too easily over metal surfaces, package-forming difficulties will occur, resulting in line down-time.

(2) Freedom from Block—When laminates are pre-coated with sealing materials, self-sealing or "blocking" can take place under roll pressure. This "blocking" effect indicates potential package-forming difficulties, resulting in line down-time.

(3) Flatness of Film—As a result of unfavourable laminating conditions, the film may show an excessive tendency to curl. Excessive curl frequency causes operating difficulties in the package-forming operations, resulting in a large amount of line down-time.

(4) Uniformity of Heat Seal Response—Since the heat sealing device is maintained within narrow temperature ranges and since the film has contact with the heat sealing device for a brief period of time, it is essential that the heat sealing response of the material be uniform within a shipment. If the sealing characteristics of the material are poor, product leakage and possible contamination of the food product occurs.

(5) Flavour and Odour Characteristics of the Film—The film must be free from objectionable flavours and odours since the flexible package must not deleteriously affect the food product.

The following list summarizes the major quality characteristics of flexible packaging materials received as roll stock:

(1) Visual examination of rolls for off-colour or off-register printing and decoration

(2) Width of rolls: go/no go gauging

(3) Weight of rolls: this is an indication of average item count.

Bags which are preformed by the packaging material supplier arrive at the food packer plant in packages, bales, or bundles. The packer in his incoming acceptance sampling procedures is concerned primarily with a visual examination of the bags. The proper basis weight, strength of material, the permeability and moisture resistance of the raw material and the quality of workmanship are specified prior to bag fabrication and it is the legal and moral responsibility of the producer to supply a product conforming to the customer's specification.

The following is a summary of significant visual quality characteristics for incoming inspection of bags:

(1) Detection of improperly sealed bottoms, back or side-seams.
(2) Reliable counts for short-run filling operations.
(3) Off-register printing, and correct printing and decoration.
(4) Ease of opening for filling in automatic filling equipment.

D. Container Closures

As stated in Section 2, container closures in 1962 accounted for approximately 3·6% (0·2 billion dollars) of the total monetary value of packaging materials in the U.S.A. used for food products. This percentage is divided among caps and crowns as follows:

Caps	2·2%
Crowns	1·4%

Closures will be discussed in this section in the above order.

1. Caps

In the U.S.A., the cap fabricator guarantees his product to conform to the food processor's requirements. He therefore has a legal and a moral obligation to see that the specified materials are used in the fabricating operations and that the quality of the workmanship is satisfactory.

In general, the inherent design of the closure determines whether or not a satisfactory fit between the cap and the bottle or jar will result when the container-cap combination is assembled at random. The critical quality characteristics of caps in this instance are functional, and for previously stated reasons it is not possible to apply simple incoming sampling procedures to functional characteristics, although it is possible to make pre-production runs when these are required.

It is important for the food processor and the cap fabricator to work closely together on these quality problems and to use the same defect definitions. The quality assurance of caps, therefore, is generally a cooperative venture with the fabricator working closely with the food processor.

The critical quality characteristics of cap closures which can be detected on incoming inspection are summarized as follows:

(1) Compound liner "skips"—Incomplete coverage of cap lining compound (a "skip") is a rare occurrence but the presence of a "skip" means that an incomplete seal between cap and jar will be obtained, resulting in product leakage or microbial contamination of the food product.
(2) Physical damage to the cap—This can occur during the fabricating process but more frequently it is the result of shipping damage. The result of a severe dent is an incomplete seal with the consequences to the packed food product as stated above.

The following visual quality characteristics of caps can be appraised on incoming sampling at the food processors plant:

(1) Off-register decorating and printing.
(2) Off-colour lithography.
(3) Scratches on lithographed surface.
(4) Excessive amounts of dust, dirt, and other foreign material.

2. *Crowns*

In the U.S.A., a crown specification generally includes both the shell and the liner requirement. The shell specification includes metal plate thickness, plate type, plate temper, plate coating, shell diameter, and shell height. The liner specification states the nature and the thickness of the liner. If a cork liner is specified, then the customer requirement also specifies the diameter of the liner and the nature of the disc material. The supplier, therefore, has the responsibility of certifying that the shipments of crowns meet the specifications, of guaranteeing the quality of workmanship, and of stating that the materials used will not affect the flavour of the product.

Incoming acceptance sampling procedures can be profitably established for visual defects such as:

(1) Loose or missing liners—also double liners.
(2) Mixed decorations.
(3) Die scratches on metal surface.
(4) Off-register printing or missing decoration.
(5) Off-centre spots when cork liners are specified.
(6) Off-colour lithography.

The major functional quality characteristics of crowns is leakage. This characteristic is appraised either from a pre-production run or after the bottles are packed and capped. In either case, a random sample of packed bottles is evaluated for crown leakage. If excessive leakage occurs, this is considered to be a critical defect. If a quality investigation indicates that the crown fabrication is responsible for the leakage, the supplier is penalized for the quality failure.

4. LEGAL RESTRICTIONS AND REGULATORY REQUIREMENTS FOR FOOD PACKAGING MATERIALS

In addition to meeting the standards of performance for good packaging materials a manufacturer or converter of these materials has a moral and ethical responsibility not to use substances which may constitute a public health hazard. In most countries of the free world, governmental regulations of one sort or another have been enacted in order to control potential health hazards from foods and/or packaging materials. New regulations are now

TABLE 1. Summary of Legal Restrictions and Regulatory Requirements for Food Packaging Materials

Country	Government regulation of food packaging materials		Regulations covers all types of materials (glass, metal, plastics, etc.)		Government department responsible for enforcement	Published Government documents relative to regulations
	Yes	No	Yes	No		
Argentina	X		X		National Ministry of Social Assistance and Health (National Direction of Chemistry)	National Food Regulations (1953)
Australia	X		Various reg. cover acceptability of food products		Public Health Authorities	Health Acts of the various states of Australia
Belgium	Some		Partial coverage		Ministry of Public Health	Law followed by ministerial order[a]
Brazil	X		X		State Departments of Health	National and State Laws[a]
Canada	X		X		Dept. of National Health and Welfare (Food and Drug Directorate)	National Law[a]
Columbia	X		X		Ministry of Public Health (Province Sec. of Public Health and Municipal Sec. of Public Health)	Resolution No. 00917 (28 Aug. 1963)—Ministry of Public Health
Denmark	X		X		Public Health Authorities	Order of 22 April 1913—National Public Health Service General Food Law 28 April 1950
Finland	X		X (with a few exceptions)		Ministry of Trade and Industry	Foodstuffs Decree of 21 Nov. 1952 (No. 508/52), 16–17
France	X		X (with a few exceptions)		Service de la Repression des Fraudes—Ministère de l'Agriculture	Journal Officiel de la Republique Francaise—Repression des Fraudes–Materiaux Au Contact Des Ailments Et Denrees Destines A L' Alimentation Humaine (30 Juin 1963)

Country		Coverage	Inspection authority	Food law / regulation
West Germany	X	X	No information available to the authors	German Food Law—1927 redrafted 1936 amended—21 December 1958
Great Britain	X	Various reg. cover acceptability of the food product	No information available to the authors—probably Public Health Inspection	No information available to the authors—probably British Food Drug Act
India	X	Not applicable	Not applicable	Not applicable
Italy	X	X	Ministry of Health	Ministerial Decree of 19 Jan. 1963, published in Official Gazette No. 64 (7 Mar. 1963), pp. 18–19
Jamaica	X	X	Public Health Inspectors examine imported food stuffs	Probably related British Food and Drug Act
Japan	X	Partial coverage	Welfare Ministry	Ministry regulations pertaining to Food Sanitation
Federation of Malaya and Singapore	X	X	Ministry of Health	Federation of Malaya—Sale of Food and Drugs Ordinance 1952 (No. 28 of 1952) Also Sale of Food and Drugs Regulations 1952
		X	Ministry of Health	Federation of Singapore—Sale of Food and Drugs Ordinance (No. S-252- Chapter 148) 1957 and Subsequent Amendments
Mexico	X	Applies to acceptability of product / X	Secretary of Public Health	No information available to the authors
Netherlands	X	X	Ministry of Public Health	Netherlands Food Law[a]
New Zealand	X	Applies to acceptability of product / X	This information is not clear	Food and Drug Act and New Zealand standards Bulletin[a]
Norway	X	X	Ministry of Fishery and Ministry of Health	Norwegian Food Law[a]
Peru	X	Probably covers all types	Instituto De Normas Tecnicas	Peru Food Law, published in November 1963
Spain	X	X (in process for 1964)	No information is available to authors	Not published

TABLE 1. Summary of Legal Restrictions and Regulatory Requirements for Food Packaging Materials—(Contd.)

Country	Government regulation of food packaging materials		Regulation covers all types of materials (glass, metal, plastics, etc.)		Government department responsible for enforcement	Published Government documents relative to regulations
	Yes	No	Yes	No		
U.S.A.	X		X		Food and Drug Administration, Dept. of Health, Education, and Welfare	1958 Food Additives Amendment of the Federal Food, Drug and Cosmetic Act (1938)

a No specific details are available.

being issued at a greatly accelerated rate but the applicability of the regulations to packaging materials is highly variable and may take a number of forms. In some countries, there is little more than a code dealing with sanitation. In others, laws prohibit the use of specified materials. In still others, notably the United States, only materials listed in highly codified regulations are acceptable for use.

Obviously, volumes could be written about the changing legal restrictions and regulatory requirements that packaging materials must meet. Although this Section represents considerable correspondence with associates throughout the world, it is not claimed to be a comprehensive list of all current governmental regulations, nor to represent official expressions of government policy. A summary of the information gathered from our private, unofficial sources is presented in Table 1.

In the United States, the keystone legislation was passed by Congress in 1958 as the Food Additives Amendment of the Federal Food Drug and Cosmetic Act (1938) with enforcement of its provisions assigned to the Food and Drug Administration of the Department of Health, Education and Welfare. Basically, if a substance is added to a food, or can reasonably be expected to migrate to a food, then the substance must be cleared for safety before it is used. Such clearance may take several forms:

(1) Exemption by virtue of a prior sanction granted before 1958.
(2) Exemption by reason of being "Generally Recognized as Safe".
(3) Conformity with a regulation prescribing the conditions under which such direct or indirect additive may safely be used. This is by far the most common form of clearance and it is estimated that some 6,000 substances have been cleared to date.

Although there were naturally many growing pains following enactment of the Food Additives Amendment and promulgation of the necessary rules and regulations, procedures have settled down to fairly well delineated paths. It has become almost routine for the purchaser of packaging materials to demand evidence of compliance with legal regulations from the manufacturer or fabricator of these materials. In turn, a fabricator will request assurance from the supplier of the raw materials that these materials are legally acceptable for the intended purpose. If a substance is not covered by a regulation, then steps must be taken to demonstrate its safety to the Food and Drug Administration and to petition for either a new regulation or for an amendment to an existing regulation.

Table 1 (pp. 398–400) is a summary of the limited information obtained by correspondence with associates in regard to government regulations on packaging materials.

5. SAMPLING INSPECTION SYSTEMS FOR INCOMING PACKAGING MATERIALS
A. Introduction and Discussion of Basic Principles

In previous sections of this chapter, the major quality characteristics of packaging materials have been classified into three general categories: (a) functional characteristics, (b) dimensional characteristics, and (c) visual characteristics. Many functional and visual characteristics are classified as *attributes*, i.e. the sample units are categorized as either defective or non-defective. Dimensional characteristics are classified as *variables* and are measured on a continuous scale. The basic principles discussed in this intro-duction apply both to sampling inspection by attributes and to sampling inspection by variables. However, only attribute sampling systems will be described in this chapter. These are more widely used in the food packaging industry than variables sampling systems because (a) some significant quality characteristics of packaging materials do not meet the statistical require-ments of the variables sampling plans* and (b), in general, the cost of data analysis, the cost of training inspection personnel, and the cost of administer-ing variables sampling plans is greater than the cost of corresponding attri-bute plans.

Before discussing the significant characteristics of various incoming sampling systems, the following words and phrases must be "translated" from the food technology vocabulary into the statistical quality control vocabulary.

(1) The *container fabricator*, *container manufacturer* or *material converter* is semantically equivalent to the *vendor, producer*, or *supplier*.

(2) The *food processor* or *packer* is semantically equivalent to the *consumer* or *user*.

(3) The *Producer's Risk* is defined as the *fabricator's* or *convertor's risk* of having a shipment *rejected* when it should be *accepted*.

(4) The *Consumer's Risk* is defined as the *food processor's risk* of *accepting* a shipment of objectionable quality when it should be *rejected*.

It is important to evaluate packaging material for visual and for functional quality characteristics because (a) *esthetic characteristics* such as colour, size, shape, and general appearance of the package persuade the ultimate con-sumer to make his initial purchase and (b) *end-use functional characteristics*, such as ease-of-opening, frequently persuade consumers to repeat purchase. Unfortunately, the majority of end-use and in-plant functional defects in packaging materials cannot be discovered by examining incoming ship-ments. The food processor, therefore, is forced to concentrate his incoming sampling of packaging material shipments upon simple dimensional and

---

* For a complete discussion of acceptance sampling by variables, refer to Bowker and Goode (20) or to the U.S.A. Military Standard 414 (21).

visual characteristics, knowing that these characteristics are sometimes responsible for only a small proportion of the total quality loss.

The food processor, in many instances, must rely upon the integrity of the container or packaging material supplier in order to have a high degree of assurance that incoming shipments contain only a small proportion of functional defects. This means that the consumer sometimes accepts incoming shipments and uses containers in his plant with no formal appraisal of incoming quality. In these instances, he is basing his acceptance of the shipment upon the producer's established record of satisfactory quality.

This practice is actually informal vendor certification. When this procedure is followed, the food processor "spot-checks"—draws a few small sample groups from occasional shipments—in order to up-date the information on the quality performance of the producer.

When shipments of packages or packaging materials are classified as acceptable or rejectable by formal acceptance sampling procedure, both the producer and the customer must recognize this fact: JUDGEMENT TO ACCEPT OR TO REJECT A SHIPMENT IS BASED PURELY UPON INFORMATION OBTAINED FROM SAMPLES DRAWN AT RANDOM FROM THE SHIPMENT AND, THEREFORE, THE RESULTING QUALITY DECISION IS MADE WITH A DEGREE OF UNCERTAINTY OR RISK. In statistical systems of sampling inspection, there are two kinds of risks: the Producer's Risk and the Consumer's Risk. The first quality risk is associated with the result of an *optimistic* sample while the second is associated with the result of a *pessimistic* sample. The salient point of statistical sampling is this principle of CALCULATED RISK. In fact, all sampling systems contain an element of risk, but only a *statistically* designed system is based upon a *calculated* or known risk.

The characteristics of an adequate acceptance sampling system are stated in the following summary suggested by Cowden:[22a]

The system must:

(1) Protect the producer against having a shipment rejected when his product is consistently satisfactory in regard to quality level.
(2) Protect the food processor against accepting a shipment of objectionable quality.
(3) Provide long-run protection to the food processor when non-destructive testing is possible.
(4) Encourage the producer to keep his fabricating or converting process in control.
(5) Minimize the cost of sampling, inspection, and administration.
(6) Provide information concerning quality of the product in order to appraise the supplier's quality performance.

The so-called "100% inspection" system is not a practical method for acceptance sampling of containers or packaging materials because: (a) this system is more expensive to operate than a sampling system, (b) the "100%" inspection" system gives no insurance that, after the inspection is completed, the product is 100% free of defective units because of inspector fallibility, and (c) when inspection tests are destructive, the "100%" method obviously cannot be used.

The primary purpose of acceptance sampling systems is to protect the customer without unduly penalizing the producer. If the plan is too stringent it can result in the rejection of normally usable product. Rejected shipments, in this instance, may contain a small proportion of defective product produced by the normal operation of a high-speed continuous process. Customers

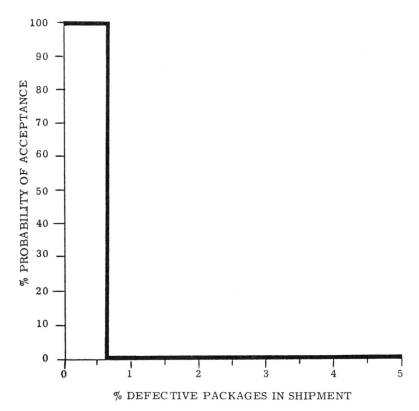

FIG. 1. Operating characteristic (OC) curve of the *ideal* inspection system.

who consider that this small proportion is objectionable and who force suppliers to accept unreasonably stringent sampling systems eventually may pay for this stringency. In order to meet an unreasonable quality demand, the producer must often install unnecessarily expensive process control and in-plant inspection systems. As Moroney aptly comments, "Stringency, like all other virtues, can be undesirable in excess."[23]

In order to protect the food processor, a sampling plan must accept shipments of desirable quality much more frequently than shipments of undesirable quality. In other words, a satisfactory plan must have adequate quality discrimination. Figure 1 shows the Operating Characteristic (OC)

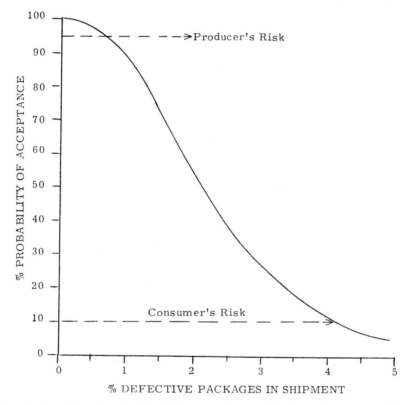

FIG. 2. Operating characteristic (OC) curve of a sampling inspection system. (Sample size 125, acceptance no. 2.)

Curve for a plan with *perfect* discrimination. All shipments containing *0·65% or more* defective packages will be *rejected 100%* of the time. Although the plan discriminates perfectly between "good" and "poor" quality, it is not a realistic sampling system because it requires a *sample size equal to the size of the shipment*. The OC Curve shown in Fig. 1, illustrates the ideal operation of a theoretical "100% inspection" system, the fallacies of which have already been pointed out.

Figure 2, on the other hand, illustrates the probability discrimination of a realistic sampling system. Observe that the percent defective that was accepted 100% of the time by the plan shown in Fig. 1 is now accepted only 95% of the time by the plan shown in Fig. 2. Notice also that the sharp break shown in Fig. 1 between "good" and "poor" quality does not occur in Fig. 2. The OC Curve shown in Fig. 2 indicates that there is a wide quality range and that the proportions of defective material within this range have varying probabilities of being accepted.

In this discussion of sampling systems, it is assumed that defective packages are distributed at random within a shipment. This is generally true for high speed continuous fabricating processes when extensive materials handling operations are present between the origin of defective materials and preparation of the product for shipping. An industrial experiment was run in which 50 colour-coded metal bodies, simulating a sequence of defective containers, were placed in the fabricator's conveyor system immediately after the body-forming operation. After extensive normal materials handling operations such as application and drying of spray lacquer, leakage testing operations, and casing operations, the original sequence of 50 colour-coded containers was found to be distributed throughout an interval of 41 cases (24 cans per case). Random sampling is acknowledged to be a more efficient method for collecting quality data than any other sampling method when defectives are randomly distributed throughout a lot. For this reason, the sampling systems discussed in this section assume (a) that defective containers are distributed at random throughout a shipment and (b) that the samples are drawn at random from the shipment.

B. Classification of Incoming Sampling Systems by Sampling Methods

Sampling systems are classified by sampling methods into three general categories: single, double, and sequential methods. Detailed descriptions of these plans are given in standard texts on statistical quality control such as those published by Grant and by Duncan; reference may also be made to work by Steiner.[24a, 25, 26] A summary of the salient features of these three sampling methods is given below.

1. Single Sampling Plans

The operational procedure for a single sampling plan is as follows:

Draw a single group of packages *at random* from the incoming shipment. This group must consist of a pre-calculated number of sample units. If the number of defective packages in the group exceeds a precalculated number, the shipment is classified as rejectable—otherwise it is accepted.

The advantages and disadvantages of single sampling systems are summarized as follows:[24b, 25, 28b]

Advantages

(1) Single sampling plans are relatively easy to design.
(2) These plans are easily explained to inspection personnel.
(3) Single sampling plans are simple to administer and the single sampling administration costs are the lowest of the three kinds of plans.
(4) The data obtained from a random sample can be used to appraise a fabricator's quality performance, provided that *all* of the sample units are inspected.

Disadvantages

(1) When destructive testing is required and when the package is expensive, single sampling is costly.
(2) When the test procedure is intricate and time-consuming, single sampling is costly.

2. Double Sampling Plans

The operational procedure for double sampling plans is as follows:

A smaller number of packages than the number required by the corresponding single sampling plan is drawn *at random* from the shipment. If the number of defective packages in this first group is equal to or less than a precalculated limit the shipment is accepted. If the number of defective packages is equal to or greater than a second precalculated limit, the shipment is classified as rejectable. If the number of defective packages found in this first sample lies between the two precalculated limits, then a second group of samples, equal in size to the first,[27] is drawn *at random* from the shipment and examined for the presence of defectives. When resampling is required, the decision regarding the disposition of the shipment is based upon the combined results of the two groups. In this instance, when the combined number of defective packages exceeds a precalculated limit, the shipment is classified as rejectable—otherwise it is accepted.

Advantages

(1) When the quality level of an incoming shipment is *very good* or *very poor*, double sampling plans require 10–50% fewer samples than corresponding single sampling plans.[5e]
(2) Since all of the sample packages in the first group is always inspected, the data from this initial sample can be used to appraise the quality performance of the supplier.

Disadvantages

(1) Double sampling plans require more samples than the corresponding single sampling plans when the quality level of the shipment is at the "indifference" point, i.e. it is neither very good nor very poor.

(2) The use of these plans results in a variable inspection load. This means that the administration costs will be higher than those for the corresponding single sampling system.

(3) In commercial practice, it is advisable to draw all of the sample packages from the shipment at one time. For this reason, the sampling costs of a double sampling system are expected to be higher than those of the corresponding single sampling system.

3. Sequential Sampling Plans

(a) Item-by-Item Sequential Plan. In this sampling system, samples are drawn *at random* from a shipment and are examined one at a time. After each sample is inspected, one of three quality decisions is made, based upon the accumulated number of defectives found in the total number of samples examined up to that point: (1) to accept the shipment, (2) to classify the shipment as rejectable, and (3) to continue sampling. In theory, this procedure must be repeated until either the first or the second decision is reached or until *all* of the samples in the shipment have been examined. However, for practical purposes, truncation of item-by-item sequential inspection when the *single sample size* is reached is recommended. When this procedure is followed, the shipment quality decision is based upon the acceptance and the rejection criteria of the single sampling plan if the shipment quality is at the "indifference" level.

A detailed description of an item-by-item sequential plan for incoming sampling of metal containers is given by Way and Weimerskirch.[8] Based upon 12 years experience with item-by-item sequential inspection, the use of this system is strongly recommended when food processors install formal acceptance sampling systems for packaging materials.

Advantages

(1) When the quality level of an incoming shipment is *very good* or *very poor*, item-by-item sequential inspection requires only 30–50% as many samples as single sampling inspection.[5a]

(2) When tests are destructive and when sample units are expensive, the inspection costs for this system will average less than those for single sampling systems.

(3) When the quality level of the shipment is at the "indifference" point, the total number of samples inspected cannot exceed the single sample size if the sequential inspection procedure is truncated at this point.

Disadvantages

(1) Item-by-item sequential inspection results in a highly variable inspection load.

(2) Administrative costs for item-by-item sequential inspection are higher than those for single sampling systems.

(3) It is difficult to evaluate the quality performance of a supplier from inspection data normally resulting from item-by-item sequential inspection. Special sampling procedures must be used for this purpose.

(b) Multiple Sampling Plans. These plans are natural extensions of double and of item-by-item sequential sampling systems. However, their use in incoming inspection of packaging materials appears to be very limited. For the basic principles of this system, consult Grant, Duncan, and other statistical quality control textbooks.

4. *Advantages and Disadvantages of the Three Sampling Methods*

Duncan makes an excellent comparison of single, double and sequential sampling systems.[25] This comparison is given with a few modifications in Table 2.

TABLE 2. Comparison of single, double and sequential sampling systems

Factors to be considered	Type of sampling method		
	Single	Double	Sequential
Protection against undesirable acceptance and rejection of shipments	All methods are approximately equal		
Total cost of inspection	Most	Intermediate	Least
Variability of inspection load	Constant	Variable	Variable
Sampling costs when all samples are drawn at one time	Least expensive	Most expensive	Equal to single sample if terminated at single sample size
Accurate estimation of lot quality (rating of supplier)	Best	Intermediate	Worst
Amount of record-keeping	Least	Intermediate	Most
Psychological: "Gives supplier more than one chance"	Worst	Intermediate	Best

C. Cost Comparison of Single, Double and Sequential Systems having the same OC Curve

The total costs of an incoming inspection system is composed of three different parts.[22b, 28a]

1. Overhead Costs

These costs include administrative costs, inspector training costs, cost of conveying samples from sampling area to inspection area, and cost of storing the sample packages until they are inspected.

2. Sampling Costs

When shipments of containers are sampled, it is advisable, because of materials handling problems, to draw the maximum sample size from the shipment at one time and to store the samples for subsequent inspection. This means that the truncation point of sequential inspection systems must be calculated in advance.

3. Inspection Cost

This cost depends upon the average number of samples inspected and, for other than single sampling, this average inspection load varies with the quality level of the submitted shipment. For this reason, the sample calculations of inspection costs presented in this section are based upon the average sample size required (a) when the shipment quality level is equal to the acceptable quality level (AQL) and (b) when the shipment quality level is equal to the "indifference" quality.

For the conditions stated above, the estimated total cost of a particular sampling method can be expressed by the following relationship:[22b]

$$C_T = C_O + C_S\, n_m + C_I\, \bar{n}$$

n_m = Maximum number of sample packages selected per shipment

Where: C_T = Total cost
C_O = Overhead cost/Shipment
C_S = Sampling cost/Package
C_I = Inspection cost/Package
$\bar{n}$ = Average number of packages inspected per shipment

To illustrate the utility of the above relationship for selecting an economical sampling system under specified quality conditions, we shall calculate the total costs for four different sampling methods, using the quality conditions specified by the OC curve shown in Fig. 2.*

* This is also the same as the OC curve specified for Plan K, Normal Inspection, MIL-STD-105D (27).

Acceptable Quality Level (AQL) = 0·65% Producer's Risk (α) = 5%
Objectionable Quality Level (LTPD) = 4·26% Consumer's Risk (β) = 10%
In order to compare the estimated total cost of these four different sampling systems, we need only estimate the relative values of overhead, sampling, and inspection costs. The cost category bearing the relative value of "one" is the smallest of the three. As an example, let us assume the following relative values:

	Relative value
Inspection/Container	1
Sampling/Container	5
Overhead cost/shipment:	
Single sample inspection	20
Double sample inspection	30
Multiple sample inspection	40
Item-by-item sequential inspection	50

The following table shows the maximum numbers of containers to be drawn from each shipment and also the average number of containers expected to be examined if the shipment quality level is (a) equal to the AQL or (b) equal to the "indifference" point:

	Maximum number of containers sampled per shipment	Average number of containers examined at*	
		AQL	Indifference Point
Single sample inspection	125	125	125
Double sample inspection	160	111	130
Multiple sample inspection	224	90	107
Item-by-item sequential inspection	125	76	88

* Calculated from ASN Curves, some of which are given in MIL-STD-105D [27].

It is assumed that the maximum number of samples is selected at one time from the shipment and stored pending inspection.

When the total cost is calculated for each of the systems using the cost function specified on page 410; the total relative costs of the sampling inspection systems per shipment are as follows:

| | Relative costs per shipment at (*) | | | | | | | |
| | AQL | | | | Indifference point | | | |
	Over-head cost	Samp. cost	Insp. cost	Total cost	Over-head cost	Samp. cost	Insp. cost	Total cost
Single sample inspection	20	625	125	770	20	625	125	770
Double sample inspection	30	800	111	941	30	800	130	960
Multiple sample inspection	40	1120	90	1250	40	1120	107	1267
Item-by-item sequential inspection	50	625	76	751	50	625	88	763

* 1 Unit of relative cost = Actual monetary cost of inspecting an individual container.

Observe that, under the quality conditions specified by the OC curve shown in Fig. 2 and based upon the previously stated relative cost values, the item-by-item sequential system has the least total relative cost. However, it is only 7 to 19 relative cost units less than the single sampling system. The double and multiple sampling inspection systems show considerable higher total relative costs than the single sample and item-by-item sequential systems. When inspection costs are low, therefore, and when the total number of sample packages must be selected from the shipment in advance and stored pending inspection, it is apparent that double and multiple sampling procedures are too costly for use in acceptance sampling of packaging materials. Under these circumstances, it is advisable for the food processor to use single sampling inspection methods or item-by-item sequential inspection, terminating at the single sample size. When the testing method is destructive or when it is expensive, the total relative cost advantages of item-by-item sequential inspection are even more apparent.

D. Classification of Incoming Sampling Systems by Type of Protection

A very brief classification of incoming sampling systems in regard to the type of protection is given below. A complete discussion of this subject will be found in the statistical quality control text-books those published by Grant, Duncan, Peach, Cowden, and other authors.[22, 24, 25, 28]

1. Dual Protection

This classification is based upon the requirement that the OC curve pass through two specified points such as (a) the AQL at the Producer's Risk and (b) the Objectionable Quality Level (LTPD) and the Consumer's Risk. This kind of plan provides protection for both the fabricator and for the food processor. If either the Producer's or the Consumer's Risk is small, the sample size will be large. Similarly, if fine discrimination is desired, i.e. if the ratio LTPD/AQL is close to 1·0, the sample size will be large.

2. Single Protection

This classification is based upon the requirement that the OC Curve pass through one specified point. Moreover, additional but independent conditions are specified for the plan. The Dodge-Romig plans fall into this category since they specify the Consumer's Risk and the Objectionable Quality Level (LTPD).[29] The additional conditions required by these plans are the specification of the Average Outgoing Quality Limit (AOQL) and minimization of inspection.

The USA MIL-STD-105 sampling tables are also based upon this type of protection. The MIL-STD-105 tables specify the AQL and the Producer's Risk on the OC curve.[27] In addition, they provide for increasing or decreasing the severity of inspection, depending upon the past history of the supplier's quality level.

REFERENCES

1. Hoskins, F. J. (1955). "Quality Control Techniques Used in the Food Industry". National Convention *Transactions*, American Society for Quality Control. Ninth Annual Convention, pp. 293–297.
2. Stier, H. L. (1959). "How Statistical Quality Control is Used in Food Processing Industries". National Convention *Transactions*, American Society for Quality Control. Thirteenth Annual Convention, pp. 663–674.
3. Brokaw, C. H. and Kramer, A. "Quality Control in Processing Foods", *Perspective and Projections in Food Technology*, **18**, no. 9 (September, 1964), pp. 73–78.
4. Judge, Edward E. (1963). "The Almanac of the Canning Freezing, Preserving Industries," 48th Ed., p. 316, 324–358, 423–432. (Westminster, Maryland).
5. Juran, J. M., Seder, L. A. and Gryna, F. M. (1962). "Quality Control Handbook". (McGraw-Hill, N.Y.). (a) pp. 3–54 to 3–56; (b) pp. 3–62 to 3–65; (c) pp. 3–52 to 3–56; (d) pp. 12–16 to 12–18; (e) p. 13–77.
6. Brighton, K. W.; Riester, D. W.; and Braun, O. G. (1963). "Technical Problems Presented by New Containers and Materials". *Food Technology*, pp. 22–28.
7. "Modern Packaging Encyclopedia". (Modern Packaging, 770 Lexington Avenue, New York 21, New York).
   (a) Reynolds, O. C., "Growth and Change in Packaging—Value of Packing Materials, 1939–1962", Vol. 37 (1964), pp. 22–25.
   (b) "Standard Tests for Packaging Materials", Vol. 35 (1961), pp. 30–31.
8. Way, C. B. and Weimerskirch, R. I. (1956). "A Mutual Approach to Quality Control by Can Manufacturer and Food Processor". National Convention *Transactions*, American Society for Quality Control. Tenth Annual Convention, pp. 313–321.

9. Soog, B. E. (1953). "Some Applications of SQC in Paper Boxboard and Printing Industries". National Convention *Transactions*. American Society for Quality Control. Seventh Annual Convention, pp. 605–641.

10. Benson, R. E. (1957). "Developing Quality Standards and Rating in Folding Carton Manufacture". National Conventions *Transactions*. American Society for Quality Control. Eleventh Annual Convention, pp. 111–118.

11. Allen, E. E. (1960). "A Program for Defining and Controlling Visual Defects in a Multiplant Operation". National Convention *Transactions* American Society for Quality Control. Fourteenth Annual Convention, pp. 349–353.

12. Lang, Karl F. (1957). "Problems and Pitfalls in Acceptance Sampling of Glass Containers". National Convention *Transactions*, American Society for Quality Control. Eleventh Annual Convention, pp. 119–130.

13. Tarver, Mae-Goodwin.
    (a) (1962) "SQC in the Food and Allied Industries", *Proceedings*, 1962 Rochester (N.Y.) QC Clinic, American Society for Quality Control, pp. 31–42.
    (b) (1957). "Special Statistical Methods Applicable to Metal Container Research and Manufacture". 12th Midwest Conference Proceedings, American Society for Quality Control, pp. R–1 through R–16.

14. Packaging Institute (1955). "Glossary of Packaging Terms". (Packaging Institute, Inc. 342 Madison Avenue, New York 17, N.Y.). (a) p. 88; (b) p. 87; (c) p. 187.

15. Hartford-Empire Division of Emhart Mfg. Co. "Glass Defects—Causes and Corrections". (Emhart Mfg. Co., Hartford 2, Connecticut (1957).)

16. American Society for Testing Materials Standards (1961). Part 5. Published by American Society for Testing Materials, 1916 Race Street, Philadelphia 3, Pa.
    (a) C-147-59T Tentative Method of Internal Pressure Test on Glass Containers—Issued 1959 (pp. 708–710).
    (b) C-149-50 Standard Method of Thermal Shock Method on Glass Containers—Revised (1950), pp. 725–727.

17. American Association of Railroads, W. S. Flint, Tariff Pub. Officer, One Park Avenue at 33rd Street, New York 16, N.Y. Uniform Freight Classification Ratings, Rules and Regulations.

18. National Motor Freight Association, T. C. Freund Issuing Office, 1616 P Street, N.W., Washington 36, D.C., National Motor Freight Classification.

19. Society of Plastics Industries (U.S.A.): Plastics Container Division, Report No. 1—Bottle Standards (29 August 1963), 250 Park Avenue, New York 17, N.Y.

20. Bowker, A. H. and Goode, H. P. (1952). "Sampling Inspection by Variables". (McGraw-Hill Book Co., New York, N.Y.).

21. U.S.A. Department of Defense (11 June 1957), Military Standard 414: Sampling Procedures and Tables for Inspection by Attributes—U.S. Government Printing Office, Washington, D.C. 20402, 29 April 1963, MIL-STD-105D.

22. Cowden, Dudley, J. (1957). "Statistical Methods in Quality Control". (Prentice-Hall, Englewood Cliffs, N.J.). (a) pp. 488–497; (b) pp. 582–584.

23. Moroney, J. J. (1956). "Facts from Figures". p. 132. (Penguin Books, Baltimore, Maryland).

24. Grant, E. L. (1964). "Statistical Methods in Quality Control". 3rd Ed. (McGraw-Hill Book Co., New York, N.Y.). (a) pp. 403–430; (b) pp. 328–372.

25. Duncan, Acheson J. (1952). "Quality Control and Industrial Statistics", pp. 131–172. (Richard D. Irwin, Inc., Homewood, Illinois).

26. E. H. Steiner (1967). Statistical Methods in Quality Control. In: "Quality Control in the Food Industry", Vol. I. (Ed. S. M. Herschdoerfer). (Academic Press Inc.).

27. U.S.A.—Department of Defense, Military Standard 105: Sampling Procedures and Tables for Inspection by Attributes—U.S. Government Printing Office, Washington, D.C. 20402. 29 April 1963: MIL-STD-105D.

28. Peach, Paul (1947). "An Introduction to Industrial Statistics", 2nd Ed. (Edwards & Broughton Co., Raleigh, N.C.). (a) pp. 110–112; (b) pp. 36–42.

29. Dodge, H. F. and Romig, H. G. (1959). "Sampling Inspection Tables". (John Wiley and Sons, Inc., New York, N.Y.).

Automatic Control

H. A. SLIGHT

British Food Manufacturing Industries Research Association
Leatherhead, Surrey, England

1. INTRODUCTION

At a recent national industrial conference with speeches from union leaders and top management there was no argument as to whether automation was a good or bad thing. It was agreed that automation was essential if Britain was to survive as a major industrial nation and the conference concentrated on ways to speed its introduction.

Some food manufacturers consider that automation will inevitably result in a product of inferior quality. This is a fallacy, since such a situation can only arise when insufficient thought has been given to the correct application of automatic techniques. When automatic control is used correctly a far more consistent quality can be maintained than is possible with human control; the basic requirement of a control system, as will be described later, is the automatic correction of any deviation from a pre-set value.

Although this is not the place for a detailed discussion it should be mentioned that as well as giving a more consistent quality there are a number of other economic advantages in the use of automatic control, some of which are:

(1) A reduction in process and laboratory labour requirements.
(2) A closer control of, for example, moisture content which will allow working nearer to an upper limit.

17

(3) An increased throughput.

(4) Reduced power costs.

(5) Higher process plant utilization.

Automatic control can be applied with advantage to batch as well as continuous processes but it must be stressed that automatic control should be considered as an essential part of the scheme when a continuous process is being designed. If this is not done the invariable result is an inefficient process, and a major re-design will be required to improve the efficiency. This situation often arises during the conversion of a batch to a continuous process.

It is appreciated that, with many existing processes, complete automatic control is not economically viable but such a decision should be made only after careful study of all the available information. Too often a control scheme is dismissed solely on the capital cost of the equipment without serious consideration being given to the savings that would result.

An automatic control system consists basically of a measuring device, a regulating device, and a controller that uses the measured information to control the regulating device.

Although these three parts will be discussed separately, in a practical application they should be considered together as a complete system.

2. MEASUREMENT

A. Temperature

There are few food manufacturing processes that do not involve a change in temperature and the accurate control of process temperatures can be vital to the quality of the product. Many people consider that the measurement of temperature is simple but it is not an easy matter to obtain an accurate and meaningful reading and it is important that the right type of sensor should be used for a particular application.

The temperature sensors described in this section are those that are of particular interest to the food industry, namely, filled bulb, thermocouples and electrical resistance types.

1. Filled Bulb Thermometers

Filled bulb measuring and controlling instruments fall into two main categories: those that respond to a change in volume and those that respond to a change in pressure. These instruments consist of a metal bulb which is connected to a measuring element by a capillary tube, the whole system being filled with either a gas or a liquid or a combination of both. The measuring element, which transforms a change in volume or pressure into the movement of a dial pointer, is commonly a Bourdon tube but can be a bellows or diaphragm assembly.

(a) *Volumetric types.* The bulb, capillary and measuring element are completely filled, under pressure, with an organic liquid. When the temperature of the bulb is raised the liquid expands and the increased volume actuates the calibrated measuring element.

The temperature limits within which a liquid system can be used range from approximately $-50°C$ to $+400°C$, and spans of about $15°C$ up to $150°C$ are obtainable. A span greater than $150°C$ becomes non-linear.

The use of a mercury-filled system will increase the upper temperature limit to approximately $550°C$ and the minimum span to about $25°C$.

(b) *Pressure types.* The system is partially filled with a volatile liquid. A rise in temperature will increase the vapour pressure and the increased pressure actuates the calibrated measuring element.

There are a number of different classes of vapour pressure instruments designed for specific temperature ranges, the principal difference being the ratio of liquid to vapour used.

The temperature limits of a vapour pressure instrument are more restricted than those of a volumetric system ($-15°C$ to $+250°C$) and the response is non-linear, the graduation being wider at the higher temperature end of the scale. Thus, at the top end of the scale a higher discrimination can be obtained, which for a particular application can be advantageous.

Gas-filled systems will cover a wide range of temperatures from about $-200°C$ to $+550°C$ but the minimum span is restricted to about $50°C$.

(c) *General considerations.* Compared with electrical temperature measuring devices the sensor is considerably larger and the bulb can vary from about $\frac{3}{8}$ in diameter $\times 2$ in long to $\frac{3}{4}$ in diameter $\times 10$ in (9.5×51 mm–19×254 mm). The actual size is governed by the temperature span required and the filling medium used. This comparatively large size will limit its application and will also increase the response time.

In case of leaks or breakages the type of filling medium that is used must be considered and Table 1 gives a list of those which may be found in commercial instruments.

The maximum length of the capillary tubing can vary from a few feet to more than 200 ft (61 m) and depends upon the type of instrument and the application.

The overrange, i.e. the excess temperature that can be tolerated without damage to the filled system, is generally of the order of 100% except for the vapour pressure instrument which has a very small overrange. This is of particular importance where in-place cleaning or sterilizing systems are used.

Unless special compensated systems are used, wide changes of the ambient temperature conditions surrounding the capillary and measuring element of the volumetric type can cause considerable errors. Thus the siting of these components adjacent to boilers or other sources of high temperature should be avoided.

The advantages of a filled bulb temperature system are that it requires no external power supply, is generally robust and is comparatively inexpensive although failure usually means a new complete system.

TABLE 1. Temperature bulb filling mediums.

Volumetric	Vapour Pressure
Alcohol	Toluene
Xylene	Iso-propyl alcohol
Mercury	Ethyl alcohol
Creosote	Sulphur Dioxide
	Methyl Chloride
	Ethane
	Propane
	Methyl Ether
	Ethyl Chloride
	Chlorobenzene
	Freon
	Methyl Bromide
	Butane

2. Thermocouples

If two dissimilar metals or alloys are joined at two points to form a circuit a current will flow if the two junctions are at different temperatures. A thermocouple temperature measuring system consists basically of two insulated dissimilar metal wires joined together at the active end while the other end is connected to an instrument that will measure millivolts.

Since a thermocouple measures the difference between the temperature at the measuring junction and that at the reference, or cold, junction connected to the instrument, it follows that the reference junction must be kept at a constant temperature. In the laboratory the reference junction is often placed in melting ice and the e.m.f. generated by thermocouples over a temperature range are referred to 0°C in the standard tables used.

For industrial use the reference junction is either placed in an electrically heated oven of known constant temperature or ambient changes at the junction of the thermocouple with the measuring instrument are automatically, mechanically or electrically, compensated.

The metals used for thermocouples can be divided into two groups consisting of base metals and rare metals (the rare metals such as platinum and rhodium are more suitable for high temperatures, above say 500°C). The principal base metal thermocouples used in food processing applications are Copper/Constantan, which can be used over a temperature range of from

−250°C to +400°C (although continuous use at temperatures above about 300°C will result in a shorter life owing to copper oxidization), Iron/Constantan and Chromel/Constantan which have a range of from −200°C to +850°C. Chromel is the generally used name for a Nickel/Chromium alloy.

The temperature e.m.f. characteristics of the base metal thermocouples are almost linear above ambient but vary in sensitivity; for example, at 100°C a Copper/Constantan couple generates approximately 4·2 mV, Iron/Constantan 5·3 mV and Chromel/Constantan 6·3 mV, with a 0°C reference junction.

Although most manufacturers supply thermocouples well within the tolerances set out in the appropriate British Standard Code (B.S. 1041) it is as well to note that the latter quotes tolerances of ±1°C from 0 to 100°C, ±3°C from 0 to 300°C and ±3°C from 0 to 400°C for the above mentioned thermocouples. For accurate temperature measurement the suppliers will, at additional cost, either use selected lengths of wire or provide a calibration certificate.

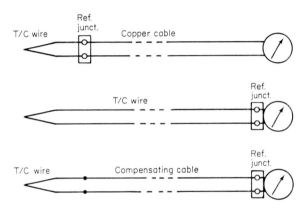

FIG. 1. Connections where the thermocouple is remote from the measuring instrument.

A bare, fine gauge wire thermocouple will have the quickest response time to temperature changes but for reasons of hygiene and protection from damage most industrial couples are either sealed in a metal sheath or placed in pockets which project into the measured medium. Any such protection will increase the thermal time-lag and result in a longer response time.

A number of suitable instruments may be used to measure the thermocouple mV, varying from a simple moving coil galvanometer to an electronic servo potentiometric recorder controller.

Where the measuring instrument is at a considerable distance from the thermocouple the reference junction can be situated near to the couple and copper wired cable used to complete the circuit from the reference to the instrument. Alternatively, special compensating cable may be used to connect the couple to the reference junction at, or within, the instrument (Fig. 1) Both copper and compensating cables are of low resistance to reduce losses and can have thick robust insulation to resist mechanical damage.

3. Electrical Resistance Thermometers

The principle of this type of thermometer is the measurement of the electrical resistance of a conductor which varies with temperature. Two types of sensor will be considered, the resistance bulb and the thermistor.

(a) *Resistance Bulb.* This consists of a length of wire wound on a bobbin or former and usually enclosed in a sealed metal sheath or bulb for protection against corrosion and mechanical damage. Wire of pure platinum or nickel is generally used because of the high degree of stability and reproducibility obtained with these metals.

Nickel wound sensors are suitable for temperatures from about $-230°C$ to $+350°C$ and platinum up to $600°C$. Under certain conditions special platinum sensors can be used to extend the range to above $1000°C$.

Industrial sensors are generally encased in a hermetically sealed stainless steel sheath of $\frac{1}{4}$ in (6·35 mm) diameter and in a range of standard lengths from 3 in to 36 in (76–914 mm) long. The sensitive part of the sensor is usually the first inch from the tip. For certain applications sensors about $\frac{1}{8}$ in (3·18 mm) diameter and $\frac{1}{2}$ in (12·7 mm) long are obtainable.

The response time can vary from about 1 sec upwards depending upon the size and type of encapsulation.

British Standard 1904 quotes two grades of accuracy. For example, with Grade I at $100°C$ the tolerance should be equivalent to approximately $\pm0·2°C$ and and with Grade II $\pm0·5°C$.

The change of resistance resulting from the temperature change of the sensor is usually measured by a Wheatstone bridge circuit. Most industrial instruments use either a moving coil galvanometer to measure the out-of-balance current of the bridge or a servo self-balancing system. The latter system senses the out-of-balance condition and automatically adjusts the bridge to restore balance, the required adjustment being displayed on an indicator or recorder chart as a temperature reading.

The sensor and measuring instrument may be hundreds of feet apart, being connected by normal rubber- or plastic-covered copper cable. With the basic circuit shown in (Fig. 2a), the connecting cable is included in the resistance measurement of the sensor, thus temperature variations along this cable would result in a varying resistance which would be erroneously indicated as a change in sensor temperature. The effect of varying lead resistance can be eliminated by using a 3 or 4 wire system where the leads are connected in opposite arms of the bridge network (Fig. 2b).

(b) *Thermistor.* The thermistor is a temperature sensitive resistor manufactured from metal oxides. It has a negative temperature coefficient, i.e. the resistance decreases with increase in temperature, but has a non-linear response, obeying an exponential law.

The thermistor is manufactured in a number of different forms and for temperature measurements can range from a bead, barely visible to the naked eye, to a disc element of ½ in diameter or more. The bead is hermetically sealed by encapsulating in glass or epoxy resin and may be fitted into a large variety of probes. The small size of the thermistor can result in a short response time but this is modified by the encapsulation and type of probe.

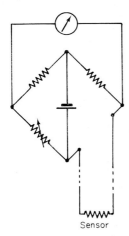 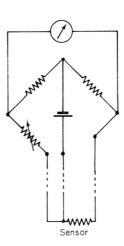

FIG. 2a. Basic 2 wire resistance bulb system.   FIG. 2b. 3 wire system.

The operating temperature range extends from −100°C to over +300°C but certain types of thermistors are restricted to 150°C. The thermistor is an extremely sensitive device and, for a restricted range temperature, differences of less than 0·001°C can be measured.

Resistance values can range from tens of ohms to tens of millions of ohms although for general temperature applications values of from 1 to 10 KΩ are more commonly used. This comparatively high resistance allows considerable flexibility in the length and type of connection between sensor and measuring instrument.

In the last few years very considerable advances have been made in the accuracy and stability of the thermistor, and beads are now available which have repeatable resistance/temperature characteristics to a tolerance of

±0·25% (thus obviating the need to calibrate replacement probes), and a stability equivalent to better than 0·1°C per annum can be expected.

The measuring instrument invariably takes the form of a Wheatstone bridge circuit similar to that used for resistance bulbs.

Although the thermistor has a non-linear response the measuring instrument can be designed to give a linear output over a limited range. For most applications this range is limited to about 50°C for an acceptable accuracy and sensitivity although recent work using a multi-sensor probe has shown that a high degree of linearity over a range of 100°C is possible.

B. Flow Metering

The main types of liquid flow meters can be classified by their operating principles into the following groups:
1. Positive Displacement Meter
2. Velocity Meter
3. Differential Pressure Meter
4. Variable Area Meter

1. Positive Displacement Meters

In these flow meters precise and separate quantities of the liquid are counted as they pass through the meter. This type is the most widely used flow meter in the food industry. It can be considered, in principle, as a pump that is being driven by the flowing liquid instead of driving it. The moving member can be a piston, lobe, vane or disc and may rotate, oscillate or nutate; the movement is transmitted either mechanically by a shaft or electrically by a magnetically operated system.

Owing to their mechanical construction and the fine clearances involved, positive displacement meters are not suitable for metering slurries unless the solid matter is of very small particle size.

Since this type of meter counts specific quantities of liquid, it is very suitable for batch dispensing systems.

2. Velocity Meters

The velocity meter measures the velocity of the flowing liquid, the volume passed being equal to the velocity times the cross-sectioned area of the flow p ath.

The most widely known velocity meter is the turbine. It consists of a rotor mounted on bearings such that its axis lies in the direction of flow and the force of the flowing liquid on the helical blades of the rotor causes it to rotate. The speed of rotation can be measured either electronically or mechanically and indicated on a dial calibrated in rate of flow or integrated on a revolution counter.

Although this is not recommended, the turbine meter can be used with slurries providing a loss of accuracy can be tolerated.

A meter that can be used with slurries and pastes, as well as with liquids, is the electromagnetic flow meter and it is also unaffected by variation in viscosity and density. It employs the same magnetic principles as the dynamo, i.e., an e.m.f. is generated in a conductor that is moving through a magnetic field.

The meter consists of a short length of pipe lined with insulating material and the magnetic field is produced by current fed to coils fitted to the outside of the pipe. The liquid, a conductor, flows through this magnetic field and generates an e.m.f. which is detected by two electrodes fitted in the lining of the pipe, at diametrically opposite positions. The e.m.f. is amplified and fed to an indicator or recorder and can be used for control purposes. A major advantage of this meter is that it affords an unobstructed passage to the flowing liquid.

3. Differential Pressure Meters

The differential pressure meter measures the pressure drop or differential across a restriction in a pipeline. On passing through the restriction the liquid is forced to accelerate by the reduction in bore and this causes a drop in pressure on the downstream side of the restriction.

The most common form of D.P. meter uses an orifice plate which consists of a thin metal plate, the order of $\frac{1}{8}$ in (3·18 mm) thick, having a central hole which has a chamfered edge. This plate is clamped between flanges such that the hole is concentric with the bore of the pipe. Small holes are drilled at specified distances upstream and downstream of the orifice plate and small bore pipes connect these holes, or pressure tappings, to a differential pressure detecting device.

The orifice plate is not suitable for slurries, as a build-up of solid matter at the plate will alter the flow pattern and cause inaccurate readings.

The Venturi flow meter may be considered as an orifice plate having conical sections on both sides of the orifice or throat. The conical sections reduce the energy loss caused by turbulence and thus there is less pressure loss than with a simple orifice plate. Providing the suspended solids are of a form that will not deposit on the sides of the conical sections the Venturi may be used for slurries.

The orifice plate and Venturi are basically steady state devices and because of the square-root relationship between the differential pressure and the rate of flow, the average of a fluctuating differential pressure does not give a true measurement of flow.

The differential pressure is converted into an electric or pneumatic signal by the use of a diaphragm or bellows type transducer.

4. *Variable Area Meters*

In the differential pressure meter there is a fixed restriction or orifice and the flow is measured by the differential pressure across it. In the variable area meter there is a variable annular orifice and a relatively constant pressure differential. A movable restriction takes up a position that depends on the equilibrium of a retaining force and the force due to the flow of liquid.

The most widely used meter of this type is more generally known as a "Rotameter" and consists of a float contained in a tapered tube which is mounted vertically with the wider end to the top. The float takes up a position in the tube such that the upward force of the liquid flowing through the annular orifice equals the downward gravitational force of the float and for this reason the meter should always be mounted in a vertical position.

In the smaller types the tube is made of glass and the position of the float can be read off a scale calibrated in units of rate of flow. When the liquid is opaque and the float cannot be observed. or when a recording or control signal is required, a magnetically linked follower can be connected to a suitable transducer.

Slurries can be metered providing the solids are in a finely divided state and in a form that will not build up a deposit on the float or tube.

C. Weighing

The efficient control of the weight of an ingredient or product invariably requires the use of a transducer to provide an electrical or pneumatic signal related to that weight. The transducer can either be designed as an integral part of the weighing mechanism or can be attached to an existing system.

Any attachment to a weighing machine must not restrict or load the mechanism to a degree that will impair the required accuracy. A photoelectric device, being a non-contacting transducer, is used successfully for this purpose and is fitted to the dial of a weighing machine so that the scale pointer obstructs the beam of light when the required weight is indicated. A number of these devices can be fitted at various positions on the scale and the resulting signals used to start or stop the material feed mechanisms. Transducers such as magnetically operated reed switches, inductive proximity switches or pneumatic devices can be used in place of the photo-electric method.

Another method is to fit a low friction precision rotary potentiometer or variable resistor to the pointer shaft of the weighing machine. The wiper blade of the potentiometer will follow the pointer and the change in electrical resistance will correlate with the indicated weight. An electrical signal can be obtained from the resistance change and can be used to operate feed devices.

The most commonly used direct weight transducer is the strain gauge load cell from which can be obtained an electrical signal that is proportional to the weight or load applied to it.

A strain gauge consists of a grid of very fine resistance wire bonded on to a thin impregnated paper backing and when the grid is subjected to tension or compression the resistance of the wire changes.

The load cell consists of a steel billet or ring that is deformed (elastically) by the force applied to it. Two pairs of strain gauges are firmly bonded to the billet so that they are compressed or elongated by the deformation that results from the applied weight. The unit is enclosed in a very robust hermetically sealed casing.

The strain gauges are electrically connected in the form of a Wheatstone bridge and for industrial use a self balancing servo system is incorporated which drives an indicator dial and provides an electrical control signal. This type of load cell is capable of weighing to an accuracy of better than 0·25 %.

Other types of load cells measure the pressure developed within a pneumatic or hydraulic capsule by the applied weight.

The metering by weight of materials into a vessel may be carried out automatically and continuously in a number of ways. Perhaps the simplest method is the use of a container mounted on a weighing machine, or load cells, such that when the material flowing into the container has reached a pre-set weight the feed is cut off and a valve in the base of the container opens to deposit the contents. When the container is empty, as determined either by a time control or by weight, the valve is closed and the feed restarted for another batch.

By starting and stopping different feed valves at specified container weights a number of ingredients of varying weights may be metered into the container before emptying.

Where the metering of ingredients from a number of large hoppers is required, a weighing machine under each hopper and feeding on to a conveyor belt can be used. To save on the number of weighing machines an automatic system comprising a weigh trolley, which runs underneath the hopper outlets, has been used. The trolley stops at each hopper sequentially, controls the operation of the feed valves and automatically empties its load at the end of the cycle.

In the direct weighing of a vessel and its contents the tare weight of the vessel will affect the accuracy to which the contents may be weighed and should be kept as low as possible. For example, if with a load cell system capable of weighing to an accuracy of $\pm\frac{1}{2}\%$ 50 lb (22·7 kg) of product is contained in a vessel weighing 100 lb (45·4 kg), the obtainable accuracy is $\pm\frac{1}{2}\%$ of 150 lb ($\frac{3}{4}$ lb) and not $\pm\frac{1}{2}\%$ of 50 lb ($\frac{1}{4}$ lb).

The dispensing of a specific quantity of a foodstuff into a container may require very accurate weight control and a large number of filling machines incorporate a weighing system for this purpose. Poor weight control can arise from variations in the weight of the empty container. To overcome this difficulty automatic systems are available which measure the tare weight of the container and control the filling machine by deducting this weight from the weight of the filled container. Such a system can also be used to avoid inaccuracies caused by product spillage and build-up on a weigh platform.

Where a continuously metered flow of powder or granular material is required a weigh belt feeder may be used. A common example of this machine consists of a short conveyor belt that is supported, complete with its rollers, on knife edges at the centre line of the discharge end pulley. The material to be metered falls on the belt from an overhead chute or hopper and the load on the belt is transmitted through a lever to a scale beam which is counterbalanced by adjustable poise weights. Movement of the scale beam about the balance position is detected by photo-electric units which transmit signals to a mechanism that controls the feed rate of the material falling on to the belt. Control of the feed rate may be achieved by varying the opening of a hopper gate, by varying the speed of the belt, or by varying the current to an electromagnetic vibrator attached to a (near horizontal) chute.

Weigh belt feeders are capable of supplying a metered flow of material to an accuracy of better than $\pm 1\%$.

D. Level Detectors

The level of a material in a vessel or hopper may be required for a number of reasons. For example: level indication for stock control of material in silos or large hoppers; to prevent under- or over-fill of a container; to meter specific quantities of different materials into a mixing vessel.

A number of level detectors can be used with liquids or solids although the use of a level detector for a quantitative measurement of solids is limited because of the variable surface configuration that usually results under filling or emptying conditions.

The most commonly used method of liquid level control is a float actuated valve or switch. When used in the right application it is very reliable and is capable of controlling the level to a high degree of accuracy.

For use with solids the equivalent to a float switch is a device which consists of a lightly driven paddle-wheel fitted inside the vessel. Whereas the wheel will turn freely in air the resistance of a solid will prevent rotation and this latter action is transmitted as an alarm or control signal.

Another simple on–off level detector for solids is a diaphragm pressure switch fitted in the wall of the vessel. The pressure of the material forces in the diaphragm against a light spring or counterweight and this movement actuates a microswitch.

The pressure owing to the hydrostatic head of a liquid can be used to indicate continuously the level existing within a vessel. A sensitive direct pressure gauge can be used with open vessels, and a differential pressure system for a closed or pressurized vessel. This type of level detector is only suitable for liquids of constant specific gravity.

Where the temperature of a liquid is above or below ambient a temperature sensor can be used for on–off level indication or control. The sensitive yet simple thermistor probe indicator is being used successfully in this application.

The electrical conductivity of a liquid is utilized to control the level at one or more specific points. The vessel is fitted with one or more electrodes at different levels and the liquid completes a low voltage circuit to operate a control system. The electrodes are installed vertically from an insulated support so that their lower ends are situated at the required levels. If made of metal the vessel itself can be used as a common return path for the electrical circuit.

The electrical capacitance type level probe is being used increasingly both for discrete and for continuous systems.

In the simplest system a metal probe forms one plate of a condenser and the wall of the vessel the other plate. For discrete level control a short probe projecting from the side of the vessel, can be used whereas for continuous measurement the probe is mounted in a vertical position and is sufficiently long to cover the depth over which the measurement is required. Let us consider a continuous system and a non-conducting material; with the vessel empty, or with the probe uncovered, the capacitance between probe and vessel is low, being dependent upon the dielectric constant of air. As the level in the vessel rises the air between probe and wall is gradually replaced by a material of higher dielectric constant and the capacitance is thus gradually increased. This increase is measured electrically and the resultant signal displayed as a measurement of level. With a conducting liquid the probe is covered with an insulating coating but the working principle is effectively the same as above. Modern capacitance level detectors have the transistorized electronics built into the head of the probe, thus allowing the indicators to be hundreds of yards away and probes of 100 ft (30 m) or more in length are used for continuous level measurement in silos. These long probes usually take the form of an insulated steel cable anchored at the top and bottom of the silo.

The obstruction of a beam of energy by the material is a well known method of level detection and sources of light, ultrasonic sound and nuclear radiation are commonly used in these detectors.

A system consisting of a lamp, focusing lenses and photoelectric cell is low priced and is capable of a high degree of discrimination of level but it is not suitable for dusty, dirty or steamy ambient conditions.

An ultrasonic generator and receiver is more costly but is only affected by extreme ambient conditions. The generator alone can be used by employing the damping effect caused by the presence of material on the vibrating surface of the head.

A radioactive system is relatively expensive but has the advantage that, particularly when used to detect the level of dense material, both source and detector can be installed outside the walls of the vessel and is thus unaffected by high temperatures or corrosive conditions that may exist within the vessel.

By suitable positioning of source and detector both the light and ultrasonic systems can be used to measure the level within a vessel by detecting reflected energy from the surface of the material.

E. Moisture

The measurement and control of the moisture content of most foodstuffs is of great importance and until recent years there were very few reliable and accurate continuous measuring installations.

The methods of moisture measurement that can give an almost instantaneous reading and are thus suitable for use in a continuous measuring system fall into two main categories:

(1) Electrical methods
(2) Absorption methods

1. Electrical Methods

The electrical characteristics of a substance are altered by a change in moisture content and the two that have been used for moisture measurement are conductivity and capacitance.

(a) Conductivity. The electrical conductivity of a foodstuff increases with an increase in moisture content but unfortunately the conductivity is influenced by other constituents; changes in the salt or acid content, for example, will have a very large effect. However, provided a high order of accuracy is not required it is possible to measure the conductivity of a flowing liquid and to relate this measurement to the moisture content.

In the simplest form a source of constant voltage is connected to two electrodes between which the material is flowing, and the resultant current, which is dependent upon the conductivity, is measured. With this form of measurement it is essential that the electrodes are in good electrical contact with the flowing material and for this reason the method is more suitable for liquids than for powders or granular material.

An alternative method of measuring the conductivity of liquids or slurries that avoids the possible fouling or corrosion of the electrodes is the use of two coils surrounding a non-conducting length of pipe. The coils are spaced apart and act in a similar manner to an electrical transformer with the liquid acting as the conducting "iron" core. Thus if an alternating current is passed through one coil a similar current will be induced in the second coil and the value of the induced current is dependent upon the conductivity of the liquid between them.

Since the conductivity of a material is temperature sensitive, a constant temperature or automatic compensation is required.

(b) *Capacitance.* The principle of the capacitance moisture meter is based upon the difference in dielectric constant of a material in its dry and moisture-containing states.

Whereas the dielectric constant of most organic materials is in the range of 2–5, in the dry state, the value for water is approximately 80. Thus a small addition of water to the dry material will make a considerable difference to its dielectric constant.

As its name implies the capacitance moisture meter measures the electrical capacitance of the material placed between the metal plates of a measuring cell. In the most common form of meter the cell is connected in an arm of a capacitance measuring bridge network that is energized by a radio frequency oscillator.

For a given configuration of the cell plates the capacitance depends upon the dielectric constant of the material between the plates. Thus:

$$\text{Capacitance} = C\,K\,A/D$$
$$\text{where } C = \text{a constant}$$
$$K = \text{dielectric constant}$$
$$A = \text{area of plates}$$
$$D = \text{distance between the plates}$$

The meter must be calibrated against samples of known moisture content.

In a continuous measuring system the cell plates may be fitted in opposite walls of a duct or pipe made of electrical insulating material. Alternative types of cell configuration are plates formed as spaced rings round a pipe or flat concentric ring plates over which passes a flowing stream of powder or granular material. An interesting development is the Foxboro-Yoxall sensing head (Fig. 3) shaped like a ski which rides on the surface of granular material being conveyed on a belt. One plate is horizontal and lies on the top of the material and the other is vertical, like the keel of a yacht, and is immersed in the material.

The conductance of the material being measured will influence the reading of a capacitance moisture meter but the effect will depend upon the quantity and variation of the electrolyte present in the material.

As a general rule the accuracy of a capacitance meter tends to deteriorate at moisture content levels of above 20–25%.

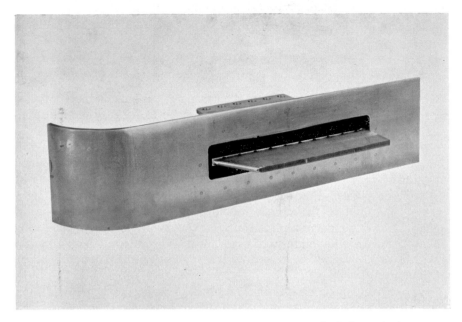

FIG. 3a. Foxboro-Yoxall "ski" moisture measuring head. Underneath view.

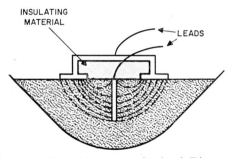

FIG. 3b. Foxboro-Yoxall "ski" moisture measuring head. Diagrammatic cross-section.

As the dielectric constant of most materials will change with temperature, suitable precautions must be taken.

2. Absorption Methods

Over the past few years considerable work has been carried out on methods that measure the quantity of a specific form of radiated energy that is absorbed by the moisture contained in a foodstuff. The most successful are those using microwaves and infra-red radiation where accurate and reliable continuous measuring systems have been developed.

(a) *Microwave.* The microwave region of the radio frequency spectrum lies at the higher frequency end where the wavelength is measured in centimetres.

The disposition of the electrons of a water molecule are such that it can be considered as a dipole having a positive charge at one end and a negative charge at the other. If placed in an electric field the dipole will orient itself such that the negative end of the dipole faces the positive side of the field and vice versa. When the electric field is alternating the dipole will change its orientation at the same frequency and the energy required to overcome molecular friction is absorbed by the electric field. In a low frequency field the dipoles follow the alternations easily and very little energy is absorbed, but as the frequency is increased more and more energy is absorbed until a maximum is reached in the microwave frequency band at a wavelength of approximately 3 cm. If the frequency is increased still further the dipole is unable to follow the rapidly changing field and the absorbed energy gradually decreases.

The unit of attenuation, which is a measure of the energy absorption, is the decibel (db) and is defined as:

$$db = 10 \log_{10} \frac{\text{input energy}}{\text{output energy}}$$

The attenuation of water is much greater than that of most dry materials and this is the basis of the microwave method of moisture determination.

The whole spectrum of radio frequencies is divided into internationally agreed frequency bands which are allocated for communication and industrial uses. Two frequency bands are used for moisture meters, namely X band covering 8·2 to 12·4 GHz/s and S band covering 2·6 to 3·95 GHz/s, where 1 GHz $= 10^9$ Hz.

The relation between wavelength λ in cm and frequency f in cycles per second is given by $\lambda = (3 \times 10^{10})/f$, thus a wavelength of 3 cm corresponds to a frequency of 10 GHz/s.

The moisture measurement is carried out by transmitting a beam of microwave energy, from an oscillator of constant frequency and power output,

18

through the moisture containing material to a receiver. The degree of attenuation is displayed on an indicator or recorder connected to the receiver output.

To avoid confusion with microwave heating application it should be noted that powers of 20–30 milliwatts are used in moisture measuring systems, which is approximately one-fiftieth of that required to light a torch bulb.

Fig. 4. B.F.M.I.R.A. microwave cell for use with liquids.

Microwave energy cannot be transmitted through ordinary wire conductors, and waveguides, which are hollow metal pipes of rectangular section, are used to connect the transmitter and receiver to the measuring cell.

The measuring cell can take a number of different forms which, although apparently simple, can involve complex design considerations for an efficient system. A cell (Fig. 4) that has been used successfully for liquid products consists of a pipe section with waveguides attached at diametrically opposite positions. "Windows" made of material that is transparent to microwave radiation, such as PTFE or Perspex, prevent the liquid in the pipe from entering the waveguide.

Another cell (Fig. 5) used for granular materials consists of a metal duct of rectangular section having waveguide horns set in its narrow sides. The horns spread the microwave radiation over a greater area to cover a larger sample of the product. The cell is lined on its longer sides with a special material that absorbs spurious reflected microwave radiation which could give rise to incorrect results. Perspex windows are used to prevent the material from entering the horns.

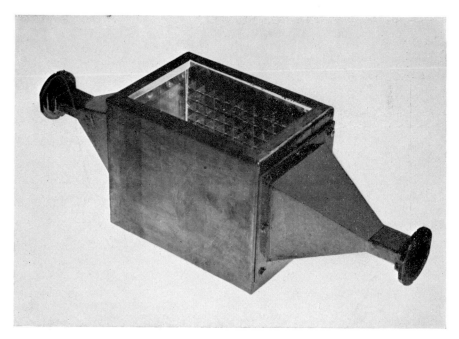

FIG. 5. B.F.M.I.R.A. microwave cell for use with granular materials.

A microwave system must be calibrated with samples of known moisture content and since the attenuation is temperature dependent, temperature compensation must be applied. The British Food Manufacturing Industries Research Association has designed a control unit that will automatically compensate for temperature variations over a very wide range and which also has range expansion facilities to enable the important section of the moisture content range to be displayed.

Microwave systems can continuously measure the moisture content of a wide variety of liquid and granular foodstuffs and are capable of measuring changes of $0\cdot1\%$ moisture content.

Although theoretically it is possible, using microwave, to measure moisture contents from parts per million up to 100%, there are practical limitations at both ends of the scale. To obtain an acceptable accuracy of measurement there are upper and lower limits to the amount of water that the microwave system can measure. This means that with materials having a low moisture content the sample thickness is large and for high moisture it is small. In addition the design of a cell for continuous measurement at high moistures is very complex and present systems are limited to about 45% moisture content. However, development work, using different microwave measurement techniques, is being carried out in order to extend considerably this upper moisture limit.

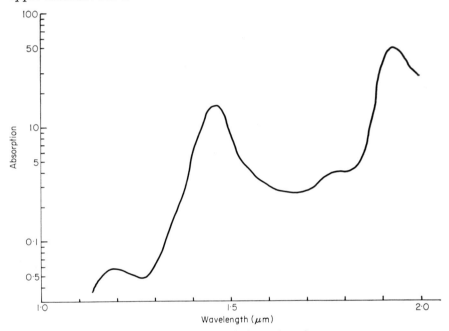

FIG. 6. The near infra-red absorption of water.

The laboratory measurement of discrete samples is less restricted and moisture contents between the range of 0·05% and 80% have been measured.

(b) *Infra-red.* In the 1–2 μm band of the infra-red spectrum there are wavelengths that are strongly absorbed by water (Fig. 6), one of the principal wavelengths being 1·93 μm. The basis of the infra-red method of moisture determination is the measurement of the quantity of radiation absorbed by the water contained in the material under test.

A beam of radiation of 1·93 μm wavelength is projected on to the materia and the proportion that is reflected from the surface will depend upon the amount absorbed by the water. The reflected radiation is measured by a photo-cell and after amplification a signal is displayed on an indicator or recorder. As the surface optical characteristics of the material will affect the degree of reflection a similar measurement is also carried out at a wavelength (1·7 μm) that is not absorbed by water and the two measurements are compared to give a reading that can be calibrated with reference to samples of known moisture content.

As the infra-red penetrates to only a short distance (the actual value depending upon the density of the material) a consistent moisture distribution through the sample is essential for an accurate determination.

The instrument (Fig. 7) consists of a separate measuring head and control unit connected by a cable. Thus the control unit with its indicator or recorder

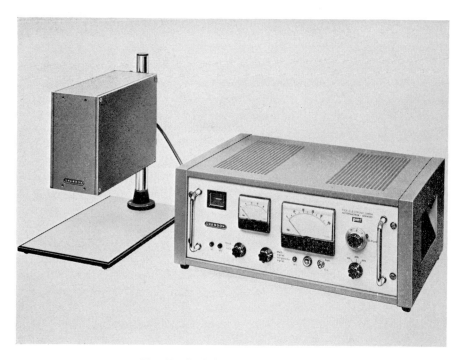

FIG. 7. Pier infra-red moisture meter.

can be situated at a central control point with the head situated some distance away on the process line.

A typical application of the instrument is its use with a conveyor belt where the hermetically sealed measuring head is mounted approximately $4\frac{1}{2}$ in (114·3 mm) above the surface of the material on the belt. Immediately in front of the head it is usual to fit a "plough" which levels off the material to the correct height and presents freshly exposed material for measurement.

The infra-red moisture meter has been found to be most successful with powdered materials such as starch, icing sugar and dried soup powders where a discrimination of better than 0·1 % moisture can be obtained. It can cover a range of moisture contents from approximately 0·5% to 25% and by the use of different infra-red wavelengths, moisture contents in excess of 25% can be measured.

The moisture meter is not suitable for very dark materials or for those having a highly reflecting surface.

F. Humidity

The three principal methods of measuring humidity are the use of a psychrometer, a hygrometer and a dew-point meter.

1. Psychrometer

The psychrometer consists of two thermometers, one exposed to the atmosphere and the other with its bulb enclosed by a wet wick. When a stream of air is blown over the bulbs the temperature of the wet bulb is lowered owing to the cooling effected by the evaporation of water. The wet and dry bulb temperatures can be converted to a relative humidity reading by referring to a psychometric chart.

In the continuous reading instrument manufactured by the Foster Instrument Co. (Fig. 8) resistance bulb sensors are used to measure the temperatures, one being covered by a wick which is kept continuously wet by a reservoir of distilled water. A small electric fan draws a continuous sample of air through a non-hygroscopic filter and across the sensors. The resistance bulbs are connected to a remote recording/control unit that automatically computes the relative humidity and displays this reading and the dry bulb temperature on a continuous strip chart recorder. As it is essential for accurate results that the wick is kept clean, a variety of different washable filters are available.

Up to six measuring heads may be connected to one multi-point recorder and any head and the recorder can be hundreds of feet apart.

2. Hygrometer

The term hygrometer originally referred to an instrument that depended for its operation on a change in length of a hygroscopic material such as hair or animal membrane. Today this term is used for a measuring instrument that utilizes any hygroscopic material that exhibits a change in state with a change of relative humidity. The hair hygrometer, although a robust instrument when used carefully within its limitations, is not suitable for automatic control.

By using the change in conductivity or capacitance that occurs when a hygroscopic substance absorbs moisture, instruments can be designed to give an electrical output signal. A conductivity element can take a number of different forms but all consist basically of noble metal electrodes between which is an insulator coated with a salt, usually lithium or calcium chloride. The salt becomes more conductive as its absorbs moisture from the air and a thin coating of large surface area is used to achieve a rapid response. The element is temperature sensitive and should therefore either be used at a constant temperature or temperature compensation must be applied.

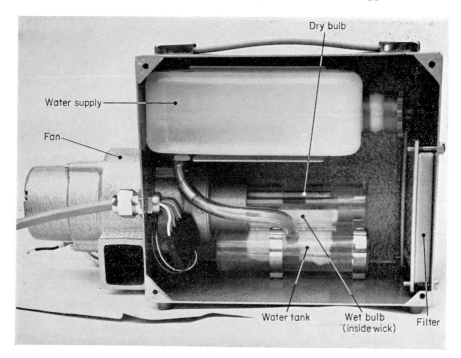

FIG. 8. Foster Instrument Co. R.H. measuring head.

A capacitance element consists of two electrodes and a hygroscopic dielectric. The dielectric material is a very thin layer of aluminium oxide that is formed on to a pure aluminium electrode. The other electrode is usually a thin porous coating of an electrical conducting material such as graphite. When the oxide absorbs or gives up moisture the capacitance of the element changes and this change is measured and calibrated in terms of relative humidity.

As both the conductivity and capacitance elements are very sensitive to contamination, regular checking and calibration is necessary. Both elements can be used with self balancing bridge instruments having recording and control output signals.

3. Dew Point

The dew point is the temperature at which air is saturated with water vapour, i.e. in vapour-pressure equilibrium. It derives its name from the temperature at which a drop of water condenses on to a polished surface that is being gradually cooled.

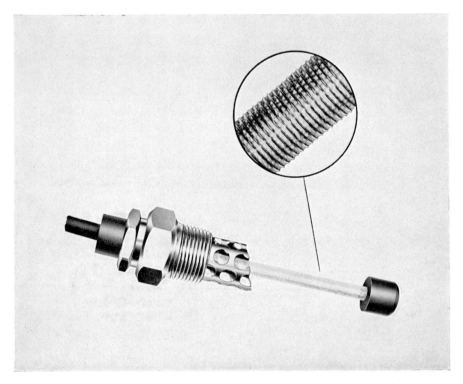

FIG. 9. Foxboro-Yoxall "Dewcell" element.

Although continuous reading instruments using electrical methods of determining the presence of the water droplet have been designed they are not very suitable for industrial applications.

The Foxboro-Yoxall "Dewcel" (Fig. 9), although similar in construction to a conductivity element, measures the "dew point" temperature at which the vapour pressure of a saturated solution of a hygroscopic salt is in equilibrium with the atmosphere. As the equilibrium temperature for a salt solution will be higher than that of the atmosphere this unit is heated, instead of cooled as in the mirror dew point meter.

A resistance bulb temperature sensor is enclosed in a tube which has a woven glass wick, saturated with a lithium chloride solution, wrapped around it. A pair of parallel gold or silver metal wires is wound round the surface of the wick and supplied with 25 V A.C. The heat generated by the current flowing through the salt solution raises the temperature. When the equilibrium temperature is reached the water in the solution evaporates but as the loss of water reduces the conductivity of the solution the current and heat generated is also reduced. Thus a stable condition is reached where the heat input is just sufficient to evaporate the moisture absorbed from the atmosphere. This temperature is measured and the resulting signal used for recording and control.

G. Density, Specific Gravity

The hydrometer float, universally used for the measurement of the specific gravity of liquids, has been adapted for continuous measurement. The float is enclosed in a constant head sampling chamber and the vertical movement

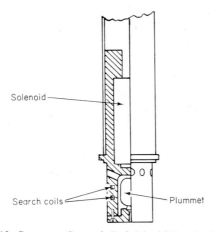

FIG. 10. Sangamo Controls Ltd. Liquid Density Meter.

of the float is measured inductively. At one end of the float is fixed an iron core which forms part of a differential transformer. Vertical movement of the core alters the magnetic coupling of the transformer coils and the resultant signal is amplified before being used to operate a recorder or control system.

Alternatively the movement of the float can be measured with a photoelectric device where a vane attached to the float varies the amount of light passing from a lamp to a photocell.

18*

A sophisticated adaptation of the float principle has been developed in an instrument manufactured by Sangamo Controls Ltd. (Fig. 10) which measures the force required to hold a plummet in a precise position, against the forces acting upon it owing to changes in density.

The spherical, gold plated, ferrous plummet is totally immersed in the liquid to be measured and its density is arranged to be slightly greater than the liquid so that it will always tend to sink. Total immersion prevents errors caused by surface tension. Two search coils fed with a high frequency supply are contained within an epoxy resin baffle surrounding the plummet. The plummet is prevented from sinking by the electromagnetic force of a D.C. solenoid situated directly above it and the search coils, via electronic circuitry, control the current in the solenoid such that the plummet is maintained centrally between the two coils. Thus, if the plummet tends to sink, owing to a decrease in the liquid density, the change is immediately sensed by the search coils which increase the solenoid current to restore the plummet to its original position. The change in solenoid current is measured, amplified and used for recording or control purposes.

Zero suppression and automatic temperature compensation is available and the instrument is suitable for tank or pipeline installations. A by-pass is usually required for pipeline use since, in order to avoid errors caused by liquid flow forces on the plummet, the throughput is limited to a maximum of 15 gal/h (68·2 litres/h).

One of the simplest methods of measuring the specific gravity of a liquid under atmospheric conditions is the use of an air bubbler. This consists of a small bore pipe projecting into a sampling chamber or vessel where a constant liquid level is maintained. The pipe is connected to a regulated air supply and the pressure required just to bubble air into the liquid, as measured on a pressure gauge, is equal to the pressure head of the liquid at the end of the pipe. This pressure is equivalent to the weight of a constant volume of liquid and can be calibrated in terms of specific gravity.

Where a constant liquid level is not possible two pipes can be used, immersed to different depths, and the difference in pressure between the pipes is measured.

The air bubbler is not generally suitable as a method of measuring a narrow range of specific gravity, as such a range constitutes a very small proportion of the total pressure, but this situation can be improved by the use of a range suppression chamber.

An instrument that is widely used in some sections of the food industry is the continuous weighing density meter which under certain conditions is suitable for slurries as well as liquids. It consists of a loop of stainless steel tube, through which the liquid flows, pivoted about flexible connections at the "open" ends of the loop. The loop is connected to a weigh-beam and counterbalanced by adjustable poise weights. A change in specific gravity of the liquid results in a change in the weight of the loop and its contents which is measured by a force-balance system giving an electrical or pneumatic control signal.

The flexible connectors are usually stainless steel bellows which allow pressures of up to 150 p.s.i.g. (1·034 MN/m²) to be used but where hygienic considerations predominate, smooth bore silicone rubber connectors can be used which reduce the sensitivity and limits the pressure to 40 p.s.i.g. (275·8 KN/m²).

Slurries must be pumped through the meter at a rate high enough to prevent the deposition of solids in the loop.

The nucleonic or gamma-ray density gauge was one of the first industrial applications of radioactive isotopes (in 1947) and it operates by measuring the amount of radiation that passes through a constant thickness of the material under test. The measured radiation varies inversely with the density.

A radioactive source, consisting of a radioisotope fitted in a shielded container, and a detector are mounted opposite each other on the outside of a vessel or pipe. The detector may use a Geiger counter, a scintillation counter, or an ionization chamber, depending upon the degree of accuracy required. A Geiger counter detector is the least accurate but, as it requires only simple electronic circuitry, is relatively inexpensive.

As the nucleonic density gauge can usually be clamped on to a pipeline its installation, or removal, requires no disruption of an existing process and there are no cleaning or hygiene difficulties. Today nucleonic instruments achieve a high standard of reliability and stability and require minimum maintenance but periodic calibration is necessary, as the radiation from a source decays at a known and specific rate. The useful life of a source can vary from approximately 2 to 50 years depending upon the radioisotope used.

H. Viscosity

The continuous measurement and control of viscosity is an important factor in the manufacture of a wide range of foodstuffs but until very recently a suitable instrument was not available. The oil industry has used continuous process viscometers for some years but with few exceptions they do not meet the requirements of the food manufacturer. These viscometers have been designed for Newtonian liquids of comparatively low viscosities and generally would not meet the requirements of the food industry with regard to hygienic construction. Most applications of continuous viscosity measurement in the food industry require an instrument that is robust, easily cleaned and designed for non-Newtonian liquids having viscosities ranging from a few poises up to over a thousand poises. Although a few foreign instruments are stated to be suitable for foodstuffs they have been rejected by a number of the larger British food manufacturers for their small sample size and inability to withstand factory conditions. They appear to be adapted laboratory instruments.

Perhaps the three most commonly used methods of measuring the viscosity of discrete samples are:

(a) The time taken for a specific quantity of liquid to flow from a given cup or vessel which has a standard hole or orifice in its base.

(b) The time of descent of a standard size steel ball through the sample.

(c) The measurement of the torque required to rotate the inner cylinder or bob of a co-axial system.

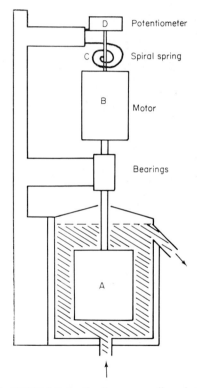

Fig. 11. B.F.M.I.R.A. Continuous reading viscometer.

Since (a) and (b) are not suitable for continuous measurement method (c) has been used in the recent development of a continuous reading viscometer designed for factory use.

This instrument (Fig. 11) consists of a bob or inner cylinder (A) which is rotated at a constant speed, or shear rate, by a motor (B). The motor is mounted such that the motor body is free to rotate on its own longitudinal axis. The motor body is restrained from rotating, owing to reaction torque, by a spiral spring (C) and takes up a position such that the forces from the torque and the spring are balanced. The angular deflection of the motor is measured by a precision potentiometer (D) and the electrical signal obtained from the potentiometer can be used for recording and control and is calibrated in terms of apparent viscosity.

The liquid to be measured flows through the annulus between the inner and outer cylinders, entering at the bottom inlet pipe. The viscometer is kept at a constant temperature by water flowing through the jacket surrounding the outer cylinder but automatic temperature compensation is available to cope with wide variations in the process liquid temperature.

The viscosity range of such an instrument can cover from 0–25 poises up to 1000 poises at a shear rate of any specific value between 10 and 100 sec^{-1}. The accuracy of measurement is approximately $\pm 1\%$ of full scale and a flow rate of up to 2 gal/min (9·08 litres/min) can be accommodated.

A multi-shear rate version of the above viscometer has been developed using an infinitely variable speed motor and an electronic torque transducer fitted in the shaft of the inner cylinder. Viscosities from a few poises up to several thousands can be measured.

I. pH

A pH measuring system consists basically of a measuring electrode, a reference electrode and an instrument to measure the potential between the electrodes.

The measuring electrode consists of a tube having a thin-walled bulb at the bottom made of a special glass. A potential will be developed between the inner and outer surfaces of the bulb if the pH of the liquids in contact with them are different. The inner surface is kept at a constant pH by filling the electrode with a buffer solution, and electrical connection is made through a silver wire coated with silver chloride.

The most commonly used reference electrode consists of a tube containing a saturated solution of potassium chloride. Electrical connection is made through a platinum wire, mercury, and a paste of calomel (mercurous chloride) and potassium chloride. A porous plug in the bottom of the tube completes the connection to the process liquid.

The measuring instrument consists essentially of a stable millivoltmeter having a very high input resistance or impedance. The glass pH electrode has a very high resistance which can be more than 100 MΩ and to avoid any shunting effects the input resistance of the measuring instrument must be at least 1000 times this value to obtain accurate results. This high resistance must be maintained in the insulation of all the electrical connections which include plugs, sockets and interconnecting cables.

As the electrodes are invariably earthed through the process liquid the maintenance of high insulation conditions is essential in an industrial pH installation. The high impedance system is also prone to pick-up of electrical interference signals and care should be taken in the positioning of the electrodes and their connecting cables.

The e.m.f. developed by the electrode system is temperature dependent but automatic temperature compensation is available covering a wide temperature

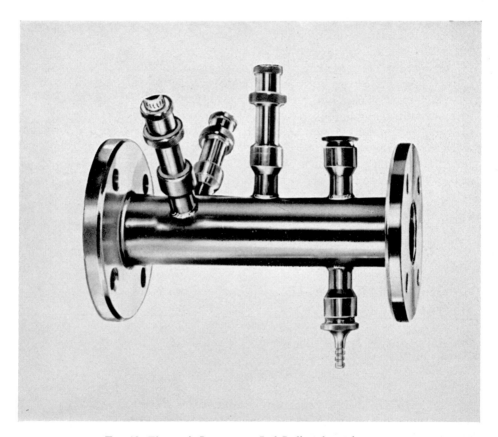

FIG. 12. Electronic Instruments Ltd. In-line electrode system.

range. The temperature is usually measured with a resistance bulb sensor mounted adjacent to the electrodes.

Dip tube electrode assemblies are available to measure the pH of liquids contained in tanks, and to ensure a representative reading the electrodes must be positioned in an area of turbulence, and it is preferable to use an agitator or stirrer to ensure good mixing.

For pipeline installations in-line electrode systems (Fig. 12) can be used which will withstand working pressures of up to 100 p.s.i.g. (689·5 KN/m²).

The deposition of solids on to the electrodes will cause a loss of sensitivity. This coating can sometimes be avoided or reduced by careful positioning of the electrodes within the process and it is usually advantageous to place them in a fast-moving stream of liquid.

Where rapid coating of the electrodes cannot be avoided by other means, ultrasonic in-place cleaning is used and such systems can increase the period for removal of electrodes for cleaning from every 24 h to two or three times a year.

3. REGULATION

A. Actuators

In order to control a process, action must be taken in accordance with the control signal initiated by the measuring system and in the majority of cases this entails the use of an actuator to transform the electrical or pneumatic

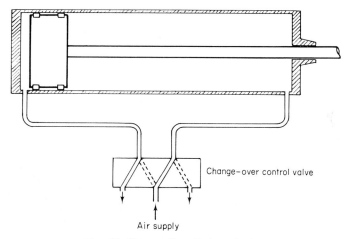

Change–over control valve

Air supply

FIG. 13. Pneumatic cylinder actuator.

signal into a mechanical motion. An exception is where the regulating or control device uses electricity directly, such as an electric heating element. In this case a small electrical signal can, by using thyristors for example, control many kilowatts of electrical heating power without the intervention of any mechanical device.

The power required to operate the actuator may be electric, pneumatic or hydraulic, but as hydraulic actuators are normally used to provide very large forces they will not be considered here.

Actuators can be classified into two categories—those that normally have only two positions, for example one that opens or closes a valve, and those that can be controlled to any intermediate position within their range.

The energy most widely used to operate an actuator is pneumatic power and a common form of two-position actuator, producing a linear motion, is the pneumatic cylinder (Fig. 13). Compressed air, entering at one port, will drive the piston to the other end of the cylinder and when air is supplied to the other port the piston will be driven back. The change-over valve can be operated from a pneumatic or electric control signal.

The vane type two-position actuator (Fig. 14) produces a rotary motion, usually of 90° for rotary valve operation. This is a small, powerful, yet simple

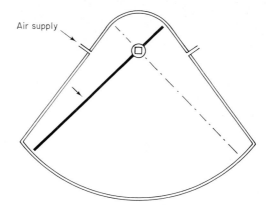

Fig. 14. Vane actuator.

actuator that provides a rotary action without recourse to couplings or gears. The torque obtained is approximately proportioned to the air pressure.

Both the cylinder and vane actuator can be fitted with a spring such that it returns to its de-energized position on removal of the air pressure. The spring return is ideally suited for conditions when an actuator must return to a "fail safe" position on failure of the air supply.

The actuator most extensively used with automatic control valves is the pneumatic diaphragm operator shown in Fig. 15. It consists essentially of a flexible diaphragm, usually made of Neoprene, which divides a pressure-tight circular casing. Attached to the diaphragm is a metal plate into which is fitted an operating shaft or stem. A spring forces the diaphragm assembly to one end of its travel. When a pneumatic control signal (air at 3–15 p.s.i.g. is the usual control range) is fed to the upper section of the casing it drives the diaphragm down until the force is balanced by the spring. Hence the diaphragm and shaft will take up a position that is dependent upon the control signal pressure. The limits of travel are usually arranged to correspond to the upper and lower values of the control signal. By a suitable arrangement of the spring a reverse-acting motion can be achieved such that air pressure on the underside of the diaphragm will lift the shaft. A springless type of diaphragm actuator is also available where the diaphragm takes up a position that depends upon the differential pressure of signals fed to the upper and lower sections of the casing.

Where high friction in a valve, or other actuator-driven device, causes hysteresis and dead band, or where the precise position of the shaft is critical a "valve positioner" is recommended. The valve positioner is, in effect, a controller that compares the actual position of the shaft with the control signal and takes appropriate action if they differ.

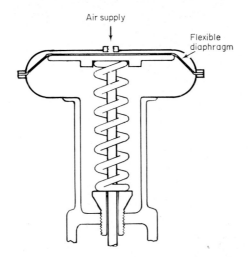

Fig. 15. Diaphragm valve operator.

For the control of pneumatic actuators by an electrical signal, electro-pneumatic transducers are available which will convert an electrical control signal into a pneumatic equivalent.

Electrically powered actuators fall into two categories—solenoid operated types and electric motor driven types.

Solenoid actuators consist of an electro-magnet and an armature and are usually energized with alternating current. They are two-position devices with a comparatively short travel and for this reason are commonly used to operate on–off valves. They are normally spring loaded and can thus be arranged to "fail safe".

By the use of suitable gears and levers the electric motor actuator can produce any rotary or linear motion. As a suitable motor can be stopped or reversed at will, this type of actuator is very suitable for precise position control. On power failure this actuator usually stays at the position it is at, but on the smaller devices a spring return mechanism is often supplied.

B. Valves

There are many different types of valves available for industrial use (the British Valve Manufacturers Association enumerates 39 basic types suitable for fluids), but this section will deal with some of those final control elements that have a wide application to food processing.

The plug valve (Fig. 16) consists of a plug having a hole or port which, when turned through 90°, lines up with ports in the valve body to allow liquid

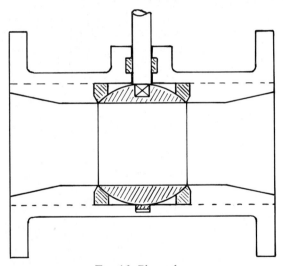

FIG. 16. Plug valve.

to pass. The plug may be of parallel, taper or spherical shape and can have a variety of different port areas and shapes. The plug valve is suitable for high pressures and temperatures and may be steam or water jacketed.

The diaphragm valve (Fig. 17) is well known to the food industry as it is of hygienic design and can be used with liquids, slurries and pulps. Downward pressure forces the flexible diaphragm down on to the valve seat making a tight seal. The body and diaphragm may be lined with rubber, PTFE or other materials.

The pinch valve (Fig. 18) is of simple design, hygienic and especially suitable for handling foodstuffs with the minimum of damage to solids contained in liquids. Foodstuffs such as diced vegetables and jams are typical examples.

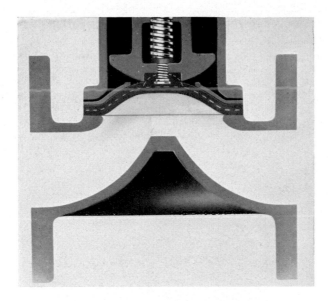

FIG. 17. Saunders diaphragm valve.

The valve consists of a flexible rubber tube contained in a cast metal body. Compressed air, or water, fed into the space between the tube and body compresses the tube to reduce or stop the flow of material. The tube is easily removed for replacement or sterilization.

Another valve that is of particular value to the food industry is the Mucon flexible diaphragm iris-type valve (Fig. 19) that is suitable for handling free-flowing powders, granular materials and slurries. The principle of operation

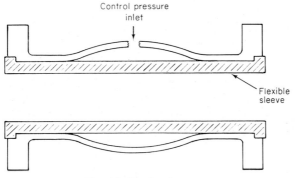

FIG. 18. Pinch valve.

can be appreciated by considering a sleeve of flexible material having metal rings fixed at both ends. If one ring is rotated relative to the other the sleeve will twist, closing up the aperture through the sleeve until at 180° rotation the aperture is completely closed. Nylon is the standard sleeve material but coated fabrics or rubber materials are available. The Mucon valve is limited to a pressure of 15–20 p.s.i.g. (103–138 KN/m²).

The APV Zephyr valve (Fig. 20) is a self-contained unit having both the piston type pneumatically operated actuator and the valve in one stainless steel casing. It is of hygienic design, has been specifically developed to handle

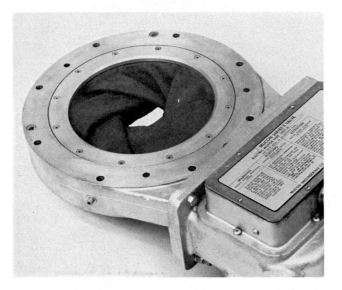

Fig. 19. Mucon iris type diaphragm valve.

liquid foodstuffs and is constructed such that it can be easily dismantled for cleaning or maintenance. The valve head consists of a resilient reinforced rubber disc that ensures a complete seal on to the valve seating.

For a wide range of industrial applications the process control valve (Fig. 21) is used to control automatically, to fine limits, the flow of liquids and gases. Vertical movement of the valve stem, driven from an actuator such as that shown in Fig. 15, varies the size of the orifice through which the fluid can flow. Under conditions of high pressure a considerable force may be required to lift the valve head off its seat and the double-ported valve has been designed to overcome this problem. In this type (Fig. 22) as the pressure acts on both the lower face of one head and the upper face of the other the two forces tend to cancel out. A disadvantage of the double-ported valve is that,

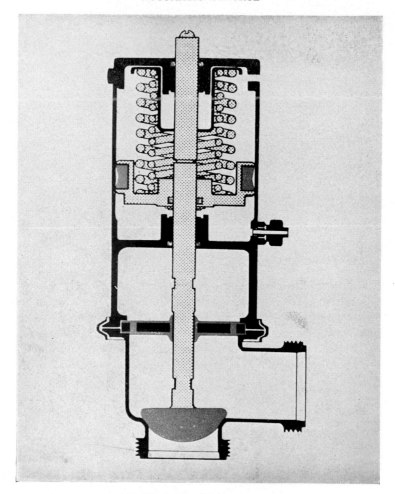

FIG. 20. A.P.V. "Zephyr" valve.

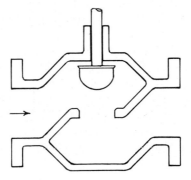

FIG. 21. Single port control valve.

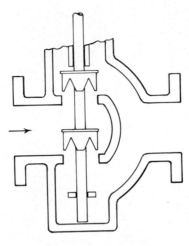

FIG. 22. Double port control valve.

in practice, it is difficult to obtain a tight shut-off. Although the valve heads and seats can be ground to give a tight seal at normal temperature the valve body will expand when it gets hot and a complete seal may no longer be possible. Depending upon the operating conditions this trouble may be overcome by the use of seat inserts of PTFE or other resilient materials. The flow characteristic of a control valve can be defined as the flow rate that results

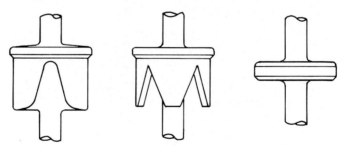

FIG. 23. Control valve heads.

from a specific change or lift of the valve head under conditions of constant pressure drop, both flow rate and valve lift being measured as a percentage of the maximum value. This relationship is usually plotted graphically. The three main control valve characteristics are: equal percentage, linear, and quick-opening and these are principally obtained from the shape of the valve head. Typical heads are shown in Fig. 23. The optimum type of valve characteristic for a particular application will depend upon the control system used and the range of flow rate.

The correct sizing of a control valve is complex, and ideally full knowledge of the flow conditions are required. A common error is the use of a control valve of the same size as the connecting pipeline, whereas for proper control the valve size should very often be smaller than the pipeline. The advice of the valve manufacturer or an experienced control engineer should be obtained before specifying a control valve for a particular application.

4. CONTROL

This section deals with the methods that must be provided to control automatically the regulating device from signals received from the measuring sensor.

Consider the example of an automatic control system shown in Fig. 24 where a heat exchanger, consisting of a steam jacketed tank, is required to maintain a flowing supply of sugar syrup at 150°F (66°C). The temperature of the syrup flowing out of the tank is sensed by, for example, a resistance bulb, which is connected to a controller whose set-point has been adjusted to 150°F. If the temperature of the syrup falls below 150°F the controller senses the difference between the measured temperature and the set-point value and

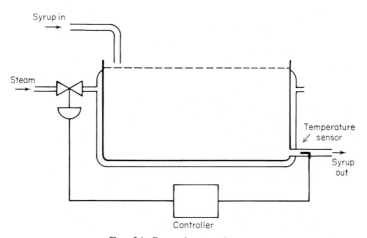

FIG. 24. Syrup heat exchanger.

feeds back an error signal to the actuator which opens the steam valve. Similarly if the temperature of the syrup rises above 150°F the steam valve closes. A control system such as this is called a feedback control loop where the syrup is the controlled medium, the temperature of the syrup the controlled variable, the resistance bulb the primary element and the steam valve the final control element.

In practice the basic control system as described above may not be sufficient, as process characteristics can affect the control action. The most important of these is process lag, i.e. the time taken for the system to stabilize after a change in process conditions. Consider the situation that would arise if the demand for syrup were suddenly increased by an appreciable amount. Initially the temperature at the tank outlet would remain at 150°F as the tank acts as a reservoir of heated syrup. After a time dependent upon the degree of mixing within the tank, the temperature will start to drop. This drop will be sensed by the resistance bulb and the steam valve will open, but, owing to the increased throughput, there is a greater quantity of syrup to heat and this will take extra time. Thus, as a result of these time lags a quantity of syrup will have passed that was at a lower temperature than that specified.

The degree and effect of process lag will depend on the quantity of syrup held in the tank. A large quantity, relative to the throughput, will tend to even out small variations but large changes in the conditions will be more difficult to control. As well as a change in throughput other changes, such as a sudden drop in steam pressure, perhaps caused by a heavy demand in another part of the factory, or a change in temperature of the incoming syrup from a fresh or different supply, will also affect the control. Another temperature process lag is caused by poor thermal conductivity. If for example a steam jacket has a thick coating of scale the heat from the steam will take longer to reach the product. The thermal conductivity of the product must also be considered.

There are a number of different types of control action which vary in complexity according to the application and the degree of accuracy required. The more common modes of control are two-position, proportional, reset (integral) and rate (derivative). A combination of the last three modes can be used, i.e. proportional plus reset, proportional plus rate, or proportional plus reset plus rate, the latter usually being referred to as three-term control, but the rate (derivative) mode cannot be used on its own.

Two-position mode. In two-position control, more commonly known as on–off control, the final control element is moved to either of its extreme positions whenever the controlled variable deviates from the set-point by a specific amount. Between these two positions there is a dead band or neutral zone in which there is no control action. In Fig. 24 two-position control could be arranged such that if, for example, the temperature dropped to 145°F (63°C) the steam valve opens and if it rises to 155°F (68°C) the valve closes. The valve would remain open from 145°F to 155°F and closed from 155°F to 145°F.

With this form of control the temperature will never remain at set-point but will cycle about this value, the upper and lower limits being determined by the width of the dead band. Ideally the temperature would cycle between the dead band values but process lag will cause the temperature limits to extend beyond these values to an extent determined by the process conditions.

Proportional mode. The proportional controller moves the final control element to a specific position for each value of the controlled variable and the relationship is linear. Referring to our syrup heat exchanger the position of the steam valve with regard to temperature could be as that shown in Fig. 25

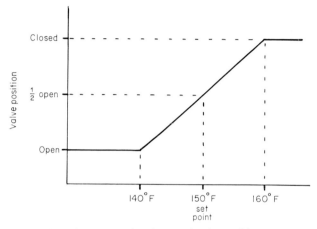

FIG. 25. Proportional control valve positions.

where at 160°F (71°C) the valve is closed, at 140°F (60°C) it is fully open, and at any intermediate temperature the valve takes up a position proportional to that temperature.

The proportional band is the range of the controlled variable over which the proportional action operates and is usually expressed as a percentage of the full scale range of the controller. Thus, in our example, the proportional band is 140°F–160°F, i.e. 20 Fahrenheit degrees, and if the full scale range is 60°F–260°F (16°C–127°C), i.e. 200 Fahrenheit degrees, the proportional band expressed as a percentage would be 20/200 or 10%.

Unfortunately proportional action cannot control load changes as the following explanation will demonstrate. If the throughput of syrup in our example is increased, more steam is required and the steam valve will have to take up a new, more open, position to maintain the temperature at the setpoint. The increased throughput will result initially in a drop in measured temperature and as the temperature drops the valve will open to a degree that depends upon the proportional band characteristics. The temperature will then start to rise but in doing so it will cause the valve to start closing again and this in turn will cause the temperature to drop. Thus there are two opposing conditions which will balance out with the valve taking up a position that results in a final controlled temperature lower than the set-point. This deviation from the set-point is called offset and, other conditions being equal, the wider the proportional band the greater will be the offset. It can be removed manually by resetting the set-point to bring the controlled temperature to the required value.

Reset (*Integral*) *mode.* The reset mode moves the final control element for corrective action at a speed or rate that is determined by the amount that the controlled variable deviates from the set-point. The rate of reset is adjustable and for a given setting the rate is proportional to the deviation. Thus the greater the deviation the faster the control element will move and vice versa, but as it will always move while a deviation exists it will only stop when the controlled variable returns to the set-point value.

As the reset mode carries out automatically the manual action required for proportional control under load change conditions it is frequently used in conjunction with the proportional mode.

Rate (*Derivative*) *mode.* A controller employing a rate mode moves the final control element to a position that is proportional to the rate of change (first derivative) of the deviation. Thus, in our example, the faster the temperature of the syrup changes the more the steam valve is moved to correct this change. The rate mode ensures that rapid corrective action is taken as soon as a deviation occurs and leaves the proportional or proportional plus reset modes to bring the control valve to its final position.

General considerations. To decide on the mode of control required for a particular application requires experience and as much information as possible of the process characteristics. If in doubt it is better to use a controller having more facilities than less. For example, if for a particular application it is considered that proportional plus reset modes may be sufficient it would be wise to use a three term controller to ensure efficient control. The extra cost can be small compared with the results of poor control. It should also be borne in mind that the added rate mode may be essential if at some future date the process is modified.

The following notes are given as a general guide to the process characteristics with which the various control modes, and combinations of these modes, may be used.

Two-position: Minimum process lag time.
Slow and small changes of throughput or load.

Proportional: Small to moderate process lag time.
    Small changes in load.
Proportional plus Reset: Small to moderate process lag time.
    Large, but slow, changes in load.
Proportional plus Rate: Long process lag time.
    Small changes in load.
Proportional plus Reset plus Rate: Long process lag times.
    Large, and fast, changes in load.

Automatic controllers may use pneumatic or electronic operation. Both types of controller have their advantages for particular applications and should be considered in conjunction with the type of sensor and actuator used.

Pneumatic controllers are less expensive but for the smaller installation the cost of producing a clean, dry air supply must be taken into account. Electronic controllers are faster in operation and electric cabling is generally easier and cheaper to instal than pneumatic tubing. This is also important where distance and centralization of instruments at a control panel is concerned. As, at present, the majority of actuators are pneumatically operated an electro-pneumatic converter is required for the electronic system. There is evidence from the larger users of automatic control equipment that there is less maintenance and plant "down" time with electronic systems. Plug-in replaceable electronic units can result in rapid fault clearance and the use of less skilled maintenance staff.

5. FACTORY INSTALLATIONS

Some food manufacturers have appreciated the advantages that can result from the judicious use of automatic control and the following is a brief description of three such cases.

The extensive system recently installed by a biscuit manufacturing company controls the whole mixing process from the bulk storage of ingredients to the mixed dough, and after the selection of the required recipe the operation of the process is automatic. Signals from weighing and flow metering equipment are received at a central control unit which controls the routing and timing of each ingredient. The quantity of each ingredient is automatically recorded and total consumption figures are logged. The plant operation and state of the bulk ingredient stores are displayed on a mimic diagram. The weighing of solids is carried out by the use of load cells fitted to hoppers or by transducers fitted to weighing machine scales and fluids are controlled by flow meters or positive displacement metering pumps.

A large manufacturer of ice cream has used automatic control systems in his factory wherever possible and the following are some of the areas that have been covered. The ice cream ingredients are stored in temperature controlled vessels and the flow of liquids, both into and out of these vessels, is controlled by the use of positive displacement flow meters that give an electrical signal pulse for every 0·1 gal (0·45 litres) that has passed. As there are a large number of alternative recipes for the basic types of mix, the blending of the ingredients is carried out in a continuous batch system. The required ingredient quantities are set up on programme control equipment and the blend is then executed automatically. After passing through an H.T.S.T. pasteurizer and a homogenizer the mix is held, for a predetermined time, at a high temperature by the use of a controller that measures the temperatures of both the mix and the heating medium to ensure accurate control. After packaging the ice cream is passed to a very large cold store where the temperature throughout the store is controlled to an accuracy of $\pm 1 \cdot 0°F$ ($0 \cdot 56°C$). The changeover from manual to automatic control has resulted in an annual saving of £40,000.

Wheat is conditioned by damping it with water to obtain the optimum condition for milling. Thus an automatic method for correctly controlling the moisture content of his wheat is of importance to the miller. The Flour Milling and Baking Research Association and the S.I.R.A. Institute have, in a joint project, designed an automatic control system that has been operating successfully in a mill since mid-1969. The system uses the microwave absorption technique of moisture measurement and a signal derived from measurements taken of both the dry and damp wheat are used to operate a control valve in the water spray line. The moisture content of the wheat is being measured with an accuracy of better than $\pm 0 \cdot 25\%$, when compared with standard oven drying determinations, and the increased flour extraction rate is a considerable economic advantage.

BIBLIOGRAPHY

B.S. Code 1041. "Temperature Measurement".

B.S. 1904. "Industrial Platinum Resistance Thermometer Elements."

Giles, A. F. "Electronic Sensing Devices." (George Newnes Ltd. London).

"The Instrument Manual." (United Trade Press, London).

Research Report No. 152. "The Application of Infra-Red Absorption Techniques to Moisture Measurement using the Pier Moisture Meter." (B.F.M.I.R.A., Leatherhead, Surrey).

Scientific and Technical Survey No. 52. "Liquid Flow Meters." (B.F.M.I.R.A., Leatherhead, Surrey).

Symposium Proceedings, 1969. "Relative Humidity in the Food Industry." (B.F.M.I.R.A., Leatherhead, Surrey).

Technical Circular No. 421. "Continuous Moisture Measurement, The Microwave Absorption Technique Applied to Golden Syrup." (B.F.M.I.R.A., Leatherhead, Surrey).

Technical Circular No. 426 "Continuous Moisture Measurement, The Microwave Absorption Technique Applied to Soya Beans." (B.F.M.I.R.A., Leatherhead, Surrey).

Technical Circular No. 441. "Continuous Moisture Measurement, The Microwave Absorption Technique Applied to Bread Crumbs." (B.F.M.I.R.A., Leatherhead, Surrey).

Technical Circular No. 451. "Evaluation of the B.F.M.I.R.A. In-Line Viscometer using Tomato Ketchup." (B.F.M.I.R.A., Leatherhead, Surrey).

Thomas, H. A. "Automation for Management." (Gower Press, London).

"Valves for the Control of Fluids." (The British Valve Manufacturers Association, London).

Young, A. J. "An Introduction to Process Control System Design." (Longmans, Green & Co. Ltd., London).

Author Index

Numbers in parentheses are the reference numbers and are given to assist locating in the text references where the authors' names are not given. Numbers in italics are the pages on which the references are listed.

Subject Index